Using Microcomputers

Using Microcomputers

D. G. Dologite

Baruch College
City University of New York

R. J. Mockler

St. John's University

PRENTICE HALL, Englewood Cliffs, New Jersey 07632

Library of Congress Cataloging-in-Publication Data

Dologite, D. G. (Dorothy G.) (date).
  Using microcomputers.

  Includes index.
  1. Microcomputers.   I. Mockler, Robert J.   II. Title.
QA76.5.D637   1988   004.16   87–36115
ISBN 0–13–940743–x

Editorial/production supervision: Barbara Grasso
Interior design: Lee Cohen
Design supervision: Lorraine Mullaney
Cover design: Lorraine Mullaney
Manufacturing buyers: Barbara Kittle and Margaret Rizzi
Page layout: Debbie Toymil and Karen Salzbach
Photo research: Teri Stratford
Photo editor: Lorinda Morris
Cover photo: International Business Machines Corporation

TO

Irene, Mel, Nick, Gail, Bonnie, Colman,
Joanna, MaryAnn, Jack, and Chris

our family support network

Printed in the United States of America

10 9 8 7 6 5 4 3 2 1

ISBN 0-13-940743-X   01

Prentice-Hall International (UK) Limited, *London*
Prentice-Hall of Australia Pty. Limited, *Sydney*
Prentice-Hall Canada Inc., *Toronto*
Prentice-Hall Hispanoamericana, S.A., *Mexico*
Prentice-Hall of India Private Limited, *New Delhi*
Prentice-Hall of Japan, Inc., *Tokyo*
Simon & Schuster Asia Pte. Ltd., *Singapore*
Editora Prentice-Hall do Brasil, Ltda., *Rio de Janeiro*

Overview

Contents

③ Application Software   80

④ System Software   114

Module II: Personal Productivity Applications

⑤ Spreadsheet and Financial Modeling Packages   150

⑥ Graphics Packages   186

7 Word Processing, Integrated, and Related Packages   220

8 Database and File Management Packages   264

9 Industry-Specific and Accounting Packages   300

Module IV: Data Communications

Module V: Special Topics

13 Desktop Publishing   408

14 Knowledge-Based Systems and Other Applications   458

Appendix A—History and Social Impact of Computing   495

Letter to the Student

Dear Student:

This book was written for you. It is designed to help you learn about microcomputers. Microcomputers are often called "personal computers" or simply "PCs."

The book focuses on the microcomputer as a tool to get a job done. Where necessary, it gets down to the nitty-gritty details that ultimately separate the microcomputer literate from everyone else. It does this in a way that is easy for complete novices to understand.

As the title suggests, you are especially encouraged to *use* microcomputers. That is the best way to know them well. They are sturdy machines that will let you experiment as long as you like. (If your school has a lab, you will probably have restrictions about how long you can use a microcomputer at any one sitting.)

There are so many ways that a microcomputer can help you accomplish current and future tasks. Examples include producing written assignments, like term papers (using word processing), to preparing a company's annual budget (using an electronic spreadsheet).

Be open minded about exploring the rich storehouse of programs available. Programs are also called "software" or "applications." They make the microcomputer perform useful tasks, such as word processing. There is an endless variety of software available to support school, work, home, and even entertainment purposes.

Hopefully you will be motivated to pursue a study of microcomputers beyond this book. Chapter 1 offers some ideas about how to do this.

If there is any topic concerning this book that you would like to express an opinion about, we would like to hear from you. You can write to us using the following address:

Prof. D. G. Dologite
Baruch College—CUNY
Box 513
17 Lexington Avenue
New York, NY 10010

We hope that this book provides you with a rich and rewarding study of microcomputers.

Best regards,
D. G. Dologite
R. J. Mockler

Letter to the Instructor

Dear Instructor:

    This text and supplementary package are designed to support your introduction to computing/data processing courses that are taught from a microcomputer perspective.

    Some highlights incorporated in the text to support this include:

- *Uses a friendly, comfortable, nonthreatening style.* The book shows people learning to use microcomputers in much the same way your students will be. This helps students to realize that their learning experience is a commonly shared one. It intentionally avoids an approach that threatens the student with a feeling of computer ignorance.

  It is an approach pioneered in two earlier books, *Using Small Business Computers* (D. G. Dologite, Prentice-Hall, 1984) and *Using Computers* (D. G. Dologite, Prentice-Hall, 1987). They helped instructors at hundreds of schools to bring microcomputers into the classroom. This book, *Using Microcomputers,* integrates the best of the earlier books and adds a wealth of new microcomputer information. It gets down to the nitty-gritty details that separate the microcomputer literate from everyone else—in a way that is easy for complete novices to understand.
- *Puts microcomputers in perspective.* Where appropriate, this book shows how microcomputers function in an organization with a mix of hardware. It does not leave students with the incorrect notion that microcomputers exist in isolation. Chapter 12, as an example, shows how large organizations link their microcomputers into mainframes to give employees the best of both worlds.
- *Makes extensive use of case studies.* Students like to read about *people* going through experiences with which they can identify. The text is designed to hold reader interest by presenting numerous mini-case studies showing how different types of people—such as a film writer, a real estate agent, a stock broker, a journalist, a lawyer, an accountant, a farmer, a marketing manager, a teacher, and a hospital administrator—learn to use and actually do use their microcomputers in order to become more productive.

  One major case study is threaded throughout the text to integrate the material in a natural real-life way. It concerns Interstate Distributing Company and its marketing manger, Frank Nelson.

  Special case studies, with discussion questions, appear at the end of all chapters. They add an entirely new dimension to the chapters or show a familiar topic from a new perspective.
- *Focuses on applications.* The book focuses on the microcomputer as a tool to get a job done, rather than as an engineering marvel. The application orientation covers
  - using personal productivity applications, such as word processing, spreadsheets, and graphics (Chapters 5, 6, and 7)
  - using database and accounting applications (Chapters 8 and 9)
  - using data communications, including local area networks (Chapters 11 and 12)

— using specialized applications, such as desktop publishing and knowledge-based systems (Chapters 13 and 14)

· *Provides a flexible format.* After the introductory chapter, any major module, and in some cases, any chapter, may be studied without loss of continuity.
· *Offers software independence.* The book is independent of any particular brand of software. This allows instructors to choose among alternative microcomputer software offerings. A separate "software tutorial" supplement, however, is available for use with *Using Microcomputers.*
· *Includes supplements.*
For purchase by students:
— *Student Study Guide and Workbook,* by D. G. Dologite and R. J. Mockler
— *Application Software,* by D. Curtin, a software lab manual. It includes coverage of hardware, DOS, WordPerfect, Twin/Lotus, and dBASE III Plus. A WordStar version is also available.
— Software (for student purchase or site licensing)
— *Using BASIC,* by D. G. Dologite and R. J. Mockler, a structured BASIC programming supplement. It follows the process that a student, who is a part-time worker, goes through while learning how to program. The student uses a miniature example of the employer's customer report and file. The book has bound into it a student "Study Guide and Workbook" on BASIC with answers.
For instructors (free to adopters):
— *Instructor's Guide*
— Computerized test bank
— Floppy disk of all BASIC programs in *Using BASIC*
— Color transparencies and transparency masters
— EXSYS, a program "shell" that allows users to create their own expert (knowledge-based) system

If you would like to offer comments on the text, supplements, or the introductory course they support, please write to us as follows:

Prof. D. G. Dologite
Baruch College—CUNY
Box 513
17 Lexington Avenue
New York, NY 10010

We would like to hear from you.

Best regards,
D. G. Dologite
R. J. Mockler

Acknowledgments

Appreciation is gratefully extended to:

- The following companies for furnishing software and other materials for research: Aldus Corporation, Ashton-Tate, Borland International, Inc., General Optimization Inc., Generic Software, Inc., IBM Corporation, Lifetree Software, Lotus Development Corporation, MicroData Base Systems, Inc., MicroPro International Corporation, MicroRIM, Inc., Open Systems, Inc., RightSoft, Inc., SPSS Inc., STSC, Inc., Texas Instruments Inc., WordPerfect Corporation.

- Contributors of material for the end-of-chapter case studies: Cahners Publishing Company, Consumer Software, Inc., CW Communications, Inc., Hayden Publishing Company, Inc., M & T Publishing, Inc., Texas Instruments, Inc., *The New York Times,* Warner Books, Yourdon Press, Ziff Communications Company.

- Manuscript reviewers for this book or portions of it that appeared earlier in *Using Computers,* D. G. Dologite, Prentice-Hall, 1987: Rosann Webb Collins, University of North Carolina; John W. Fendrich, Bradley University; Madison K. Finley, Dutchess Community College; Elaine Haight, Santa Monica College; Cynthia J. Kachik, Santa Fe Community College; Richard Lee Kerns, East Carolina University; Kenneth E. Martins, University of North Florida; as well as colleagues and students at Baruch College—City University of New York for reviewing and criticizing the text, including B. Loerinc Helft, Samuel Ryan, David Stephan, William Ferns.

- Research and student assistants for helping to construct this, or earlier portions of the manuscript: Swee-Lim Chia, Dean Hannotte, Ted Jaye, Maxwell Lown, Mary Ann Vasaturo, Nancy Ward, May-Mei Wong.

1

Introduction to Using Microcomputers

AFTER READING THIS CHAPTER, YOU SHOULD BE ABLE TO

- Give examples of how individuals use microcomputers
- Explain the fundamental technical details of working with computers
- Identify sources where computer topics can be explored further

The microcomputer is probably the most significant productivity tool of our time. In the coming years, business professionals who do not harness its capability will be functioning at a disadvantage.

Figure 1-1 illustrates common business-use microcomputers, which are widely called personal computers (the two terms are interchangeable in this book). Small shops and individuals can use such computers as easily and cheaply as can large companies.

This chapter explores how some enterprising individuals use personal computers. Some of their computers are linked into large computers which are called mainframes or mainframe computers. Mainframes as well as medium-sized minicomputers continue to play significant roles, along with the microcomputer, in today's computing environments.

People who use computers are frequently called *end-users*, or simply *users*. Examples of innovative and traditional computing users and uses are the concern of the first half of this chapter. The examples should

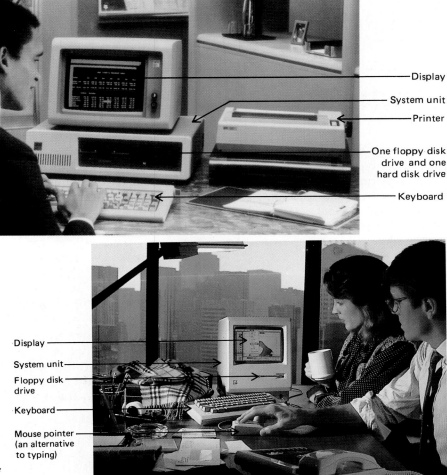

FIGURE 1-1
Typical personal computers: the IBM Personal Computer—XT (top) and the Apple Macintosh (bottom)
(*Top: courtesy of IBM; bottom: courtesy of Apple Computer, Inc.*)

be regarded as an introduction or overview to computing uses that are covered in detail in the remaining chapters of this book. The examples reflect the kinds of computing today's computer literate individuals do everyday.

The remaining part of the chapter covers some fundamental technical details of working with computers. A closing section encourages a further exploration of computing topics through magazines, conferences, user groups, and other sources.

To draw attention to concepts that are important to this study of microcomputers, certain terms are emphasized with bold or italic typefaces. In this chapter, no attempt is made to provide formal definitions of all important terms. It is more important to grasp the general "flavor" of these introductory concepts than it is to focus on precise definitions of terms. Most of the important concepts and terms used in this chapter are repeated and given full-chapter treatment later in this book.

COMPUTER DISTINCTIONS

A traditional classification of computers is

- **Microcomputers** (small computers)
- **Minicomputers** (medium-sized computers)
- **Mainframe computers** (large computers)

Figure 1-2 provides a brief comparative description of these computers in terms of typical users, uses, and cost.

At one time it was easy to tell one computer from the other. But technology has been narrowing the gap rapidly in terms of capability. For example, a small desktop **personal computer,** technically called a microcomputer, is as powerful today as a mainframe was 20 years ago.

More expensive computers generally support several users at once, as diagrammed in Figure 1-3, on what is called a **multiuser computer.** In such an environment, users often use terminals. **Terminals,** like the one in Figure 1-4, look and behave very much like personal computers. But they do not have a system unit as shown in Figure 1-3. The **system unit** does the processing work in a computer. In a multiuser system, everyone shares one system unit, which usually is then called a **processor.**

At National Bank, for example, a large mainframe processor is located on the seventh floor of the headquarters building. Hundreds of user terminals are linked by wire cables to the bank's mainframe processor. Bank users who prefer personal computers can also link them

FIGURE 1-2
Brief comparison of computers

TYPE	TYPICAL USERS AND USES	COST
	General	
Microcomputer	One user; personal and business use	Up to $7,000
Multiuser microcomputer and minicomputer	Multiple users; business and other uses	Up to $400,000
Mainframe	Multiple users; business and other uses with large volumes of data	Up to $8 million
	Special	
Supercomputer	Multiple users; research, scientific, and business use; handles very large volumes of data at extremely fast speeds	Up to $18 million

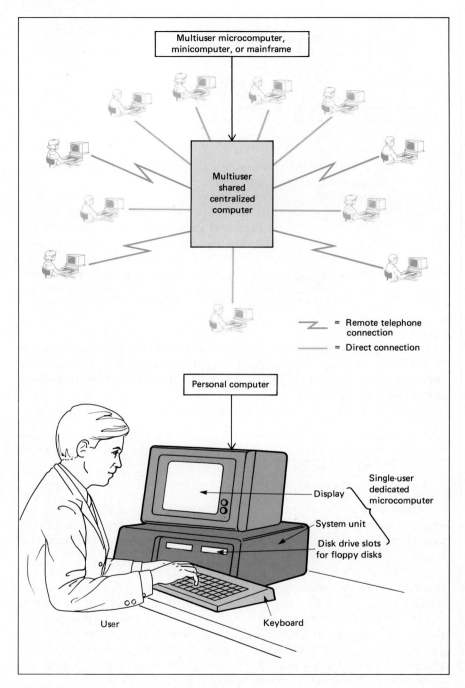

FIGURE 1-3
Comparison of single-user and multiuser computers
(*D. G. Dologite*, Using Small Business Computers, © *1984, p. 6. Reprinted by permission*
of Prentice-Hall, Inc., Englewood Cliffs, NJ.)

Display

Keyboard

FIGURE 1-4
A typical terminal often found in
multiuser computer installations
(Courtesy of Lear Siegler, Inc.)

to the company's mainframe. This gives personal computer users the best of both worlds. They have their own local personal computing capability as well as access to the company's more powerful mainframe computing capability.

IMPORTANCE OF SOFTWARE

Hardware is the physical part of a computer. It contrasts with **software,** which is the nonphysical part. Software is another term for the **programs** that tell hardware what to do. Without software, hardware is useless.

Software can be compared to music residing on cartridge tapes or records. A music lover may want a certain song by a certain vocalist and so buys a record to have a copy of it. In a similar way, a copy of desired software is acquired by buying it on various media, like the floppy disk shown in Figure 1-1. An example of software is a word processing program that helps a computer user to produce letters and reports. Anyone who wants to do word processing buys a floppy disk with a copy of a desired word processing program on it.

Figure 1-5 lists major application software categories. A user's main concern generally is with **application software.** As the term implies, this software *applies* a computer to a specific user task.

APPLICATION CATEGORY	SOFTWARE EXAMPLES
Personal productivity	Spreadsheet Word processing Graphics
File-based application development	File management systems Database management systems
Routine accounting and related operations	Accounting systems Industry-specific systems
Communications	Wide- and local-area networking (linking) of computers Communication services, like on-line databases and electronic mail
Special-purpose	Desktop publishing systems Knowledge-based systems
Others	

FIGURE 1-5
Application software categories

Typical reasons users give for acquiring a computer include the following:

- To improve personal productivity
- To computerize files and create file-based applications
- To automate routine operations, such as accounting and related processing tasks
- To transmit and receive (communicate) computer-based information with other computers, and to benefit from communication services, such as electronic mail and on-line databases
- To benefit from special-purpose applications, such as desktop publishing and knowledge-based systems

One person may have all these reasons for using a computer. Such a person would probably use lots of application software. However, only one computer is necessary. The many separate software applications would all work on the same "black box," as many people call the computer hardware.

Large organizations with large computers inevitably have software to serve all these purposes and more. Generally they have a resident computer department staffed with computer specialists and programmers. This professional staff creates some of the organization's main programs that help to run the business.

By contrast, individuals and smaller organizations usually buy ready-made, or **packaged, software** for their microcomputers and minicomputers. Generally, they do their computing without the aid of computer professionals.

COMPUTER USES AND USERS

It is enlightening to explore how individuals and organizations use computers to serve their application purposes.

The following examples of traditional, as well as innovative, uses and users provide an insight into contemporary computing. Two of the many examples covered are recalled in other chapters of the book. They help to contrast computing in a small- to medium-sized company, Interstate Distributing Company, with computing in a very large organization, National Bank. Their different approaches to computing cover the range of cases typically encountered in contemporary computing environments.

Although examples are grouped by the following major categories:

- Improving personal productivity (with word processing, spreadsheet, and graphics software)
- Creating file-based applications (with file and database management software)
- Automating routine operations (with accounting and industry-specific software)
- Communicating with other computers (with networking and other software)
- Using special-purpose applications (such as desktop publishing and knowledge-based system software)

many examples overlap. Today's computer uses and users defy simplistic categorization.

IMPROVING PERSONAL PRODUCTIVITY

A writer, a campaigner, and a manager are no different from everyone else who tries to make every minute of the workday count. The following examples focus on the software that these professionals use. In all cases, computing is regarded as a tool to help boost personal performance.

Writer

Mike Hoover, an independent writer, film producer, and director, depends on a computer to maintain a high level of personal productivity wherever he is.[1] He believes he can take his portable personal computer anywhere—Yosemite, Afghanistan, the Soviet Union, or the passenger

---

[1] Karen Springen, "Covering Sharks to Soviets," *Infoworld*, April 29, 1985, p. 71.

seat of an airplane. It was in a plane that Mr. Hoover used his personal computer to write the script notes for *Up*, a film documentary on flying. The documentary earned him a second Academy Award.

Mr. Hoover uses several common application packages to organize his notes, research, and files. One of them is a word processing package. Its display screen resembles the example shown in Figure 1-6, which allows him to see his notes on one part and to write his story on another part.

The **word processing package** helps to improve his personal productivity mainly because it allows him to type text and electronically edit it by moving paragraphs around and making other needed changes. In addition, once a story looks right, he types a few keys to have it effortlessly printed. He can print as many original copies as desired.

When Mr. Hoover films in Afghanistan, or other remote places, he uses a solar-cell panel, as shown in Figure 1-7, to recharge the portable computer's batteries. They run up to ten hours. His special recharging scheme is crucial because he counts on computing in places that lack electrical power.

FIGURE 1-6
Split-screen display feature in a word processing package
(Software: Microsoft Word. Reprinted by permission of the copyright owner Microsoft Corporation.)

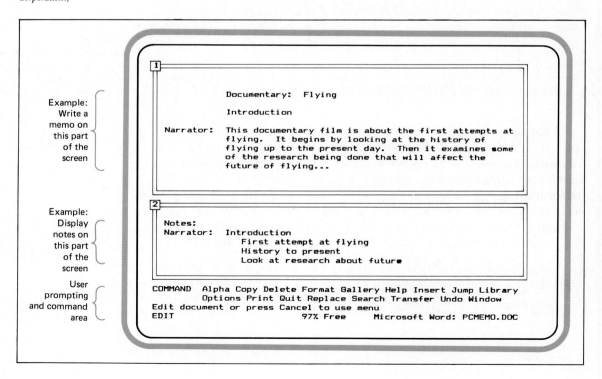

Portable
computer

Solar
panel

FIGURE 1-7
Mike Hoover powers his portable computer with solar panels when visiting remote places, like Afghanistan.
(Courtesy of Mike Hoover Productions, Inc.)

Campaigner

While Mr. Hoover uses general packages, Thom Serrani, a politician, uses a specialized package to boost his personal effectiveness.[2] In one political campaign, he had two advantages the opponent lacked: a personal computer and a software package called the "Campaign Manager."

When the votes were counted, Mr. Serrani had wrested the nomination away from the better-financed party leader's choice. He said, "It's tough to put a numerical figure on what the computer is worth in votes, but I can't think of another factor itself that was more important."

The main menu and other displays of the software that helped him to organize a winning campaign are shown in Figure 1-8. Mr. Serrani

---

[2] Michael Muskal, "A Victory for Campaign Manager," *PC Magazine*, March 6, 1985, pp. 201–206.

FIGURE 1-8
*Main menu and other displays of a
program to support political campaigners*
(*Software: adaptation of Campaign Manager,
courtesy of Aristotle Industries*)

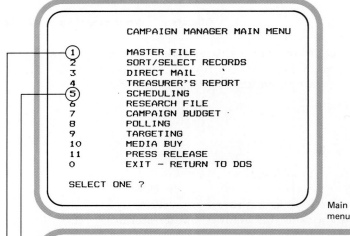

```
                    CAMPAIGN MANAGER MAIN MENU

         1         MASTER FILE
         2         SORT/SELECT RECORDS
         3         DIRECT MAIL        `
         4         TREASURER'S REPORT
         5         SCHEDULING
         6         RESEARCH FILE
         7         CAMPAIGN BUDGET  ·
         8         POLLING
         9         TARGETING
        10         MEDIA BUY
        11         PRESS RELEASE
         0         EXIT - RETURN TO DOS

         SELECT ONE ?
```

Main
menu

Scheduling
option helps
to keep
track of
details
about
upcoming
campaign
events

```
                    CAMPAIGN MANAGER - SCHEDULE          CURRENT
                                                         10-17-198X
                                                         13:33
       DATE       :07-02-8X
       EVENT      :JULY 4TH PARADE
       LOCATION   :MAIN STREET
       ARRIVE     :11:00AM
       LEAVE      : 2:00PM
       SPONSOR    :TOWN FATHERS
       CONTACT    :MAYOR GREENE
       TELEPHONE  :2039495959
       STAFF      :JOE, SAMMY, MARIUSH, AND SARAH
       DRIVER     :SARAH  .
       CAR        :BELGRANO
       SUPPLIES   :TABLOIDS, LAPEL PINS, BALLOONS
       PRESS Y/N  :Y
       SPEECH     :OUR AMERICAN HERITAGE
       V.I.P.'s   :MAYOR GREENE, SENATOR BODD
       NOTES      :THIS ONE WILL BE A PIECE OF CAKE, TRY TO BE NICE TO BODD.
       DIRECTIONS:YOU KNOW HOW TO GET THERE

       1PREV   2NEXT   3     4     5     6     7DELETE  8MENU   9EXIT   OSAVE
```

One
typical
record
in the
master
file of
campaign
contributors

```
                    CAMPAIGN MANAGER - MASTER FILE
       LAST NAME : Armstrong_____
       FIRST NAME: Dean_____        TEL(H): 2038536686
       SALUTATION: Dean_____        TEL(O): 8002434401
       MAIL NAME : Dean Armstrong_____  CODES : EE IG GA_____
       ADDRESS   : 3 Outer Road_____
       CITY      : Norwalk_____ STATE: CT ZIP: 06854

       EMPLOYER  : Aristotle Ind._____        _____
       OCCUPATION: V.P._____         :          NOTES           :
                                                 : This guy has big bucks___ :
       SOURCE    AMOUNT       DATE      ELECTION LTR SENT : He is a V.I.P._____ :
       flf      10000.00    09/04/8X     GEN       A      : _____ :
       glg      __200.00    10/17/8X     CON       B      : _____ :
       ---      -----·--    __/__/__     ---       -      : _____ :
       ---      -----·--    __/__/__     ---       -      : _____ :
       ---      -----·--    __/__/__     ---       -      : _____ :
       ---      -----·--    __/__/__     ---       -      : _____ :
       ---      -----·--    __/__/__     ---       -      : _____ :
       ---      -----·--    __/__/__     ---       -      : _____ :
       ---      -----·--    __/__/__     ---       -      :_____:
       1thankA  2thankB   31tr.1  41tr.2  51tr.3  61tr.4  7DELETE  8RESTAR  9EXIT  OSAVE
```

used the software to track campaign contributors, whose names are stored in the program's master file. As the example in Figure 1-8 indicates, the software also helped in scheduling and budgeting and in a host of other campaign management tasks.

Manager

Frank Nelson, a marketing manager at Interstate Distributing Company, works in a traditional company environment. He, like Mr. Hoover, uses common off-the-shelf packages to help improve his productivity. The standard packages he uses are the same that many computer-literate professionals make use of every day:

Package	*Purpose*
Word processing	To help prepare written documents
Spreadsheet	To help calculate numbers for decision making
Graphics	To help make presentations to an audience and to convert spreadsheet numbers into easy-to-understand charts

Figure 1-9 shows what his computer display looks like when using these applications.

As implied from the difference in a comparison of Figures 1-6 and 1-9, users have a choice of word processing software packages. Hundreds of different brands of packages exist in many application areas.

FIGURE 1-9
Three common personal productivity packages

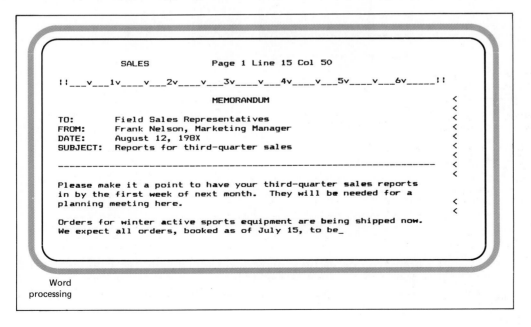

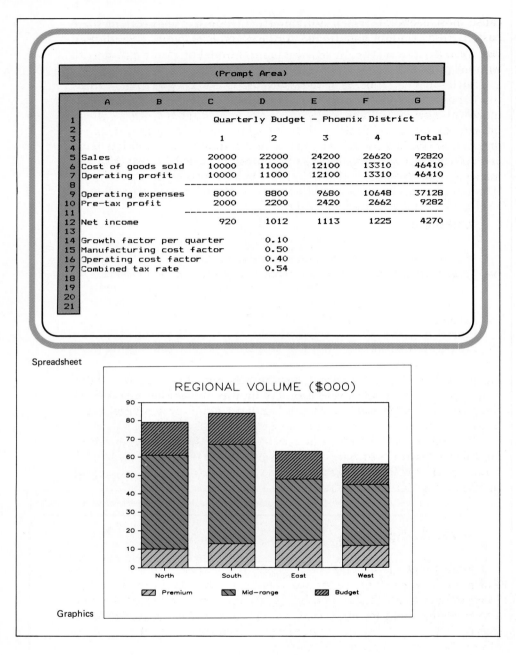

Spreadsheet

Graphics

FIGURE 1-9 (continued)

CREATING FILE-BASED APPLICATIONS

Many computer users have ideas about how the computer could be more useful to them. This generally happens as soon as a new user becomes more experienced and more comfortable with computing. Because most users are not programmers, how do they implement their custom ideas on the computer? One answer is with *file and database management software*. It helps users to create custom file-based applications without programming.

Such software is liberating more and more computer users to harness the computer's power for their own needs. As this software becomes more "user-friendly," anyone with an application idea will be able to implement it on a computer, without programming. The following paragraphs describe how a marketing manager, an apartment building owner, and an employee in a large personnel department use their own database management software.

Marketing

Mr. Nelson, the marketing manager at Interstate Distributing Company, uses a database package to create computer files for

- Salespeople
- Expenses
- Business contacts
- Prospective customers

He prints a variety of reports from the files depending on his needs. One report lists prospective customers by the salesperson assigned to the account. The printed report tells him immediately which salespeople need help to turn over new accounts quicker.

Mr. Nelson established all the files by himself without programming. He followed helpful prompts on menulike screens to set up his files. A report generator feature of the software allows him to create any report he likes using data in the files.

Tenant Billing

Irene Jones initiated a more ambitious database project. It began with a file of tenants who rent apartments in a building she owns. Ms. Jones generates a rent roll and other reports from the tenant file. She also wanted to produce individual rent statements. That required learning the database programming language. She had to invest a few evenings of her spare time to learn the language.

Ms. Jones found a database language simpler to learn and use than normal computer programming languages. When done, she estimated that it took about one-tenth the time to produce rent statements than if she had used a normal programming language.

As its name implies, **database management software** helps users to set up, maintain, and manipulate data. Data reside in computer *files* that usually consist of many uniform *records*, as shown in the example in Figure 1-10.

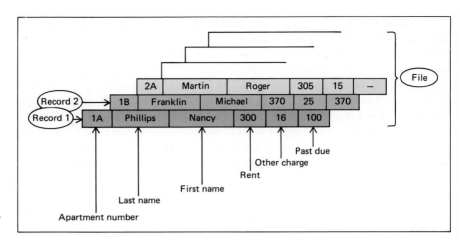

FIGURE 1-10
Many uniform records make up a database file

Large Organizations

Database software is used in large organizations as well as small ones. Loretta Carlson finds National Bank's mainframe database software is not much different, conceptually, from the first database package that she used on her personal computer. Her organization eventually distributed microcomputer versions of the mainframe database software to employees. This software enables Ms. Carlson, a loan department manager, to extract selected loan records from the mainframe customer loan file and process them on her microcomputer.

The customer loan file that Ms. Carlson accesses on the mainframe is an institutional, or company, file. A person called the **database administrator** controls a company's database files in a large organization. User access to the files is controlled by security traps in the software. Users have freedom, nonetheless, to generate personal applications with the data made available to them.

AUTOMATING ACCOUNTING AND RELATED OPERATIONS

Small- to medium-sized companies purchase **accounting** and **industry-specific packages** to automate routine day-to-day operations. Such operations could involve, as they do at Interstate Distributing Company, processing volumes of sales orders, sending customer bills, and receiving customer payments. This software generally also produces management information. It usually runs on microcomputers and minicomputers.

For years, mainframe computers have supported the day-to-day accounting and other routine operations at large organizations. The software that runs the day-to-day operations in large organizations is often called a *data processing system*.

Large organizations usually supplement their data processing systems with *management information system* (MIS) software. This software generates management-level information from the same data used by the data processing system. Usually all this software is custom built from scratch and runs on mainframes. More recently, some of this custom software has been scaled down to department size and programmed to run on microcomputers and minicomputers.

Examples of businesses as varied as distribution, farming, retailing, banking, and health care, which have installed microcomputer systems to automate their operations, are described in the paragraphs that follow.

Distribution

To run its business, Interstate Distributing Company bought an industry-specific package designed for distributors. The company distributes sporting goods to wholesalers and retailers. It is a small- to medium-sized business without a resident professional computer staff. The hardware consists of personal computers.

The software handles such jobs as

- Order entry
- Customer billing
- Inventory control
- Payments to suppliers
- General ledger accounting

The company requires two goals from its computing efforts:

1. Expediting routine operations
2. Providing management information as a by-product of routine operations

Management information appears in computer screen displays and printed reports for things like

- Unfilled orders over 10 days old
- Unpaid customer accounts older than 30, 60, 90, and 120 days
- Fast-moving and slow-moving products

This kind of critical information enables management to take action to reverse negative trends and to capitalize on positive ones.

Because the software that Interstate Distributing Company uses has applicability beyond the distribution industry, it is repackaged and sold as a general accounting package to others. Over 200,000 copies of the software are being used by various organizations that do order entry, customer billing, and other standard office tasks.

Farming

To help run her family's farm, Amy DeWitt uses a farm management software package. It has accounting as well as swine and crop production control programs.

The goal of one part of the software is to maintain control over farm production costs. If known early enough, the family can lock in profits with marketing techniques like "forward contracting." In forward contracting, buyers agree to purchase a farmer's crops at a set price prior to the actual harvest. If the DeWitts know they can produce corn at $3 a bushel, for example, they can sign a contract selling the crop at $3.40 a bushel and lock in a profit. "Knowing exact production costs," claims Ms. DeWitt, "takes much of the gamble out of crop marketing."

Retailing

Esprit, the women's clothing company that made sweatshirts chic, put just as much style and effort into its use of personal computers.[3] It developed its own software from scratch with in-house programmers and software designers. Retail industry observers say the company developed one of the most advanced personal computer-based retail operations anywhere.

Instead of cash registers, Esprit uses microcomputers at its own stores, as shown in Figure 1-11. The personal computers are custom painted black and have a cash drawer and printer below the countertop. A credit card reader attaches to the keyboard.

Joan Hemsley, manager of retail systems for the company, says that the firm can program "a tremendous number of contols into the personal computer." Some include tallying up sales and totals for purchases that include items priced at various discounts.

Esprit's in-house programmers wrote custom point-of-sale software in three months. It took a few more months to write software to link

FIGURE 1-11
Personal computers help to run the Esprit retail business.
(Courtesy of Tim Davis Photography)

[3] John Greitzer, "The Easy Sell," *PC Week*, May 14, 1985, pp. 55–60.

all the personal computers to a centralized minicomputer. A minicomputer in each store contains the inventory item prices and discount offers.

Periodically, each store's minicomputer sends summary totals and control information to the distant corporate mainframe computer over telephone lines.

Banking

National Bank is a large organization that also uses all kinds of computers. Its large data processing system runs on mainframes and processes mainly bank teller transactions. But many branch banking operations and specialized administrative applications were programmed from scratch to run on microcomputers and minicomputers.

One microcomputer application was custom designed and programmed for the headquarters-office personnel department. It keeps track of recent job applicants who have specialized skills that the bank may require.

Another microcomputer application is programmed to extract selected records of mortgage account customers from the company's mainframe. When the records are available to the microcomputer, a mortgage loan officer processes them for decision-making purposes.

Health Care

St. Barnabas Medical Center, the largest hospital in New Jersey, also is a mainframe computer organization.[4] In addition, it uses microcomputers to help process all patient and hospital administrative tasks. Patient summaries and financial management reports can be printed on a daily basis, if administrators need them. The hospital computer staff programs some software itself and buys some.

Some organizations in the health care industry are installing microcomputers to process patient medical cards, as shown in Figure 1-12. The card itself was developed by three enterprising young people.[5] One was 19-year-old Douglas Becker, and two were 23-year-olds, Eric Becker and Christopher Hoehn-Saric. The medical card carries 800 pages of a patient's medical history. Using videodisk technology, they created the card to carry, among other things, a person's

FIGURE 1-12
Card encoded with a person's medical history
(Courtesy of LifeCard International, Inc., a subsidiary of Blue Cross & Blue Shield of Maryland, Inc.)

- · Photograph
- · Facsimile of a signature
- · Description of health insurance
- · Copy of an electrocardiogram
- · Chest X ray
- · List of medicines taken
- · Name of physicians who have provided treatment

---

[4] Barbara Call, "St. Barnabas Medical Center: PCs Help Hospital Stabilize Costs," *PC Week*, May 20, 1986, pp. 79–82.

[5] Irvin Molotsky, "Insurance Cards to Detail Medical Histories," *New York Times*, May 7, 1985, p. A1.

The innovative card is used by hospitals and doctors to determine patient treatment and to avoid unnecessary procedures. It can be a lifesaver in an emergency. The card processing programs provide management and research information to administrators and doctors.

COMMUNICATIONS

Automating an organization's business may involve installing **communication software.** It allows cooperating computing devices to transmit and receive data. At National Bank, for example, it helps to link branch microcomputers to the headquarters' mainframe. The main reason for linking, or **networking**, computers is for sharing

- Data, like those in the customer database files
- Resources, like computer printers

For less than $500, any microcomputer user can buy a *modem*, as shown in Figure 1-13. A modem is to a computer what a telephone is to a person. With a modem and communication software in place, a user's telephone line is available to dial into vast stores of research and special-interest *on-line databases*. The Dow Jones and other financial databases are popular with many individual, as well as corporate, users. Public communication services offer a host of other options, for a fee, like *electronic mailboxes* and *electronic bulletin boards*.

Some examples of communication uses and users follow. The first examples concentrate on personal use. The concluding examples highlight networking.

Personal Use

Mr. Hoover, the film writer and producer, depends on communication for two reasons. One is for general transmission services to send news stories. While in Afghanistan covering the war, for example, he used a modem to send updated information to another microcomputer at CBS News' main offices in New York City. Because no phones were available in Afghanistan, information was transmitted from Pakistan.

"Before," Mr. Hoover recalls, "you would write an article on a yellow legal pad and give it to a runner." The runner would deliver it to the nearest wireservice bureau. The bureau would wire it to the destination.

Now a floppy disk and a modem deliver articles directly to their destination, with no intermediaries. He claims that deliveries "are far more accurate. You're getting every keystroke right into CBS."

A second reason Mr. Hoover uses communications is to call the DIALOG on-line database service in California to do research. The database contains one of the largest computerized bibliography collections anywhere.

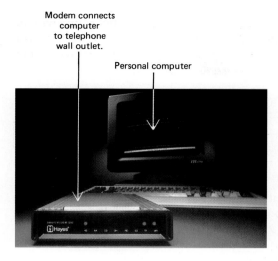

Modem connects
computer
to telephone
wall outlet.

Personal computer

FIGURE 1-13
Personal computer with a modem for
communication
(Courtesy of Hayes MicroComputers
Products, Inc.)

Another researcher, Mary Ann Malone, uses the LEXIS on-line database for lawyers. As a corporate lawyer for a large electronics firm, she does on-line research for her cases using a microcomputer. Material she locates helps her to construct legal arguments.

Henry Surdez, an independent insurance agent, sends new insurance policy information, using his microcomputer and a modem, to company headquarters. In some cases, while a customer is still in the office, headquarters returns a copy of the policy for on-the-spot printing in his office.

Networking

Networking enables many users to share common computer files and resources. "Wherever there is more than one computer user, the environment is ripe for sharing," claims Lazlo Nagy, manager of National Bank's computer center. At the bank, for example, an officer using a microcomputer to approve a new loan may need access to a customer's account. A teller using a special teller-terminal may need access to the same account. A computer center operator using a terminal may have access to the same account to prepare a monthly printed customer statement.

Traditionally, the multiuser computer has been the normal way to share both the company's database and expensive disks and printers. A more recent approach is largely a phenomenon of microcomputers, called *local-area networking*. Figure 1-14 diagrams a local-area network of microcomputers in a manufacturing environment. A similar network is eventually installed at Interstate Distributing Company.

In a **local-area network**, a high-speed cable, or communication line, connects microcomputers or other computers and related computer equipment. Everyone on the line can share files and printers and can exchange electronic mail.

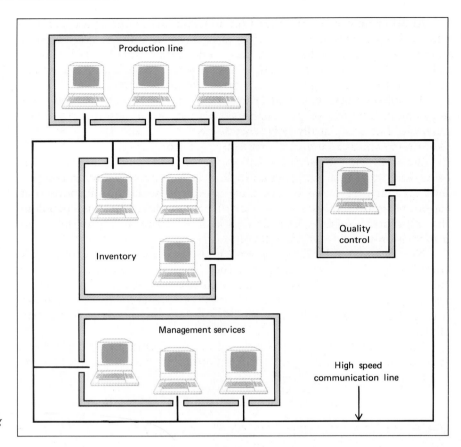

FIGURE 1-14
A local-area network in a manufacturing environment

NEWER USES

Reasons already given for using microcomputers include

- Improving personal productivity (with word processing, spreadsheet, and graphics software)
- Creating file-based applications (with file and database management software)
- Automating routine operations (with accounting and industry-specific software)
- Communicating with other computers, sharing files, and exchanging electronic mail (with networking and other software)
- Using special-purpose applications (such as desktop publishing and knowledge-based system software)

Newer uses include harnessing the microcomputer's power to prepare newsletters, brochures, direct mail pieces, and other items for publication. The computer industry calls this application **desktop publishing.**

Another newer use includes a diesel locomotive maintenance expert who is about to retire. By capturing and recording some of his expertise in computer software, he can share his knowledge with others he leaves behind. The captured knowledge is transferred to a knowledge-based system software package that runs on a microcomputer.

A different case exists where jobs too dangerous for humans are automated. The job of passing materials into a flaming-hot oven, for example, has successfully been transferred to a robot. The robot looks like a mechanical arm and is driven by a microcomputer.

Both *knowledge-based systems* and *robotics* are branches of *artificial intelligence* research, which promises many innovative ways to use microcomputers. In many cases, such uses have profound social implications that cannot be ignored. Most such uses involve unemployment. It is a problem that all mature societies face as they convert from an industrial to an information-based social structure.

Newer uses also include implanting miniaturized computers in every conceivable kind of consumer product, from toys to automobiles, as shown in Figure 1-15. These uses build on the tradition of creating special-purpose computers and instruments to do everything from monitoring chemical plants to processing laboratory tests in various medical clinics.

Little doubt exists that computing has a profound impact on society. It requires computer-literate individuals to realize its full potential without creating damaging social side effects.

FIGURE 1-15
Automobile dashboard with a computer
touch-sensitive display screen
(Courtesy of Chrysler Corp.)

USING A COMPUTER

Most people buy packaged software to use with their personal computers. Typical users, like Mr. Nelson, who is Interstate Distributing Company's marketing manager, walk into a computer retail store and leave with one or more software application packages. Its main contents, shown in Figure 1-16, are

- One or more **floppy disks** that contain the software
- A **User Guide** with instructions about how to use the software

The *User Guide* instructs Mr. Nelson about how to put the floppy disk into the computer disk drives, like those shown in Figure 1-1. It explains what happens after the computer power is turned on and the first menu, like the one in Figure 1-8, appears. It details what each menu option is for and what typing, or alternate action, a user is expected to do.

Mr. Nelson wondered what was "floppy" about a floppy disk. The ones he bought were small 5¼-inch squares. They had a cardboard

FIGURE 1-16
A typical software package bought from a retail store contains a User Guide *and one or more floppy disks.*
(*Courtesy of Satellite Software International*)

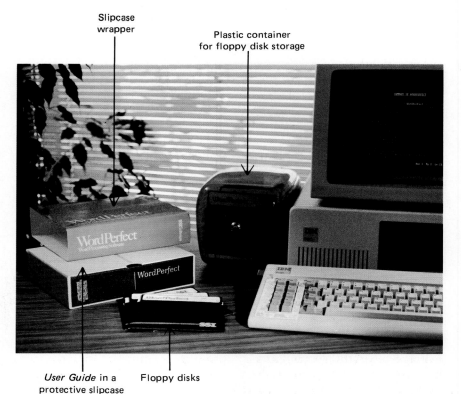

Slipcase wrapper

Plastic container for floppy disk storage

User Guide in a protective slipcase

Floppy disks

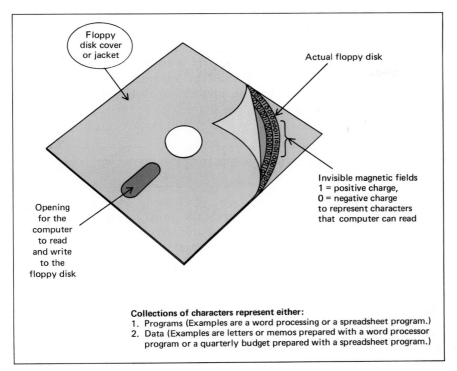

Floppy disk cover or jacket

Actual floppy disk

Invisible magnetic fields
1 = positive charge,
0 = negative charge
to represent characters
that computer can read

Opening for the computer to read and write to the floppy disk

Collections of characters represent either:
1. Programs (Examples are a word processing or a spreadsheet program.)
2. Data (Examples are letters or memos prepared with a word processor program or a quarterly budget prepared with a spreadsheet program.)

FIGURE 1-17
Cutaway view of a floppy disk

jacket with a hole in the middle, as shown in Figure 1-17. Some smaller 3½-inch disks have rigid plastic jackets.

The computer salesperson explained that jackets cover the thin floppy disk housed inside it. The disk material feels like a thin layer of recording tape used in tape recorders. It is covered with invisible magnetized areas that the computer can read. The magnetized areas represent program instructions and data to the computer.

After Mr. Nelson uses his spreadsheet software to prepare budgets, he saves the budgets on floppy disks. They are saved as *data files*. His spreadsheet program is also stored on a floppy disk as a *program file*.

He soon learned that everything stored on a disk is called a *file*. He also discovered that a disk usually holds only two types of files:

· **Program files** (example: word processing program file)
· **Data files** (example: business letter file created with the word processing program)

Operating system software keeps one type of file separate from another, without user assistance. The **operating system** is special software that manages everything that happens inside the computer. In some cases it is like a traffic cop controlling the direction and flow of everything over the proper electronic roadways.

Mr. Nelson's operating system is called **DOS** (rhymes with "floss"), for **Disk Operating System.** It came in a package just like the one in Figure 1-16. Usually his DOS disk is put in a floppy disk drive and then removed after the computer power is turned on. The DOS disk prepares his hardware to accept whatever application he desires. After he replaces the DOS disk with an application disk, he is ready to do some serious computing.

WHAT IS A SYSTEM?

Anyone studying computing finds the word *system* used over and over again. The word generally refers to interrelated items considered as a unit. In a **computer system,** the interrelated items, as diagrammed in Figure 1-18, are

- Hardware
- Software
- People
- Procedures

If any of these ingredients is ignored, computing is usually a failure.

Computer professionals often find people who claim to "need a computer." While these people have hardware in mind, they remain unaware that it is only one of several elements necessary to computerize.

In addition to selecting hardware, users must knowledgeably select software. Then they must learn how to use the software or train someone else to use it. Inevitably new software means new ways of doing things or new procedures to follow. Where does the information come from that is to be entered into the computer? What happens when errors

FIGURE 1-18
Interrelated items in any computer system

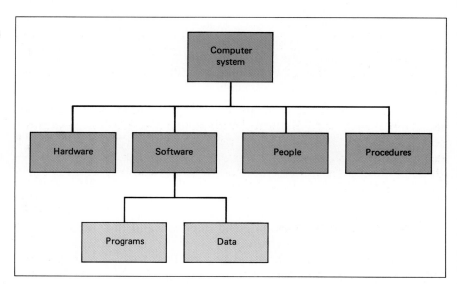

occur? If the power goes off, how are programs and data backed up for safety purposes? Who should have access to file information? How often should reports be printed?

To stress the interrelated nature of all elements that make computing possible, hardware and software suppliers often attach the term *system* to product names:

Type	Examples of Product Names
Hardware	IBM System 370 DEC System 2060
Software	Business Graphics System Micro Data Base System

In these cases, hardware generally consists of many interrelated equipment parts. Likewise, the software consists of a collection of interrelated programs.

The word *system* is also often used to classify hardware and software categories:

Type	Examples of Category Name
Hardware	Microcomputer systems Minicomputer systems Mainframe systems
Software	Database systems Accounting systems Operating systems

When Ms. Jones first studied computing, she felt uneasy about seeing the term *system*. As she gained computer experience, she learned that *either* software or hardware is at the heart of any "system" encountered. That simplified things somewhat.

UNDER THE HOOD

Ms. Jones found that it helps to understand what goes on, as she says, "under the hood." Knowing fundamental concepts like input, processing, and output clears up how all computers work. The concept of storage clears up why users buy floppy or other disks. Finally, by learning about bits and bytes, it is easy to understand the salesperson who quotes a computer's capacity in bytes.

Input, Processing, and Output

Ms. Jones found that **input** and **output** are computer jargon for putting something into a computer and getting something out. Between

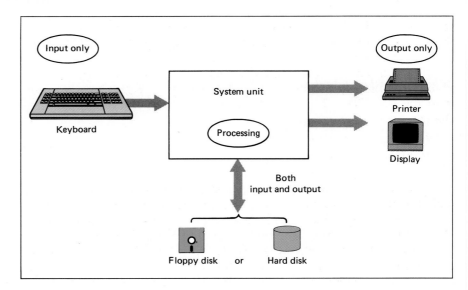

FIGURE 1-19
Fundamental computer input,
processing, and output operations

input and output, as shown in Figure 1-19, **processing** occurs to transform input into output.

For example, Ms. Jones may input, or type, a command to find those tenants in the file who have overdue rent balances. During the processing stage, the tenant file on the floppy disk is searched. Every

FIGURE 1-20
A computer's memory is only a temporary
workspace for programs and data, which
are permanently stored on disk.

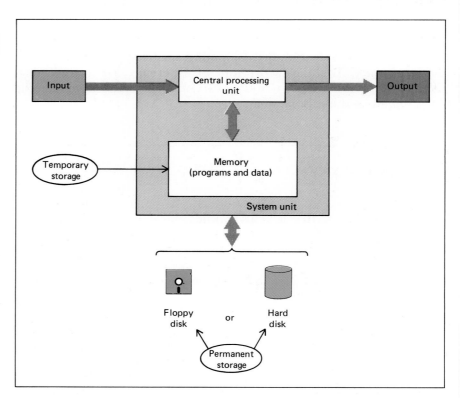

record is examined to see who has a past due balance. As records meeting the search criterion are found, they are output or displayed. It all happens at lightning speed.

If her intention is to *update* the tenant file, say, add $20 to the Phillips's monthly rent, she must first input, or type, 20. Then output is to the disk file. The Phillips's record on the disk must reflect the change.

Storage

As Figure 1-20 shows, permanent disk **storage** for computer program and data files is necessary because the computer's **memory** is temporary, or volatile, storage that is used only while processing is in progress. When the power goes off, everything in memory disappears.

This is why users start a computer session by first placing floppy disks into the disk drives. A copy of the disk program and related data are loaded into memory. They give the **central processing unit,** which is equivalent to the computer's brain, something to work on, or "process."

Bits and Bytes

Everything in the computer's memory is represented by an on or off electronic pulse. This limited two-state situation is called a **binary system,** as indicated in Figure 1-21. One *binary* dig*it* is called a **bit.** To

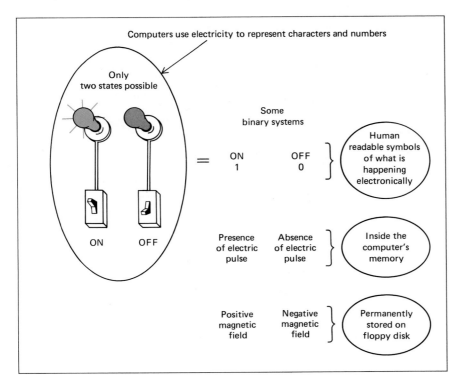

FIGURE 1-21
The two-state limitation of representing data with electricity

ASCII 7-BIT CODE	MEANING
100 0001	A
100 0010	B
100 0011	C
100 0100	D
100 0101	E
100 0110	F
100 0111	G
100 1000	H
100 1001	I
100 1010	J
100 1011	K
100 1100	L
100 1101	M
100 1110	N
100 1111	O
101 0000	P
101 0001	Q
101 0010	R
101 0011	S
101 0100	T
101 0101	U
101 0110	V
101 0111	W
101 1000	X
101 1001	Y
101 1010	Z
011 0000	0
011 0001	1
011 0010	2
011 0011	3
011 0100	4
011 0101	5
011 0110	6
011 0111	7
011 1000	8
011 1001	9

FIGURE 1-22
Example of bit patterns in the ASCII code

UNITS	COMPOSED OF	NUMBER OF CHARACTERS IT CAN STORE
bit	1 or 0	none
byte	8 bits	1
Kbyte	1,000 bytes (or 1,024 bytes unrounded)	1,000
64 Kbytes	64,000 bytes	64,000
Mbytes	1,000,000 bytes	1,000,000
Gbytes	1 billion bytes	1 billion

Abbreviations:

K = kilo, a thousand

M = mega, a million

G = giga, a billion

FIGURE 1-23
Bits and bytes

overcome the limitation and to store meaningful information requires grouping several pulses together. The computer industry standardized on grouping seven binary digits together. Examples of specific groupings and their meaning are given in Figure 1-22. Whenever Ms. Jones types an "A" on the keyboard, for example, what really gets sent to the computer's memory for processing is 1000001. A special check bit, called a parity bit, is first added to each 7-bit grouping, which results in a total of 8 bits. Eight bits equals one **byte** (pronounced "bite").

The computer industry calls this bit arrangement the *American Standard Code for Information Interchange*, or **ASCII** (pronounced "as-key"). While the ASCII code dominates microcomputer and minicomputer hardware, another code dominates mainframes. It is called *Extended Binary Coded Decimal Interchange Code*, or EBCDIC (pronounced "ebsee-dick").

An eight-bit byte is the fundamental unit computers work with. The chart in Figure 1-23 clarifies the bit and byte relationship.

Computer memory and disk storage capacity are usually quoted in bytes. Generally, the higher the byte capacity, the more powerful and expensive the product.

BECOMING INFORMED

Many sources exist to help anyone studying computing to become more informed, especially about microcomputers. They include books, periodicals, user groups, shows, exhibitions, and conferences, among other sources.

Books

Many computer books focus on buying hardware and specific products. Some cover both hardware and software. The card catalog of the library is an ideal source to locate books on computing topics. Books are also sold in computer retail stores.

Periodicals

One of the best sources of information is computer magazines or periodicals. Most are available at local computer stores and libraries. Some useful general publications are

Personal Computing
Desktop Computing
Business Computer Software

Many periodicals are dedicated to individual computer products and product lines. They cover hardware and software topics and assume that a reader is somewhat familiar with the products endorsed. They aim at a more sophisticated reader and include the following:

Publication	Product
PC Magazine	IBM products
PC World	IBM products
MacWorld	Apple Macintosh products

Another category of publications aims at a computer-literate reader but is not product specific. Some of these publications are

Computerworld
Byte
Infoworld
Mini-Micro Systems
Datamation
Computer Decisions

The last three in this list are free to qualified subscribers. Qualifying subscribers usually belong to organizations using several computers and have the purchasing power to support the magazine's advertisers.

User Groups

Local community **user groups** that began years ago as hobbyist clubs have matured sufficiently to offer monthly meetings where business people can swap problems and share solutions. Often groups are formed around specific personal computer brands.

Groups usually have speakers at monthly meetings. Some invite hardware and software vendor representatives to talk about their products.

Groups often form subgroups known as special-interest groups (SIGs). SIGs on communications, corporate uses, word processing, graphics, new users, and others reflect the special interests of members. SIGs carry on in much the same way as the parent organization. They have regular meetings with speakers and often offer tutorial courses for other members. A user-group newsletter keeps members informed of organization and SIG activities, officers, and meeting notices. Some newsletters resemble regular periodicals with ads and articles.

Members often contribute software to the group. It is offered free to other members, except for the cost of distribution and the floppy disk (often under $10). It is called **public domain software,** and it frequently travels from group to group. Much of it is not commercial quality and is of interest only to programmers and hobbyists.

Companies of all sizes have adopted the idea and sponsor their own user groups. Managers responsible for the smooth integration of microcomputers into their organization have also banded together to form local groups. They swap ideas on how to manage the evolution of microcomputers into their formerly all-mainframe-oriented organizations. They also look for common and shared solutions to buying, tutorial classes, and other concerns.

Product-specific periodicals usually carry directories listing user groups. They also give contact information. Some give group news items. Other user group information is usually available from local computer stores.

Shows, Exhibitions, and Conferences

Computer shows, exhibitions, and conferences are often held on local, regional, and national levels. They are a good way to see a collection of the lastest hardware and software available. Usually entrance fees for vendor- and user-group-sponsored events are nominal. Conferences or seminars usually feature speakers followed by audience question-and-answer sessions. Some events sponsor all-day workshops and tutorials. Fees for these services often are several hundred dollars.

Computer periodicals often include lists of shows, exhibits, and conferences.

Other Sources

Hardware and software manufacturers have free literature available to anyone who writes for it. Publications often have insert postcards for requesting free vendor-advertised literature. Free literature is also available at local computer stores and shows.

While vendor literature presents the vendor's product bias, such literature can be informative. Often it includes technical specifications which can be challenging to nontechnicians.

Hardware suppliers also publish directories of software and provide toll-free 800 numbers for user support. Their directories often include software produced by third parties. **Third party** is a computer industry term for independently developed products and services.

The medical, printing, construction, wholesale, retail, and other industries inform members of computer-related topics. They do this through trade publications, professional associations, conferences, shows, and exhibits, among other outlets. No better contact exists for a new computer user than someone in a similar industry who already is an experienced computer user.

CASE STUDY: The Smart Way to Learn Computing

Any new job brings anxiety—without the added pressure of having to learn how to use a computer. But Lisa Figoli faced both situations when she began working at National Semiconductor last year. Figoli was given an IBM Personal Computer with a hard disk and was told, in so many words, to "get computing." The department had no formal training program, but had standardized on a few packages, such as WordStar for word processing and the Condor for data base management software.

"I was told I'd be using WordStar and they gave me this big book to learn it. My boss spent a few minutes with me to get me started," recalls Figoli. "But the documentation was ridiculous."

First-Time Users.   Computers can be intimidating for many of the reasons the above case illustrates, especially for the first-time user "required" to use one. Unfortunately, many companies minimize the importance of training people in the rush to "computerize" operations. As one computer instructor puts it: "I've hardly ever seen an office where learning is a priority."

For starting out, getting help from someone with experience can speed the learning process immensely. When you're just familiarizing yourself with the computer, for example, someone can show you how to insert a disk, power up, and begin entering information in a minute's time. Trying to figure out the same things, if you're a beginner, can take a lot longer and make your first experience with computers frustrating.

If you are already putting your computer to good use, you've probably found yourself in the position of unofficial guru to friends and associates still new to the personal computing game. That is exactly the position Jackie Crews, a manager of technical documentation at McCormack and Dodge, a mainframe software developer in Natwick, Massachusetts, found herself in after she purchased her first personal computer.

Experienced User.   "I've had some friends call me who are absolutely terrified of using a personal computer," which Crews attributes in part to their not having experienced anything quite like it before. "I know if I don't know something I can always look it up. My friends who are new to it have this compulsion to try to learn everything they can. They do things like make lists of the commands from the documentation and try to memorize them." In fact, your time can often be spent more effectively understanding the concepts of how a computer or program works than memorizing procedures.

"Proficiency in personal computing means essentially that you're able to do things in a reasonable amount of time," notes Dr. Jay Sedlick at National Training Systems in Santa Monica, California. In many cases, it's "inefficient to become an expert," says Sedlick. "As a user, you're not like a fighter pilot who has to know everything there is to know about operating the plane because survival depends on it. There's no penalty for looking something up in the manual."

Computing or Skiing.   Then there is the question of how much time to invest in learning a given program. The amount of time for mastery is going to vary depending on the program itself and your own capacity for, and interest in, learning it. As a general rule of thumb, you should get enough grasp of a program to be able to use it productively if you spend a weekend learning it—with about the same intensity you approach a ski weekend.

But don't fear. There is hope for those who would rather go skiing on weekends than curl up to a Lotus 1-2-3 manual. Training courses and tutorial software abound. However, the usefulness of such courses and materials varies greatly.

Like the applications they are designed to explain, tutorial software packages range from introductory programs, designed to teach the fundamentals of computing, to ones focused on the more sophisticated applications, such as Lotus's Symphony and Ashton-Tate's Framework integrated packages.

Instructional software is cheap (programs are typically in the $50 to $75 range) and can be used in the privacy of your home, office, or wherever your computer is.

But even the best instruction is only a partial solution. Nobody is going to teach you everything there is to know about computing and how you should best use your personal computer.

Lisa Figoli, who had to learn WordStar on her own as part of her job, found her own solution. A trip to the bookstore resulted in the purchase of a handy reference for learning how to do specific tasks such as boilerplating paragraphs using WordStar.

She was also aided by a series of interactive training disks, which she used at home on her husband's IBM PC-compatible Compaq computer. "I liked the (training) software because it gave me an idea of how to do word processing. It got me excited about computing," says Figoli. As she discovered, the smart way to learn computing is the way that best suits you.

(*SOURCE: Reprinted with permission from Personal Computing, June 1985, pp. 101–106. Copyright 1985, Hayden Publishing Company.*)

SHORTCUTS FOR EASIER LEARNING

1. *Try to Grasp Universal Concepts*.   Loading a program into memory and saving data to disk are concepts common to all programs. Program-specific commands will be learned more readily once you have an overall comprehension of common operations.

2. *Don't Presuppose Complexity*.   A fear among some people new to computing is that they won't be able to learn because they aren't "computer-oriented" (which probably means they got a "C" in high school algebra). But relatively few of the popular applications require extensive mathematical knowledge or training. Word processing surely doesn't.

3. *Be as Good as You Have to Be*.   You don't have to be a computer expert—or even an expert of a particular application—to make good use of a program. To perform certain complex operations in

some programs, try opening the manual and simply following the procedures without trying to memorize them. If you use any function enough, you'll remember it.

4. *Conquer the Keyboard.*   If you don't know how to type, everything you do on the computer is going to seem awfully slow compared to those in the office who do. Even though they may only know how to run one program, they know where to find the keys. If you're using the computer mainly as a decision-support tool and/or to do number-crunching, it may not be important for you to learn how to type well. But if you're going to be doing a lot of text-oriented work, it becomes a priority to be at ease with the keyboard. A number of low-cost software packages teach typing.

5. *Diagnose Your Input Errors.*   The cliché "garbage in, garbage out" dates back to the early days of mainframe computers, but it can be applied just as readily to any computer on the market today. Just as software, or the set of instructions that programs a computer, gives hardware its smarts, so will giving bad or false information make any computer look dumb. Operator error is the most frequent cause of a problem.

6. *Look for On-screen Help.*   Most of the early personal computer enthusiasts learned how to use their computers the hard way, by plowing through difficult, often poorly organized documentation. That's no longer necessary. On-line help screens are available and easily accessible in even the most powerful business/professional applications.

7. *Find the Right Software.*   If you find that a program is too difficult to learn and help is not readily available, try a different one. Many relatively easy-to-use programs cover the most common personal computer applications—word processing, database, spreadsheet analysis, graphing, and communications—comprehensively enough so they'll accomplish much of what most people want to do. Don't buy the most complicated (and expensive) programs unless you know you will really need them.

DISCUSSION QUESTION

1. Defend the statement "For most of us, becoming an expert is not the primary goal in computing; it is developing enough understanding to get the job done."

2. Because few employers provide the uninterrupted, relaxed time necessary to learn how to use a computer, what advice would help a potential job hunter?

CHAPTER SUMMARY

- People who use computers are frequently called *end-users*, or simply *users*.
- A traditional classification of computers is: *microcomputers* (small computers), *minicomputers* (medium-sized computers), and *mainframes* or *mainframe computers* (large computers).
- A small desktop-sized *personal computer* is technically called called a microcomputer.
- A *multiuser computer* supports several people simultaneously.
- *Terminals*, unlike microcomputers, have no system unit, or ability to do their own processing. They are used with multiuser computers.
- *Hardware* is the physical part of a computer.
- *Software* is another term for the programs that tell the computer what to do. Without software, hardware is useless.

- *Application software* applies a computer to a specific user task.
- *Packaged software* is ready-made software.
- A writer might improve personal productivity with word processing software. A manager might use spreadsheet software to help calculate numbers for decision making.
- *File* and *database management software* enables users to set up, maintain, and manipulate data, as well as to create custom file-based applications without programming.
- Purchased *accounting* and *industry-specific* software *packages* automate day-to-day operations in small- to medium-sized organizations. The packages generally also produce management information.
- *Communication software* allows cooperating computing devices to transmit and receive data. It also

enables the use of *on-line databases* of information and other services, like *electronic mail*.

- *Networking*, or linking computers, allows the sharing of data, such as customer files, and resources, such as printers.

- *Local area networking* is a recent approach to sharing a company's database and expensive disks and printers by using mainly microcomputers.

- Newer uses of microcomputers include *desktop publishing* and *knowledge-based systems*.

- A purchased software package typically contains *floppy disks* of programs and a *User Guide* of instructions for how to use the programs.

- Disks contain two types of files: *program files* (an example is a spreadsheet program file) and *data files* (an example is a budget file created with the spreadsheet program).

- *DOS* is an acronym for *disk operating system*. It is special software that manages everything that happens inside the computer.

- A *computing system* consists of interrelated hardware, software, people, and procedures.

- *Input* is computer jargon to put something in a computer. *Output* is to get something out. Between the two, *processing* occurs to transform input into output.

- Computer *memory* offers only temporary *storage*. That is why users begin a computer session by loading memory with programs and data from disk *storage*.

- Everything inside the computer's memory is represented by a *binary system* of on or off electronic pulses.

- A *bit* is one binary digit. Eight bits are called a *byte*.

- A *byte* is the fundamental unit with which a computer works.

- *ASCII* is an acronym for *American Standard Code* for *Information Interchange*. It is a 7-bit code that is a computer industry standard for minicomputers and microcomputers.

- Sources to learn more about computers include books, periodicals, user groups, shows, exhibitions, and conferences.

KEY TERMS

Accounting package	Floppy disks	Processor
American Standard Code for Information Interchange (ASCII)	Graphics package	Program files
	Hardware	Programs
Application software	Industry-specific package	Public-domain software
Binary system	Input	Software
Bits	Local-area network	Spreadsheet package
Bytes	Mainframe computer	Storage
Central processing unit	Microcomputer	System unit
Communication software	Minicomputer	Terminals
Computer system	Multiuser environment	Third party
Database administrator	Networking	User
Database management software	Operating system	User groups
Data files	Output	*User Guide*
Desktop publishing	Packaged software	Word processing package
Disk operating system (DOS)	Personal computer	
File management software	Processing	

REVIEW QUESTIONS

1. What is a traditional classification of computers?
2. Differentiate between a microcomputer and a terminal. Where are terminals used?
3. Contrast hardware and software.
4. What is application software?

5. Give examples of how users improve their personal productivity with computers.

6. What is database software used for?

7. What kind of software is used to automate routine day-to-day operations at small-to-medium-sized companies?

8. Why do users buy communication software?

9. What are the typical contents of a software package bought at a computer store?

10. Identify two types of files typically found on a disk. Give an example of each type.

11. What is DOS?

12. What is a computer system?

13. Draw a diagram to show the relationship of input, processing, and output.

14. Why do users begin a computer session by placing floppy disks in disk drives?

15. Compare bits and bytes.

16. Identify sources that can help a person to learn more about computers.

EXERCISES

1. *C. Davidson Case.* After Charles Davidson bought a microcomputer, he found many computer publications that were of interest. Instead of subscribing to all of them, he asks you to investigate which ones are available at the library.
   a. Make a list of all the computer periodicals your library subscribes to.
   b. Classify the periodicals according to the following categories:
      · General publications
      · Product-specific publications
      · Computer-literate audience publications
   c. Examine one periodical from each category and identify article topics that overlap across publications.
   d. Pick one topic and read it in all three publications. Make a summary of your investigation that specifies for each article
      · Publication examined and article title.
      · A short summary with a list of things you did not understand. Indicate which of the three you found to be the most helpful and explain why.

2. *C. Davidson Case.* Mr. Davidson liked your library investigatory work and has asked you to do another project. This involves finding out about the local computer user group.
   a. Visit a local computer user group meeting. Write a report on what transpires there. Make a list of what you did not understand.
   b. At the end of your computer study, review the list to see how many items you can answer yourself.

3. Visit a local computer show, exhibition, or conference. Make a written or oral report about your field trip. Include in the report
   · Hardware you liked the best and why
   · Software you thought was especially interesting and why

2

Microcomputer Hardware

AFTER READING THIS CHAPTER, YOU SHOULD BE ABLE TO

- Identify the basic input, output, and processing hardware components of a business-use microcomputer

- Differentiate between the "PC and compatibles standard" and the new emerging standards

- Initiate a systematic evaluation of microcomputer hardware to make a buying or upgrade decision

This chapter is about **hardware,** the physical part of a computer. Figure 2-1 illustrates some of the basic hardware components of a business-use personal microcomputer. Components include the keyboard, display, printer, disk drives, and system unit. They are all discussed in this chapter. Discussions of hardware related to use of communications, graphics, and desktop publishing applications are reserved for separate chapters in this book.

This chapter traces how Frank Nelson, a marketing manager at Interstate Distributing Company, systematically approaches the hardware-buying decision. He is a new computer user at a modest-size company who decides that his best choice is a traditional, well-established, microcomputer. He considers all the input, output, and processing components that make up a microcomputer's hardware.

FIGURE 2-1
THE IBM Personal Computer
(*Courtesy of IBM*)

The discussion begins by examining the "PC standard" as well as new emerging standards that dominate the microcomputer hardware industry. It concludes with discussions of new microprocessor technology and hardware-buying evaluation considerations.

Informed buyers determine the software needed *first*, then they select the hardware *second*. Software discussions occupy most of the chapters in this book. To understand the software discussions, it helps to be familiar with hardware fundamentals.

BUSINESS STANDARDS

Mr. Nelson's buying research convinced him of the need to buy a standard business-use, instead of home-use, personal microcomputer. At the time he bought, an IBM Personal Computer (IBM PC), shown in Figure 2-1, or one compatible with it, was considered the **personal computer (PC),** or **PC standard.** The term indicates that, as Figure 2-2 shows, there are more IBM and compatibles in use than any other type of microcomputer by an overwhelming proportion.

The major microcomputers in the IBM PC family, which generated the "PC standard," are identified in Figure 2-3. When the "PC standard"

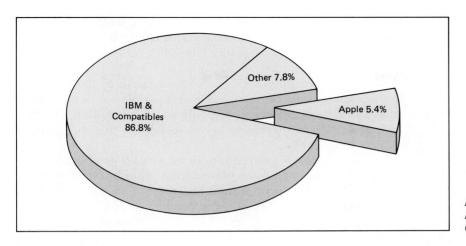

FIGURE 2-2
Installed microcomputers by brand
(Source: International Data Corp., May 1987)

FIGURE 2-3
Major microcomputers in the IBM PC
family which generated the "PC standard"

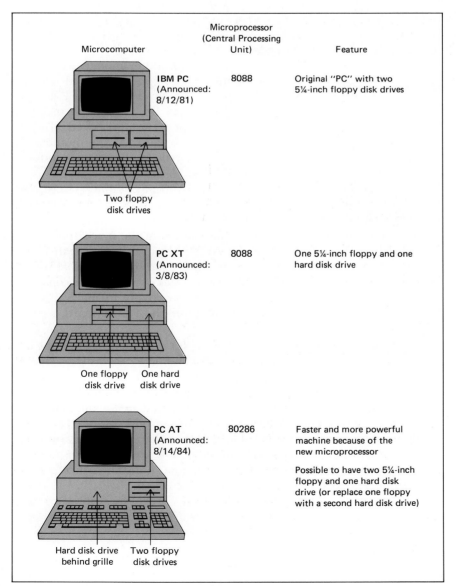

is emulated, or copied, by other manufacturers, their products are called **compatibles,** or **clones.** Compatibles manufacturers usually advertise that their products meet, for instance, the "PC AT standard" or the "PC standard."

Because IBM copyrighted a critical component in its hardware, no compatible computer can be completely compatible—at least legally. So manufacturers attempt to attain compatibility while including features, such as portability or an alternative keyboard design, that differentiate their products from IBM's.

Mr. Nelson's approach assured him of an already established computer support environment. Over 3,000 business programs were available for the PC standard. This is important because not all programs work on all computers. Only a PC standard computer could take advantage of this wealth of available programs. No other computer product had anywhere near the same selection.

In addition, hardware service was available from the PC standard manufacturer, as well as from many independent companies. A community user group existed that could bail him out if he had a problem. These considerations influenced his buying decision.

Many desktop and portable personal computer models were available when he shopped. Most claimed to be compatible with the PC standard. A list of some available products is given in Figure 2-4.

Mr. Nelson was on his own. He worked for a small- to medium-sized sporting goods distributor that had not yet computerized. His purchase would start a long-term automation project. At the moment, he felt confident in following a generally acknowledged computer industry standard.

Although some more technologically advanced computers were available, they would first have to prove themselves in the business marketplace. It takes several years for business standards to evolve.

One personal microcomputer that came into the marketplace after the IBM Personal Computer is the Apple Macintosh, shown in Figure 2-5. It had nothing in common with the PC standard. None of the PC standard programs worked on it. Its original lack of widespread consumer acceptance encouraged its manufacturer eventually to make a model that could run all the software available for the PC standard, such as the one shown in Figure 2-6.

Probably the most important reason for a company to adopt one standard, versus several, is that programs and data can easily be shared. *Sharing* may simply mean carrying a floppy disk from one personal computer to another. If the two computers are compatible, the data can be read by either. If they are not, it could mean no sharing or possibly reentering data from scratch on the second computer.

If hardware and software all adhered to the same standard, there would be no problem. Computer-literate people are aware that potential problems exist when dealing with mixed, or nonstandard, computer products.

PRODUCT	MODEL
Desktop Models	
Advanced Logic Research	Access 386
AST Research	Premium
AT&T	7300
	6300 Plus
Apple	Macintosh II
	II
	IIe
Compaq	Deskpro
Computer Direct	CD/286
Epson	Equity
Hewlett-Packard	Vectra
	Touchscreen
IBM	Personal Computer
	Personal Computer XT
	Personal Computer AT
	Personal System/2
ITT	Xtra
Kaypro	286i
Leading Edge	Model D
Multitech	Accel
NCR	PC Model 8
NEC	APC IV PowerMate
Olivetti	M28
PC Designs	GV-386
PC Limited	386
Proteus Technology	286 Standard
Sperry	PC/microIT
Tandy	3000
	4000
Texas Instruments	Business Pro
Unisys	PC/HT
Zenith	ZW-248
Portable Models	
Apple	Macintosh
	Macintosh SE
	IIc
Compaq	Portable
Data General	One
Datavue	Spark
	Snap
Grid	Grid
Hewlett-Packard	Portable Plus
IBM	PC Convertible
Kaypro	2000
NEC	MultiSpeed
Panasonic	Executive Partner
Sanyo	MBC
Sharp	PC-7100
Tandy	1400
Wang	Laptop
Zenith	183

FIGURE 2-4
A sampler of personal microcomputers

9-inch display

System unit

Slot to insert one 3½-inch floppy disk

Keyboard

Mouse

FIGURE 2-5
The Apple Macintosh microcomputer
(Courtesy of Apple Computer, Inc.)

FIGURE 2-6
The Apple Macintosh II, which can run all the software that runs on a
PC standard microcomputer (Courtesy of Apple Computer, Inc.)

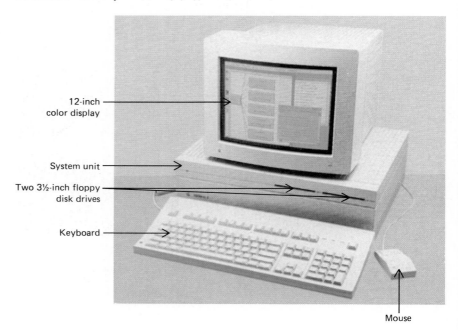

12-inch color display

System unit

Two 3½-inch floppy disk drives

Keyboard

Mouse

EMERGING STANDARDS

IBM introduced a successor to the PC standard in 1987. The new line is called the **Personal System/2** (a short form is **PS/2**). It represents a new generation of computers, and potentially a new standard. Figure 2-7 shows one of the computers, a floor-standing version, from this new line.

The Personal System/2 uses a 3½-inch floppy disk, which is incompatible with the PC standard's 5¼-inch floppy disk. Figure 2-7 demonstrates a solution to deal with such a mixed standard. An optional device, such as the 5¼-inch external disk drive shown, could be used to swap old PC standard data or programs between the machines. Other swapping solutions exist, but most require some kind of conversion process.

Figure 2-8 shows a desktop computer from the new PS/2 line, which resembles the earlier computers. The PS/2 line is **downward compatible,** which means it will run all the software that runs on PC standard micro-computers using the Disk Operating System (DOS).

But the PS/2 hardware is best exploited by a new operating system called **Operating System/2** (a short form is **OS/2**). Software vendors must rewrite their software to tap the power of OS/2. New application software that works with OS/2 is expected to evolve over time.

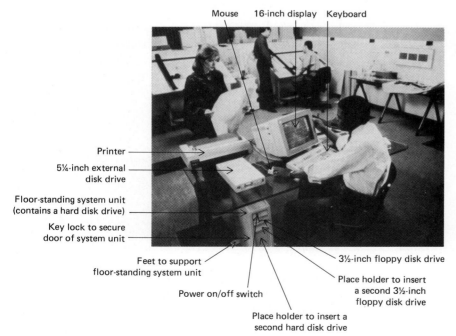

FIGURE 2-7
The IBM Personal System/2 Model 80,
a floor-standing microcomputer
(Courtesy of IBM)

12-inch display

System unit

3½-inch floppy disk drive (and one concealed hard disk drive)

Keyboard

FIGURE 2-8
The IBM Personal System/2 Model 50, which resembles an original IBM PC (Courtesy of IBM)

Users only reluctantly abandon their old comfortable application software to upgrade. It is costly to buy new software and to spend time learning how to use it.

The earlier PC standard, some computer industry analysts predict, is far from dead. Over 10 million have been installed, and they will probably continue to serve well for many more years. Users usually keep a microcomputer, at least a first one, for three or more years. They rarely attempt quick changeovers.

Investing in the new standard does have benefits, though, that cannot be ignored. They arise from new hardware technology built into the PS/2 line. Most of it is not visible. The new technology is addressed, whenever appropriate, in the following sections that cover each component in a typical microcomputer system:

- Input hardware—keyboard and other devices
- Output hardware—displays and printers
- Storage hardware—floppy and hard disks
- Processing hardware—microprocessor chips and related hardware, such as memory chips

KEYBOARD INPUT

A **keyboard** is the traditional way to get input into a computer. The keyboard that comes with Mr. Nelson's microcomputer resembles the one shown in Figure 2-9. It is a typical keyboard on a business-use microcomputer. Part of it looks like a familiar typewriter keyboard. This similarity helps to shorten the learning curve for those new users, like Mr. Nelson, who already know how to type a little.

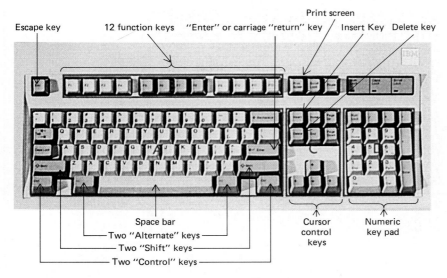

Escape key   12 function keys   "Enter" or carriage "return" key   Print screen   Insert Key   Delete key

Space bar
Two "Alternate" keys
Two "Shift" keys
Two "Control" keys

Cursor control keys

Numeric key pad

FIGURE 2-9
Typical keyboard with function keys, numeric keypad that incorporates cursor control keys, and auxiliary keys (Courtesy of IBM)

If completely unfamiliar with typing, he could have used one of several disk tutorials on keyboarding. Many applications do not, however, require a great deal of keyboarding skill. Word processing is an obvious exception.

The separate **numeric keypad** is for speeding data entry in numeric-oriented applications. The **cursor control keys,** also called **arrow keys,** are another separate bank of keys. They allow cursor manipulation. The **cursor** is the tiny underscore, often set to blinking, on the display, as shown in Figure 2-10. It always indicates the position where the next typed character will appear. It is usually found after a **prompt,** which is a message for some user action, as shown in the example in Figure 2-11. It indicates that a keyboard entry is required.

When doing word processing, Mr. Nelson uses the arrow keys to move the cursor right, left, up, and down around the screen. He holds an arrow key down longer than one stroke timing to zoom the cursor to the place in the text where a change is to be made.

An unfamiliar group of keys Mr. Nelson learned about are the **function keys.** They are also called *program function keys* and are referenced as F1 or PF1, or whatever number applies. Programmers call them *soft keys* because their functions are controlled by software.

Mr. Nelson's word processing software uses the F8 key to underline text and the F10 key to save text. Another application uses the same keys differently. It gets confusing at times. To help remember function key assignments, some users attach labels to keys as reminders. Computer stores sell cardboard **keyboard templates** that overlay function keys and have a place to write memory-jogging labels for function key actions.

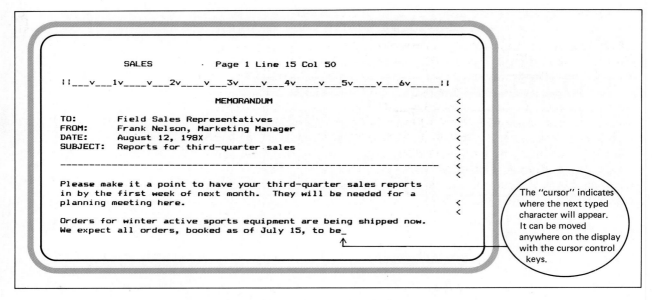

FIGURE 2-10
A cursor as it appears in a word processing memo

FIGURE 2-11
Often a cursor is found after a user prompt for a keyboard entry.
(Adaptation of Volkswriter software with permission of Lifetree Software, Inc.)

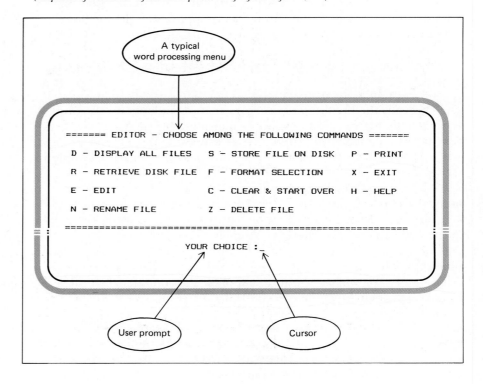

Keyboard Alternatives

Alternatives to keyboarding include a pointer device called a *mouse*, *touch-sensitive displays*, and *voice*. All require specialized software to integrate with a given computer and application.

The **mouse** is a pointing device that functions much like the cursor control arrow keys. It is a standard input device on the Macintosh microcomputer, as shown in Figure 2-12. As the mouse is physically moved around the desktop, a mouse **pointer** on the display moves.

In Figure 2-12, the pointer is directed at a menu item. The menu is called a **pull-down,** or **drop-down, menu** because it appears only in response to the selection at the top of the menu list. Selecting an item requires a click of the mouse's button. At the moment, the pointer indicates selection of the "change" function to alter word processing text on the display.

FIGURE 2-12
Using a mouse to make menu selections
(*Macintosh microcomputer and MacWrite software,*
courtesy of Apple Computer, Inc.)

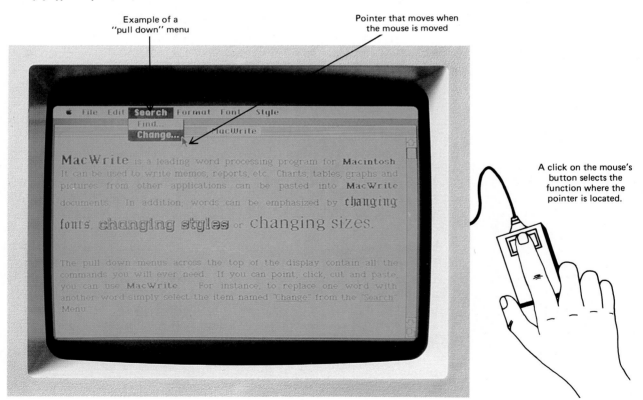

Example of a
"pull down" menu

Pointer that moves when
the mouse is moved

A click on the mouse's
button selects the
function where the
pointer is located.

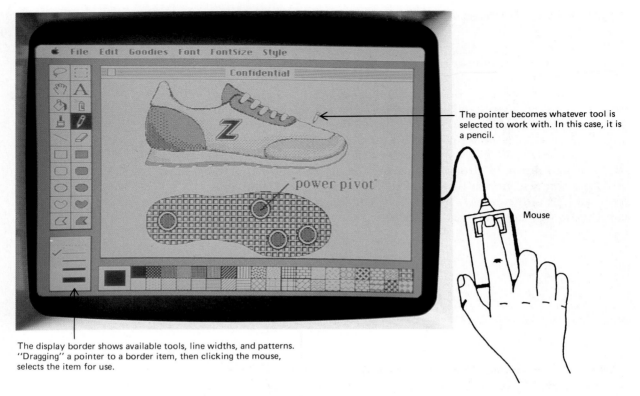

The pointer becomes whatever tool is selected to work with. In this case, it is a pencil.

Mouse

The display border shows available tools, line widths, and patterns. ''Dragging'' a pointer to a border item, then clicking the mouse, selects the item for use.

FIGURE 2-13
Using a mouse to move a "pencil tool" for free-form drawing
(Software: Macintosh microcomputer and MacPaint, courtesy of Apple Computer, Inc.)

The Macintosh screen pointer can assume another shape. As the example in Figure 2-13 demonstrates, it has become a pencil with which to draw a product image on the screen. Specialized software makes the pointer change shapes.

Some users find any diversion of their hands from the keyboard disruptive. The mouse, nonetheless, is gaining popularity as an input device, especially with software that is fashioned in the so-called "Macintosh style."

Touch-sensitive displays are another alternative to keyboards for entering data into a computer. Hewlett-Packard's Touchscreen Personal Computer, as shown in Figure 2-14, is activated by touching the screen and blocking light beams, as diagrammed in Figure 2-15. Some futurists predict that the touchscreen will replace the mouse for professional and occasional use. Its use already is important in educational and graphic applications.

Voice recognition, another alternative to keyboards, uses a microphone for sound input, as shown in Figure 2-16. It remains limited in interpreting human words accurately and requires large amounts of computer memory to process.

FIGURE 2-14
A touch-sensitive display
(*Courtesy of Hewlett-Packard*)

Most voice systems available today are speaker dependent: each operator must train the system to recognize his or her voice pattern. This involves repeating words or phrases three or more times. The words are digitized and stored as data on disk. Later, when a word is spoken as a command to the computer, its sound pattern must match one of those previously stored. After a match, the program continues to perform whatever it was designed to do.

FIGURE 2-15
A grid of hidden infrared light beams surrounds the outside of some touch-sensitive screens.

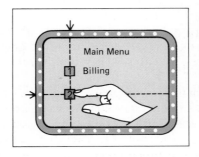

FIGURE 2-16
Using voice-recognition input
(*Courtesy of Texas Instruments*)

Many voice systems are called *discrete word recognizers* because a user must pause very slightly between words or phrases. Inputting command words or phrases can involve awkward repetition and mismatches.

Some researchers predict that efficient voice recognition devices are years away from serious commercial use. At least one computer vendor, however, demonstrates its voice-recognition progress by showing a researcher using plain spoken English to command a computer to take dictated letters.

DISPLAY OUTPUT

When he bought his computer, Mr. Nelson had to select a TV-like **display,** which is also called a **monitor.** It is one of the normal devices for viewing computer-processed output. Initially Mr. Nelson had to decide whether he wanted a monochrome or a color display.

Monochrome

Monochrome displays present only one color, usually green, amber, or black, against a solid background on the screen. Because they are the least expensive choice, with some costing under $100, monochrome displays are the most popular type used. They are preferred for text applications, like word processing. Text is usually displayed in 80 columns by 25 rows, as shown in Figure 2-17.

Figure 2-17
Text displays divide a screen into 80 columns by 25 rows.

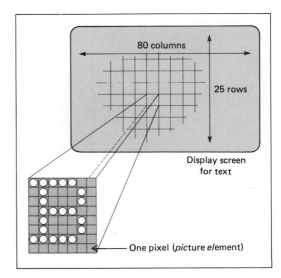

80 columns

25 rows

Display screen for text

One pixel (*pic*ture *el*ement)

Resolution

Monochrome displays usually have *high resolution*. **Resolution** refers to the number of distinguishable points or dots on the display. The higher the resolution, the more precise the image.

One manufacturer divides its screen into 960 columns by 240 rows. This gives the screen 230,400 points, or pixels. **Pixel** is a term for one *pic*ture *ele*ment. Through appropriate software, each pixel can be turned on or off. Each can also be assigned a color.

When displaying ordinary character text, the greater the number of pixels forming each individual character, the more solid each character appears on the screen. For graphics, more pixels mean sharper images.

Color

Mr. Nelson thought seriously about buying a color display because most new software packages make use of color. Research shows that color conveys ideas and impressions faster than words or numbers alone. Columns of numbers showing negative amounts in red are an example of conveying information through color.

If the choice is for a color display, then a decision must be made between a *composite* or an *RGB monitor*. Less expensive color displays, called **composite monitors,** are like ordinary television sets. They use a simple composite video color signal. **RGB monitors** use a refined color separation technology to produce high-quality color images. The RGB acronym stands for red, green, and blue. Generally, the more expensive the color display, the better the image quality.

To examine quality on RGB monitors, Mr. Nelson used a standard test method by filling the screen with one letter in one color, say "H." It is done by pressing the "H" key and holding it down. Then he checked the display, especially around the edges of the screen. The presence of other colors indicates poor quality or screen problems.

Then he moved the cursor across the screen at maximum speed by holding down the space bar. One display showed a trail or smear behind the cursor. The trail could prove unpleasant in applications with rapidly changing images. Flickering images on another model produced eyestrain.

Despite the effectiveness of these tests, he decided that the most important test was his own viewing comfort. He stared at screens, both alone and in side-by-side comparisons, to see if he liked what he saw. Are the colors right? Is the resolution adequate? Do ordinary text characters look good?

Display Connection

Mr. Nelson had to buy a separate piece of hardware to enable the display to "talk to" the computer. The hardware is called a number of things, such as a **display, graphics,** or **video**

- **Adapter**
- **Board**
- **Card**
- **Interface**
- **Circuit board**

An example of this hardware is given in Figure 2-18. It must be inserted, as shown in Figure 2-19, into a slot in the computer's system unit. The *system unit* of a computer houses its main electronic circuitry. A cable physically connects the display to the circuit board once it is "seated" in the computer's system unit.

Circuit boards are a common way to attach so-called "peripheral" devices such as displays, printers, and disk drives to the computer's system unit. All circuit boards look similar, regardless of the function they serve.

The display circuit board must match one of several available graphic capabilities of the computer. The capabilities are known as graphic "standards" and are discussed in Chapter 6, "Graphics Packages."

While the PC standard computer requires a circuit board to connect the display to the system unit, the PS/2 computers do not. They have the necessary circuitry already built in. Only a display must be selected. The display uses analog signals that produce many more color gradations than the digital displays used on the PC standard. The difference between the two can be compared to a light dimmer and a light switch. A light dimmer is an analog device and can produce many various shadings of light. By contrast, a light switch is a digital device. It can produce

FIGURE 2-18
An example of a circuit board
(Courtesy of AMDEK Corporation)

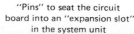

"Pins" to seat the circuit board into an "expansion slot" in the system unit

Keyboard

Cover of system unit

Display

Circuit board being inserted into an "expansion slot" in the system unit

System unit pulled out from its cover

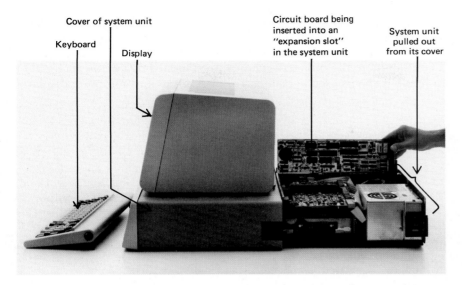

FIGURE 2-19
Inserting a circuit board into an
expansion slot in the system unit
(Courtesy of Anderson Jacobson)

no shadings. It is either on or off. Displays using digital technology usually produce fewer colors at a time than their analog counterparts.

Flat-Panel Displays

Flat-panel displays often come on small portable microcomputers, like the one shown in Figure 2-20. One of the display technologies used is the familiar *liquid crystal*, such as that used in an ordinary wristwatch.

Flat panel display

FIGURE 2-20
Using a portable computer with a flat-
panel display
(Radio Shack portable computer, courtesy of
Radio Shack, a Division of Tandy Corp.)

Flat-panel displays often cost more than standard displays and have less clarity. Some are difficult to read when viewed from a side angle. Nonetheless, they enable designing portability into a microcomputer. They eliminate the bulk associated with standard *cathode ray tube* (*CRT*) technology that is used in ordinary television sets and computer displays.

PRINTED OUTPUT

Not all computer output is displayed. A good deal of it is also printed. Microcomputer printers can

- Print text at a speedy 700 characters per second
- Produce characters of perfect quality
- Dazzle with color graphics
- Cost less than a portable typewriter

Unfortunately, no one printer has all these characteristics combined. Trade-offs are inevitable, and Mr. Nelson had to make a choice. He also had to do some preplanning about print quality, speed, and the software that would be used.

As a first step, he had to decide what primary job the printer would be used for. Would it mainly print text or graphic images? He also had to decide where printed documents would be used. Printed material sent outside the company had to be of a higher quality than that sent inside the company. Most companies like to project a quality image to customers and others through their printed material.

Then he had to estimate his printing volume and speed. He could print material at slow characters-per-second to faster pages-per-minute speeds. Typical speed requirements come from estimating the lines of printing done each workday, divided by a printer's speed. The result gives the time necessary to complete a printing task. Tasks should finish in the time planned for them, or the printer is too slow for the job.

In many cases, while printing is going on, the computer cannot be used for anything else. If printing takes three hours, the computer cannot be scheduled for any other use. But programs are available that allow printing and other tasks to occur simultaneously.

Still another consideration is software and printer interfacing: Will they "talk" to each other? Printers have specific commands that move margins, change line spacing, and the like. Most software packages list the printers with which they work. For the most part, popular software works with popular printers.

Once the necessary preplanning of printer quality, speed, and inter-face is completed, it is time to compare individual models. Before reaching that stage, Mr. Nelson learned the basics about the main printer types available:

- Letter quality
- Dot matrix
- Ink jet
- Laser

Letter-Quality Printers

Letter-quality printers produce high-quality, correspondence-level printing that is appropriate to send outside a company. Their characters are formed by *daisy wheel* or *thimble* elements, as shown in Figure 2-21. Characters are molded, one on each petal of the daisy wheel. The little 4-inch diameter wheel constantly spins. When the correct character at the end of the spoke reaches the 12 o'clock position, it is hammered

FIGURE 2-21
A formed-character letter-quality printer.
Such printers use either a daisy wheel
or a thimble element to produce fully
formed characters.
(*Top left*: *courtesy of NEC Information Systems,*
Inc.; *top right*: *courtesy of ITT Qume, San*
Jose, CA; *bottom*: *courtesy of Hewlett-Packard*)

Thimble element   Daisy wheel element

onto an inked ribbon which strikes the paper. A *thimble* works much like a daisy wheel.

A letter-quality daisy wheel printer changes character style by physically changing the daisy wheel. Wheels slip in and out of their protective housing in the printhead.

Letter-quality printers print slowly, often under 100 characters per second. They are being displaced by more flexible dot-matrix printers.

Dot-Matrix Printers

For flexible printing requirements, from rough drafts to company correspondence and graphics, users often get a **dot-matrix printer.** These printers compose characters with dots arranged in a matrix, much like the pixels on a display. Characters are produced by software-controlled pins that are activated against an inked ribbon, as shown in Figure 2-22. A comparison of dot-matrix and letter-quality characters appears in Figure 2-23.

Like daisy wheel printers, dot-matrix printers are noisy, but they are faster, are usually less expensive, and offer more capabilities. Some can print up to 700 characters per second.

A dot-matrix printer's capability becomes apparent when preparing wide spreadsheets. A 12-month spreadsheet normally is too wide to fit across a standard 80-column-wide personal printer. One solution is to print the spreadsheet in sections and glue them together. A better solution with a dot-matrix printer is to use a program that rotates the spreadsheet 90 degrees. When printed horizontally instead of vertically, the spreadsheet fits neatly on one piece of paper. Such a solution is impossible with a letter-quality printer.

Some printers are 132 columns or characters wide, a carry-over from the standard width of mainframe computer printers. This width is often useful for wide spreadsheets, accounting, and other reports. Continuous-form computer stock paper, as shown in Figure 2-24, is available for printers either 80 or 132 characters wide.

FIGURE 2-22
(A) A dot-matrix printing head. (B) Building a solid-looking character. These dots show the letter "B" being formed by a dot-matrix printer after one pass and after multiple passes.

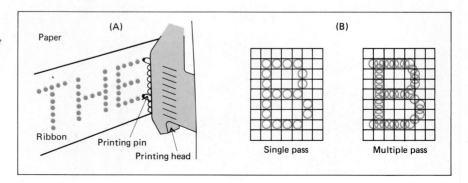

LETTER-QUALITY

"Script"-style daisy wheel print example:

ABCDEFGHIJKLMNOPQRSTUVWXYZ abcdefghijklmnopqrstuvwxyz
1234567890

"Roman"-style daisy wheel print example:

ABCDEFGHIJKLMNOPQRSTUVWXYZ abcdefghijklmnopqrstuvwxyz
1234567890

DOT-MATRIX

Condensed print example:

ABCDEFGHIJKLMNOPQRSTUVWZYX abcdefghijklmnopqrstuvwxyz
1234567890

Standard print example:

ABCDEFGHIJKLMNOPQRSTUVWXYZ abcdefghijklmnopqrstuvwxyz
1234567890

Expanded print example:

ABCDEFGHIJKLMNOPQRSTUVWZYX
abcdefghijklmnopqrstuvwxyz
1234567890

FIGURE 2-23
Comparison of letter-quality and dot-matrix print

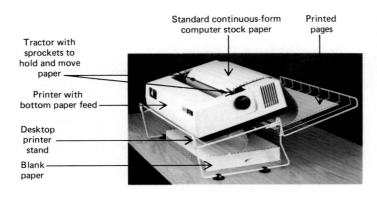

Standard continuous-form computer stock paper

Printed pages

Tractor with sprockets to hold and move paper

Printer with bottom paper feed

Desktop printer stand

Blank paper

FIGURE 2-24
Example of standard continuous-form
computer stock paper
(Courtesy of Global Computer Supplies)

Example of
graphic
capability

Example of
four different
type styles

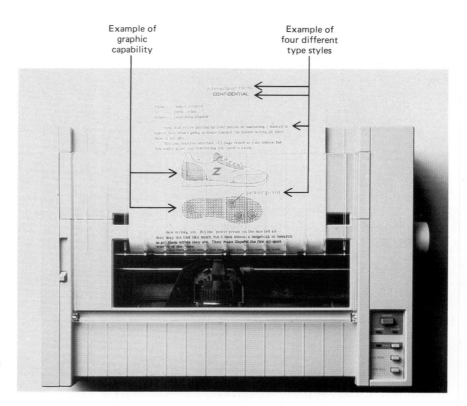

FIGURE 2-25
Print possibilities with a dot-matrix
printer
(Courtesy of Apple Computer, Inc.)

Another example of a dot-matrix printer's capability appears in Figure 2-25. Graphics mix with ordinary text of various type styles. Printing is entirely controlled by software.

Some dot-matrix printers, which are called **near letter-quality printers,** provide even more capabilities. These printers produce both rough-draft- and letter-, or correspondence-, quality output. High-quality print is accomplished with repeated printhead passes and various pinhead arrangements, such as those shown in Figure 2-26. Specifications for one example printer include the following:

Quality	Dot Matrix	Speed in Characters per Second
Letter	18×48	100
Rough draft	9×7	290

FIGURE 2-26
Examples of dot-matrix pin head layouts

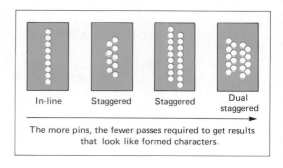

The print quality possible from a near letter-quality printer is fast making the daisy-wheel printer obsolete.

Ink-Jet Printers

Ink-jet printers, like the small one in Figure 2-27, project drops of ink onto the paper's surface. Ink-jet printers can produce high-quality output at 30–270 characters per second.

Like dot-matrix printers, software controls printing. It enables a wide choice of type styles as well as graphic images to be printed. Some versions can produce print in color but cost more. One color version is claimed to produce "near-offset-quality." It is treading on the polished "typeset" look offered by laser printers.

Laser Printers

Mr. Nelson learned that **laser printers,** such as the one in Figure 2-28, print on paper like ordinary copy machines. Internally a laser printer projects a beam of laser light to form character or graphic images on a rotating drum. The images are covered with ink, like copy toner, before they are transferred to plain paper. At least one company markets a dual-function laser printer/copier. Laser printers can cost several thousand dollars and print more than five pages per minute. They are considered volume printers and are smaller versions of page-printing systems used in large organizations.

FIGURE 2-27
An ink-jet printer
(*Hewlett-Packard Thinkjet printer, courtesy of Hewlett-Packard*)

Laser printer

FIGURE 2-28
A laser printer
(Hewlett-Packard LaserJet Series II printer,
courtesy of Hewlett-Packard)

Laser printers surpass many others because they can produce images that resemble not just typewriter quality, but professional typeset quality. An example of this print quality appears in Figure 2-29. It is a quality favored by companies that do their own in-house desktop publishing. A separate discussion in Chapter 13, "Desktop Publishing," considers the laser printer's publishing role.

FIGURE 2-29
This newsletter is an example of laser-
quality printing. (LaserWriter printing,
courtesy of Apple Computer, Inc.)

PRINTER TYPE	EXAMPLE OF SPEED
Letter quality	12–100 characters per second
Dot matrix	40–700 characters per second
Ink jet	30–300 characters per second
Laser	5–28 pages per minute

FIGURE 2-30
Some personal printer choices

A summary of personal computer printer choices appears in Figure 2-30.

STORAGE

Computers lose everything in memory when the power is shut off. To preserve both programs and data from destruction, Mr. Nelson's computer comes with disk drives for more permanent storage. The drives can house floppy or hard disk storage media.

Drives and Disks

The personal computer Mr. Nelson bought came with one built-in floppy disk drive, much like those in Figure 2-1. A **disk drive** is a unit that houses, and physically provides access to, disks during use by a program.

Disk drives work with either floppy or hard disks. **Disks** are magnetic storage media for data and programs. They contain an invisible coating which is stamped during use with positive and negative fields, represented

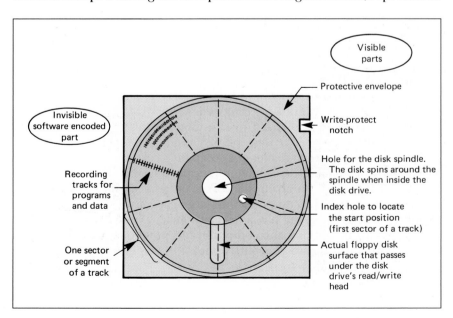

FIGURE 2-31
Floppy disk

Visible parts

Protective envelope

Write-protect notch

Invisible software encoded part

Hole for the disk spindle. The disk spins around the spindle when inside the disk drive.

Recording tracks for programs and data

Index hole to locate the start position (first sector of a track)

One sector or segment of a track

Actual floppy disk surface that passes under the disk drive's read/write head

Evolution of Floppy Disks

Characters (or bytes of storage)

K = thousand
M = million

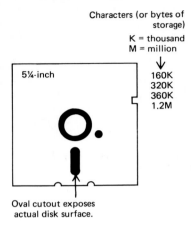

5¼-inch   160K
320K
360K
1.2M

Oval cutout exposes
actual disk surface.

Metal cover
automatically slides
over to expose disk
only when inside a
disk drive.

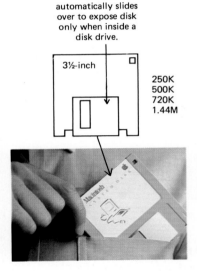

3½-inch   250K
500K
720K
1.44M

FIGURE 2-32
As the size of a floppy disk decreases, its
storage continues to grow.
(Courtesy of Apple Computer, Inc.)

by 1's and 0's as shown in Figure 2-31. Groups of 1's and 0's make up the coded characters of programs or data. All can be erased and reused.

A read/write head in the disk drive, which is similar to one in a record player, is positioned over a specific track of the disk. Once positioned, it can either read information stored there or write it.

Floppy Disks

Floppy disks are small portable computer storage media. They can be carried anywhere. By contrast, hard disks are mounted inside the disk drive and generally cannot be separated from the disk drive itself. Once a floppy disk is placed, by hand, inside a floppy disk drive slot, it works the same as a built-in hard disk.

An example of the 5¼-inch floppy disk used by Mr. Nelson's microcomputer appears in Figure 2-32. It is shown along with a 3½-inch floppy disk. The IBM Personal Computer and compatibles use a 5¼-inch floppy disk while the newer IBM Personal System/2, as well as all the Apple Macintosh computers, use a 3½-inch floppy disk.

If a user glues a label over the *write-protect notch* of a floppy disk, it signals the disk drive not to accept write-overs that would destroy stored data. Mr. Nelson write protects original copies of program disks to avoid inadvertently erasing his investment.

A standard 5¼-inch floppy disk holds 360,000 characters or bytes. A high-density 5¼-inch floppy disk, used on the IBM PC AT shown in Figure 2-33, holds 1,200,000 characters.

The floppy disk drive shown in Figure 2-33 is called a *half-height* or *thinline* disk drive. It takes up half the space of a regular 5¼-inch disk drive. The increased disk capacity and reduced size of the drive reveal trends toward even higher storage capacities in more miniaturized space.

Hard Disks

Mr. Nelson found that **hard disks,** also called fixed disks, were faster and more expensive than floppy disks. They are built right into the disk drive, so they cannot be removed. One IBM PS/2 model offers 314 million characters of hard disk storage. Adding another optional hard disk drive gives it a total of 628 million characters of storage. This amount supports large files of a company's customers, orders, inventory, and other data. It is capable of supporting the storage needs for many users at once as a group file server on a local-area network.

Because a powerful computer with large-capacity disk storage usually supports several users, it has a security lock. The lock prevents any casual user from working the computer and potentially damaging data on the hard disk. It also prevents removal of expensive circuit boards or other internal hardware.

A hard disk drive is located in the center of the system unit behind the ventilation grille.

Half-height floppy disk drives

Security lock

FIGURE 2-33
Half-height floppy disk drives are used on the IBM Personal Computer AT. (Courtesy of IBM)

Hard disks, Mr. Nelson learned, do not eliminate the need for a floppy disk drive. It serves as a transfer device to get software, purchased on floppies, onto the hard disk. Most software is currently sold on floppy disks.

Figure 2-34 shows a cutaway photo of a hard disk drive. Disk platters are rigid metal. An access arm moves to the track where requested data are located and its read/write head takes over. Data are automatically read or written in response to program commands.

Some manufacturers have miniaturized hard disks to fit on the side of a circuit board, such as the one shown earlier in Figure 2-18. This version is called a *hard card*. It must be mounted in an empty slot in the system unit, like any other circuit board.

The problem with a hard disk is that it cannot be removed for safekeeping elsewhere, as a floppy disk can. This can create a *backup* problem.

FIGURE 2-34
A cutaway photo of a hard disk drive
(*Courtesy of Microscience International Corp.*)

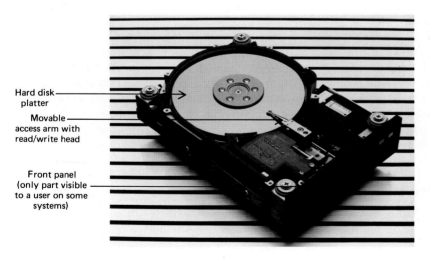

Hard disk platter

Movable access arm with read/write head

Front panel (only part visible to a user on some systems)

Personal computer
system unit

Backup tape cartridge drive

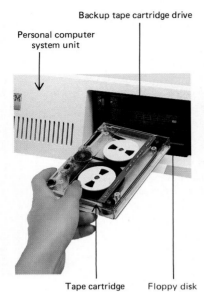

Tape cartridge   Floppy disk
                        drive

FIGURE 2-35
Tape cartridge is often used on personal
computers to back up hard disk files.
(Courtesy of Archive Corp.)

FIGURE 2-36
This 5¼-inch optical disk stores 550
million characters.
(Courtesy of MacWorld and F. B. Stimson,
San Francisco)

Backup

Why is disk backup such a critical issue? Mr. Nelson was told, by every computer-literate person he met, that it is vital. Disk drives sometimes fail, destroying precious data or programs stored there. Only a safely stored duplicate, or **backup copy** of a disk, can restore the data formerly contained on the wiped-out disk.

More often than not, backups are required because of simple human error. An entire disk or just one file might inadvertently be erased. If the erased file contains a mailing list that took two weeks to enter, and no backup exists, the entire effort must be repeated. These are the usual problems that make backing-up disks a vital concern to computer users.

One of many ways to back up a hard disk is with a *tape cartridge,* as shown in Figure 2-35. On one microcomputer with a built-in tape cartridge, it takes a little over one minute to back up every 1,000,000 characters. Alternatively, selective file backup onto floppy disks is possible. This is time consuming and error prone because of the need to use many floppy disks to do the job.

Optical Disks

Optical disks, like the one shown in Figure 2-36, are emerging as a new personal computer storage medium. They are often called **laser disks** because a laser beam is used to read and write to them. They come in three varieties.

The first is called a CD ROM (compact disk read-only memory) or an OROM (optical read-only memory). A CD ROM's main advantage is economy. Manufacturers can build relatively inexpensive optical drives by using parts from audio compact disks (CDs) and hard disk drives. One 5¼-inch disk holds about 550 million characters of storage.

Since a CD ROM disk is pressed at the factory, information cannot be recorded on it by a personal computer. This disadvantage limits its use to the distribution of large collections of data. As an example, the catalog of the United States Library of Congress is available on a CD ROM for a personal computer. The disk costs a few thousand dollars.

A second type is a WORM (write once, read many times) disk. While data can be written to the disk by a personal computer, they cannot be erased. The lack of erasability can be an advantage. A WORM disk containing bank records, for example, provides an indestructible audit trail. It makes the disk ideally suited to office storage systems.

A third and final type of optical disk is an erasable optical disk. It has the potential to replace hard disks with such added benefits as the following:

· Provides vastly improved storage capacity
· Offers the potential to combine data, video, and audio information in a single medium

· Permits the removal of a disk from its drive, which simplifies data backup and security procedures, and encourages the collection of databases

SYSTEM UNIT

The **system unit,** as shown in Figures 2-1, 2-5, 2-6, and 2-7, is the housing unit for components that perform the actual processing in a microcomputer. The following main components work together to do the processing:

· *Central processing unit (CPU)*, also known as a *microprocessor*
· *Random access memory (RAM)*, also known as *memory*
· *Read-only memory (ROM)*

Chips

All these components are **integrated circuit (IC) chips,** as shown in Figure 2-37, which illustrates a central processing unit (CPU) or micro-processor chip. Chips engineered for special purposes are manufactured by etching thousands of electronic components onto a tiny surface of silicon. Silicon is a compound made from sand. Sometimes the chip is called a *silicon*, or *semiconductor*, *chip*.

After a chip is manufactured, it is placed and concealed inside a plastic housing, called a **carrier.** The carrier sometimes resembles a centipede with tiny pins that stick out underneath to plug it into a circuit board. The circuit board shown in Figure 2-18 has dozens of special-purpose chips on it. Pins connect chip circuitry to the electronic

FIGURE 2-37
A microprocessor chip (*Left: courtesy of Raytheon Co.*)

Relative size of a microprocessor chip, also called an integrated circuit (IC) chip

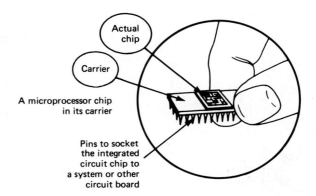

Actual chip

Carrier

A microprocessor chip in its carrier

Pins to socket the integrated circuit chip to a system or other circuit board

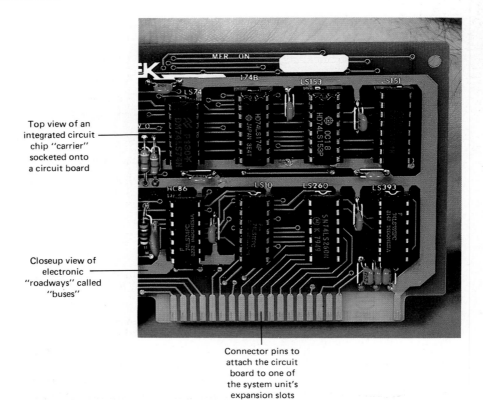

Top view of an
integrated circuit
chip "carrier"
socketed onto
a circuit board

Closeup view of
electronic
"roadways" called
"buses"

Connector pins to
attach the circuit
board to one of
the system unit's
expansion slots

FIGURE 2-38
*An "add-on" circuit board populated
with integrated circuit chips*
(Courtesy of AMDEK Corporation)

FIGURE 2-39
*Relationship of the system board to the
rest of the computer's hardware*

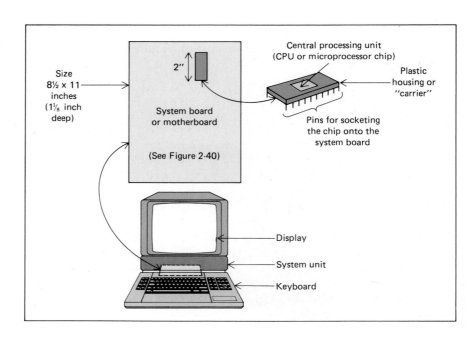

Size
8½ x 11
inches
(1⅛ inch
deep)

2"

Central processing unit
(CPU or microprocessor chip)

Plastic
housing or
"carrier"

System board
or motherboard

Pins for socketing
the chip onto the
system board

(See Figure 2-40)

Display

System unit

Keyboard

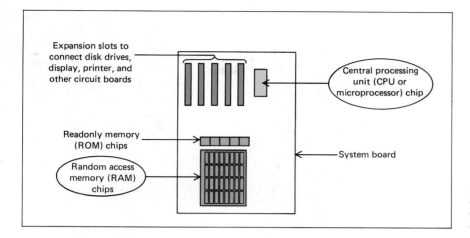

Expansion slots to
connect disk drives,
display, printer, and
other circuit boards

Central processing
unit (CPU or
microprocessor) chip

Readonly memory
(ROM) chips

Random access
memory (RAM)
chips

System board

FIGURE 2-40
Diagram of selected integrated circuit (IC)
chips and expansion slots on the system
board of the IBM Personal Computer

roadways, called **buses,** that are etched into the circuit board. Figure 2-38 illustrates a close-up of chips and buses on a circuit board.

Some circuit boards include chips without pins, called *surface-mounted chips.* Such chips provide less bulk and other advantages that result in more finely engineered boards.

The main circuit board inside the system unit is called a **system board** or **motherboard.** It is about twice the size of the circuit board shown in Figure 2-18, and it resides on the floor of the system unit that Mr. Nelson eventually acquired. Figure 2-39 diagrams the relationship of the system board to the rest of the computer's hardware. Figure 2-40 diagrams the distribution of the main chips on the system board.

Microprocessor

The **central processing unit (CPU),** also called a **microprocessor,** is the "brain" of the computer. It does the processing in the three-part input-processing-output cycle of a computer's operations. It works hand-in-glove with special software called the operating system. Chapter 4 covers operating systems and details how the central processing unit carries out its "processing" tasks. Operating system software is always programmed to work directly with a specific microprocessor chip or family of chips, such as those identified in Figure 2-41.

As Figure 2-37 shows, the central processing unit consists of one tiny thumbnail-sized chip. Its small size earns it the name "micro" processor. Mr. Nelson finds it awesome that such a tiny "engine" drives his complete computer. He tries to remember that the *microprocessor* is only one component, but the most important one, in a *microcomputer.* A *microcomputer* also requires input and output components, in addition to a processing component.

| MANUFACTURER | MICROPROCESSOR CHIP | | PERSONAL COMPUTERS THAT USE THE CHIP |
	Product	Size in Bits	
Intel	8086	16	AT&T Personal Computer 6300
	8088	16	IBM Personal Computer
	80286	16	IBM Personal Computer AT
			IBM Personal System/2—Models 50 and 60
			AT&T Personal Computer 6300 Plus
			Compaq Portable II
	80386	32	Selected by over 100 manufacturers for new hardware designs, including IBM Personal System/2—Models 70 and 80 Compaq Deskpro PC Limited
MOS Technology	6502	8	Apple II
Motorola	68000	32	Apple Macintosh
	68010	32	AT&T Personal Computer 7300
	68020	32	Apple Macintosh II

FIGURE 2-41
A sampler of microprocessor manufacturers and products

Mr. Nelson's computer is called a 16-bit computer because the microprocessor chip processes information 16 bits at a time. It is more powerful than a computer that processes only 8 bits at a time. The number of bits a computer processes is a classic way to chart the rapid advances in computer technology. One *Computerworld* ad sums up the evolution this way: "If the auto industry had done what the computer industry has done in the last 30 years, a Rolls-Royce would cost $2.50 and get 2 million miles per gallon."

In the computer industry, more bits mean more advanced state-of-the-art products. More advanced state-of-the-art computers and related software translate into such observable things as the following:

· Programs usually run faster.
· More color, combined with text and graphics features, is possible in programs.
· Command sequences or procedures are easier to master, as programs assume more of the routine work.

Memory

Mr. Nelson had to decide how much memory to buy. **Random access memory (RAM),** also simply called **memory,** is the place in the computer where programs and data must reside before they are processed by the central processing unit. The amount of memory he bought depended, in part, on the largest application program to be resident there.

Memory is temporary storage. If the computer power is turned off, everything in it is lost. That is why programs and data are permanently stored on floppy and hard disks. Whenever a program is needed, a copy of it is first loaded from a disk into memory and then processed.

Mr. Nelson intended to use one package that required 512,000 bytes of memory. Memory requirements are published with software packages. The computer he bought came with less, so he had to purchase the remainder as add-on memory.

Memory that comes with the computer purchase price is located right in memory chips on the system board, as shown in Figure 2-40. The remainder can come on an add-on circuit board, like the one shown in Figure 2-18. The new circuit board must be placed, as shown in Figure 2-19, in one of the expansion slots on the system board.

Expansion slots provide a place to connect circuit boards to the system board. Connector pins, like those shown in Figure 2-38, connect any add-on circuit board to the system board. Some users buy multifunction boards to conserve precious expansion slots. A **multifunction board** provides on one board the functions of several separate boards.

Every byte in random access memory, as the name implies, is randomly addressable. The central processing unit can instantly access any one of the 512,000 locations that Mr. Nelson's program requires. Each location stores 8 bits, or the equivalent of one character.

Unlike random access memory, **read-only memory (ROM)** offers permanent storage. It consists of a few special-purpose chips on the system board. They come preprogrammed with instructions that do not disappear when the power is turned off. Usually read-only memory contains utility programs that

- Put images on the screen
- Give the keyboard keys their special control capabilities
- Start the computer

Starting the computer from scratch is referred to as a **cold boot.** The phrase comes from the old expression to "pull yourself up by your bootstraps." Read-only memory contains the *bootstrap program*. A **warm boot** refers to restarting a program with the machine already powered on.

ARCHITECTURE

In computing, **architecture** refers to the overall design of how a computer is built to handle its input-processing-output functions. With the introduction of IBM's Personal System/2 line, microcomputers are taking on some of the characteristics of their older minicomputer and mainframe cousins. One of the outward signs of this is the move from desktop to larger floor-standing system units. Figure 2-42 shows the

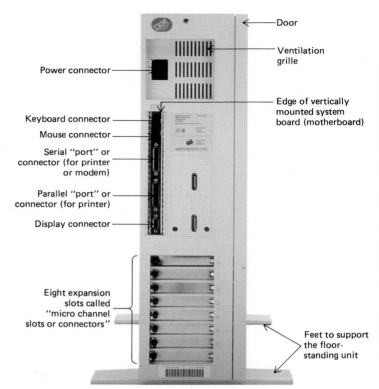

Door

Ventilation grille

Power connector

Keyboard connector

Mouse connector

Serial "port" or connector (for printer or modem)

Parallel "port" or connector (for printer)

Display connector

Edge of vertically mounted system board (motherboard)

Eight expansion slots called "micro channel slots or connectors"

Feet to support the floor-standing unit

FIGURE 2-42
Rear of IBM's Personal System/2
Model 80
(Courtesy of IBM)

rear view of the same floor-standing microcomputer system unit shown in Figure 2-7.

The most important part of Figure 2-42 is the expansion slots. They are called **micro channel connectors** in the PS/2 line. They borrow the name "channel" from the mainframe world. Channels, in a mainframe, tether various components, like disk and communication controllers, to the processor unit. The processor unit houses the central processing unit (CPU). Each mainframe **controller** is a separate specialized computer in its own right. Each is designed to off-load some of the processing burden from the central processing unit (CPU).

This same architecture is implemented, in a more miniaturized way, in the newer microcomputers, as is evident in Figure 2-43. The new so-called **micro channel architecture (MCA)** allows other processors, in addition to the central processing unit (CPU), to coexist and perform various processing tasks. Every micro channel processor controls its own "private" resources that are located on its own circuit board. Each also has a chance to access "public" resources, such as disk storage and printers, through the micro channel bus. A built-in "fairness algorithm" prevents any one processor from monopolizing the bus at the expense of any other device.

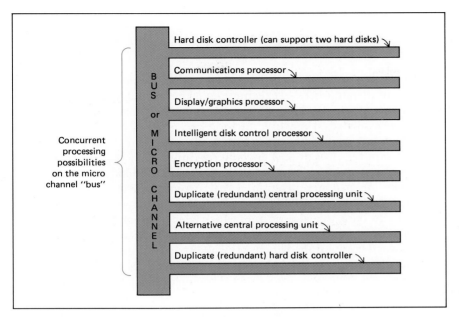

FIGURE 2-43
Diagram of the micro channel connector slots filled with optional circuit boards

By comparison, in the older PC standard architecture, there is no way for multiple microprocessors to effectively work together on the same bus.

Some of the possibilities of using the micro channel architecture are

- **Multiuser computing,** which allows more than one user to share the computer's resources. The microcomputer's function is then indistinguishable from that of a minicomputer or mainframe.
- **Fault-tolerant computing,** which kicks in a duplicate hardware component the instant a failure is detected in a primary component.
- **Parallel processing,** which harnesses the power of several coprocessors for a single computing task. In its simplest form, the main central processing unit (CPU) can off-load, for instance:
- Screen display tasks to the display processor
- Disk input/output tasks to the disk controller while it moves ahead to process the next step in a programmed sequence of steps. In its most extended form, this is the architecture theory behind modern supercomputers that are also called "parallel processors." In effect, it is possible to develop a personal supercomputer.

This architecture also facilitates **multitasking,** which allows a user to conduct several computing sessions simultaneously, with no performance degradation. An example is illustrated in Figure 2-6 where several applications are being juggled at once. But such multitasking has long been possible with older architectures and sophisticated software that simulate the effect of having many coprocessors.

MICROPROCESSOR TECHNOLOGY

Users of older microcomputers can update them to gain the advantages of new state-of-the-art technology. The advantages of upgrading, for instance, from an 8088 microprocessor-based machine to an 80386 microprocessor-based machine include executing programs faster. The clock that acts as a metronome timing all actions in the original 8088-based computer runs at 4.77 megahertz (millions of cycles per second), while it may run at 16 or more megahertz in an 80386 computer. This can make an ordinary program written for the 8088 run from 15 to 20 times faster on an 80386 machine. Most users of faster machines refuse to go back to a slower one, which seems sluggish by comparison.

A major design goal of the 80386 microprocessor was to be **downward** or **backward compatible,** which is the ability to run previous applications without alteration. It does this in what is called its **real mode,** which mimics an old 8088 microprocessor. This includes a limitation to address only one megabyte of memory, as listed on the comparison chart in Figure 2-44. Traditionally, this means running only one old DOS application at a time.

But the 80386 is evolutionary and introduces two other modes of operations, called

- Protected mode
- Virtual 86 mode

Protected mode makes multitasking, the ability to execute concurrently two or more tasks, possible. This is a superset of a similar mode first introduced in the 80286 microprocessor. *Protection* refers to preventing two or more applications from trespassing on each other's territory. Protected mode can address up to 4 gigabytes (billions of bytes) of memory. The newer Operating System/2 (OS/2) runs in this mode. A disadvantage is that a user must buy and learn new application software to benefit from this feature.

The third **virtual 86 mode** duplicates the first real mode but does it many times over. Instead of one DOS application, a user can run many of them. This mode allows a user to continue to use all the old software with a master control program such as Windows/386 or DesqView.

Operating system software, which works hand-in-glove with a microprocessor, is the key that opens the new technology for useful applications. Consequently, this microprocessor technology is reviewed once again from the operating system viewpoint in Chapter 4, "System Software."

Upgrade Alternatives

Many users with investments in older computers want to upgrade. They also want the benefits of speed, multitasking, and the newer applications available for 80286 or 80386 or other newer microprocessor-based

	MICROPROCESSOR: INTEL MODEL NUMBER		
	8088	80286	80386
Clock speed (in megahertz, millions of clock cycles per second)	4.77 MHz	10–16 MHz	16–20+ MHz
Operating system optimized for the microprocessor	DOS	OS/2	Windows/386 (control program)
Multitasking	No	Yes	Yes
Processes data at one time	16 bits	16 bits	32 bits
Memory size (bytes it can work with, or "address," directly)	1 megabyte (although DOS only addresses 640 kilobytes)	16 megabytes	4 gigabytes
Virtual memory size (bytes it can address indirectly; "virtual" memory uses the disk as a substitute for real memory)	None	1 gigabyte	64 terabytes

Note:

Kilobyte = One thousand bytes, or 1Kbyte
Megabyte = One million bytes, or 1Mbyte
Gigabyte = One billion bytes, or 1Gbyte
Terabyte = One trillion bytes, or 1Tbyte

FIGURE 2-44
Evolution of a microprocessor

machines. One obvious solution is to get rid of the old hardware and buy a newer computer. But other, less expensive, alternatives exist. Only two of several other solutions are identified here.

One solution involves buying a so-called **accelerator board** or **card,** which is simply a circuit board with the new microprocessor on it. In effect, it puts the old microprocessor to sleep while it takes over.

Another solution involves replacing the entire old motherboard with a new one containing the new microprocessor. This is a more expensive and laborious alternative. It is also more effective because the old restrictive circuitry is replaced with circuitry appropriate to the microprocessor served.

Any upgrade must be carefully examined for the compromises that must inevitably be made. Generally, the trade-offs are worth the effort to move up to the next generation of computers.

EVALUATION

After evaluating hardware, Mr. Nelson bought a microcomputer with one floppy and one hard disk, a color display, and a near letter-quality printer. Because of careful shopping, his system accommodated all his requirements, such as more add-on memory, without problems.

A checklist, like the Hardware Evaluation Checklist in Figure 2-45, guided his systematic evaluation and selection. The first part helps to evaluate general concerns, like hardware cost and maintenance. The second part helps to evaluate specific hardware components, like the system unit.

FIGURE 2-45
Hardware evaluation checklist

PART ONE: GENERAL CONDITIONS

General

Is hardware compatible with the personal computer business-use standard?
Is it easy to use?
Is a large number already in use?
Are current users happy with the hardware?
Is the *User Guide* easy to follow?
Are the manufacturer's reputation and length of time in business significant?
Is the warrantee period reasonable?
Is a diagnostic self-test available?
Are delivery and related costs reasonable?
Is the delay between order placement and delivery acceptable?

Installation

Who does the hardware installation at the user site?
Are required power supply and number of outlets in place?
Are other supplies, like cables, known and available?

Maintenance

Is service provided by the hardware manufacturer or another company with
    a good service reputation?
Are acceptable service contracts available, like on-site, carry-in, or other
    options?
Are local user references about service favorable?
Is loaner hardware provided if a service emergency arises?

PART TWO: SPECIFIC HARDWARE

System Unit

Is the microprocessor chip used considered state of the art?

To give an example of use, when Mr. Nelson evaluated different computers, he used Part One of the checklist to guide the evaluation of a computer's reputation. The list helped him to remember to find out if 50 or 50,000 other users owned the computer. He did not want to be among the first to use a new brand or model of computer. New computers are notorious for problems with insufficient testing for defects in manufacture or design. He checked the market and financial position of the manufacturer to be sure it would still be in business in three to five years to upgrade and service his unit.

He also investigated computer repair or *maintenance service*. First he tried the carry-in service to his local computer store. But his second disk failure took three trips, each costing a lost half-day of work. It convinced him to have the complete service burden taken off his shoulders with on-site servicing as needed.

Are memory increments possible (in what increment size and cost per increment)?

Are enough expansion slots provided (number available, number required for basic functions, number of disk types and drives supported, number of printers supported, number of communication ports supported)?

Keyboard

Does it have a familiar key arrangement?

Does it include a numeric keypad and programmable function keys?

Are keyboard alternatives available?

Display

Is the screen size of the display acceptable?

Does the display screen have an antiglare surface?

Are the color and resolution satisfactory?

Printer

Does print quality meet or surpass requirements?

Is speed satisfactory?

Is it compatible with the other hardware and software to be used?

Does it accept continuous-form and single-sheet paper?

Does it handle desirable paper sizes (minimum/maximum dimensions)?

Does it print carbon copies (maximum possible)?

Does it handle graphics?

Are character styles adequate?

Are changing paper and ribbon easy to do?

Is the noise level acceptable, or is a noise shield available?

Disk

Is disk storage capacity adequate?

Are backup devices available with software included?

CASE STUDY: Buying a Personal Computer

I have made no attempt to recommend any specific computer: Even if I could magically pick the best personal computer in the world (which would be difficult without knowing what you intend to use it for), it would probably be replaced by a better computer next month.

Though I won't tell you what you should buy, I can give you some general guidelines that should be helpful.

Ask for Help.   Many people feel terribly alone when they venture into a computer store to buy their first machine. This is understandable, but not really necessary. You should be able to find several sources of information to help you make a wise choice. Friends, teachers, and business colleagues are probably the best source of information. They can tell you about their experiences, and give you advice about how your specific needs would best be met by a personal computer.

Visit your local magazine shop and buy a handful of popular computer magazines. Look for a *Consumer Reports* evaluation of popular computers. Check the newspaper for information about computer shows, conferences, or fairs that may be appearing in your city.

Never Trust a Personal Computer Salesperson.   You've probably learned over the years to be slightly suspicious of used car, real estate, insurance, and other salespeople. There is no reason why you should be any more trusting of the salespeople in the retail computer store from which you will probably buy your first personal computer. *Always remember: salespeople are in business to sell a consumer product*, not to provide a solution to your particular problem.

The turnover rate in a computer store is so high that at any given moment, you're likely to be dealing with a salesperson who knows only a little more about the computer than you do. As these people work in stores that almost certainly concentrate on one or two particular brands of personal computer, they emphasize them and make unfavorable remarks about all other types.

Never Buy Your First Computer from a Mail-Order Company, or from a Discount Dealer.   Mail-order is *terrific* if you know exactly what you want, and if you don't expect to need any help or service after the sale. If you are buying your first computer, I would suggest that you go straight to a retail outlet that is willing to spend a lot of time answering your questions both before and after you buy your computer. This doesn't mean that you should unilaterally trust the answer you get from the salespeople in these stores, either—but at least you can ask them questions!

Many of the discount stores participate in what's known as the "gray market." They buy merchandise at distress-level discounts from reputable computer stores that find themselves stuck with excess inventory. If you buy your computer from a "discount house" like Wacky Willie's Wild and Wooly Camera, Stereo, Computer and Lawn Care Shop, you may find yourself in great trouble if you need repair work done. Wacky Willie won't want to do it. If your warranty is still valid, he'll suggest that you send your computer back to the manufacturer. It means that you won't see it for a month or two. If you take your ailing computer to the repair shop of your local computer repair store, you'll find that the already high labor charges have been tripled for all computers purchased from Wacky Willie—or you may find that they simply refuse to touch it.

Don't Concentrate on the Hardware Features. Find Out What Software You Want First, Then Find Out What Hardware Will Accept That Software.   The most important thing is to determine what kind of software you need *first,* and then choose your hardware *second.* Most of the popular software packages will run on virtually any personal computer, but some of the more exotic ones will not.

(*SOURCE: Edward Yourdon,* The Perils of Personal Computing, *Yourdon Press, New York, 1985, pp. 113–116. Adapted with permission.*)

DISCUSSION QUESTIONS

1. Before buying a personal computer, how can one take advantage of buying experience that already exists?

2. What are some sound shopping tips to give a first-time personal computer buyer?

CHAPTER SUMMARY

- The basic hardware components of a business-use personal microcomputer include *keyboard, display, printer, disk drives,* and *system unit.*

- An IBM Personal computer (IBM PC), or one compatible with it, is considered the *personal computer (PC)* or *PC standard.*

- When other manufacturers emulate or copy the PC standard, their products are called *compatibles* or *clones.*

- Buying a widely accepted personal computer assures a user of an already established computer support environment.

- An important reason for a company to adopt one standard, versus several, is that programs and data can easily be shared.

- IBM's *Personal System/2 (PS/2)* succeeds the IBM PC and represents a new generation of computers, and potentially a new standard. It uses a 3½-inch floppy disk which is incompatible with the 5¼-inch floppy disk on the PC standard. The hardware is *downward compatible,* which means it will run all the software that runs on the PC standard. It is best exploited by a new operating system called *Operating System/2.*

- A keyboard is the traditional way to get input into a computer. It consists of a *numeric keypad, cursor control keys* (also called *arrow keys*), and *function keys.*

- Alternatives to *keyboarding* include a pointer device called a *mouse, touch-sensitive displays,* and *voice.* All require specialized software when used.

- A *pull-down* or *drop-down menu* appears only in response to a selection at the top of the menu list.

- TV-like screen *displays* are also called *monitors.* They are the normal device for viewing computer-processed output.

- *Monochrome* displays present only one color, usually green, amber, or black, against a solid background. They are inexpensive and are preferred for text applications, like word processing.

- *RGB monitors* are expensive, quality, color displays.

- *Circuit boards* are a common way to attach devices such as displays, printers, and disk drives to the computer's system unit.

- Before buying a printer, preplanning print quality, speed, and software interface requirements is necessary.

- The four main personal computer printer types are *letter quality, dot matrix, ink jet,* and *laser.*

- *Near letter-quality dot-matrix printers* produce both rough-draft and letter-quality documents.

- A *disk drive* is a unit that houses, and physically provides access to, disks during use by a program. *Disks* are magnetic storage media for data and programs. They can be either *floppy* or *hard* disks.

- A *backup copy* of a disk, which is a duplicate copy, is critical to restore any data or programs lost on a wiped-out disk.

- *Optical disks,* also known as *laser disks,* are emerging as a new personal computer storage medium.

- The *system unit* is the housing unit for components that perform the actual processing in a microcomputer, such as the central processing unit, random access memory, and read-only memory. These components are *integrated circuit (IC) chips.* They reside on the main circuit board inside the system unit which is the *system board* or *motherboard.* Chips are housed in *carriers* and connect, by pins, to electronic roadways on circuit boards called *buses. Surface-mounted chips* have no pins.

- *Integrated circuit chips* have thousands of electronic

components etched on their surface of *silicon*. They are engineered to perform various functions.

- A *microprocessor* is a miniature *central processing unit* (*CPU*) on a single integrated circuit chip. It is the "brain" of a microcomputer. It does the processing in the three-part input-processing-output cycle of a computer's operations.

- *Random access memory* (*RAM*) is the place in the computer where programs and data must reside before they are processed by the central processing unit. Any RAM location is randomly available, or accessible, to the central processing unit. It is temporary, or volatile, storage.

- *Expansion slots* provide a place to connect circuit boards to the system board. They are called *micro channel connectors* in IBM's PS/2 line.

- *Read-only memory* (*ROM*) offers permanent storage. It contains utility programs that do not disappear when the power is turned off.

- *Architecture* refers to the overall design of how a computer is built to handle its input-processing-output functions. *Micro channel architecture* (*MCA*), in IBM's PS/2 line, allows other processors, in addition to the central processing unit (CPU), to coexist and perform various processing tasks, such as *multiuser computing*, *fault tolerant computing*, *parallel processing*, and *multitasking*.

- The 80386 microprocessor was designed with *downward* or *backward compatibility*, which is the ability to run previous applications without alteration. It does this in *real mode*, which mimics an old 8088 (or 8086) microprocessor.

- *Protected mode* makes multitasking possible on an 80386 or 80286 chip.

- *Virtual 86 mode* duplicates the real mode but does it many times over.

- An *accelerator board* is a hardware upgrade alternative to a new machine. It is a circuit board with a microprocessor on it different from the original one.

- A systematic hardware evaluation considers general cost and maintenance factors, as well as specific technical detail about hardware, like display size and disk storage capacity.

KEY TERMS

Accelerator board (card)	Display	Micro channel architecture (MCA)	Pixel
Architecture	Dot-matrix printer	Micro channel connector	Pointer
Arrow keys	Downward compatible	Microprocessor	Prompt
Backup copy	Drop-down menu	Monitor	Protected mode
Backward compatible	Expansion slots	Monochrome	Pull-down menu
Bus	Fault-tolerant computing	Motherboard	Random access memory (RAM)
Carrier	Flat-panel display	Mouse	Read-only memory (ROM)
Central processing unit (CPU)	Floppy disk	Multifunction board	Real mode
Circuit board	Function keys	Multitasking	Resolution
Clones	Hard disk	Multiuser computing	RGB monitor
Cold boot	Hardware	Near letter-quality printer	System board
Compatibles	Ink-jet printer	Numeric keypad	System unit
Composite monitor	Integrated circuit (IC) chips	Operating System/2 (OS/2)	Touch-sensitive display
Controller	Keyboard	Optical disk	Virtual 86 mode
Cursor	Keyboard template	Parallel processing	Voice recognition
Cursor control keys	Laser disk	PC standard	Warm boot
Disk	Laser printer	Personal computer (PC)	
Disk drive	Letter-quality printer	Personal System/2 (PS/2)	
	Memory		

REVIEW QUESTIONS

1. What are the basic components of a business-use personal computer?

2. Give two reasons for buying a widely accepted standard computer.

3. Describe the IBM Personal System/2 (PS/2) in relation to the PC standard.

4. What are the function keys and cursor control keys used for? *function keys- provide command with one stroke. cursor- moves all around the screen*

5. Give examples of alternatives to keyboarding for getting information into a computer.

6. Describe the trade-offs between screen displays sold as monochrome and RGB monitors.

7. What is a circuit board?

8. Before making a printer purchase, what preplanning is necessary?

9. Describe the four main types of printers used with microcomputers. *LETTER QUALITY, LASER JET INK, DOT MATRIX*

10. Compare floppy, hard, and optical disks.

11. Why is backup such a critical issue? *SO YOU DON'T LOSE WHAT YOU HAVE IF THE COMPUTER IS*

12. What is the system unit of a microcomputer? *SHUT DOWN*

13. What is a microprocessor? Is it the same as a microcomputer?

14. Differentiate between random access memory *TEMPORY STORAGE* (RAM) and read-only memory (ROM). *PERMANT STORAGE*

15. Define the following terms:
    a. Architecture
    b. Micro channel architecture (MCA)
    c. Multiuser computing
    d. Fault-tolerant computing
    e. Parallel processing
    f. Multitasking
    g. Downward or backward compatibility
    h. Accelerator board

16. Identify at least four items that should be carefully investigated when evaluating personal computer hardware for purchase.

EXERCISES

1. Learn what hardware your microcomputer lab has installed. The components and examples listed below can serve as a guide:
   a. System unit manufacturer (examples: IBM, Apple)
   b. System unit model (examples: Personal Computer, Macintosh)
   c. Display manufacturer (examples: IBM, Amdek)
   d. Keyboard arrangement in relation to the example shown in Figure 2-9 (examples: function keys on left, cursor control keys incorporated into numeric keypad)
   e. Alternative input devices (example: mouse)
   f. Printer manufacturer (examples: IBM, Epson)
   This information is often visible on individual hardware components. If not, ask a lab consultant or ask to see the *User Guide* or *User Manual* for the hardware component in question.

2. To become more familiar with your hardware, examine the various *User Guides* or *User Manuals* that come with components. Your micro lab probably makes them available for student use. Find answers for the following:
   a. Microprocessor chip used for the central processing unit and size (bits it can process at one time)
   b. System unit clock speed (in megahertz)
   c. Memory or random access memory (RAM) storage capacity

   d. Floppy disk drives
      · Number installed
      · Disk size (example: 5¼-inch)
      · Disk storage capacity (example: 360 Kbytes)
   e. Hard disk drives
      · Number installed
      · Disk size
      · Disk storage capacity
   f. Display
      · Type (digital or analog)
      · Size of screen
      · Color range
   g. Expansion slots
      · Number available
      · Number used—and for what (example: one for display and one for expanded memory)
   h. Printer
      · Type (example: dot matrix)
      · Width (example: 80 columns)
      · Speed (example: 120 characters per second)
      · Capabilities (examples: condensed type, graphics)

3. Many disk-based tutorials are available that can help you "Get to Know Your Hardware." If any are available in your micro lab, ask to run one. It should come with instructions for use, from power on to power off.

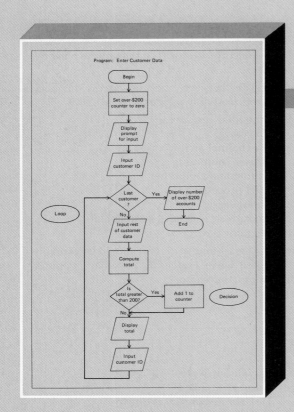

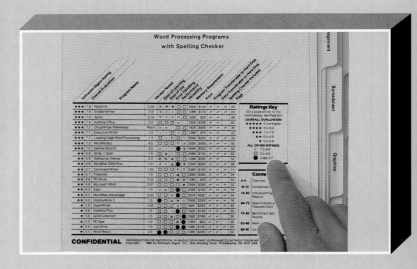

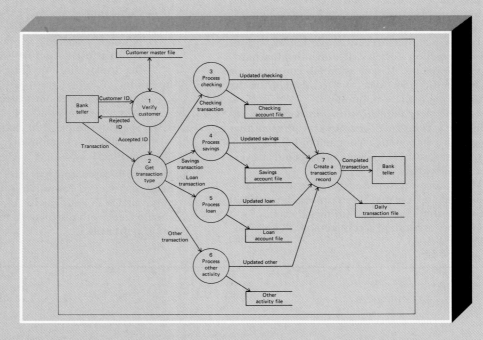

3

Application Software

AFTER READING THIS CHAPTER, YOU SHOULD BE ABLE TO

- Identify five application categories and give examples of software found in each category

- Identify how users acquire application software

- Describe how applications are created from scratch

- Initiate an evaluation of packaged applications

Application software is the most important ingredient of any computer system. It makes the hardware perform a meaningful user task, like word processing or payroll processing. It is so important that informed personal computer users shop for application software first. Then they buy the hardware on which the software runs.

Most of the chapters in this book are devoted to application software. This chapter serves as either an introduction to, or a summary of, all the application software chapters that follow.

It begins with a discussion of the various microcomputer application software categories, which are identified in Figure 3-1. Then it discusses ways to acquire application software, including buying it packaged or creating it from scratch.

All applications, even packaged ones, had to be created from scratch at some point in time. A section is included that describes the multistep process to develop application software from scratch. This section also covers newer methods that have evolved for creating so-called "user-developed systems."

Today, most microcomputer application software is bought as ready-made "packages." A concluding section describes a systematic approach to evaluate application packages.

APPLICATION SOFTWARE AND CATEGORIES

The term **application software** comes from the fact that such software *applies* the computer to real-world user tasks. Common microcomputer categories of application software include those identified in Figure 3-1. Although this breakdown focuses on microcomputers, much of the software can be found on microcomputers, minicomputers, and mainframe computers. It is even possible to find one product, like a vendor's database management software, available for all three types of hardware.

Most microcomputer application software is bought already programmed as a ready-made **package** for immediate use. This contrasts with application software that is used on mainframe computers. Organi-

FIGURE 3-1
Breakdown of computer software into categories

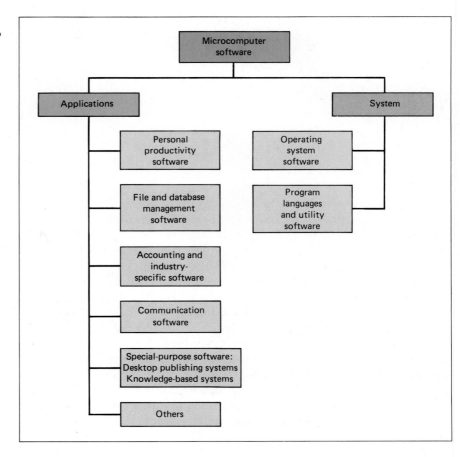

IMPORTANT

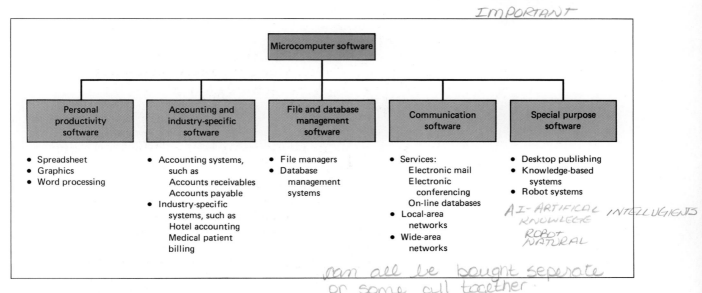

FIGURE 3-2
Detail of application software categories

zations that use mainframes typically have a large staff of in-house computer professionals. They are responsible for creating, from scratch, much of the organization's application software. Creating applications from scratch is also done, but to less extent, in microcomputer- and minicomputer-based organizations.

The main microcomputer application categories covered in this book are

· Personal productivity software
· File and database management software
· Accounting and industry-specific software
· Communication software
· Special-purpose software, such as desktop publishing and knowledge-based systems

These categories can be further broken down into the detailed application areas identified in Figure 3-2. To exploit applications in all these areas, users need a sense of what the software can do for them.

Personal Productivity

Personal productivity applications are those generally retailed over the counter at local computer stores. They are designed to help users accomplish some of their most important everyday professional tasks. Figure 3-3 identifies the three most common personal productivity applications—spreadsheet, graphics, and word processing—as well as some uses of them.

APPLICATION	EXAMPLES OF USE
Spreadsheet	Analyze numbers for decision-making purposes
Graphics	Visually simplify numbers to reveal trends or patterns and to present information to others
Word processing	Produce reports and other documents

FIGURE 3-3
Personal productivity applications

Personal productivity applications for microcomputer use are sold singly or in combination. Single applications are called **stand-alone packages.** They usually cost under $500. Packages that contain several applications are called **integrated packages.** They usually cost more than one stand-alone package, but the cost per application is lower.

New applications that aim to improve a person's personal productivity arrive in computer stores regularly. Most have not yet penetrated the established base of users that the "big three" applications (word processing, spreadsheet, and graphics) have.

Some newer packages expand the range of tasks covered by the big three. As an example, financial modeling packages are used in decision-making tasks where spreadsheets seem inadequate. These packages and other related software are covered in Chapters 5–7, which discuss personal productivity software in detail.

Because of the popularity of personal productivity software on microcomputers, software developers have re-created the big three packages for minicomputers and mainframes.

Accounting and Industry-Specific

Small- to medium-sized companies generally buy **accounting** and **industry-specific packages** to

- Improve day-to-day operations, like order progressing and customer billing
- Produce information with decision-making value as a by-product of processing

Figure 3-4 gives examples of some of the kinds of packages that they buy. When accounting software is generalized enough to be used by many industry types, it is often called a *general, horizontal,* or *cross-industry accounting package*. An example is an accounts receivable package that can be used by a manufacturer as well as by a contractor.

Industry-specific packages are tailored to the needs of a specific industry segment. Many examples of specific industries where such packages exist are given in the bottom of Figure 3-4.

If several stand-alone accounting packages are combined, the product is generally sold as an **integrated accounting system.** An integrated accounting system for microcomputer use can cost well over $10,000,

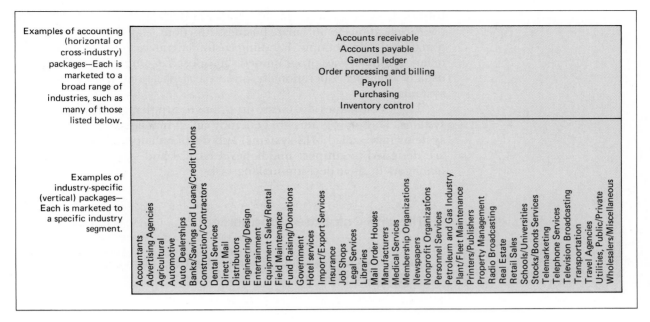

FIGURE 3-4
Accounting and industry-specific packages

while individual *stand-alone packages* can cost from $50 to $2,000 each. This software costs more for minicomputer use.

To give some perspective, Figure 3-5 compares software in this micro-computer application category with comparable software used on main-

FIGURE 3-5
Accounting and industry-specific applications compared on microcomputers and mainframes

MANAGEMENT LEVEL	MICROCOMPUTER AND MINICOMPUTER EXAMPLES	MAINFRAME EXAMPLES
Operational (production)	Accounting packages Integrated accounting system packages Industry-specific packages (for example, hotel or medical services)	Data processing, production, or operational systems (specific-task oriented, for example, accounts payable or bank teller collections)
Tactical	Same as above	Management information systems (specific business-function oriented, for example, marketing)
Strategic	Financial modeling packages	Decision support systems

frames. Large organizations, like National Bank, program most of their own applications to automate business functions, especially at the operational level. For example, handling customer transactions through bank-teller terminals was programmed "in-house." Computer professionals usually call such operationally oriented applications **data processing systems.**

Large companies also create programs to supplement data processing systems. These programs are generally called **management information systems** (also called **MIS systems**) and **decision support systems.** They are designed to support middle-level tactical and upper-level strategic managers in their decision-making tasks.

File and Database Management

From a user viewpoint, **file** and **database management packages** are invaluable to keep records that must be

- Shuffled, or sorted, into a different order
- Searched for a specific record or records
- Combined into useful lists or reports

Today's **file** and **database management software** does all this and more. It allows users to, in effect, create their own file-based applications, often without programming. Built-in programs do the work after answering a menu of questions or entering special commands.

The simplest packages for microcomputers are called *file managers* or *file management* packages. Everyone from office helper to manager can use these packages to keep electronic files of such things as correspondence, equipment, and names and addresses.

More advanced, and often more difficult to use, packages are called *database management systems*. They are available for microcomputers, minicomputers, and mainframes. They can help to create almost any kind of database file, form, or report desired. Often advanced uses require learning a database programming language. Such languages are often simpler to learn than common programming languages like BASIC and COBOL.

Sometimes database management software serves both personal and institutional purposes, as the diagram in Figure 3-6 indicates. At Interstate Distributing Company as well as at National Bank, a designated employee or computer professional oversees special institutional problems, like database security and data integrity. Because the company database is the source of management information, garbage data must not be allowed to pollute the database. To repeat the shopworn computer phrase, "Garbage in means garbage out."

Database management software costs a few hundred dollars for microcomputers, compared with sometimes over $100,000 for a mainframe version.

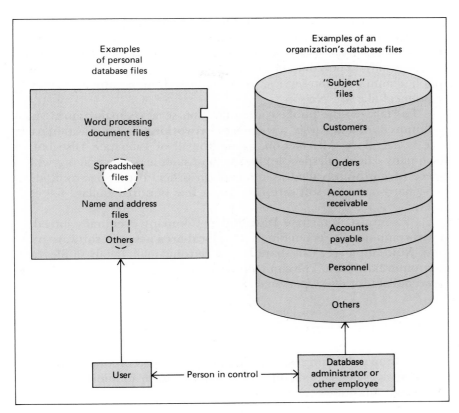

FIGURE 3-6
Personal versus organizational databases

Communication

Communication software enables a microcomputer user to benefit from such modern communication services as the following:

Communication Service	Application
Electronic mail	Replaces the manual sending and receiving of mail with instant electronic methods using a computer
Electronic conferencing	Eliminates face-to-face conferencing with computers and allows conferees to be in any place and to participate in an ongoing conference at any time
On-line databases	Allows an electronic search and retrieval of libraries of information using a computer

These communication services are widely available at large **public communication services.** They are like a public utility that charges users a fee for such services.

Frank Nelson, who works at Interstate Distributing Company, a relatively small organization, uses communication software to send electronic mail to salespeople. They, in turn, send him expense and activity reports electronically. The company retains an electronic mailbox at a large public communication service that uses a mainframe computer to service customers like Mr. Nelson.

To "talk" to the public communication service's mainframe, which is hundreds of miles away, a **wide-area networking** communication package is necessary. Mr. Nelson, as well as all of Interstate Distributing Company's field salespeople, had to buy such a package along with a piece of hardware called a "modem" in order to use electronic mail. The hardware and software can cost a few hundred dollars for each user.

By contrast, Interstate Distributing Company eventually linked all microcomputers in its building with a **local-area network** software package. Now employees can share local electronic mail, database files, and computer hardware. The company's local-area network cost several hundred dollars for every personal computer connected to the network.

Desktop Publishing

Desktop publishing enables the computer-aided production of documents such as newsletters, brochures, and forms. In addition to a desktop microcomputer, it usually also requires

- A word processing package
- A graphics package
- A page composition package
- A laser printer

It also assumes that a user has the graphic and production skills to create and lay out an eye-pleasing, publishable document. It can require a considerable amount of skill to get high-quality results, and to coordinate the interrelated workings of all the software and hardware.

Although desktop publishing is a specialized application, some computer industry analysts predict that it will become as common as word processing is today.

Desktop publishing enables users to bypass traditional publication channels. The savings realized by avoiding professional typesetting costs alone, in many cases, can make the $10,000 or so initial cost of getting started in desktop publishing seem like a minimal investment.

Knowledge-Based Systems

Today's advanced systems often emerge from artificial intelligence research. As the tree diagram in Figure 3-7 implies, there is *no* software called **artificial intelligence (AI).** AI is an umbrella term that describes

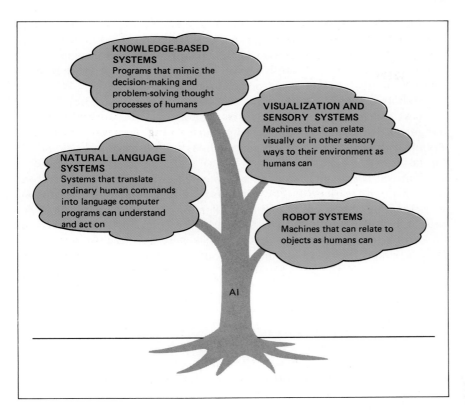

FIGURE 3-7
Artificial intelligence family tree

a group of technologies aimed at making computers imitate aspects of human behavior. AI research has spawned

- Knowledge-based systems
- Robot systems, often with visualization and other sensory subsystems
- Natural language systems

Knowledge-based system software can capture, magnify, and distribute access to judgment. It can function as an assistant, colleague, or expert. It allows an expert to pass along years of accumulated, specialized knowledge to others. In one case, a cook at a large soup company transferred his special expertise to a knowledge-based system before retirement. Businesses are finding knowledge-based systems a salvation to ensure that the company's expertise does not die when somebody leaves the organization.

The heart of such a system is its knowledge base. It has similarities to a database but consists of rules and facts related to a specific problem area. Some knowledge-based systems are helping decision makers to improve their own decision-making skills.

Robot systems combine hardware and software to serve a function in the workplace, which is usually a factory assembly line.

Specially designed software enables a robot to "learn" the task it must tirelessly repeat. The ability of the mechanical robot to learn a task gives it humanlike characteristics. It appears to be intelligent, although every move is carefully driven by a program written by a human that frequently runs on a microcomputer.

Robots do boring, repetitious tasks without a groan. They free up humans for more challenging tasks. Robots also do work that is too dangerous for humans, like removing parts from a flaming-hot furnace. Robots with visualization system capabilities can perform more demanding tasks.

Natural language system software enables users to carry on a computer dialogue in plain English. It is usually found attached to database management systems. It makes it simpler for occasional computer users to search and manipulate data stored in the company's database files.

Applications with artificial intelligence were once confined to mainframes. Today they exist on microcomputers and minicomputers as well.

Other

A host of other software falls into assorted categories, like

- Health care
- Research, education, and training
- Home-use tax, accounting, and financial planning
- Music and art
- Sports and entertainment

This partial list could easily be expanded with all the innovative products that regularly enter the application software market.

APPLICATION ACQUISITION CHOICES

After a user decides that one or more applications will meet personal or organizational needs, the software must be acquired. Application acquisition choices, ordered in terms of the best investment of user time and money, are as follows:

1. Buy a packaged application
2. Modify an existing package (sometimes possible with accounting and industry-specific applications)
3. Develop a custom application with the aid of a packaged database management system
4. Develop a custom application from scratch using traditional methods

Buy a Package

NOTE

Since application software costs less to buy than to program from scratch, most users buy it packaged. A major disadvantage of packaged software is that it probably is not an exact fit to user needs. Faced with such a situation, there are several possibilities. One advocates that if 80 percent of the package fits, use it and adjust the remaining 20 percent requirement to make the package work. With most inexpensive retailed software, this is highly realistic.

A word processing package under $500, for example, may fit "must have" requirements but fall short on the "would like to have" requirements. Compared with the benefits computerized word processing can bring to any writing effort, the trade-off decision is not hard to make.

Modify a Package

Most packaged software is sold "as is," so there is no possibility of modifying the package. Packages in the accounting and industry-specific category are an exception. With some, however, the cost of modifying that last 20 percent could cost more than building the software from scratch.

Use a Database Package

Many desirable applications are not available in a package. This motivates users to develop unique **custom applications** for their exclusive use. Often this is accomplished by using a database management system package. While this software can be used by novices, it still requires the technical design of

- Database record content
- Display or report output content

Sometimes professional assistance is needed for this work. But results can be obtained in far less time than would be required if a traditional programming language, like BASIC or COBOL, is used.

Develop from Scratch

Generally, large organizations maintain a staff of computer professionals to design custom applications from scratch for their unique data processing and management information system needs. They now also have a staff of microcomputer specialists who can design and program microcomputer applications.

Organizations that do not have computer professionals on the payroll will often contract with a freelance programmer-analyst or a "software house" to do the highly detailed technical development work required for a new application.

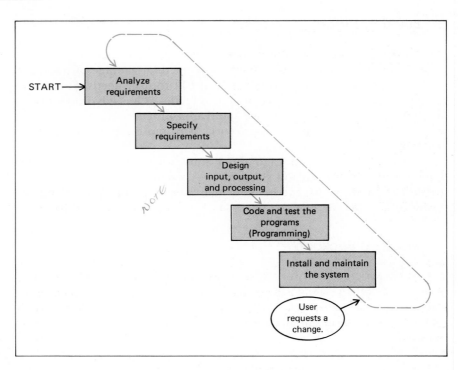

FIGURE 3-8
System development life cycle

Computer professionals often follow the **system development life cycle** when preparing custom applications. It is the computer industry's formalized method to create new applications, usually called "systems," from scratch. It consists of steps, identified in Figure 3-8, to

- Analyze system requirements
- Specify requirements
- Design a system's input, processing and output
- Write or code the new system's programs, enter the code into the computer, and test the programs
- Install and maintain the system

As soon as a custom application is implemented, revisions are inevitable. This leads to respecifying requirements and beginning the cycle over again.

Figure 3-9 compares the features of packaged application software with custom application software. Custom software is flexible, since it is designed solely to please one user. Usually custom software is also more efficient because it is not encumbered with options designed to please a broad user population.

On the other hand, packages are less expensive and can be installed for use quicker than can custom applications. Generally, a *User Guide* is also available to guide installation and use.

Typically, no computer professional staff is required to install and run a package on a microcomputer. By contrast, custom applications

CRITERIA	CUSTOM	PACKAGE
Cost	–	+
Time to install	–	+
Flexibility	+	–
Software efficiency	+	–
Computer professional staffing required	–	+
User Guide or other documentation available	–	+

FIGURE 3-9
Comparison of application software (+ favorable, – not favorable)

require someone who knows the intricates of the new software to help install it and train people to use it. This requirement could be reduced if supporting documents, like a *User Guide*, accompanied a custom application. Unfortunately, in custom application situations, it is usually a case of "there was no time to do it."

APPLICATION DEVELOPMENT

All application software had to be prepared from scratch, at one time or another, even if it is now resold thousands of times as a packaged software product. This section examines the stages in the system development life cycle to give some perspective to how application software evolves.

In large organizations, and in companies devoted to developing new software (called **software houses, software development companies, software suppliers,** and **software venders**), many computer professionals and others participate in the development of a single software product. In small organizations, sometimes one person develops the software desired on a one-shot contract basis.

Most professional software developers follow one of many versions of the system development life cycle, such as the one shown in Figure 3-8. Figure 3-10 gives a brief description of each step in the cycle. Steps represent a formal set of guidelines and procedures for taking a system problem from beginning to end. In effect, new applications are born, developed, and die or are reborn through change.

The investigation of *what* has to be done is commonly called the **system analysis** phase. The definition of *how* to do it is commonly called the **system design** phase. Tasks accomplished in these phases pave the way for the actual coding of system programs.

STEP	DESCRIPTION
Analysis	A user identifies new system requirements.
	A system analyst investigates the need for a new system and prepares a feasibility report.
Specification	A system analyst creates formal specifications for the new system using a diagramming or other technique.
Design	A system analyst or designer prepares formal design documents, including: Output report and screen layouts (output definition) Database record content Input screen and form layouts (input definition) Program organization or hierarchy chart Program logic specifications (processing definition) Hardware specficiations, if needed
Program	Computer programmers write program code, enter it into a computer, and test the programs.
Installation and maintenance	A system analyst coordinates installation of programs at the user's site and conducts user training. Users operate the installed system. System analysts and programmers work with users throughout the life of the system to maintain and upgrade it.

FIGURE 3-10
Format steps to develop and program a new information system

Requirements Analysis

The system development life cycle begins with **requirements analysis,** which is an investigatory stage. In this case, assume that Anchor Bank, a smaller company version of National Bank, contracts with a software house to develop a custom microcomputer application. Anchor Bank wants, among other things, to send each customer one statement that consolidates all of that customer's bank business for the month. Currently, a customer gets only a checking account statement. It does not record either loan or savings account activity.

Anchor Bank's management also wants more information on fees received from all bank services, among other things.

It is up to **system analysts** like Ms. Eleanor Beyer, an employee of the software house, to perform all new system analysis and design work. She begins by investigating the present system to see what has to be done to resolve current problems. She interviews key people, observes procedures, and examines relevant documents. She concludes this first step with a written *feasibility report*.

A formal **feasibility report** spells out what the investigation of user requirements reveals. It also details the economic, technological, and operational feasibility of the requested system:

· *Economic feasibility* answers the question of whether benefits exceed the costs of the new system.

- *Technological feasibility* answers questions about whether hardware and software are available to build the new system.
- *Operational feasibility* answers questions about the ability of the organization to develop and support a new system.

Anchor Bank management's review of the written, and often orally presented, feasibility report ends in a "go/no-go" decision. The decision determines whether or not the remaining phases of the system development life cycle are pursued.

Specification

The second phase in the system development life cycle involves specifying what the new system must do. To specify the new system, Ms. Beyer draws data flow diagrams, such as the one in Figure 3-11.

FIGURE 3-11
A data flow diagram—overview level

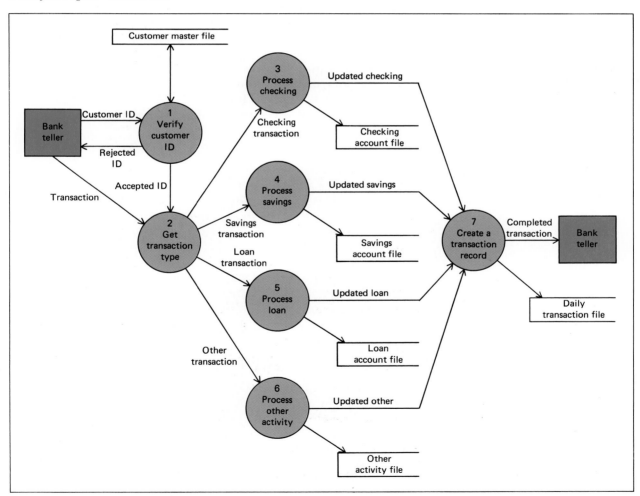

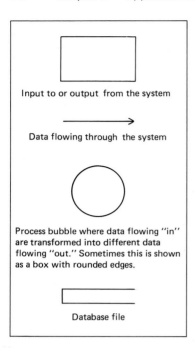

FIGURE 3-12
Data flow diagram symbols

Figure 3-12 identifies the meaning of the four symbols used to draw data flow diagrams.

A **data flow diagram** is a graphical model of a system. Ms. Beyer makes the analogy that her data flow diagrams are like an architect's blueprint of a new building. They represent on paper what the real system will be like when designed and in use. Creating the data flow diagrams from scratch, she finds, is especially useful to help conceptualize the flow of data throughout the system. This feature gives the technique its name.

Having a model of the system makes it easy to add, change, or delete parts of the system. Usually such changes would be unthinkable in a real system. A pair of scissors and some glue enables shifting the so-called *bubble diagram* around at will. It is even easier when using a computer with graphics software that facilitates the creation and modification of data flow diagrams.

Data flow diagramming is the first of several so-called **structured methods** used in the analysis and design of computer systems. These methods are called "structured" because they begin by looking at the "big picture." From there, they become systematically decomposed into more and more refined detail. Each bubble on the data flow diagram in Figure 3-11, as an example, is further decomposed into another data flow diagram that details the processing going on inside the bubble.

Some analysts prefer to use other methods when specifying a new system. One older method is *system flowcharting*. Figure 3-13 shows an example of a system flowchart. This method requires the use of a specified set of symbols, some of which are given in Figure 3-14.

FIGURE 3-13
System flowchart of Anchor Bank's customer transaction processing

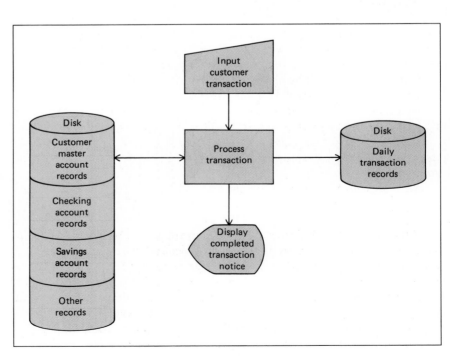

A **system flowchart** is a graphic model of the flow of control through a system. For example, in Figure 3-13 control passes from a computer keyboard to a program that processes transactions. Some disk files are updated and a new transaction file is created.

Ms. Beyer sketches flowcharts every now and again for a variety of purposes. But she prefers to draw a full system model with data flow diagrams to help her focus on the data interface between processes. These critical links must be in place for a system to succeed. Many system failures can be traced to processes that did not correctly integrate with each other.

While system flowcharts and data flow diagrams are tools that Ms. Beyer uses to help model a new system, the tools do not help her decide what goes into the model. No tool can help her to do that. Ms. Beyer learned how to analyze and model a new system mostly from experience. As a trainee, she worked with system analysts to learn from them while supporting their work. She also attended analysis and design courses and examined past successful and unsuccessful systems. This preparation as a trainee took about two years. It came after she spent a few years in programming jobs.

Design

Once *what* will be done is specified, Ms. Beyer concentrates on designing *how* it will be done. The design step of the system development life cycles moves toward creating a physical reality out of the paper (or logical) model. Output screens and printed reports, as well as input screens and database record content, are designed in this phase.

The major output of any new system usually includes printed and displayed reports. The bank system's new output is mainly a printed consolidated customer statement, like the example in Figure 3-15. Ms. Beyer's statement design is considered a *custom form* because it has printing already typeset on it before the computer prints on it. Most companies use a custom format when a document goes to people outside the organization. Companies that use laser printers, which can print forms along with data, avoid the expense and trouble of preprinted forms.

Most computer reports do not go outside a company. They are designed for internal company use and are printed on plain computer stock paper.

Some output takes the format of a screen display. Loan officers, for example, want to be able to view a customer profile, like the example in Figure 3-16.

Once output is designed, it is easy to work backward to determine what must go into a system to get the desired result out. Output is created from data stored in a company's database files. Using output as a guide for what data are needed, database file content is designed next. A simple example of how database files are designed is covered in Chapter 8, "Database and File Management Packages."

After all the files are designed, the next step is to design input. Input mainly concerns getting data into the database, usually through

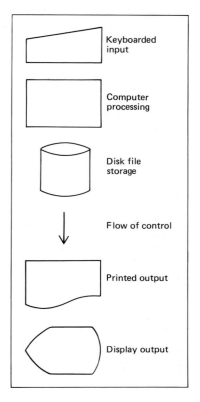

FIGURE 3-14
Common system flowchart symbols (These are a few of many symbols available.)

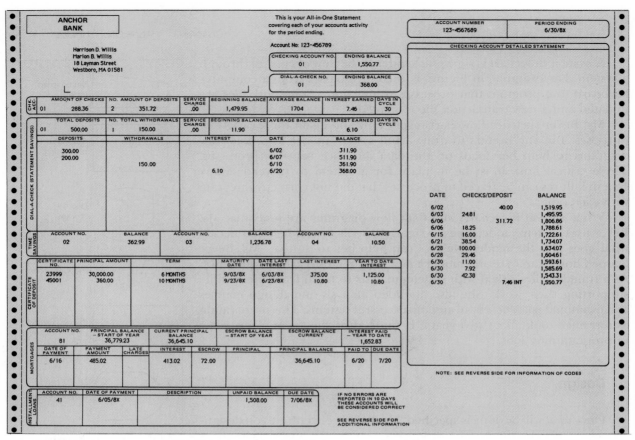

FIGURE 3-15
Output designed for printing on custom computer forms

FIGURE 3-16
Output designed for screen display

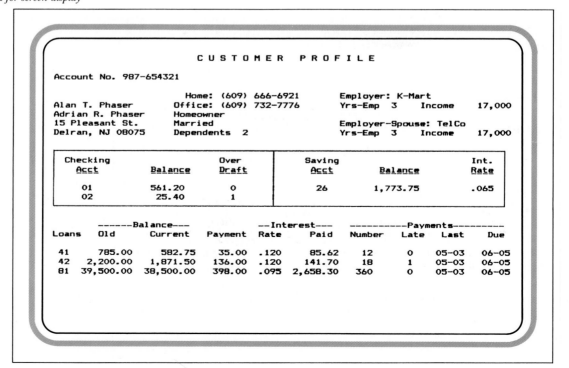

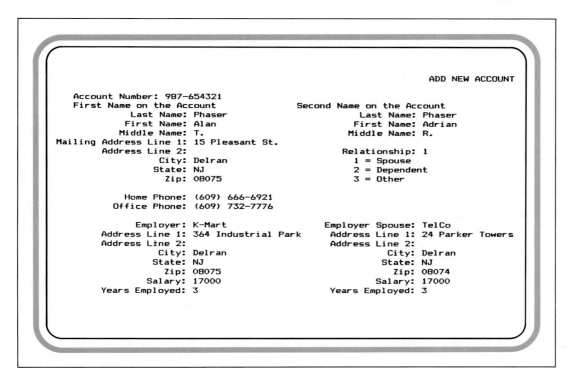

FIGURE 3-17
A screen designed for data input

data-entry screens. The example in Figure 3-17 shows one of several data-entry screens that Ms. Beyer designs. With the screen, a user can get a new account established in the customer database.

Ms. Beyer also designs menu screens, like the one in Figure 3-18, to simplify use of the new system.

In the design phase, it may also be necessary to specify and order hardware if none is already available.

FIGURE 3-18
Menu screen design

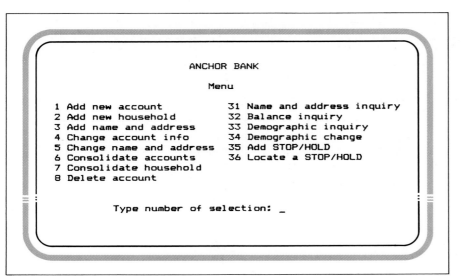

Programming

At this point in a system development project, the step-by-step procedure to get input into the computer, process it, and generate output must be defined. This processing logic is implemented in a computer **program.**

To create a computer program is a multistep process, as shown in Figure 3-19. Generally, a computer program begins with an overall plan, which can take the visible form of a *hierarchy chart*, such as the one shown in Figure 3-20. Then the detailed logic for each module of the plan is defined.

Defining the detailed processing logic of a program can take many visible forms. The examples in Figures 3-21 and 3-22 show complete,

FIGURE 3-19
Programming is a multistep process.

COMMON TERM	STEP	VISIBLE RESULT
Program design	1. Design the overall program structure	Program "hierarchy" or organization chart
	2. Design the detailed processing logic	Process logic specifications prepared using pseudocode, program flowcharts, or some other technique
Coding or programming	3. Write the code in BASIC or COBOL or another program language that will make the computer execute the logic desired	Handwritten program code
	4. Type the code into the computer using the COBOL, BASIC, or another language processor	Often these two steps are combined by programmers who write code while sitting at a personal computer
		Computer-printed lists or displays of program code (for example, see Figures 4-16, 4-17, 4-21, 4-22, and 4-23).
Testing or debugging	5. Remove code syntax and logic errors ("debug" the program)	Progress from problem to error-free program execution
	6. Test the program	Correctly printed reports and displays of any input and output programmed

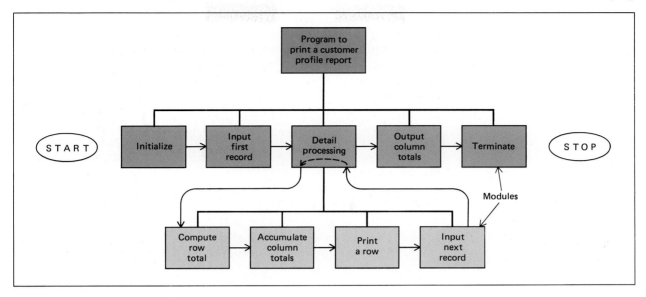

FIGURE 3-20
A hierarchy chart graphically depicts the overall processing plan for a computer program.

although trivial, computer programs in order to illustrate two methods used to define processing logic. They are called *pseudocode* and *program flowcharts*. Figure 3-23 shows the meaning of the program flowchart symbols used. Program flowcharting usually involves symbols that differ from those used for system flowcharting.

The design of a program's overall structure and detailed processing logic is often called **program design.** Program design precedes **program coding,** which is writing computer programs using the code and rules of a chosen program language, such as BASIC or COBOL. An example of program excerpts, coded in several different programming languages, appears in the next chapter.

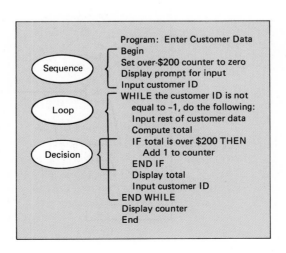

FIGURE 3-21
Pseudocode is one way to describe the processing logic that must be coded into a program.

Coded programs must be typed into the computer, one line of code at a time. The code instructs a computer how to perform its step-by-step processing in any application's particular case.

FIGURE 3-22
A program flowchart is another way to describe
the processing logic that must be coded into a program.

FIGURE 3-23
Program flowchart symbols

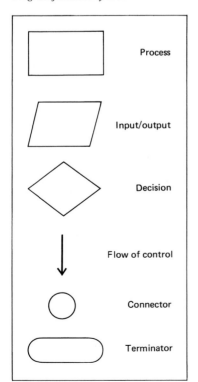

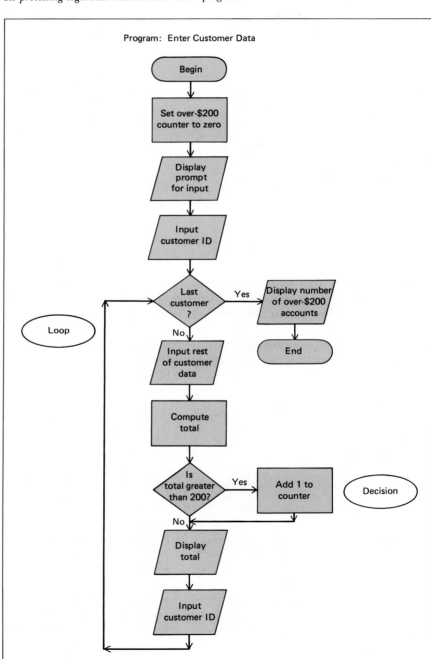

Rarely is any computer program designed, coded, or entered into the computer perfectly the first time. Because of this, both the design and code must usually be fixed and retested many, many times before a new program runs correctly. Removing errors from a computer program is called **debugging** the program. It is a normal part of a program's evolution.

Many people incorrectly think that coding is all there is to programming. But coding cannot occur without having an idea of what the code is supposed to do.

Program coding and designing are separate and distinct jobs. Often a system analyst, like Ms. Beyer, creates a program's design. Then she passes her designs to a person called a **computer programmer,** who specializes in coding and debugging programs. In some smaller organizations, a single person performs all program design and coding work. Dual-function professionals are often called **programmer-analysts.**

Finally, programs must pass tests for performance accuracy. In the Anchor Bank case, Ms. Beyer planned performance tests that were executed prior to the formal user acceptance tests. Once the user "signs off" that a system works as expected, it is ready to be installed at the user's workplace.

Installation

Installing new system hardware and software at a user site involves setting up the physical computer, ordering supplies, training users and managers about how to run the system, converting data to computer format, running tests, and monitoring ongoing system performance. Managing these steps for any system installation is a major task. In a large project, a project leader must coordinate the activites of

- Hardware vendors to ensure on-time equipment delivery
- Contractors to prepare new hardware sites
- Purchasing managers to acquire equipment and supplies
- Training specialists to organize and conduct training sessions for both users and managers
- Technical writers to prepare training and user guides
- Programmers to design and write programs
- System analysts and trainees to provide necessary analysis and design support

Ms. Beyer, as the Anchor Bank system project leader, handled most tasks herself, with the support of computer programmers. She also prepared **system documentation,** which is a collection of all the documents created to develop and install the new system, plus a few others. Documentation provides an essential reference source to smooth the long-term maintenance of the system.

As latent program bugs emerge, and as new requirements occur, *program modifications* to the existing system are inevitable. Ms. Beyer designed a Program Modification Request form for initiating changes. Essentially, the form starts the system development life cycle all over again.

USER-DEVELOPED SYSTEMS

User-developed systems are applications developed by users for their own benefit. Larger organizations encourage user-developed systems through their **Information Centers,** which provide staffs of computer professionals to assist users. Professionals work directly with users to help them satisfy their own computer requirements without the need for formal system development life-cycle procedures.

To help users help themselves requires that an organization provide user-oriented software tools. These tools include ordinary microcomputer database management system software.

The tools are used, first, to create quick **prototypes,** or rough versions of user applications. The **prototyping approach** involves a computer professional who works with individual users, showing them interim application results and refining the results repeatedly until the users are happy. In some cases, the method eliminates the laborious job of preparing requirement documents and system specifications. In general, the method eliminates a formal adherence to the system development life cycle.

Prototyping is becoming more widespread because it

- Gets the application into operation quickly
- Provides more precise definition of user requirements, since a user actually works with the application
- Controls user expectations because of the user's involvement in actually building the application
- Eliminates user training
- Has a low-risk, high-payoff benefit to an organization

Application development software packages, like those listed in Figure 3-24, are mostly database management system packages. Many are available to automate application development and usually require

FIGURE 3-24
Application development software
packages for microcomputers

SOFTWARE	VENDOR
Microcomputers	
Condor	Condor
dBASE	Ashton-Tate
Knowledge Man	Micro Data Base Systems
MDBS	Micro Data Base Systems
PC/FOCUS	Information Builders
R:base	MicroRim
Revelation	Cosmos
RL-1 Relational Database Management	ABW Corp.
Savvy PC	Excalibur Technologies

the skills of a programmer or system analyst. But in some cases, users have themselves become proficient in using application development software.

One application development package, as an example, works with a fill-in-the-blanks technique. While sitting at a microcomputer, an analyst is prompted to fill in one form that describes screen layouts and input flow. A second form is used to describe files. A third form is used to describe the transfer of data from one file to another.

A prototype of an application can be created from 10 to 50 times more efficiently than using conventional development methods. After the application works, making changes takes under one hour. In some cases, prototyped applications are used as the model for applications that are programmed in more hardware-efficient conventional programming languages, like BASIC or COBOL.

Nurturing user-developed systems, in most organizations, results in innovative applications. But problems with user-developed systems include

- Overlapping applications, or duplication of effort. This occurs when one group creates an application that is already available in another part of the company.
- Diverted employees. This occurs when employees get overly engrossed in an application development project and ignore their primary job responsibility.
- Problem applications. This occurs when applications are not well designed or tested because professional guidance is ignored.
- Morale problems. This is evident when personnel feel left out of new application efforts. This is especially prevalent in large organizations where new microcomputer applications are making old mainframe computer professionals feel superseded.

In some companies, computer department employees feel helpless in the face of proliferating user-developed microcomputer systems.

EVALUATING PACKAGED APPLICATIONS

Today, most microcomputer applications are not developed from scratch. They are bought ready-made, or packaged. To help conduct a systematic evaluation of packaged application software, checklists are often used. They are included in the chapters of this book devoted to the various applications. For example, Chapter 5 has a Spreadsheet Evaluation Checklist which is used for spreadsheet software.

If a package meets application checklist requirements, then the General Software Evaluation Checklist in Figure 3-25 can be used for a follow-up evaluation. Like many other evaluation checklists, those found in this book are designed to be modified to meet individual needs. They function best as a departure point for thoughtful investigation and analysis.

It should be remembered that there is no right or wrong order to evaluate packages. The checklists simply help to ensure that all important evaluation areas are covered.

FIGURE 3-25
General software evaluation
checklist

PART ONE: GENERAL CONDITIONS
(No computer needed)

Package

Are published evaluations and reviews available?

Are recommendations of others favorable?

Are hardware requirements satisfactory (like computer brand supported, minimum memory required, display required, number and type of disk drives required, printers supported)?

Are required add-on hardware/software available at a satisfactory cost?

Is the correct operating system available?

Are file exchanges with other software possible?

Documentation

Does the *User Guide* contain an index and procedures for start-up and disk backup?

After-Sale Support

Is service available from the purchase or package source?

Is a service charge, if any, appropriate?

PART TWO: HANDS-ON TEST
(Need a computer)

Ease-of-Use

Does overall operation feel comfortable or confusing?

Does data entry move along at a good speed (or are there unsatisfactory idle periods between entries)?

Do screen formats appear clear, uncluttered, and consistent?

Are HELP and EXIT routines provided?

Are ERROR correction messages understandable and solvable?

Do errors deadlock processing?

Are file or disk backup procedures complicated?

Support Tools

Are the disk-based tutorial and *User Guide* helpful?

Application Function

Does the software meet all the items identified as "must have" on the application Evaluation Checklist? (For example, see Spreadsheet Checklist in Figure 5-19, or Word Processing Checklist in Figure 7-19.)

General Considerations

Part One of the General Software Checklist helps to weed out unusable packages. It encourages a check of published reviews or articles about an application. Often they shed insight on package performance and ease of use.

If reviews are uniformly dismal, it may save a hands-on test entirely. Uniformly good reviews, however, are not uncommon, even for bad software. Reviewers have publication loyalty and other biases influencing judgment. So while reviews are helpful, they should be regarded as opinion and not as fact.

Public communication services provide on-line databases of published articles and reviews. Some give only summaries of articles. Based on summaries, one could decide if a thorough reading of source articles would be informative.

Current application users can provide valuable recommendations and insights about after-sale support. Do competent people respond to service calls?

Product literature and *User Guides* provide helpful information. Usually they can be examined for free at computer stores. But as one dealer warns, "If you can't understand a *User Guide* after reading it for fifteen minutes at the store, it won't make any more sense if you try to use it later."

Some *User Guides* can be purchased separately for a seriously considered package. Companies deduct the cost from the price of software if later purchased.

User Guides should include an index and examples of use. Evidence of a written tutorial is good, but an on-screen one is even more helpful. Step-by-step procedures for start-up, operations, and backing up disks should be clear. The *Guide* should list operating system and hardware requirements as well as any limitations.

Program backup copy procedures can be important if the application is distributed on disks that are **copy protected** or uncopyable. This is designed to inhibit the illegal proliferation of proprietary software. A legitimate purchaser of application software, however, should do everything possible to prevent any downtime occurring from faulty program disks.

Testing Services

Several independent organizations test and rate software. They issue periodic updates, often in loose-leaf binders, as shown in Figure 3-26. Such a service can cost about $200 a year. Computer professionals and some libraries subscribe to these services.

One service claims that its comparative tests are unbiased because it accepts no advertising from any software supplier. It puts all comparable packages through the same tests under controlled conditions.

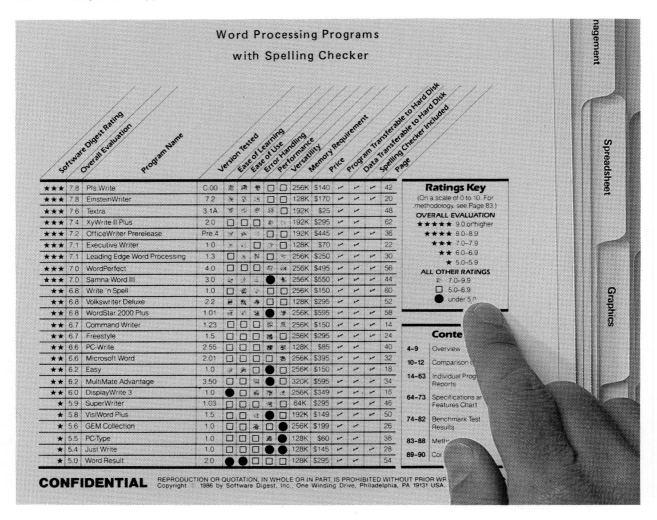

Word Processing Programs with Spelling Checker

Software Digest Rating	Overall Evaluation	Program Name	Version Tested	Memory Requirement	Price	Program Transferable to Hard Disk	Data Transferable to Hard Disk	Spelling Checker Included	Page
★★★	7.8	Pfs:Write	C.00	256K	$140	✓	✓	✓	42
★★★	7.8	EinsteinWriter	7.2	128K	$170	✓	✓	✓	20
★★★	7.6	Textra	3.1A	192K	$25	✓	✓		48
★★★	7.4	XyWrite II Plus	2.0	192K	$295	✓	✓		62
★★★	7.2	OfficeWriter Prerelease	Pre 4	192K	$445	✓	✓		36
★★★	7.1	Executive Writer	1.0	128K	$70	✓	✓		22
★★★	7.1	Leading Edge Word Processing	1.3	256K	$250	✓	✓	✓	30
★★★	7.0	WordPerfect	4.0	256K	$495	✓	✓	✓	56
★★★	7.0	Samna Word III	3.0	256K	$550	✓	✓	✓	44
★★	6.8	Write 'n Spell	1.0	256K	$150	✓	✓		60
★★	6.8	Volkswriter Deluxe	2.2	128K	$295	✓	✓		52
★★	6.8	WordStar 2000 Plus	1.01	256K	$595	✓	✓	✓	58
★★	6.7	Command Writer	1.23	256K	$150	✓	✓	✓	14
★★	6.7	Freestyle	1.5	256K	$295	✓	✓	✓	24
★★	6.6	PC-Write	2.55	128K	$85	✓	✓		40
★★	6.6	Microsoft Word	2.01	256K	$395	✓	✓	✓	32
★★	6.2	Easy	1.0	256K	$150	✓	✓	✓	18
★★	6.2	MultiMate Advantage	3.50	320K	$595	✓	✓	✓	34
★★	6.0	DisplayWrite 3	1.0	256K	$349	✓	✓	✓	16
★	5.9	SuperWriter	1.03	64K	$295	✓	✓	✓	46
★	5.8	VisiWord Plus	1.5	192K	$149	✓	✓	✓	50
★	5.6	GEM Collection	1.0	256K	$199	✓	✓		26
★	5.5	PC-Type	1.0	128K	$60	✓	✓		38
★	5.4	Just Write	1.0	128K	$145	✓	✓		28
★	5.0	Word Result	2.0	128K	$295	✓	✓		54

Ratings Key

(On a scale of 0 to 10. For methodology, see Page 83.)

OVERALL EVALUATION
★★★★★ 9.0 or higher
★★★★ 8.0-8.9
★★★ 7.0-7.9
★★ 6.0-6.9
★ 5.0-5.9

ALL OTHER RATINGS
▨ 7.0-9.9
☐ 5.0-6.9
● under 5.0

Conte[nts]
4-9   Overview
10-12   Comparison
14-63   Individual Prog... Reports
64-73   Specifications a... Features Chart
74-82   Benchmark Test Results
83-88   Meth...
89-90   Co...

FIGURE 3-26
A comparative report from a software testing and rating service
(*Service*: Software Digest Ratings Newsletter, *courtesy of Software Digest*)

Users find these services useful for the following reasons:

- They help to eliminate packages that are not worth further investigation.
- They help to identify packages that should be investigated further.
- They save time by not having to seek out individual reviews.

Hands-On Test

If the application package passes the criteria in Part One of the General Software Evaluation Checklist, it could justify a hands-on test. A **hands-on test** is actually using the candidate software on a computer to check it firsthand. Part Two of the General Evaluation Checklist guides the hands-on test.

Many software products are poorly designed, making them tedious and costly to use. Hands-on testing helps to avoid being encumbered with awkward software. It also helps to verify that the software does, or does not, work as advertised.

A package should feel comfortable to use. If it feels confusing or sluggish, it might never be used after purchase. To avoid a lost investment, especially of learning time, the hands-on test could prove invaluable.

CASE STUDY: Report: PCs Don't Always Improve Worker Productivity

Using personal computers does not necessarily lead to productivity increases. That's the conclusion of two Wall Street reports—one from First Boston Corp., the other from Morgan Stanley—that used recent data from the U.S. Commerce Department to explore the link between high-technology purchases and productivity.

Both reports found a disquieting lack of—and in some cases decline in—productivity in the white-collar sector of the economy, where 80 percent of the high-technology purchases have been made in the last 15 years. High-tech investments in the manufacturing sector, on the other hand, resulted in dramatic increases in productivity, according to the Morgan Stanley report.

One Up, One Down.   The author of the Morgan Stanley report, senior economist Stephen Roach, found that despite the PC investments, white-collar productivity declined 2.6 percent over the past 10 years. The productivity of manufacturing workers, however, increased 46 percent. Productivity levels were determined according to government measurements. "The presumption that high-tech offers a guaranteed productivity payback is a luxury the U.S. economy can no longer afford," said Mr. Roach.

William Sahlman of the Harvard Business School, however, disputed the researchers' findings. He said the productivity measurements used by the government are insufficient to register the gains made by high-technology products. "We would have to pay attention to what would have happened without the introduction of technology," Mr. Sahlman said. "You can't just measure simple statistics on output. You have to measure quality, too."

On a personal level, computers have made work less taxing and more accurate, he maintained. Nationally, the economy could be paralyzed without the assistance of computers that handle the ever-increasing volumes of information being generated, he said. "Maybe we didn't gain much ground, but we sure kept up with the mess," he said. "We've gone from zero PCs to 12 million in six years. We still don't know how to use PCs productively. We are still in the neophyte stage of this cycle of technology."

But Rosanne Cahn, the economist who authored the First Boston report, said she has heard those arguments before. To an extent, she agreed with Mr. Sahlman. "Without computers, productivity growth would have been even lower," she said.

Whatever the case, the question remains: Has business gotten its money's worth?

Both Ms. Cahn and Mr. Roach thought not. "The stock of computers has grown rapidly, [yet] there has been no noticeable impact on any economy-wide measure that might be expected to be positively affected by computerization," Ms. Cahn wrote in her report.

Future Payoff. But that payoff may yet be coming—at the end of the decade. From the industrial revolution, the analyst said, productivity enhancements wrought by technology investments have taken decades to show up in national economies.

"A lot of technology has been indiscriminately acquired and hasn't matched the demands and needs of office workers who end up using mainframes for narrow tasks," said Mr. Roach. "Corporate America has presumed that technology offers opportunities of improved productivity."

Networking, improved information management, software that solves specific business problems, reductions in computer-support (MIS) staffing and standardization within organizations will all help productivity, said Mr. Roach. "The applications of high-technology have not been all that well thought-out by management," he said, which has "had open-ended technological acquisition programs for a decade and a half while hoping that, by osmosis, the payback would rise to the surface."

(*Source*: Reprinted with permission from *PC Week*, June 17, 1987, p. 115. Copyright © by Ziff Communications Company.)

DISCUSSION QUESTIONS

1. Opposing positions are argued in the above article about workers and their productivity when using computers. Which position would you support and why?

2. Some solutions are offered in the article to "help productivity." Why do you agree, or not agree, with the solutions offered? Can you recommend others?

CHAPTER SUMMARY

- *Application software* makes the hardware perform a meaningful user task, like word processing or order processing.

- Five categories of application software are: personal productivity, file and database management, accounting and industry-specific, communications, and special-purpose (like desktop publishing and knowledge-based systems).

- *Personal productivity* applications, like word processing, spreadsheets, and graphics, help business professionals accomplish some of their most important everyday professional tasks.

- *Stand-alone packages* are single applications. *Integrated packages* contain several applications.

- Small- to medium-sized organizations buy packaged accounting and industry-specific packages to improve day-to-day operations and produce information for decision making as a by-product of processing.

- An *accounting package* that is generalized enough to be used by many industry types is called a *general, horizontal,* or *cross-industry* package.

- An *industry-specific package*, also called a *vertical package*, is tailored to the needs of a specific industry segment.

- An *integrated accounting system* combines several stand-alone accounting packages.

- Large organizations program most of their own applications to automate their businesses. So-called *data processing systems* handle the day-to-day operations. So-called *management information systems* and *decision support systems* support middle- and upper-level managers in their decision-making tasks.

- *File and database management software* allows users to create their own unique file-based applications, often without programming. *File managers* are simpler and easier to use than *database management systems*.

- *Communication software* links remote computing devices together in *wide-area* and *local-area networks*.

It also enables a user to benefit from services like *electronic mail*, *electronic conferencing*, and *on-line databases*. Services are widely available from *public communication services* for a fee.

- *Desktop publishing* enables the computer-aided production of documents such as newsletters and brochures. It requires the use of a desktop microcomputer, page composition software, and a printer, among other possible components.

- *Artificial intelligence* is an umbrella term for systems that mimic human behavior like *knowledge-based systems*, *robot systems*, and *natural language systems*.

- *Knowledge-based system software* can capture, magnify, and distribute access to judgment. It can function as an assistant, colleague, or expert.

- *Robot systems* combine hardware and software to serve a function in the workplace, which usually is a factory assembly line.

- *Natural language system software* enables users to carry on a computer dialogue in plain English.

- Application acquisition choices, ordered in terms of the best investment of user time and money, are: buy a package, modify a package, create a custom application with a database package, and develop a custom application from scratch using traditional methods.

- A *custom application* is unique and is developed for a person's or an organization's exclusive use.

- The *system development life cycle* is the computer industry's formalized method to create new applications, usually called "systems," from scratch.

- Companies devoted to developing new software are called *software houses*, *software development companies*, and *software suppliers* or *vendors*.

- *System analysis* refers to the investigative phase of *what* has to be done in a new application. *System design* refers to the definition of *how* it will be done.

- A *requirement analysis* is an investigatory stage that begins the system development life cycle. It involves interviewing key people, observing procedures, and examining relevant documents.

- A *system analyst* performs all system analysis and design work identified with the system development life cycle.

- A *feasibility report* details the economic, technological, and operational feasibility of a proposed system development project.

- A *data flow diagram* is a graphical model of a system.

- A *system flowchart* is a graphical model of the flow of control through a system.

- A *program* defines the processing logic to get input into a computer, process it, and generate output.

- *Program coding* is writing computer programs using the code and rules of a chosen program language, such as BASIC or COBOL.

- *Debugging* is removing errors from a computer program.

- A *computer programmer* specializes in coding and debugging programs.

- A *programmer-analyst* is a dual-function computer professional who can do both system analyst and programmer projects.

- *User-developed systems* are applications developed by users for their own benefit.

- Large organizations provide *Information Centers*, staffed with computer professionals, to help users create "user-developed systems."

- A *prototype* is a quickly produced, rough version of a user application.

- The *prototyping approach* involves a computer professional who works with a user to create a user-developed application. The approach eliminates a formal adherence to the system development life cycle.

- Evaluating an application begins with checking whether all application requirements have been met. If they have been, it continues with an evaluation of general package considerations and a hands-on test. Often checklists are used to guide a systematic evaluation process.

- Testing services are independent organizations that test and rate software.

- A *hands-on test* is actually using candidate software on a computer to check it firsthand.

KEY TERMS

Accounting package
Application development software
  package
Application software

Artificial intelligence
Communication software
Computer programmer
Copy protected

Custom application
Database management system,
    software, or package
Data flow diagram
Data processing system
Debugging
Decision support system
Desktop publishing
Electronic conferencing
Electronic mail
Feasibility report
File management package
Hands-on test
Horizontal package
Industry-specific package
Information Center
Integrated accounting system
Integrated packages
Knowledge-based system software
Local-area network
Management information system
    (MIS system)
Natural language system software
On-line databases
Packaged application

Personal productivity application
Program
Program coding
Program design
Programmer-analyst
Prototype
Prototyping approach
Public communication service
Requirements analysis
Robot systems
Software development company
Software house
Software supplier or vendor
Stand-alone packages
Structured methods
System analysis
System analyst
System design
System development life cycle
System documentation
System flowchart
User-developed systems
Vertical package
Wide-area network

REVIEW QUESTIONS

1. What is application software?

2. Identify five application categories and give examples of software found in each category.

3. Differentiate between a stand-alone and an integrated application.

4. Differentiate between accounting and industry-specific packages.

5. What are a user's choices in acquiring application software? Which is the best and why?

6. Identify the steps in the system development life cycle.

Compare the following:

7. · System analysis with system design

8. · System analyst with computer programmer

9. · System flowchart with program flowchart

10. · Program coding with program design

11. · Prototype with prototyping approach

Define the following:

12. · Software house

13. · Feasibility report

14. · Debugging

15. · User-developed system

16. · Information Center

17. Before a "hands-on test" of application software is made, what items should be evaluated?

EXERCISES

1. *Amalgamated Industries Case.* The manager of the Information Center at Amalgamated Industries is responsible for keeping up to date about new microcomputer applications. She asks for your support and wants you to visit a library and research the latest application products in any two of the

five possible categories presented in this chapter. Use computer periodicals published only within the last six months. Use the General Software Evaluation Checklist in Figure 3-25 as a guide for what to report about each product.

2. *Bethesda Nursing Home Case.*   Bethesda Nursing Home wants to automate its manual patient billing system. It purchased a microcomputer for about $10,000 to do this, which was its first venture into computing. However, after one year of trying to program the application, Bethesda gave up on the whole project. During that year, it spent an additional $15,000 on fees to a freelance programmer-analyst for programs it never used. Discuss alternative strategies Bethesda could have used when originally deciding to automate its patient billing.

3. Prepare an oral or written report on the concept of "prototyping" new applications. You might want to check the resources listed under "prototyping" in the *Computer Literature Index*. It is a useful bibliography for computer researchers.

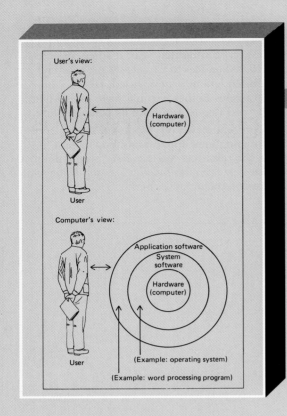

User's view:

User

Hardware (computer)

Computer's view:

User

Application software
System software
Hardware (computer)

(Example: operating system)

(Example: word processing program)

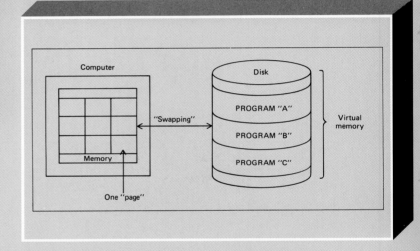

Computer

Memory

One "page"

"Swapping"

Disk

PROGRAM "A"

PROGRAM "B"

PROGRAM "C"

Virtual memory

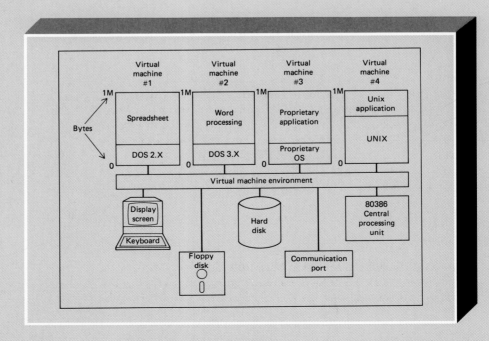

Virtual machine #1	Virtual machine #2	Virtual machine #3	Virtual machine #4

1M

Bytes

0

Spreadsheet

DOS 2.X

Word processing

DOS 3.X

Proprietary application

Proprietary OS

Unix application

UNIX

Virtual machine environment

Display screen

Keyboard

Floppy disk

Hard disk

Communication port

80386 Central processing unit

4

System Software

AFTER READING THIS CHAPTER, YOU SHOULD BE ABLE TO

· Describe what an operating system does

· Describe the purpose of disk housekeeping utilities

· Explain what program language processors are and why they are used

Users typically view their interaction with a computer as a very direct link to hardware, as shown in Figure 4-1. Hardware is the visible part of a computer system so the view is natural. Logically, the user is several layers removed, from the computer's viewpoint, as also shown in Figure 4-1. Two layers of software intervene, the application and system software layers. This chapter concerns the system software layer.

As shown in Figure 4-2, **system software** is an umbrella term for a collection of software that consists of

· Operating systems
· Utility programs
· Program language processors

Users of packaged applications often have little direct interface with system software, except for utility programs. Anyone who writes computer programs from scratch knows the three system software levels well.

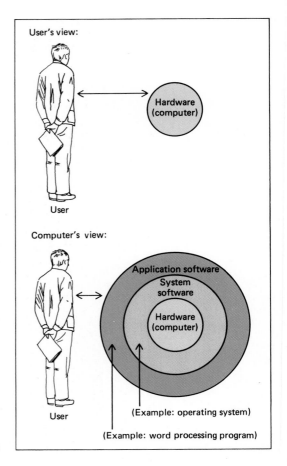

FIGURE 4-1
Different views of user-computer interaction

Because the operating system is the dominant component, popular microcomputer system software packages are often simply called "operating systems." Examples are *DOS* (*Disk Operating System*) and *OS/2* (*Operating System/2*).

System software seems to be more complex for users to work with or to try to understand than most application software. The reason for this is easy to comprehend. While application software is designed to service a user need, most system software is not. It is designed to service the computer itself. Since the computer is technologically a complex machine, so is the software that supports it to make it function.

OPERATING SYSTEM FUNCTIONS

The **operating system** is the centerpiece in the collection of programs known as system software. It acts as a buffer between an application and the computer's hardware. It enables the application to run (or execute) on the computer's hardware by relieving the application from the job of managing

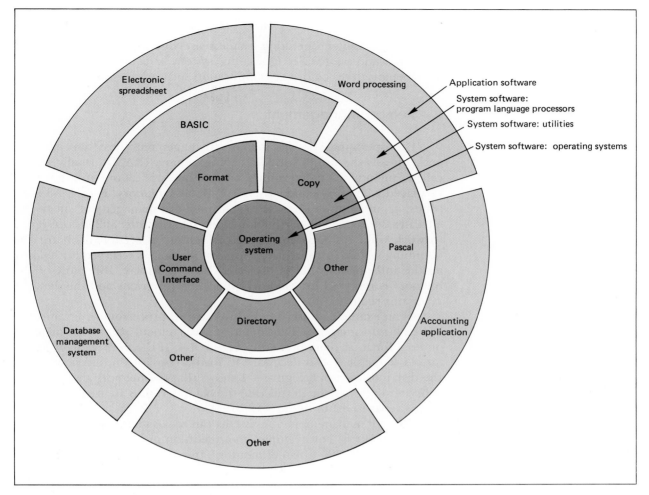

FIGURE 4-2
Detailed view of the three system software levels in relation to application
software

- · Memory (random access memory)
- · Data input and output
- · Program execution

Each operating system is optimized to run with a specific microprocessor, or central processing unit. For example:

Operating System	Microprocessor (Central Processing Unit) Which the Operating System Is Optimized to Support
DOS (IBM and Microsoft versions)	Intel 8086 and 8088
OS/2 (IBM and Microsoft versions)	Intel 80286
Apple Macintosh	Motorola 68000
Apple Macintosh II	Morotola 68020
DOS plus Microsoft 386 Windows	Intel 80386

Microcomputer operating systems are distributed on a disk, just like application software. Operating system software must be loaded into memory first, before any application software.

Memory Management

The operating system's memory management subsystem allocates and controls the use of random access memory (RAM), usually simply called "memory." It determines where the application program is to be placed when it is loaded into a computer's memory. Figure 4-3 illustrates, as an example, how the OS/2 memory management subsystem allocates the 16 megabytes (million bytes) that the Intel 80286 is designed to work with. As apparent, some of memory is sectioned off for the operating system software itself. Some of memory is reserved for holding all the information that is projected on the display. But most of the memory is reserved for holding application programs and the data the programs require.

As an example, a user might load a word processing program from the disk into memory. The memory management subsystem allocates an area for it, as diagrammed in Figure 4-4. If the user wants to revise an old letter, it is also necessary to load a copy of the old letter from the disk into memory. Figure 4-4 shows that the memory management subsystem places data, in this case the old letter, into an area of memory that is separate from the program.

Memory management subsystems can make memory appear larger than it actually is. For example, an application may be sold as requiring 640 Kbytes (640,000 bytes) of memory. In reality, the program requires one megabyte (1,000,000 bytes is the rounded form for 1,024,000 bytes). To execute in a 640-Kbyte memory space, some memory management techniques are required.

The **program overlay** technique allows a programmer to write programs that chain, or link, one program segment to another. For example, one program might begin by displaying a menu and asking the user for a menu choice. Depending on the user's choice, a new program segment may be brought from the disk into memory. It could execute until, perhaps, instructed to chain to another program segment. This program overlay technique can repeat as needed.

A **memory bank** technique partitions memory into sections, called "banks," and switches among them, as needed. It is used to support multiple users. Another technique, called *virtual memory*, is described in a later section of this chapter.

Input and Output Management

A major job of the operating system is to manage the flow of data traffic in and out of the computer over the proper electronic roadways.

The traffic control of data into and out of the computer is handled by a special suite of programs called **BIOS** (pronounced "bye-ose" for **Basic Input/Output System**). The operating system BIOS is coordinated to work with the hardware BIOS chips. Together they form the link that enables all the hardware peripherals to function in a microcomputer. This BIOS subsystem knows the correct signals for data routing and makes it easy for an application program to distribute data to a disk drive, the display screen, the printer, or any other peripheral connected to the computer.

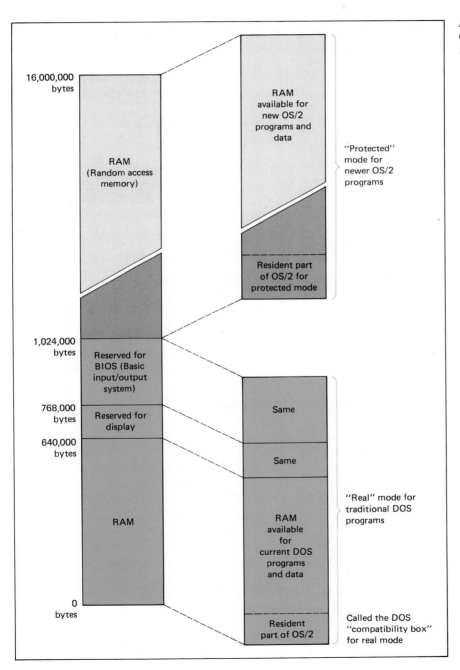

FIGURE 4-3
OS/2 memory (RAM) allocation of 16 megabytes

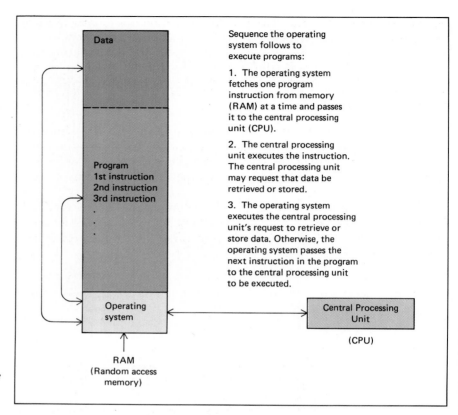

FIGURE 4-4
Programs and data are placed in separate areas of memory (RAM). The sequence of program execution is outlined.

In the word processing example, the BIOS subsystem does the actual retrieval of the old letter from the disk. It also places the letter in the spot that the memory management subsystem allocates for it in memory.

Program Execution Management

One of the main functions of the operating system is to orchestrate everything that happens inside the computer. The **executive subsystem** acts like the conductor of a symphony orchestra. It must make all the hardware and software work harmoniously or cacophony will result.

As an example, when an application in process needs data, such as the old letter called by the word processing program, the executive subsystem directs its retrieval through the BIOS subsystem. First, the executive halts program processing temporarily until the record is retrieved. If a nonexistent data file is asked for, it notifies the application to take corrective action. If no error control is programmed into the application, the executive takes over and usually suspends execution. It then notifies the user of the problem.

Figure 4-5 provides a much more detailed example of how a program is executed inside a computer. Execution occurs through the executive subsystem of the operating system working in close coordination with the central processing unit. The two major components of the central processing unit are identified

- *Control unit*—carries out program instructions.
- *Arithmetic/logic unit*—calculates and compares data when instructed by the control unit. Arithmetic operations are normal addition, subtraction, multiplication, and division.

Figure 4-5 shows how the central processing unit works in tandem with memory, which the operating system has sectioned off into locations with addresses. **Memory addresses** are like mailboxes where the addresses never change, but content varies every time a new program or data are loaded and processed.

The figure also shows how a customer's new charge of $200 is added to the old balance of $400. The example assumes that previous processing put the customer's old balance in the arithmetic/logic unit. The remaining steps to process the transaction are

- First, a program instruction is brought by the operating system from its memory location and is temporarily stored in the control unit. In the example,

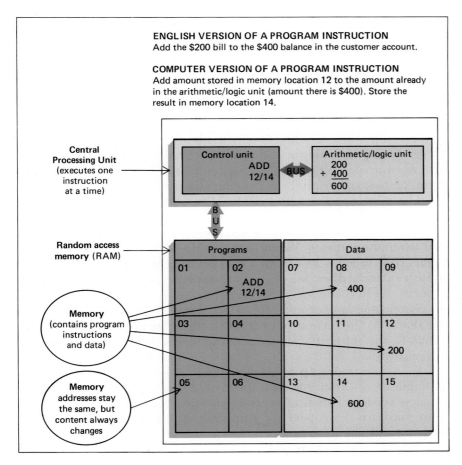

FIGURE 4-5
How a computer executes a program instruction

the instruction is ADD, and the memory address 12 holds the data to be added.

- Next, data are brought by the operating system from memory location 12 and are temporarily placed in the arithmetic/logic unit. In the example, the value 200 is retrieved.
- Next, the central processing unit takes over to process the operation specified in the instruction, which is an "add" operation. In this example, the new amount in the arithmetic/logic unit is added to the amount already resident there.
- Finally, the result, 600, is transferred by the operating system to memory location 14.

A later program instruction makes the operating system store the data on an external disk for future reference and processing. The example is greatly simplified. In addition, all program instructions and data are really processed as strings of 1's and 0's, or on and off electronic pulses. Nothing would be understandable in English.

OPERATING SYSTEM ENVIRONMENTS

Major differences in how the operating system exercises its management functions are evident in single-tasking, multitasking, and multiuser computer environments.

Single Tasking

A **single-tasking operating system** is the kind Mr. Nelson uses. It accommodates one user and is only used on personal microcomputers. He can do only one thing at a time, whether it is an electronic spreadsheet, or a word processing project, or whatever. If he wants to print a document, he has to wait until the printing task is done to resume work.

The most popular single-tasking operating system for microcomputers is called DOS or **MS–DOS,** which is designed to work with Intel's 8086 and 8088 microprocessors. MS stands for Microsoft, the company that wrote the software. When IBM put MS–DOS on its Personal Computer, IBM called it **PC–DOS.** This operating system is considered an **industry standard** because of its widespread use on millions of microcomputers.

System and application software are usually sold by version number, like DOS 3.3. The version number reflects different upgrades or improvements to the software. Some operating system versions are identified in Figure 4-6.

If anyone trades up to a new version of an old operating system, all application software written for the old version should be usable on the new version. This is called **compatibility.** It is highly desirable, and more software developers are emphasizing this feature in their ever-evolving and maturing products.

Otherwise, to upgrade to an incompatible operating system requires

OPERATING SYSTEMS	MAJOR FEATURES
DOS Versions	
DOS 1	Basic single-tasking operating systems for an 8088/8086 microprocessor-based computer with 5 ¼-inch floppy disk drive support
DOS 2	Hard disk support
DOS 3	Local area network support
DOS 3.2	3 ½-inch floppy disk drive support
DOS 3.3	Adds new commands and other features
OS/2 Versions	
OS/2 1 Standard Edition	Basic multitasking operating system for an 80286 microprocessor-based computer
OS/2 1.1 Standard Edition	Adds a windowing capability called "Presentation Manager" or "Windows"
OS/2 1.1 Extended Edition	IBM proprietary extension that adds communication and database support

FIGURE 4-6
Operating system versions

buying new application software to work with it. In effect, it means trashing all old software. Users with heavy investments in application software and learning do not willingly change to an incompatible operating system.

Users of DOS applications can upgrade to OS/2 and continue to use old DOS software. As Figure 4-3 shows, it will execute in the first 640,000 bytes of memory (known as "the DOS 640 Kbytes barrier"). Only one DOS program can run there at a time in the so-called **real mode.**

Multitasking

Multitasking operating systems can run several applications (also called programs, tasks, or sessions) concurrently, as shown in Figure 4-7. This is the kind that Mr. Nelson eventually acquired. Multitasking operating systems are available on all types of computers, from microcomputers to mainframes.

Business professionals typically do several things or tasks at once. Microcomputers usually use windows, as shown in Figure 4-7, to display all the tasks that are active at the same time. A **window** is one area of a divided display screen. Each window has all the capabilities of a single display. A user can edit a document with a word processor in one window,

System menu box
(upper) left corner of each window)

Caption bar
(1st line in each window)

Menu bar
(2nd line
in each
window)

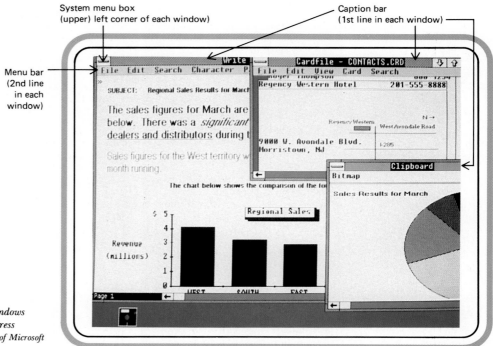

FIGURE 4-7
*A multitasking system with windows
showing three sessions in progress
(Software: Windows 2.0, courtesy of Microsoft
Corporation)*

examine a spreadsheet in another, and create a bar chart with a graphics application in a third.

By moving the cursor into a window, a user indicates which of several active processes is intended for use. Output from one window can be directed to another window to carry out multiple functions.

OS/2, or **Operating System/2,** is a single-user multitasking operating system designed to work with Intel's 80286 microprocessor. It was created by Microsoft Corporation under a joint marketing agreement with IBM Corporation. The operating system breaks the DOS 640-Kbyte barrier. It provides up to 16 megabytes of memory for running programs. The added memory enables programs to offer more functionality and ease of use than older DOS programs.

Each program that runs in the memory region above 640 Kbytes is called a **protected mode** program. The operating system, in effect, erects fire walls around programs so that they do not interfere with each other. Should one crash, it could not bring down all the others.

All application programs that take advantage of the protected mode must be programmed from scratch. This part of OS/2 is not compatible with DOS.

Proprietary Goal

For IBM, OS/2 is one of many products that manifest the firm's goal to make all its diverse computers "talk to one another." **Systems Application Architecture (SAA)** is the name of the plan to get IBM and its customers to that goal. While it may sound like the ultimate in corporate computing, IBM officials claim it may be years before users see full-scale implementation. The OS/2 part of the plan includes the following.

OS/2 Version	Contribution to SAA
OS/2 1.1 Standard Edition	Provides users with a window interface (called the "Presentation Manager" on OS/2) which is to be duplicated on all other of the firm's computer systems from personal computers to mainframes. This aspect of the grand plan is called "Comon User Access."
OS/2 1.1 Extended Edition	Provides users with a · Database Manager that is based on the firm's mainframe database management system Database 2 (DB2) and Structured Query Language (SQL). · Communication Manager that provides communications to virtually every system supported by the firm, including local-area as well as wide-area networks. This OS/2 version is only offered by IBM, but it does not preclude other suppliers from including equivalent functions in their products.

Window Package

In many cases, the system software that puts multiasking windows on the display is an add-on product to the operating system itself. It adds a new layer of software that functions as a buffer between the application software and the operating system, as shown in Figure 4-8. This software is variously called

· A window environment
· A control program

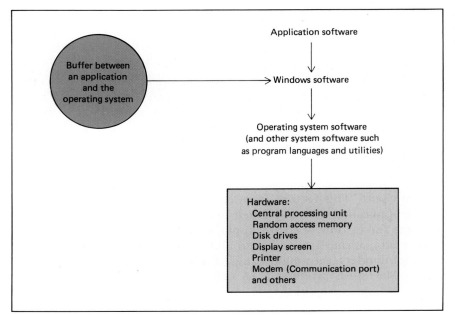

FIGURE 4-8
A windows package creates a new software layer

- An operating environment
- An application manager
- A multitasking environment manager

All names are appropriate to describe this software. It manages what a user sees on the screen or enters on the keyboard or with a mouse. It is also called a **graphic user interface.**

Probably the simplest name to use for this software is **window package.** Some window packages are Microsoft Windows, Graphics Environment Manager (GEM), DesqView, and TopView. IBM's Presentation Manager is the Microsoft Windows package remarketed under the IBM name.

Applications written to run with a window package all have a common "look and feel." The example in Figure 4-7 shows a **caption bar** across the top of each window which indicates the currently loaded program name. The system menu box at the upper left corner of each window allows the resizing, moving, or closing of a window, among other options.

Below the caption bar is a **menu bar.** Menu items are selected by using a mouse or by pressing selected keys. Some menu items invoke dialog boxes. **Dialog boxes** are also called **pop-up windows.** They may contain lists of options, among other possibilities.

A window package allows two applications to exchange data easily through a mechanism called the **clipboard.** An exchange involves the same steps, regardless of the applications involved. It works like this from a user's viewpoint:

- In one window, first block out the data for transfer. Then select "copy" from the menu. This copies the blocked data to the clipboard inside the computer's memory.
- Go to the second application window and select "paste" from the menu. This selection retrieves the data from the clipboard in memory, and places it into the second window application.

Graphics can be transferred this way as easily as text.

While the clipboard is convenient for "manual" transfers of data from one application to another, the **dynamic data exchange (DDE)** feature automates data transfers between applications. The most common example involves a "server" application that is programmed to receive stock quotations, possibly through an electronic link over the telephone. The "client" application is a graphics application. It is programmed to receive the incoming stock quotations from the server. Then it displays the changing prices of the stock through its graphs. All of this data exchange takes place without human interaction only if an application is programmed to take advantage of the dynamic data exchange feature.

A window package also provides a **device independent** interface to such hardware as display, keyboard, mouse, printer, and data communication port. This feature frees users from worry about whether or not an application will run on their hardware. If a user installs a window package successfully, then any application that is advertised to run with it will automatically interface with all the hardware used.

MultiFinder is the multitasking operating system that works on newer Apple Macintosh products. The original Apple Macintosh computer has a single-tasking Finder operating system that has the "look and feel" of a multitasking operating system. Some developers have created window software that makes the PC–DOS single-tasking operating system also "look and feel" like a multitasking operating system.

Virtual Machines

Window packages designed to run with the Intel 80386 microprocessor (central processing unit), such as Microsoft's Windows 386, can create **virtual machines.** This makes one computer perform as if it were many computers running many different operating systems simultaneously. *Virtual* means "being in essence or in effect, but *not* in fact." The technique gives a user the same illusion that multitasking gives. It appears that several computers are working, when in fact, there is only one real machine.

The memory allocation scheme to create Intel's 80386 virtual machines (called "virtual 86 mode") is given in Figure 4-9. As Figure 4-10

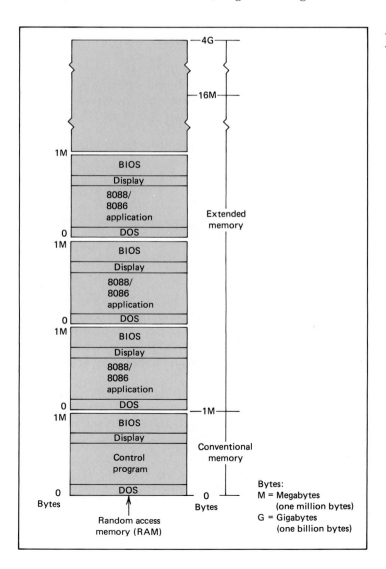

FIGURE 4-9
Memory (RAM) allocation for Intel's 80386 "virtual machines"

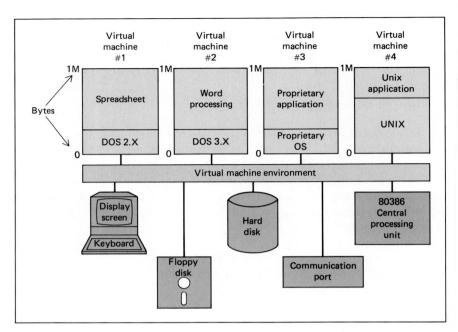

FIGURE 4-10
Each virtual machine could run a
different operating system.

shows, each virtual machine could run a different operating system. It does not necessarily have to be DOS. But when using the virtual machine feature, the operating system must be one that was originally designed for the Intel 8086 or 8088 microprocessor.

This virtual machine technique is a familiar one on large mainframe multiuser systems.

MULTIUSER OPERATING ENVIRONMENTS

All system software, especially the operating system, is far more complex in a multiuser environment. Reasons for the complexity are simple. In a multiuser installation, many users share one computer and all need support for a variety of different applications. Many of them require special input and output devices. Since all these functions require expensive hardware resources, the allocation and monitoring of resources becomes a gargantuan task.

A **multiuser operating system** must not only provide numerous services to users, hardware, and application programs but also see that programs "get along" with one another. This includes preventing a program from locking out specific records from shared files. It must also prevent the lockout of an entire disk.

On the other hand, the operating system must lock out unauthorized users. One way it does this is to require users to log on to the computer by asking for an identification number and a password. Entries are matched with files of all authorized user IDs and passwords. Only after verifying that a user is legitimate can applications be run.

One microcomputer multiuser operating system software product is **Unix,** which provides both multitasking and multiuser capability. The Unix operating systems has spawned many derivatives, like Xenix. Unix is especially prevalent in scientific and engineering environments. It was developed by Bell Laboratories and is promoted by AT&T.

Time Sharing

Multiuser operating systems support many users by loading everybody's program into memory. Then it slices up central processing unit time among all user programs, as diagrammed in Figure 4-11. Computer professionals call this **time sharing.**

Because time slices switch at blinding speed, a user is never conscious of what is happening "under the hood." Users each believe they are the only one using the computer.

As Figure 4-11 shows, multiple programs are resident in memory at once. For this reason, some computer professionals call it a *multiprogramming* operating system. The concept, whether called multiprogramming or time sharing, is fundamental to multiuser, as well as multitasking, computer operating systems.

Virtual Memory

Sometimes memory is not big enough to accommodate all the programs users require. Some operating systems then use disk space as an extension of computer memory, as shown in Figure 4-12. Since disk space is not actual memory but virtually acts as memory, the concept is called **virtual memory** or *virtual storage*. It only gives the operating system the illusion of more memory. Memory management involves sectioning memory into "pages." Sections of programs currently in use occupy real memory *pages*. When no longer in use, they are "paged out" or "swapped" for new pages from the disk.

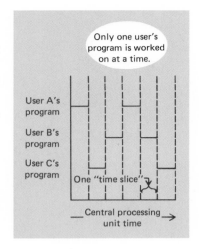

FIGURE 4-11
Time sharing or "slicing" enables one computer to support many users.

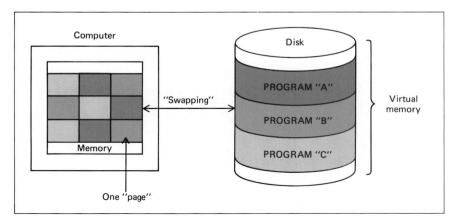

FIGURE 4-12
"Virtual memory" operating systems expand memory by using disk storage space.

If the system load gets high, and swapping is frequent, certain pages might be "paged out" and back again incessantly. Such behavior, called *thrashing*, can be a problem when not enough real memory underlies virtual memory.

UTILITY PROGRAMS

A wide range of utility programs are packaged with operating system software or can be bought separately. **Utilities** are a collection of programs that mainly help

· To keep track of disk files
· To perform disk housekeeping chores

With his simple microcomputer system, Mr. Nelson learned how to use the utility commands to *format* and *copy* disks as well as to view a *directory* of disk files.

To begin working with utility programs, Mr. Nelson places the DOS disk in the left, or "A," disk drive and then powers up the computer. Soon A> appears on the display screen as the operating system prompt for user input. The "A" in the prompt identifies the current active disk drive.

Format

One of the first utility programs Mr. Nelson tries is called **format.** Blank disks are unusable until formatted. The process of formatting, also called *initializing*, a disk partitions it into *sectors* and *tracks*. It is analogous to marking streets before building a housing development. Whenever a file is saved, the operating system first checks to find unused sections, or sectors, to store the file in.

The command to format a disk is FORMAT B:. The "B" indicates the disk drive that holds the blank disk to be formatted. After a few seconds of whirring and clicking, the display indicates that formatting is complete, as shown in Figure 4-13.

During this housekeeping chore, the operating system checks the entire disk for damaged sectors. If it finds any, it lists the amount of unusable disk space. The operating system automatically knows how to ignore bad sectors.

Mr. Nelson finds formatting disks a tedious process. He does a whole box of ten floppy disks at a time to get it over with.

Diskcopy

One reason Mr. Nelson uses the DISKCOPY utility is to make backup disks of programs and data. He never uses original program disks. He stores them in a safe palce away from the computer. Instead he uses a

FIGURE 4-13
*Some utility program commands
and responses*

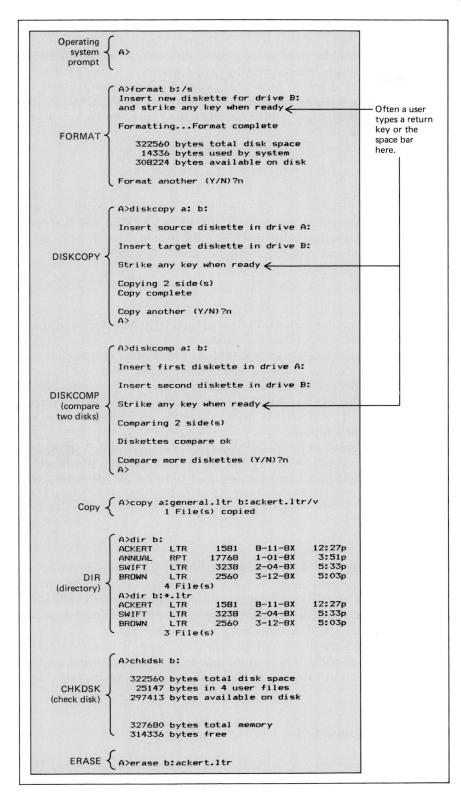

```
Operating
 system    { A>
 prompt

           { A>format b:/s
             Insert new diskette for drive B:
             and strike any key when ready

             Formatting...Format complete

  FORMAT       322560 bytes total disk space
                14336 bytes used by system
               308224 bytes available on disk

           { Format another (Y/N)?n


           { A>diskcopy a: b:

             Insert source diskette in drive A:

             Insert target diskette in drive B:

 DISKCOPY  { Strike any key when ready

             Copying 2 side(s)
             Copy complete

             Copy another (Y/N)?n
           { A>


           { A>diskcomp a: b:

             Insert first diskette in drive A:

             Insert second diskette in drive B:

 DISKCOMP  { Strike any key when ready
 (compare
 two disks)   Comparing 2 side(s)

             Diskettes compare ok

             Compare more diskettes (Y/N)?n
           { A>


    Copy   { A>copy a:general.ltr b:ackert.ltr/v
                   1 File(s) copied


           { A>dir b:
             ACKERT    LTR    1581    8-11-8X    12:27p
             ANNUAL    RPT   17768    1-01-8X     3:51p
             SWIFT     LTR    3238    2-04-8X     5:33p
    DIR      BROWN     LTR    2560    3-12-8X     5:03p
 (directory)       4 File(s)
             A>dir b:*.ltr
             ACKERT    LTR    1581    8-11-8X    12:27p
             SWIFT     LTR    3238    2-04-8X     5:33p
             BROWN     LTR    2560    3-12-8X     5:03p
           {       3 File(s)


           { A>chkdsk b:

               322560 bytes total disk space
                25147 bytes in 4 user files
               297413 bytes available on disk
  CHKDSK
 (check disk)
               327680 bytes total memory
           {   314336 bytes free

   ERASE   { A>erase b:ackert.ltr
```

Often a user
types a return
key or the
space bar
here.

"working copy" of the original in case the disk goes bad or becomes damaged.

The command he uses to copy one entire disk to another is DISK-COPY A: B:, which is interpreted as copy whatever is in disk drive A onto the disk in drive B. More disk whirring and clicking noises tell him the copying is taking place. Another command, DISKCOMP, verifies that one disk compares with or matches the other. Problems, if any, are displayed.

Copy

Should he need to copy one file, instead of an entire disk, he uses the COPY demand. As an example, COPY ACKERT.LTR B: copies the ACKERT.LTR file in disk drive A to the disk in drive B. The copied file is given the same name. It could be renamed, if desired.

Directory

Another frequently used utility program is DIR, **directory.** It displays a list, or directory, of files stored on a disk.

File names can be eight characters long followed by a three-character extension. Mr. Nelson always uses the extension LTR or RPT for his word-processed documents to distinguish letters from reports. As an example, the file called ACKERT.LTR holds the letter he recently wrote to Jim Ackert. The ANNUAL.RPT file holds his contribution to the company's annual report.

He can display only selected parts of the directory. Typing DIR A:*.LTR, for example, retrieves only the LTR items from the directory. The asterisk is known as a *wild card* and retrieves all file names with LTR extensions.

Erase

To delete unwanted files, he uses the utility program called ERASE. It immediately deletes the file name from the directory. The file content physically gets wiped out whenever the operating system needs space and writes over it. But no simple way is provided to retrieve a mistakenly erased file. That is why backup disks are so important.

Some separately sold utility packages do things like recover erased files. One also provides a menu of available DOS utility programs, such as the one shown in Figure 4-14. Often utility programs are called *DOS commands*.

Other Capabilities

As he becomes more experienced, Mr. Nelson uses some other DOS utilities. As Figure 4-15 shows, he could declare *subdirectories*. To reach the Ackert letter, for example, he declares the *pathname* by typing

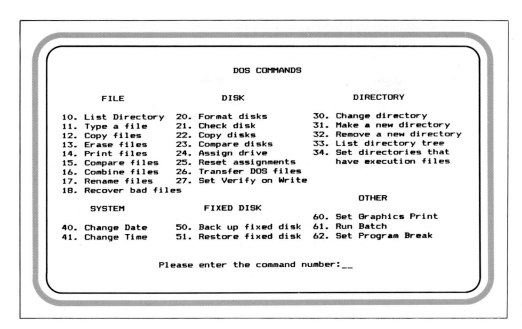

FIGURE 4-14
Menu of utility programs
(*Courtesy of Software Solutions, Inc.*)

FIGURE 4-15
Examples of a tree directory for files stored on a disk

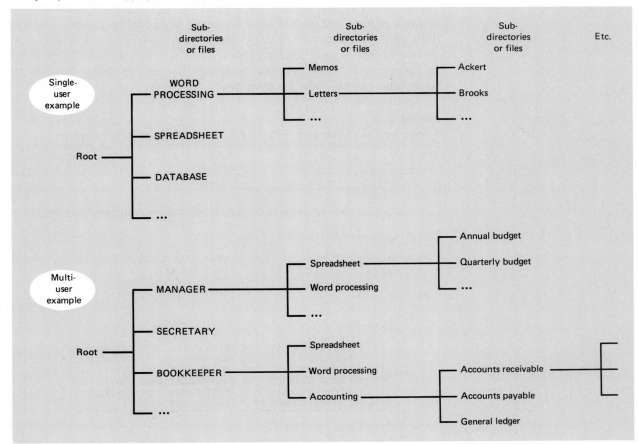

\WP\Letters\ACKERT. Each subdirectory is a refinement of the one before it.

Figure 4-14 shows how the directory structure is ideal for multiuser environments. It is also useful for hard disk users who have a large number of files to manage.

Another advanced capability allows him to *pipeline* tasks. Mr. Nelson could, for example, type DIR ¦ SORT to sort a directory list into alphabetic order. The output of DIR becomes the input to SORT. The output of SORT gets sent to the display.

In this example, the vertically split bar ¦ is called a *pipe*, and the programs named on either side of it are called *filters*. A filter theoretically gets input, then modifies or filters it, and sends the result to an output device. In some instances, pipes and filters can be strung out to do a complete series of tasks.

Utility programs that resemble those used on Mr. Nelson's microcomputer can be found on minicomputers and mainframes. The more elaborate the software and hardware instllation, the greater the need for housekeeping utility software.

PROGRAM LANGUAGES

A final part of system software concerns program languages. Figures 4-16 and 4-17 illustrate excerpts from computer program listings and show a variety of program languages, some of which are briefly described in Figure 4-18. Each program language has its own rules for how to write (also called "code") a program.

FIGURE 4-16

A single line of COBOL program code compared with two other programming languages
(*Source: T. J. O'Leary and Brian K. Williams,* Computer and Information Processing, *Benjamin Cummings, 1985, p. 171.*)

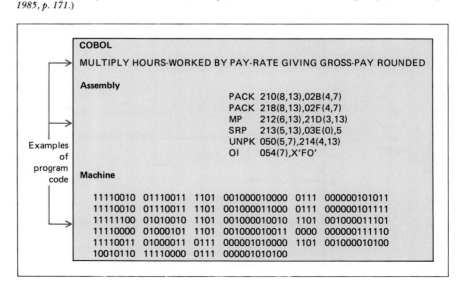

```
main ( )
{
char*name;
  printf("What is your
  name?");
  scanf("%s",name);
  printf("Hi,%s\n",name);
}
```

This "C" program asks a user
"What is your name."

```
MODULE Main; (* Modula-2 source *)

  MODULE RandomNumbers;
    IMPORT TimeOfDay;
    EXPORT Random;
    VAR Seed : INTEGER;

    PROCEDURE Random : INTEGER;
    BEGIN
      Seed := ((Seed * 21) + 13)
              MOD 256);
      RETURN Seed;
    END Random;


  BEGIN
    Seed := TimeOfDay;
  END RandomNumbers;


BEGIN (* Main *)


  WriteInt(Random,3);


END Main.
```

This "Modula 2" program
generates a random number.

```
PROGRAM averagescore (infile,outfile);

VAR score, sum, average, count : real;
    infile, outfile : text;

BEGIN
    sum:=0.0; count:0.0;
    REPEAT
        read(infile,score);
        sum:=sum + score;
        count:=count + 1.0
    UNTIL eof(infile);
    average:=sum/count;
    write (outfile, ' Average score is', average)
END.
```

This "Pascal" computes the
average (arithmetic mean) of
a group of numbers.

FIGURE 4-17
A sampler of code from three programming languages
(*Sources*: *Top, G. B. Shelley and T. J. Cashman*, Computer Fundamentals, *Anaheim Publishing, Anaheim,
Calif., 1984, p. 13.7; bottom, James A. O'Brien*, Computers in Business Management, *Richard D. Irwin,
Homewood, Ill., 1985, p. 333.*)

Ada. Developed in 1980 under the sponsorship of the U.S. Department of Defense and (named for Lady Augusta Ada Byron, considered the world's first programmer) intended to be a standard language for weapons system, although it also has commercial applications.

APL (*A Programming Language*). Introduced by IBM in 1968; is useful for processing large tables of numbers.

BASIC (*Beginner's All-purpose Symbolic Instruction Code*). Developed in 1964 at Dartmouth College. It is the most popular computer language and can be used by beginners as well as experienced people. BASIC is an interactive, procedure-oriented language that permits user and computer to communicate with each other directly.

C. A structured language developed by Bell Laboratories as part of the Unix operating system. It resembles assembler language and is becoming increasingly important for microcomputer and system programming.

COBOL (*COmmon Business-Oriented Language*). Developed in 1959. It is the most frequently used programming language in business. Writing in COBOL is like writing a paper: one writes sentences that tell the computer which operations to perform. COBOL has several advantages: (1) It is easy to understand. (2) It is self-documenting. (3) It can be used for almost any business programming task. COBOL also has some disadvantages: (1) It is wordy. (2) It is not well suited for mathematics. (3) It is not as speedy as other languages.

FORTH. Developed in the early 1980s by an astronomer to control his large telescopes. It requires little computer memory but does need a sophisticated and skilled programmer to write code properly.

FORTRAN (*FORmula TRANslation*). Introduced by IBM in 1954 as the first high-level language. It is the most widely used scientific-mathematic language.

LISP. Developed at the Massachusetts Institute of Technology in 1958 to write programs for artificial intelligence applications. It processes characters and words rather than numbers.

FIGURE 4-18
Several programming languages and their main characteristics

The program language called **machine language** is like talking to a computer in its native 1's and 0's, or off and on electronic pulses. Programming in machine language can be a nightmare to do or to correct. Imagine a programmer finding a single 1 among thousands that should be a 0.

To make programming the computer a more humane task, **program languages** evolved, as identified in Figure 4-19. As they become more readable by humans, they become less readable by hardware. The translation process from a human-readable language to a machine-readable language takes time. The higher the language, the less efficient it is in terms of processing speed. More translation steps must go on to reduce higher languages into 1's and 0's.

Language Processors

The program that accepts a programmer's code and translates it into 1's and 0's is technically called a **language processor.** Language processors use two methods to translate code. They either interpret or

Logo. Developed at the Massachusetts Institute of Technology as a dialect of LISP and is known as "turtle graphics." It is used to command a triangular pointer, called a "turtle," on a video screen to plot graphic designs. Logo is useful teaching the fundamentals of programming, especially to children.

Modula-2. Developed in 1977 by Nicklaus Wirth, the author of Pascal. It combines the strengths of Pascal with the flexibility of C. It is designed to produce programs that work correctly the first time and that are easy to maintain.

Pascal (named after the seventeenth-century French mathematician and philosopher Blaise Pascal). Developed in the mid-1970s. It takes advantage of structured programming concepts. It is relatively easy to learn, and it is frequently available on microcomputer systems. It is excellent for scientific and systems uses and has good graphics capabilities. Pascal's main drawback is that it has limited input and output capabilities.

PILOT (*Programmed Inquiry, Learning Or Teaching*). A language designed as a special-propose language to develop CAI (computer-aided instruction) programs. It is a simple interactive language that enables a person with minimal computer experience to develop and test interactive CAI programs.

PL/1 (*Programming Language One*). Introduced by IBM in 1964 as a language that combines the features of COBOL, FORTRAN, and other languages.

Prolog. Invented in France and is heavily used in European artificial intelligence research projects. The Japanese have chosen Prolog as the language for their well-publicized project to build large-scale knowledge processing systems by 1990.

RPG (*Report Program Generator*). Introduced by IBM in 1964. It is a problem-oriented language that is limited to generating business reports.

Smalltalk. Invented by Xerox Corporation and designed to support an especially visual computer system. Most commands are accomplished with the use of a mouse. The principles of Smalltalk were adapted by Apple Computer in its Macintosh computers.

GENERATION	EXAMPLES OF PROGRAM LANGUAGES	UNITS OF TIME TO COMPLETE A PROGRAM
First generation	Machine Language	500 to 1,000
Second generation	Assembly Language	50 to 100
Third generation (*High-Level Language—HLL*)	BASIC, PASCAL, C, COBOL	5 to 10
Fourth generation (*Very-High-Level Language—VHLL*)	dBASE, FOCUS, and found in database management system packages and specialized packages	1

FIGURE 4-19
Computer programming languages
(*Source: G. Schussel, "Fourth Generation Productivity Tools," Data Management, October 1984, p. 42. Adapted with permission.*)

compile it. These methods give language processors their more common names of interpreters or compilers.

An **interpreter** takes human-readable program code and changes it into machine code during the actual step-by-step execution of a program. If the program is run seven times a day, the program code is reinterpreted seven times. Ordinary microcomputer BASIC is usually interpreted BASIC.

From 4 to 50 times faster than interpreted code is compiled code. COBOL is a compiled language and several versions of compiled BASIC are available. A **compiler** takes programmer-created statements, called **source code,** and goes through the language translation stage once. The translation stage is called "compiling the program," as shown in the diagram in Figure 4-20. The machine code is saved as a program file ready for execution at any time desired. The executable program file is called the **object code.**

Compiled programs are more difficult to work with and to debug. **Debugging** is the process of removing errors from programs. When a "program doesn't run," a programmer must correct the source code. Then the source code must be recompiled.

Many commercially distributed BASIC programs are not ordinary interpreted BASIC. They are compiled BASIC. Software developers usually use the interpreted version to simplify the debugging phase. Then they compile their programs for commercial distribution.

When Interstate Distributing Company bought its packaged accounting software, it received compiled BASIC programs. They were speedy enough, but when a hidden program bug appeared, there were problems. Since Interstate had no copy of the source code, its program could not be fixed on site. The software developer had to be contacted about the problem. Then the developer went through the stages diagrammed in Figure 4-20. When repaired object code was available, a copy of it had to be sent to Interstate to replace the faulty program.

Interstate's packaged software is supported with a maintenance con-

FIGURE 4-20
Entering and compiling a BASIC program produces both source and object code.

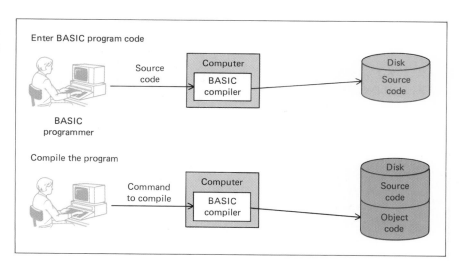

tract that covers program bug problems. But many commercial packages do not provide any repair or maintenance service. This is especially true of computer retail store packages.

BASIC

BASIC is the most popular language used with micrcomputers. The term BASIC is an acronym for *Beginners All-purpose Symbolic Instruction Code*. An extended introduction to the BASIC language and programming is available in *Using BASIC*, a structured BASIC programming supplement to this book.

An example of a microcomputer BASIC coded program appears in Figure 4-21. The example is comparable to a program that a beginning BASIC student might prepare.

As Figure 4-21 implies, a programmer types coded statements into a computer using a BASIC language processor. The "OK" on the programmer's display is a signal that the BASIC language interpreter is prepared to respond to the programmer's bidding. First, each line of program code is typed. Lines must precisely follow rules of the program language used. Some BASIC language program characteristics are shown in Figure 4-22.

After typing lines of code, which are called **program statements** or **instructions,** a programmer has several options. In the example, the

FIGURE 4-21
A BASIC program shown from the user and programmer views

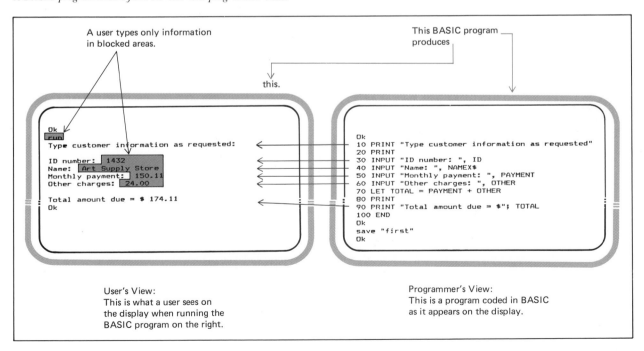

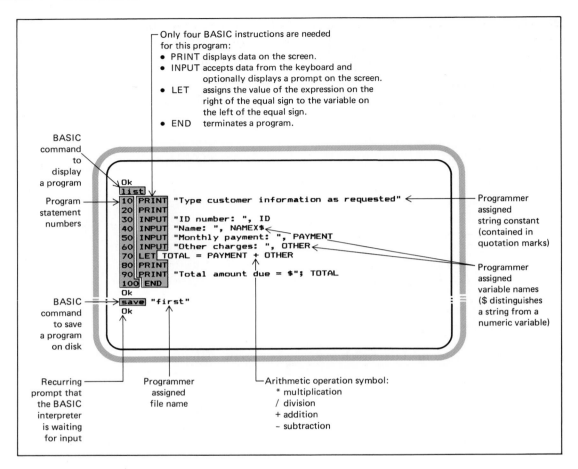

FIGURE 4-22
BASIC program characteristics

programmer chooses to SAVE the program. It becomes a disk file that will be called "First" for "first" exercise. Typing SAVE "FIRST" is all that it takes to store a BASIC microcomputer program on a disk as a program file.

To execute the program, a programmer or user simply types RUN. The RUN command executes the program immediately.

To get a printed copy of the program code, called a **program listing,** a programmer types LLIST. A listing is the only human-readable evidence and documentation that a program exists. Otherwise, the real executable program exists as magnetic fields of ones and zeros stored on the disk. To prevent a disaster, programmers make a copy of their program onto another safety or backup disk.

Figure 4-21 shows how the BASIC program requires a user to interact with the program during execution of lines 30 to 60. Whenever a user interacts with a program during execution, the program is called an *interactive* program.

Most BASIC programs are interactive, except those that print reports.

Whenever a user does not have to interact, as in report printing, the program is called a *batch* program. The term comes from early computer systems when everything was done in *batches*, without any user interaction whatsoever.

Many different versions of the BASIC language exist. Figure 4-23 shows a version called True BASIC. It was developed by the inventors of the original BASIC language. Other newer versions are Turbo BASIC and QuickBASIC.

Any BASIC programming project can quickly become more complex if it requires data file handling code. An example is a file of customer records. A program that uses the data file requires more than beginner

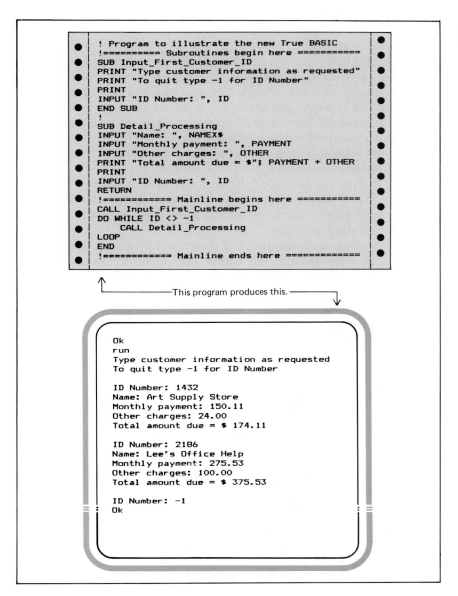

FIGURE 4-23
A True BASIC Program

programmer skills. Some experienced programmers agree with at least one software expert who claims that BASIC can become as difficult as COBOL when dealing with advanced projects.

Data File Fundamentals

Two general ways to store data records on a disk file are called

- Sequential access
- Random access

Sequential access means that any processing of the file begins with the first record and progresses sequentially through the entire file. A classic use of sequential files is for reports that require one line for every record in the file.

For applications that process records in a random order, a better method is needed. An example is an application that must respond quickly to specific customer requests for an account balance. The **random access** method is more suitable here. It allows specific records to be extracted at random. Two random access methods are briefly described here, called direct and indexed access.

In **direct access,** as long as the record number is known, any record can be retrieved, as shown in Figure 4-24. Customer records, for example, are available instantly by typing the desired record number. One disadvantage is that if only customers in record slots 1 and 100 are active, the file management subsystem automatically reserves record slots 2 to 99, which is wasted disk space.

Another obvious disadvantage of direct access is that a record's key field must be numeric and fall within the range of available record numbers. Often this is not convenient, such as when trying to access a record based on the first three letters of a customer's last name. To find a record with an alphabetic identifer or key, an indexed access is used.

With **indexed access,** a separate index file is created of only key

FIGURE 4-24
Direct access to records in a random access file

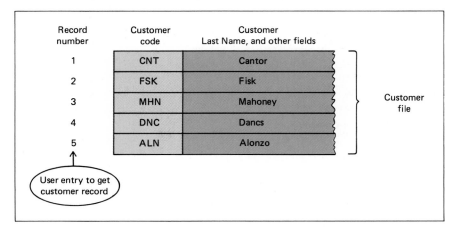

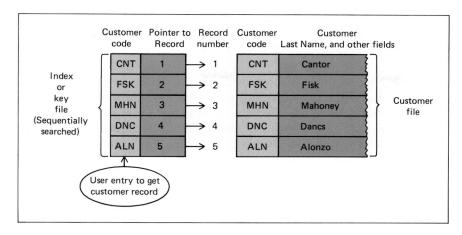

FIGURE 4-25
Indexed access to records in a random access file

fields. The index file is sequentially searched to locate a record based on its key field.

Using the example given in Figure 4-25, assume that a user enters customer code MHN. First the index file, containing only alphabetic customer codes and record numbers, is sequentially searched for "MHN." When MHN is found, the record number becomes known. It now is possible to make an immediate direct access to the full record. In effect, the *index* or *key file* is a "lookup" file to the master file.

Some program languages, like COBOL, offer a built-in feature called **indexed sequential access method (ISAM).** It works like the indexed method just described.

Programmer Tools

System software usually includes program tools to facilitate writing program code. Tools include **editors,** which are crude versions of commercial word processors. Their objective is to facilitate the typing and correction of lines of program code. Some programmers ignore the built-in editor and develop code with a favorite word processor. Most word processors are able to produce a file that most program language processors can read.

Some programmer tools or productivity aids are available as optional purchases. One example is a file manipulation package that can free a programmer from writing the code to create an index file. Another example is a screen formatting package that can free a programmer from writing the code to display anything on the screen. Both tools help to reduce application development time and may help design better applications.

Newer **fourth-generation program languages** are making older programming languages obsolete. Some let untrained users create new applications through writing in languages resembling normal English. Some require no language because they create applications based on responses to simple menu choices. The chapter on database management illustrates this trend in more detail.

EVALUATION

Some advocate that it is impossible for a novice to evaluate system software. Mr. Nelson felt it certainly was not as straightforward as evaluating applications. Since initially he wanted a single-user system, he spent no effort on evaluation. Hardware vendors included the most appropriate operating system with their hardware offering. For example:

Hardware	Single-User Operating System
IBM PC or compatible	DOS
Apple Macintosh	Apple Macintosh Finder

He acquired a PC-compatible computer system which was not powerful enough to handle the multitasking that he later desired.

Users of PC-compatible computers with DOS who want to upgrade to multitasking have to evaluate which alternative suits their needs. Some are listed below.

Microprocessor on the IBM PC or PC-Compatible Hardware in Use	Multitasking Alternative
Intel 8086 or 8088	DOS with a DOS window package (such as Microsoft's Windows 2.X)
Intel 80286 or 80386	As above, or OS/2 with an OS/2 window package (such as IBM's Presentation Manager)
Intel 80386	As above, or DOS with a DOS windows package (such as Microsoft's 386 Windows)

Initially, Mr. Nelson began with DOS and a DOS window package. Unfortunately, he found performance sluggish on his old 8088-based computer. His application seemed to slow down to a snail's pace. He eventually upgraded to a faster, more powerful, 80386 microprocessor-based computer and a compatible window package. The performance difference was like night and day.

Some of the criteria he used to select an operating system and a compatible window package are given in the System Software Evaluation Checklist that appears in Figure 4-26. By far, the main factor driving his decision was the availability of a wide variety of application software packages. While thousands of application packages were available for DOS, fewer were available for the OS/2 operating system. But applications written for the newer OS/2 operating system were easier to use and more sophisticated than their DOS counterparts. The decision required study.

Many claim that OS/2 is not for everyone. For users of older 8088-based hardware, it requires a considerable investment for

· An Intel 80286 or 80386-based computer or other hardware alternative

Is there a wide variety of application packages available to run with the operating system or operating system and windows package combination?

Can the operating system or operating system and windows package combination perform the desired number of tasks required (single-tasking or multitasking)?

Does the operating system meet long-term single-user or multiuser requirements?

Are the utility programs adequate?

Are there desirable program language processors with appropriate file-handling methods available if program development is planned?

(Figure 3-25, General Software Evaluation Checklist, is necessary to complete this evaluation.)

FIGURE 4-26
System software evaluation checklist

- A hard disk
- More than one megabyte of memory (RAM)

This hardware investment is in addition to the cost of upgrading to the new operating system, windows package, and all new OS/2 application software. For former DOS users, this out-of-pocket cost may pale when considered next to the cost, in terms of the time and trouble it takes, for learning any new software.

Once an operating system is to be used in a multiuser environment, the intensity of an evaluation effort must escalate considerably. Some of the problems faced in such an environment are discussed in Chapter 12, "Networking."

CASE STUDY: This Program Has a Defect

The Lotus Development Corporation said yesterday that thousands of copies of a new version of its Symphony, an integrated business software program, had a serious flaw that could cause users to lose large amounts of data.

This appears to be the first time the company, the leading manufacturer of business software for personal computers, has been forced to correct a significant programming mistake in one of its key software packages.

Lotus officials said yesterday that beginning next month, users of the new program, called Symphony 1.1, would receive a floppy diskette that would enable them to correct the problem. Starting next week, they said, copies of the flawed program on dealers' shelves would be replaced. . . . Ron Scott, a company spokesman, said that all of the copies sold so far include the error. "We are not certain how the glitch slipped in, but the important thing now is to get the corrective disk out."

Other Companies' Troubles.   Troubles with the early releases of programs are not uncommon in the software industry, especially among small software houses. Lotus' arch rival, the Microsoft Corporation, had a similar embarrassment last year when a major mistake was discovered in Microsoft Word, a word processing program.

But the Lotus situation is unusual—the problem is severe, and it is happening to the maker of some of the most widely used programs in the industry. The situation is also mysterious: programs like Symphony are tested extensively by a sampling of users before being marketed.

"It doesn't come at a partularly auspicious time," said William Shattuck, a software securities analyst at Montgomery Securities. . . . Lotus is scheduled to introduce its newest program, Signal, a stock market tracking system, at a press conference this morning in New York.

Complaints from Users. Lotus said it became aware of the Symphony problem after users—primarily managers in large corporations—complained that some data disappeared when they performed common tasks on the program's spreadsheet, a type of electronic ledger. The trouble-plagued tasks include inserting data into columns or rows of the spreadsheet, deleting data, or moving numbers between sections.

The company recommended that until the program was fixed, users "save" their worksheets . . . before performing any of these operations. Lotus officials acknowledged that taking such precautions would drastically slow the work being done.

"If they can demonstrate that they really solved the problem, they should be able to slide by without a lot of trouble," Mr. Shattuck said. "But it sure doesn't look good."

At Lotus, Mr. Scott said that "the important thing is that we caught this early and solved it."

(*SOURCE*: David E. Sanger, *"Lotus Program Has a Defect,"* New York Times, *September 17, 1985, p. D4. Adapted with permission.*)

DISCUSSION QUESTIONS

1. Assume that you have just read the same article in the newspaper and that you are one of the users of the defective software. Describe your actions to control the problem and your reactions about owning defective software.

2. Comment on these thoughts from James Martin, one of the dominant futurists in the computer industry: "Human beings can invent, conceptualize, demand improvements, and create visions. They can write music, start wars, build cities, create art,

fall in love, go to the moon, and colonize the solar system, but they cannot write program code which is guaranteed correct. . . . Program coding is an inhuman use of human beings because it asks them to do something beyond their capabilities—produce perfect, intricate, complex logic. . . . That is a task for computers, not human beings." (Source: James Martin, *System Design from Provably Correct Constructs*, Prentice-Hall, Englewood Cliffs, N.J., 1985, p. 56.)

CHAPTER SUMMARY

- *System software* is an umbrella term for a collection of software that consists of an operating system, utility programs, and program language processors.

- The *operating system* buffers the application from the hardware by managing memory, data input and output, and program execution.

- The operating system's *memory management subsystem* allocates and controls the use of random access memory (RAM).

- The operating system's *basic input/output system* (*BIOS*) handles all data traffic control in and out of the computer.

- A *single-tasking operating system* accommodates one

user solving one task at a time and is only used on microcomputers. *PC–DOS*, also known as *MS–DOS*, is a single-tasking operating system.

- *Multitasking operating systems* can run several applications concurrently. *Operating System/2 (OS/2)* is a multitasking operating system.

- A *window package* is software that divides the screen to display multiple tasks in progress. It is also called a *graphic user interface*. It provides a common "look and feel" among applications through devices like a *caption bar*, *menu bar*, and *dialog boxes*.

- A *clipboard* allows the manual exchange of data from one application to another that is running with a window package.

- *Virtual machines* make one computer perform as if it were many computers running many different operating systems simultaneously.

- A *multiuser operating system* provides services to many users who share one computer.

- In *time sharing*, a multiuser operating system slices up central processing unit time to accommodate many users at once.

- *Virtual memory* is the use of disk space as an extension of computer memory.

- *Utilities* are a collection of programs that mainly help to keep track of disk files and to perform disk housekeeping chores. Examples of utility commands in DOS are: format, diskcopy, copy, directory, and erase.

- *Program languages* evolved to make programming the computer a more humane task. A *language processor* accepts a programmer's code and translates it into 1's and 0's, which is called *machine language*.

- An *interpreter* takes human-readable program code and changes it into machine code during the actual step-by-step execution of a program. A *compiler* takes programmer-created statements, called *source code*, and goes through the translation stage once, during which executable *object code* is created.

- *Debugging* is the process of removing errors from programs. A line of program code is called a *program statement* or *instruction*. A printed copy of a program's code is called a *program listing*.

- *BASIC* is the most popular programming language used with microcomputers.

- Two general ways to store data records on a disk file are called sequential access and random access. *Sequential access* means that any processing of the file begins with the first record and progresses sequentially. The *random access* method allows processing of records in a random order. Two random access techniques used are direct access and indexed sequential access method (ISAM).

- *Programmer tools*, such as *editors*, facilitate writing program code.

- *Fourth-generation program languages* are making older programming languages obsolete.

KEY TERMS

Arithmetic/logic unit
BASIC
Basic input/output system (BIOS)
Caption bar
Clipboard
Compatibility
Compiler
Control unit
Debugging
Device independence
Dialog box
Direct access
Directory
Diskcopy

Disk Operating System (DOS)
Dynamic data exchange (DDE)
Editor
Executive subsystem
Format
Fourth-generation program languages
Graphic user interface
Indexed access
Indexed sequential access method (ISAM)
Index file
Industry standard
Interpreter

Language processor
Machine language
Memory addresses
Memory bank
Menu bar
MS–DOS
Multitasking operating system
Multiuser operating system
Object code
Operating system
Operating System/2 (OS/2)
PC–DOS
Pop-up windows
Presentation Manager
Program language
Program listing
Program overlay
Program statements (or
   instructions)

Protected mode
Random access
Real mode
Sequential access
Single-tasking operating system
Source code
Systems Application Architecture
   (SAA)
System software
Time sharing
Unix operating system
Utilities
Version number
Virtual machines
Virtual memory
Window
Window package

REVIEW QUESTIONS

1. What is system software?

2. What is an operating system?

3. What do each of the operating system's three sub-systems do?

   Compare the following:

4. · Single-tasking and multitasking operating systems

5. · Virtual memory and virtual machines

6. · Interpreter and compiler

7. · Source code and object code

8. · Sequential and random access

9. What is a window package?

10. What is a multiuser operating system?

11. What are utilities? Describe three of them.

12. What is the purpose of a program language processor?

13. Describe
    · Debugging
    · BASIC
    · Programmer tools
    · Fourth-generation lanaguages

EXERCISES

1. *Kristen Company Case.* The Kristen Company is installing a multiuser operating system and needs an appropriate hierarchical directory structure. Using Figure 4-15 as a guide, lay out a structure that would be suitable for supporting three vice-presidents. Each is responsible for two managers. All users maintain separate directories for word processing and spreadsheet files.

2. Read three recent articles about microcomputer multitasking operating systems. All three articles could be about one operating system or several. For each operating system, list the features available in each system software layer. If several are used, compare features to make a determination about which one is the superior product.

3. Locate and run a disk-based tutorial for the DOS or another operating system. Make an outline of the steps in the learning sequence followed. Prepare an oral or written report on what you learned and how you learned it. Conclude the report with your evaluation of the learning experience.

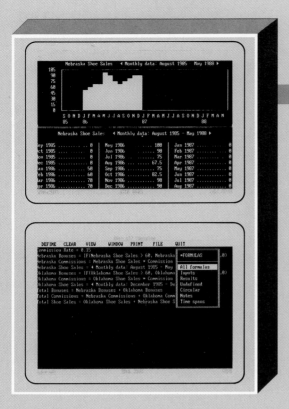

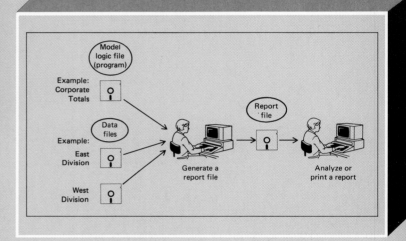

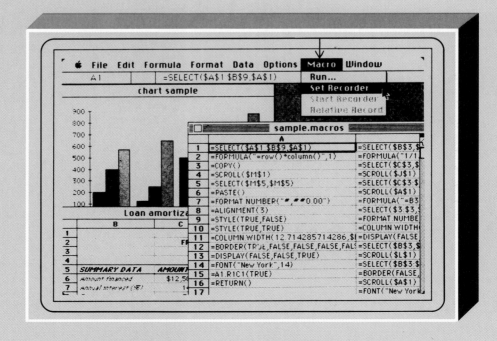

5

Spreadsheet and Financial Modeling Packages

AFTER READING THIS CHAPTER, YOU SHOULD BE ABLE TO

- Describe uses for a spreadsheet package and initiate an application evaluation
- Identify the value added to spreadsheets by add-on accessory packages
- Describe issues to consider when many users share spreadsheets
- Describe uses for financial modeling packages

This chapter "walks through" how a decision maker uses an electronic spreadsheet to help solve number-oriented problems. In doing so, it illustrates this computer age tool's impact on improving personal productivity. Spreadsheet features, problems, and guidelines for evaluation are examined.

Spreadsheet software is a mature industry. Many add-on and add-in, or accessory, packages proliferate. They add value to basic spreadsheet functions. Some of these add-on products are examined. Also examined are some issues to consider in environments where many users share spreadsheet files.

Finally, the chapter considers financial modeling packages. This is the type of software used when a spreadsheet package no longer seems adequate.

FIGURE 5-1
Scratch pad spreadsheet prepared with pencil and a calculator

SPREADSHEET CHARACTERISTICS

Both a scratch pad and an electronic **spreadsheet** are convenient tools to explore problems that can be defined numerically in row and column format. To compare manual and automated techniques of problem analysis, suppose that Frank Nelson, a marketing manager at Interstate Distributing Company, prepares a table of sales projections for one of the company's sports lines of baseball bats. Figure 5-1 shows the table using conventional scratch pad, calculator, and pencil.

Now suppose that Mr. Nelson uses any one of a number of electronic spreadsheets to do the projections. What differences would there be? The answer is that initially, except for numbers in the total column, none. In other words, the burden of developing the planning model is the planner's. Primary numbers in the spreadsheet have to be manually entered into the computer. In addition, the planner must precisely define relationships between numbers on the spreadsheet.

In Figure 5-1, totals reflect the result of units times price. The relationship of the two columns is important to the spreadsheet. It gets typed into the computer as a simple $A \times B = C$ formula. The formula stays hidden while a result flashes on the computer's screen.

This ability to memorize entered relationships gives the electronic spreadsheet its power. Whenever changes affecting stored relationships are made, the program instantly recalculates and redisplays updated values.

To use an example, assume that Mr. Nelson wants to know what effect there will be on totals if sales of baseball bats, type-3, fall to 300 units. With an electronic spreadsheet, typing the number for the new units is all that is needed. Instantly the total and grand total appear updated. This immediate feedback to "what if" questions makes an electronic spreadsheet a powerful, flexible analysis tool.

CREATING A SPREADSHEET

Looking over Mr. Nelson's shoulder, one observes how to enter a spreadsheet on the computer. After the computer's power switch is turned on, he slips a floppy disk containing the spreadsheet program into the disk drive. Instantly the computer's screen looks like Figure 5-2, a blank spreadsheet with labeled columns and rows.

The spreadsheet program loaded from the disk into the computer's memory could have been any one of many available. This one happens to be Lotus 1-2-3. All commands described relate to this particular example.

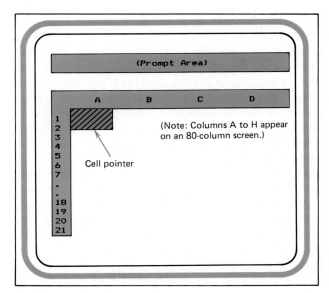

FIGURE 5-2
First screen of a typical spreadsheet
(*D. G. Dologite*, Using Small Business Computers, © *1984, p. 133. Reprinted by permission of Prentice-Hall, Inc., Englewood Cliffs, New Jersey.*)

Figure 5-2 illustrates only a small portion of what often is an enormous sheet of electronic paper. Undisplayed columns and rows can be scrolled into the display area by typing the cursor control or "arrow" keys.

At the intersection of column A and row 1, called **coordinate** or **cell** A1, is the cell pointer. The **cell pointer** indicates which cell is currently activated or being considered for use.

To enter the spreadsheet shown in Figure 5-3, Mr. Nelson types the down arrow key to move the cell pointer to cell A2. After typing

FIGURE 5-3
A spreadsheet of sales projections

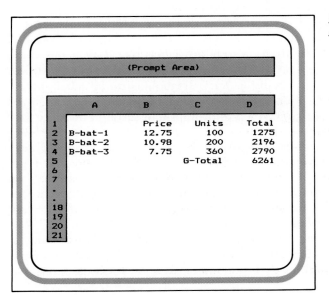

B-bat-1, the down arrow key is used again to move to the next cell, and the next, for the following two entries.

The up and right arrow keys get Mr. Nelson to the top of column B. There, he types in a column description, then uses the down arrow key to arrive at cell B2. In this, and the next two cells, he types prices. He repeats the column B arrow movement and typing procedure for column C. He concludes column C entries by typing a label, G-Total.

Descriptive labels, numbers, or formulas can be typed into any cell. Column D requires the entry of formulas to calculate total amounts. Totals are the result of price multiplied by units.

Multiplication is indicated by an asterisk (*) key. So Mr. Nelson types +B2*C2 into cell D2. The extra plus sign in front of B2 tells the program to read B as a formula instead of as a label. The result instantly appears in D2. The formula, meanwhile, remains in the computer's memory as cell information and is not displayed. The rest of the column is typed substituting 3, then 4, for the 2 in the formula.

The last item in the total column is the sum of all the items above it. Special functions like summation are invoked with an "@" key, as in @SUM(D2.D4). The range from cell D2 to cell D4 is summed and the result displayed.

The spreadsheet entry is complete. To make it look a bit neater, a **command** is entered to right-justify labels. Mr. Nelson found command entry to be relatively easy to master, even though it required hitting the arrow keys and the enter, or carriage return, key many times. As an example, if the enter key is symbolized as a bracketed [E], he had to type /→[E]→[E]→[E]A1.D5[E] to right-justify labels on his spreadsheet.

What do all the right arrows and [E]'s mean? They follow an initial slash (/) key that starts a command entry. It brings a **menu line** of command names to the prompt area, as shown in Figure 5-4. The **menu pointer** highlights the first of several command choices. Mr. Nelson types all the right arrow keys to move the menu pointer to desired choices. Then he types the entry key to indicate a command selection.

The specific commands he selects are /RANGE LABEL–PREFIX RIGHT. They tell the program to adjust labels that appear anywhere within the cell range of A1 to D5. The labels should be *right* justified. Previously they had a left-justify *prefix* symbol, as do all label entries. Fortunately, nothing more than arrow and the enter keys had to be typed. The menu line functioned to prompt him through the necessary command sequence.

Other commands save a spreadsheet on a disk as a file for later use. The command sequence is /FILE SAVE. Mr. Nelson also types any eight-character file name he desires. To print a spreadsheet on paper, he uses the command sequence /PRINT PRINTER RANGE (cell range) GO. The **cell range** is the first and the last cell coordinates that mark the extreme boundaries of his spreadsheet.

As is obvious, the upfront work of spreadsheet entry is often as labor intensive as doing the job manually. In addition, a planner has to learn about cell and menu pointer movement, formula entry, and

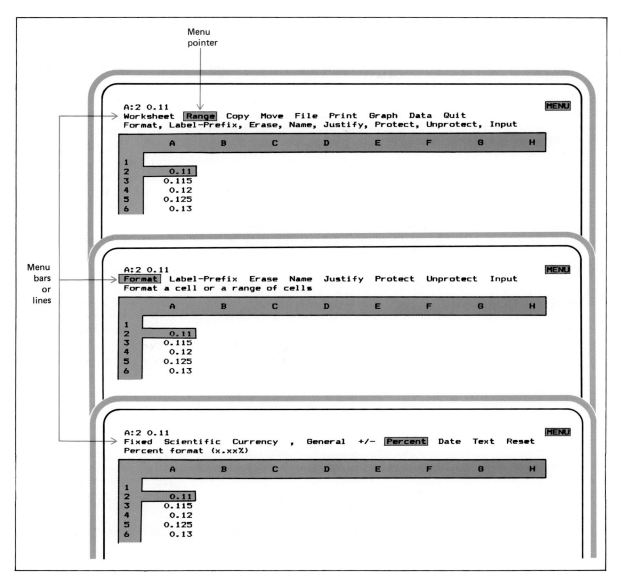

FIGURE 5-4
A menu bar and pointer in a keyboard-oriented spreadsheet
(*Software: Lotus 1-2-3®, courtesy of © Lotus Development Corporation, 1986. Lotus is a registered trademark of Lotus Development Corporation. Used with permission.*)

commands from a *User Guide*. While the learning effort requires time, it does not require previous computer experience.

"WHAT IF" QUESTIONS

The payoff for all the initial effort comes in asking "what if" questions. To get a response to the "what if" question posed earlier, Mr. Nelson simply changes the units for baseball bats, type-3, from 360 to 300.

This requires moving the cell pointer and typing the new units amount. Totals across and down instantly display the reduced figures.

Mr. Nelson further explores whether a price-cutting strategy is worth pursuing. "What if" the price of type-1 baseball bats drops to $11.99, causing sales to climb to 150 units? Entering the new dollar and sale figures quantifies this assumption. The instantly available bottom line recommends that the strategy is worth more serious investigation.

Another planner calculates quarterly sales on the basis of a growth rate from a base figure. The spreadsheet is shown in Figure 5-5. By moving the pointer to the cell in which the growth rate is displayed and changing the figure, the program automatically recalculates projected sales for each period. All expense and profit figures are also automatically changed.

But a spreadsheet is capable of more complex analyses. One investment manager uses it to create five-year income statements for real estate ventures. The statements are based on about 50 revenue and cost assumptions. Any change in assumptions takes only seconds to recalculate.

Users find, from working with a spreadsheet, that assumptions once believed to be important are often demonstrated to be not as crucial as others. In one manufacturing company case, overhead costs proved to be more critical to profit fluctuations than material cost assumptions. To the planner, getting that kind of understanding about the situation is worth the spreadsheet investment of learning time and money.

FIGURE 5-5
A spreadsheet of a quarterly budget

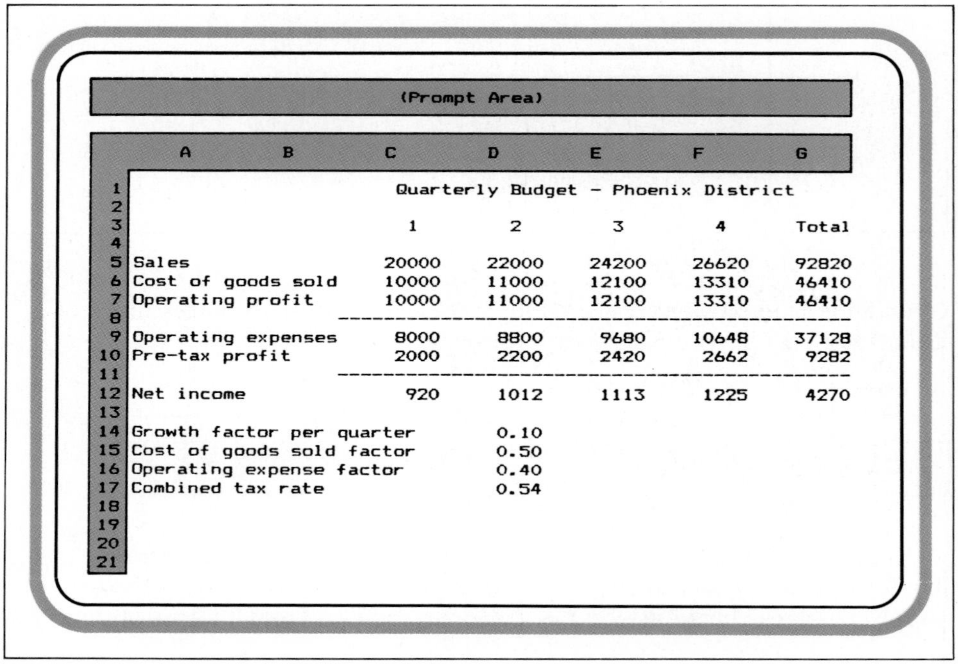

	(Prompt Area)					
	A	B	C	D	E	F	G
1			Quarterly Budget — Phoenix District				
2							
3			1	2	3	4	Total
4							
5	Sales		20000	22000	24200	26620	92820
6	Cost of goods sold		10000	11000	12100	13310	46410
7	Operating profit		10000	11000	12100	13310	46410
8							
9	Operating expenses		8000	8800	9680	10648	37128
10	Pre-tax profit		2000	2200	2420	2662	9282
11							
12	Net income		920	1012	1113	1225	4270
13							
14	Growth factor per quarter		0.10				
15	Cost of goods sold factor		0.50				
16	Operating expense factor		0.40				
17	Combined tax rate		0.54				
18							
19							
20							
21							

PRODUCTIVITY FEATURES

Spreadsheet packages, like those listed in Figure 5-6, share a basic set of features or commands. All help to enhance a user's personal productivity.

A **copy** feature, in particular, automatically duplicates cells across a range of rows or columns. A business forecaster preparing a ten-year plan, for example, enters figures for only the first year's column. With a few keystrokes, subsequent columns replicate the same or incremented figures in a matter of seconds. This copy feature is a great timesaving device when preparing more elaborate spreadsheets.

Equally useful are features to *insert*, *delete*, or *move* entire rows and columns. They can be especially helpful when a spreadsheet is finished and it is discovered that an important calculation was omitted.

A **format** feature controls the way in which spreadsheets are displayed. Formatting specifications might include

- Expand the width of a column
- Put two decimal places in numbers
- Position information in a column flush with the right or left margin, or centered

FIGURE 5-6
A sampler of spreadsheet software packages for personal computers

STAND-ALONE PACKAGES

Boeing CALC	PFS:Professional Plan
CalcIT	Planning Assistant
Easyplanner	PractiCalc
Harmony	Silk
Mathplan	SQL Calc
Multiplan	The Smart Spreadsheet
OmniCalc	The Spreadsheet
PC–Calc	VP Planner
PeachCalc	

INTEGRATED PACKAGES WITH A SPREADSHEET

Ability	KnowledgeMan
Aura	Lotus 1-2-3
Electric Desk	Microsoft Works
Enable	Open Access
Ensemble	PC Excel
Excel	PFS:First Choice
Framework	Quattro
Integrated 7	SuperCalc
Jack2	Symphony
Javelin	The Twin
Jazz	Word Perfect Executive

- Show negative numbers with a preceding minus sign, surrounded by parentheses, or displayed in red

A host of other possibilities exist to define the format for individual cells, columns, rows, or blocks of cells.

Users working with large spreadsheets find the *split-screen window* feature helpful. A vertical **split screen,** as shown in Figure 5-7, juxtaposes different sections of a spreadsheet. It can be valuable for comparative analysis. Horizontal splits are also possible.

A related feature, often called **titles,** locks in a row or column on the display. The secured title area, usually at the top or left edge of the screen, remains in place regardless of which rows or columns are selected for viewing.

Built-In Functions

The availability of **built-in functions,** like summation, further supports a user's personal productivity. Functions are equivalent to prepared formulas. They eliminate the need to create common formulas from scratch. In addition to *sum*, *average*, and *count*, generally *minimum* and *maximum* are available. Financial functions, such as *internal rate of return* and *net present value*, are also common. Some include functions like *variance*, *standard deviation*, and *frequency distribution*. A small example

FIGURE 5-7
A spreadsheet with a vertically split screen

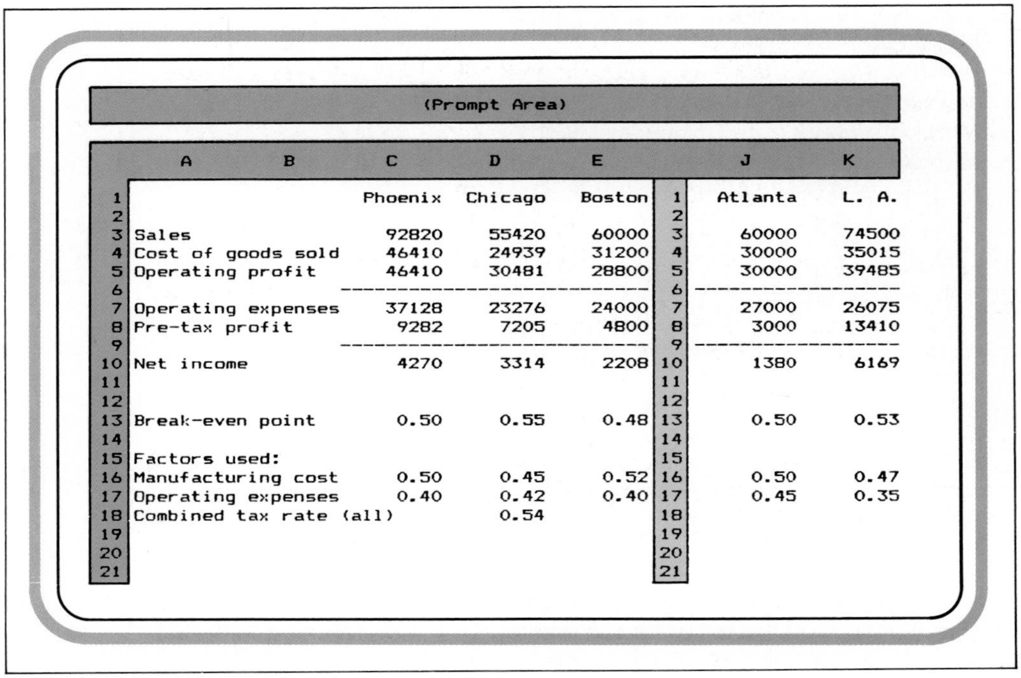

	(Prompt Area)						
	A	B	C	D	E	J	K
1			Phoenix	Chicago	Boston	Atlanta	L. A.
2							
3	Sales		92820	55420	60000	60000	74500
4	Cost of goods sold		46410	24939	31200	30000	35015
5	Operating profit		46410	30481	28800	30000	39485
6			------	------	------	------	------
7	Operating expenses		37128	23276	24000	27000	26075
8	Pre-tax profit		9282	7205	4800	3000	13410
9			------	------	------	------	------
10	Net income		4270	3314	2208	1380	6169
11							
12							
13	Break-even point		0.50	0.55	0.48	0.50	0.53
14							
15	Factors used:						
16	Manufacturing cost		0.50	0.45	0.52	0.50	0.47
17	Operating expenses		0.40	0.42	0.40	0.45	0.35
18	Combined tax rate (all)			0.54			
19							
20							
21							

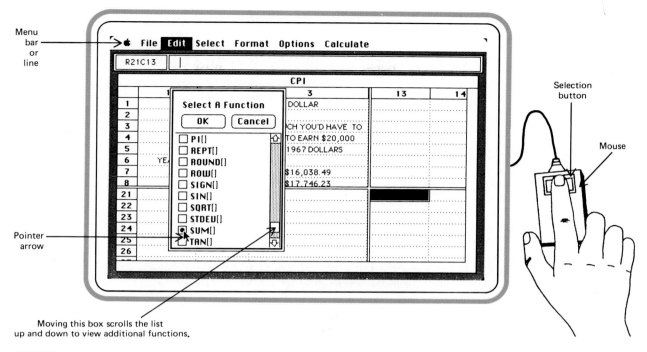

Menu bar or line

Pointer arrow

Selection button

Mouse

Moving this box scrolls the list up and down to view additional functions.

FIGURE 5-8
Selecting the "SUM" function from a list of available functions. The list pointer arrow is moved by the mouse.
(*Software*: Multiplan, *courtesy of MacWorld*)

of some available functions appears in Figure 5-8. It shows the common SUM function being selected.

Unlike Mr. Nelson's spreadsheet, the one in Figure 5-8 uses a mouse to move the pointer to list choices. Hitting the mouse button selects whatever function the pointer is resting on. By contrast, Mr. Nelson must type the "@" key to signal a function selection, then type the function name, like @SUM.

The *lookup* function proves useful to anyone, like a tax preparer, who has to "look up" tables of numbers. When the lookup function is used in a cell, it causes a search for a value in a previously entered table. For example, a lookup command can dictate a search through a tax table to find the tax rate for a specific year.

SPECIAL FEATURES

As spreadsheet users become more experienced using their software, they often demand increased functionality. Some special features used are protection, linking, integration, and macros.

Protection

Professional people often use spreadsheets to help manage their personal or business investments. Ann Leiboff, a lawyer with a private practice, developed the **protected spreadsheet** that appears in Figure 5-9. It computes the worth of her investments on a daily basis.

The first level of protection requires entry of a password just to display the spreadsheet. Only she can access or update the spreadsheet, because no one knows her password. The spreadsheet displays without row or column numbers or letters.

Another level of protection locks in ranges of cells that do not need daily updating. Unprotected cells are highlighted and underlined on the display. The cursor moves from one unprotected cell to another whenever the return key is typed. It simplifies updating the spreadsheet. It also helps to prevent accidental changes.

Linking and Naming

Daniel Meixell, a stock broker, has other spreadsheet requirements. He manages many client portfolios at once. He requires a way to summarize client accounts into a master control account. One solution is a spreadsheet that provides links between master and subordinate spreadsheets. **Linking** is a natural way to combine things like quarterly reports into an annual report.

One spreadsheet product requires assigning a name to a cell or range of cells that are to be linked. A command must also be issued to declare this name as a link item. Using Figure 5-9 to give an example, the three totals collectively might be named "TOTALS." After that, whenever a master spreadsheet is loaded into memory, it can access "TOTALS" from subordinate spreadsheets containing cells named "TOTALS."

Integration

Having a package that integrates a spreadsheet with other applications solves many problems for Patrick Cunningham. He prepares cost estimates for construction projects. As Figure 5-10 shows, his proposal requires integrating spreadsheet, graphics, and word processing functions.

"I put a lot of numbers into the text of my proposals," Mr. Cunningham says, "and the text always has to match the numbers in my supporting spreadsheets. My problem was that I'd get a proposal just about done, and then one of the numbers in the spreadsheet would change." With a stand-alone spreadsheet package, he claims it was easy enough to recalculate the spreadsheet. But then he also had to find the affected numbers in the text of his proposal and change them. "It was a cut-and-paste quagmire," he says. So he acquired a program that offered several integrated functions. Many packages exist, as evident from the

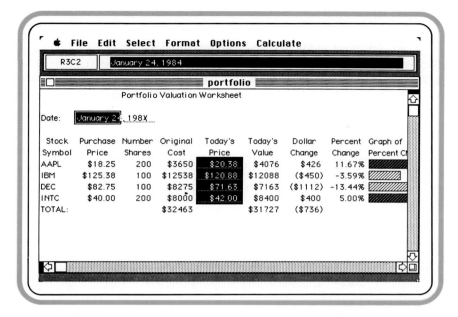

FIGURE 5-9
A protected spreadsheet displayed without row and column numbers or letters (Software: Multiplan, courtesy of MacWorld)

list in Figure 5-6. His package automatically updates all data that are active in the word processor whenever changes are made to a related spreadsheet or graphic.

Macros

At National Bank, loan officers have a different problem. They want to create a sophisticated spreadsheet for reuse by others. To do this, they require a spreadsheet with a macro capability. A **macro** capability

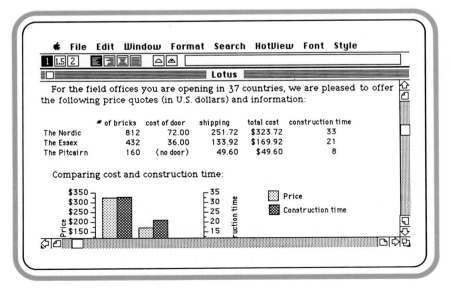

FIGURE 5-10
An integrated package that updates all information in the word processor when changes are made to spreadsheets and graphs (Software: Jazz, courtesy of Lotus Development Corporation)

means a programming capability. It is frequently used to create a "fill-in-the-blanks" spreadsheet, as shown in Figure 5-11. Programmers and experienced spreadsheet users do not find such macro creation intimidating. After a programmer prepares the master spreadsheet, called a **template,** it is copied for circulation to users.

A user types only a keystroke or keyword to activate a macro when

FIGURE 5-11
A hand-coded macro named SETUP
(*Software: Lotus 1-2-3, courtesy of* PC World, *555 DeHaro St., San Francisco, CA 94107*)

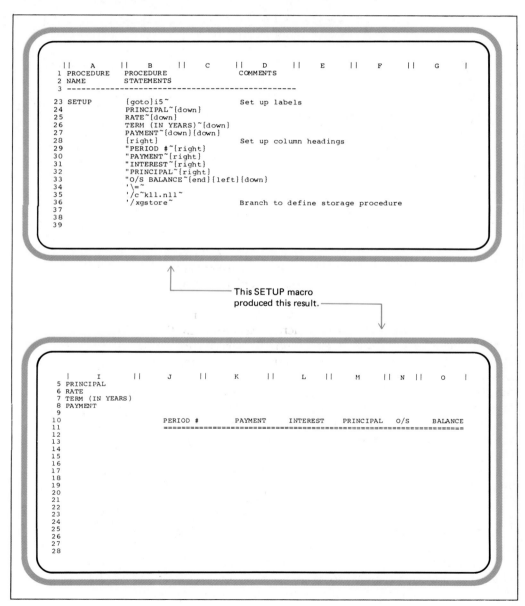

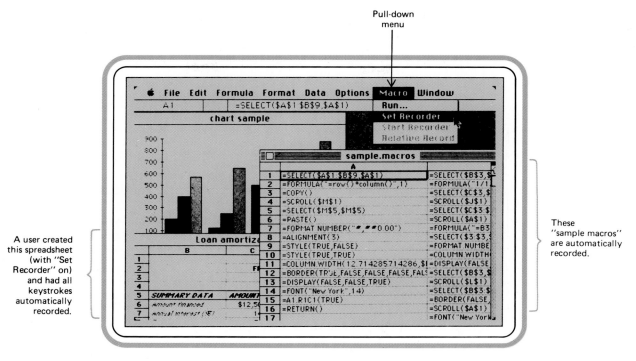

FIGURE 5-12
Creating macros automatically by selecting "Set Recorder" from the menu
(Software: Excel, courtesy of Microsoft)

filling in the spreadsheet. This is why macros are sometimes called "the typing alternative." They allow a user to replace a block of keystrokes with a simple key entry.

One spreadsheet package, tested by loan officer Henry Marshall, allows the effortless creation of macros. As shown in Figure 5-12, it has one menu item called "macro" and another called "Set Recorder." By selecting both menu items, every keystroke is translated into the program's macro language and saved for later reuse. Mr. Marshall never has to learn the macro language, because the macros are automatically created for him. Sample macros created by the "recorder" appear in the "sample macro" window of Figure 5-12. The recorded macros create a loan amortization spreadsheet. A completed loan amortization spreadsheet appears in Figure 5-13.

One computer consultant finds that spreadsheet programmers often inappropriately try to use a spreadsheet's macro capability to create every conceivable kind of application. He calls this the "shoehorn syndrome." "It occurs," he suggests, "because they only know one program language, their spreadsheet macro language. But is the spreadsheet macro language the best one to develop all other applications?"

Many think it is not. Instead, they recommend that users buy professionally prepared packaged software, like a payroll package to do payroll and a project management package to do project management.

```
|   I      ||    J    ||   K    ||   L    ||   M    || N ||   O    |
5 PRINCIPAL         10,000.00
6 RATE                  15.00
7 TERM (IN YEARS)        1.00
8 PAYMENT              902.58
9
10               PERIOD #    PAYMENT   INTEREST   PRINCIPAL   O/S   BALANCE
11               ===============================================================
12
13                                                                  10,000.00
14                 1.00      902.58     125.00     777.58            9,222.42
15                 2.00      902.58     115.28     787.30            8,435.11
16                 3.00      902.58     105.44     797.14            7,637.97
17                 4.00      902.58      95.47     807.11            6,830.86
18                 5.00      902.58      85.39     817.20            6,013.66
19                 6.00      902.58      75.17     827.41            5,186.25
20                 7.00      902.58      64.83     837.75            4,348.50
21                 8.00      902.58      54.36     848.23            3,500.27
22                 9.00      902.58      43.75     858.83            2,641.44
23                10.00      902.58      33.02     869.57            1,771.87
24                11.00      902.58      22.15     880.43              891.44
25                12.00      902.58      11.14     891.44                 .00
26               --------------------------------------------------------------
27                        10,831.00     831.00  10,000.00                 .00
28               ===============================================================
```

FIGURE 5-13
Completed loan amortization spreadsheet
(*Software: Lotus 1-2-3, courtesy of* PC World, *555 DeHaro St., San Francisco, CA 94107*)

Templates

A template is a spreadsheet without actual numbers or data. It is often created by using a spreadsheet's macro capability. All the formulas and data relationships are in place, ready to calculate as soon as there is something other than zeros to enter. Mr. Marshall's loan amortization schedule is a template. A blank one is always ready to be reused the moment a new loan customer comes into National Bank.

Internally developed templates create two spinoff advantages. One is that they can be used to standardize company policies and methods. At the bank, copies of Mr. Marshall's template are used by all loan officers. Because of this, the bank's management knows that loan negotiations will all be based on the correct amortization formula in the template.

The second advantage of a template is that it captures expertise that can be shared. In a large organization all managers may not know how to handle a certain aspect of a quarterly report. A template can capture this expertise so that it can be passed around. As a result, it automatically raises the general level of competence in the organization.

Commercially sold templates are available in three basic categories: financial, real estate, and scientific or statistical. Often they complement more comprehensive stand-alone applications in these areas.

DOCUMENTATION

When presenting a spreadsheet to others, the assumptions used to arrive at its conclusion are usually explained or documented. As a general practice, the spreadsheet itself should display, rather than conceal, assumptions built into formulas. Dedicating a section of the spreadsheet to a list of assumptions should be an essential part of the spreadsheet design process.

Examples of spreadsheets with an area dedicated to listing assumptions and factors used include the following:

Figure	Area Dedicated to Spreadsheet Assumptions and Factors
5-5	Rows 14–17
5-7	Rows 16–18
5-13	Rows 5–8

A host of products have emerged to support further documentation of a spreadsheet. DocuCalc, The Spreadsheet Auditor, and the Cam-

FIGURE 5-14
Examples of spreadsheet documentation products
(*Top software*: DocuCalc, courtesy of *Micro Decision Systems*; *bottom software*: *SmartNotes, courtesy of Personics Corp.*)

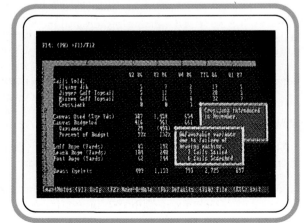

A grid report of spreadsheet formulas in rows and columns

A pop-up window for attaching notes to any spreadsheet cell

bridge Spreadsheet Analyst, as examples, are useful to produce reports that make it easier to find errors in a spreadsheet. Such products can

- Print a grid report of all formulas used in a spreadsheet, as shown in the top of Figure 5-14
- Generate a list of all the cells in a spreadsheet that refer to a specified cell
- Display a suspect cell and probe other cells linked to it in any way desired to trace a problem to its roots

Another type of product, such as Note-It and SmartNotes, lets a user attach brief notes to any cell. To create a note, as illustrated on the bottom of Figure 5-14, a so-called *pop-up window* appears. Anything typed in the window becomes cell reference information, which can be recalled whenever needed. Some products also allow notes to be attached to the entire spreadsheet file.

ADD-ON PRODUCTS

Both the documentation aids and commercially sold templates are known as "add-on" products. **Add-ons** or **add-ins,** in the software industry, are packages created to add value to other, more widely used, packages. In the spreadsheet market, most of this software is written to add value to the Lotus 1-2-3 package.

Many add-on packages are actually *patches* to improve weaknesses in the original product. In many cases, the value they add eventually gets incorporated into the original product.

The Lotus 1-2-3 product has generated a whole industry of add-ons. These add-ons generally fall into the following categories:

Category	Comment
Applications	To add industry-specific functionality to a spreadsheet (usually sold as templates)
Auditing	To annotate spreadsheets and to test for accuracy
File utilities	To compress spreadsheet file storage, increase usable memory, recover corrupted or lost spreadsheet files
Graphics	To enhance or add graphic features
Macro recorders	To simplify macro creation
Printing utilities	To rotate a spreadsheet 90 degrees for printing horizontally on one continuous sheet of paper
Report writers	To format a spreadsheet into a polished report complete with page header and footer lines on multiple pages with margins and mixed type styles
Word processors	To provide text-editing features in the familiar spreadsheet environment

Two add-on products require special attention:

- English-language command interface
- Goal-seeking capability

English-Language Command Interface

One add-on package called HAL (for Human Process Language) allows a user to type commands instead of using Lotus 1-2-3's menu line. The resemblance of these commands to English has led many to describe the product as a natural-language interface, or an **English-Language command interface,** in this case for Lotus 1-2-3.

Figure 5-15 gives an example of the command language interface. The backslash (\) key brings up the "request box" on top of the normal menu line. With the cursor in cell B3, the command "Enter Jan to Dec down" creates the first column, with month names spelled in full. After 25125 is typed in cell C3, the command "project down by 2%" automatically increments the value down the column. A final command formats column C by eliminating decimal places and adding commas to the numbers.

If desired, the command "total income" would produce a total for column C. The simple command "graph this" would present the spreadsheet in a bar chart.

In the package's 2,000-word vocabulary, "this" means an entire table, or spreadsheet. Such a command seems to give the software artificial intelligence characteristics. Yet, a user must fully understand the command vocabulary, or it could mean errors. As an example, to issue the command "delete this" would wipe out an entire spreadsheet. If a user wanted to delete only one cell, the command should have been "delete this cell." In addition, commands must be issued in a prescribed order, beginning with a verb.

Fortunately, an **undo** feature cancels a mistake or change of mind. Some other features that are built in to add value to the original package are the following:

- Records macros automatically for playback. Since macros are in English, they are self-documenting.
- Makes more extensive use of assumptions when executing complex commands (for example, the command "graph this" produces a single vertical bar chart).
- Highlights cells that are dependent on other cells to simplify auditing a spreadsheet or isolating a problem.
- Simplifies entry of sequential data (including month names and days of the week).

While such a product can simplify spreadsheet use for an experienced user, it does not provide an easy path for beginners to master the intricacies of the spreadsheet program itself.

Goal-Seeking and Optimization

Some spreadsheet add-on packages allow "executing formulas backwards," as one user describes it. This feature is widely used in financial modeling packages and in mainframe decision support system packages, where it is called **goal-seeking.**

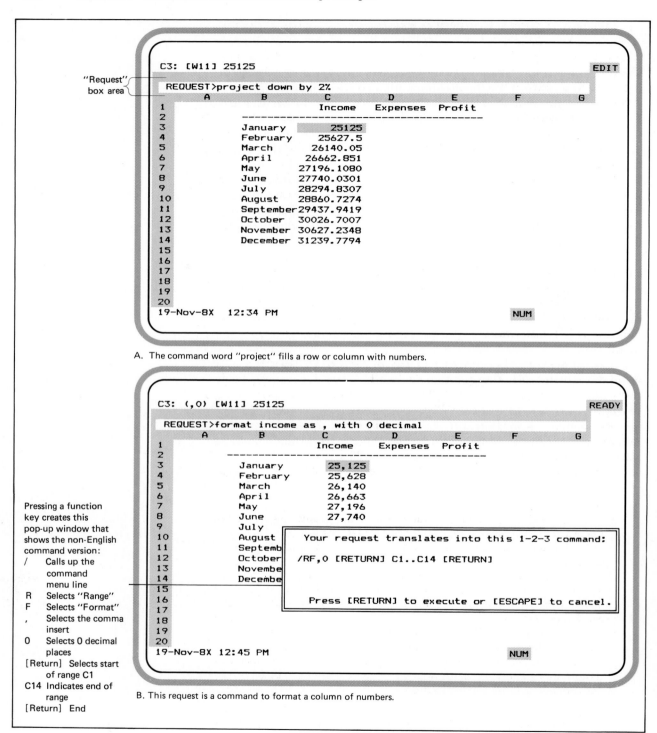

A. The command word "project" fills a row or column with numbers.

B. This request is a command to format a column of numbers.

FIGURE 5-15
Using an English-language command interface
(*Software*: *Lotus 1-2-3 and HAL, courtesy of Lotus Development Corporation*)

To give an example, assume that a spreadsheet user has a common formula, such as Profits = (Unit Price × Number of Units Sold) − Expenses. Whenever unit price is changed, profits change. But what if the spreadsheet user wants to know the unit price necessary to achieve a particular profit? While it is easy enough to change the result of a formula, by changing a constant value, it is impossible to go the other way. Spreadsheets normally cannot handle going backward to show what supporting numbers would have to be in order to produce a desired result. Packages such as Goal Solutions and microCUBE help to overcome this kind of spreadsheet dilemma.

The example in Figure 5-16 demonstrates how optimization software, such as What's Best, can be applied. **Optimization** software helps a user to select the "best" option from a series of "what if" possibilities. Although this is a linear programming problem, an advanced college degree is generally not necessary to use the software effectively.

In this case, assume that restaurateur Alex Seymour develops a spreadsheet to help solve what he calls the "Sunday night specials problem." His restaurant is open every day except Monday. He must use up as many perishables as possible by Sunday night, because by Tuesday the remaining meat and vegetables will not be fresh enough to serve. Like any other restaurateur, he tries to create "specials" to use up the perishables.

The question is, "How many servings of each dish must he sell by Sunday night to earn the greatest profit while keeping spoilage to a minimum and using only the available ingredients?" The spreadsheet in Figure 5-16 illustrates the basic relationships involved here.

To determine the greatest possible profit, given the kinds of dishes and the ingredients on hand, the restaurant owner could plug numbers into the spreadsheet until the value in cell A20 is sufficiently high. It is far easier to identify the "ABC" cells and let spreadsheet add-on software handle it. The ABC cells are

A = "Adjustable" cells. They are variable cells that would normally have data plugged into them during a manual "what if" session. (With optimization software, their content dynamically changes as the limits of the "C constraint" cells are tested.)

B = "Best" cell. It holds the result of all the tested combinations funneled into one cell that reflects the maximum profit, minimum resources used, or whatever is the purpose of the spreadsheet. In the example case, it is maximum profit.

C = "Constraint" cells. They contain the formulas (in this case: In-stock minus Used Ingredients) that are repeatedly varied in order to arrive at a "best" solution. (Note: In the example, the total number of units used is the quantity in row 6 multiplied by the units-per-serving in each ingredient row.)

Any problem where "ABC" cells can be identified could benefit from optimization software. The software will churn through the spreadsheet, running repeated calculations—essentially performing a multitude of "what if's"—until it finds the best solution. While sifting through the

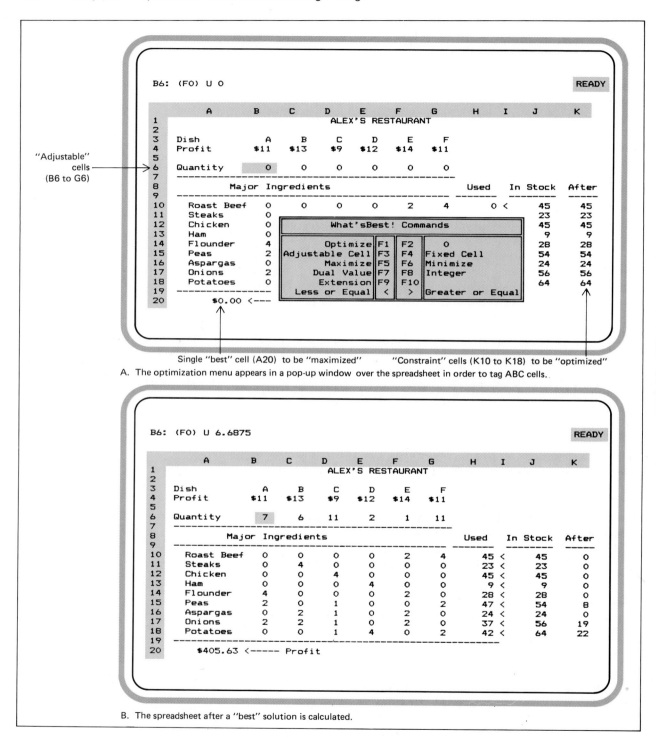

"Adjustable" cells (B6 to G6)

Single "best" cell (A20) to be "maximized"   "Constraint" cells (K10 to K18) to be "optimized"

A. The optimization menu appears in a pop-up window over the spreadsheet in order to tag ABC cells.

B. The spreadsheet after a "best" solution is calculated.

FIGURE 5-16

Before and after applying optimization to a spreadsheet

(*Software*: What's Best, *courtesy of General Optimization, Inc.; example and photos,*
courtesy of PC World)

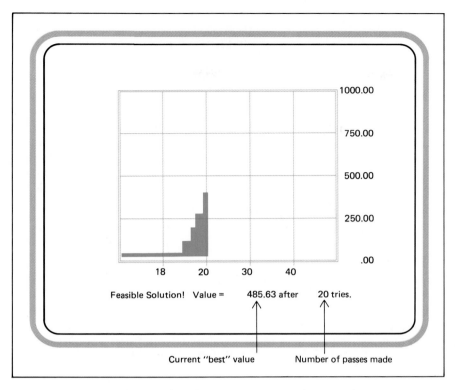

FIGURE 5-17
Display on screen after entering ABC cells and before displaying a solution
(*Software: What's Best, courtesy of General Optimization, Inc.; example and photo, courtesy of* PC World)

possibilities, one package displays the bar chart, shown in Figure 5-17, indicating the number of passes taken through the data and the current "best" value. In the example case, in less than 15 seconds the software made 20 passes through the spreadsheet and arrived at the best answer, a maximum profit of $485.63 is possible.

The example is a typical "product mix" problem. Scheduling problems are also appropriate, like finding the least expensive way to staff an institution while keeping the required minimum number of personnel on duty at all times. One midwestern hospital reportedly reworked its nursing schedule and discovered it could save $80,000 a month in salaries.

MULTIUSER

When many users can access and use a centralized spreadsheet at one time, it is known as a **multiuser spreadsheet package.** Such spreadsheets are found on local-area networks, minicomputers, and mainframes. Some representative packages are listed in Figure 5-18. Many of them are also used in single-user environments.

One package allows users who have access to the spreadsheet to retrieve a copy of it. The copy can be manipulated as desired, but it must be saved under a new file name. This is known as **file locking.**

20/20 Calc	Future Calc
Boeing Calc	Mancalc
Calc	Maxicalc
CICS/Calc	Megacalc
Data Porte	Nyplan
Dynaplan	OmniCalc
Easy Calc	Oxycalc
ESS	Saturn-Calc
ExecuCalc	SQL Calc
Financial Planning	Supercomp
Spreadsheet	VAX DECalc
FOCCALC	

FIGURE 5-18
A sampler of multiuser spreadsheet software packages

Only the designated "owner" of the spreadsheet has permission to destroy it by saving a new spreadsheet in its place. A file-locking feature ensures that everyone is working from the same spreadsheet data. In addition, it places control for the spreadsheet numbers with a single source.

Large as well as small organizations use multiuser spreadsheets to create "consolidations." For example, at Interstate Distributing Company, all managers were eventually given access to a centralized spreadsheet. Each manager retrieves a copy of it to prepare the department budget. When all budgets are done, they are combined or merged into one **consolidated,** or summary, spreadsheet for company analysis and report purposes.

Consolidations are simplified with a spreadsheet that has a **multidimension** feature. This feature is usually available on multiuser spreadsheets. A typical spreadsheet is two dimensional, since it is composed of rows and columns. By contrast, a three-dimensional spreadsheet has rows, columns, and pages. Using the same example, if there are five departmental managers, each department budget would be on a separate page representing a third dimension to a consolidated summary. That is what additional dimensions do—they allow the organization and analysis of data by whatever criteria are appropriate. A common organization is budget category (1st dimension or rows), time category (2nd dimension or columns), and departments (3rd dimension or pages).

Some spreadsheets allow more than three dimensions. Each dimension is considered a subset of a single multidimensional spreadsheet.

Some organizations have no centralized spreadsheet software but have employees who need to share spreadsheet files. If everybody uses the same spreadsheet package, data sharing is accomplished by swapping disks with a copy of the spreadsheet file on them.

This requires that an organization "standardize" on a single spreadsheet product. **Standardizing** on software means that all employees who need a spreadsheet, as an example, use the same package. It simplifies data sharing and enables an organization to benefit from corporate buying discounts, as well as common training and maintenance support.

If several different spreadsheet packages are in use, a **file conversion** or **translation** feature is usually necessary to share data. The *conversion* feature **exports** a copy of the file in a format for use on a foreign spreadsheet. The foreign spreadsheet may have to use an **import** function to retrieve the file and convert it into its native format before it can be used. Common formats for spreadsheet file exchanges include the following:

File Format	Comment
DIF (Data Interchange Format)	A general file exchange format
ASCII (American Standard Code for Information Interchange format)	A general file exchange format
WKS and **WK1**	Lotus 1-2-3 file format

Spreadsheet files translated into ASCII, for example, can also be used in many word processing projects. The import of an ASCII file into a spreadsheet, however, requires some work to make it usable by the program.

SPREADSHEET EVALUATION

Before acquiring a spreadsheet package, individual requirements that must be met by the application should be specified. The Spreadsheet Evaluation Checklist, given in Figure 5-19, helps identify requirements and provides a systematic tool for the evaluation process.

FIGURE 5-19
Spreadsheet evaluation checklist

SPREADSHEET

Are the maximum number of rows and columns adequate?
Is the maximum cell size adequate?
Can cells be named?
Is the recalculation speed adequate?
Does recalculation occur in a natural order?
Is it possible to turn off automatic recalculation?
Are built-in functions adequate?
Is formatting adequate?
Can spreadsheets be linked or consolidated?
Can files be transferred into and out of the program?
Are split-screen windows provided?
Is password protection possible?
Does the spreadsheet have a mouse or keyboard orientation?
Does it have a macro capability?

(Figure 3-25, General Software Evaluation Checklist, is necessary to complete this evaluation.)

Such checklists are best used as a point of departure for more intense analyses. This is especially true if an acquisition involves a new computer that will be used to run more than the spreadsheet package.

Most of the checklist items have already been covered. Those that have not include style and spreadsheet size.

Style

Although most spreadsheets perform the same functions, packages differ significantly in style. Style choice is between spreadsheets that are either

- **Mouse oriented** with pull-down menus (as evident in Figures 5-8 to 5-10 and 5-12
- **Keyboard oriented** with menu bars and commands (as evident in Figure 5-4 and related figures)

Some practice is needed to get the right hand-eye coordination to move the pointer with a mouse. Many who have tried it like the power and convenience that this style brings to spreadsheet work.

The mouse pointer changes shape depending on where it is. It requires getting used to but provides convenient visual guides to what is happening on the display. Examples of various pointer shapes used by one spreadsheet on the Apple Macintosh computer are listed in Figure 5-20.

Keyboard-oriented spreadsheets have similar menu bars. They require a lot of cursor control arrow key typing to reach and activate a menu option. Some experienced users skip the arrow key typing and enter commands directly. In most cases, commands are activated with a single character:

Examples of Keyboard Commands	*Action*
C	Column-width
F	Format
W	Window split
T	Titles (freeze rows/ columns on screen)
D	Delete rows/columns

FIGURE 5-20
Mouse-oriented spreadsheet: example of screen-pointer shape changes

SCREEN POINTER SHAPE	SCREEN AREA WHERE USED	ACTION
Arrow	Menu bar	Pulls down menus
Cross	Worksheet body	Activates cells
I-Beam	Formula creation area	Indicates where typing will take place
Wristwatch		Marks time for an action that requires a few moments to complete

Other Criteria

In addition to style, spreadsheet evaluators might want to review the following:

- What is the maximum spreadsheet size, in columns and rows? It is important to be sure the largest spreadsheet intended for the program can be accommodated.
- Can the automatic recalculation feature be turned off? This improves efficiency while making extensive spreadsheet changes.
- Does recalculation occur in a natural order? It ensures that all cells affected by a change are automatically updated. Some only recalculate from the change forward, which can be troublesome.

FINANCIAL MODELING PACKAGES

Many computer consultants recommend to users who outgrow spreadsheet packages that they move up to a financial modeling package, such as those listed in Figure 5-21. A **financial modeling package** is used to handle problems that have more dimensions and complex formulas than can easily be handled by the present generation of spreadsheet packages. But the line between the two is starting to blur. More and more of the functionality, once found only in financial modeling packages, is appearing in spreadsheet packages. This includes the capability to do multidimensions and goal-seeking.

Financial modeling software has its origin in mainframe software. It has been available for years to financial specialists at large corporations.

FIGURE 5-21
A sampler of financial modeling software packages

MICROCOMPUTERS

Control/PC
Encore
ESCA-Decision Support System
FCS–EPS
IFPS Personal
Javelin
Micro-DSS Analysis
MicroForesight
Micro/PROPHIT
MindSight
Oz:Management Control

MAINFRAMES

Econometric Modeling System (EMS)
Empire
Express
FCS–EPS
Interactive Financial Planning System (IFPS)
Xsim

Corporations either bought the software, sometimes at a cost of over $100,000, or paid a hefty fee for its use (over telecommunication lines) to a computer time-sharing service bureau.

Comparable packages for microcomputers can cost $1,500 or less. Some large corporations are using them to eliminate time-sharing service fees.

Corporate users typically are financial analysts who spend considerable time learning how to become proficient with the software. It requires learning how to program.

Even though the output from a financial modeling package looks like a spreadsheet, the cells are not active. They can be changed only by writing a program. A program is also necessary to load cell content, as the example in Figure 5-22 shows. To spreadsheet users, this requires an adjustment. Working on a cell-by-cell basis is replaced with programming on a line-by-line basis. Another adjustment is calling the result, which looks like a spreadsheet, a **model.**

Modeling

Modeling is a process of representing, through mathematical equations and logical expressions, aspects of an organization's business activities. In other words, a **model** is a simulation of an activity.

A spreadsheet's rows and columns are good for building two-dimensional models. But it is common to see three- and four-dimensional models that analyze important organizational problems. For example, when the activities of a company are viewed by

- Product line
- Geographic area
- Time range
- Specific business variables (like sales and depreciation)

a four-dimensional problem exists.

A model usually represents important parts of the organization and possibly the competitive and external environments in which it operates. It is able to support a careful study and analysis of alternative courses of action. Such models often require multidimension and consolidation features beyond those normally found in spreadsheets.

Modeling languages, such as the one shown to write the program in Figure 5-23, are used to create, or program, models. Generically they are called "fourth-generation programming languages." To users, this means that they are easier to work with than third-generation languages such as BASIC or COBOL.

Some modeling languages are similar to English-like macro or command languages found in spreadsheet packages. Others are not, such as the example shown in Figure 5-24.

Usually separate files are created for a model's logic and data, as shown in Figure 5-25. The ability to reuse logic models with different or changed data files is one of the strengths of such software. In addition, many separate data files can be processed against the same model logic for the easy creation of consolidations, such as the one shown in Figure 5-26.

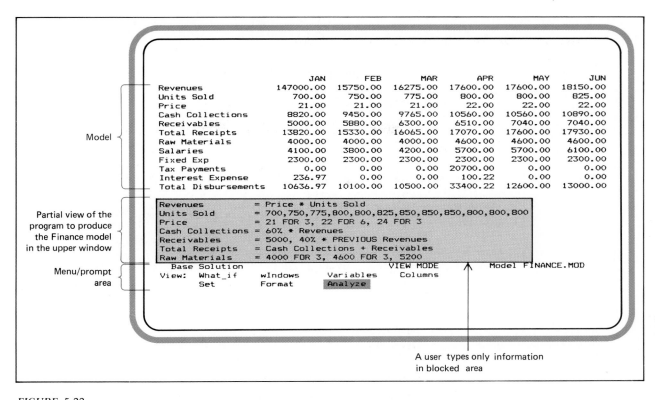

Model {

	JAN	FEB	MAR	APR	MAY	JUN
Revenues	147000.00	15750.00	16275.00	17600.00	17600.00	18150.00
Units Sold	700.00	750.00	775.00	800.00	800.00	825.00
Price	21.00	21.00	21.00	22.00	22.00	22.00
Cash Collections	8820.00	9450.00	9765.00	10560.00	10560.00	10890.00
Receivables	5000.00	5880.00	6300.00	6510.00	7040.00	7040.00
Total Receipts	13820.00	15330.00	16065.00	17070.00	17600.00	17930.00
Raw Materials	4000.00	4000.00	4000.00	4600.00	4600.00	4600.00
Salaries	4100.00	3800.00	4200.00	5700.00	5700.00	6100.00
Fixed Exp	2300.00	2300.00	2300.00	2300.00	2300.00	2300.00
Tax Payments	0.00	0.00	0.00	20700.00	0.00	0.00
Interest Expense	236.97	0.00	0.00	100.22	0.00	0.00
Total Disbursements	10636.97	10100.00	10500.00	33400.22	12600.00	13000.00

Partial view of the
program to produce
the Finance model
in the upper window {

```
Revenues        = Price * Units Sold
Units Sold      = 700,750,775,800,800,825,850,850,850,800,800,800
Price           = 21 FOR 3, 22 FOR 6, 24 FOR 3
Cash Collections = 60% * Revenues
Receivables     = 5000, 40% * PREVIOUS Revenues
Total Receipts  = Cash Collections + Receivables
Raw Materials   = 4000 FOR 3, 4600 FOR 3, 5200
```

Menu/prompt
area {

```
   Base Solution                        VIEW MODE        Model FINANCE.MOD
View:  What_if    wIndows     Variables    Columns
       Set        Format      Analyze
```

A user types only information
in blocked area

FIGURE 5-22
Split-screen view of a model and program produced by a financial modeling package that runs on microcomputers and mainframes.
(*Software*: IFPS/Personal, courtesy of Execucom Systems Corporation)

FIGURE 5-23
Example of a financial modeling package's programming language (*Software*: IFPS/Personal, courtesy of Execucom Systems Corporation)

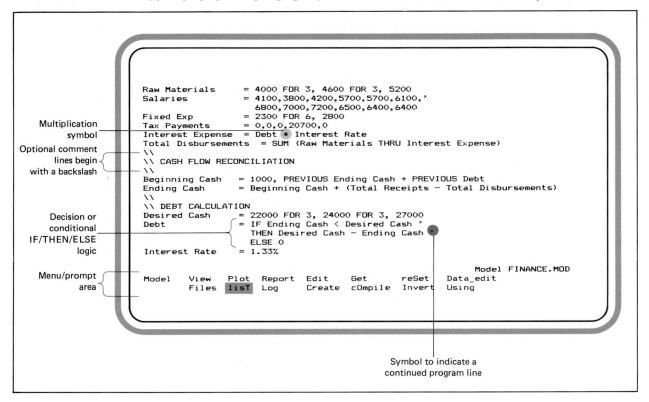

```
Raw Materials     = 4000 FOR 3, 4600 FOR 3, 5200
Salaries          = 4100,3800,4200,5700,5700,6100,'
                    6800,7000,7200,6500,6400,6400
Fixed Exp         = 2300 FOR 6, 2800
Tax Payments      = 0,0,0,20700,0
Interest Expense  = Debt * Interest Rate
Total Disbursements = SUM (Raw Materials THRU Interest Expense)
\\
\\ CASH FLOW RECONCILIATION
\\
Beginning Cash    = 1000, PREVIOUS Ending Cash + PREVIOUS Debt
Ending Cash       = Beginning Cash + (Total Receipts - Total Disbursements)
\\
\\ DEBT CALCULATION
Desired Cash      = 22000 FOR 3, 24000 FOR 3, 27000
Debt              = IF Ending Cash < Desired Cash '
                    THEN Desired Cash - Ending Cash
                    ELSE 0
Interest Rate     = 1.33%

                                           Model FINANCE.MOD
Model    View    Plot   Report    Edit    Get      reSet  Data_edit
         Files   lisT   Log       Create  cOmpile  Invert Using
```

Multiplication symbol

Optional comment
lines begin
with a backslash {

Decision or
conditional
IF/THEN/ELSE
logic

Menu/prompt
area {

Symbol to indicate a
continued program line

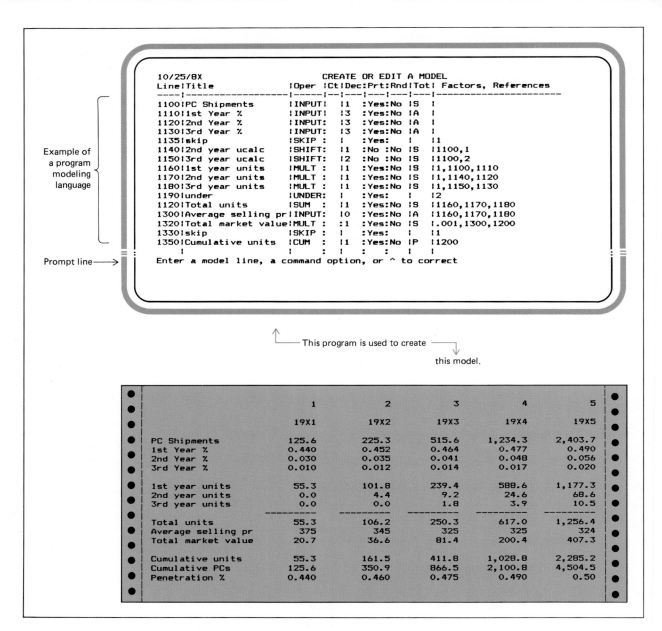

```
10/25/8X                    CREATE OR EDIT A MODEL
Line!Title                 !Oper !Ct!Dec:Prt:Rnd!Tot! Factors, References
----!-------------------!-----!--!---!---!---!---!-----------------------
1100!PC Shipments          !INPUT! !1 :Yes:No !S !
1110!1st Year %            !INPUT! !3 :Yes:No !A !
1120!2nd Year %            !INPUT! !3 :Yes:No !A !
1130!3rd Year %            !INPUT! !3 :Yes:No !A !
1135!skip                  !SKIP : ! :Yes:    ! !1
1140!2nd year ucalc        !SHIFT! !1 :No :No !S !1100,1
1150!3rd year ucalc        !SHIFT! !2 :No :No !S !1100,2
1160!1st year units        !MULT : !1 :Yes:No !S !1,1100,1110
1170!2nd year units        !MULT : !1 :Yes:No !S !1,1140,1120
1180!3rd year units        !MULT : !1 :Yes:No !S !1,1150,1130
1190!under                 !UNDER! ! :Yes:    ! !2
1120!Total units           !SUM : !1 :Yes:No !S !1160,1170,1180
1300!Average selling pr    !INPUT! !0 :Yes:No !A !1160,1170,1180
1320!Total market value    !MULT : !:1 :Yes:No !S !.001,1300,1200
1330!skip                  !SKIP : ! :Yes:    ! !1
1350!Cumulative units      !CUM : !1 :Yes:No !P !1200
    !                      !     : ! :   :   ! !
Enter a model line, a command option, or ^ to correct
```

Example of a program modeling language

Prompt line →

— This program is used to create —

this model.

	1	2	3	4	5
	19X1	19X2	19X3	19X4	19X5
PC Shipments	125.6	225.3	515.6	1,234.3	2,403.7
1st Year %	0.440	0.452	0.464	0.477	0.490
2nd Year %	0.030	0.035	0.041	0.048	0.056
3rd Year %	0.010	0.012	0.014	0.017	0.020
1st year units	55.3	101.8	239.4	588.6	1,177.3
2nd year units	0.0	4.4	9.2	24.6	68.6
3rd year units	0.0	0.0	1.8	3.9	10.5
Total units	55.3	106.2	250.3	617.0	1,256.4
Average selling pr	375	345	325	325	324
Total market value	20.7	36.6	81.4	200.4	407.3
Cumulative units	55.3	161.5	411.8	1,028.8	2,285.2
Cumulative PCs	125.6	350.9	866.5	2,100.8	4,504.5
Penetration %	0.440	0.460	0.475	0.490	0.50

FIGURE 5-24
Using a financial modeling package to write a program to create a model
(*Software: MicroPROPHIT, courtesy of* Business Software)

FIGURE 5-25
Logic, data, and reports are usually kept in separate files when using a financial modeling package
(*Software: IFPS/Personal, courtesy of* Execucom Systems Corporation)

Model logic file (program)

Example: Corporate Totals

Data files

Example:

East Division

West Division

Generate a report file

Report file

Analyze or print a report

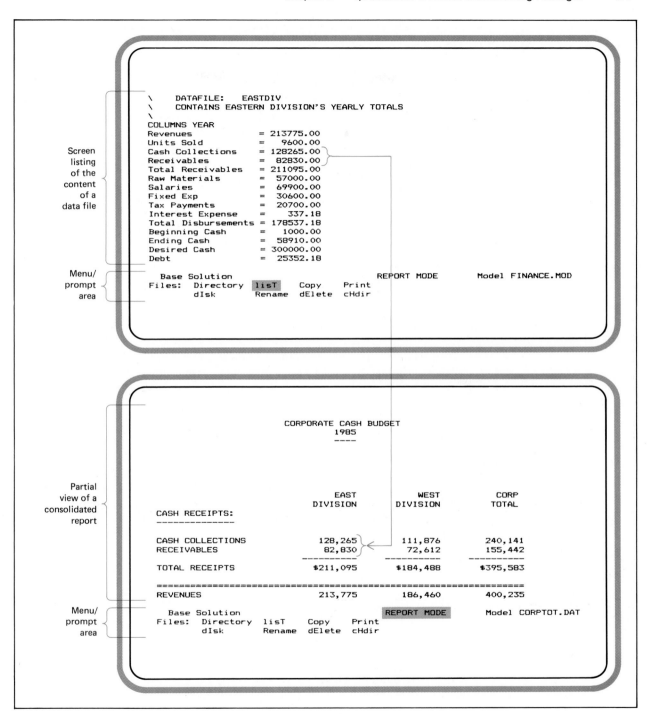

```
\     DATAFILE:    EASTDIV
\     CONTAINS EASTERN DIVISION'S YEARLY TOTALS
\
COLUMNS YEAR
Revenues              = 213775.00
Units Sold            =   9600.00
Cash Collections      = 128265.00
Receivables           =  82830.00
Total Receivables     = 211095.00
Raw Materials         =  57000.00
Salaries              =  69900.00
Fixed Exp             =  30600.00
Tax Payments          =  20700.00
Interest Expense      =    337.18
Total Disbursements   = 178537.18
Beginning Cash        =   1000.00
Ending Cash           =  58910.00
Desired Cash          = 300000.00
Debt                  =  25352.18

  Base Solution                          REPORT MODE       Model FINANCE.MOD
Files:  Directory   lisT    Copy    Print
        dIsk        Rename  dElete  cHdir
```

Screen
listing
of the
content
of a
data file

Menu/
prompt
area

```
                        CORPORATE CASH BUDGET
                               1985
                               ----



                              EAST           WEST          CORP
                            DIVISION       DIVISION        TOTAL
CASH RECEIPTS:
---------------

CASH COLLECTIONS            128,265        111,876        240,141
RECEIVABLES                  82,830         72,612        155,442
                         ----------     ----------     ----------
TOTAL RECEIPTS             $211,095       $184,488       $395,583

=================================================================
REVENUES                    213,775        186,460        400,235

  Base Solution                        REPORT MODE       Model CORPTOT.DAT
Files:  Directory   lisT    Copy    Print
        dIsk        Rename  dElete  cHdir
```

Partial
view of a
consolidated
report

Menu/
prompt
area

FIGURE 5-26
Creating a consolidated report using a separate data file
(Software: IFPS/Personal, courtesy of Execucom Systems Corporation)

Decision Support

National Bank maintains a Decision Support Center that is staffed with technical support specialists who are knowledgeable about modeling. They are trained to help users, and they usually design and program models for top-level decision makers.

Because decision makers are the main consumers for this type of software, both financial modeling and spreadsheet packages are often called **decision support tools.** Such modeling tools are at the heart of any computer-based decision support system, which is usually found in large organizations.

Only a few managers learn how to build models, but most learn how to manipulate models. There are some who delegate all model use and manipulation to a senior staff person who is referred to as a "coach" or "chauffeur."

HYBRID PACKAGES

The maturing spreadsheet and financial modeling software industry is producing hybrid packages that encourage a user to

- Carefully structure spreadsheet problems
- Separate formulas from the spreadsheet grid
- Document assumptions

The packages intrinsically assume that a spreadsheet, or model, will have to be explained to others.

Javelin, as an example, offers a spreadsheet as only one of ten possible "views" of its data. Other views, some of which are shown in Figure 5-27, include

- Table View: Used to enter data by name (like "Nebraska Shoe Sales") and time periods (like August to May 198X). Data are stored in a so-called "central information base." The base can be produced in any other "view" desired.
- Graph View: Used to view data in graphical form or, by moving a cursor on the graph, to change data in the central information base.
- Diagram View: Used to see a visual representation of how data items relate to each other.
- Formulas View: Used to trace a model's underlying assumptions. Formulas are normally built in the Table View.
- Worksheet View: Used to see a spreadsheet image of data. If data are changed in one cell, all views reflect that alteration to the central information base.

Other hybrid packages have similarities but are more database-manager package oriented, such as reflex and VP Planner. They are covered in Chapter 8, "Database and File Management Packages."

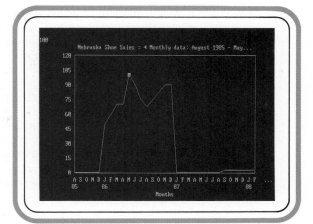

The chart and table views are synchronized to display the same time periods.

Simply moving a cursor around on the graph view allows data to be entered into the central information base.

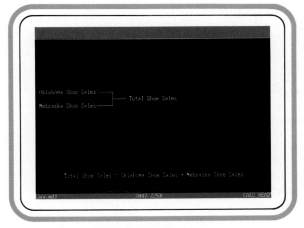

The diagram view tracks the logic and structure of a model.

The formula view documents assumptions and logic behind a model.

FIGURE 5-27
A powerful financial analysis and modeling tool (*Software: Javelin, courtesy of Javelin Software*)

CASE STUDY: Avoiding Spreadsheet Disaster

While the spreadsheet affords tremendous productivity gains, it also may open a Pandora's box, its spirits looming darkly over the bottom line. The problem is simple, yet elusive: The computer's remarkable power to get more work done faster also creates the opportunity to make more mistakes and multiply them more rapidly.

Spreadsheet Sharing.   Errors can creep into calculations in many ways. A common mistake occurs when one person tries to adapt a spreadsheet built by another, perhaps without fully understanding the model's structure. In doing so, the second user may change or overwrite a crucial formula, introducing an error into the calculations. With luck, the error will be obvious. Occasionally, though, the error escapes detection.

This kind of spreadsheet sharing often arises as part of the "initial excitement of using spreadsheets," says John Haner, partner with Arthur Andersen & Co. in Chicago. "One person tends to turn to another for help. It's difficult to control this kind of informal sharing. It's important to have a healthy skepticism of what's in these spread-sheets."

Sharing of spreadsheets can have another pitfall, says Rick Richardson, partner with Arthur Young & Co. in New York. "When individuals come up with a great template and share it with others, they often end up performing a staff function—training and coordinating the others who want to adopt the spreadsheet. They lose whatever productivity gain the spreadsheet helped achieve in the first place."

Formal Policies.   Accounting firms, attuned as they are to financial controls, have developed some of the earliest formal spreadsheet policies and procedures. Arthur Young, for example, treats spreadsheet templates like computer programs: Each requires a manual. "My advice to clients is to centralize the coordination of spreadsheet sharing," Richardson says. "That includes technical review, documentation, and dissemination of templates."

Corporations are starting to follow the accountants' lead in instituting spreadsheet controls. Last fall, General Instrument Corp. introduced its "personal computer documentation/programming standards," says Jonathan Yarmis, personal computer analyst for the New Jersey company. Under this policy, all spreadsheets must be accompanied by a written narrative explaining how the model works.

"There was some initial resistance on the part of some people," Yarmis says. "They said writing documentation would take away their initial productivity gains." Yarmis challenged them by betting that if he examined five of their spreadsheets, he could find mistakes in at least two of them. Several people took up Yarmis on the challenge—and lost.

He also encourages people to include a printout of the spreadsheet model, made with a program called Spreadsheet Auditor. The $99 package prints all the equations from a spreadsheet template in a form that the programs themselves don't: in a table in the same relative position they occupy in the spreadsheet.

Other Problems.   But some say policies such as those at General Instrument may not solve all the potential problems. Although people may document their spreadsheets, "Documentation never gets read," says Alan Gross, Head of the Microcomputer Managers Association of New York.

Brian Smolens, product manager for accounting software at Entre Computer Centers of Vienna, Virginia, finds another problem exists. "Lotus 1-2-3 is very seductive. Once people learn it they want to use it for everything. Many companies," he says, "may be pushing spreadsheet software to accomplish tasks that other programs can do better."

(*SOURCE: By permission of Jack Grushow, Consumer Software, Inc., Vancouver, B.C., June 1986.*)

A FEW SPREADSHEET TIPS

1. Create a separate data input area.   It should show assumptions or factors, opening balances, base figures, and other data. The best place for the input area is the upper left corner of the worksheet. The body of the worksheet should contain only formulas and references to data input area cells. That way you can easily see what assumptions results will be based on.

2. Use templates.   Setting up a basic model of a spreadsheet and saving a copy of the model with no data (template) will allow you to use the model again and again without wasting time re-creating

	A	B	C	D	E	F	G
1		Jan-Mar	Apr-Jun	Jul-Sept	Oct-Dec	Annual	Cross-check
2	Food	1200	1320	1452	1597	5569	
3	Rent	2100	2100	2100	2100	8400	
4	Utilities	450	495	545	599	2088	
5		--					
6		3750	3915	4097	4296	16058	16058
7							0
8							

FIGURE 5-28
Spreadsheet with a cross-check
(*Courtesy of* PC World, *555 De Haro St.,
San Francisco, CA 94107*)

it. Just load the file holding the template you've created, key in the data, and save the resulting worksheet under a unique name. Leave room at the top of the template for the date and notes about what data it contains.

3. *Include cross-checks.*   A prudent spreadsheet model should calculate important values more than one way to cross-check the results, as shown in Figure 5-28.

4. *Experiment.*   It's easy to change values and watch the results. Do it often and you will get a better feel for spreadsheet software. Substitute some wildly optimistic or pessimistic values for your assumptions. You may gain insight into the way your model works that wouldn't come out under normal circumstances.

DISCUSSION QUESTIONS

1. "Dependence on spreadsheet programs can leave an organization vulnerable if a template designer leaves the company or is temporarily unavailable." Why could this statement be true?

2. Describe organizational spreadsheet problems and solutions.

CHAPTER SUMMARY

- Electronic *spreadsheets* are convenient tools to explore problems that can be defined numerically in row and column format. A spreadsheet user is responsible for developing a spreadsheet model, entering primary numbers, and defining relationships among numbers.

- *Cells* hold numbers, labels, and formulas. They are activated by the presence of a *cell pointer* that is moved around the display by cursor control arrow keys, or by a mouse.

- Spreadsheet *commands* include those to select a range of cells, right-justify labels in a cell or cell range, save a spreadsheet file, and print a spreadsheet, among others.

- To ask a "what if" question requires moving a cell pointer and typing a new amount in a cell. Totals across and down instantly display the changed figures.

- Spreadsheet features that enhance a user's personal

productivity include an ability to *insert, delete, move, copy,* and *format* a cell, range of cells, or entire rows or columns. *Split-screen windows* are also helpful.

- *Built-in functions* are equivalent to prepared formulas. They eliminate the need to create common formulas from scratch, like sum, average, count, minimum, maximum, and others.

- A *protected spreadsheet* has certain cells locked to prevent them from being changed.

- A spreadsheet integrated with other applications allows combining, for example, word processing and graphic functions in the same document.

- A *macro* is a block of program code. Only a keystroke or keyword is used to activate the program code.

- A spreadsheet *template* is a spreadsheet without numbers or data. It is often created with macros to simplify the work of template users.

- *Add-ons,* or *add-ins,* in the software industry, are

packages created to add value to other, more widely used, packages. Add-on packages are available for the Lotus 1-2-3 package, for example, in application, auditing, file utility, graphic, macro recorder, printing utility, and other categories.

- An *English-language command interface* allows a user to type commands that resemble natural-language English. An example is to command a spreadsheet to "graph this."
- An *undo* feature cancels a mistake or change of mind.
- A *goal-seeking* feature allows a user to indicate a result that is desired, then identify the numbers that can and cannot be manipulated in order to achieve the desired goal. Optimization software helps a user to select the "best" option from a series of "what if" possibilities.
- A *multiuser spreadsheet* is a centralized spreadsheet that allows many users access at once. A *file-locking* feature keeps users, except the file owner, from destroying the file.
- A *consolidation* feature allows for the combination or merging of several spreadsheets to get a summary spreadsheet, which is often used for analysis and report purposes.
- A *multidimension* feature allows for the organization and analysis of spreadsheet data by whatever criteria are appropriate, such as budget category, time period, and departments.
- *Standardizing on software* means that all employees who need a spreadsheet, as an example, use the same package. This facilitates exchanging files, as well as software training and maintenance, in an organization.
- A *file conversion* or *translation* feature is necessary to share files if different spreadsheet packages are in use. Files are *exported* from one spreadsheet and *imported* into another using common file formats, such as ASCII.
- Criteria used to evaluate spreadsheets include style, cell capacity, ease of file transfer, recalculation, and many other details.
- A *financial modeling package* is used to handle problems that have more dimensions and complex formulas than can easily be handled by a spreadsheet package.
- *Modeling* is a process of representing, through mathematical equations and logical expressions, aspects of an organization's business activities. A *model* is a simulation of an activity.
- *Modeling languages* are used to program models.
- Both financial modeling packages and spreadsheets are considered *decision support tools*.

KEY TERMS

Add-ins
Add-ons
ASCII (American Standard Code for Information Interchange)
Built-in functions
Cell
Cell pointer
Cell range
Command
Consolidation
Coordinate
Copy
Decision support tool
DIF (Data Interchange Format)
Electronic spreadsheet
English-language command interface
Export
File conversion
File locking
Financial modeling package
Format

Goal-seeking
Import
Keyboard oriented
Linking
Macros
Menu line
Menu pointer
Model
Modeling
Modeling language
Mouse oriented
Multidimension
Multiuser spreadsheet package
Optimization
Protected spreadsheet
Split screen
Spreadsheet
Standardizing
Template
Titles
Translation
Undo
WKS and WK1

REVIEW QUESTIONS

1. Describe some characteristics of electronic spreadsheets.
2. What is a "cell"? How is a "cell pointer" used?
3. Give examples of common spreadsheet commands.
4. Describe how to ask a spreadsheet "what if" questions.
5. Identify three common spreadsheet productivity enhancement features.
6. What are built-in funtions? Give examples.
7. How can a spreadsheet be protected?
8. What is the benefit of software that integrates a spreadsheet with other applications?
9. Differentiate between a macro and a template.
10. What are add-on packages? Give some examples.
11. What is goal-seeking?
12. What is a multiuser spreadsheet? a multidimensional spreadsheet?
13. Why would an organization standardize on software?
14. List criteria to consider when evaluating spreadsheet software.
15. When is a financial modeling package useful?
16. What is modeling?
17. Give two examples of computerized decision support tools.

EXERCISES

1. *Phoenix District Case.*   Assume that you are the corporate financial officer in charge of designing a "fill-in-the-blanks" spreadsheet template for all district offices. Use the Phoenix District spreadsheet in Figure 5-5 as a prototype of the result you want from each district.
   a. Which cells would be field protected?
   b. Which cells would contain formulas?
   c. Which cells would contain fixed numeric information?
   d. Which cells would require "fill-in-the-blanks" manual entry?

2. *Allied Industries Company Case.*   Assume that you are the microcomputer manager of Allied Industries' home office and that it is a job responsibility to keep up to date on spreadsheet and other microcomputer applications. Examine as many articles as you can about spreadsheets that appeared in the last three months. Prepare a report that reviews recent topics in the spreadsheet area.

3. Try to arrange a demonstration of a mouse-oriented and a keyboard-oriented spreadsheet. If possible, try to hands-on test them yourself. Make a determination about which style is easier to learn. Explain your reasons in a report.

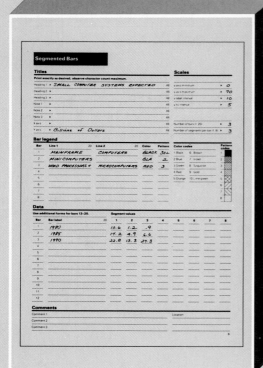

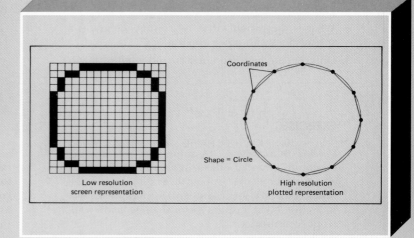

Coordinates

Low resolution
screen representation

Shape = Circle

High resolution
plotted representation

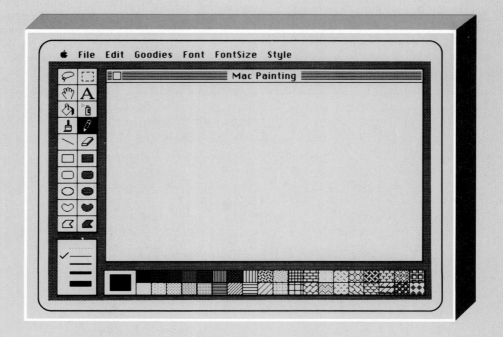

6

Graphics Packages

AFTER READING THIS CHAPTER, YOU SHOULD BE ABLE TO

- Describe uses for business graphics packages and initiate an application evaluation
- Describe uses for painting, imaging, computer-aided design, and animation software

"I can't see the forest because of all the trees," Frank Nelson says to himself more than once after looking at a spreadsheet. Masses of numbers sometimes hide important facts and figures. At this point he decides to convert a spreadsheet into graphical form. It reveals trends and patterns that enable him to pinpoint potential problem areas.

Using graphics for personal data analysis is called **analytic graphics.** Sprucing up the same graph for presentation to others often requires a different **presentation graphics** package. Some even use painting and image processing packages to spruce up business graphics.

This chapter examines the wealth of graphics software available to personal computer users. First, it looks at **business graphics,** which is the general classification for analytic and presentation graphics packages, as shown in Figure 6-1. Then, after a review of painting and image processing software, the chapter concludes with a look at computer-aided design (CAD) and animation graphics.

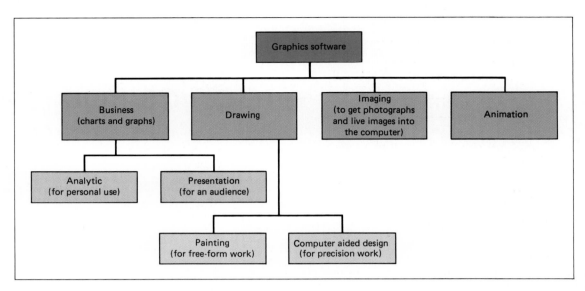

FIGURE 6-1
Categories of graphics software packages for personal computers

ANALYTIC GRAPHICS

Analytic graphics help a decision maker to analyze a problem, discern a trend, assess relationships, or investigate any of many other decision-related possibilities. This type of graphics software comes with all the integrated packages identified in Figure 5-6. It produces charts that are usually viewed as **soft copy** on a display only by the spreadsheet creator. If a printed or **hard copy** is desired, a standard dot-matrix personal printer is adequate. It gives black-and-white hard copy that is useful for reference, like the example in Figure 6-2.

The example in Figure 6-2 did not require much work. To create it, Mr. Nelson typed /G to invoke the Graph function in his integrated package. When the graphics main menu appears, he types the following sequence:

Typed Key(s)	Action
T	Selects the "type" menu option to choose a graph type
S	Chooses a "stack-bar" chart
X	Indicates that the bar labels on the X-axis are to be entered
A2.A5	Uses the labels in cells A2 to A5 as bar labels
A	Indicates that the first range of data is to be entered
B2.B5	Enters the cell range containing the data
B	Indicates that the second range of data is to be entered
C2.C5	Enters the cell range containing the data
C	Indicates that the last range of data is to be entered
D2.D5	Enters the cell range containing the data

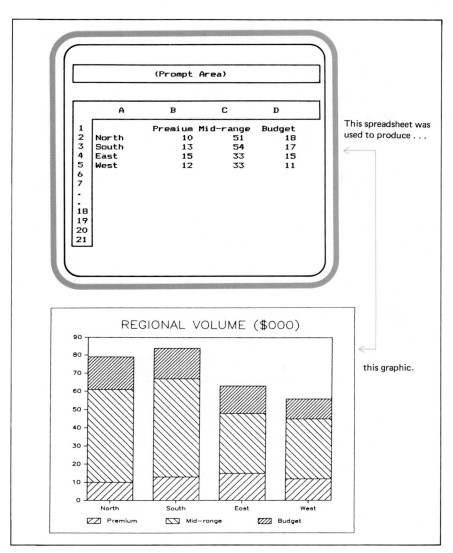

FIGURE 6-2
A spreadsheet converted into a graphic that is printed
on a dot-matrix printer
(Software: Lotus 1-2-3®, courtesy of ©Lotus Development Corporation,
1988. Used with permission.)

After he types the last cell range, he types V to view the graph. The displayed result resembles Figure 6-2. A few more entries are required to add the extra description lines on the top and bottom of the graph.

Now Mr. Nelson can see how figures "look." They are for a new line of baseball bats that are sold in three qualities: top-of-the-line or premium, midrange, and budget categories. The vertical bars instantly highlight differences in how each sales region is performing in relation to others.

His integrated package allows him to revise the spreadsheet and have the changes instantly reflected in the graph. By contrast, with stand-alone spreadsheet software, some disk swapping would be necessary. The spreadsheet program would have to be closed down, and the program disk would have to be replaced with the graphics program disk. Sometimes the time and trouble involved in changing to the graphics package outweigh the benefit provided.

FIGURE 6-3
Examples of computer-generated presentation graphs produced on a plotter
(*Software: Graphwriter, courtesy of Lotus Development Corp.*)

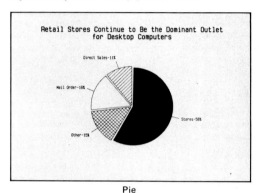

Pie

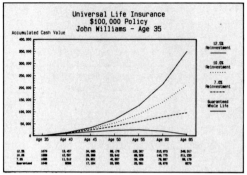

Line-table

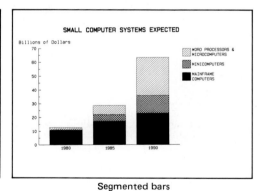

Scatter

Segmented bars

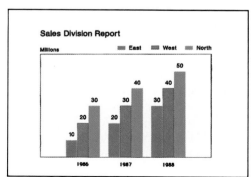

Clustered bars

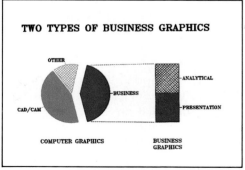

Pie-bar combination

PRESENTATION GRAPHICS

Analytic graphics serve Mr. Nelson's decision-making needs well. But sometimes he requires presentation-quality graphics for

- Reports
- Business meetings
- Customer presentations

Presentation quality usually means refined color charts, such as the ones in Figure 6-3. They have none of the "computerese" look of the chart in Figure 6-2.

To get presentation quality usually requires an investment in more software and hardware. Presentation graphics packages, such as some of those listed in Figure 6-4, can cost a few hundred dollars. Graphics output devices, which include plotters like the one shown in Figure 6-5, can cost hundreds of dollars more. **Plotters** do more than print paper charts. They also print on plastic sheets, called **overhead transparencies,** for use in an overhead projector, like the one shown in Figure 6-6.

Eventually Mr. Nelson's company acquired presentation graphics software. The company also acquired an inexpensive plotter.

Some conclusions derived from a Wharton Business School study convinced the company to make the graphics investment. The study showed that an audience is twice as likely to be persuaded by a presentation with visuals than without them. It indicated that speakers with visuals appeared

- More professional
- Better prepared
- More persuasive
- More credible
- More interesting

BPS Business Graphics	Graphwriter
Business Graphics System	Harvard Presentation Graphics
Chart-Master	Hypergraphics
ChartStar	Infographics CHOICE
Colography	Instant Replay
dGraph	Microsoft Chart
Diagram-Master	PC Presents
EnerGraphics	Perspective
Executive Picture Show	PFS:graph
Executive Presentation Kit	PictureIt
Fast Graphs	Picture Perfect
Freelance Plus	Presentation Master
GEM Graph	ShowIt
GrafTalk	Show Partner
Graphix partner	SlideWrite
GraphPlan	VCN Concorde

FIGURE 6-4
A sampler of business graphics software packages for personal computers

FIGURE 6-5
A typical plotter used for presentation graphics
(Courtesy of Hewlett-Packard)

FIGURE 6-6
This overhead projector displays a graph that is printed on a clear plastic "overhead transparency."
(Courtesy of Hewlett-Packard)

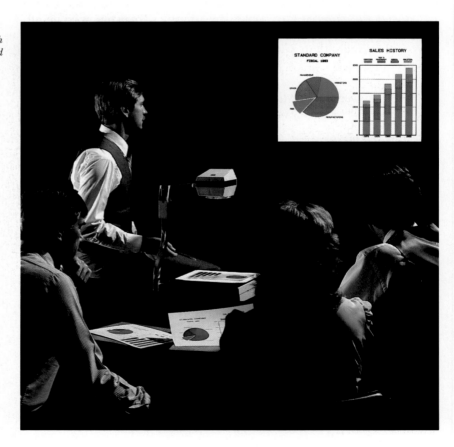

Keep graphs uncluttered.
Keep them brief.
Make only one point with one graphic.

Pie Charts
Use to emphasize the relationship of the parts to the whole.
Consider pulled-out slices for special emphasis.

Bar Charts
Use for data arranged in segments (by month, year, etc.).
Use vertical or horizontal bars.
Show complex facts clearly by using multiple or segmented bars.

Line Graphs
Use to display trends or continuous data.
Select baseline and scale for maximum effectiveness.

Word Charts
Use key words only.
Use bullets and color to highlight key points.
Break up information to make a series of graphs (a progressive or "build" series). Use color to show the new line added to each chart. Do not try to enhance word charts with graphic decorations.

FIGURE 6-7
Selected presentation graphics guidelines

Other studies show that when visuals are used, an audience remembers about 90 percent of the information compared with only 10 percent without them.

On the other hand, Mr. Nelson's packages came with warnings about not to overdo it. Bad graphics can do more harm than good if they are oversimplified and irrelevant to the points being made. The list in Figure 6-7 covers some guidelines about creating presentation graphics.

The graphics package that Mr. Nelson uses is the same one that is being used in companies of all sizes. As an example, a vice-president and other professionals at National Bank, a mainframe organization, use the same package to make graphics. They make many formal reports, both written and oral. Their graphics needs encouraged the bank to supply them with a personal computer, graphics software, plotter, and slide-making hardware. They call it their shared **graphics workstation.** Five other departments in the bank have similar graphics workstations.

Creating Graphs

One graphics package that the bank acquired comes with 23 prepared *input forms*, one for each type of chart, like the example in Figure 6-8. Theresa Fordham, a vice-president of the bank, took a company-sponsored seminar that showed her how to use the software and the input forms. Consequently, she makes some charts herself. After creating and storing graphs, Ms. Fordham gives the disk to an assistant to run off on the plotter.

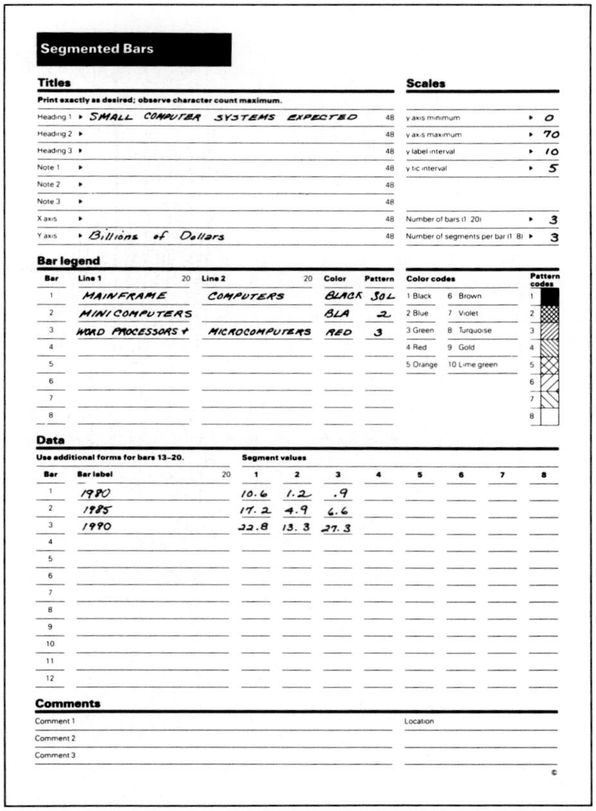

Segmented Bars

Titles

Print exactly as desired; observe character count maximum.

Heading 1 ▸	SMALL COMPUTER SYSTEMS EXPECTED	48
Heading 2 ▸		48
Heading 3 ▸		48
Note 1 ▸		48
Note 2 ▸		48
Note 3 ▸		48
X axis ▸		48
Y axis ▸	Billions of Dollars	48

Scales

y axis minimum ▸	0
y axis maximum ▸	70
y label interval ▸	10
y tic interval ▸	5
Number of bars (1 20) ▸	3
Number of segments per bar (1 8) ▸	3

Bar legend

Bar	Line 1 (20)	Line 2 (20)	Color	Pattern
1	MAINFRAME	COMPUTERS	BLACK	SOL
2	MINICOMPUTERS		BLA	2
3	WORD PROCESSORS +	MICROCOMPUTERS	RED	3
4				
5				
6				
7				
8				

Color codes

1 Black	6 Brown
2 Blue	7 Violet
3 Green	8 Turquoise
4 Red	9 Gold
5 Orange	10 Lime green

Pattern codes 1 2 3 4 5 6 7 8

Data

Use additional forms for bars 13–20. **Segment values**

Bar	Bar label (20)	1	2	3	4	5	6	7	8
1	1980	10.6	1.2	.9					
2	1985	17.2	4.9	6.6					
3	1990	22.8	13.3	27.3					
4									
5									
6									
7									
8									
9									
10									
11									
12									

Comments

Comment 1 Location
Comment 2
Comment 3

©

FIGURE 6-8
Sample input form for the segmented bar chart shown in Figure 6-3
(*Courtesy of Lotus Development Corp.*)

Standard **input forms** simplify graphic production for a novice user. Forms contain answers to prompts from the graphics program. Once formats become familiar, users find input forms unnecessary.

A chart element guide, like the one in Figure 6-9, helps users to learn graphics jargon. It is necessary to prepare chart forms.

Entering Data

To prepare a chart, Ms. Fordham selects "Execute a Format" from a main menu. She can enter new data from the keyboard or input data automatically from a spreadsheet, among other options. She elects to enter new data.

Because the chart is specific, menu choices and prompts are also specific. The technique eliminates extraneous prompts required by more generalized approaches to graph creation.

Keyboard entries, given in Figure 6-10, follow the form Ms. Fordham filled out earlier (see Figure 6-8). Only selected entries are shown in Figure 6-10 to give a flavor of the entry procedure. Style options are chosen from the chart provided in Figure 6-11. A list of these and other options is available anytime by pressing a help key.

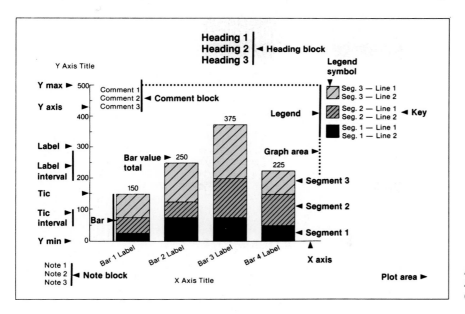

FIGURE 6-9
Segmented bar chart elements
(Courtesy of Lotus Development Corp.)

FIGURE 6-10
Selected keyboard entries for segmented bar chart

DISPLAYED PROMPTS	KEYBOARD ENTRIES
(Compare sample entries with Figures 6-8 and 6-9)	
Enter new heading 1:	SMALL COMPUTER SYSTEMS EXPECTED
Enter new Y axis title:	Billions of dollars
Enter new Y axis minimum:	0
Enter new Y axis maximum:	70
Enter Y axis label interval:	10
Enter Y axis tic interval:	5
Enter new number of bars:	3
Enter new number of segments:	3
Enter bar legend line 1 (segment 1):	MAINFRAME
Enter bar legend line 2 (segment 1):	COMPUTERS
Segment 1 color is . . . red	
Enter new segment 1 color:	BLACK
Segment 1 fill is . . . solid fill	
Enter new segment 1 fill:	(Return key reselects the one recommended, SOLID)
Enter new bar 1 label:	1980
Enter new bar 2 label:	1985
Enter new bar 3 label:	1990
Enter segment 1 values for:	

Bar #	Label	New Value
1	1980	10.6
2	1985	17.2
3	1990	22.8

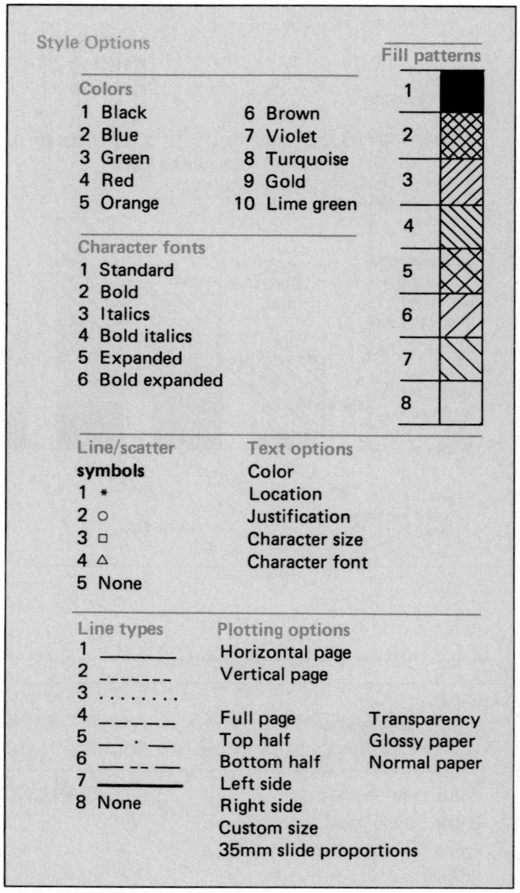

Style Options

Fill patterns

Colors
1 Black   6 Brown
2 Blue   7 Violet
3 Green   8 Turquoise
4 Red   9 Gold
5 Orange   10 Lime green

Character fonts
1 Standard
2 Bold
3 Italics
4 Bold italics
5 Expanded
6 Bold expanded

Line/scatter   Text options
symbols   Color
1 *   Location
2 ○   Justification
3 □   Character size
4 △   Character font
5 None

Line types   Plotting options
1 _____   Horizontal page
2 - - - - - -   Vertical page
3 . . . .
4 _ _ _ _ _   Full page   Transparency
5 _ · _   Top half   Glossy paper
6 _ _ · · _ _   Bottom half   Normal paper
7 _____   Left side
8 None   Right side
                    Custom size
                    35mm slide proportions

FIGURE 6-11
Style options
(*Courtesy of Lotus Development Corp.*)

The keyboard entry procedure in Figure 6-10 reveals *default* selections, like colors and fill patterns. **Defaults** are common in many software packages. They are preselected choices. In graphics packages they reflect a trend toward so-called *smart charts*. They are model charts prepared by graphics experts, like those Ms. Fordham uses. Only customized data value entries must be keyboarded to produce professional looking results.

Another type of package, like Infographics CHOICE, has built-in design intelligence. After a user answers questions about input data, the software selects the best type of chart to represent the data.

Some software asks a user to choose color mood. Based on a choice like "spring" or "winter," it chooses a pleasing set of colors. This feature is becoming more important as software packages offer hundreds of colors to select from.

When all data entry is complete, a menu option enables Ms. Fordham to *preview* the chart on the display. **Previewing** is a common and necessary feature with graphics. It allows a user to examine and revise things like color, fill pattern, and other selections. When satisfied with the result, she sends the graphic to the plotter for a printed copy.

COLOR DISPLAY HARDWARE

Previewing is done on a high-resolution red-green-blue (RGB) monitor, or color display. Some confusion reigns in the world of color display hardware because of the proliferation of so-called **graphic standards,** as evidenced in Figure 6-12. Even after an attempt is made to sort the standards out, the sheer number of options can be overwhelming.

GRAPHIC STANDARD	DISPLAY/MONITOR TYPE		
	Monochrome	Color	Enhanced Color
Analog			
Multi-Color Graphic Array (MCGA)	Text and graphics 640 × 480 pixels 64 shades of gray	Text and graphics 320 × 200 pixels 256 colors	
		Text only 640 × 400 pixels 16 colors	
Video Graphics Array (VGA)		Text and graphics 320 × 200 pixels 256 colors 640 × 480 pixels 16 colors Text only 720 × 400 pixels 16 colors	
Advanced			Same as VGA, plus Text and graphics 1024 × 768 pixels 256 colors
Digital			
Monochrome Display Adapter (MDA)	Text only		
Hercules Graphics Card (Hercules)	Text and graphics 720 × 348 pixels		
Color/Graphics Adapter (CGA)		Text and graphics 320 × 200 pixels 4 colors	Same as CGA
Enhanced Graphics Adapter (EGA)	Text and graphics 640 × 350 pixels	Text and graphics 320 × 200 pixels 16 colors	Same as EGA color, plus Text and graphics 640 × 350 pixels 16 colors

FIGURE 6-12
Common display combinations with selected graphic standards

Essentially, there are two groups of standards. The newer group belongs to the **analog graphic standards,** established by IBM with its newer line of Personal System/2 hardware. The older group belongs to the **digital graphic standards,** established by IBM with its older line of Personal Computer hardware.

Analog Displays

Newer analog monitors display as many as 256 colors simultaneously from a selection of over 262,000 color possibilities. This range of colors would not be practical using digital technology.

Digital and analog technologies can be compared to an ordinary light switch and a light dimmer. The light switch is a digital device. It is either on or off. There is no in-between variation.

This contrasts with a dimmer, which is an analog device. Turning the dial on the dimmer produces any number of in-between shadings of light. This wide range of light variations parallels the color possibilities available with the analog display.

Figure 6-12 indicates that three analog and four digital graphic standards are common. The dominant characteristics of the analog standards is the ability to display 256 colors simultaneously. By contrast, the digital graphic standards can display only 16 colors simultaneously.

The IBM Personal System/2 line of computers has either a Multi-Color Graphics Array (MCGA) or Video Graphics Array (VGA) standard already built into the system unit. The "Advanced" capability is available only through additional hardware. The hardware is a display circuit board, similar to the one in Figure 2-18, that fits into an expansion slot in the system unit.

Digital Displays

In general, digital displays require a separate circuit board, called a **graphics board** or **graphics adapter,** to function. If the display and circuit board are not compatible, no image will appear on the screen, and the display hardware might be damaged. For example, connecting a Color/Graphics Adapter (CGA) to a monochrome display results in a strange noise that is soon followed by acrid smoke. This kind of problem does not occur with newer analog displays. Their built-in graphics adapter automatically detects which display is attached and adjusts accordingly.

Figure 6-13 shows a cutaway section of both color and monochrome displays. Both use ordinary **cathode ray tube (CRT)** technology, which is the same display technology used in ordinary television sets. The monochrome display uses one **color gun,** while a color display uses three color guns, red, green, and blue.

Color is created when one color beam turns on its corresponding color phosphor, which coats the back of the screen. Each screen pixel is made up of a collection of tiny **phosphor** dots, which glow when

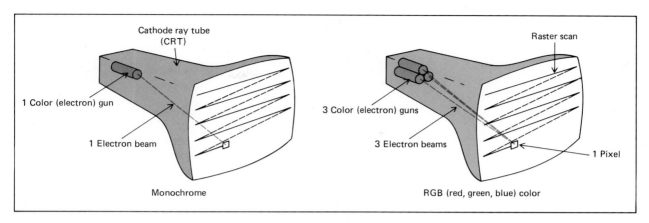

FIGURE 6-13
Comparison of monochrome and RGB color displays

struck by the appropriate light beam. Because the phosphor's glow quickly fades, it must be refreshed 15 to 70 or more times each second. Refreshing the screen is called a **raster scan.**

If only every other line of pixels on the screen is refreshed in one pass, it requires two passes to fully refresh the entire screen. This is called an *interlaced* display. It sometimes causes a slight flickering effect and is less desirable than a *noninterlaced* display.

Each graphic standard has a different primary scanning rate. So, if the display is built to accept a Color/Graphics Adapter (CGA) horizontal scan rate of 15.75 kilohertz (thousands of cycles per second), and is attached to a display circuit board that scans at the Enhanced Graphics Adapter (EGA) rate of 21.85 kilohertz, problems occur.

So-called **multiscan monitors** or **multisync monitors** help solve the graphics compatibility problem. They accept a range of graphics standard scan rates from various graphic display boards. Multiscan monitors cost more than other types of displays. Generally, a color display can cost a few hundred dollars to well over $1,000, depending on features and resolution desired. Graphic display boards are an additional cost and often double the cost of acquiring a graphics capability.

Some packages require a user to indicate what digital display and board combination are being used. The software wants "to know" what kind of devices are attached so that it can send proper signals to "drive" them to perform.

Newer operating system software products, like window packages, allow software to run without being concerned about which display is used. This allows for the creation of **device independent software.** It not only simplifies use of the software but also simplifies its development. Software developers no longer have to write a "driver" program for every possible display board and display, such as those listed in Figure 6-14, that will be used with their products.

DISPLAY (MONITOR) SUPPLIERS

Amdek
Compaq
IBM
Mitsubishi
NEC
Princeton Graphics
Quadram
Sony
Taxan

DISPLAY BOARD SUPPLIERS

AST Research
Chips and Technologies Inc.
Emulex/Persyt
Everex
Genoa Systems
Graphics Software Systems
Hercules Computer Technology
IBM
Mylex
Paradise Systems
Quadram
Sigma Designs
STB Systems Inc
Tecmar Inc.
Tseng Laboratories
Video 7

FIGURE 6-14
A sampler of display hardware suppliers

OTHER GRAPHICS HARDWARE

Once a graphic is displayed, it might be sent to a color graphics plotter. An eight-pen plotter, like the one shown in Figure 6-5, costs over $1,000. It produces a color chart in a few minutes. Producing a batch of charts will often tie up the plotter and graphics workstation for hours.

To create slides for presentation requires different hardware, as shown in Figure 6-15. The hardware costs over $1,000 and consists of a 35-millimeter camera attached to a recording device. It converts the computer image to the camera image. A separate shoe-box size piece of equipment is used to mount the film, produced by the recorder, on plastic mounts.

Some believe that only slides represent top-of-the-line presentation-quality graphics. Professional slide-making service bureaus produce slides with a resolution of 4,000 by 4,000 dots, or pixels, per slide. By contrast,

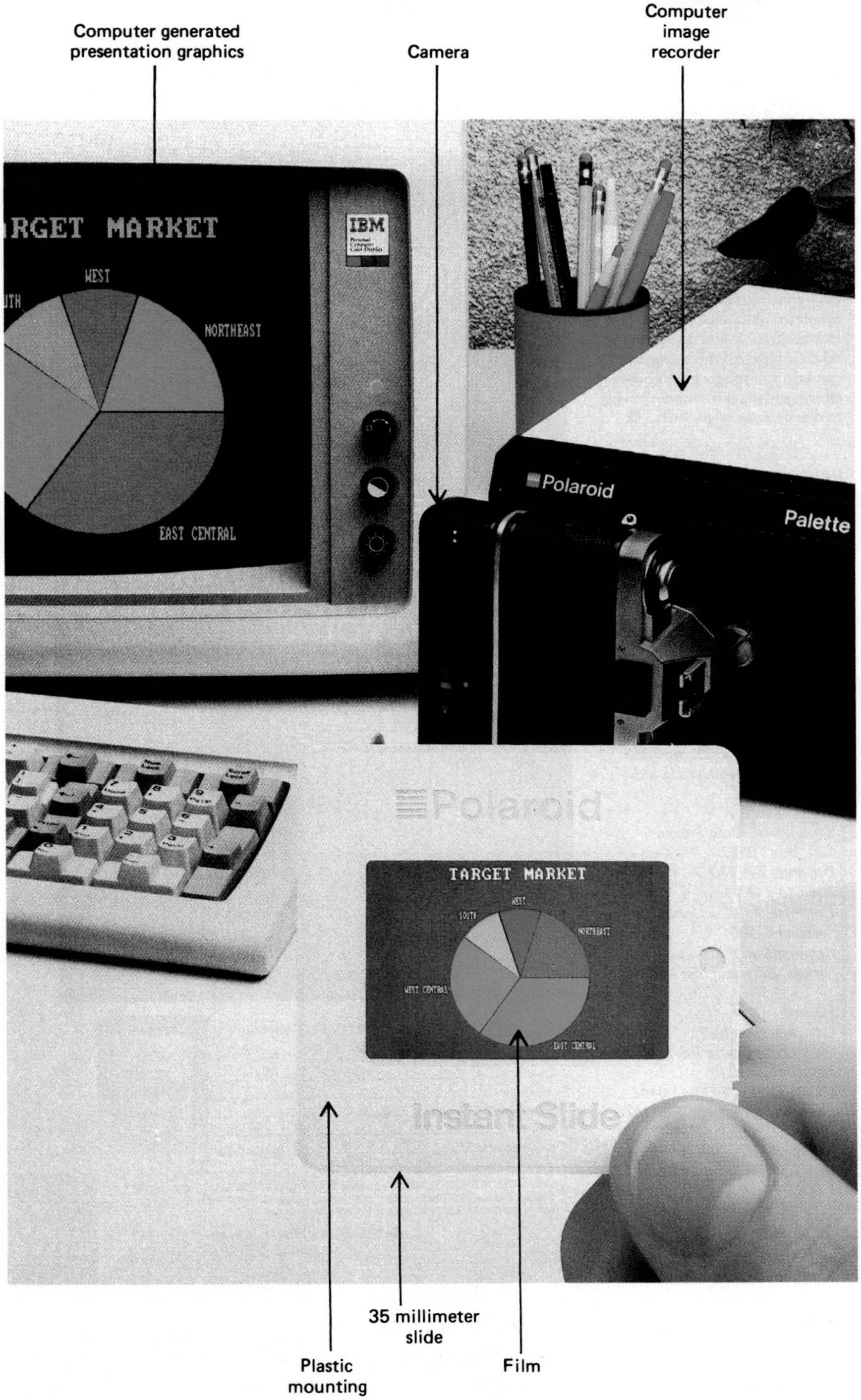

FIGURE 6-15
Computer-generated slides
(Polaroid Palette, courtesy of Polaroid Corporation)

one desktop computer slide machine offers only double the resolution that appears on the display. If a color display resolution is 640 by 350 pixels, the final slide is 1,280 by 700 dots.

Some graphics packages, like PC Presents, let users telecommunicate their graphics to any of a nationwide network of graphic service bureaus. Some slide, transparency, or paper print orders are delivered the next day. Slides generally cost less than that charged by neighborhood graphic services.

SLIDE SHOWS

Some companies and individuals have eliminated slides by using slide-show software and a personal computer. Mark Levine is one of them. He trains technicians for a major consumer electronics company. He uses a **slide-show** program for training purposes. When his training classes are small, viewers sit around the personal computer display, which he uses as a projection device. If the audience is large, he plugs the display into a direct-connect projection device, such as the one shown in Figure 6-16. The large-screen device costs several thousand dollars.

His slide show effectively is a list of picture files stored on disk. To create a slide show, Mr. Levine types the name of one or more files where graphics are stored. He also indicates the "slide" sequence and length of time a "slide" should remain on the display. He can request a special fadeout or dissolve effect to separate one graphic from the next.

Whenever desired, he can run the slide show. It could be set to run automatically. He can also manually advance "slides" or reverse them at the touch of a key. Slide-show packages include VCN ExecuVision, Show Partner, and PC Storyboard.

His package also includes clip art. **Clip art** refers to prestored symbol libraries ready for electronic cutting and pasting into any chart, as shown in Figure 6-17. Some packages offer prestored images of world famous figures and have a "straight from the art department" look.

FIGURE 6-16
Using a personal computer with a large screen projection device to present a "slide show"
(*Electrohome Projection System, courtesy of Electrohome Limited*)

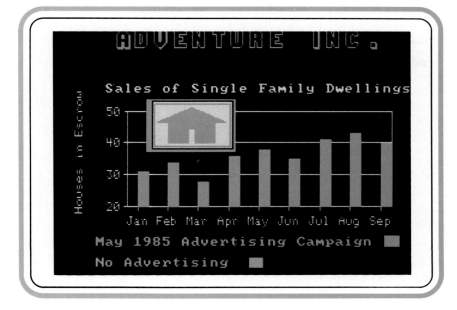

FIGURE–6-17
A graphic enhanced with a clip-art image of a house. The graphic is also rescaled, and shading, colors, and additional text are added.
(*Software: Lotus 1-2-3 and Grafix Partner, courtesy of Lotus Developmemt Corporation*)

Mr. Levine's software is like Hypergraphics Presentation Graphics System, which contains an *authoring language*. It allows him to include graphics with text for student questions.

EVALUATING PRESENTATION GRAPHICS

A list of criteria to help evaluate business graphics appears in Figure 6-18. Evaluators tell of many quirks in individual packages, like ones that

· Print, but do not save, plotted graphics
· Allow only three data values on one axis
· Provide only black-and-white graphs

Serious graphics shoppers take their most complex chart for a hands-on test of candidate software and hardware. They do an "eyeball" examination of the results.

Graphic output, on whatever device desired, should meet personal image quality standards for

· Smooth line and edge definition (avoiding a "jagged" or "stair-stepped" appearance)
· Solid area fills (free of streaks and voids)
· Accurate colors

In addition, evaluating the speed of graphic printing helps to determine if one chart takes 5 or 20 minutes to produce. The hard-copy device used may lock the computer out of use for other work.

BUSINESS GRAPHICS

Are standard bar, pie, and line charts available?

Can data be input automatically from popular programs?

Can data be input directly from a keyboard?

Are all other required charts provided, for example, word charts, organization charts, scatter charts, combination charts, three-dimensional charts?

Are enhancement features available, for example, free-form drawing, animation, slide shows, symbol libraries, text styles, and size options?

Can the software drive the specific graphic hardware products required, including color displays, plotters, printers, cameras, digitizers, and large-screen projectors?

Are image quality and speed requirements met or exceeded?

(Figure 3-25, General Software Evaluation Checklist, is necessary to complete this evaluation.)

FIGURE 6-18
Business graphics evaluation checklist

PAINTING

Ever since the Apple Macintosh personal computer appeared with the attractive MacPaint package, the appeal of electronic painting surges ahead. Some regard electronic **painting,** where the display is used like a canvas, as enormous fun but not very useful.

Others, like Jeri Laizure, think differently. Ms. Laizure is a partner in Laizure/Woodward and Wise, an eight-person ad agency in North Carolina. She tells about using a painting program to do an ad for a shoe manufacturer that ran in a major national newspaper. "The way the ad looks is directly influenced by something you can do with painting software," she claims. "We had the idea to show lots and lots of shoes with the caption 'What are all those tongues wagging for?' So we drew one and then used the COPY capability to make a whole collection of them on screen. We must have saved a day's work on that one ad alone."

When using painting software, Ms. Laizure sees a screen that resembles the one in Figure 6-19. Icons symbolizing artist tools border part of the screen. The paintbrush "tool" is highlighted. It is selected by a click of the mouse button. Other items, like brush size and color, are selected the same way. The pointer changes shape to resemble the paint brush icon as it gets "dragged" into the drawing area. Figure 6-20 demonstrates pencil drawing in action and compares it with a paintbrush stroke.

Figure 6-21 illustrates some typical icons and their function in painting packages.

Figure 6-22 shows one of the outstanding features of painting software, the ability to clean up drawings at the dot level. To improve detail, a **zoom** or *magnify* function causes an enlarged dot-by-dot pattern

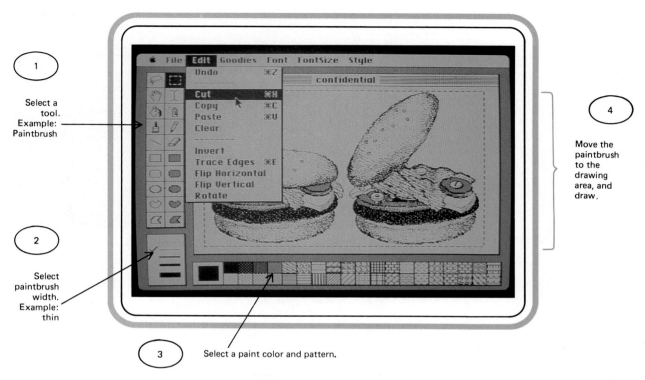

① Select a tool. Example: Paintbrush

② Select paintbrush width. Example: thin

③ Select a paint color and pattern.

④ Move the paintbrush to the drawing area, and draw.

FIGURE 6-19
Sample artwork using a painting package
and steps used to create artwork
(Software: PC Paintbrush,
courtesy of IMSI)

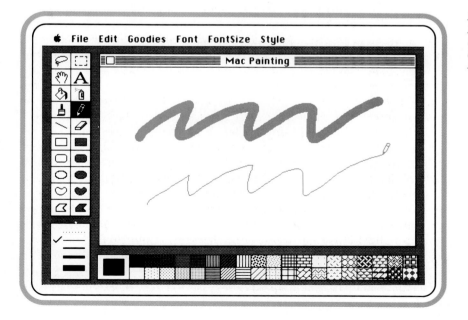

FIGURE 6-20
Free-form lines drawn with a pencil
(bottom line) and a paintbrush (top line)
(Software: MacPaint, courtesy of MacWorld,
Apple Computer, Inc.)

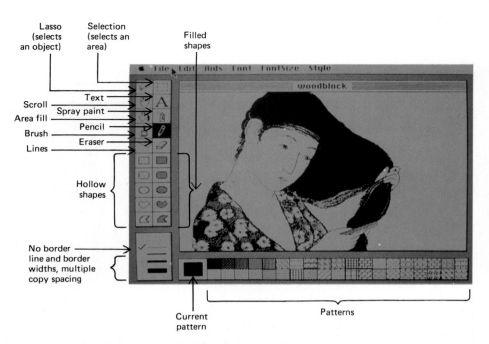

Lasso
(selects
an object)

Selection
(selects an
area)

Filled
shapes

Text

Scroll
Area fill
Brush
Lines

Spray paint
Pencil
Eraser

Hollow
shapes

No border
line and border
widths, multiple
copy spacing

Current
pattern

Patterns

FIGURE 6-21

*Icons and their meaning in the
MacPaint package*
(*Software: MacPaint, courtesy of
Apple Computer, Inc.*)

of a drawing section to display. The success or failure of dot insertions
or deletions can be watched in the insert screen in the corner.

Painting packages, such as those listed in Figure 6-23, are being
used in business to create ads, letterheads, company insignias or "logos,"
and a host of other original projects. Some use them to spruce up business
announcements, mailers, promotions, newsletters, and in-house publications. The slick magazine *MacWorld* uses MacPaint to do the bulk of
its artwork.

FIGURE 6-22

*The magnify feature enables cleaning up
a drawing at the single-dot level*
(*Software: MacPaint, courtesy of Apple
Computer, Inc.*)

Section
of a drawing

Same section
magnified for
refinement at the
dot level

FIGURE 6-23

*A sampler of painting software packages
for personal computers*

Aurora
Dr. Halo
Lenipen
Lumena
MacPaint
PC Illustrator
PC Paint
PC Paintbrush
Picture Marker
PYXEL Visuals
TelePaint

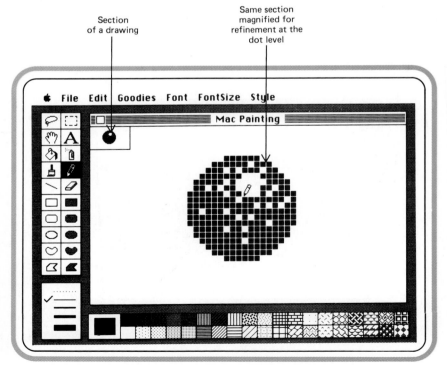

IMAGING SYSTEMS

Imaging systems complement painting packages. Instead of painting an image, a favorite photograph can be used instead. To get an image into the computer requires additional hardware.

For under $250, a product like ThunderScan, shown in Figure 6-24, digitizes any printed image. This scanner turns a printer into a scanner by replacing the ribbon cartridge with a scanning cartridge de-

FIGURE 6-24
Image processing created with a dot-matrix printer ribbon replacement cartridge
(Thunderscan®, courtesy of ThunderWare®, Inc.)

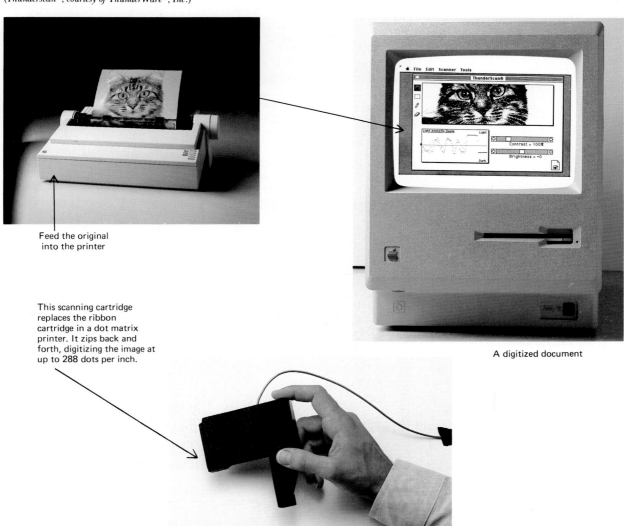

Feed the original
into the printer

This scanning cartridge
replaces the ribbon
cartridge in a dot matrix
printer. It zips back and
forth, digitizing the image at
up to 288 dots per inch.

A digitized document

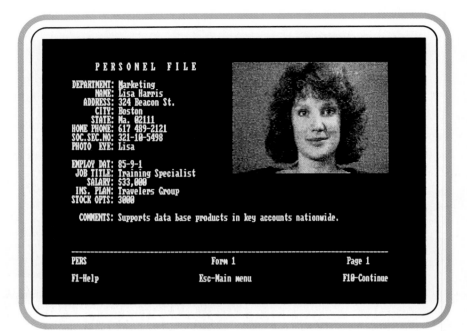

Personnel
record

Real estate
record

FIGURE 6-25
Photographs added to the database records with an imaging system
(*Software*: PC Eye, *courtesy of Chorus Data Systems*)

Display of
image

Image being
photographed

Camera kit

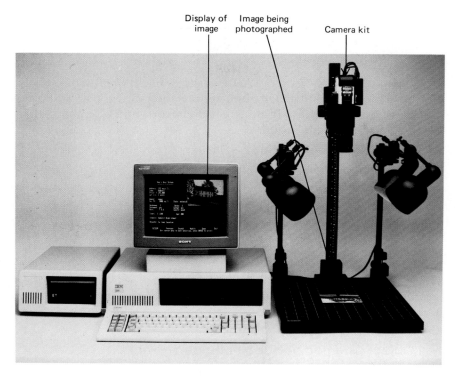

Figure 6-26
A camera-based imaging system
(*Software: PC Eye, courtesy of Chorus Data Systems; imaging hardware: Integrated Imaging System, courtesy of Datacopy*)

vice. As an alternative, separate scanners are available, and are discussed more fully in Chapter 13, "Desktop Publishing."

Digitizing means to re-create an image into a series of dots. Then each dot can be stored as a binary digit and manipulated just like any other computer data. Things that can be digitized include

- Forms
- Photographs
- Mechanical drawings
- Maps
- Company logos
- Floor plans
- Signatures

Images can be black and white or color originals.

Figure 6-25 shows digitized photographs inserted in database records for personnel and real estate applications.

Some imaging systems cost close to $10,000 and come with a digitizing camera and software, like the one shown in Figure 6-26. They can digitize live pictures as well as video cassette recorded images.

The Smithsonian Institute uses a camera product for storage and retrieval of its sensitive, decaying archival materials. Hewlett-Packard, the computer manufacturer, uses a similar imaging system to help illustrate technical manuals.

Anvil 1000MD
AutoCAD
CADKEY
CAD Master
CADplan
CADVANCE
DR Draw
EXECADD
GEM Draw
IBM Drawing Assistant
MacDraw
MicroCAD
PC Draw
RapidCAD
The Drawing Processor
Versa CADD
Windows Draw

FIGURE 6-27
A sampler of computed-aided design software packages for personal computers

COMPUTER-AIDED DESIGN

Computer-aided design (CAD) packages, like those listed in Figure 6-27, are used to create and manipulate precision-drawn objects. Professionals whose jobs involve drawing precise objects and assembling them into composite designs include

- Architects
- Civil, mechanical, electrical, and electronic engineers
- Landscape designers
- Theatrical designers
- Television and film animators
- Furniture and jewelry designers
- Model makers
- Illustrators and artists

These and other professionals who must draw objects, move them around, take them apart, and put them back together again might productively use a computer-aided design package.

Object Oriented versus Bit Mapped

The difference between a CAD package and a painting package lies in how an image is produced and stored. A CAD package produces **object-oriented images,** which are also called **vector images.** To sketch a square on the computer screen, as the example in Figure 6-28 illustrates, the mathematical formula describing the path an imaginary pencil point takes to produce that square is stored by the software in the computer's memory, or on the disk, as an indivisible unit. The object's shape, in this case a square, along with other information, is saved, rather than the image itself.

One advantage of object-oriented images is that they are always sharp and clear, even when enlarged. Because they are stored as formu-

FIGURE 6-28
Creating an object-oriented image

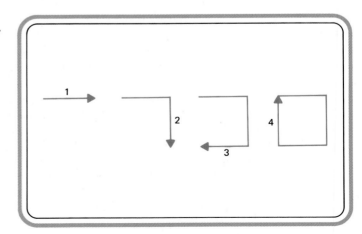

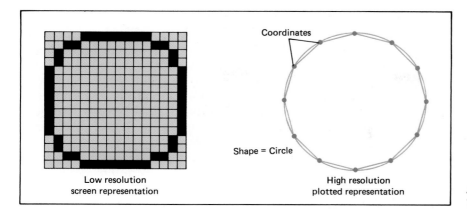

Low resolution
screen representation

Coordinates

Shape = Circle

High resolution
plotted representation

FIGURE 6-29
Two versions of an object-oriented image

las, aspects of them are easily altered. For example, it is a simple matter to change a square into a rectangle. All that is required is that the length of the two sides described in the original formula be adjusted by the software.

Another advantage of object-oriented images is that they can be printed out even more clearly than their screen representations. Using a high-solution printer or plotter, a jagged circle on the screen will appear in print with a smooth circumference, as illustrated in Figure 6-29.

Painting packages, on the other hand, store **bit-mapped images.** The location of each dot making up an image is recorded by the software. The entire screen image is stored with one screen pixel represented as one or more bits of data.

One advantage is that since every pixel is treated as a separate entity and defined positionally, every one of them can be manipulated individually. An image can be edited or created dot by dot. By contrast, this cannot be done with an object-oriented image.

The main disadvantage of bit-mapped graphics is that quality deteriorates whenever an image is enlarged. If a one-inch line is drawn with a 72-dots-per-inch screen, and that line is then enlarged to 10 inches, the new, larger image will be composed of only 7.2 dots per inch.

A comparable object-oriented image can overcome its screen limitation of 72 dots per inch with a printer that can print a version having a resolution as high as 300 dots per inch or more. But the image produced by the bit-mapped graphics will never be better than the original constructed on screen.

The disadvantage of the object-oriented approach to graphics is that it only deals with complete visual objects, such as a square or circle. It cannot be manipulated at the dot level.

Many graphics users have purchased both types of graphics packages to cover all the bases. But newer packages, like SuperPaint and VCN Concorde, now handle both drawing methods. The main advantage is to combine pixel-by-pixel drawing abilities of bit-mapped graphics with the flexibility to print an image at a higher resolution, as is possible with object-oriented graphics.

Design Example

To design the floor plan shown in Figure 6-30, architect Allan Lerch uses a computer-aided design package. It displays a menu down the right side of the screen. He uses a mouse to move the cursor to a desired menu item, then clicks the mouse selection button to make a choice.

The cursor in the drawing area appears as a cross. A faint grid appears in the background. He sets the grid to any scale, like 1 inch equals 1 foot. It helps to keep his floor plan scaled exactly to size.

To draw a line on the screen, he simply locks in the begin and end points with clicks of the mouse button. The line automatically snaps to the closest grid line in perfect alignment. As an alternative, he can type in actual line points like 0,0 and 5,5. Such a line might go from the lower left corner of the screen to the middle of the screen, depending on the scale used.

Mr. Lerch's CAD workstation consists of two displays. One larger color monitor displays his design. A smaller monochrome display acts as a dialogue center to enter commands and otherwise interact with the program. It is a typical CAD workstation.

Drawing a circle is similar to drawing a line. It involves locating the circle's center point and another point on the circle itself. After the points are indicated, the circle instantly appears. He can also draw arcs, traces (a fat line), and solids (filled-in, closed areas).

Mr. Lerch often reuses drawings that he designed and stored in a **symbol library,** which is also called an **object library.** They include drawings of a staircase and a bathtub. He copies them wherever needed in his new designs.

He also can place, sketch, shrink, scale, and rotate any symbol on the screen. By joining symbols he can create new images for storage in the symbol library.

FIGURE 6-30
A multilayered architectural plan prepared with a CAD package
(*Software: AUTOCAD, courtesy of Autodesk, Inc.*)

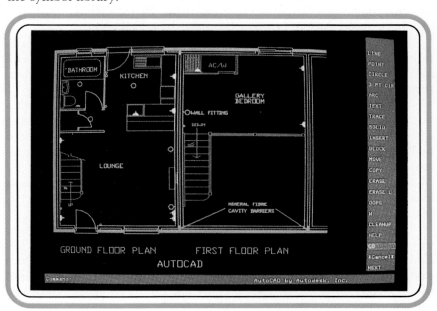

Layer 1

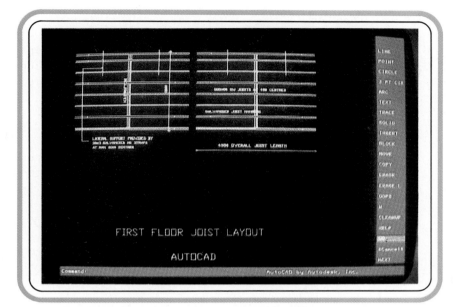

Layer 2

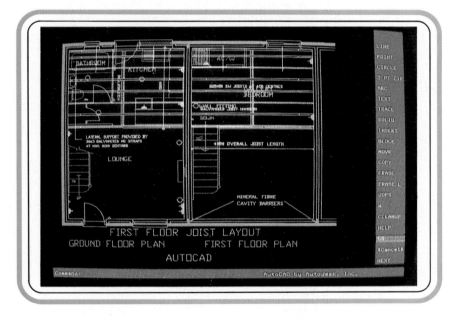

Combined
Layers 1 and 2

FIGURE 6-30 (continued)

The floor plan in Figure 6-30 is composed of multiple layers. Large jobs require many separate layers drawn for each engineering discipline involved in construction, including

- Heating
- Plumbing
- Electrical and fire protection

FIGURE 6-31
Three-dimensional views provided by a
CAD package
(*Software: MicroCAD, courtesy of* PC World,
555 DeHaro St., San Francisco, CA 94107)

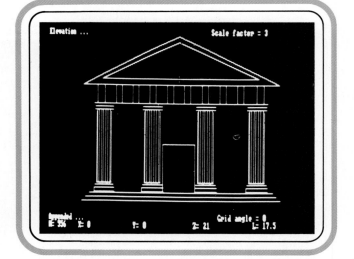

Elevation view, as
if standing in front
of an object

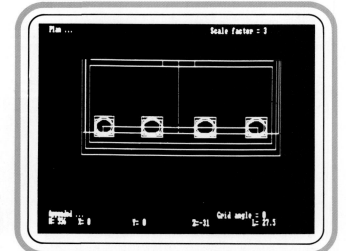

Plan view, as if
viewing an object
from above (like a
floor plan)

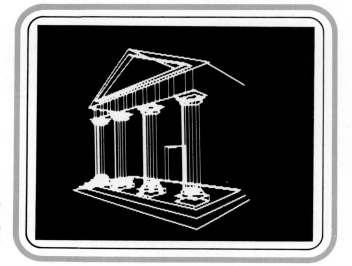

Perspective view, as if
viewing an object from
a particular reference
point

214

Mr. Lerch stores each layer in a different color. He also plots layers in different colors on transparencies for presentation to clients.

Three Dimensions

Katherine D'Angelo, another architect, uses a different CAD package. It enables her to define three-dimensional images. Like the example in Figure 6-31, images can be viewed from several angles.

When she starts her CAD package, she defines not only the length and width dimensions of her working grid but the depth as well. So when she defines new objects, she must declare X, Y, and Z coordinates, instead of just X and Y coordinates, as Mr. Lerch does.

Every image created on the screen is saved in a database as an object with its attendant characteristics of

- Shape
- Size
- Proportion
- Location

The database can be used by another program to develop a list of materials needed to construct the designed objects. Cost information can also be produced.

Benefits

To a casual observer, creating a drawing with a CAD package might appear to be just as time consuming as the manual drafting process. Initially it is, until a library of reusable symbols is created. Sometimes old drawings supply ready-made symbols. As shown in Figure 6-32, a **digitizer tablet** is a common way to get prepared images into computer form. The tablet contains a grid. Anytime the drawing device crosses a grid line, it sends an X–Y coordinate to the computer.

Other benefits CAD users claim include the following:

- The clarity, precision, and accuracy of a CAD-generated drawing are far superior to those of a manually produced drawing.
- Multiple copies of similar or identical drawings are easily produced.
- Changes mandated by clients and engineers can easily be accommodated.
- Drawing objects to scale is simpler.
- Using library objects not only saves time but also standardizes details from drawing to drawing.

As Gordon Brooks, an electronics designer, would argue, "The benefits do not come cheap." It cost him about $30,000 to set up a fully equipped personal computer-based CAD workstation. It cost considerably less, however, than a traditional minicomputer-based CAD workstation. Large organizations are known to spend up to $300,000 for similar minicomputer-based computer-aided design support.

FIGURE 6-32
Using a digitizer tablet
(Courtesy of Houston Instruments)

ANIMATION

Personal computer-based **animation,** or continuous movement graphics, systems also cost $30,000 to $60,000. After adding a professional quality video tape recorder, these systems can cost from $2,000 to $30,000 more. They are like sophisticated CAD workstations. But the cost compares favorably with the cost of buying one outside-produced video, which generally costs as much as the entire PC-based 3-D animation system.

The most popular creative application is television station break commercials. Others include Anheuser-Busch Corporation's use of a PC-based animation system to design business presentations, promotions, logos, and other art-based projects. Its system enables Mike Culley, senior art director at Busch Creative Services (a subsidiary of Anheuser-Busch of St. Louis, Missouri), to produce 10- to 20-second sequences for under $10,000 in production costs. He claims "that's at least one-third to one-half the cost of going to an outside production facility."[1]

One of his in-house promotions is an animated video on the process of making beer. The video is made up of a series of still-frames, like the examples in Figure 6-33, shown in rapid succession. In the examples, the bird's wing position moves down in frames 1 to 4 and up in the

FIGURE 6-33
Selected frames from an animated video

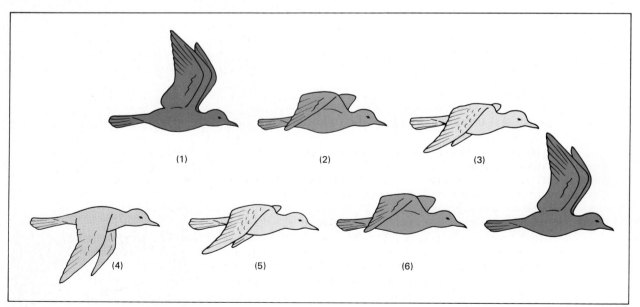

(1)   (2)   (3)

(4)   (5)   (6)

[1] Gerald Kimkel and G. Heather Luchak, "Animating Corporate Presentations," *PC Magazine,* October 28, 1986, p. 229.

other frames. The last three frames are copies of the first three frames. When these frames are moved at a fast pace, the bird seems to fly. An hour's worth of animation might require more than 80,000 frames. Until the advent of computer animation, each frame had to be drawn, colored, and photographed by hand.

The four-step animation process is essentially the same, whether it is done manually or with a computer:

1. Design a character or object

2. Develop a "script sheet" of key frames for movement

3. Create a "pencil test" (outlines) for viewing the flow of movement

4. Create a fully rendered set of images for recording on film or video

In computer animation, each of these steps represents one program.

Creating computer animation is a surprisingly complex process. An understanding of video technology is essential.

CASE STUDY: *Tools of the Trade*

Marty Smith, of Williams/Lyons in Houston, Texas, was never able to justify the cost of hiring an artist to create graphics for his sales presentations. He could, however, justify a one-time purchase of Microsoft Chart. And even though the program does not create highly sophisticated graphs, merely having the ability to produce a basic bar chart has been a revelation for Smith and a boon to his work.

As a dairy specialist for food broker Williams/Lyons, Smith regularly attends annual meetings with presidents of the clients he represents. "My job is basically sales," says Smith. "In sales, you need every aid you can get, so charts become tools of the trade. You especially need them if other people have them; and if others don't have them, then you have a leg up."

Most of Smith's attention is directed toward finding the correct graph style and making sure the data are clear, rather than concentrating heavily on design characteristics. For instance, Smith has learned that to show detailed statistics, he should use a line chart instead of a bar chart.

Even though most of his effort goes into creating a clear, accurate graph, Smith still spends some time adding small touches. To give a graph a professional, typeset look, Smith uses Chart's optional fonts to create labels and headings; he never settles for the default fonts, preferring his own designs.

One thing Smith has discovered, however, is that no matter how professionally done the charts may be, some people cannot be swayed by them. "Some people could care less about a chart," says Smith. "They are more interested in the personal relationship they have with you. They'll buy something because they trust you."

Other people distrust charts entirely. "This person figures you've gone to a lot of trouble to make this chart, so you must be trying to manipulate the data," says Smith. "They still need to see the numbers. You really need to know the person you are dealing with."

(*Source: Cheryl Spencer, "Visual Decision Making,"* Personal Computing, *January 1987, pp. 93–97.*)

DISCUSSION QUESTIONS

1. What negative responses are possible when people are shown graphics during a sales presentation? How would you react to these responses?

2. Should salespeople be required to learn how to create and generate their own computer graphics for sales presentations? Defend your answer.

CHAPTER SUMMARY

- *Business graphics* include analytic and presentation graphics.

- *Analytic graphics* are used for personal data analysis. They help a decision maker to analyze a problem, discern a trend, assess relationships, or investigate any of many other decision-related possibilities.

- *Presentation graphics* are used for presentation to others. They have a refined, versus "computerese," look.

- Display computer output, especially graphics, is called *soft copy* and contrasts with printed computer output, which is called *hard copy*.

- *Plotters* are hardware that print presentation graphics on paper or plastic sheets. Plastic sheets are called *overhead transparencies* and are used with overhead projectors for large audience presentations.

- A Wharton Business School study showed that an audience is twice as likely to be persuaded by a presentation with visuals than without them.

- Bad graphics can do more harm than good if they are oversimplified and irrelevant to the points being made.

- A *graphics workstation* might include a personal computer, graphics software, a plotter, and slide-making hardware.

- *Input forms* simplify graphics production for a novice user.

- *Defaults* in many software packages are preselected choices that simplify data entry.

- *Previewing* allows a user to examine and review a graphic before printing a final copy of it.

- Many *graphic standards* exist for color display hardware.

- The *analog graphic standard* is distinguished by a display of 256 simultaneous colors.

- The older *digital graphic standard* is distinguished by a display of 16 simultaneous colors. All digital displays require a compatible display circuit board, also called a *graphics board* or *graphics adapter*.

- Displays use *cathode ray tube* (*CRT*) technology,

which is the same technology used in ordinary television sets.

- *Phosphor* coats the back of the display screen. Its glow quickly fades and must constantly be refreshed by a *raster scan*.

- *Multiscan* or *multisync monitors* help to solve the graphics hardware compatibility problem.

- *Device independent software* does not require specific peripheral hardware, like a particular display, to function.

- *Slide-show software* is an alternative to more expensive slide presentations.

- *Clip art* refers to prestored *symbol libraries* that hold images ready for electronic cutting and pasting into any graphic.

- Criteria used to evaluate business graphics software include types of charts available, image quality, data input flexibility, and compatibility of hardware and software.

- *Painting* software allows for the free-form creation of images used to create ads, letterheads, "logos," and a host of other original projects.

- *Imaging* software allows for the digitization of a photograph or any printed (and sometimes live) image.

- *Digitizing* means to re-create an image into a series of computer-readable dots. Digitized images are used just like any other computer data.

- *Computer-aided design* (*CAD*) software is used to create and manipulate precision-drawn objects.

- *Object-oriented images* are produced by CAD packages, and stored as formulas which are always sharp and clear when enlarged.

- *Bit-mapped images* are produced by painting packages. The location of each dot making up the screen image is stored by the software. These images lose quality when enlarged.

- A *three-dimensional graphic package* can display an object's length, width, and depth characteristics.

- *Animation* is continuous movement graphics.

KEY TERMS

Analog graphic standard
Analytic graphics
Animation
Bit-mapped image
Business graphics
Cathode ray tube (CRT)
Clip art
Color gun
Computer-aided design (CAD)
Defaults
Device independent software
Digital graphic standard
Digitizer tablet

Digitizing
Graphic standards
Graphics adapter
Graphics board
Graphics workstation
Hard copy
Imaging software
Input forms
Multiscan monitor
Multisync monitor
Object library
Object-oriented image
Overhead transparency

Painting software
Phosphor
Plotter
Presentation graphics
Previewing
Raster scan
Slide show
Soft copy
Symbol library
Vector image
Zoom function

REVIEW QUESTIONS

1. Differentiate between analytic and presentation graphics.

2. Identify some graphic hardware devices.

3. What are the two groups of graphic standards? What distinquishes each?

4. What is the purpose of a raster scan?

5. What is a symbol, or object, library?

6. Explain the terms "defaults" and "previewing."

7. List criteria to consider when evaluating business graphics software.

8. Describe uses for painting, imaging, computer-aided design, and animation software.

9. What does "digitizing" mean?

10. What distinguishes object-oriented from bit-mapped images?

11. What characterizes three-dimensional graphics?

EXERCISES

1. *Modify a Graph.*   Modify the sample input form in Figure 6-8 of a segmented bar chart. Assume that
  · A fourth bar is added for 1995 with the amounts 25.4, 15.7, and 35.2
  · The *Y* axis is changed to "Billions of $"
Use the element chart in Figure 6-9 as a guide.

2. *Create a Graph.*   Create your own segmented bar chart using pencil and paper. Assume that the school registrar has asked you to present a chart that shows your cost for school and books for the last two terms. You decide that two bars (one for each term), each with two segments (one for book costs and another for school tuition costs), will be appropriate. It will be implemented with Mr. Nelson's graphics package. You can use the segmented bar chart input form in Figure 6-8, with the element

chart in Figure 6-9, as a guide. Use the style options listed in Figure 6-11 to customize your graphics.

3. *Lark Enterprises Case.*   Lark Enterprises wants to develop an in-house graphics capability. The company needs both appropriate hardware and software. You are asked to do a computer periodical literature search and write a report about your preliminary findings for the following:

a. A graphics package that is designed for novice users who intend to create business charts and graphics, especially spreadsheet-based charts. Use the evaluation checklist in Figure 6-18 as a guide. If possible, do a hands-on test, or get a demonstration, of the recommended software.

b. Hardware that supports the software and includes a color display and an inexpensive flatbed plotter.

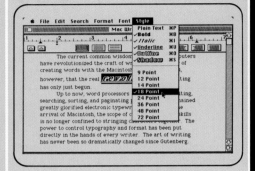

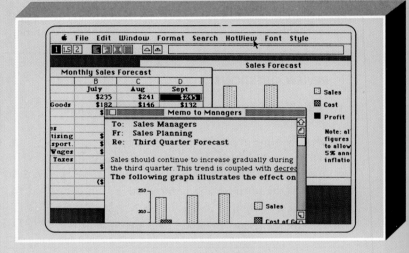

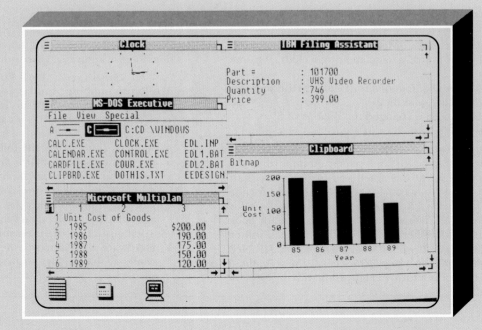

Word Processing, Integrated, and Related Packages

AFTER READING THIS CHAPTER, YOU SHOULD BE ABLE TO

· Describe word processing features and initiate a package evaluation

· Identify four ways to achieve application integration

· Describe uses for packages such as outliner and desktop organizers

According to many studies, more personal computer users own a *word processing* package than any other application.

This chapter explores the phases a word processing document passes through. It also looks at such word processing features as personalized form letters and spelling checkers. It also considers package evaluation guidelines.

Word processing is often one of the applications combined in an *integrated package*. This chapter examines all-in-one integrated packages as well as alternative ways to achieve application integration.

Personal computer users gravitate to other applications that help them become more productive. Some use *outliners* and *desktop organizers*. The chapter includes a review of these and other related packages.

WORD PROCESSING CHARACTERISTICS

A **word processing package** provides for the automated manipulation of words. Like a spreadsheet package, it requires as much upfront work as doing the job manually. Someone has to create the words to be processed. Whether these words form a contract, a letter, or a manuscript, typing them into the computer is not much different from typing the same document on a typewriter.

It may require, in fact, learning a new command language. Even if the application is part of an integrated package with common commands throughout, learning word processing features and vocabulary, as shown in Figure 7-1, is preliminary to use.

Like an electronic spreadsheet, the payoff comes when changes are needed. The ability to print a fresh original document after typing a

FIGURE 7-1
Sample word processing pages with features described
(Courtesy of MicroPro International Corp.)

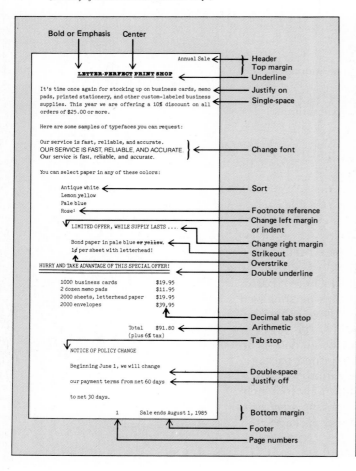
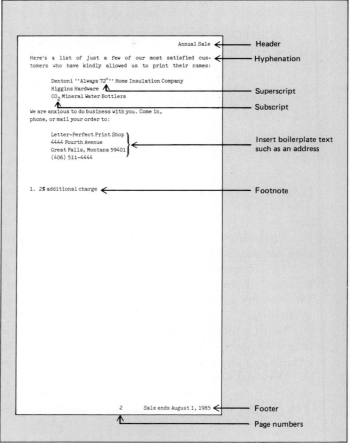

few changes immeasurably reflects on productivity. Time saved can be spent on other tasks.

Because of the ease of producing revised drafts, changes to upgrade documents can be made more freely. Proofreading is reduced to just the changes. This encourages revision to produce even better crafted documents.

Final printing is left to the computer. The improved visual quality of printed work enhances the professional image of an individual or a company.

Some word processing tasks still remain more appropriate for a typewriter. As an example, filling in forms sometimes is not an efficient activity on a computer.

Most other things, from a conventional business letter to a full-length manuscript, can usually be done faster and cheaper with a word processing application.

Standard word processing is divided into five phases related to a document's life cycle, as follows:

Phase in Document Life Cycle	User Action
1. Create a document	Type text on keyboard
2. Edit a document	Make corrections
3. Format a document	Insert print instructions
4. Print a document	Start printing
5. Save a document	Use document/file handling functions

DOCUMENT CREATION

Frank Nelson and most staff members at Interstate Distributing Company use word processing software. They create documents such as catalogs, contracts, product specifications, mailings to prospective customers, and ordinary business correspondence.

The package he uses is one of several popular word processing packages. Many organizations, both large and small, use it as an internal company "standard" for word processing. Having everyone use the same package promotes document file swapping and the concentration of company training and support. It also reduces software costs because of volume buying discounts.

When Mr. Nelson wants to produce a memo, or any typed document, he loads the word processing software, then begins to type. During document creation his screen looks like the one in Figure 7-2. He types the text as if using an ordinary typewriter. His typing technique falls into the hunt-and-peck category. Nonetheless, he finds he can produce rough-draft copy without assistance using the computer.

When creating text Mr. Nelson hits an *enter key*, sometimes known as the *return key*, only at the end of a paragraph. The computer automatically performs a word wrap at the end of each line. The **word wrap** function moves any word that crosses the right-hand margin to the

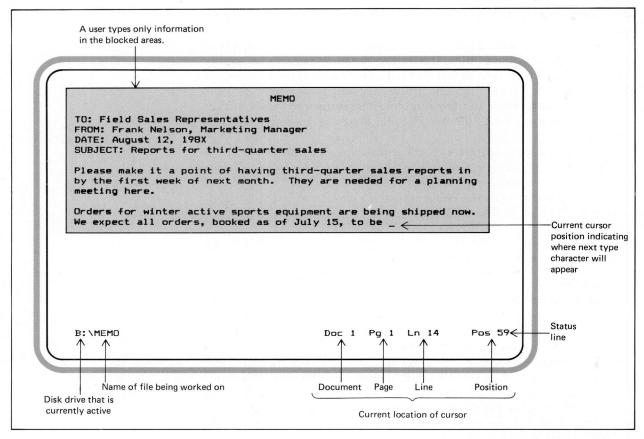

FIGURE 7-2
Creating a document
(*Software*: WordPerfect, courtesy of WordPerfect Corporation)

FIGURE 7-3
Keys that activate cursor control and other functions
(*Keyboard*: IBM Personal Computer, courtesy of IBM)

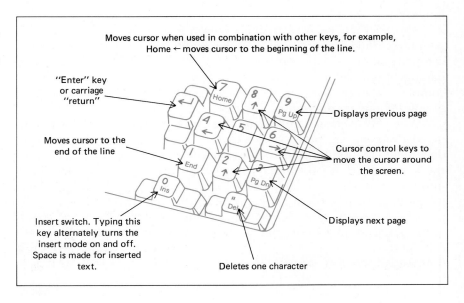

next line. This feature speeds composition because there is no need manually to control end-of-line word placement.

Document creation is further simplified by built-in scrolling and cursor control functions. They are activated by keys shown in Figure 7-3. **Scrolling** moves text up and down so that desired portions appear in the display. **Cursor control,** or **arrow, keys** move the cursor around the current display for text creation and editing anywhere on the screen.

EDITING

Revising or correcting a document is called **editing.** It is where word processing software earns its reputation as a major productivity enhancer. Whenever Mr. Nelson thinks of a better way to phrase something, he simply moves the cursor to the place in the text where the change is to be made and types the new text. Space is automatically allocated for anything he inserts, such as words, phrases, or paragraphs. The new text automatically pushes aside the old.

Deleting old text, character by character, requires pressing the DEL delete or the backspace keys. To delete a block of text requires first turning the block feature on, using the ALT alternate and F4 function keys, as shown in Figure 7-4.

Then the down arrow key is used to move the cursor over the line to be deleted. As the cursor passes over each line, it becomes highlighted on the screen. After highlighting the block, pressing the DEL delete key causes a prompt to appear that asks, "Delete block? (Y/N)." This prompt confirms that a deletion is desired. It is a normal way to give a user a second chance to avoid wiping out text. Pressing the Y for a "yes" answer causes the marked block of text to disappear from the screen.

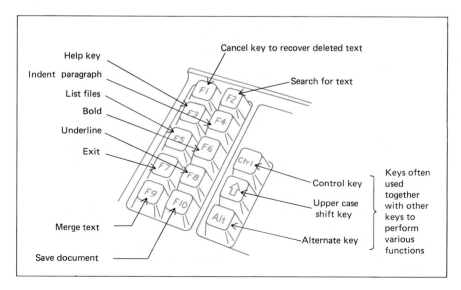

Help key
Indent paragraph
List files
Bold
Underline
Exit
Merge text
Save document

Cancel key to recover deleted text
Search for text

F1
F2
F3
F4
F5
F6
F7
F8
F9
F10

Ctrl
Control key
Upper case shift key
Alt
Alternate key

Keys often used together with other keys to perform various functions

FIGURE 7-4
Function ("F" keys) and other key actions
(Keyboard: IBM Personal Computer, courtesy of IBM)

Should a change of mind occur after a delete is executed, all is not lost. An **undo,** also called *cancel* or *undelete*, feature restores the last deletion made. Packages usually restore from one to three or more previous deletions.

Function Keys

As illustrated in Figure 7-4, **function keys** are a separate part of the keyboard. They are often called *soft keys*. Their function varies according to the software used. Each application software package can program what function keys will do.

Each function key in Mr. Nelson's software performs a different action if used together with the ALT **alternate, shift** (big up arrow), and CTRL **control keys.** Figure 7-5 lists the action performed by the various key combinations. For example, the ALT alternate and F4 function keys turn the block feature on. The CTRL control and F4 function keys display a menu of block options.

The **block** function is used to define or mark a block of text. It is preliminary to doing an operation such as moving, copying, or deleting it.

To move a block of text, also called a **cut and paste** operation, Mr. Nelson first presses ALT F4 to turn on the block function. A reminder flashes at the bottom of the screen "Block on." Then he moves the cursor control arrow keys to make the cursor pass over the lines he wants to move. As the cursor passes over a line, it is automatically highlighted on the screen. Pressing ALT F4 a second time turns the block function off.

Pressing the CTRL F4 retrieves a menu of block options at the bottom of the screen. Option 1 is "Cut Block," the first step of the cut and paste operation. When Mr. Nelson selects 1 for the "Cut Block" option, the highlighted block disappears from the screen. It is temporarily

FIGURE 7-5
Function key actions alone and when used with other keys
(*Software: WordPerfect, courtesy of WordPerfect Corporation*)

KEY	ALONE	+ CTRL	+ SHIFT (BIG UP ARROW)	+ ALT
F1	Cancel	Go to DOS	Super/Subscript	Thesaurus
F2	Forward Search	Spell	Backward Search	Replace
F3	Help	Screen split	Switch Document	Reveal Codes
F4	Indent Left	Move Text	Indent Both Sides	Block
F5	List Files	Text In/Out	Date	Mark Text
F6	Bold	Tab Align	Center	Flush Right
F7	Exit	Footnote	Print	Math/Columns
F8	Underline	Print Format	Line Format	Page Format
F9	Merge Text	Merge/Sort	Merge End	Merge Codes
F10	Save	Macro Define	Retrieve	Macro

stored in the computer's memory, waiting to be reassigned. Then he uses the arrow keys to move the cursor to the location where he wants to reposition the cut block. With the cursor in place, he resummons the block menu by pressing CTRL F4 again. This time he selects the "5 Text" option to "paste" the text into its new position. Instantly, the cut block reappears in its new location and all the remaining text shifts down to make room for it.

A similar sequence is used to copy a block of text—paste a copy of text in another location and leave the original in place. A block of marked text could also be moved into its own file using the F10 function key to "save" it.

The function key approach to editing takes time to learn. Mr. Nelson uses a "template" that fits over the function keys to help him remember which keys to use for what. His **template** is a little plastic cutout of memory-jogger labels for the function keys, as shown in Figure 7-6. It came packaged with his word processing software when he bought it.

Alternately, he can press the F3 function key to get "on-line" help. **On-line help** is the equivalent of having a reference manual in the computer always ready to pop into instant service on the screen. Mr. Nelson often used the on-line help while he was learning.

Some word processing packages have novice, intermediate, and advanced help levels, unlike Mr. Nelson's package which has only one kind of on-line help. In addition, some packages have "context-sensitive" help. **Context-sensitive help** provides assistance appropriate to the action the word processor "senses" is causing the user to seek help. This is highly desirable in any package, not just in word processing packages.

Alternative Approaches

Approaches to editing a word processing document include using function keys, command keys, and a mouse with pull-down menus. Variations depend on the software used.

Function keys duplicate the approach used on dedicated word processors. *Dedicated word processors* are expensive, single-purpose small computers that are being phased out and replaced by general-purpose per-

Ctrl

Shift

Alt

Template

FIGURE 7-6
A function key template
(Courtesy of WordPerfect Corporation)

sonal computers. Some support several word processing specialists at once and cost up to $100,000.

Large organizations that switch to personal computers prefer packages that duplicate dedicated word processors. It saves retraining expenses. Some personal computer packages and the dedicated products they emulate are the following:

Dedicated Word Processors	Personal Computer Package Emulation
Wang	Multimate
	Samna
IBM DisplayWrite	IBM DisplayWrite

These software packages are included in the list in Figure 7-7. The list covers only a handful of the over 400 word processing packages available.

Experienced touch typists often prefer a **command key** approach. This allows them to avoid having to press distant function keys in order to issue commands. The CTRL control key (symbolized by a caret ^) triggers command key sequences. Figure 7-8 shows the Editing Menu with the keys required to activate various editing functions using a command key approach on another word processing package.

Some commands require several keystrokes. For example:

Keystroke	Meaning
^	CTRL control key to trigger command key sequence
B	Retrieves the *B*lock menu
B	Marks the *b*eginning of the block

FIGURE 7-7
A sampler of word processing software packages for personal computers

Bank Street Writer	MacWrite	Spellbinder
Brown Bag Processor	Microsoft Word	Sprint
DisplayWrite	MindReader	Textra
Easy Extra	MindWrite	Volkswriter
Electric Pencil	MultiMate	Wang Word Processing
Executive Secretary	My Word!	Webster's New World Writer
Executive Writer	OfficeWriter	
Friendly Writer	Palantir	Word
Gem Write	Paperback Writer	Word Handler
HabaWord	PC-Write	WordMARC
IBM Writing Assistant	Perfect Writer	WordPerfect
JustWrite	PFS: Professional Write	WordStar
Laser Quill	Q&A	WriteNow
Leading Edge	RWord	XyWrite
Lotus Manuscript	Samna	

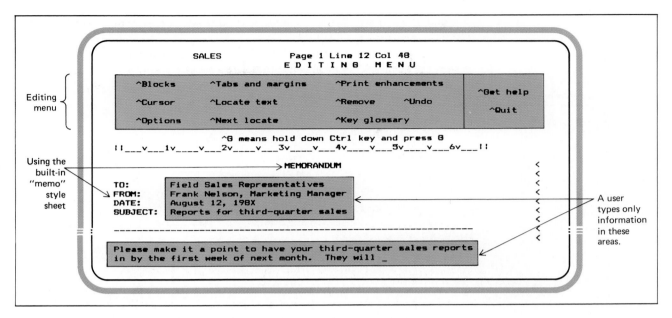

FIGURE 7-8
Creating a document with the editing command menu displayed
(Software: Wordstar 2000, courtesy of MicroPro International Corp.)

By holding down the CTRL control key and pressing the B key once, a Block Menu replaces the similar Editing Menu on the screen. The second time the B key is pressed, it marks the *beginning* of the block of text. The beginning of the block is wherever the cursor is located. A marked block of text can be moved, copied elsewhere, or deleted. These actions require additional keystrokes.

Keystrokes are **mnemonic,** or easily remembered, combinations. Experienced users memorize most command sequences. When this happens, they have the option to turn off menus to make room for more text on the screen, similar to the example in Figure 7-2. Even though menus are deleted from the screen, the commands are still operating and available for use whenever needed.

One word processing package generates eight subordinate command menus. Most users leave all subordinate menus active until they gain confidence without them. Some packages with many subordinate menus do not have a *menu deletion* feature. Instead, they have a menu bypass feature. By typing command sequences very quickly, it is possible to skip over subordinate menu displays. Menus tend to slow the processing speed of experienced users.

Mouse

Unlike command keys, using a *mouse* requires moving one hand off the keyboard to grasp and move the mouse device. It usually involves pointing to selections on a *pull-down menu*, as shown in Figure 7-9. All pointer movement is controlled by moving a mouse around a desktop.

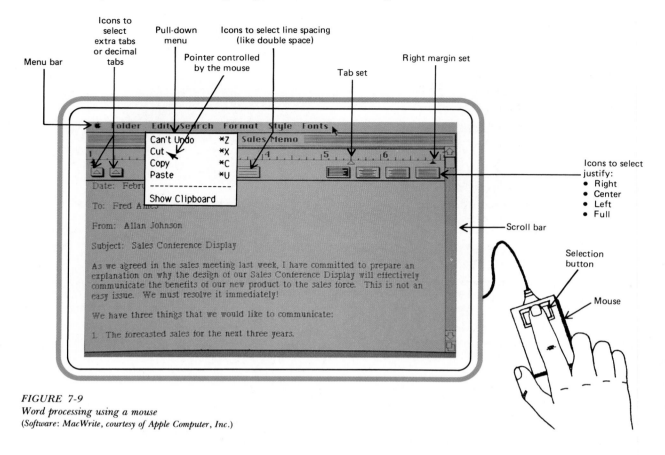

FIGURE 7-9
Word processing using a mouse
(Software: MacWrite, courtesy of Apple Computer, Inc.)

To do a block move, or *cut and paste*, works as follows:

· First, highlight the block of text to be moved. Begin by pressing down the mouse button once the pointer is positioned at the beginning of the block. Keep holding down the mouse button to drag the pointer over successive lines. At the end of the block of text, release the button.
· Next, move the pointer to the menu bar. Press the mouse button to select the "Edit" pull-down menu. Keep holding down the mouse button to drag the pointer to "Cut"; then release the mouse selection button.
· Next, move the special text insert pointer to the place in the text where the block should be moved.
· Finally, once again retrieve the "Edit" pull-down menu to select "Paste." The block instantly moves from its old location to its new location.

This approach has its own style and appeals to different types of users.

SEARCH AND REPLACE

Like block moves, **search and replace** operations to find and change text are common word processing tasks. Assume, for example, that "third" should be "fourth" in the memo that appears in Figure 7-2.

Mr. Nelson makes the change by pressing the ALT F2 keys to indicate the beginning of a text search task. Then he responds to the following prompts:

Prompt	Typed Response and Function Key
→ Srch:	third F2
Replace with	fourth F2

If "third" is replaced by "fourth" throughout a document, it is referred to as a **global** change. Alternatively, it is possible to stop at every occurrence to make whatever individual change is desired before continuing to the next occurrence.

The search and replace feature is a staple of the legal profession. It makes a standard contract for John Doe, as an example, easily changeable to one for Harrison Samuels.

Many word processing applications also provide **wild card,** or ambiguous text, searches. If unsure whether Product-ABC or Product-XYZ is included in a contract, a search for "Product-???" will retrieve the answer. The question marks signify ambiguous, or wild card, characters. Every place in the document that has a match on the characters "Product-," regardless of what characters or how many are after the hyphen, is displayed. Mr. Nelson's software uses the CTRL X key combination, instead of question marks, to identify wild card characters.

FORMATTING

Formatting a document concerns specifying its appearance on the printed page. The memo format used in Figure 7-8 comes prepared, along with other formats. Word processing packages call them *stored format* or **style sheets.** They can be used over and over again.

Alternatively, users can customize as many original formats as desired. To use the prepared memo format requires typing MEMO-FORM.FRM when beginning a word processing project. After the format is retrieved, the memo form can be filled in. Figure 7-10 shows some of the choices Mr. Nelson makes in his software to set up a format from scratch. His software does not provide prepared style sheets.

Some word processing programs require that special commands be typed right in the body of the text to control formatting:

Example of Format Commands That Appear in Body of Text	Action Generated During Printing
^BSUBJECT:^B	**Boldface** the text between the ^B characters
.MT15	Set the *m*argin to begin 15 lines down from the *t*op
.OP	*O*mit *p*age numbers

Embedding format controls makes visual review of text difficult. Some packages compensate with a **preview** option. This removes command characters temporarily to let a user see how a document will look when it is printed.

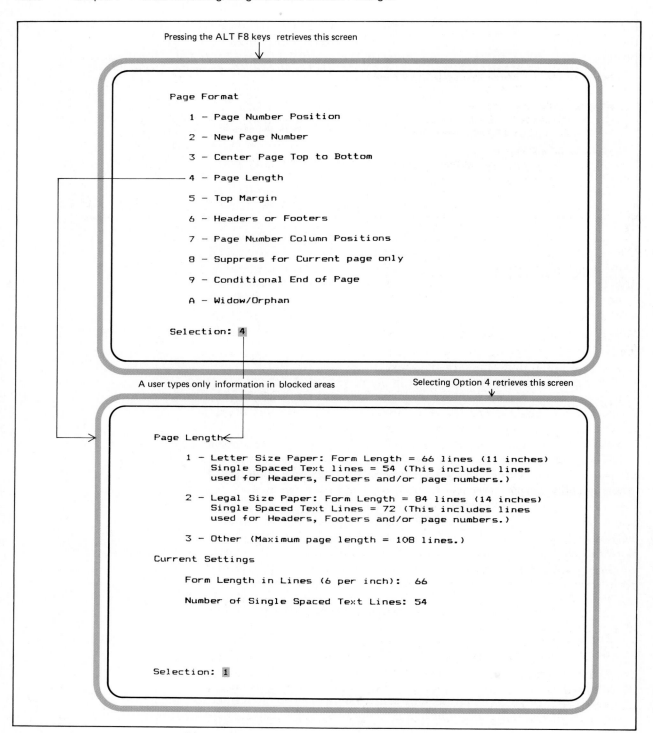

Pressing the ALT F8 keys retrieves this screen

Page Format

    1 - Page Number Position

    2 - New Page Number

    3 - Center Page Top to Bottom

    4 - Page Length

    5 - Top Margin

    6 - Headers or Footers

    7 - Page Number Column Positions

    8 - Suppress for Current page only

    9 - Conditional End of Page

    A - Widow/Orphan

Selection: 4

A user types only information in blocked areas   Selecting Option 4 retrieves this screen

Page Length

    1 - Letter Size Paper: Form Length = 66 lines (11 inches)
        Single Spaced Text lines = 54 (This includes lines
        used for Headers, Footers and/or page numbers.)

    2 - Legal Size Paper: Form Length = 84 lines (14 inches)
        Single Spaced Text Lines = 72 (This includes lines
        used for Headers, Footers and/or page numbers.)

    3 - Other (Maximum page length = 108 lines.)

Current Settings

    Form Length in Lines (6 per inch): 66

    Number of Single Spaced Text Lines: 54

Selection: 1

FIGURE 7-10
Setting up a format
(*Software*: WordPerfect, *courtesy of WordPerfect Corporation*)

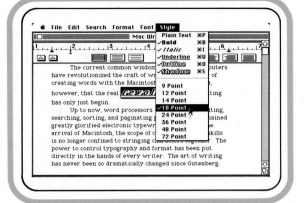

FIGURE 7-11
Examples of type font and style options
(Software: MacWrite, courtesy of MacWorld)

Mr. Nelson's package works the exact opposite. It suppresses all format control codes. Instead, he has a "Reveal Code" function using the ALT F3 keys. Seeing the format codes is necessary to delete things such as unwanted underlined or bold text.

Setting up a format is different in many mouse-oriented packages. As apparent from Figure 7-9, **icons** or symbols indicate formal settings. To change a setting requires moving the pointer to a desired icon and clicking the mouse button. Format changes instantly display on the screen.

A feature in some packages is fancy type font and style selections, such as those shown in Figure 7-11. Packages that treat text as graphics mix any and all type styles and fonts on a single page. They also add graphic inserts into text documents.

PRINTING A DOCUMENT

To get a printed copy, Mr. Nelson presses the shift F7 keys. A line of print options appears on the bottom of the screen. He types a 1 to select option "1 Full Text," and his document is printed.

If he wanted, he could start a new word processing project while the printing is going on. This feature is called **print spooling.** Technicians would say that the printer is working in the "background" while some other task can be going on in the "foreground."

Generally, Mr. Nelson saves a document file before printing it. This provides insurance if something goes wrong during the print operation. If a printer malfunction locks up his screen, or should some other unforeseen event occur, he can always recall the saved file and start the printing again.

To save a document, he presses the F10 key. A prompt asks for a file name. After the file name is typed, the file is saved to disk. He makes a second "backup copy" of the file for safety purposes before ending his project.

Others who use the same word processing package also like the file **document header** feature shown in Figure 7-12. It allows users to describe a document and list the date created, author, typist, and any relevant comments desired.

Document Review

Separate, stand-alone **document review packages,** such as ForComment, allow multiple reviewers to create and attach notes in an organized manner to an original word processing document. As shown in Figure 7-13, each time a reviewer creates a note or revision in the lower window, it is automatically linked to a specific location in the text, stamped with the reviewer's initials, and dated. Reviewers are empowered by the document's author to add only comments or to make text revisions. Reviewers can comment on the comments of other reviewers.

Authors can collate multiple review comments into a single document and make changes accordingly. The original is preserved, and the com-

FIGURE 7-12
A document summary
(*Software*: *WordPerfect, courtesy of WordPerfect Corporation*)

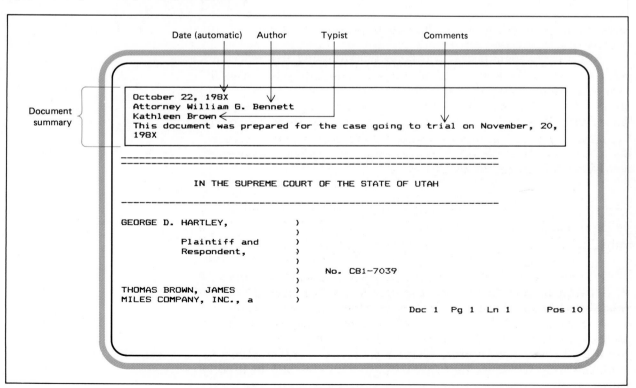

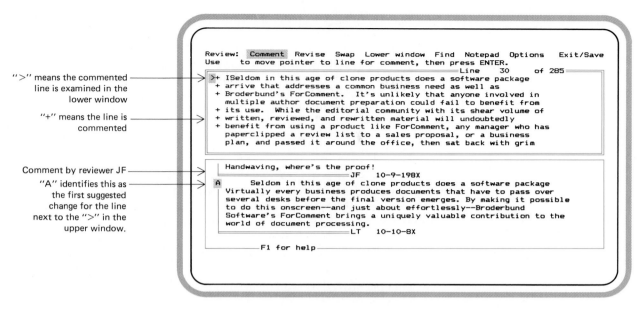

Review: [Comment] Revise Swap Lower window Find Notepad Options Exit/Save
Use   to move pointer to line for comment, then press ENTER.
───Line   30   of 285═══
">" means the commented line is examined in the lower window

">+ ISeldom in this age of clone products does a software package
  + arrive that addresses a common business need as well as
  + Broderbund's ForComment. It's unlikely that anyone involved in
    multiple author document preparation could fail to benefit from
  + its use. While the editorial community with its shear volume of
  + written, reviewed, and rewritten material will undoubtedly
  + benefit from using a product like ForComment, any manager who has
    paperclipped a review list to a sales proposal, or a business
    plan, and passed it around the office, then sat back with grim

"+" means the line is commented

    Handwaving, where's the proof!
  ════════════════════JF   10-9-198X
  A   Seldom in this age of clone products does a software package
    Virtually every business produces documents that have to pass over
    several desks before the final version emerges. By making it possible
    to do this onscreen--and just about effortlessly--Broderbund
    Software's ForComment brings a uniquely valuable contribution to the
    world of document processing.
  ════════════════════LT   10-10-8X

Comment by reviewer JF

"A" identifies this as the first suggested change for the line next to the ">" in the upper window.

  ──────F1 for help──────

FIGURE 7-13
Adding reviewer's comments to a word processing document
(Software: ForComment, courtesy of Broder-
bund Software)

ments are maintained as an audit trail throughout the history of the document.

Such a feature is useful in electronically networked common work groups. It can facilitate the review of in-house publication and corporate communications.

Some users, however, resist automating the document review process. They feel limited by the amount of the document in view on the screen. In addition, an author may be reluctant to switch back to the word processing package to implement suggested changes in cases where a separate document review package is used.

MACROS

Denise Palmeri, an administrative assistant in National Bank's personnel department, uses the same package that Mr. Nelson does. The large bank she works for selected the package as its standard word processing software. In time, she has become a sophisticated user of the word processing software and feels comfortable creating "macros."

The **macro** feature is similar to the same feature in other packages, especially spreadsheet packages. It enables her to record keystrokes, both text and function or command key combinations, under one name and play them back exactly as they were recorded. She finds this feature saves a great deal of time and reduces the incidence of keyboard input errors.

She creates all macros the same way. The following procedure is used:

- Begin defining the macro
- Enter the name of the macro
- Type the keystrokes to be recorded in the macro file
- End defining the macro

As an example, she defined the name of an envelope printing macro to be the ALT and the letter E keys. Now, whenever she needs to type an envelope, she types ALT E and the macro file is automatically played out to

- Search the content of a letter for the recipient's address (the letter's "inside address")
- Mark the address as a block of text
- Send the marked block to the printer (which has been loaded with an envelope)
- Print the address on the envelope

This macro saves her from repeating the same keystroke procedure every time she needs to type an envelope.

One PC consultant sets up the following word processing macros for his clients in New York City:

Client *Must Type*	*Macro Action Performed*
ALT N	Prints the last line of the inside address on letters to be mailed locally: "New York, New York 100___." Only the last two digits of the zip code must be typed. It saves 20 keystrokes each time it is used, and it is used hundreds of times each day.
ALT R	Prints a document on a laser printer so the first page is on top and the last page is on the bottom. Some laser printers stack their output backwards. This saves enormous time and trouble manually restacking printed output.

These macros, on the simplest level, spare one the worst sort of typing tedium. At their most sophisticated, they make a major contribution to office productivity.

Occasionally Ms. Palmeri uses her word processing package's **type-through** or *typewriter* feature for typing envelope addresses. It enables her to type directly to the printer, as if using an ordinary typewriter. This feature is useful to fill out forms and to address randomly needed envelopes.

Ms. Palmeri belongs to a community personal computer users group.

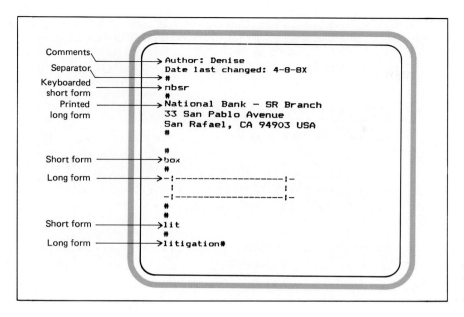

FIGURE 7-14
Example of a key glossary file
(Software: WordStar 2000, courtesy of Micro-
Pro International Corp.)

In the special-interest group (SIG) on word processing to which she belongs, a discussion ignited about the confusion between macros and key glossaries. A **key glossary,** it was pointed out, allows the retrieval of boilerplate text by using a few keystrokes, as the key file in Figure 7-14 illustrates. A macro goes beyond boilerplate text retrieval because it can actually perform word processing commands.

SPELLER AND GRAMMAR CHECKERS

Because she maintains high-quality standards for her work, Ms. Palmeri processes formal documents through a **spelling checker.** This checker matches a document's words with its over-100,000-word dictionary. It displays suspect words with suggested corrections. A single keystroke accepts a suggestion. All suggestions can be ignored. Alternatively, a substitute word can be typed.

Some people buy separate spelling checkers when word processing programs do not have them built in. Some stand-alone packages are Webster's New World Spelling Checker, Electric Webster, MacSpell, and Word-Proof. Turbo Lightning and other packages offer **on-line** or **real-time spell checking.** This feature catches spelling and typographical errors while a document is being typed. This feature often requires additional hardware, such as extra memory or hard disk capacity.

Another complementary product is a **grammar** or **style checker.** It picks out errors that a spelling checker would ignore. As an example, it correctly detects "can not" as an erroneous form of "cannot," although

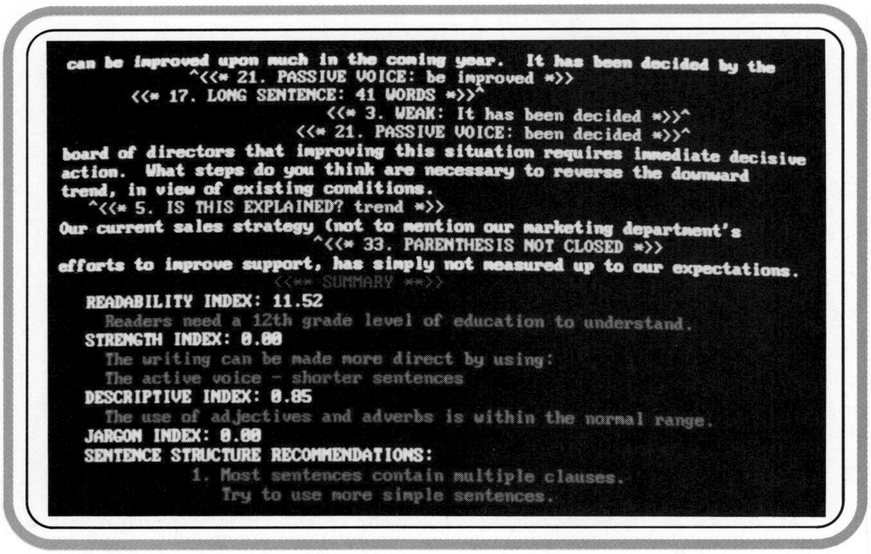

FIGURE 7-15
A style checker at work
(*Software*: *RightWriter*, *courtesy of Decision-*
Ware)

the error would pass a spelling checker. Other errors it catches include archaic words (upon instead of on), awkward usage (and/or), and redundant phrases (join together). Some packages report total word count and the frequency of each word used. Grammar checker packages include Punctuation and Style, Grammatik, and RightWriter.

As shown in Figure 7-15, the user of a grammar checker can examine a **markup copy,** which is a copy of the style-checked document with comments and suggestions inserted throughout. The original document remains intact. The program finds

- Incomplete sentences
- Passive voice
- Double words
- Redundant, clichéd, or ambiguous phrases
- Long or wordy sentences

The software even offers suggestions for replacing poorly or incorrectly worded phrases. For example, if it finds "their is," it will suggest "there is." It will recommend replacing the wordy phrase "in view of the fact that" with "since." Although it unmercifully points out any weaknesses in writing style, this electronic editor has the potential to help improve a writer's work.

Another companion product, which is also built into some word processing packages, is a **synonym finder** or **electronic thesaurus.** The thesaurus presents alternative word possibilities, or synonyms, for any word desired. Both the thesaurus and the speller can be called up for "on-line" correcting or replacing of words in a word processing document. Examples of stand-alone thesauri are Webster's New World On-line Thesaurus, Reference Set, and Word Finder.

In this reference category also appears a product like Microsoft Bookshelf, a general-purpose reference work that is available on a CD ROM optical disk. It contains the following:

- Dictionary
- World Almanac and Book of Facts
- Chicago Manual of Style
- Bartlett's Familiar Quotations
- And more

It works with over a dozen popular word processing packages. Desired material from these references can be electronically cut and pasted into a document. After each paste, a copyright notice appears within the document, noting its source. To use the package requires buying a CD ROM disk drive, interfacing circuit board, and cable.

PERSONALIZED FORM LETTERS

Ms. Palmeri often uses her word processing package to send personalized form letters. This function is often called **mail merge** and may be sold as a separate package.

National Bank's personnel department sends form letters to people who send in unsolicited job resumés that the bank cannot use. To automate the letter production process, Ms. Palmeri creates a master form letter, like the one in Figure 7-16. Her word processor calls it the "primary document."

FIGURE 7-16
A screen display of the primary file for printing personalized form letters (Software: WordPerfect, courtesy of WordPerfect Corporation)

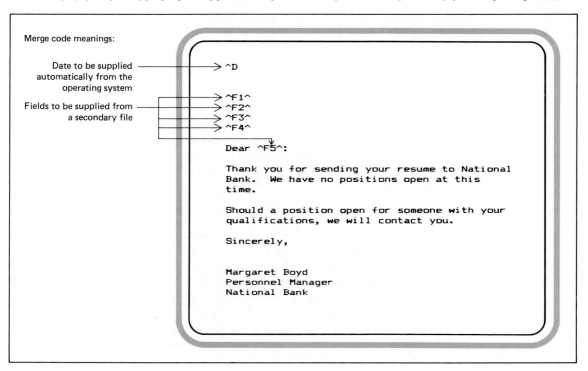

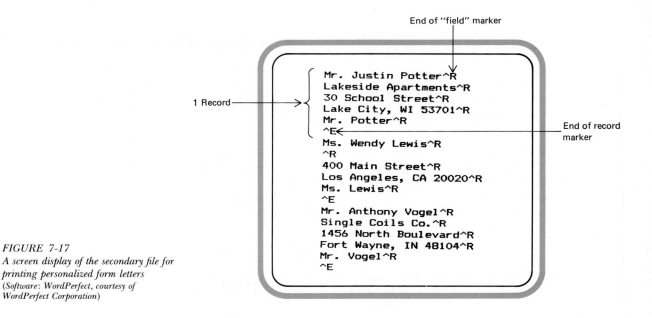

FIGURE 7-17
A screen display of the secondary file for
printing personalized form letters
(Software: WordPerfect, courtesy of
WordPerfect Corporation)

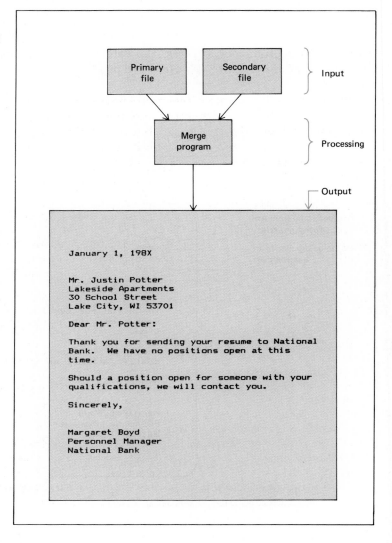

FIGURE 7-18
Using data from the first record in the
secondary file to produce a personalized
form letter

Periodically, she creates a file of names and addresses of people who are to receive a copy of the form letter. The file is called a "secondary" file. Her screen resembles the one in Figure 7-17 when creating this file. Some word processing packages use a special built-in data-entry screen to create the secondary file.

When ready to print the letters, such as the example in Figure 7-18, she begins by pressing the CTRL F9 keys. She is then prompted to type the names of both the primary and secondary files. The two files first are merged and displayed. Then another function key combination starts the actual printing. This sequence has been considerably simplified since recording it into a macro.

Some organizations keep their name and address files for bulk mailings on a database management system (DBMS). Ordinarily a DBMS handles more records and offers greater sorting flexibility than a word processing package. A file transfer procedure is then necessary to move the names and addresses out of the database package and into the word processing package. Most word processing and other packages have a *file conversion* feature to exchange files.

PROFESSIONAL-CLASS FEATURES

Professional-class word processors are powerful word engines packed with a slew of advanced formatting and editing features. They have a reputation for being difficult to use, but new designs are making them easier to master. The features that distinguish one or another of these word processing packages include the following:

- *Automatic hyphenation* uses a set of hyphenation rules to hyphenate words automatically that cross into a user-definable hyphenation zone at the right edge of the line. This feature is usually supplemented with a user-expandable dictionary for words where hyphenation does not follow normal rules.
- *Math* performs addition, subtraction, division, and multiplication. It can also add multiple rows and columns with a single command.
- *Sort* uses any column desired as the sort key to list text and tables in either alphabetic or numeric order.
- *Print queuing* allows several documents to be queued and printed in sequence while editing work can continue.
- *Proportional spacing* allocates more room for an uppercase letter "M" than for a lowercase letter "i."
- *Widow and orphan control* prevents one line from being separated on a page from the rest of the paragraph on another page.
- *Search across directories and drives* extends a text search beyond a file to all or selected files in one or more directories or disk drives.
- *Multiple document access* allows working on two or more documents simultaneously, using split screens or window overlays.
- *DOS access* allows the temporary exit to any DOS activity. It includes running a different application entirely and returning to exactly where a task was left off when the word processor is reentered.
- *Graphics* includes drawing boxes around text, as well as importing graphics from other applications and wrapping text around pictures.

In addition to these features, most word processing packages are incorporating features normally identified with desktop publishing applications. These features are covered in Chapter 13, "Desktop Publishing."

Some new features result in entirely new products. An example is voice-activated word processors that can recognize as many as 20,000 words. While one package requires users to pause about one-tenth of a second between words, another accepts sustained dictation.

ChemText is another example of a specialty word processor. It incorporates rules of chemistry so that chemists can draw rough sketches of compounds and other structures.

For foreign-language applications, a package such as International Bilingual Word Processor produces text in non-English. Packages are available for French, German, Spanish, Italian, Chinese, Japanese, Hebrew, Arabic, Persian, and many other languages. Some English-language word processors can produce text in some of these languages with the addition of specialized font software.

When there are so many powerful features at their disposal, some word processing users feel like Sunday drivers at the wheel of a 10-gear tractor-trailer. To avoid this syndrome, evaluating a word processing package before buying it is critical.

WORD PROCESSING EVALUATION

When deciding which word processing package to buy, a systematic evaluation is important to select the correct package the first time. Studies show that users usually do not switch word processing packages after learning how to use one. This remains true even though they clearly bought the wrong package or a demonstrably better package for their needs is readily available.

Users are reluctant to switch because the time and effort required to learn any new software far exceeds its purchase price. At least one package, Sprint, tries to ease the upgrade dilemma by providing a **keystroke-emulation** feature. This enables a user to make the new word processor mimic the keyboard commands of a favorite word processor.

Many first-time users become easily dazzled by all the fancy capabilities new word processing packages offer. But everyone who wants to process words has different requirements. A good way to begin is to work backward from the end product desired. What will word processing be used for?

The simplest and least expensive software will easily handle short letters and be easy to learn. A moderately powered and priced program will do form letters, short papers, and articles and be more difficult to learn. The elaborate packages will do most complex word processing tasks and provide advanced features like those listed in the Word Processing Evaluation Checklist in Figure 7-19. Two items on the list, text-based data managers and outline processors, are discussed in the next section.

	BASIC	INTERMEDIATE	ADVANCED
File organization	Renames file Deletes file	Writes block to new file Reads file into document File size limited only by memory Mail merge Makes/reads ASCII files	Automatic index/table of contents Uses disk as virtual or extended memory Continually saves to disk Splits screen or window overlays Moves blocks between files Text-based data management Outline processor Key glossaries Multiple document access
Input and editing	Insert and replace Block copy and move Search and replace Page, row, and column display Tab ruler display Cursor movement by character, line, and screen Deletes by character, line, and block What you see is what you get	Deletes by word and sentence Deletes to end of line Deletes word to left Undo delete Decimal tabs Search and replace/ignores case Search and replace/backward Horizontal scrolling Cursor movement by page, sentence, paragraph; to beginning and end of line or document; to specified line or specified page	Spelling checker Grammar checker Thesaurus Math Macros Mouse support Wild-card search and replace Transposes characters Changes (upper and lower) cases Column move Sort Search across directories and drives Context-sensitive help and tutorial Hidden comments
Formatting	Adjusts margins Adjusts line spacing Centers text	Superscript and subscript Justified margins Underline Boldface Headers and footers Block indentation Automatic reformatting Automatic page numbering	Automatic footnoting Automatic hyphenation Style sheets Widow and orphan control Proportional spacing
Printing	Automatic pagination	Prints multiple copies Prints selected pages Extended character set	Automatic envelope addressing Print queuing Print spooling Printer pause for text entry Laser printer support

(Figure 3-25, General Software Evaluation Checklist, is necessary to complete this evaluation.)

FIGURE 7-19
Word processing evaluation checklist
(*Source*: PC World, *555 DeHaro St., San Francisco, CA 47107. Adapted with permission.*)

Users occasionally make the mistake of buying a package so powerful and complex to learn that they never use it. On the other hand, buying a package with so little power that it cannot grow as need and skill level increase is also a problem. To avoid either extreme, a careful evaluation process is critical.

Word processing software that features a "what you see is what you get" display, also known by the acronym "WYSIWYG," is desirable. Alternatives may not, as an example, display justified, proportionally spaced, finished page formats complete with heading and page number. With such software, a user has no idea of what a page will look like until a trial print is made.

Because most word processing time is spent entering and revising documents, the speed and convenience of basic editing is critical. Comparative hands-on testing reveals such glaring differences between packages as 22 versus 4 seconds to scroll through a seven-page double-spaced document.

Some word processing packages restrict document size to available memory size. One allows documents up to only ten double-spaced pages. Size restrictions require dividing longer documents into smaller segments or files. Editing divided documents may be time consuming and awkward.

Some word processing software handles documents larger than memory. To do this it swaps text to and from the disk. The technique is called *virtual memory*. Swaps theoretically are invisible to a user. Floppy disk swaps, however, are often noticeably sluggish. With such software, document size limit becomes the total available disk capacity.

Like document length, document width may be a limitation with some word processing software. Eighty-column-wide document processing is standard. One goes to 240 columns wide. If wide documents are to be processed, the *horizontal scrolling* feature should be examined.

For a hands-on test, many use the longest and most complex representative document possible. Nearly all packages seem easy when working on a single paragraph. It takes a more demanding test to see where the frustrations are hidden.

COMPUTER-AIDED WRITING

Some begin the writing process by making a rigid outline. Others begin by jotting down random notes and organizing them later. Computer-aided writing packages, called *outline processors* and *text-based data managers*, can help both types.

The main difference between these packages is how they aid the writing process:

Package	Distinguishing Characteristic
Outline processor	A writer must begin with an outline.

Text-based data managers   A writer does not have to begin with an outline. Instead, a writer can scribble notes and organize them later.

Both provide a way to overcome a computer-age writer's biggest dilemma, facing a blank screen. Both packages may require a transfer to a full-featured word processing package to finish a writing project.

Another package related to both outliners and word processors, called hypertext, is also covered in this computer-aided writing section.

Outline Processors

For individuals in technical and detail-oriented fields, outlining has always made sense. So-called *outliners*, *outline processors*, or *idea processors*, such as those listed in Figure 7-20, make it all the more practical.

Ronald Geer, a Washington, D.C.-based attorney, thinks "it's like having a dynamic yellow pad. I learned to outline on a yellow pad long before I had a computer for writing briefs or presentations." Mr. Geer's outlines generally run three or four levels deep. The lowest-level heading usually represents one complete paragraph. "If suddenly the wording of a paragraph crystalizes in my mind, it's nice that I can include that right there," he adds. "Otherwise, I prepare the outline," like the one in Figure 7-21, "to the paragraph level, and then actually write the document with a word processor."

Mr. Geer starts his outline by listing five major categories shown in the first outline in Figure 7-21. "Most briefs will follow the same basic structure," he says. As he fleshes out the details in lower levels of the outline, he often finds he needs to change the introduction to reflect the organization he is building. The task is made easy by the ability to edit, erase, and copy electronically. So far, all this can be done by any word processor.

An outliner, however, has the ability to expand and collapse the outline to show hierarchical levels to the depth he wants. "My outlines on paper used to get as long as 10 to 15 sheets," says Mr. Geer. "Sometimes I would get lost because it would be so difficult to go back through the outline to see what I had already done. More than once I discovered I was repeating things. With the outline processor, I can get the level view I need and can still see the broad context. It's easier to keep the flow of ideas in order."

To move blocks of text from one part of the outline to another requires only moving the heading. The program automatically moves the text under the heading.

Users of outline processors include traditional word processing-oriented professionals like lawyers, researchers, and writers. They also include managers and decision makers who like to have extensive hierarchical "to do" lists or control sheets. An outliner provides a convenient place to collect and store the details of projects such as assembling the annual report or setting up a regional sales meeting. It is one way to monitor or "watch" over a project to be sure nothing "falls through the cracks."

FactCruncher
Framework
Freestyle
Idea!
Kamas
MaxThink
More
PC-Outline
Ready!
Symphony Text Outliner
ThinkTank
Voila!

FIGURE 7-20
A sampler of outline processor software packages for personal computers

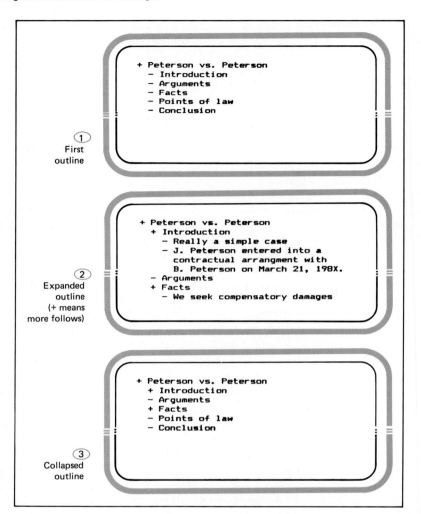

FIGURE 7-21
Displays from an outline package
(Software: ThinkTank. ThinkTank is a trademark of Symantec Corp., Living Videotext Division, 117 Easy St., Mountain View, CA 94043.)

Hypertext

Related to both outliners and word processors are so-called "hypertext" packages. **Hypertext** is an electronic system for organizing and presenting information nonsequentially. An example of reading a hypertext document helps to understand how it works:

A student sits in front of his personal computer, studying the electronic edition of the *Marine Manual Guide*, as illustrated in Figure 7-22. Not entirely confident of the meaning of "amphibious," the student clicks a mouse button and a definition window appears on the screen (Figure 7-22A). Returning to the main text, he desires more in-depth information about identifying individual mammal species. He clicks the mouse button on "seal-like" and is presented with a new level of information (Figure 7-22B). While reading the new screen, he decides to explore more about the sea-lion's "visible external ears." Again he clicks the mouse over the text in question and is

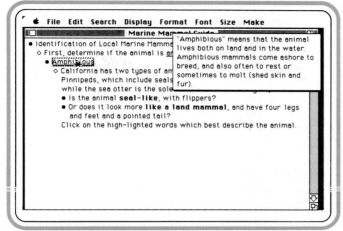

A. The word "amphibious" is a *note* button
that produces the definition in the window

This screen was
produced as a
replacement
button for the
word "seal-like"
above.

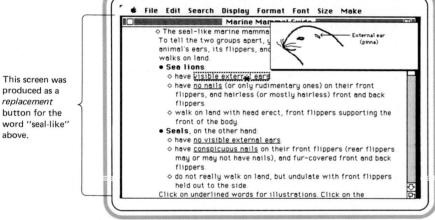

B. The phrase "visible external ears" is a *note* button
that produces the graphic in the window

FIGURE 7-22
Reading a hypertext document
(Software: Guide, courtesy of OWL Interna-
tional)

presented with another window of detail. This time it is a pictorial representation of the text in question. . . .

In this example, the hypertext is used for self-paced instruction. More and more detail is revealed as the reader's understanding and interest increase.

To create such a document is as much related to building as to writing. After a block of text is created, it must be labeled. One software product, Guide, calls the labels "buttons." The window in Figure 7-22A, as an example, is the result of a clicking on a "note" button. As long as the mouse button is depressed, the note remains on the screen. All the text in Figure 7-22B, as another example, is assigned to the word "seal-like" as a "replacement" button. It replaces any text currently on the screen.

Although the concept of hypertext is 20 years old, applications of it are just emerging. Apple Computer calls the concept a "software erector set" and their product HyperCard. The company expects software developers to use such products to create "stackware" (a play on the word "software") applications. A powerful *scripting language*, which is the equivalent of a programming language, can be used to customize applications that link together text, graphics, video and sound.

Some hypertext software developers warn of potential problems. In some cases, text entry is awkward, and formatting is next to impossible. Another potential problem is that a hypertext reader needs a personal computer and a copy of the software to read the document. It is possible authors will have no assurance that their work will not be altered. In addition, authors may have no control over the appearance of the finished product.

Text-Based Data Manager

Barbara Unangst, a professor of environment and industrial health at a prominent midwestern university, prepares scientific papers and lectures. She writes notes first and organizes them later. Text-based data manager packages, such as those listed in Figure 7-23, do not require her to change her work habits.

Figure 7-24 diagrams how her software works. She types research notes whenever she is inclined to and marks any special "keywords" that are in the notes. She identifies each note with a unique name. This step resembles what anyone does when manually making notes on stacks of 3″ by 5″ index cards.

The difference occurs when Ms. Unangst wants to make order out of seeming chaos. She simply asks to find all the notes that contain desired tags, or "keywords." Instantly, all notes containing the keywords are retrieved and are placed at her disposal.

If a keyword search does not find a specific note, she can request a special search of the entire text of every note. This process can be time consuming as the pool of notes grows.

The whole idea behind a text-based data manager package is flexibility. It is as though a user could scribble hundreds of notes on hundreds of pieces of paper and toss them all in a box, and then, like magic, only the one slip of paper wanted at any given time could be pulled out of the box.

Later, a collection of keywords can be used to create an outline for organizing note collections into coherent formal documents.

Text-based data manager packages share characteristics with database management software. Both offer information search and retrieval. But most database management packages require a rigid predesignated record format, like the one in Figure 8-7. A text-based data manager package, by contrast, requires no format or preplanning.

Many professionals find text-based data manager packages useful. Doctors especially like them to keep a descriptive file for each patient without worrying about codes, forms, rules, or character restrictions typically found in database management packages.

FIGURE 7-23
A sampler of text-based data manager software packages for personal computers

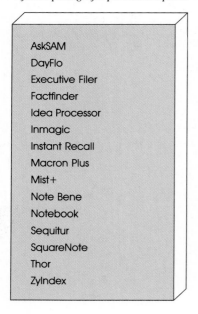

AskSAM
DayFlo
Executive Filer
Factfinder
Idea Processor
Inmagic
Instant Recall
Macron Plus
Mist+
Note Bene
Notebook
Sequitur
SquareNote
Thor
ZyIndex

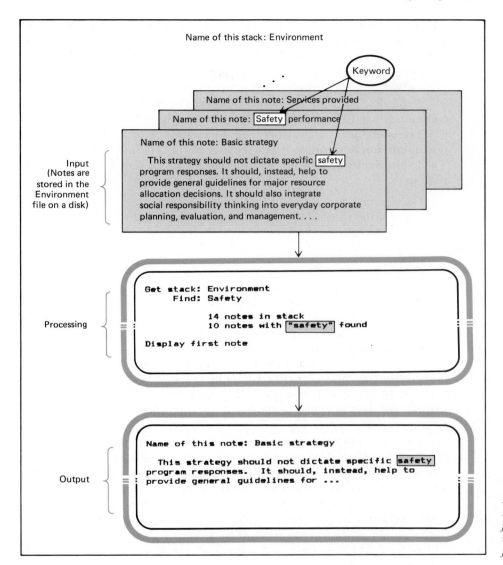

FIGURE 7-24
*Performing a search
for the keyword "safety"
in a collection of stored free-
form notes*

INTEGRATED PACKAGES

Word processing comes bundled in many of the integrated packages listed in Figure 5-6. An **integrated package** combines several functions. Generally, they are

- Word processing
- Spreadsheet
- Graphics
- Database management
- Communications

These "all-in-one" packages appeal to professional users who are not single-task "production" workers. In the course of a day such users will write memos (word processing), send the memos electronically (communications), look up names and addresses (database management), plan a budget (spreadsheet), and put together a presentation (graphics).

Typically, with an all-in-one integrated package, only one set of commands has to be learned. All applications use them similarly.

Transferring a spreadsheet file to include it in a word-processed document might require a few keystrokes in an integrated package. To do the same thing with stand-alone packages requires more work, such as

- Copying the spreadsheet file into another file format that is acceptable to the word processing package
- Closing down the spreadsheet package and starting the word processing package
- Opening the new spreadsheet file with the word processing package
- Editing the spreadsheet once it is in the word processor, because many times it comes in with garbage attached

Exchanging Files

Exchanging files among stand-alone applications is a user problem, since there is no such thing as a universal file format. This is partly because software developers like to restrict their product and file designs. It is also because some file designs are better for some tasks and other designs are better for other tasks.

Most sophisticated spreadsheet and database software uses a compact *binary* file design. Some word processors and many simple database file managers use an *ASCII* (*A*merican *S*tandard *C*ode for *I*nformation *I*nterchange) file design. (An ASCII character table is shown in Appendix C.) ASCII is the most common format used to exchange files with other applications, as well as with mainframes and communication services. This type of file contains only standard ASCII characters with each field separated from the next by a comma.

If an ASCII file is to be exchanged between two different word processors, as an example, first the file is converted to an ASCII file for transfer, or *export*, to the second word processor. It usually is first stripped, in a *conversion* program, of all formatting control characters. This requires formatting to be manually reinstated after the ASCII file is *imported* at the second word processor.

Many word processing packages have built-in routines to import files, without ASCII conversion, directly from other popular word processing and other packages. All foreign format codes are automatically replaced by the word processor's native code during the import operation.

The word processing industry seeks a standard format for document exchange. Some consider IBM's internal standard, **Document Content Architecture** (DCA), to solve the file exchange problem. It is, however, only an intermediary document structure that requires two conversions.

When a document is moved from one system to another, it is first translated out of native format into the DCA format. On receipt, it is translated out of DCA and into the format of the receiving system.

DCA comes in two flavors:

- *Revisable Form Text (DCA RFT)* is designed for the exchange of documents that will be altered after they are revised.
- *Final Form Text (DCA FFT)* is a display- or print-only form of DCA. Such files are not meant to be edited after receipt.

DCA is expected to mature and enable, eventually, the creation and distribution of documents containing various data types, such as text, image, and graphics.

Another promising standard for file exchange is Microsoft's **Rich Text Format (RTF).** It is the standard for information moved from one application to another through the Microsoft Windows package. It means formatting information is not lost if both sending and receiving applications support RTF.

Users of all-in-one integrated packages avoid all such file exchange problems.

Styles

Displays of several all-in-one integrated packages appear in Figure 7-25. Each has a very different style of operation. Framework, as an example, treats the screen as a collection of *frames*. Each frame can be thought about as a window that can be expanded or reduced to any size. A frame can contain text, a graphic, a spreadsheet, a database file, or an outline.

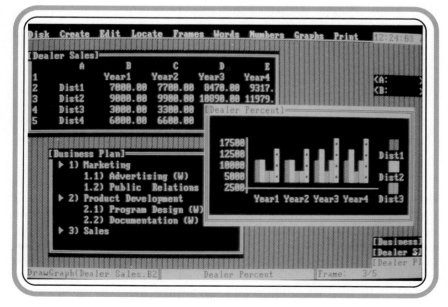

FIGURE 7-25
Examples of all-in-one integrated packages that allow several applications to be active
(*Top: courtesy of Ashton-Tate; middle and bottom: courtesy of Lotus Development Corporation*)

Framework

Symphony

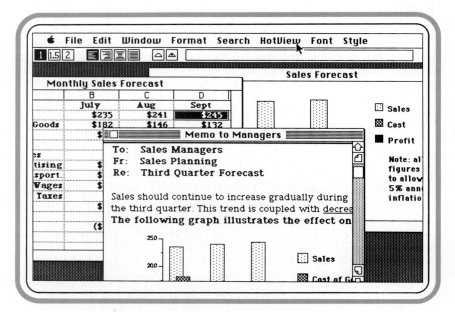

Jazz

FIGURE 7-25 (continued)

As shown in Figure 7-26, the outliner application is expected to be the controlling device for a collection of frames. A single outline subheading can instantly be expanded to include text, a spreadsheet, a graph, or any combination of numbers, graphs, or text.

An integrated product like Framework might appeal to anyone who works with outlines and words. The package contrasts with one like Symphony, which appeals more to anyone who works with numbers. It treats the screen as one enormous spreadsheet that can contain, within

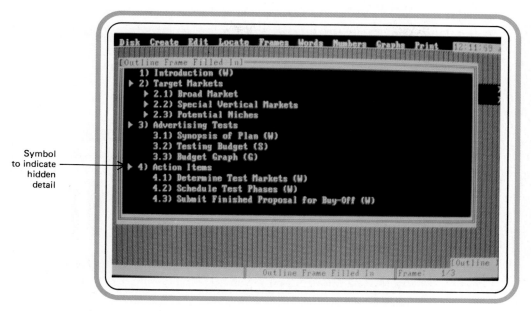

FIGURE 7-26
An outliner that expands or collapses to show varying levels of detail
(Software: Framework, courtesy of Ashton-Tate)

its cells, smaller spreadsheets, text, graphics, and database files. A user must organize what goes where and keep track of cell allocation.

A different integrated package like Jazz offers mouse control with pull-down menus and icons. This technique became popular with the Apple Macintosh computer and is generally known as the "Mac style." It is more intuitive than other computer interface approaches.

In an ideally integrated package, any change made to a spreadsheet number should ripple through and automatically change a letter that contains the same number reference. If the same number is represented in a graph, the graph should also instantly reflect the change. Not all packages achieve this ideal.

Some other disadvantages of integrated packages are the following:

· Users cannot choose a preferred mix of applications.
· Users cannot start with one application and add another when desired.
· The number of features in one or more basic application is often less than in comparable stand-alone packages.

Windows

An alternative solves these limitations. It is a software product that performs only the integration with whatever stand-alone packages a user desires. The product is the same **window package** that is described in Chapter 3. The name describes what the packages does: It creates windows, as shown in Figure 7-27, which are viewing ports to observe different applications. When used, the package looks exactly like any

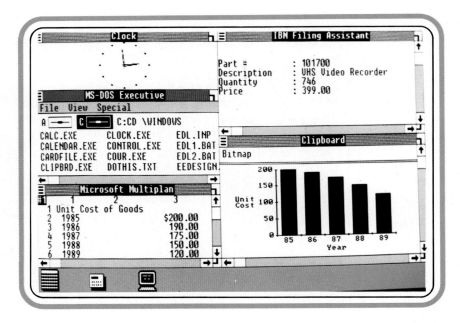

System menu box
(upper) left corner of each window)

Caption bar
(1st line in each window)

Menu bar
(2nd line
in each
window)

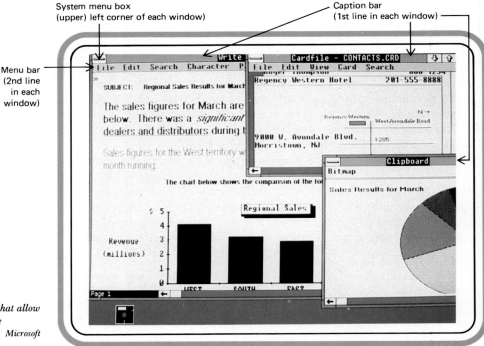

FIGURE 7-27
Examples of window packages that allow
several applications to be active
(*Software*: *Windows*, *courtesy of Microsoft*
Corp.)

integrated package. Comparing Figures 7-27 and 7-25 demonstrates the similarity.

A window package performs only a service function. The diagram in Figure 7-28 illustrates how it adds a new layer of software. Its advantages and disadvantages, when compared with an all-in-one integrated package, are summarized in Figure 7-29.

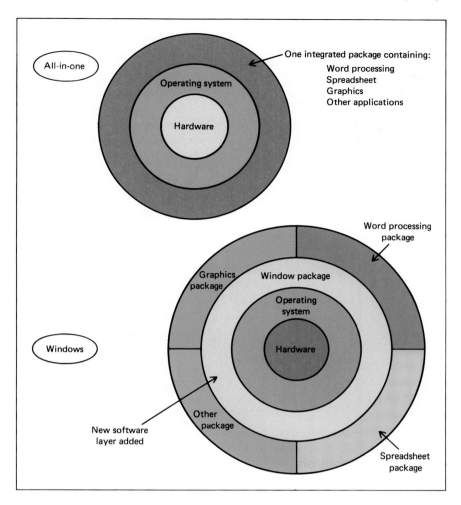

FIGURE 7-28
Difference between an all-in-one integrated package and a window package that integrates several different applications

FIGURE 7-29
Comparison of integration techiques (+ Favorable, − Not favorable)

	ALL-IN-ONE INTEGRATED PACKAGE	WINDOW INTEGRATING PACKAGE	FAMILY OF STAND-ALONE APPLICATIONS
User can choose applications to integrate	−	+	−
User can add applications as needed	−	+	+
Common command structure throughout applications	+	−	+
Cost per function	+	−	−
Number of features per application	−	+	+

PRODUCT FAMILY	STAND-ALONE PACKAGES	
IBM Assistant Series:	IBM Writing Assistant	
	IBM Planning Assistant	
	IBM Graphing Assistant	
	IBM Filing Assistant	
	IBM Reporting Assistant	
IT Software:	CallIT	LinkIT
	AskIT	SortIT
	WriteIT	PassIT
	CalcIT	EditIT
	ShowIT	StatIT
	KeepIT	
Smart Software System:	Smart Word Processor	
	Smart Spreadsheet with Graphics	
	Smart Data Manager	
	Smart Communications	
	Smart Time Manager	
WordPerfect Library:	WordPerfect	
	Math Plan	
	SSI Data	

FIGURE 7-30
A sampler of stand-alone packages produced as a family of products for personal computers

Family of Products

Stand-alone packages produced as a **family of products** are another solution to integrating applications. They require swapping disks, on a floppy-disk-based system, when switching from one application to another. They do, however, provide file compatibility among applications. A word processing application, for example, can read a spreadsheet file and integrate the content into the text.

A family of products has another advantage associated with integrated packages. Only one set of commands has to be learned. They are uniformly used throughout the suite of application packages. Other advantages and disadvantages appear in the comparison in Figure 7-29. A sampler of family products is given in Figure 7-30.

DESKTOP ORGANIZER

So-called *power users*, people who are experienced personal computer users, often use a **desktop organizer** package as a sort of application and file integrator. As Figure 7-31 demonstrates, such a package can be used to replace such desktop accessories as the following:

- Notepad
- Appointment book
- Clock
- Calendar
- Calculator
- Rolodex, or index, card file
- Telephone directory and automatic dialer

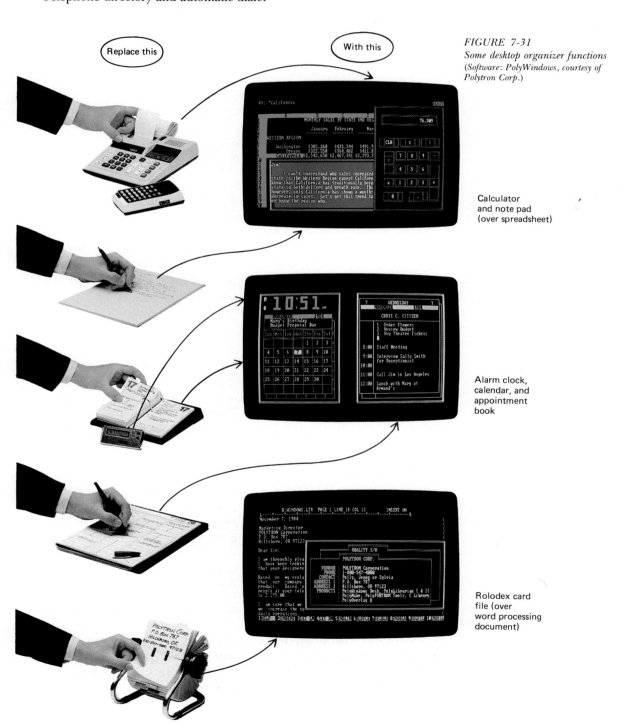

Replace this

With this

FIGURE 7-31
Some desktop organizer functions
(Software: PolyWindows, courtesy of
Polytron Corp.)

Calculator
and note pad
(over spreadsheet)

Alarm clock,
calendar, and
appointment
book

Rolodex card
file (over
word processing
document)

Calendar/1	Higgins	Personal Datebook II
Calendar Management	Homebase	Personal Secretary
Calendar Plus	HQ	PolyWindows
Daymaster	IntelPlan	Pop-Up Calendar
Desk Organizer	Lotus Metro	Pop-Up Deskset
DeskSet Plus	MicroMinder	Resident
Execu Time	Office	Shoebox
Executive Organizer	Partner PC	Sidekick
Front Desk	PC-Desk	Time Manager
Get Organized!	PC-Desk Team	

FIGURE 7-32
A sampler of desktop organizer packages for personal computers

This electronic desktop software is relatively simple to install and use. Generally it is loaded into memory first, before anything else. The software "hides" in the background while running any other application. When needed, sometimes only one keystroke can call up a function. It could be put aside as eaily without disrupting the main task. Some available packages, which are often called **memory-resident utilities,** are listed in 7-32.

Features

The **notepad** or **clipboard** feature allows a user to "cut and paste" data from one application to another. This is a feature also built into window packages and some family-type software.

Figure 7-33 shows how Lee Sharpe, who is a longtime personal computer user, incorporates data from a spreadsheet into a memo:

- Figure 7-33A shows the spreadsheet on the screen with the desktop organizer prepared to "capture" the desired information.
- Figure 7-33B shows the results of Mr. Sharpe's reentering the word processing program and calling up the desktop organizer to "paste" in the spreadsheet data.
- Figure 7-33C shows the resulting memo.

In some cases, this procedure solves the application integration problem.

Gerald Lopez, an office manager, uses another desktop organizer feature. It is the automatic telephone dialer that eliminates the need for dialing, or pressing touch-tone, phone numbers. It also includes a code feature that lets him highlight special calendar conditions. An asterisk (*), for example, codes top-priority calendar items. These items automatically appear on the calendar each day until removed.

A. Running the "clip from screen" function, the user highlights part of a spreadsheet, copies this data to a notepad module, then exits both applications.

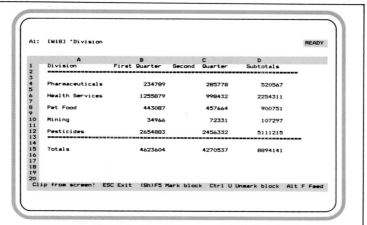

B. In the memorandum in the background, a note marks the spot where the user will insert the captured spreadsheet in the notepad module shown to the right. With a single keystroke, the user clears the notepad from the screen and pastes the captured data into the word processor.

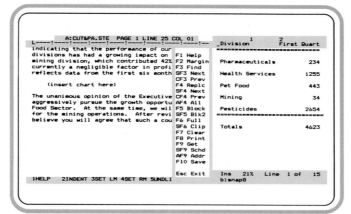

C. The final form of the memorandum, complete with spreadsheet data imported using the desktop organizer's clipboard function.

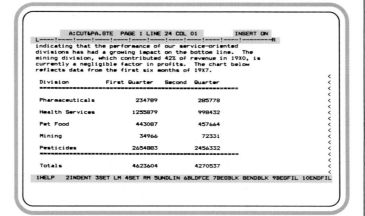

FIGURE 7-33
Using the notepad to transfer data from a spreadsheet
into a word processor
(Software: Pop-Up DesksetPlus, courtesy of National Software
Testing Laboratories, Inc.)

Sometimes in the middle of using the word processor, his telephone rings. It may be a customer who wants to meet tomorrow at 2:00 P.M. to discuss an important matter. Without leaving the personal computer, Mr. Lopez presses a few keys to replace the word processing document with a list of appointments for the next day. According to the appointment book, a 2:30 meeting is scheduled, but 1:00 P.M. is open. A new entry is typed into the appointment book. An alarm clock is also set to go off a half-hour earlier as a reminder. After hanging up, pressing a few keys restores the word processing document. The cursor is even positioned exactly where it was before the telephone rang. This scenario is standard for personal computer users of desktop organizer packages.

Some products in this category focus only on the calendar and appointment functions. One controls the schedule of up to 100 people at once and ably supports an office receptionist. With a built-in code system, it tracks everyone by activity and location.

Limitations

Major problems of such packages are that they may

- Be memory hogs
- Disrupt an otherwise working main application

Other problems may become evident in a package evaluation. As an example, one product fails to alert a user of a conflict in appointments and will book two, say three o'clock meetings. Another restricts notepad jotting to a limiting 12 lines of 65 characters each.

As this software matures, it is expected to become more flexible. It is also expected to become an inclusive part of integrated, as well as stand-alone, packages.

CASE STUDY: The Word Processing Companion

Sandi Joubert had a reason for coupling a database package with her word processing package: tired fingers. Joubert, who divides her time between secretarial duties at an architectural firm and a budding business of her own in Bozeman, Montana, says that she finds WordPerfect's mailing list format and control-key codes tough on the typist—her. And her new business, a promotion mailing service for local resorts called The Tourism Company, requires her to enter hundreds of names and addresses.

"I like WordPerfect, and I knew that it did mail-merge, but I also knew that it would probably be easier to enter everything in a database," she says.

The small conveniences of using a database, such as dBASE III, she points out, mean a lot when they're multiplied by hundreds of records. One example: dBase automatically progresses to the next field when one is filled.

Of course, the big conveniences help, too. Searching and sorting through her dBase records is "really simple," according to Joubert. She can quickly narrow her list to a hundred or so items, sort the records by zip code to get a discount on bulk mailings, and save the results as a text file for WordPerfect to convert into its own mailing list format. The form letters she then creates in WordPerfect will draw on these selected records, in the order they were sorted, and print out accordingly.

A database also enables you to create printed reports of your entered information, sorted by whatever criteria you select and arranged on paper as you see fit. A word processor often lets you print your mailing list only as it appears on the screen—no columns or tables in alphabetical order.

Can you live with a word processor's inflexible mailing list structure? For a few dozen names and addresses, certainly; but not if your list is growing into the hundreds.

(SOURCE: Christopher O'Malley, *"The Data Base Alternative,"* Personal Computing, *May 1987, p. 103.*)

DISCUSSION QUESTIONS

1. What might be limitations in a word processing package's mail-merge feature?

2. Creating personalized form letters can be a lot of work. Defend instances where you think it is worth the effort.

CHAPTER SUMMARY

- A *word processing package* provides for the automated manipulation of words.

- Word processing requires as much "upfront" work as an electronic spreadsheet does. The payoff comes, in both applications, when changes are required.

- The five phases of a word-processed document's life cycle are create, edit, format, print, and save a document.

- The *word wrap* function moves any word that crosses the right-hand margin to the next line.

- *Scrolling* moves text up and down so that desired portions appear in the display.

- *Cursor control arrow keys* move the cursor all around the current display for creating or editing text anywhere on the screen.

- *Editing* a document means to revise or correct it.

- *Function keys* are a separate part of the keyboard that perform various tasks, depending on the software used.

- *Mnemonic* commands are easily remembered keystrokes that perform built-in functions, for example, P to print a document.

- Using a *mouse* to edit a word-processed document requires moving a hand off the main keyboard to grasp the mouse device. The mouse activates a pointer that is used to make selections on a *pull-down menu.*

- *Search and replace* are the functions used to find a word or phrase in a word-processed document and replace it with another word or phrase. Replacement can occur automatically throughout a document.

- *Formatting* concerns a document's appearance on the printed page.

- *Document review packages* allow multiple reviewers to create and attach notes in an organized manner to a word-processed document.

- *Macros* permit the recording of keystrokes, both text and function or command key combinations, under one name and play them back exactly as they were recorded.

- A *spelling checker* matches words in a document with words in its dictionary for mismatches. It displays suspect words and suggested corrections.

- A *grammor* or *style checker* picks out errors a spelling checker would ignore, like selected spellings (example: cannot), archaic words, awkward usage, redundant phrases, and others.

- Creating *personalized form letters* involves setting up two files: a primary form letter file and a secondary file. They are merged in processing, which is often called a *mail-merge* application.

- When evaluating word processing applications, it is important to consider the end product desired. Other considerations are the desirability of a "what you see is what you get" display, and the speed and convenience of basic editing tasks.

· An *outline processor* helps to organize thoughts on a screen in outline form. Hierarchic outline levels can be expanded or collapsed as desired.

· *Hypertext* is an electronic system for organizing and presenting information nonsequentially.

· A *text-based data management* package allows a user to write notes marked with keywords for later search, retrieval, and organization.

· An all-in-one *integrated package* generally includes word processing, spreadsheet, graphics, database management, and communications. It provides easy movement among applications.

· Alternative approaches to integration are *window packages* and a *family* of stand-alone packages.

· Functions found in a *desktop organizer* application include appointment book, clock, calendar, calculator, index card file, and notepad.

KEY TERMS

Alternate key
Arrow keys
Block
Clipboard
Command key
Context-sensitive help
Control key
Cursor control keys
Cut and paste
Desktop organizer
Document Content Architecture (DCA)
Document header
Document review package
Editing
Family of products
Formatting
Function keys
Global
Grammar checker

Hypertext
Icons
Integrated package
Key glossary
Keystroke emulation
Macro
Mail merge
Markup copy
Memory-resident utilities
Mnemonic
Notepad
On-line help
On-line spell checking
Outline processor
Preview
Print queuing
Print spooling
Proportional spacing
Real-time spell checking
Rich Text Format (RTF)

Scrolling
Search and replace
Shift key
Spelling checker
Style checker
Style sheets
Synonym finder
Template
Text-based data managers
Thesaurus
Type-through
Undo
Widow and orphan control
Wild card
Window package
Word processing package
Word wrap
WYSIWYG

REVIEW QUESTIONS

1. Identify the five phases in a word-processed document's life cycle.

2. Describe the terms *word wrap* and *scrolling*.

3. Give examples of some things function keys do in a word processing application.

4. Give examples of mnemonic commands and their function in a word processing application.

5. Give an example of using a mouse to edit a word-processed document.

6. What is search and replace used for?

7. What is a document review package used for?

8. Give two examples of how macros can enhance word processing productivity.

9. Compare speller with grammar checker packages.

10. Diagram how to create personalized form letters with a word processing mail-merge application.

11. What are three important guidelines when evaluating word processing packages?

12. Compare outline processors with text-based data management packages.

13. What is hypertext?

14. What is an integrated package?

15. Describe alternative ways to achieve application integration.

16. What functions are typically found in desktop organizer packages?

EXERCISES

1. *Brighton Company Case.*   Assume that the Brighton Company marketing manager has asked you to research recent computer periodicals and to prepare a report on the most appropriate word processing package for general department use. All except one in the department are hunt-and-peck typists. They will need to produce
   · Company memos
   · Customer correspondence
   · Marketing reports (five pages maximum)
   Budget is no problem. The report should compare three word processing packages. Use the evaluation checklist in Figure 7-19 as a guide to desirable features. Pick one package that you think is the best for Brighton's marketing department personnel. Justify your recommendation.

2. *Brighton Company Case.*   A full evaluation of a word processing package for the Brighton Company project requires a hands-on test of the package. Assume whatever word processing package that you have access to is a candidate package. Use the document in Figure 7-1 as the test document to evaluate how well the word processing package can perform all the features illustrated. Write a report on the results of this test.

3. An acquaintance who uses word processing decides that a grammar checker will improve his prose and eliminate misspellings forever. Write a short response that you would offer to enlighten this person.

Execute the command
Specify scope
Construct a field list
Build a search condition
Build a scope condition

= Equal
<= Less Than or Equal To
< Less Than
> Greater Than
>= Greater Than or Equal
<> Not Equal To

Enter a numeric value: ⬚0

No more conditions
Combine with .AND.
Combine with .OR.

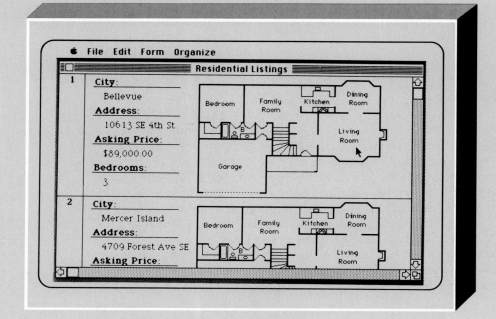

```
                              ─Current Query Context─
      list the salespeople with salary greater than average
      which of those are in california
      are there any poor performers


      Did not understand: poor performers
      Please enter a synonym or change spelling.
      R>salespeople with sales less than plan

      Do you want to make this a permanent definition? (Y/N)...............▊
```

 File Edit Form Organize

Residential Listings

1 **City:**
    Bellevue
   Address:
    10613 SE 4th St
   Asking Price:
    $89,000.00
   Bedrooms:
    3

   Bedroom   Family Room   Kitchen   Dining Room

   Living Room

   Garage

2 **City:**
    Mercer Island
   Address:
    4709 Forest Ave SE
   Asking Price:

   Bedroom   Family Room   Kitchen   Dining Room

   Living Room

Database and File Management Packages

AFTER READING THIS CHAPTER, YOU SHOULD BE ABLE TO

- Describe the steps necessary to develop a custom application using a database package

- Distinguish between a file management package and a database management system package

- Initiate a systematic evaluation of database software for personal computer use

Database software helps users to create custom applications without programming. This chapter begins with a step-by-step "walkthrough" of how a database package is used to create an application for keeping a tenant file. The file becomes the foundation of a plan to automate a small-size business that is owned by and operated by one person.

A **database** is a collection of related files, as shown in Figure 8-1. A file consists of records that hold data.

Either a file manager or database management system package could be used for the tenant application described in the first part of this chapter. Simple packages are called **file managers.** They work on one file at a time. Fancier packages are called **database management systems (DBMS).** They can work on several files at one time.

The chapter describes how the tenant file begins as a file manager application and grows into a database management system application. This process highlights features that distinguish file manager from data-

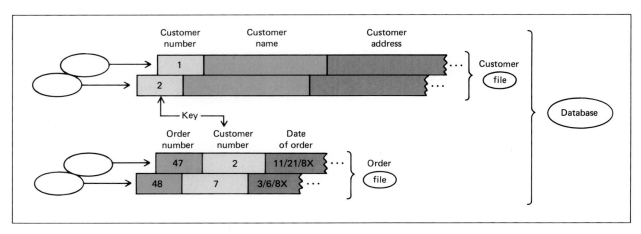

FIGURE 8-1
A collection of related files is called a database. A file consists of records.

base management system packages. The upgrade shows how applications with more than one file are designed and manipulated. It also shows an example of a DBMS program language.

One concluding section is about using natural language, or plain English, to conduct a dialogue with database software. Another section looks at microcomputer versions of mainframe packages. An evaluation section closes the chapter.

FILE MANAGERS

File managers or **file management packages** work on only one file at a time. They can be thought of as a single-file segment of a database management system package. Anyone who has ever had to make an organized list of anything would find them useful. Frank Nelson of Interstate Distributing Company uses a very simple file manager. He stores the names of contacts at companies where he buys merchandise. Denise Palmeri at National Bank uses a similar package to store lists of the bank's job titles and salary ranges. Others use file managers to store inventory lists, fund-raising lists, mailing lists, customer name and address lists, employee lists, and office equipment control lists, among many other things. Some file management packages for personal computers include those identified in Figure 8-2.

Irene Jones needed some kind of database software to store her tenant list. Ms. Jones once worked for a real estate firm. Now she manages an apartment building of her own.

Instead of a file manager package, she bought a database management system package. She felt certain her needs would outgrow a simple file manager. Nonetheless, initially she started slowly and used her database software as if it were an ordinary file manager.

FIGURE 8-2
A sampler of file management software packages for personal computers

Data Base Manager II
DB Master
Friday!
Microsoft File
Notebook
Nutshell
Perfect Filer
Q & A
Versaform

All database software, including file managers, help a user to

- Create a file
- Add records to the file
- Search the file
- Sort the file
- Produce reports

But what should go in the file?

In a popular computing magazine, Ms. Jones found a helpful article about the "Two-Step Way to a Custom Application." It suggested that a user

1. Draw a **layout,** or illustrated plan, of the report wanted

2. Use the report as a guide to set up the file

It seemed simple enough, so she decided to pursue her project the "two-step" way.

Step 1: Draw Layout

Ms. Jones wants a monthly list of tenants on a Rent Roll Report, as shown in Figure 8-3. She uses the report as a control sheet. When rent checks arrive, they are manually checked in on the Rent Roll Report.

Drawing a *report layout* of the Rent Roll Report is easy. Ms. Jones now uses something similar which is prepared by hand each month. She looks forward to transferring the report preparation and calculation chore to the computer.

Step 2: Use Report to Set Up Files

The next step requires setting up what the file will contain. The "two-step" technique uses the report content as the best guide to what should be in the file.

Following the procedure, Ms. Jones circles all the constant data contained in the report, as shown in the example in Figure 8-4. **Constant**

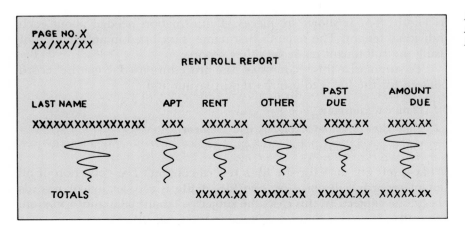

FIGURE 8-3
A rough hand-drawn layout of the Rent Roll Report

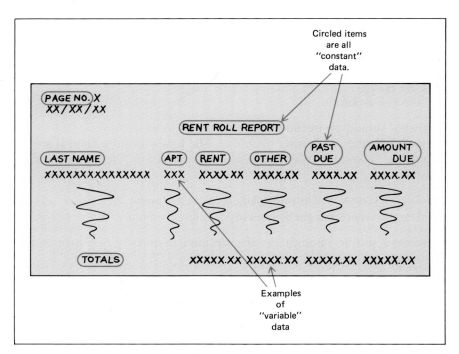

FIGURE 8-4
"Constant" data never change; "variable" data always change.

FIGURE 8-5
Content of each tenant record

Apartment number
Tenant last name
Tenant first name
Rent amount
Other charges amount
Past due amount

data, like headings, do not change from report to report. They are not included in the file. Uncircled items are variable data.

Variable data can change each time the report is run. Variable data can be split into primary and secondary data. Any variable that can be computed from other variables is considered **secondary data.** In Figure 8-4, the secondary data are totals. For example, total amount due is the number that results from adding three other primary data: rent amount, other charges amount, and past due amount.

Primary data cannot be computed. They are the usual items included in a file except for repetitious, or redundant, items. In Figure 8-4, repetitious variables are date and page number. Ms. Jones did not have to worry about these because the package generates them automatically.

After page number and date are eliminated from the primary data, what is left are data for the tenant record. Record content is identified in Figure 8-5. It shows six pieces of information needed about each individual tenant. The tenant's first name is included in anticipation of using the full tenant name on other reports.

To summarize this second step, the procedure used to get the record content for the file is to use the report layout and

1. Eliminate constants
2. Eliminate computed secondary data elements
3. Eliminate redundant data elements

What is left are data for the file's record content. The collection of all tenant **records** will make up one file. A **file** is a collection of records about one subject. In this case, the subject is tenant billing information.

This simple method suffices for many personal computer applications. More complex applications with several files require still another procedure that is described in the "Multiple Files" section.

With the report layout and file record content in place, Ms. Jones is ready to use her personal database software as a tool to create a custom application.

Create the File

Ms. Jones creates the tenant file aided by a series of screens, such as the one in Figure 8-6, that help beginners to use the package. She selects "Create" from the **menu bar** of command selections. It has the **menu pointer,** or **highlight,** over it. She just has to hit the enter, or carriage return, key to select "Create."

Any selection from the main menu bar results in the appearance of a pull-down menu of options. A second highlight appears on the pull-down menu. It is over the "Database file" option. Again Ms. Jones hits the enter key to select the option to create her database file. Then a so-called *dialogue or information box* appears with a request for the name of the file. Ms. Jones decides to call it TENANT and types the letters into the spaces provided.

A new screen, like the one in Figure 8-7, appears. It assists her entry of the tenant record. A record is divided into **fields** that are slots to hold data. To her, a "field" name is another term for the name of a column heading on the Rent Roll Report. The field names she types are restricted to ten characters each.

FIGURE 8-6
The menu pointer moves by pressing arrow keys to select a menu item on the menu bar.
(Software: dBASE III Plus, courtesy of Ashton-Tate)

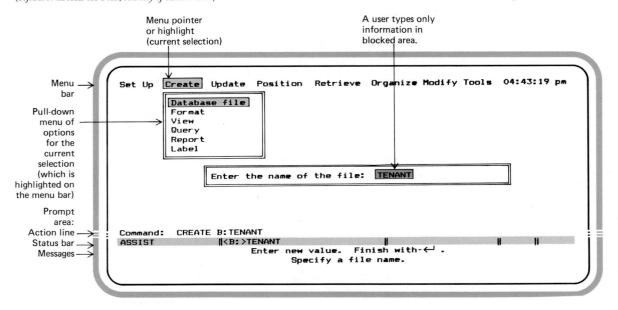

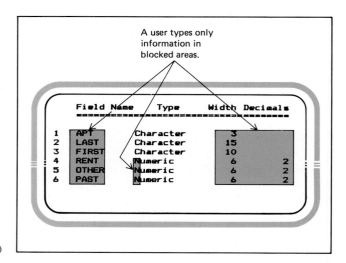

FIGURE 8-7
Setting up the TENANT record content
(Software: dBASE III Plus, courtesy of Ashton-Tate)

If a field contains character data, it is considered a "character" type. This includes data like name and zip code, because they are *not* normally used in arithmetic calculations. Hitting the enter key accepts the already filled-in phrase "Character." If a field contains numbers that will be used in arithmetic calculations, it is considered a "numeric" type. Ms. Jones types an "N" to indicate a numeric type. The rest of the word "Numeric" is automatically filled in. For all numeric fields, there is an option to enter the number of decimal positions required, if any.

Once the record fields are established, an automatic data-entry form, like the one in Figure 8-8 appears. Ms. Jones fills in the form by typing tenant billing information. This data-entry process continues as one after another tenant record is loaded into the file.

If desired, she can create a custom screen form for data entry. Compa-

FIGURE 8-8
The first record filled with data
(Software: dBASE III Plus, courtesy of Ashton-Tate)

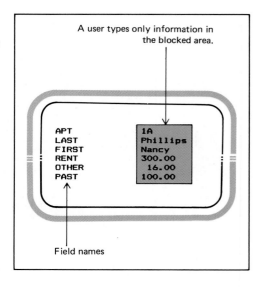

nies with many records to enter often create custom entry screens. They also hire data-entry operators to load and maintain files. Once a file is completely loaded, or built, it can be searched.

Search the File

When she wants to do a file **search** of selected records, Ms. Jones selects the "Retrieve" item from the main menu bar, as shown in Figure 8-9. Then a series of menus help her to specify the nature of the file search or retrieval. The complete set of menus for one search, of all tenants who have a past due balance, is given in Figures 8-9 and 8-10.

Hitting the enter key to select special words, like "LIST" and "PAST," slowly builds the command structure displayed on the bottom of the screen. It takes seven menus with selections to get a result.

After a while, Ms. Jones found it tiresome to view all the menus. Instead, she learned the commands from the action line on the bottom of the screen. Soon she typed the command herself as a quicker alternative method to search the file. The examples in Figure 8-11 show this alternative way to do searches. The command to do the same search is typed "LIST FOR PAST > 0." It also shows the result displayed.

Many software packages provide beginner and advanced methods of use. The **menu mode** with lots of screens is slower, but helpful, for beginners. The absence of menus is called the **command mode.** It requires that a user master the commands desired. Experienced users like the command mode to speed through all computer interaction.

FIGURE 8-9
Using a series of menus to search or retrieve all records where the
past due amount is greater than zero
(Software: dBASE III Plus, courtesy of Ashton-Tate)

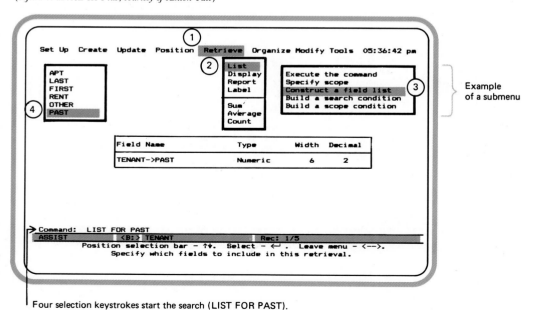

Four selection keystrokes start the search (LIST FOR PAST).

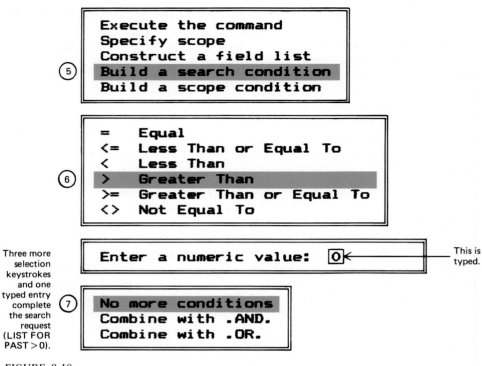

FIGURE 8-10
The remainder of the series of menus required to retrieve all records where the past due amount is greater than zero
(Software: dBASE III Plus, courtesy of Ashton-Tate)

FIGURE 8-11
Examples of searching a file
(Software: dBASE III Plus, courtesy of Ashton-Tate)

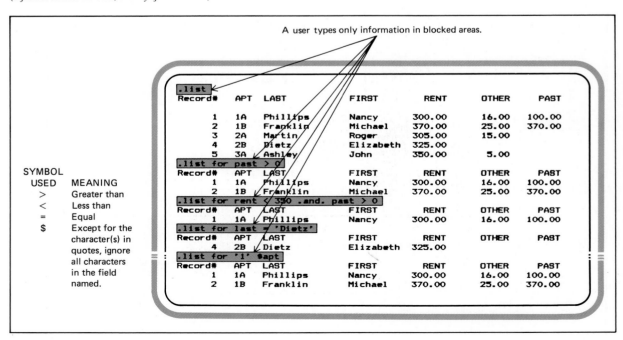

The examples in Figure 8-11 give an idea of the built-in flexibility to search a file. "Greater than" and "less than" searches are possible by entering appropriate ">" and "<" symbols.

Ms. Jones can perform a search even if only partial information is known. A "$" symbol is used to indicate that only partial information is given. This feature helps, as an example, to find the names of all tenants in first-floor apartments. By typing LIST FOR '1' $APT, she indicates that as long as '1' exists in the apartment number field, a record meets the search criterion. All other characters in the apartment number field are ignored.

Sort the File

Ms. Jones can use the **SORT** command to put records in any alphabetic or numeric order she chooses, as shown in the examples in Figure 8-12. One example is for a numeric sort by rent amount in descending

FIGURE 8-12
Examples of sorting a file
(Software: dBASE III Plus, courtesy of Ashton-Tate)

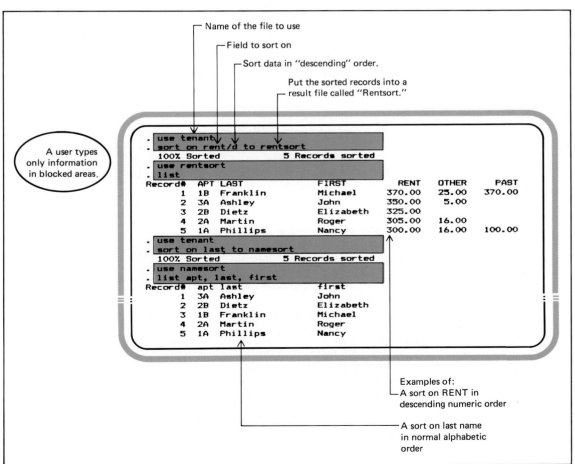

order. It requires typing the name of the field to sort on. It also requires typing the name of a new file that will hold the sorted records. When a sort is complete, a USE command activates the sorted file. Using the sort feature can quickly result in an unwieldy number of redundant files.

To speed up sorting and searching and to eliminate redundant files, database software provides for the creation of an index. An index to a file is much like an index to a book. Readers often do not read through an entire book to find a particular item. They look up the item in an index, note the page number, and turn right to it.

Database software can provide the same service. Ms. Jones indexes her tenant file on last name as shown in Figure 8-13. The *INDEX* command creates a separate **index file** containing only the last name, or key field, and the record number where the full record can be found. A **key field** is usually any important lookup item in a record. One record may have several keys. Each one can be a separate index file.

Now instead of a *SORT* on the last name, Ms. Jones gets the same result faster by using the original tenant file along with its index file. She creates other indexes on other fields. It eliminates all sorting and a lot of duplicate files.

Creating a Report

To create the Rent Roll Report shown in Figure 8-14, Ms. Jones goes back to using the menu-assist method. It is simpler than using commands to create a report. After selecting "Create" from the main

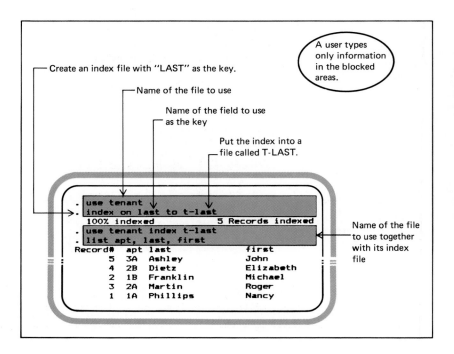

FIGURE 8-13
Indexing a file eliminates time-consuming sorts.
(Software: dBASE III Plus, courtesy of Ashton-Tate)

```
Page No.        1
05/27/8X
                        RENT ROLL REPORT

LAST NAME          APT       RENT       OTHER       PAST      AMOUNT
                                                    DUE        DUE

Phillips           1A      300.00       16.00     100.00      416.00

Franklin           1B      370.00       25.00     370.00      765.00

Martin             2A      305.00       15.00       0.00      320.00

Dietz              2B      325.00        0.00       0.00      325.00

Ashley             3A      350.00        5.00       0.00      355.00

*** Total ***
                          1650.00       61.00     470.00     2181.00
```

FIGURE 8-14
A report prepared without programming using a database package

menu bar, and "Report" from the pull-down menu, she types RENT-ROLL. RENTROLL is the name she gives to the file that will hold the report format she is about to create.

She types the report heading into the highlighted area on the next screen, as shown in Figure 8-15. Centering is automatic and is done later during actual report printing.

She next types what goes into each report column. A new screen appears to get column information, as shown in Figure 8-16. As each new column is entered, it is added to the report format and displayed below the data-entry area.

FIGURE 8-15
Creating a report without programming
(Software: dBASE III Plus, courtesy of Ashton-Tate)

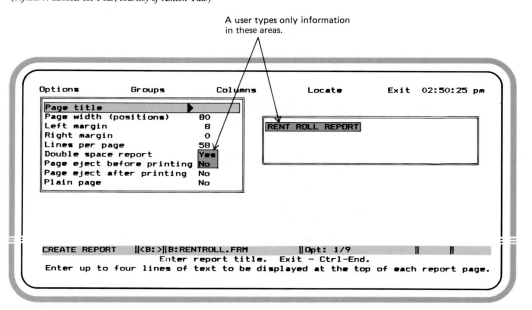

A user types only information
in these areas.

```
Options          Groups          Columns          Locate        Exit   02:50:25 pm

Page title                    ▶
Page width (positions)    80
Left margin                8                    RENT ROLL REPORT
Right margin               0
Lines per page            58
Double space report      Yes
Page eject before printing No
Page eject after printing No
Plain page                No



CREATE REPORT    ||<B:>||B:RENTROLL.FRM        ||Opt: 1/9      ||       ||
                      Enter report title.  Exit — Ctrl—End.
        Enter up to four lines of text to be displayed at the top of each report page.
```

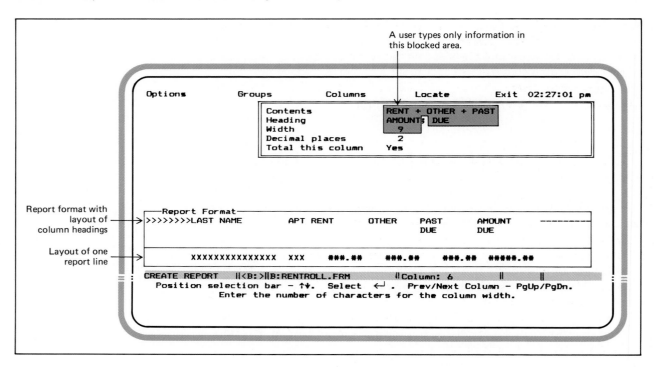

FIGURE 8-16
Last screen to create the Rent Roll Report without programming
(*Software*: *dBASE III Plus*, *courtesy of Ashton-Tate*)

It takes only a few minutes to create a report. The report format is automatically saved. It can be changed, if desired. To use it, Ms. Jones selects "Retrieve" from the main menu bar and "Report" from the pull-down menu. After identifying the format file name, RENT-ROLL, the report is printed.

Packages usually provide report options. They include automatic calculation of the average, minimum, or maximum for a column or row.

No program code had to be written to get the Rent Roll Report. It is produced with the standard **report generation** feature built into database software.

Interface with Other Applications

Ms. Jones's package provides commands to transfer files into and out of her package. She transfers database files into her word processing package. There she manipulates records as ordinary text for inclusion in correspondence.

Some users want to transfer files into their database applications. As an example, John Frazer put a simple mailing list on a word processing package. As the list grew, he wanted to sort it by state and zip code to do selective mailings. First, he transferred the word processing file into the database package. There he sorted the file as he liked. Then he transferred the resulting file back to the word processing package to create customized form letters.

By contrast, users of integrated software packages do not have to transfer files into and out of various applications.

DATABASE MANAGEMENT SYSTEM

Everything just described can be done with both file manager and database management system packages. Everything described in the following section, however, relates to the additional features found in a DBMS package, such as those listed in Figure 8-17. They mainly are

- An ability to relate several files to each other through a key field, as shown in Figure 8-18
- A built-in language to program special application requirements

The program language feature is not present in all DBMS packages. But it is not needed by all DBMS users. Both features require more skill to use. Some individuals and companies hire consultants with expertise in a special DBMS product to help them implement a custom application.

PROGRAMMABLE	NOT PROGRAMMABLE
Codor	Btrieve
dBASE III	Cornerstone
dBASE III Plus	DataFlex
DataEase	Enrich
Filevision	Formula IV
GOLDATAbase	NutShell
Informix-SQL	Palantir Filer
KnowledgeMan	PC-File
Metafile	PFS:Professional File
MDBS III	Personal Pearl
Oracle	PowerBase
PC/FOCUS	Q&A
Paradox	RapidFile
R:base	VP Info
Revelation	
SAVVY PC	

FIGURE 8-17
A sampler of database management software packages for personal computers

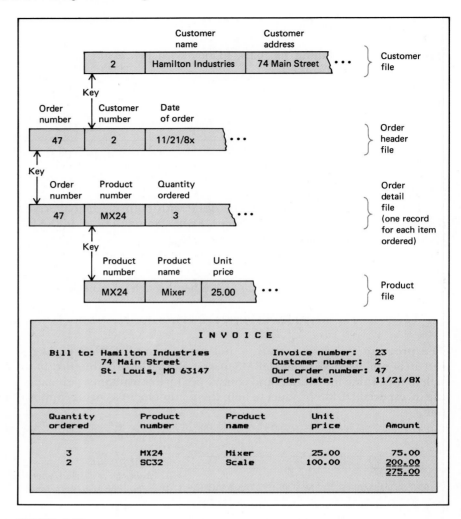

FIGURE 8-18
Using data from four linked files to create
one customer bill

Relate Files

Ms. Jones had no immediate need to relate files but expected the feature would be needed eventually. For example, if she bought a new building, she would need to relate tenants to specific buildings. If she started to itemize other charges, she would need to relate other charges to specific tenants. She also planned to maintain a separate lease file.

She visualized how her files would relate to each other by examining examples of others. One example, illustrated in Figure 8-18, shows an ordinary situation where four files are used to create one customer bill. One file relates to another in a linked chain.

DBMSs that provide for relating files are called **relational DBMS systems.** In Ms. Jones's DBMS, one of several commands used to relate

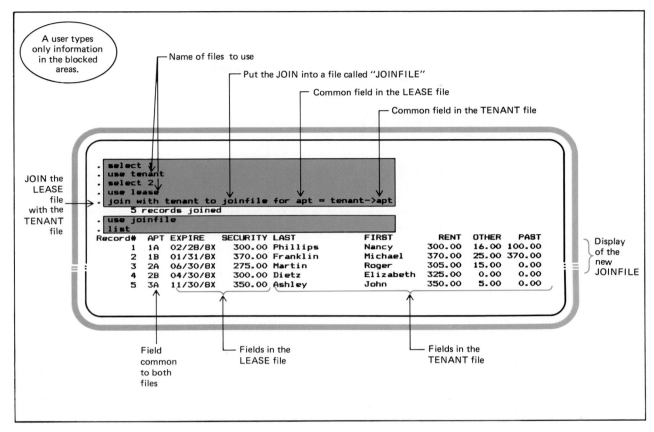

FIGURE 8-19
An example of JOINing the LEASE and TENANT files

one file to another file is JOIN. It is a common command word for the relate function. An example of joining a simple lease file with the tenant file apears in Figure 8-19. Ms. Jones decided to keep lease expiration date and security deposit amount separate from tenant monthly billing information. The lease file later grew to include the name of the future occupant (or lessee) of an apartment, new lease start date, and so on.

Different packages use different techniques to relate one file to another. One package provides a fill-in-the-blanks screen to identify relationships, as shown in Figure 8-20. Another requires setting up "zoom links." They enable instantaneous navigation among related files, as diagrammed in Figure 8-21.

Ms. Jones's package optionally relates files through the menu-assist method and through an alternative "SET RELATION" command. Both result in "views," which function like indexes to the linked files. They do not create duplicate files, as JOIN does.

Because file manipulation is so flexible with a relational DBMS, applications can start simply and grow as needed. This is not true of file manager packages, which cannot link files.

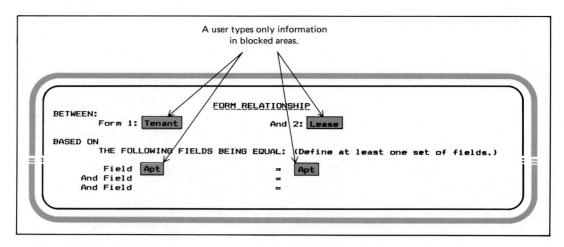

FIGURE 8-20
Using a fill-in-the-blanks screen to link two files
(*Software*: *DataEase, courtesy of Software Solutions, Inc.*)

FIGURE 8-21
Using a "zoom" function to cross-reference
database information
(*Software*: *PowerBase, courtesy of Power-base Systems, Inc.*)

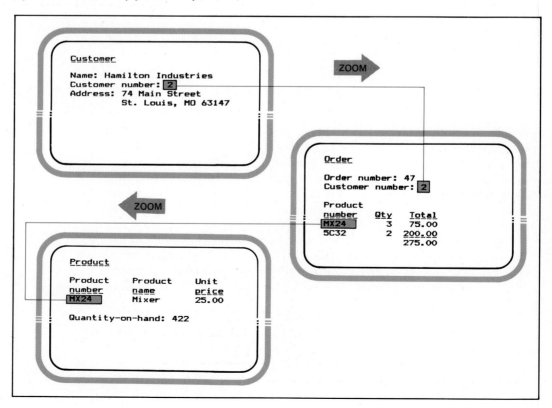

Multiple-File Design

To set up and maintain a smooth-running DBMS with several related files requires good file design. The several files used to create the invoice in Figure 8-18 are well designed. They were created by following two basic rules which are illustrated in Figure 8-22:

1. Eliminate any repeating groups of fields. Make each group a separate record.

2. Eliminate fields that do not depend entirely on the record key.

The example in Figure 8-22 shows how a bad file design is converted into a good file design. To avoid repeating fields, the order file is split into two smaller files. The split solves two rule violations. One new order detail record is equal to one row on an invoice.

Sometimes users forget to keep files organized by one subject. A good example of the "one-file, one-subject" concept appears in Figure 8-18. The three subject files there are

- Customers
- Orders (separate header and detail files)
- Products

FIGURE 8-22
Splitting one long record into two smaller records

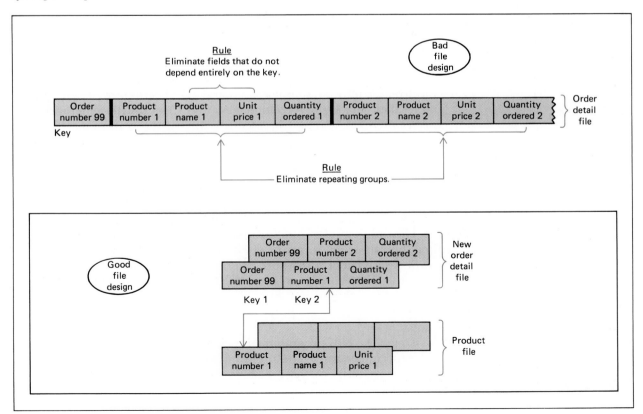

To avoid overlapped subject files, a third rule is necessary:

3. Eliminate fields that belong to another subject file.

Often following the first two rules also solves third rule violations. It does in Figure 8-22. There the repeating product data must be removed from the order detail file. It automatically resolves the inherent violation of rule 3.

The smaller files that result, from following these three rules, can easily be modified with

- Additions
- Changes
- Deletions

For example, if the unit price is wrong for product MX24, it must be changed in only one place, the product file. But if files remain poorly designed, the unit price change creates a serious problem. Every order with product MX24 would have to be located in the bad file and individually changed.

The three rules just covered are called **normalizing files.** Relational DBMS users rigorously follow them, as do professional database designers.

DBMS Program Language

A built-in DBMS programming language gives any user complete application design flexibility. The price for this flexibility is to learn how to use the programming language. DBMS program languages are often called *very-high-level languages* (VHLL), or **fourth-generation languages** (4GL). The other three generations progress from machine language, to assembler language, to ordinary *high-level languages* (HLL), like BASIC and COBOL.

Ms. Jones learned to use the DBMS program language in her package when she decided to replace her monthly hand-prepared rent bills with computerized bills. Unfortunately, the report-generation feature of her DBMS could not produce the bill she designed, as shown in Figure 8-23. The only way she could produce computerized bills was to program them herself or get someone else to do it.

She once had a BASIC programming course, which eased her learning of the DBMS program language. Almost all programmers who know a third-generation language find that DBMS program languages are easy to master. Even nonprogrammers find them manageable after some study.

To get the bills programmed took Ms. Jones a few evenings of study and experimentation. The program code she wrote appears in Figure 8-24. An example of the rent bills produced by the program appears in Figure 8-25.

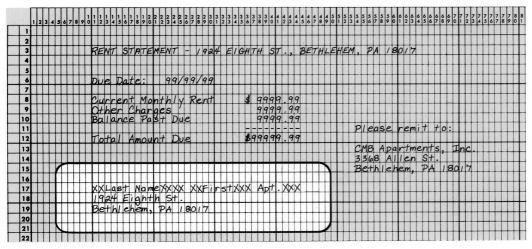

FIGURE 8-23

*Computer spacing layout chart of a rent statement designed to fit in a
window mailing envelope. One square on the grid paper matches one
printer space.*

FIGURE 8-24

The DBMS program language code used to produce the rent statement in Figure 8-25
(Software: dBASE III Plus, courtesy of Ashton-Tate)

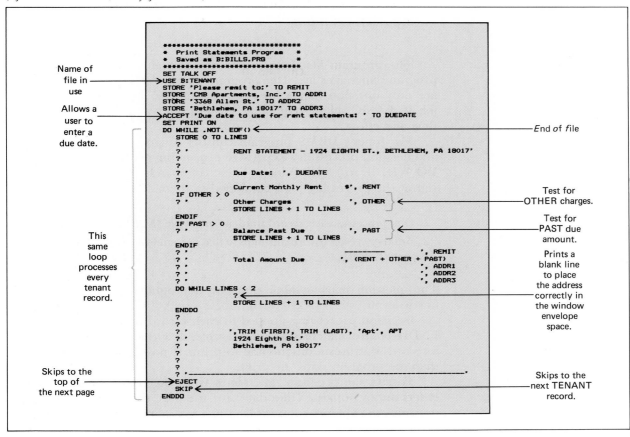

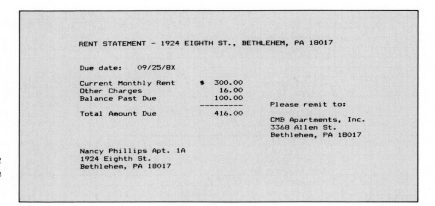

```
        RENT STATEMENT - 1924 EIGHTH ST., BETHLEHEM, PA 18017

        Due date:   09/25/8X

        Current Monthly Rent       $   300.00
        Other Charges                   16.00
        Balance Past Due               100.00
                                    ----------    Please remit to:
        Total Amount Due               416.00
                                                  CMB Apartments, Inc.
                                                  3368 Allen St.
                                                  Bethlehem, PA 18017

        Nancy Phillips Apt. 1A
        1924 Eighth St.
        Bethlehem, PA 18017
```

FIGURE 8-25
A rent statement using data from the first record in the TENANT file. The program code that had to be written by a user to print this bill appears in Figure 8-24.

Ms. Jones decided not to use preprinted forms. She planned to retain the simplicity of her hand-prepared bills while adding the convenience of using a window envelope. A window envelope lets the mailing address show through a cutout. It eliminates the need for a separate program to print mailing labels.

Program Example

The program Ms. Jones wrote demonstrates how efficient DBMS program languages are. Her program consists of 46 lines, 10 of which are only question marks, or print commands. By contrast, the same job in BASIC might require about 140 lines and a great deal more time and effort.

Ms. Jones's DBMS program consists of procedures for repetitive and decision processing. **Repetitive processing** occurs inside a so-called DO WHILE to ENDDO loop. These commands cause the program to repeat the processing logic contained in them. Two loops are needed:

1. One processes each record until an *end-of-file* (EOF) condition is reached.
2. Another creates extra blank lines so that the window envelope address placement is exact.

The question mark symbol alone on a program line causes a blank line to print.

Decision processing applied to each record is indicated by IF and ENDIF control statements. For example, if "Other Charges" appear in a record, it causes a unique line to print. If no "Other Charges" exist, then the program skips the print.

To run the program, Ms. Jones types the command DO BILLS, enters an appropriate "due date" for the bills, then waits for printing to complete. The program is saved in a file called BILLS.

PACKAGE VARIATIONS

When she shopped for database software, Ms. Jones found a variety of packages available. The types of text-based data manager packages she found are covered in Chapter 7 under "Computer-Aided Writing." But packages that offered graphics and specific data features are covered here, as are hybrid packages.

Graphics

One package that Ms. Jones looked at stored graphics as well as text in its database, as shown in Figure 8-26. A real estate agency uses this feature for its database of residential properties for sale. The graphics capability enables storing a floor plan of a property along with its description. Someone manually traces the floor plan on a digitizer tablet to get the image into the file. Sometimes the image is drawn freehand. Some packages even work with imaging software and hardware, as described in Chapter 7, to get images into a database.

The application makes a positive impact on potential customers coming into the agency to buy a home. They can view properties on the screen. Agents can, if needed, print a copy of the screen image for a client who wants to take the copy home for further study.

Another graphics-oriented package lets users link graphics with database files. A rabbit rancher uses such a package to track his animals, as evident in Figure 8-27. The ranch owner prepared the application, which consists of three files:

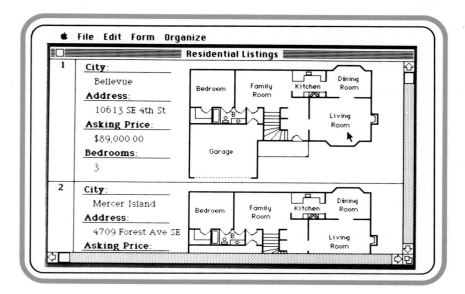

FIGURE 8-26
A real estate agency uses a file management package that stores graphics as well as text.
(Software: Microsoft File, courtesy of Microsoft Corp.)

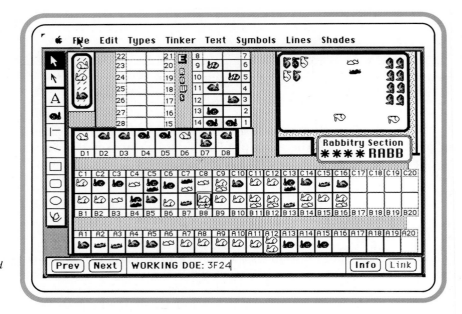

FIGURE 8-27
A rabbit rancher uses a graphics-oriented
database package to track his animals.
(*Software: Filevision, courtesy of Telos
Corporation*)

1. The architectual layout of the rabbit ranch
2. The content and status of individual rabbit hutches
3. The pedigrees of the rabbits

The rancher links all three files to enable interrogation of information at the ranch, hutch, or rabbit level of detail.

Data Features

Many database software packages allow for the creation of custom-designed forms. The process of designing a form on a blank screen is called **screen painting.** As an example, one user created the data-entry screen shown in Figure 8-28 by typing on a blank screen whatever she

FIGURE 8-28
A screen-painted form

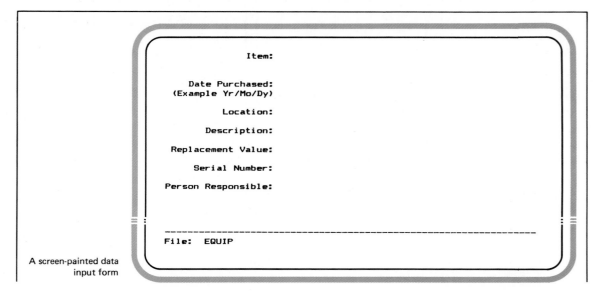

A screen-painted data
input form

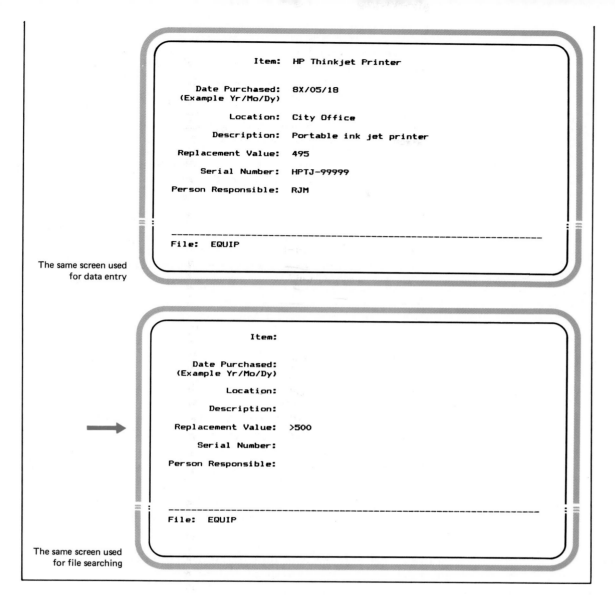

The same screen used for data entry

The same screen used for file searching

FIGURE 8-28 (*continued*)

desired. Each name followed by a colon automatically becomes a field name.

When a user wants to use the custom input screen for data entry, it is displayed with highlighted field names. The same screen is also used to search a file. Search criteria are typed into the form as shown in the same figure. The simplicity of using this particular package is offset by the fact that it is limited to manipulating one file at a time. It is a file manager. Also, the package requires an add-on package to generate reports.

Many database packages provide features to validate the accuracy of data as they are entered. Typical data-entry checks might include the following:

- This is a mandatory field; data must be entered before proceeding.
- This field must contain numeric data only.

287

- Only uppercase characters are allowed in this field.
- Data in this field must be within preset minimum and maximum numeric range limits.
- Only specific values are allowed in this field, such as CA, TX, or NY (for California, Texas, and New York).
- Data in the "part number" field of an order, as an example, cannot be accepted unless the number already exists in the parts file.
- Only a yes or no response is valid for this field.

Other packages offer an ability to expand a field's width as it is needed. For example, if an address requires an extra line or if an individual has two telephone numbers, the extra data can simply be typed. The field automatically expands to accommodate the addition.

Hybrid Packages

In the maturing database management software package area, there are a number of hybrid packages that focus on data analysis capabilities. VP Planner, as an example, looks like a spreadsheet package but creates database files that are in dBASE II or III format. The benefit is that a user has the data analysis and manipulation capability associated with a spreadsheet environment, without spreadsheet restrictions. A restriction often is that a spreadsheet can only be as large as memory. Memory may be 640 thousand characters or bytes. A database, on the other hand, is usually restricted only by the size of the disk, which may be 20 or more million characters or bytes if it is on a hard disk.

Several database files can be joined to create layered, or multidimensional, spreadsheet reports. To do this, the hybrid package requires a database specification screen to be filled out, as shown in Figure 8-29. It shows that four levels or dimensions are required. In this example, the spreadsheet report is to show totals by month, by account, by product, and by region. By contrast, some traditional spreadsheet packages may require a spiderweb of sheet linkages to do this.

Another hybrid package, such as Reflex, also looks like a spreadsheet, although it is more of a data analyzer. It offers users an ability to retrieve a cross-tabulation of data. One user of this feature is a stereo shop owner. He keeps a database of all customers, as shown in Figure 8-30. He uses the data to explore customer buying patterns in order to focus the store's marketing efforts.

One concern is how much customers spend based on the distance they travel to the store. He can specify that for the report, the *X* axis of the table is PRODUCT, the *Y* axis is DISTANCE, and the numbers in the center SUMS. The resulting report, shown in Figure 8-30, helps him to decide where to advertise and what products to emphasize in advertisements. His report can be turned into a graphic bar chart in a few seconds, if desired.

In theory, a user could transfer the database file to a statistics package to perform a cross-tabulation. The transfer may be time consuming and cumbersome. Having such a feature built right into the database software promotes data analysis in place of mere data retrieval.

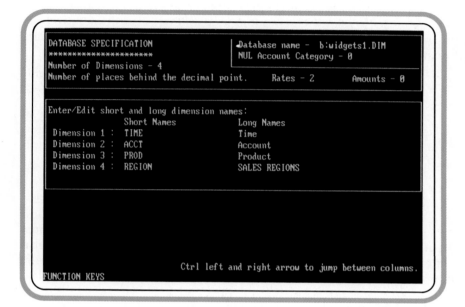

FIGURE 8-29
A specification screen for a database or spreadsheet that is to be summarized by four categories
(Software: VP Planner. VP Planner is a trademark of Paperback Software Int'l.)

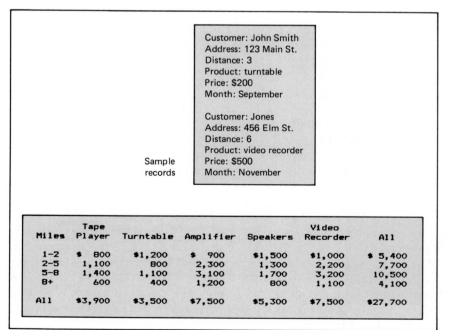

FIGURE 8-30
A "cross-tabulation" report of database records. In this application, a stereo shop owner asks how much customers spend on equipment based on the number of miles they travel to the store. The report helps the owner to focus advertising efforts.
(Software: Reflex. Copyright © 1985 by Popular Computing, Inc. Reprinted from Info-World, *1060 Marsh Rd., Menlo Park, CA 94025.)*

NATURAL LANGUAGE

In a class by itself are **natural language packages.** They are "add-on" software to some database packages and are built into others. They enable a user to ask search questions in plain English. Software products include Clout and Q&A. The second product is a combination data manager and word processing package.

These packages shield users from having to learn formal DBMS search commands. In effect, they work on the "front end" of a database package, as diagrammed in Figure 8-31.

The application shown in the figure is used by a sales manager in a large company. He imports mainframe files into his personal computer. Then he interrogates the files using the natural language accessory package with his personal database package.

Internal Dictionary

Figure 8-32 shows how simple English sentences retrieve information. The natural language package interprets a request based on an internal dictionary. One package has a built-in root dictionary of 400

FIGURE 8-31
Using plain English to make a database inquiry
(*Software*: *Clout, courtesy of MicroRim*)

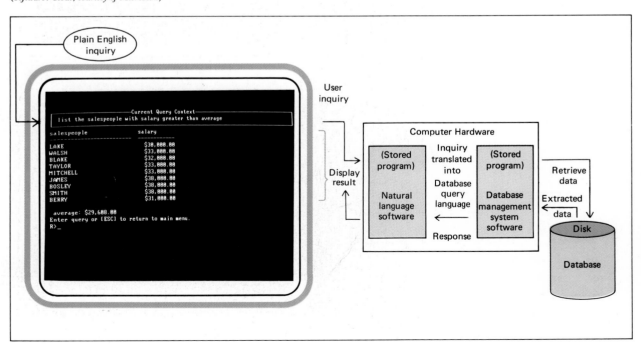

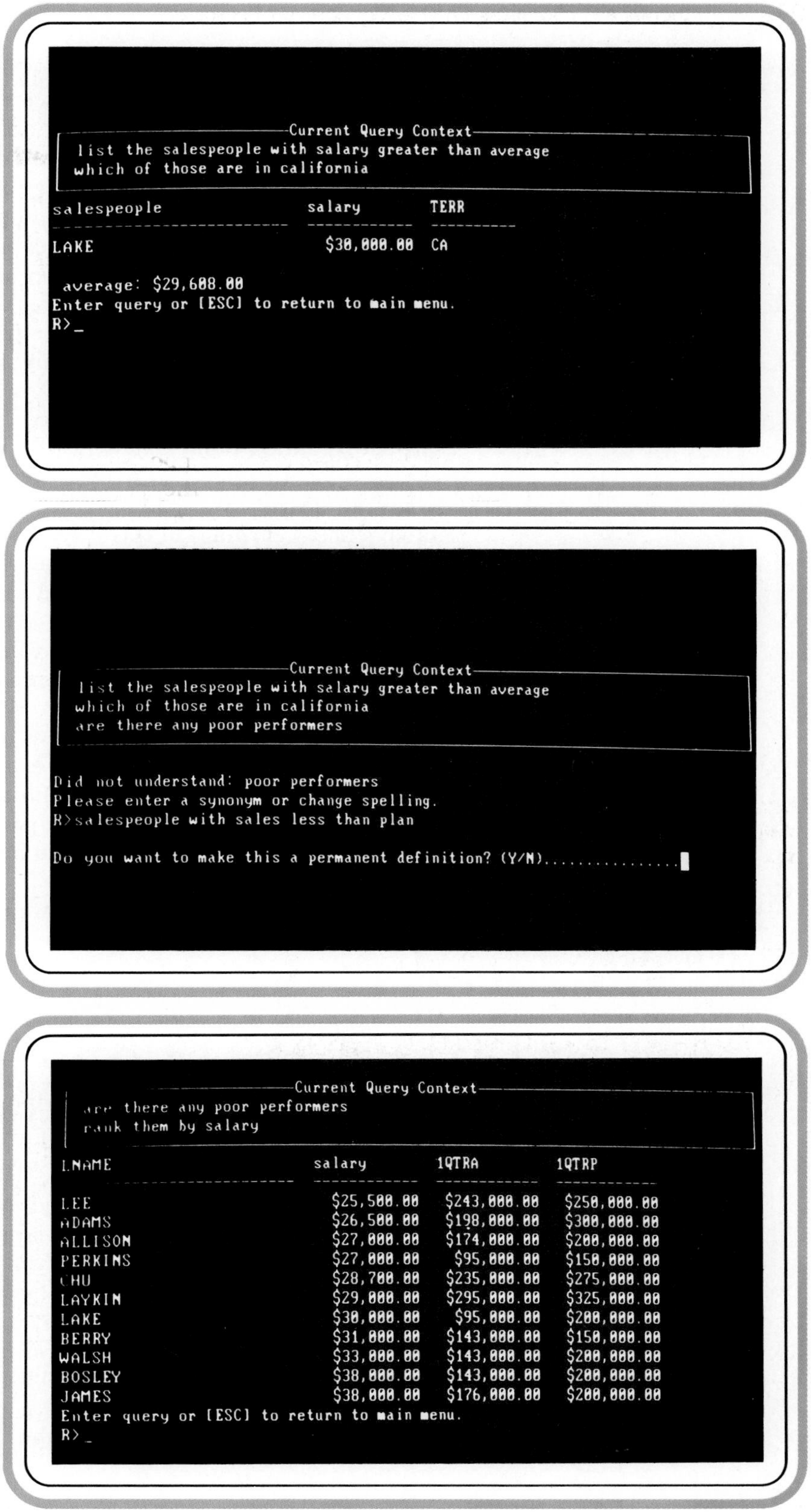

```
┌─────────────────Current Query Context─────────────────┐
│ list the salespeople with salary greater than average   │
│ which of those are in california                         │
└──────────────────────────────────────────────────────┘

salespeople              salary        TERR
───────────              ──────        ────
LAKE                     $30,000.00    CA

 average: $29,600.00
Enter query or [ESC] to return to main menu.
R>_
```

```
┌─────────────────Current Query Context─────────────────┐
│ list the salespeople with salary greater than average   │
│ which of those are in california                         │
│ are there any poor performers                            │
└──────────────────────────────────────────────────────┘

Did not understand: poor performers
Please enter a synonym or change spelling.
R>salespeople with sales less than plan

Do you want to make this a permanent definition? (Y/N)...............▌
```

```
┌─────────────────Current Query Context─────────────────┐
│ are there any poor performers                            │
│ rank them by salary                                      │
└──────────────────────────────────────────────────────┘

LNAME              salary        1QTRA          1QTRP
─────              ──────        ─────          ─────
LEE                $25,500.00    $243,000.00    $250,000.00
ADAMS              $26,500.00    $198,000.00    $300,000.00
ALLISON            $27,000.00    $174,000.00    $200,000.00
PERKINS            $27,000.00    $95,000.00     $150,000.00
CHU                $28,700.00    $235,000.00    $275,000.00
LAYKIM             $29,000.00    $295,000.00    $325,000.00
LAKE               $30,000.00    $95,000.00     $200,000.00
BERRY              $31,000.00    $143,000.00    $150,000.00
WALSH              $33,000.00    $143,000.00    $200,000.00
BOSLEY             $38,000.00    $143,000.00    $200,000.00
JAMES              $38,000.00    $176,000.00    $200,000.00
Enter query or [ESC] to return to main menu.
R> _
```

FIGURE 8-32
*Examples of plain English database
inquiries that are made possible by natural
language software*
(Software: Clout, courtesy of MicroRim)

items. A user can add more words, phrases, or even calculations and is restricted only by available disk space.

A dictionary might contain, as an example, the words "job," "occupation," "work," and "position." It can be told that they all mean the same thing when used in an inquiry. Words can also be defined as the result of computation or data manipulation. As an example, "profit" might be defined as "sales" minus "expenses." Amounts for both "sales" and "expenses" could reside in different files. The program can search in up to five files to find results to an inquiry.

Loading the dictionary is a one-time, menu-driven effort. A user must tell the program in which file and field to look to find every dictionary item.

But if a new item is encountered during an inquiry, the dictionary can be expanded immediately, as illustrated in the second example of Figure 8-32. In effect, it "learns" new information as it is used. This ability to "learn" is a characteristic of programs that display artificial intelligence. Learning, in this case, is simply the result of loading more terms to expand the internal dictionary. This is typical of many primitive programs that demonstrate artificial intelligence.

The program's main limitation is that it must be set up to respond to questions about a specific, limited field of knowledge. The dictionary for sales information is unable to answer questions, for example, about inventory status.

One advantage of the program, on the other hand, is the way it handles multilevel questions. The example in Figure 8-32 shows how each succeeding inquiry is built on those before it. This is another characterisic that makes natural language packages seem intelligent. Actually, they are programmed to assume that incomplete requests logically relate to previous requests.

It is anticipated that natural language programs will mature over time and simplify the user interface to many different types of applications.

MICROCOMPUTER VERSIONS OF MAINFRAME DBMSs

Large companies with established mainframe DBMSs are implementing microcomputer versions of their large systems. With a microcomputer version of the corporate DBMS on a user's personal computer, slices of the company's database can be downloaded from the central mainframe. At one's personal computer, the data can be manipulated and analyzed locally. No file format conversion steps are necessary, since everyone uses copies of the same DBMS.

DBMSs that function on microcomputers, as well as on minicomputers and mainframes, have advantages. They protect a user's investment because applications and data can be moved to a more powerful hardware environment. Larger hardware offers massive amounts of data storage and a multiuser capability.

Mainframe and minicomputer DBMSs downscaled for microcomputers include PC/FOCUS and Oracle among many others. Prices to implement these systems on microcomputers vary from a few hundred to a few thousand dollars per copy. Some require about three days of formal training just as they do for large computer use. The mainframe component of the link is a separate single piece of software that can cost as much as $70,000.

The trend to supply users with slices of the corporate database for their own data manipulation is helping to change the role of older corporate data processing departments. Its job is becoming more one of trustee rather than owner of the corporate database. Its job is to be sure user service requests are handled with dispatch and timely updated information. Processing has moved out of the computer center and into the local user's personal computer.

This arrangement requires that the corporate database administrator implement strong security controls. Who can get what information must be monitored. Who has the authority to update information must be extremely controlled to avoid trashing the integrity of the corporate database. These and other multiuser DBMS concerns are addressed in Chapter 11, "Communication Software and Services."

EVALUATION

Perhaps no packaged software is as difficult to evaluate as a DBMS. Perhaps none could benefit a user as much. In the end Ms. Jones concluded it was not so much finding the right package as it was not getting a limited or inappropriate one.

Limited software to her is a package without a program language or a capability to manipulate multiple files. Many file manager packages fall into this category. They usually handle only one file at a time. These packages are ideal for users with static files. All cost considerably less than a DBMS that can deal with several files at once.

Fulfilling Requirements

One thing that was very helpful to Ms. Jones when she was looking for a suitable package was to have specified her requirements. Having the following detail about her application was invaluable:

GENERAL

Can the package work with several files at once (a relational database management system package) or only one file (a file manager package)?

Is there a built-in programming language?

Is formal training required to use the package?

Can it accommodate both command and menu-driven entry styles?

Are special features provided, like graphics?

CREATE THE DATABASE

Is a data-entry form provided?

Can a custom data-entry form be designed on the screen?

Are data checks provided, like upper- and lower-range limits?

Are duplicate records allowed in a file?

Is indexing provided?

Are field types like data and dollar amounts provided?

Can a record be inserted in the middle of a file?

Can a deleted record be recalled?

DATABASE INQUIRY

Are missing character and range searches provided?

Are automatic features like count, mean, minimum, maximum, variance, and standard deviation available?

Can retrieved records be ordered by subgroups with totals both across rows and down columns?

Is a natural language package available to simplify inquiries?

GENERATE REPORTS AND FORMS

Are reports automatically formatted?

Can reports and forms be screen painted?

Can formats be saved and modified?

Are all query features enabled when generating reports and forms?

LIMITATIONS

What is the maximum number of files per database, files available at one time, character size per record, records per file, fields per record, characters per field?

What is the largest calculated number possible?

FIGURE 8-33

Database software evaluation checklist. Figure 3-25, General Software Evaluation Checklist, is necessary to complete this evaluation.

- Maximum number of files to be used
- Maximum number of records used per file
- Maximum number of fields used per record
- Maximum number of characters used per field
- Field types required:
    Character
    Numeric
    Dollar
    Date
- Largest calculated number used
- Sample of a typical report (like the Rent Roll Report)
- Sample of a typical form (like the Rent Statement)

She found that many packages had limitations in these and other areas.

To determine a package's suitability, she had to do a hands-on test. She tried to create the tenant file and to generate a Rent Roll Report and Rent Statement. The hands-on test unquestionably solves the problem of which packages are suitable. Of four she tried, only two successfully completed all tasks acceptably.

Checklist

Ms. Jones used a Database Software Evaluation Checklist, like the one in Figure 8-33, to guide a systematic approach to the evaluation process.

The hands-on portion of her evaluation helped to isolate performance, ease of use, and documentation. Performance is a critical test area, especially if large databases are planned. A file sort that takes one half-hour on one DBMS, as an example, takes minutes on another.

Every DBMS has a different approach with which a user must be comfortable over the long run. A hands-on test is the only way to uncover the potential hidden frustrations in any package. Many DBMS suppliers offer a demonstration disk at a nominal cost. The investment is well worth it if no other way exists to hands-on test a database package.

CASE STUDY: A Database Response to Tourist Inquiries

California's Monterey Peninsula draws travelers from every state and all over the world. One of the jobs of the local Chamber of Commerce is to respond to inquiries from potential visitors and supply them with information on the various attractions.

Brochure Selection Problems.   In one year, handling tourist inquiries lost the Chamber about $30,000. But in a dramatic turnaround using database software on a personal computer, the organization produced a net profit of $2,000.

Burke Pease, formerly the Chamber's executive vice president, says. "It was almost impossible to handle all the criteria for selecting which inquiries should get whose brochures." For example, a bed and breakfast inn in Carmel would want its information mailed only to those seeking overnight accommodations in that city. Inquiries relating to any other city or camping would not benefit the inn's business. Similarly, an upscale restaurant might want to specify that its brochure be mailed only to those staying in full-service hotels.

"When you have 80 or 90 subscriber businesses, each with their own criteria regarding the individuals to whom they want their brochures mailed," Pease says, "it is an untenable manual task. The Chamber couldn't offer to do it. Now we offer client businesses good value for the merchandising dollar."

The hardware used is a portable personal computer. Pease says he started out without any knowledge of computers, but was free of any phobia. Then he says, "I just started reading whatever I could get my hands on about database management systems."

False Start.   "We did try to install one database package just before the one we use now, which happens to be dBASE. We just couldn't get it to cooperate," he states. "Theoretically it was more user-friendly; it has lots of menus. The problem was, we couldn't get it to do specific functions we needed using the menus. The documentation was very difficult to work with. After a couple of months we had to scrap the software before our staff quit. The frustration level was incredible."

Inquiry Program.   Pease dove right into programming in dBASE. Working evenings and weekends, he put in an estimated 50 to 60 hours writing his first program, the response to tourist inquiries. It took about a month. "Fortunately," he says, "programs are written in a modular fashion, so you only write one little step at a time. If I had known that it was going to have 18 different modules, I'm not sure I would have done what I did. But I had fun, and there's nothing like that sense of accomplishment that comes when it works," he concludes.

The inquiry-response program, which produced the most cost savings, and has been copyrighted by Pease, matches visitors with their interests. The Chamber classifies inquiries by type, such as tourist, or convention delegate, or whatever. An alphabetic code indicates type of accommodations preferred, like full-service hotel or ocean-view lodging. Stated preferences must be compared with scheduled activities such as scuba diving, adobe tours, or winery tastings.

At the end of the day a staff person activates the program. During the night it compares request preferences with offered services. In the morning a freshly printed stack of labels, like the one shown in Figure 8-34, awaits a high school student whose part-time job it is to stuff envelopes. Across the top of each label are codes indicating which brochures are to be stuffed. Brochures are kept in cardboard bins, each labeled with a code matching the computer symbol.

FIGURE 8-34
A typical label generated by the inquiry-response program. Patrick and Jane Murphy will be getting brochures 9, 42, 43, and 61.

```
9*42*43*61

Patrick and Jane Murphy
3333 Fawn Street
Culver City, CA 90230
```

Programming Is a Drawback.   The Monterey Chamber is very satisfied with their database software and the cost saving it has made possible. Pease says the only drawback is the need to involve oneself in programming. "To really gain maximum benefit, you have to learn how to program," he explains.

Pease cautions, however, that "You've got to find an employee who takes to all this. Managers probably will not have the time to keep up with file maintenance themselves."

(SOURCE: *Helene Kane, "Tourism Made Profitable,"* Business Software, *June 1985, pp. 38–41. Adapted with permission.*)

DISCUSSION QUESTIONS

1. In addition to the inquiry-response program, what other programs do you think would help to support the Chamber's tourism job?

2. Do you think managers should also be programmers? Why?

CHAPTER SUMMARY

· A *database* is a collection of related files.

· *File managers* or *file management* packages work on only one file at a time.

· File management software helps a user to create a file, add records to it, search and sort it, and produce reports.

· Two necessary steps to create a custom application are (1) draw a layout of the report wanted and (2) use the report as a guide to set up the file.

· *Primary* data cannot be computed. They usually are included in a file. *Secondary* data can be computed from primary data. They usually are not included in a file.

· To get the record content for a file from the report layout requires eliminating constants, secondary data, and redundant data.

· A *file* is a collection of records about one subject. A collection of *records* makes up a file. A record is divided into *fields* that are slots to hold data.

· An example of a *file search* or *inquiry* is to list or display all records for tenants who have a past due balance greater than zero.

· A *sort* puts records into any alphabetic or numeric order desired.

· An *index file* speeds up sorting and searching. It contains only key fields that act as an index to full records in a main file.

· A *report generator* produces custom reports without programming.

· Two features that distinguish a *database management system* (DBMS) from a file management package are (1) an ability to relate several files to each other through a key field and (2) a built-in language to program special application requirements.

· A *relational DBMS* links files to each other through a key field. A *key field* is any important lookup item in a record.

· Three rules for designing multiple-file applications are to eliminate repeating groups of fields, fields that do not depend on the record key, and fields that belong to another subject file. These rules are called *normalizing* a file.

· *Fourth-generation language* is the name given to program languages built into DBMS packages. They are more efficient to use than third-generation languages, like COBOL or BASIC.

· Fourth-generation languages include procedures for *repetitive* (DO loops) and *decision* (IF test) processing.

· Some DBMSs provide for data checking or validating, like ensuring that data are within preset minimum and maximum limits.

- A *natural language* package enables a user to conduct a dialogue with a DBMS package using plain English.

- Some mainframe DBMS products are also available on microcomputers.

- When evaluating a DBMS package, it is helpful to have specifications like the number of files, records, and fields required, among other detail.

KEY TERMS

Command mode ~absence of menus in [software app]
Constant data item which did not change
Database Collection of related file
Database management system ~ work on many (DBMS) systems at one time
Decision processing
Dialogue or information box
Field a slot in a record.
File collect of records on one subject
File management package file manger works on one file at a time
File manager
Fourth-generation language english language.
Highlight
Index
Key field any import lookup on record
Layout

Menu bar
Menu mode
Menu pointer
Natural language package
Normalizing files
Primary data
Pull-down menu
Record
Relational DBMS
Repetitive processing
Report generation
Screen painting
Search
Secondary data a v t c b c f u v
Sort
Variable data

REVIEW QUESTIONS

1. List the things a user can do with a file management package.
2. What are two necessary steps to develop a custom application using a database package?
3. Why is a primary data element different from a secondary data element? Which one is included in a database file?
4. List the steps used to get the record content for a file from a report layout.
5. What is a field? a record? a file?
6. What is an index file?
7. Give three examples of file searches or inquiries.
8. Give an example of a file sort.
9. Give an example of how to generate a custom report without programming.

10. What features distinguish a database management system package from a file management package?
11. How does a relational DBMS link files together? Give an example.
12. What are three rules for designing a multiple-file application?
13. What is the name given to program languages that are built into DBMS packages? Explain the reason for the name.
14. List three data-entry validation checks that might be found in a DBMS package.
15. What benefits does a natural language package provide?
16. When evaluating a database package, what kind of detail is helpful?

EXERCISES

1. *CMB Apartments, Inc. Case.* Assume that Ms. Jones has asked you to research a DBMS purchase. Examine all the DBMS articles you can that appeared over the last three months. Write a report about your research. Identify two DBMSs that you would recommend evaluating further and explain why you chose the two.

2. *CMB Apartments, Inc. Case.* Selecting a DBMS package for the CMB Apartments, Inc. project requires a closer evaluation. Assume that whatever DBMS package you have access to is a candidate package. Locate a copy of the package's *User Guide* and find answers to questions on the Database Software Evaluation Checklist in Figure 8-33. Prepare a report on the results of this evaluation.

3. *Allied Industries Case.* Assume that you are the microcomputer manager for Allied Industries' home office and that it is a job responsibility to keep up to date on database and other microcomputer applications. Research recent computer periodicals for information about DBMSs that come packaged with operating systems, such as IBM's OS/2. Prepare a report of your findings.

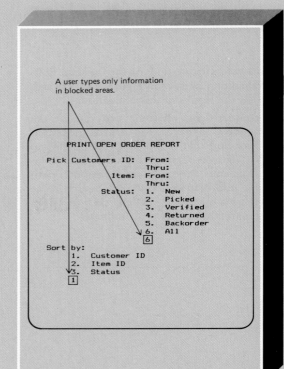

A user types only information in blocked areas.

```
PRINT OPEN ORDER REPORT
Pick Customers ID:   From:
                     Thru:
              Item:  From:
                     Thru:
            Status:  1.  New
                     2.  Picked
                     3.  Verified
                     4.  Returned
                     5.  Backorder
                     6.  All
                     6

Sort by:
      1.   Customer ID
      2.   Item ID
      3.   Status
      1
```

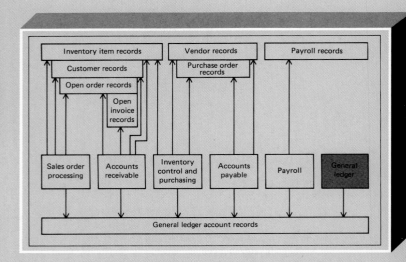

Inventory item records	Vendor records	Payroll records

Customer records

Open order records

Open invoice records

Purchase order records

Sales order processing	Accounts receivable	Inventory control and purchasing	Accounts payable	Payroll	General ledger

General ledger account records

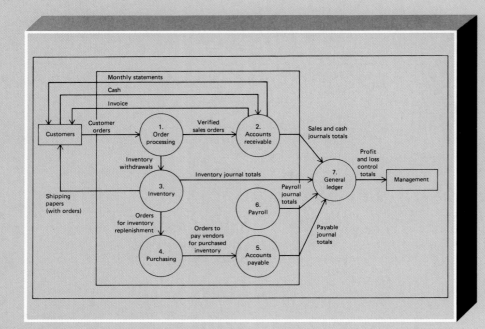

Monthly statements

Cash

Invoice

Customers — Customer orders → 1. Order processing — Verified sales orders → 2. Accounts receivable — Sales and cash journals totals →

Inventory withdrawals

3. Inventory — Inventory journal totals →

Shipping papers (with orders)

Orders for inventory replenishment

Orders to pay vendors for purchased inventory

4. Purchasing — → 5. Accounts payable

6. Payroll — Payroll journal totals →

7. General ledger — Profit and loss control totals → Management

Payable journal totals

9

Industry-Specific and Accounting Packages

AFTER READING THIS CHAPTER, YOU SHOULD BE ABLE TO

- Give an example of how an industry-specific package can be used to automate an organization
- Describe the benefits of automating routine procedures in an organization
- Identify how the general ledger application functions in an integrated accounting system package

Industry-specific and accounting packages are ready-made software to help automate an organization. These packages, listed in Figure 9-1, are usually used to

- Process volumes of raw data created by day-to-day routine tasks, such as sales order processing and accounts receivable processing
- Transform raw data into useful management information

Small- and medium-sized organizations are the primary users of these packages. Large organizations, by contrast, use custom-designed and programmed software to do similar tasks. This chapter begins with an overview of both these approaches to automating an organization. The main part of the chapter consists of "walking through" how

ACCOUNTING PACKAGES

Stand-Alone

Accounts payable
Accounts receivable
General ledger
Inventory control
Payroll
Purchasing
Sales order processing

Integrated Accounting System Packages

Combine several packages from the above list.

INDUSTRY-SPECIFIC PACKAGES

Advertising agency
Agriculture management
Church management system
Construction job costing and estimating
Distributor management
Engineering/design
Financial services
Hotel management
Insurance property and casualty agency management
Law enforcement management system
Law office management system
Licensed animal management system
Manufacturers
Medical office management system
Mortgage loan management
Personnel agency management
Property management
Restaurant management
Travel agency
Utility billing system

FIGURE 9-1
Industry-specific and accounting packages

an industry-specific package is used to automate the business routine at Interstate Distributing Company. It also considers the benefits derived from automation.

The chapter concludes with a discussion of integrated accounting packages. It focuses on the general ledger application, the main link in an integrated accounting package.

SOFTWARE TO AUTOMATE AN ORGANIZATION

The software used to automate an organization may vary depending on the size of computer used, as indicated in Figure 9-2. Small- to medium-sized organizations generally buy packaged software that works on a microcomputer or minicomputer.

This contrasts with large organizations that use mainframe computers. They generally have a large staff of computer professionals to custom design and program the software necessary to automate the organization.

FIGURE 9-2
Software that helps to automate an organization.

Goals of Automation		Software That Accomplishes the Goals	
		Mainframes	Microcomputers and Minicomputers
Process volumes of raw data Level 1	Examples of Raw Data • Orders and bills • Accounts receivable checks • Accounting transactions • Tenant bills	General Software Categories • Data processing systems • Production or operations information systems Specific Software Examples • Billing systems • Accounts receivable systems	Accounting • Stand-alone accounting packages, such as sales order processing and accounts receivable packages • Integrated accounting system packages, which combine several stand-alone accounting packages
Transform raw data into useful management information Level 2	For all the above tasks, produce: • Summary reports • Control reports • Exception reports	General Software Category • Management information systems Specific Software Examples • Marketing information systems • Personnel information systems • Customer information systems	Industry-Specific Packages such as: • Advertising agency packages • Property management packages • Hotel management packages
Make information more efficient for decision making Level 3	Provide data manipulation, inquiry, and report generation, to suit an individual's personal decision-making style	General Software Categories • Decision support systems (for modeling) • Database management systems (for inquiry and reporting)	General Software Categories • Spreadsheet, financial modeling, and other packages (for modeling) • Database management system packages (for inquiry and reporting)

FIGURE 9-3
Typical management hierarchy

Figure 9-2 shows that whatever the computer's size, the software that accomplishes the automation has similar goals:

· To process volumes of raw data
· To transform raw data into useful management information

These goals are roughly associated with the lower and middle levels of the **management hierarchy** found in most organizations, as shown in Figure 9-3.

Operational-level managers experience day-to-day burdens, such as getting out volumes of sale invoices (bills) in a timely fashion. In a small- to medium-sized organization, the package that the operational manager purchases to do the bills could be either

· A **stand-alone accounting package** (which performs one function, such as sales order processing)
· An **integrated accounting system package** (which combines several stand-alone accounting functions, such as sales order processing and accounts receivable processing)

Packages in the above general accounting categories are often called **"horizontal" packages** because they can be used by many industry types, possibly without change. Their usefulness cuts across many industrial categories.

An **industry-specific package** is often called a **"vertical" package** because it cuts one slice from the broad industrial spectrum. It is designed to be useful by one among many industries. Such packages are tailored for any one of dozens of industries, such as

· A medical patient profile and billing package
· An advertising agency package
· A property management package
· A hotel management package

By contrast, in a mainframe organization, **data processing system** is the term often used to reference the computer systems that do the routine volume processing tasks, like daily sales order processing or accounts receivable processing. These systems are usually supplemented with **management information systems** (MIS), which are designed to provide useful management-level information.

The small computer environment does not have an MIS equivalent. Any of the accounting or industry-specific packages that process routine tasks usually also generates management information. This capability is already built into the package.

The mainframe systems usually function very much like their small computer counterparts. All perform basic procedures involving

· Input
· Processing
· Output

Following these common procedures, as they are done on a microcomputer at Interstate Distributing Company, demonstrates how this software helps to automate an organization.

INDUSTRY-SPECIFIC EXAMPLE

Interstate Distributing Company bought an industry-specific package designed for distributors. The company distributes sports equipment, like bicycles and tennis racquets. The package offers all the applications identified in Figure 9-4. Individual applications are sold as stand-alone accounting packages. They can be purchased separately and linked to others as needed. Linking applications through database file integration is a characteristic of all modern computer systems.

Although Interstate's applications are sold mainly to distributors, companies from other industries buy the same software. They use it as a general-purpose integrated accounting system package.

Sales Order Processing

One of Interstate's major benefits from using packaged software is improved sales order processing. Its **sales order processing application** allows orders to be entered into the computer as soon as they are received from a customer. Each order requires only a minimal amount of typing by an order processing clerk.

The application is menu driven. From the order processing menu, shown in Figure 9-5, Cynthia Morrow, an order processing clerk, selects

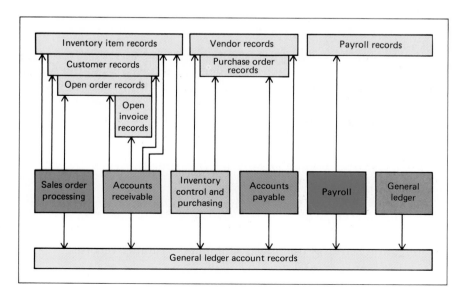

FIGURE 9-4

Application packages share database files in integrated accounting and industry-specific computer systems.

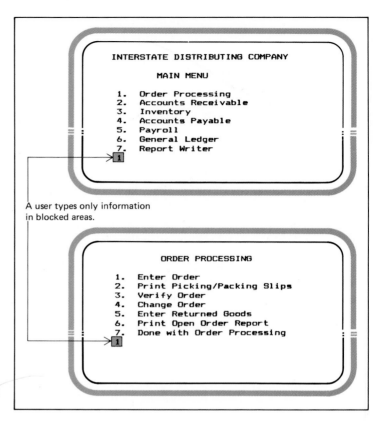

INTERSTATE DISTRIBUTING COMPANY

MAIN MENU

1. Order Processing
2. Accounts Receivable
3. Inventory
4. Accounts Payable
5. Payroll
6. General Ledger
7. Report Writer

A user types only information
in blocked areas.

ORDER PROCESSING

1. Enter Order
2. Print Picking/Packing Slips
3. Verify Order
4. Change Order
5. Enter Returned Goods
6. Print Open Order Report
7. Done with Order Processing

FIGURE 9-5
The main and second-level menus in a
sales order processing application

the option to enter an order. Another menu selection tells the computer
if the order is a

1. New order

2. Shipped order

3. Cash order

She selects number 1 to enter the order just received from the Sports
Unlimited Company. It produces the screen shown in Figure 9-6.

Order Header

The display in Figure 9-6 is known as the **order header** data-entry
screen. It accepts all order data except lines of item detail. The detail
is held for a second screen.

As Figure 9-6 indicates, a minimum amount of order header data
needs entering. Many of the data that automatically fill in on the form
come from the customer record in the database. The entry of SPRTSU
identifies and retrieves the Sports Unlimited customer record.

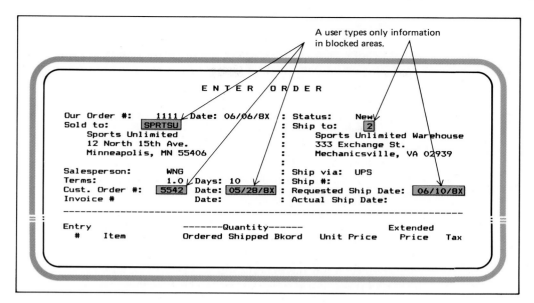

FIGURE 9-6
A data-entry screen to enter order header information

The customer database record automatically supplies the following data:

- "Sold to" name and address
- Salesperson identifier
- Terms of sale

A numeric entry identifies which one of a possible 99 ship-to addresses is used for this order. Ship-to name and address are retrieved from a separate ship-to address file in the company database.

Data unique to the order that needs typing are

- Customer order number and date
- Requested ship date

Since this is a new order, other items are not yet applicable.

The order entry date is automatic. It fills in with the date generated by the computer as today's date. The order number is also computer generated, as is the next sequential new order number.

An override of any displayed data is possible. For example, assume that this order is for "NET 30," which means that the full amount is due in 30 days after billing. Ms. Morrow can enter these "terms" as a so-called **override** to the one displayed. The "terms" displayed show a 1 percent discount if the bill is paid within ten days.

Line Items

After header data are completed, Ms. Morrow enters the **line items** which are the actual items ordered. She uses the screen shown in Figure 9-7. Each line item is automatically given an entry number. Generally, all Ms. Morrow enters are item number and quantity ordered. Data such as description and unit price are pulled from the database inventory item record and automatically displayed. Extended price is automatically calculated and displayed.

If a customer tax code exists in the customer's database record, tax is automatically calculated. Several other automatic procedures occur, among them:

- A check is made to determine item availability. If available, sufficient quantity is put in reserve for this order.
- A check is made that the order does not exceed the customer's credit limit.
- A dual-function **picking/packing slip** is printed. The warehouse uses it to gather, or *pick* items, as well as to *pack* and ship them.
- An **invoice,** or bill, as shown in Figure 9-8, is printed after the items are shipped.
- A **customer statement,** which lists all invoices, is printed once a month for mailing to customers.

FIGURE 9-7
A data-entry screen to enter, verify, or change order line items

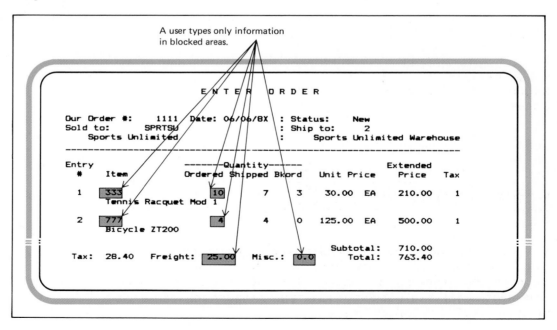

IDC

INTERSTATE
Distributing Company
9841 Cavell Ave.
Bloomington, MN 55403

INVOICE
No. 2222

INVOICE
No. 2222

Sports Unlimited

SOLD TO
Sports Unlimited
12 North 15th Ave.
Minneapolis, MN 55406

SHIP TO
Sports Unlimited Warehouse
333 Exchange St.
Mechanicsville, VA 02939

INVOICE DATE	INVOICE NO.
06/06/8X	2222

DATE	SALESP.	ORDER NO.	ORDER DATE	SHIPPED VIA	TERMS	INVOICE NO.
06/08/8X	WNG	1111		UPS	1.0%/ 10	2222

ORDERED	QUANTITY SHIPPED	BACKORDERED	ITEM NUMBER	DESCRIPTION	UNIT	UNIT PRICE	AMOUNT
10	7	3	333	Tennis Racquet Mod 1	EA	30.00	210.00
4	4	0	777	Bicycle ZT200	EA	125.00	500.00

IDC

PLEASE RETURN
THIS PORTION
OF THE INVOICE
WITH YOUR
PAYMENT.

NON-TAXABLE	TAXABLE	SALES TAX	FREIGHT	MISCELLANEOUS	INVOICE TOTAL	
.00	710.00	28.40	25.00	.00		763.40

INVOICE TOTAL
763.40

FIGURE 9-8
A computer-generated invoice using a
preprinted form

OPERATIONAL BENEFITS

Many operational-level benefits follow from these streamlined procedures. For example, data-entry clerks do not have to waste time on customer credit checking. The computer does it automatically. Customer complaints about calculation errors are virtually eliminated because the computer does all the calculations.

In addition, very little human effort is involved in the automated production of

- Picking/packing slips
- Invoices
- Customer statements

They are by-products of entering the original order. Once order data are entered, they are reused to generate all required follow-up documents. All that is required to get any of these documents is to make a menu selection.

Overall, Interstate estimates that order processing productivity has improved about 50 percent over manual methods. Such increased efficiency is measurable throughout all of its newly automated production functions.

MANAGEMENT INFORMATION BENEFITS

As a marketing manager, Frank Nelson often questions reasons for order shipping delays. The **Open Order Report,** shown in Figure 9-9, provides answers about which customers have unshipped orders. It also shows exactly what items are causing the backorder problem. The report is especially valuable

- To help avoid potential problems with customers
- To spot negative trends that may need reversing

Because all of Interstate's applications are designed to provide management information, many report variations are possible. As an example, the Open Order Report can be based on one or more of the following criteria:

FIGURE 9-9
A daily report of upshipped orders by customer account

		CUST	------DATE------			-----DESCRIPTION-----		QTY	------QUANTITY/DOLLAR------		
ORDER	STATUS	ID	ORDER	REQ'D	SHIP	ITEM NO.	PRICE	AVAIL	ORDERED	SHIPPED	BACKORDER
214	PICKED	ABLE	05/24			Ski-Rosner 190		510	8	0	0
						420	200.00		1600.00	0	.00
1114	BKORD	ABLE	06/06	06/15		Ski-Water Adult		2	10	0	10
						666	50.00		500.00	0	500.00
						------TOTAL------			2100.00	0	500.00
1111	BKORD	SPRTSU	06/06	06/10	06/08	Tennis Racquet Mod 1		0	10	7	3
						333	30.00		300.00	210.00	90.00
						------TOTAL------			300.00	210.00	90.00

06/08/8X   Interstate Distributing Company   Page 1
                        OPEN ORDER REPORT

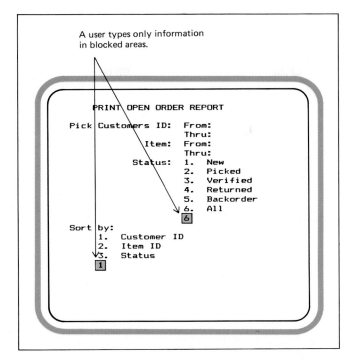

FIGURE 9-10
A completed menu of options to print the
Open Order Report in Figure 9-9

- A select group of customers
- A select item or group of items
- An order status, including new, picked, verified, returned, backordered, or all categories

In addition, the report can be sorted in various ways, as the menu in Figure 9-10 implies. Reports can also be displayed instead of printed. Most are available on a regularly scheduled, or on an "on-demand," basis.

Mr. Nelson also finds a **Sales History Report** valuable. The report can be printed in summary form, as shown in Figure 9-11, or with line item detail for selected dates, up to one year. With this report he can analyze how his marketing strategies are doing. He often sorts the report

- By item number: to identify products that are the most and least profitable. On examining this report, he asks, "Are sales efforts directed toward the most profitable products?"
- By product category: to identify groups of products that are the most and least profitable lines for the company to carry.
- By customer: to identify which customers are the most profitable. Using this summary he asks, "Does the sales staff presently spend the most time with these customers?"
- By salesperson: to identify which salespeople are the most profitable. The report answers the question, "Are the leading salespeople also the most profitable?"

```
06/08/8X                 Interstate Distributing Company              Page    1
                   S A L E S   H I S T O R Y  -  S U M M A R Y


-------------CUSTOMER-------------
     ID            NAME            COST         SALES        PROFIT        %


ABLE          Able Active Sports   26,120.25    37,252.80    11,132.55   29.9

SPRTSU        Sports Unlimited      3,805.21     5,535.40     1,729.83   31.3


         G R A N D   T O T A L S   29,925.46    42,788.20    12,862.38   30.1
```

FIGURE 9-11
An on-demand Sales History Report that
identifies profit by customer

Exception Reports

At Interstate Distributing Company, managers practice **management by exception.** The approach advocates spending time on exceptional conditions and not wasting valuable time on things that are performing as expected. To help support this style of management, Mr. Nelson prefers **exception reports.** They list only the special, or exceptional, cases that require management attention or action. As an example, he usually identifies only the most and least successful people on a salesperson report. While the most successful might be rewarded with incentives, the least successful might be scheduled for more training or other action.

The consequences of these sales reports are considerable. Mr. Nelson and other managers adjust the company's marketing strategies based on answers the reports provide.

The higher up the management hierarchy a manager moves, the less detail ordinarily appears on reports. Instead, reports become focused on the so-called "big picture." Management of the day-to-day operations is left to lower-level staff people.

A final example of a company report, with exception information on it, appears in Figure 9-12. It is the **Aged Trial Balance,** and it is critical to the company's financial officer. The report lists customer balances according to how old the balance is since the billing date.

It is used to see who owes money and who is paying late. It generates corrective action that includes everything from a gentle phone reminder for payment to placing a bad debt with a credit service for collection.

In addition to prepared reports, Interstate's software provides an inquiry and report-generation capability. It is similar to the same capabilities described in Chapter 8, "Database and File Management Packages."

While the software Interstate uses to run its business is not perfect, it provides relevant and timely information that the company never had before. It has enabled Interstate to make decisions that have reduced

```
06/30/8X                    Interstate Distributing Company                    Page   1
                A G E D   T R I A L   B A L A N C E  -  S U M M A R Y

     -----------CUSTOMER----------              --------------------AGED BALANCE--------------------
     ID           NAME          AMOUNT    CURRENT    OVER 30    OVER 60    OVER 90    OVER 120

    ABLE     Able Active Sports   5400.11      .00        .00    5400.11       .00        .00

    SPRTSU   Sports Unlimited      963.40    763.40    200.00        .00       .00        .00

        G R A N D   T O T A L S   6363.51    763.40    200.00    5400.11       .00        .00
```

FIGURE 9-12
An on-demand summary version of the Aged Trial Balance

both customer bad debts and inventory costs. These decisions alone
have more than paid for the investment in computer hardware and
software.

INTEGRATED ACCOUNTING

    The software that Interstate bought to automate its business is sold
primarily to companies in the distribution industry. Distributors usually
implement all integrated accounting functions, as diagrammed in Figure
9-13.

FIGURE 9-13
Overview of information flow in an integrated accounting system. The shaded areas are the applications at the core of every accounting system.

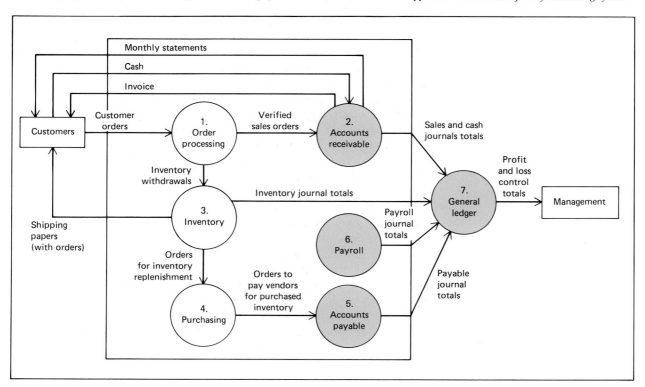

Many companies from other industries buy some of the same packages. Usually only the following four packages interest these other nondistributor companies:

- General ledger
- Accounts receivable
- Accounts payable
- Payroll

These packages are considered the core of every accounting system. They are generic functions that are useful across industry type. Some software developers sell them as "horizontal," cross-industry, packages even though they may have been designed to flesh out an industry-specific, or "vertical," package. A sampler of integrated accounting packages and suppliers is given in Figure 9-14.

FIGURE 9-14
A sampler of integrated accounting packages

PACKAGE	SUPPLIER
Accounting Software Library	SBT Corporation
Accounting-2 Series	Cougar Mountain Software
Accountmate	Sourcemate Information Systems
APPGEN Applications Environment	Software Express
Balance	Royal American Technologies
Cascade MVP	Cascade Software Inc.
DAC-Easy Accounting	DAC Software, Inc.
EasyBusiness Series	Computer Associates
Enterprise System	BPI Systems Inc.
General Business System	CYMA McGraw-Hill
Great Plains	Great Plains Software
IBM Business Adviser	IBM Corporation
LIBRA Accounting Systems	LIBRA Programming Inc.
MAS90	State of the Art
MBA	Micro Business Application
Mica Accounting Series	Micro Associates, Inc.
Net Profit	The Software Link
New Views	Q. W. Page Associates
Open Systems Harmony	Open Systems
Peachtree Complete Business Accounting System	Peachtree Software
RealWorld Accounting Version 3.1	RealWorld Corporation
RM/COBOL Accounting Package	MCBA
SAMM	Eastman Microsystems
Solomon III	TLB, Inc.
TCS	TCS Software

GENERAL LEDGER

Figure 9-13 shows that the **general ledger application** is the heart of an integrated accounting package. It is responsible for producing a company's two important financial reports, the balance sheet and the income statement. As the abbreviated samples in Figure 9-15 indicate, these documents contain summary totals of all business activity. Other applications feed summary totals to the general ledger file, as shown in Figure 9-4.

Because totals are automatically updated as transactions occur, Interstate's financial statements are always up to date and available on demand. A menu selection retrieves the document desired. Without automation, Interstate depended on professional accounting assistance to prepare financial statements once a month by hand.

```
1/31/8X
          S A M P L E   B A L A N C E   S H E E T
ACCT.
 NO.                                           AMOUNT
                 Assets
1000             Cash                          $   500
1010             Accounts Receivable             1,000
1500             Equipment                        2,000
1510             Less Depreciation              ___500
                 Total Assets                   _3,000

                 Liabilities
2000             Accounts Payable                  750
2500             Bank Loan                      ___800
                 Total Liabilities              _1,550

                 Equity
3000             Stock                            1,000
                 Net Income                     ___450
                 Total Equity                   _1,450


                 Total Liab & Equity            _3,000
```

FIGURE 9-15
Abbreviated samples of the balance sheet and income statement produced by general ledger applications

```
1/31/8X
          S A M P L E   I N C O M E   S T A T E M E N T
ACCT.                ___CURRENT MONTH___    ____YEAR TO DATE____
 NO.    DESCRIPTION   AMOUNT   % OF SALES    AMOUNT   % OF SALES

4000    Sales        $10,000     100        $10,000     100
5000    Cost of Sales __7,000     70         __7,000     70
        Gross Income  __3,000     30         __3,000     30

        Expenses
6000    Salaries     $ 1,500     15         $ 1,500     15
6010    Rent             750      8             750      8
6020    Depreciation  ___300      3          ___300      3
        Total Expenses __2,550    26         __2,500     26

        Net Income       450      5             450      5
```

The **balance sheet** is a snapshot view of a company at a fixed moment in time. It shows the net position of the company's assets and liabilities. When Interstate negotiates capital loans from a bank, the balance sheet is examined by bank officers. It lets them see at a glance what financial shape the company is in.

The **income statement,** on the other hand, is a more dynamic document. It shows Interstate's income and expenses over a period of time. It is a record of the company's performance during the period covered by the report. Changes in this document trigger management policy changes that reinforce positive trends and try to reverse negative ones.

Chart of Accounts

In order for the general ledger application to produce the balance sheet and income statement, Interstate had to set up a **chart of accounts.** This procedure assigns numbers to account names. The account number system that Interstate uses is apparent from Figure 9-15. It follows a commonly accepted numbering practice:

Account Number Range	Account Type
1000-1499	Current assets
1500-1999	Fixed assets
2000-2499	Current liabilities
2500-2999	Long-term liabilities
3000-3999	Equity
4000-4499	Sales and other income
4500-4999	Sales returns and allowances
5000-5999	Costs of sales
6000-6999	Expenses

All general ledger accounts are named as desired. For accounts that have no automatic entries from other applications, a separate program is provided for manual posting.

Interstate had to tell the application, during an initial setup procedure, how many accounting and history totals to carry for each account. Often totals are retained one or two years for comparative reporting.

DATABASE AND SPREADSHEET VERSIONS

Some accounting software is written to run on top of popular database management system (DBMS) or spreadsheet packages. In other words, a user who buys the accounting software may also have to buy a specific

DBMS or spreadsheet package. The following are example accounting packages:

Accounting Package	Also Requires This Package
Accountmate	dBASE database management system
GNP Development CPA+	Lotus 1-2-3 spreadsheet

Such accounting packages have all the advantages and disadvantages of their foundation package. In the case of one DBMS accounting package, for example, a user has a timesaving window feature to handle interruptions. To illustrate this advantage, an example of how interruptions are now handled is helpful. Suppose a sales manager brings a new customer's order that needs to ship in one hour. A new customer's record is usually set up with the accounts receivable application. This may require closing down the sales order entry application, which is in progress, in order to bring up the accounts receivable application so that the new customer record can be established. The new record is necessary before it is possible to use it to enter an order.

Once the new customer record is established, the accounts receivable application is closed down. Then the sales order processing application is started up again and the new customer's order is finally entered. This process is time consuming and frustrating to anyone doing the processing.

By contrast, with a well-designed **DBMS accounting package,** a window could be opened on the screen at any time while using the sales order processing application. It would allow the new customer master record to be established instantly. Once the new record is created, the window could be closed with a few keystrokes. The new record could then be used to process the new order. This simpler procedure is being implemented in many newer accounting packages.

Another advantage is that a user can easily modify a DBMS accounting package. Many freelance programmers know how to program in popular DBMS programming languages to serve such a need.

On the other hand, there are disadvantages also. For example, a DBMS accounting package may process transactions more slowly than other alternatives. To make the software run faster might require a user to give up access to all program code. Technically this means giving up access to the readable "source code" in order to obtain an unreadable, but faster, "object code" version of the program. The faster version is also called a "compiled" version. The problem is that if a program modification is required, a user cannot do it without access to the program "source code."

Accounting packages based on spreadsheet software tend to be less flexible for routine processing than other alternatives. They have the advantage that many programmers know the popular spreadsheet macro programming languages and could easily make custom modifications to the software, if required.

CASE STUDY: On Switching Accounting Systems

Sherry Knight, a Certified Public Accountant (CPA), spends most of her time helping companies implement micro-based accounting systems. Knight describes a conversion that helps to show how they work.

Moving Down to an Upgrade.   One firm was using an IBM System 34 minicomputer and paying IBM $6,000 year rent on General Ledger and Accounts Payable modules. When the company inquired about adding Accounts Receivable, it turned out that would cost another $6,000. Instead, the company turned to Knight for help and got a CYMA system for $2,500 outright for General Ledger, Accounts Receivable, and Accounts Payable. The consulting fees came to about $5,000.

Knight's firm did the training and wrote documentation specific to that company's needs. It also trained the company's accountant, who was new to such work. Knight went in about a month before the actual conversion started and designed the new chart of accounts.

The old chart of accounts had a single code for sales. Knight divided this to be able to report on sales by product types. Similarly, the personnel expense code was expanded to include different wage categories such as commission sales, clerical hourly wages, and fixed professional salaries.

After designing the new chart of accounts, Knight prepared a conversion chart for the data-entry people to use in transferring everything to the new chart of accounts.

The data had to be re-entered by hand. This meant entering vendor and customer names and addresses (about 700) for Accounts Receivable and Accounts Payable files, and putting the balance forwards into both of these. The company has a 600- to 700-per-month transaction volume, with about 4 million in sales per year. It took an experienced clerk in the data-entry department about 2.5 hours per module to enter these data.

Conversion.   Knight said that the biggest problem on the project was the fact that company personnel had trouble keeping to the time commitments needed to convert over expeditiously. She says this happens frequently.

She also says little things can create significant delays. For instance, supplies will be missing, such as forms for invoices and checks, which must be ordered well in advance of bringing the new system up. And forms will frequently differ from those used with the old system.

Knight and other experts agree that the mistake most paid lip service to and least observed in practice, however, is simply not following instruction procedures correctly.

(*SOURCE: Lee Thé, "On Switching Accounting Systems: Why, When, How," Business Software, February 1987, pp. 60–66. Adapted with permission.*)

DISCUSSION QUESTIONS

1. Describe how an accountant can help a company to automate its business.

2. What steps would you suggest that a company take, when switching from a manual accounting system to a computerized one, to be sure it goes smoothly?

CHAPTER SUMMARY

- Small- to medium-sized organizations generally use industry-specific and accounting packages, which work on a microcomputer or minicomputer, to automate their business.

- The goals of all software that accomplishes automation in an organization are: to process volumes of raw data and to transfer raw data into useful management information.

- In most organizations, the *management hierarchy* consists of three levels: operational (lowest), tactical (middle), and strategic (upper).

- A *stand-alone accounting package* performs one function, such as sales order or accounts receivable processing.

- An *integrated accounting system package* combines several stand-alone accounting functions.

- An *industry-specific package* is tailored to automate procedures in one type of industry. Examples of packages are: travel agency package, advertising package, and property management package.

- A *horizontal package* is a general accounting package that can be used by many industry types, possibly without change. It contrasts with a *vertical package* which is designed to be useful by one among many industries.

- *Data processing systems* automate routine day-to-day jobs in mainframe organizations.

- *Management information systems* (*MIS*) produce information to help managers make business decisions in large mainframe organizations. They are usually built on a strong data processing system foundation.

- In a *sales order processing application*, the *order header* screen accepts entry of "sold to" and "ship to" information. Most information is automatically filled in from stored database information.

- The *line item* screen accepts the detailed entry, such as item number and quantity, for each actual item ordered. Almost everything else in a line item entry is automatically filled in from stored database information.

- The benefits of automated sales order entry procedures include automatic checks for item availability and customer credit limit, automatic calculations, and the effortless production of picking/packing slips, invoices, and monthly customer statements.

- A *Sales History Report* is an example of a management information report. It can be produced many ways, such as by item number to identify the most and least profitable items, or by customer to identify which customers contribute the most to profits. Managers adjust a company's marketing strategies based on the answers to such reports.

- An *exception report* lists only special, or exceptional, cases that require management attention or action. An example is a Salesperson Report of only the most and least successful salespeople in a company. Good salespeople might be rewarded with bonuses and poor salespeople might be given additional training.

- The core applications of every accounting system are general ledger, accounts receivable, accounts payable, and payroll applications.

- The *general ledger application* is the heart of an integrated accounting package because it produces an organization's two important financial reports, the *balance sheet* and the *income statement*.

- A *DBMS accounting package* is one that is built on top of a popular database management system (DBMS) package. A user may be required to buy the DBMS package as well as the accounting package.

KEY TERMS

Aged Trial Balance
Balance sheet
Chart of accounts
Customer statement
Data processing system
DBMS accounting package
Exception report
General ledger application
Horizontal package
Income statement
Industry-specific package
Integrated accounting system
  package

Invoice
Line items
Management by exception
Management hierarchy
Management information system
  (MIS)
Open Order Report
Order header
Override
Picking/packing slip
Sales History Report
Sales order processing application
Stand-alone accounting package
Vertical package

REVIEW QUESTIONS

1. What software do small- to medium-sized organizations use to automate their business?

2. What are the common goals of all software that can help to automate a business?

3. What are the levels in the management hierarchy?

4. What is a stand-alone accounting package?

5. What is an integrated accounting package?

6. Give three examples of industry-specific packages.

7. Contrast a "horizontal" with a "vertical" package.

8. In a sales order processing application, what data are entered on the order-header and line-item screens?

9. List three operational benefits of automated sales order entry procedures.

10. What is a data processing system?

11. What is a management information system?

12. Give one example of a management information report. How is the information used?

13. What is an exception report?

14. What are the core applications in an integrated accounting system?

15. Why is the general ledger application the heart of an integrated accounting package?

16. What is a DBMS accounting package?

EXERCISES

1. *WMK Associates Case.*   Mr. Kennedy, president of WMK Associates, a distributing company, wants to automate the company's accounting procedures. Do some preliminary investigatory work by finding three reviews of integrated accounting packages in recent computer periodicals. List the applications included in each package. Write a report about the features identified for each application.

2. *WMK Associates Case.*   Write to the companies identified in exercise 1. Ask for literature that describes their integrated package. Ask especially for detailed information on the general ledger and sales order processing packages.

    When literature is available, prepare a written or oral report on the following differences in the general ledger packages:

- Chart of accounts numbering scheme
- Chart of accounts setup procedure to define the balance sheet and income statement
- Balance sheet print options
- Income statement print options

3. Use recent computer periodicals to locate articles on any three industry-specific packages. Those identified in Figure 9-1 can serve as a guide to packages in this category. Prepare a report that summarizes what each application is designed to do for the industry addressed.

To check data-entry procedures:
Enter several real new orders and save them to a file.
Retrieve some orders to enter additional items.
Enter an item quantity shipped which is less than the
item quantity ordered.

To check the screen output:
Display an unshipped customer order.
Display a backorder.

To check the printed output:
Print an invoice.
Print a customer statement.
Print a sales journal.

To check file maintenance procedures:
Add several real customer records.
Delete some customer records.
Change some customer records.
Verify changes with a printed customer list.

To check other procedures:
Simulate end-of-week/month/year entries.
Verify accuracy with appropriate printed reports.
Perform a disk backup.

			Apr '84			
Sun	Mon	Tue	Wed	Thu	Fri	Sat
1	2	3	4	5	6	7
	On	On	On	On	On	
8	9	10	11	12	13	14
	On	On	On	On	On	
15	16	17	18	19	20	21
	On	On	On	On	On	
22	23	24	25	26	27	28
	On	On	On	On	On	
29	30					
	On					

COMMAND: Activity Edit Goto Help Options
Quit Resource [Transfer] Worksheet
Select option or type command letter
CALENDAR   Microsoft Project: develop. CAL

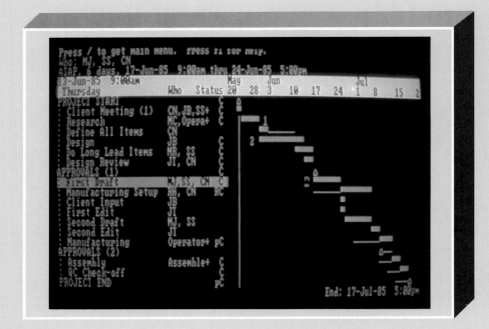

10

Automating a Business: A Case Study

AFTER READING THIS CHAPTER, YOU SHOULD BE ABLE TO

- Describe a systematic approach to analyzing an organization's packaged computer system requirements
- Explain the hardware and conversion planning required before installing a computer system

Studies show that most new jobs are being created in organizations with 20 or fewer people. When organizations this size computerize, they install packaged computer systems. Almost everyone in the organization is affected by the new computer system. Some are even enlisted as part of the team to analyze requirements for the new system and to install it.

Even departments or divisions of large organizations set up their own local computer systems. Personnel in the department or division inevitably become involved in the project.

Setting up any new computer system is a major organizational commitment. Often such a system profoundly changes the way in which business is normally done. Major job training and realignment may be necessary for both the professional and office staff. If the wrong computer system is installed, it can have disastrous results and is known to even cause business failure.

This chapter "walks through" the steps used by Interstate Distributing Company to set up its computerized system. The company bought and installed a packaged computer system. It paid a computer professional to help guide the project.

The chapter begins with an introduction to the systematic approach used by the computer professional. It then covers how each phase of the approach is executed. It concludes with a review of the hardware and conversion planning steps required to complete a successful installation of a packaged system.

SYSTEMATIC APPROACH

Figure 10-1 identifies four steps in an orderly, systematic approach to implementing a packaged computer system. It begins with specifying business requirements. This step actually sets up the criteria that will be the basis for locating and evaluating application software. Once software is selected, it often dictates the hardware required. Finally, purchased software and hardware are installed, used, and maintained.

Figure 10-2 illustrates these steps as a part of an infinite cycle. Because a business is a dynamic organization, it is wrong to think of its computerized system as static or frozen in time. Changes occur in procedures, or new business opportunities arise that motivate a renewed look at the computer system.

While using a systematic approach to setting up a packaged system provides no guarantee of success, it considerably reduces the chance of ending up with a disaster.

FIGURE 10-1
A systematic approach to implement a packaged computer system

1. Specify requirements for
    Routine business automation
    Management information
2. Locate software that comes closest to meeting requirements
    Evaluate candidate software
    Select the best
3. Locate hardware that secures the most benefit from the software
    Evaluate candidate hardware
    Select the best
4. Install the new system

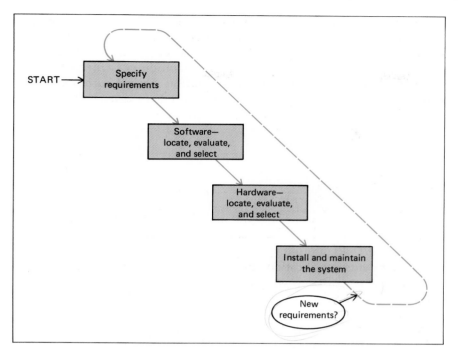

FIGURE 10-2
Cyclic nature of using packaged computer systems

PROFESSIONAL SUPPORT

Interstate Distributing Company went to its local business computer center for help. It found that the store, the Downtown Business Computer Center, was different from a typical computer retail store. Typical computer retail stores are interested in selling mainly hardware. The Center is interested in selling professional computer consulting services. It specializes in helping local companies to set up computer systems. It is paid a fee for its consulting services by clients or customers.

The computer industry considers the Downtown Business Computer Center store to be a value added reseller. **Value added resellers (VARs)** combine hardware and software, often from various manufacturers, and resell them as a **turnkey system.** Theoretically, all a user has to do to use a turnkey system is to turn the key to start it, but it does require that the user first learn how to work the system.

Sometimes these resellers are called **independent system vendors, system integrators,** and **turnkey vendors.** They are the computer industry's traditional distribution channel for *accounting* and *industry-specific packages*. The packages are also called *horizontal* and *vertical packages* by these resellers.

When invited, a turnkey vendor typically does a feasibility study.

A **feasibility study** is a formal term for analyzing a company's computing requirements. From the vendor's standpoint, it also verifies whether a user has money to pay and is ready to sign a contract for services.

Erica Grant, one of Downtown Business Computer Center's system specialists, handled the Interstate account. She worked with Leonard Angus, Interstate's accountant, and others at the client company, to help set up the new computer system.

SPECIFY REQUIREMENTS

To help specify its computing requirements, Interstate Distributing Company used prepared "requirements specification" lists, like the one for an integrated accounting system in Figure 10-3. Ms. Grant supplied the "requirements specification" list. Her company had a collection of them for a variety of packaged systems. They were prepared from researched sources like

- Company experience from working with other clients
- Software vendor literature
- Books and articles about computer systems, which often contain checklists

Ms. Grant's experience with other similar systems enabled her to understand Interstate's specific computing requirements. But Interstate's accountant, Mr. Angus, retained a healthy skepticism and asked about computer systems that ended up as failures. When he asked why they happened, Ms. Grant explained that in some cases there is a failure to identify the actual problem that needs a solution.

In one case, as an example, an order processing system was set up to speed up an order backlog problem. The system handled all the volume the user needed with room to spare. But it did not solve the problem. It turned out that the poorly maintained equipment in the machine shop was slowing down production. It caused the order backlog problem. Speeding up order processing with a computer simply helped to aggravate the situation.

Many other companies that want to computerize often do not have orderly business procedures in place. Some applications have, in fact, ended up automating inadequate procedures inherited from existing manual systems. One company first had to revise a disorderly pricing policy before any computer system could contribute to smoother operations.

These cases illustrate problems that could occur in any organization, regardless of size. Large companies have them, as well as small companies.

Budget Guidelines

After helping to specify requirements, Mr. Angus, Interstate's accountant, had to establish whether or not the company could afford

General Ledger

General ledger accounts

Digits in largest balance

Accounting periods

Periods history retained (12, 24)

Companies

Order Processing

Orders/day

Line-items/order

Days until order filled

% Line-items backordered

Days on backorder

Prices for all items

Quantity breaks for all items

Price contracts

Sales history periods retained (12, 24)

Accounts Receivable

Customers

New customers added/year

Customer ship-to addresses

Invoices/day

Cash receipts/month

Days invoices unpaid

Inventory and Purchasing

Items

New items added/year

Product classes

Issues/month

Receipts/month

Adjustment/month

Purchase orders/month

Lines/purchase order

Warehouses

Warehouse transfers/month

Accounts Payable

Vendors

New vendors added/year

Invoices/month

Days invoices unpaid

Checks/month

General distributions/invoice

Payroll

Employees

Departments

Pay periods/year

States

Special deductions/employee

Unions

FIGURE 10-3
Requirements specification form for an
integrated accounting system

the investment. Even if the firm had the funds, would it be a cost-justifiable purchase?

How much must be budgeted for a new computer system? Companies of all sizes use rule-of-thumb guidelines. Any company like Interstate in the distribution business, as an example, budgets 1 percent or more of its annual gross sales on a computer system. Ms. Grant explains that the budget covers

· Hardware
· Software
· Supplies and related expenses

Service-oriented businesses tend to spend twice as much as distributing companies.

As a simple example, assume that Interstate's gross sales are $1 million. Going by the rule-of-thumb, Mr. Angus plans a budget like

	BUDGET PLANNING	
	Minimum Plan	Maximum Plan
Gross sales	$1,000,000	$1,000,000
Rule-of-thumb allowance (1%–4%)	×.01	×.04
Total budget	$10,000	$40,000
Minus allowance for related expenses (rule-of-thumb is from 10% to 65%)	.35	.35
	$3,500	$14,000
Available for new system hardware and software	$6,500	$26,000

FIGURE 10-4
Rule-of-thumb budget planning worksheet for a new packaged computer system

the one shown in Figure 10-4. Related expenses cover things like hardware and software maintenance contracts.

Supplies like extra floppy disks and disk storage containers, computer stock paper, and printer ribbons are needed. These supply expenses, like hardware and software maintenance contracts, are ongoing expenses for the life of the system.

Other expenses that might be involved in setting up a computer system are listed in Figure 10-5.

Cost Justification

In many cases cost justification of a computer system shows a very swift payback. This enables a company to spend more than the minimum that the rule-of-thumb amount recommends.

FIGURE 10-5
Examples of related expenses

Installation costs, including hardware delivery, new office furniture, extra cables and electrical outlets, and proper lighting

Renovation costs to prepare physical site for equipment installation

Conversion cost to enter information from the old system into the new system

Personnel costs, including hiring and training expenses

Security costs for affixing hardware to prevent theft, and for renting a safety deposit box or vault to store backup copies of files and sensitive printed documents

Supplies expense for disks, disk file containers, computer paper, printer ribbons, and equipment storage cabinet

Insurance for the computer system

Finance charges if a loan is involved

Consultant fees

Legal fees if advice is needed for vendor contracts and negotiations

Ms. Grant provided the expertise to develop cost-justification figures. It often concerned reduced personnel expense. Assume, as a simplified example, that a worker spends 20 hours a month preparing customer statements. The worker also spends 20 hours a month preparing payroll deduction calculations. A computer is expected to eliminate these chores. If the worker is paid $10 an hour, there is a savings of $4,800 a year. This is called a **hard-dollar saving,** because actual dollars will not have to be allocated to these expenses.

From her experience, Ms. Grant found that most new computer installations do not result in reducing permanent staff. Instead, in office and professional environments, employee time is almost always refocused on other work activities. Usually the introduction of office automation results in freeing time for more job-enriched tasks. The computer takes over the repetitive, mundane chores at which it excels.

Improved management control is another area Ms. Grant quantifies to cost justify a new computer system. An example is inventory control. A business with good inventory controls can prevent expensive idle inventory from accumulating. A $300,000 inventory reduced by just 5 percent results in a $15,000 hard-dollar savings.

When Interstate installed its computer system, it was able to measure benefits such as

- Improved cash flow management with information supplied by the new computer system
- Increased sales because of better information that identified high-profit versus low-profit items
- Improved customer service with automated order processing
- Reduced debts with quicker billing after order shipment
- Reduced clerical time (about 50 percent less) spent on all bookkeeping tasks

Ms. Grant explained that cost justifying a computer system for professional or management workers is different. It assumes that the addition of automated systems results in performance or productivity improvement. The benefit is measured in **soft dollars,** which do not decrease a company's expenses.

As an example, assume that Interstate's marketing manager could prepare budgets in half the time it takes to do them manually. If he now spends four hours a week, automation would give him two more hours a week for other work. Assume that his annual salary, including fringe benefits, is $48,000. The soft-dollar benefit can be calculated as shown in Figure 10-6.

Salary at $48,000/year = $923/week (52 weeks)

35 hours/week = $26.37/hour

Save 2 hours/week = $52.74 savings/week

$52.74 × 52 weeks = $2,742 savings/year

FIGURE 10-6
Example of estimating savings

Often on the list of cost-justification arguments is the ability to do more things, or expand operations, because of automation. One carpet manufacturer, as an example, grew 200 percent in two years after acquiring a computer system, without adding more administrative staff. In this case, the company was free to become a more aggressive competitor. The growth was fostered by good computer production and management information system support.

Finally, justifying a new computer system usually includes intangible, or nonquantifiable, benefits. Ms. Grant identifies these to be, for example, improved employee morale and job satisfaction. In some cases, Ms. Grant recommends the use of more elaborate investment cost-benefit analysis techniques.

LOCATE SOFTWARE

Interstate decided to proceed with the computer investment, based on its cost-justification review of the project. It triggered Ms. Grant's next step to locate an appropriate software package. During the preliminary feasibility analysis phase, she had already lined up some potential packages. They were all in the microcomputer and low-end minicomputer category. This is consistent with the budget she had to work with.

Computer professionals, like Ms. Grant, locate industry-specific packages through

· Contacting other consultants
· Contacting knowledgeable associates, as well as industry-specific professional organizations
· Looking through **software directories** which list package information, like those listed in Figure 10-7
· Attending industry-specific trade shows and seminars
· Studying computer and industry trade magazines for reviews and advertisements related to the software of interest

Many printed directories cost over $100 each. They usually contain only a fraction of the software on the market and often carry out-of-date listings. Some directories are also available on-line through public

FIGURE 10-7
A sampler of software directories

Directory of Microcomputer Software, Datapro Research

Directory of Minicomputer Software, Datapro Research

ICP Software Directory, International Computer Programs

PC Clearinghouse Software Directory, PC Clearinghouse

Software Catalog: Microcomputers, Imprint Software (also available on-line through DIALOG)

Software Catalog: Minicomputers, Imprint Software

communication service companies. They tend to be more up to date and are available to anyone who subscribes to the service.

Any user or organization can check these directories if it wants to set up a "do-it-yourself" packaged computer system. Examples of typical directory listings for *industry-specific packages* appear in Figure 10-8. Listings contain information about

- What the software does
- The hardware supported
- Special software requirements
- Operating system requirements

FIGURE 10-8
Typical software directory listings for the wholesale distributor industry
(*Source*: ICP Software Directory, *54th ed., pp 345–349. Courtesy of International Computer Programs, Inc. Adapted with permission.*)

CONSUMER AND DISTRIBUTION SERVICES
Wholesale Trade/Distribution

SUPEREX WHOLESALER™
Product Type: Applications Software
Geographic Area Served: United States
Hardware Supported: IBM PC; Apple
Operating Systems: Apple DOS 3.3, PC DOS
Languages: BASIC
Number of Clients/Users: Not Specified
Narrative: The SUPEREX WHOLESALER handles order entry, inventory control billing, accounts receivable and interfaces with the SUPEREX ACCOUNTING SYSTEM. Features include: 1) Menu driven; 2) Screen prompts; 3) Inventory — over 2,500 items on double-sided/double-density disk or 20,000 item on 10MB hard disk; 4) Receiving reports; 5) Price overrides; 6) Allows discounts; 7) Automatically calculates sales tax; 8) Accounts receivable — 1,000 customers online with floppy disk or 10,000 customers online with hard disk, tracks open invoices, ages open invoices; 9) Credit management — brings customer limit to screen with each invoice, automatically flags accounts on credit hold or over limit; 10) Mailing list; 11) Prints aged receivables, transaction file, issues statements; 12) Reorders — allows minimum reorder level, writes purchase orders, tracks back orders; 13) Back orders — creates back order file, generates automatic back orders, lists back orders on each invoice; 14) Management reports — sales per item, sales per salesman, running totals by day, week, month or year; and 15) Report generation — custom reports, price lists, transaction reports, on-order reports, profit on inventory, inventory value.

Contact Data	Pricing
Superex Business Systems	$600.00
151 Ludlow Street	
Yonkers, NY 10705	
Tele. 914-964-5200	
Telex 131584	*P23561*

MSI IMPACT
Product Type: Applications Software
Geographic Area Served: United States
Hardware Supported: ADDS Mentor; IBM PC-AT
Operating Systems: PICK, PC DOS
Languages: BASIC
Number of Clients/Users: Not Specified
Narrative: MSI Impact provides customer buying history, chain discounting, matrix pricing, sales analysis, gross profit, sales support, quotations, order entry, pick ticket, back orders, inventory control, accounts receivable, accounts payable, general ledger and purchasing for wholesale/distribution operations. A 90-day warranty is included. One week of training is included.

Contact Data	Pricing
Charles F. Walz	$8,500.00—
Vice President	$25,000.00
Management Systems, Inc.	
652 Glenbrook Road	
Stamford, CT 06906	
Tele. 203-357-0280	*P26583*

IMS WHOLESALE DISTRIBUTION SYSTEM
Product Type: Applications Software
Geographic Area Served: United States, Canada, Mexico, Central South America, Australia, New Zealand, Middle East, Europe, Scandinavia, United Kingdom, South Africa
Hardware Supported: CP/M-based Hardware: MS-DOS-based Hardware
Operating Systems: PC DOS, MP M-86, CP M-80, CP M-86, MS-DOS
Languages: BASIC
Number of Clients/Users: 4,800
Narratives: The system automatically adjusts inventory levels and averages cost based on new shipments. Pre-set levels can be assigned with optional manual override at the order desk. The system prints picking tickets, packing lists, and invoices, and a stocking report flags items that should be reordered or liquidated. Numerous sales and inventory reports are available along with an accounts receivable module that ages overdue accounts on a daily basis. The system also handles purchasing and backorders. It interacts with the IMS Manufacturing Inventory Control System. Training in the supplier's office is $150.00 for two days. The manual is included in price of program and priced separately at $25.00 to $40.00. The distribution media is disk.
Special Configuration Requirements: CP/M; 64K; others; 128K; printer

Contact Data	Pricing
H. Dale McCullough	PRICE UPON
Director of Marketing	REQUEST
International Micro Systems, Inc.	
6445 Metcalf	
Shawnee Mission, KS 66202	
Tele. 913-677-1137	
Telex 437237	*P16048*

DIS-MIS DISTRIBUTOR'S MANAGEMENT INFORMATION SYSTEM
Product Type: Turnkey System
Geographic Area Served: United States
Hardware Supported: DEC PDP-11, Micro/PDP-11
Operating Systems: RSTS-E
Languages: COBOL
Number of Clients/Users: Not Specified
Narrative: DIS-MIS provides a multi-user computer system for small and medium-sized distributors/wholesalers. It includes complete order entry, inventory management, accounts receivable, accounts payable, general ledger, and payroll capabilities.
Special Configuration Requirements: 512KB memory, tape, printer, CRTs

Contact Data	Pricing
G. William Barnett	PRICE UPON
Director of Sales	REQUEST
The Computer Generation, Inc.	
3855 Presidential Parkway	
Atlanta, GA 30340	
Tele. 404-458-2371	*P24800*

- Language in which the programs are written
- Number of current users
- Pricing
- Contact information
- Geographic area serviced by the software vendor

In addition to industry packages, these directories list general *accounting system packages*, among a host of other software categories. This is evident from the sample list of subject categories given in Figure 10-9.

These directories are also a source of vendor information. Some vendors have been in the software business for years supplying packages

FIGURE 10-9
Subject categories available in a software directory
(*Source*: *Reprinted by permission of the publisher from* The Software Catalog: Microcomputer. *Copyright by Elsevier Science Publishing Co., Inc.*)

Software Subject Categories

100 COMMERCIAL
- 101 Accounting—Fixed Asset
- 103 Accounting—General Ledger
- 107 Accounting—Integrated Systems
- 111 Accounts Payable
- 114 Accounts Receivable
- 126 Data Processing
- 134 Financial
- 149 Integrated Business Systems
- 150 Integrated Office Management
- 151 Inventory
- 143 Invoicing/Order Entry
- 152 Job Costing/Control
- 154 Mailing Lists
- 163 Marketing
- 165 Miscellaneous Commercial
- 167 Operations Research
- 171 Payroll
- 174 Personnel Management
- 176 Purchasing
- 181 Spreadsheets
- 190 Spreadsheet Support
- 182 Stock Market/Commodities
- 183 Taxes
- 185 Time Management
- 186 Time/Client Billing
- 187 Word Processing
- 188 Word Processing Support

200 EDUCATIONAL
- 214 Administration
- 231 CAI—Humanities
- 233 CAI—Language Arts
- 232 CAI—Math
- 234 CAI—Science
- 237 CAI—Social Science
- 235 CAI—Special Education
- 236 CAI—Other Basic Skills
- 244 CMI—Computer-Managed Instruction
- 250 Computer Literacy
- 234 Counseling/Aptitude Testing
- 274 Library Management
- 279 Miscellaneous Educational

300 INDUSTRIAL
- 390 CAD—Computer-Aided Design
- 395 CAM—Computer-Aided Manufacturing
- 320 Engineering (Civil and Structural)
- 322 Engineering (Electrical and Electronic)
- 326 Engineering (Mechanical)
- 324 Engineering (Miscellaneous)
- 340 Inventory
- 360 Manufacturing
- 370 Miscellaneous Industrial

400 PERSONAL
- 418 Astrology and Divination
- 420 Electronic Publications
- 428 Finances
- 442 Health and Diet
- 448 Hobbies
- 450 Household Management
- 453 Miscellaneous Personal
- 456 Music
- 468 Sports

500 GAMES
- 510 Adult
- 520 Adventure
- 530 Arcade
- 534 Educational
- 536 Miscellaneous Games
- 545 Sports Games
- 540 Party
- 550 Strategy

600 SCIENTIFIC
- 615 Astronomy
- 620 Biology
- 625 Chemistry
- 635 Earth Science
- 655 Environmental Science
- 660 Mathematics
- 668 Miscellaneous Scientific
- 670 Nuclear Science
- 685 Physics
- 695 Statistics

700 PROFESSIONS INDUSTRIES
- 704 Aerospace
- 744 Agriculture
- 708 Architecture
- 712 Automotive Industry
- 714 Aviation
- 716 Banking
- 720 Chemical Industry
- 724 Communications Media
- 728 Construction Contracting
- 729 CPA
- 730 Demography (Census, Poll Taking, etc.)
- 735 Dentistry
- 740 Energy (Oil, Gas, Alternative, etc.)
- 748 Food/Restaurant
- 750 Government Municipalities
- 751 Hospital Management
- 752 Hotel/Motel
- 756 Insurance
- 758 Law
- 764 Lumber
- 760 Medicine
- 762 Miscellaneous Professions Industries
- 763 Non-Profit
- 768 Pharmaceutics
- 796 Public Utilities
- 772 Publishing
- 776 Real Estate
- 780 Retailing
- 784 Steel
- 786 Surveying
- 788 Textile
- 792 Transportation
- 797 Veterinary Practice
- 732 Wholesaling

800 SYSTEMS
- 810 Assemblers
- 825 Communications System Emulation
- 820 Compilers/Interpreters
- 827 Conversions/Cross Compilers
- 828 Data Entry
- 830 Database Management Systems
- 832 Graphics
- 833 Information Retrieval Systems
- 840 Operating Systems
- 850 Program Generators
- 853 Programming Development Aids
- 857 Report Generators
- 859 Security Encryption Systems
- 860 System Utilities

to one or more industries. Some provide turnkey services, just like that supplied by the Downtown Business Computer Center.

In many cases, packaged software in these directories can be customized. **Customizing** a package involves introducing program modifications to tailor a package for a user. It is done for a fee.

Computer retail stores carry microcomputer accounting and some industry-specific software for the do-it-yourself organization or user. An installation program is often included for a user to customize the software for a particular computer. Other options may be built in to add or delete functions to further customize such packages.

Some of these packages provide the program code that allows a user to make any modification desired. But if a user changes the code, the software supplier cannot be held responsible for the integrity of the program. Since the supplier never guarantees integrity to begin with, that may not present a problem. The license that comes with software usually says that it is sold "as is."

SOFTWARE EVALUATION

Once appropriate software is located, it must be evaluated. Does it meet all the application requirements specified?

Ms. Grant reads vendor-supplied literature to do an initial evaluation of packages. A few vendors require a nominal fee to get a *User Guide* or other evaluation literature. The fee is usually deductible from the cost of an eventual purchase.

The initial review results in two packages for more serious consideration. Ms. Grant and Mr. Angus use many application-specific checklists, like the order processing example in Figure 10-10, to guide their evaluation.

Each package is also checked using a guide similar to the General Software Evaluation Checklist in Figure 3-25. It covers such things as a hands-on test of software.

Hands-On Test

Ms. Grant initially conducts a hands-on software test with the order processing manager, Alexandra Kaye. But first she works with Mr. Angus and Ms. Kaye to identify the specific order processing entries, displays, reports, and file updates they will examine. Their list is shown in Figure 10-11.

After the list is prepared, the actual test begins. It is done at the Downtown Business Computer Center's showroom. Ms. Kaye takes along one of Interstate's order entry clerks who will use the system on a day-to-day basis. The company strategy, encouraged by Ms. Grant, is to get users involved in the system selection process. It helps to smooth the way for a friendly, versus hostile, user acceptance of the new system.

ORDER PROCESSING

Type
Prebilling
Postbilling
Cash/counter sales
Multiuser

Capacities
Customers
Ship-to addresses/customers
Items
Branches
Warehouses
Companies
Orders
Line-items/order
Prices for all items
Quantity breaks for all items
Price contracts

Interfaces
Accounts receivable
Inventory
General ledger
Report writer
Other _____

Displays Provided
Open order inquiry
Backorder inquiry
Other _____

Order Entry
Check credit before accepting
   customer order
Hold order status
Ship-to multiple addresses
Accept:
   Noninventoried items
   Returned goods/credit memo
   Debit memo
   Direct shipped order
   Future orders
Suggest substitute for out-of-stock
   items
Add special charges to order
Modify or cancel order
Enter shipped quantities

Item Pricing Options
Item identification:
   Numeric only
   Any characters or numbers
Automatic by customer type
Automatic based on quantity ordered
Entered item price override
Base unit cost plus mark-up percent
   pricing
Contract pricing
Other _____

Discounting Options
Base unit-price minus discount
   depending on customer and/or
   item type
Line item discounts
Trade discount for entire order
Other _____

Backorders
Automatically filled when inventory is
   received by:
   Customer type priority
   Other _____
Manually filled by operator who
   releases selected backorders
   (system maintains and lists
   backorders)
Original order price retained to avoid
   customer penalty
Other _____

Printed Output Provided
Picking/packing slips
Preprinted forms
Prenumbered forms
Window envelope style
Open Order Report
   Options: _____
Order acknowledgment
Shipping labels

FIGURE 10-10
Order processing checklist

To check data-entry procedures:
  Enter several real new orders and save them to a file.
  Retrieve some orders to enter additional items.
  Enter an item quantity shipped which is less than the
    item quantity ordered.

To check the screen output:
  Display an unshipped customer order.
  Display a backorder.

To check the printed output:
  Print an invoice.
  Print a customer statement.
  Print a sales journal.

To check file maintenance procedures:
  Add several real customer records.
  Delete some customer records.
  Change some customer records.
  Verify changes with a printed customer list.

To check other procedures:
  Simulate end-of-week/month/year entries.
  Verify accuracy with appropriate printed reports.
  Perform a disk backup.

FIGURE 10-11
A "to-do" list for an order processing
software package hands-on test

All are assured that the test is not done with a specially prepared demonstration version of the package. They will use the real full version of the package. Ms. Grant warns them that some demonstration packages are known to be skillfully crafted showpieces. Often such "demos" do not accurately represent true processing procedures or response timing.

Response time is the time after a user types the last key of an entry to the time the computer displays the last letter of a reply. Elapsed response time is important because if attention is allowed to flag, productivity goes down.

Where hardware is available, a package can often be tested in the convenience of one's workplace. Such packages may first require paying the full purchase price. In return there is a policy that refunds are paid within 30 or 60 days if not satisfied with the package.

With no expert guidance available, this approach could take considerable time and effort. One integrated accounting system, as an example, takes ten hours to do a sample session. The disks supplied for testing are exact copies of their originals. The only difference is that files are limited to a few records each for test purposes. They are called **crippled copies** and are completely valid for hands-on testing purposes. They do not, however, provide a clue about how processing may slow down when substantial volumes of data will be used.

Data Entry

For its test, Interstate's order processing clerk, Cynthia Morrow, learns how to power up the system. She enters a few customer and inventory records. They are necessary to provide test data for processing orders.

When orders are entered, deliberate errors are committed to test error recovery and "help" routines. Fortunately, errors are displayed in plain English and include clear instructions for recovery. Some less satisfactory software produces coded error messages. They require looking up an error recovery procedure in a manual. Some even less sophisticated software comes to a dead halt and requires expert help to resume.

The test reveals displays of **user prompts,** or messages, that are unintimidating and free of computer jargon or codes. They are logical and consistent, which also means that they are easy to follow and eventually learn.

User prompts always appear in the same screen location and require familiar responses. Responses do not shift arbitrarily, for example, from a "YES" to a "Y," to an enter key, to indicate a positive response. Once a response pattern is established, it is consistently used.

Ms. Grant explained that the effectiveness of user prompts has a strong relationship to operator training time and motivation. The longer it takes to learn an application, the less desirable the software is. Certainly the number of features and functions in a package makes a difference to learning time. But while some packages can be intuitively learned in hours, others need days and weeks.

Displays and Reports

Mr. Angus tests the displays and reports. He selects from a menu to display a customer's order. He first must keystroke through several submenus. In some systems, a menu selection can be entered so rapidly by an experienced user that the menu never actually displays. This is a desirable feature because displaying menus slows down production. Alternatively, a user can choose the level of menu help desired.

Unfortunately, the screen Mr. Angus retrieves is so cluttered that the order shipped date seems obscure. Some reports he prints are also so full of code letters and abbreviations that they are almost uninterpretable. He wants screen and report designs to be clear and easy to use.

The Sales Journal, which he prints after invoices, looks just fine. It serves as a permanent control list of all invoices printed during the last print run. Control totals on the Journal match the ones the Interstate team manually prepared to cross-check computation accuracy.

Other Tests

Continuing the test, Mr. Angus tries end-of-period routines. Ever the skeptic, he wants to be sure periodic computer totals match manual test totals. He heard a story about one innocent user who worked with an application from a July installation through December 31 only to find the year-end totaling routine never worked.

Finally, disk backup procedures are examined. This activity is a daily event with most systems and can be very time consuming. Some systems have very elaborate multidisk swapping procedures that are highly error prone. Some have built-in system controls to guard against error. A hands-on test of backing-up disks prevents any unpleasant surprises during possible future use.

When the test is completed, the Interstate team rates the package with a numeric score. Some parts of a package are weighted as more important than others for scoring. The final score for a package is used to compare it with other packages being evaluated.

Vendor Evaluation

To evaluate the software vendor's background, and special package conditions, Ms. Grant uses a Vendor Evaluation Checklist, like the one in Figure 10-12. Most of the questions are answered directly by the software vendor.

FIGURE 10-12
Vendor evaluation checklist

PART ONE: VENDOR QUESTIONS

Business Background
How long has the company been in the computer business?
Are local customer references available?
What is the size of the technical support staff?
Is a recent financial statement available to validate company stability?
Is there any bankruptcy or computer litigation history?
Are contract terms negotiable?

System
What are charges for system installation, training, system maintenance, and
    custom programming?
What is the procedure to correct program errors?
Is the program code made available to users?
Are program change requests done by the developer who wrote the software?
Is a larger computer available to run the software package as is?
Is a list of hardware requirements available that identifies present use level
    and room for growth?

PART TWO: USER QUESTIONS

Would you buy the same system again today?
Would you recommend the vendor to others?
What level of technical knowledge is required to use and maintain the system?
Did you experience any unanticipated
    Expenses?
    Problems?
    Benefits?
    Operator turnover?
Are security controls adequate?

Program Changes

One question on the list addresses program changes. Relatively inexpensive software can become costly if a user requires changes. With some packages, changes are impossible.

Since businesses operate in a dynamic environment, computer systems software must be changeable. Payroll software, as an example, is vulnerable to change, like adding a new tax. Business growth or new procedures inevitably require software changes. It is important to fix responsibility for who does changes and what are the costs.

Ideally the company, person, or people who wrote the software are in the best position to make changes. But if the software developer is no longer available, a substitute approach is required.

If a reputable software house designed and programmed the application, it can ordinarily provide competent follow-up support for its products. But if a moonlighter put together the package and has since disappeared, support can be a problem. So can custom program requests.

The question of obtaining a copy of the program code is also raised. Consider, for example, that Interstate depends entirely on the package vendor for all software maintenance. Interstate has no access to program code. Soon, new tax changes must be made in the payroll application.

Should the vendor enter bankruptcy proceedings, all assets, including the program code, could be secured. But if the code is resident with a third party, or escrow agent, the agent can determine to release it to users. With code in hand, users can find an alternative software solution.

Disaster Insurance

To insulate her client further from disasters, Ms. Grant checks out the package vendor's business. She is aware that many new companies in the computer business tend to be especially volatile and transient. They include many new ventures and start-up companies. To avoid being left with an unusable or incomplete system, she investigates the company history and financial stability.

Other disaster insurance includes checking if a vendor's software runs unchanged on a larger computer. Ms. Grant is aware that many first-time users seriously underestimate business growth. She knows one case where all computer capability was exhausted in only one year. Since no larger computer existed in the hardware product line, the user company suffered. One solution was to cut back on the number of database records stored and make do with less. The other was to abandon the investment in hardware, software, and training and start over with a more powerful computer.

User Questions

A final evaluation effort is spent cross-checking the package vendor's claims. The names of current users of the package are supplied by the vendor. So Ms. Grant is prepared for "setups," or users who have been prepared by the vendor to give all the right answers.

Some users, nonetheless, provide valuable information on the time it takes for a given volume of orders to be processed. Some also supply insights on correcting software problems.

Ms. Grant's acid test is to ask current users if they would buy the same system again today. Their answers to this and other questions about software, hardware, and vendor support are informative.

Ms. Grant and Mr. Angus round out the evaluation process by actually visiting some user sites. Seeing a candidate system in a production environment is worth the trip. On one visit, as an example, they observe an efficient order processing workflow arrangement. It was later successfully implemented at Interstate.

Mr. Angus originally asked the Downtown Business Computer Center to respond to similar questions he observes on the Vendor Evaluation Checklist. To protect Interstate, he scrutinized the financial stability of the consulting business, as well as its technical background. When everything checked out, he recommended that Interstate use the Center's services.

Selection

Ms. Grant aims for an objective selection of the best software. Usually this involves giving numeric scores to evaluation results, as evident from the Selection Summary Worksheet in Figure 10-13.

The extra step from evaluation to selection involves combining simple or weighted scores, from the various evaluations, and comparing results. A final ranking identifies which package, from the analysis, appears to be the best choice. Interstate makes the final choice from the ranking and Ms. Grant's recommendations.

Evaluation Items	CANDIDATE SYSTEMS (Scale: 1 = poor to 10 = excellent)	
	ABC System	XYZ System
Satisfies all application "must have" requirements	8	9
General software evaluation	8	9
Hands-on test	7	8
Turnkey vendor evaluation	7	7
User satisfaction	7	8
Subtotal	37	41
Divide by 5 for average score	÷5	÷5
Total	7.41	8.2
Final ranking	2	1

FIGURE 10-13
Selection summary worksheet

HARDWARE PLANNING

Usually a company or a user buys whatever hardware that the software works on, if a good software package is located. The software that Interstate found most desirable worked on several brands of hardware, from microcomputers through large-scale minicomputers. The company's choice of hardware became highly influenced by such mechanical requirements as

- The number of **workstations** required or locations where computing would be carried out
- The volume of printing required
- The amount of disk storage space required

Workstations

Since all information entered into Interstate's computer system is keyboarded, Ms. Grant had to do some planning. How many data-entry workstations must be active at one time to get the daily work done? The answer to this question came from counting keystrokes. The *User Guide* to the accounting package provided examples of input screens and descriptions of entries. By counting entries, one character at a time, a keystroke figure is available for workstation planning purposes.

As an example, one average order requires about 200 keystrokes. At 400 orders a day, that comes to 400×200, or 80,000 keystrokes. A data-entry operator can average 10,000 keystrokes an hour. If an average of 10,000 keystrokes an hour is used, it would take eight hours to enter orders every day. Since errors need correction, and operators take breaks, a 10 percent buffer is added. That makes order entry almost a nine-hour daily job for conservative planning purposes. A simplified version of Ms. Grant's keystroke planning worksheet is given in Figure 10-14.

Alternative solutions that Ms. Grant proposed to Interstate for consideration are

- One order processing workstation with two work shifts
- One order processing workstation with overload work shared with the accounting or warehouse workstation
- Two order processing workstations with two operators on the same shift.

With two workstations, one would be free several hours to process payroll, word processing, or whatever. The second workstation could function as a backup if the other malfunctions.

Ms. Grant reminded the Interstate decision makers about other planning limitations. As an example, some microcomputers cannot be used while printing is in progress. If they are used as workstations, the hours available for keyboarding have to be adjusted down by the number of print hours required. As an alternative, some print-spooler software could be acquired. This permits keyboard entry and printing to occur simultaneously, but it often slows down both operations.

KEYBOARDED TRANSACTION	DEPARTMENT LOCATION	CHARACTERS IN ONE TRANSACTION		DAILY NUMBER OF TRANSACTIONS		TOTAL KEYSTROKES
Order entry	Order processing	200	×	400	=	80,000
Inventory receipt	Warehouse	150	×	150	=	22,500
Cash payment	Accounting	100	×	100	=	10,000
Cash receipt	Accounting	110	×	300	=	33,000
						145,500

SUMMARY BY LOCATION			
	Order Processing	Accounting	Warehouse
Total keystrokes	80,000	43,000	22,500
Add 10% overhead	8,000	4,300	2,250
	88,000	47,300	24,750
Divide by 10,000 (conservative keystroke estimate per hour)	÷10,000	÷10,000	÷10,000
Total hours of work required	8.8 Hours	4.7 Hours	2.5 Hours

FIGURE 10-14
Computer workstation planning worksheet

Seasonal and other work patterns could influence workstation planning figures. If all workstations are microcomputers that are linked to a network, often more workstations can be added when the workload increases. On the other hand, a multiuser centralized computer with terminals requires careful calculations to be sure planned growth can be supported.

Disk Storage

To determine disk storage requirements, Ms. Grant followed a standard formula:

1. List all the programs and data the company will use.
2. List the disk space they occupy as a character count.
3. Sum the character counts.
4. Add an estimated growth factor to get total disk storage required.

She developed a worksheet similar to the simplified one given in Figure 10-15. Some information for the worksheet comes from *User Guides*. They give the amount of storage that programs require. They also give character counts for each record type.

Ms. Grant considers the critical step here to be translating the company's long-range plans into database expansion numbers. Is there to be a promotion to get many new customers? Is there a plan to increase inventoried items? When these and other planning issues are resolved, figures could be incorporated into the planning worksheet.

Estimating disk requirements also includes adding space for word-processed document and electronic spreadsheet storage. Document retention periods must be established when several users share disk storage.

Printer

To determine Interstate's print requirements, Ms. Grant listed every document printed. A simplified version of her planning worksheet is given in Figure 10-16. She also distinguished the quality of print required and the frequency of each document.

Information for the worksheet comes from documents and reports illustrated in *User Guides*. Counting the number of lines, including headings, on documents provides figures. Some things require estimates, like on-demand management reports which can be lumped together and listed as a daily estimate. Long-term requirements also need consideration.

Once daily print volume by location is known, alternative printer

FIGURE 10-15
Disk storage planning worksheet

FILE STORAGE	AVERAGE CHARACTERS IN ONE UNIT		NUMBER OF UNITS		TOTAL		RELATED PROGRAM STORAGE		TOTAL CHARACTERS OF STORAGE
1. *Company database records*									
Customer record	300	×	4000	=	1,200,000	+	72,000	=	1,272,000
Accounts receivable record	100	×	16,000	=	1,600,000	+	64,000	=	1,664,000
General ledger record	100	×	500	=	50,000	+	84,000	=	134,000
2. *Other file storage*									
Word processing documents	3,000	×	400	=	1,200,000	+	170,000	=	1,370,000
Spreadsheets	3,000	×	400	=	1,200,000	+	160,000	=	1,360,000
3. *System software*							200,000	=	200,000
Subtotal									6,000,000
Allowance for growth and workspace									×2
									12,000,000 characters

Disk storage space required

NUMBER OF PRINTED LINES				
	Daily		Monthly	
	Letter Quality	Draft Quality	Letter Quality	Draft Quality
Invoices	6,000			
Invoice register		75		
Customer statements			3,200	
Aged trial balance				2,000
Characters per line	×80	×80	×80	×80
Printed Lines required	480,000	6,000	256,000	160,000

Most important planning figure

FIGURE 10-16
Printer planning worksheet

solutions can be evaluated. For illustration purposes, two examples are developed and shown in Figure 10-17.

Ms. Grant evaluates and recommends all hardware the way she does software. Individual features are evaluated and scored. Those that score the best are recommended to Interstate for selection and installation.

Ms. Grant does include other factors in the final recommendation. They are the result of questions like the following:

· What size and type of disk will be a standard and available in the future?
· How will new industry trends impact future systems?
· What are major hardware firms, like IBM, planning to do that will influence, or even overwhelm, the industry with new hardware standards?

FIGURE 10-17
Print alternatives

Example 1: Letter-quality printer	
Daily total characters	480,000
Letter-quality printer working at 80 characters per second	÷80
Total seconds	6,000
Divide by seconds per minutes	÷60
Total print time required	100 minutes
Example 2: Dot-matrix printer	
Daily total characters	480,000
Dot-matrix printer working at "near letter quality" speed of 150 characters per second	÷150
Total seconds	3,200
Divide by seconds per minute	÷60
Total print time required	53 minutes

INSTALLATION

Ms. Grant advises clients to expect the best but be prepared for the worst when installing a new computer system. She suggests that if hardware is to be delivered in two weeks, plan on four to six weeks to avoid disappointment. When it does arrive, plan on extra time before it actually works.

Before new computer workstations were scheduled to arrive, Ms. Grant went over the Preinstallation Checklist, shown in Figure 10-18. She worked with Interstate to prepare the physical site with desks, chairs, electrical power, lighting, and storage cabinets. An initial six-month supply of computer paper, disks, and printer ribbons was on order.

Conversion

Conversion is the name given to the period when an organization changes from one system to another. Ms. Grant warned Interstate about the hazards of trying to "put everything on the computer at once." Experience shows that this spells disaster. Computerizing means changing the way business is done. The last thing needed in most organizations is to change all aspects of a business at once. Tasks need to be done in priority order. Ms. Grant recommended that the company begin with the least critical task first to give everyone time to adjust to the new system. But Interstate decided instead to start with the most critical function, sales order processing. It accepted Ms. Grant's recommendation to begin during a slow period in the seasonal business.

To make a smooth transition to the automated system, Ms. Grant helped Interstate to follow the Conversion Checklist shown in Figure 10-19. It covered areas such as training, data entry, and parallel operations.

Training

Ms. Grant told Interstate that where training is not handled carefully, valued employees have quit and even sabotaged new computer equipment. To prevent such negativism, she suggested involving employees as early as possible in the computerization effort.

Since management and data-entry operators at Interstate were involved in the evaluation and selection process, training progressed smoothly. Training sessions for data-entry personnel consisted of discussions and demonstrations of the computer system's operation.

A handout illustrating management reports and their use helped to orient managers about the new system. Managers only had to be trained in how to make inquiries and to generate reports. This was handled on a private basis with each manager.

PREINSTALLATION

Is desk space available for the computers, disks, displays, printers, and paper catchers?

Is a dedicated power line available for each computer, or a power line surge protector?

Are telephone jacks available for connecting modems?

Are adjustable lighting, and chairs on casters, available for computer users?

Are supplies available such as blank floppy disks, floppy disk storage containers, stock computer paper, custom preprinted paper, and printer ribbons?

Is storage space available for supplies such as *User Guides*, cartons of computer paper, extra printer ribbons, floppy disks, and disk storage containers?

FIGURE 10-18
Preinstallation checklist

Convert Data

All Interstate's customer account records, inventory item records, general ledger account records, and other company records had to be entered into the database. The task of converting files into computerized form is often a very trying period for an organization. Ms. Grant worked with Mr. Angus to determine what data were to be entered and when. Once established, actual data had to be collected, grouped, and control totaled for entry in batches. By entering small controlled groups of data, Ms. Grant could be sure that the system would not be flooded with bad information.

FIGURE 10-19
Checklist for converting from old to new system

SYSTEM CONVERSION

Training
    Orient managers about new system procedures.
    Train data-entry personnel to enter computer data.
Convert data
    Determine the source of computer data.
    Gather the data.
    Keyboard the data into the new system.
Parallel testing
    First, use the computer as a backup to manual processing.
    Next, use manual processing as a backup to computer processing.
    Cut over completely to the new system.

Parallel Testing

Once data were entered, Interstate began **parallel testing.** This is the period when the manual and computer systems function together for comparison purposes. Interstate had to ask personnel to work overtime and on weekends to accommodate the double workload. Some companies hire temporary help for parallel testing as well as for the initial data conversion work.

Ms. Grant recommended a parallel test of one to three months. But Interstate claimed it could not afford the people and financial burden of more than a few weeks of parallel operations. To compromise, it prematurely forced periodic closings and ran monthly, quarterly, and year-end reports. The procedure uncovered no problems in this critical processing. So the company was able to **cut over** completely to the new computer system.

Security and Performance Monitoring

After Ms. Grant discontinued her direct involvement with setting up Interstate's computer system, the company did its own performance monitoring and security control. Security procedures include regular off-site storage of backup disks, printouts, and system manuals. Mr. Angus conducts surprise audits and rotates data-entry personnel and tasks. Computer passwords are changed often. These procedures are normal in any well-administered computer-based organization.

Everyone working with Interstate's new system keeps a written **log book** of hardware and software problems. The log is used to help resolve maintenance problems.

Ms. Grant once explained how log books are responsible for revealing patterns that help to avoid more troublesome problems later. Problems with faulty cable connections, disks, and printers often begin with telltale symptoms. Symptoms might be anything abnormal, like repeated disk read errors. When these problems are observed and recorded, maintenance troubleshooters can often solve problems more readily.

Performance monitoring helps to determine when a system needs upgrading. As an example, backup procedures that take hours to do, and work that constantly needs overtime scheduled to complete it, are not symptoms that get recorded in a log book. When observed, they indicate problems that need attention. While some may require new computer-based solutions, others may require administrative action.

By monitoring changes in day-to-day computer activity, Mr. Angus feels he has a better chance to avoid potential problems. He also has feedback for future planning before crises occur.

When it looks as if automation might solve a new problem, or create a new opportunity, or enhance productivity in new ways, Mr. Angus begins a new cycle of specifying requirements, as shown in Figure 10-2. He believes that if a user specifies and acquires a system in the same logical manner applied to any major capital investment, it will reap the benefits later. He knows that it is a user's responsibility to make sure things go right. It is the company's money that is at risk, and it is the company that will pay if things do not go right.

PROJECT MANAGEMENT

Ms. Grant thought about the advantages of managing the Interstate computer system project with project management software. Her company just acquired a project management package that she decided to use for her next consulting assignment.

Project management software helps users to do formal planning and control of projects like installing new computer equipment or designing a new chemical plant. A sampler of available packages appears in Figure 10-20.

Project management software characteristically presents a project schedule as a chart, such as those shown in Figure 10-21. These charts and related tables enable a user to oversee a project more effectively:

· By dividing the overall project into manageable units or tasks.
· By assigning resources (people, machines, materials) to each task.
· By reassigning resources to tasks as a situation changes.

Some project managers use outline processors to help organize the initial breakdown of tasks and resources for a project. Once this information is ready, it is keyboarded into the project management software.

Scheduling

Barry Edye, a sales manager for medical X-ray equipment, uses a package that displays a project schedule in the form of a **PERT chart.** PERT is an acronym for *Project Evaluation and Review Technique.* It is a method originally developed to track the progress of large military and high-technology projects. A PERT chart, like the one in Figure 10-21, displays critical tasks along a *critical path* that must be completed on schedule. Noncritical tasks can be postponed without affecting the project completion date.

A PERT chart helps Mr. Edye's customers, mostly hospital administrators, go through the planning stage to prepare a site for X-ray installation. Building a shielded room, getting the necessary amount of metal

Advanced Pro-Path	Project Manager
Harvard Total Project Manager	Project-Master
IntelPERT	Project Schedule
MacProject	Project Scheduler/Network
Microsoft Project	Quick Plan
Milestone	SuperProject Plus
PERTMASTER	Time Line
PMS II	Vue
Primavera	

FIGURE 10-20
A sampler of project management software packages for personal computers

PERT chart, shows
interrelationship
of tasks along the critical path (double lines).

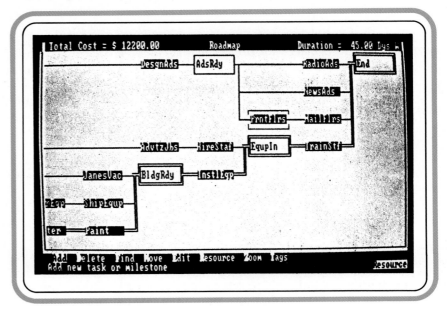

Gantt chart, shows task
beginning/ending times and sequence.

FIGURE 10-21

Common project management software
charts

(Top software: Harvard Total Project Man-
ager, courtesy of Harvard Software, Inc.; bot-
tom software: Time Line, courtesy of Break-
through Software Corporation)

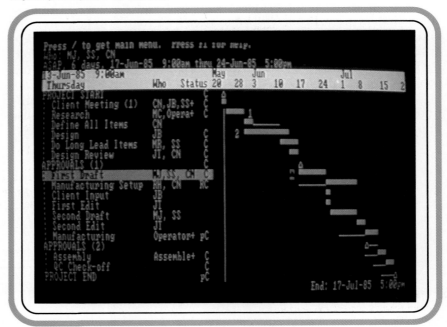

	Sun 1	Mon 2	Tue 3	Wed 4	Thu 5	Fri 6	Sat 7
		On	On	On	On	On	
	8	9 On	10 On	11 On	12 On	13 On	14
	15	16 On	17 On	18 On	19 On	20 On	21
	22	23 On	24 On	25 On	26 On	27 On	28
	29	30 [On]					

COMMAND: Activity Edit Goto Help Options
        Quit Resource [Transfer] Worksheet
Select option or type command letter
CALENDAR   Microsoft Project: develop. CAL

Calendar days can be turned "on" to indicate working days, or left blank to indicate nonworkdays.

	Resource	Capacity	Unit Cost	Per	Days to Complete	Cost to Complete
1	Forecaster	No limit	1800.00	Month	35.0	2907.90
2	Production Mngr	No limit	2550.00	Month	70.0	8239.06
3	Recruiter	No limit	2355.00	Month	32.0	3478.40
4	WP operator	No limit	55.00	Day	37.5	2062.50
5	WP equipment	No limit	26.00	Day	35.0	910.00
6	Production VP	No limit	3700.00	Month	22.0	3757.20
7	Prototype artst	No limit	235.00	Day	30.0	7050.00
8	Graphic artst	No limit	115.00	Day	65.0	7475.00
9	Production sup	No limit	2000.00	Month	20.0	1846.29
10	Marketing VP	No limit	3700.00	Month	20.0	3415.64
11	Ad writer	No limit	250.00	Day	40.0	10000.00
12	Marketing mngr	No limit	2750.00	Month	3.5	444.26
13	Ad mngr	No limit	2400.00	Month	2.5	276.94
14	Paste-up artst	No limit	75.00	Day	7.5	562.50
15	PR mngr	No limit	1900.00	Month	5.0	438.49

Cost to complete: 52864.18   Total cost of project: 52864.18

COMMAND: Activity Calendar Delete [Edit] Goto Help
           Options Print Quit Transfer View
Select option or type command letter
RESOURCE   Microsoft Project: delevop, RES

Resource list summarizes labor, material, and equipment cost and use.

FIGURE 10-22
Other project management software features
(Software: Microsoft Project, courtesy of Microsoft Corp.)

shielding shipped to the hospital, and accomplishing other tasks are preparatory to equipment delivery.

To set up a project schedule, Mr. Edye's software offers data-entry forms to:

- Identify the project.
- Set up a calendar of workdays, like the example in Figure 10-22.
- Identify tasks, including start and completion dates, among other details.
- List the resources to be allocated to the project, like the sample list shown in Figure 10-22.

Uses

Automating project scheduling and management has many uses and advantages. Mr. Edye finds that his X-ray equipment installation charts help customers to accept a more realistic equipment delivery schedule. He tells how charting "helped to save three orders that represent $5 million in X-ray equipment."

Evan Pritchard says he uses his software to "play around with a project schedule to see if the tasks can be better timed." His schedules specify steps necessary to manufacture custom integrated circuit chips. He says, "I can see where a project has some slack time. I can fill this time with another job, or call in parts sooner to shorten the time to complete the project."

At Eastman Kodak company, over 50 planners use microcomputer project management software for

- Research tracking
- New product development scheduling
- Equipment scheduling

They still use mainframe software to track very large projects.

Project management software is usable by anyone who deals with time and limited resources. Accounting and consulting firms, as an example, regularly use it to schedule their scarce resources, which are employees.

One computer industry analyst warns that if a user cannot define a project's target in advance, together with each process step and the resources devoted to each step, automation will not help.

CASE STUDY: Pursuing a Package

Finding the right vendor or value-added reseller with the right industry-specific, or "vertical," package can be time-consuming and frustrating. Contacting a retailer is often the first step. But for Mary and Dennis Courtier, owners of Pepin Heights Orchard in Minnesota, the off-the-shelf packages were unacceptable. "I must have looked at 25 different accounting packages, both for agriculture and business," she says. "But our application is so specialized, the expertise in the computer retail stores just wasn't there."

Pepin Heights Orchard uses Terra, Datasphere's agricultural cost accounting system. The software package lists for $1,995 and comprises general ledger, accounts payable, enterprise management, and asset depreciation modules. Other modules such as grower accounting and asset depreciation can be added to form computerized accounting systems geared toward packing houses, nurseries, and other agricultural businesses.

Finding Specific Software.   "We read about Terra in a trade journal, *The Goodfruit Grower*," Mary Courtier recalls. She wrote to Datasphere and asked for a demonstration of the system at an International Dwarf Tree Association symposium in Washington state. In March the Courtiers told Datasphere they would buy the system. By early May a local computer retailer delivered their $5,800 dual floppy disk IBM AT microcomputer with a 20-megabyte hard disk and amber Amdek monitor. It also included an Epson FX-100 Plus dot matrix printer. The Courtiers intend to connect IBM PC microcomputer workstations to the system and are planning to purchase a second 20-megabyte hard disk.

"When we started looking for a computer system five years ago, our business was already complex. But the software available for microcomputers wasn't sophisticated enough for what we wanted to do," Mary Courtier recalls. Minicomputer systems were too expensive. But as the minicomputer software began migrating toward microcomputers, the Courtiers resumed their search for a versatile system.

Satisfying Requirements.   The computer system they bought meets most of their requirements. It replaces what was, in effect, four separate manual bookkeeping operations. In addition to the family-held 100-acre orchard, which grosses $250,000 annually, the Courtiers operate a retail store, run a cider house, and grow 20 acres of strawberries. They pack their apples for sale to local stores and to wholesalers, and they pack some of their neighbors' apples as well.

Such a large operation requires an extremely versatile computerized accounting system. The Courtiers' new system can record the income and expenses of each profit center separately for auditing. In addition, it will consolidate the information as necessary for tax reporting and other purposes.

When their payroll suddenly expands from five employees, during the off-season, to 125 during the fall—when apples are picked, graded and shipped—the computer is essential. The fall payroll is no longer a nightmare. The payroll program conforms to agricultural regulations regarding taxes, wages, and related issues governing the operation of orchards.

Making the Impossible Possible.   The Courtiers' new computer system also provides cost accounting information that was difficult, if not impossible, to obtain with their manual bookkeeping system. It tracks expenses related to the retail operation on the basis of its August to February "season year." It also keeps records based on crop years, which begin in one calendar year but end in the next. "It was almost impossible to get good accounting figures before the computer," says Mary Courtier.

She now plans to use the system to analyze apple sales. The Orchard does most of its business with 20 stores. Mary Courtier plans to track sales at individual stores in order to spot—and remedy—soft sales.

Sales analysis, payroll, cost accounting, and the other accounting tasks the Courtiers' new computer system is being called on to perform are found in every business. They are not unique to agriculture. But the details of government regulations, the impact on record-keeping of a work force that increases 2,500 percent for a brief period each year, and the need to track a business through the cycles of the seasons, as well as through the fiscal year, earmark agriculture as a vertical market with unique requirements.

(*SOURCE: Ken Mayo, "Pursuing Verticals,"* Business Computer Systems, *September 1985, pp. 70–79.*)

DISCUSSION QUESTIONS

1. What steps would you recommend that a user pursue to locate industry-specific software?

2. A new entrepreneur, who knows the details of his business intimately, knows that he needs a computer to help his company prosper. But he finds mind boggling "the whole idea of having to identify software and hardware, then buy it, and install it with a reasonable degree of safety." Would you recommend that this entrepreneur acquire and install a computer system on his own or hire professional help? Why?

CHAPTER SUMMARY

- The four steps in an orderly, systematic approach to implementing a packaged computer system are: specify requirements; locate, evaluate, and select software; locate, evaluate, and select hardware; and install the new system.

- *Value added resellers* (*VARs*) combine hardware and software, often from various manufacturers, and resell them as a *turnkey system*. They also provide consulting services for a fee.

- A *turnkey system* is a combination of hardware and software packaged for sale by a value added seller. Theoretically, all a user has to do to use a turnkey system is to turn the key and go. It does require that a user first learn to work the system.

- A *feasibility study* is a formal term for analyzing a company's computing requirements.

- Some computer systems fail because there is a failure to identify the correct problem that needs a solution. As an example, a new computer system may speed up an order backlog problem. But it does not help if the real problem is faulty machinery that creates the order backlog.

- A "rule-of-thumb" amount to budget for a computer system is 1 percent or more of annual gross sales.

- Related expenses include the cost of floppy disks, computer stock paper, printer ribbons, and hardware and software maintenance contracts.

- One way to *cost justify* a new computer system is to calculate savings realized from reduced expenses. A good inventory system, for example, can enable management to avoid expensive idle inventory accumulations and so help to reduce expenses.

- Intangible benefits of a new system could be improved employee morale and job satisfaction.

- *Software directories* contain information about software packages, including what the software does, hardware supported, operating system requirements, pricing, number of current users, contact information, and geographic area serviced by the software supplier.

- *Customizing* a package is introducing program modifications to tailor a package for a user.

- A hands-on test of a computer package should include, among other things, an evaluation of response time, error recovery, and user prompts.

- A vendor evaluation should include checks on a vendor's business and financial background, how program changes can be implemented, and who owns program code.

- Three mechanical requirements that influence hardware planning are workstation locations, printing volume, and disk storage requirements.

- One hazard of converting from a manual to a computer system is the desire to "put everything on the computer at once." Experience shows that this spells disaster.

- *Conversion* is the term given to converting from one system to another.

- *Parallel testing* is a period when manual and computer systems function together for comparison purposes. When the test is over, there is a *cut-over* to the new system.

- A *log book* is a record of computer system malfunctions. It often helps to resolve maintenance problems when they occur.

- Project-management software enables overseeing a project more effectively by helping a user to divide a task into manageable units, assign resources to tasks, and reassign resources as a situation changes.

KEY TERMS

Accounting system packages
Conversion
Crippled copy *disk by man. for pot buyers limited records*
Customizing
Cut-over
Feasibility study
Hard-dollar saving
Independent system vendor (ISV)
Industry-specific packages
Installation
Log book
Parallel testing

PERT (Project Evaluation and
    Review Technique) chart
Project management software
Response time
Soft-dollar saving
Software directories
System integrator
Turnkey system
Turnkey vendor
User prompts
Value added reseller (VAR)
Workstations

REVIEW QUESTIONS

1. What are the steps in an orderly, systematic approach to implementing a packaged computer system?

2. What does a value added reseller sell?

3. What is a turnkey system?

4. Give an example of why some computer systems fail.

5. What is a rule-of-thumb amount to budget for a computer system?

6. What are related expenses?

7. Give an example of how to cost justify a new computer system.

8. Give an example of an intangible benefit of a new computer system.

9. What can be learned from a software directory listing?

10. What is "customizing" a package?

11. Give three examples of things to look for in a hands-on test of a software package.

12. Give three examples of things to look for in a vendor evaluation. *error recovery, evaluation response time*

13. What mechanical requirements influence hardware planning? *workstations, disk, storage printer volume* *user prompts*

14. What is a hazard of converting from a manual to a computer system?

15. What is parallel testing?

16. What purpose does a log book serve?

17. Describe how a project management package helps a user to oversee a project more effectively.

EXERCISES

1. *WMK Associates Case.*   Mr. Kennedy suggests that you continue to research the availability of integrated accounting packages for the wholesale/distribution trade. This time you review software directories for listings. Report on the number of wholesale/trade distribution applications listed. For two listings report: name of application, geographic area served, hardware supported, operating systems the application runs on, language the package is programmed in, number of clients/users, applications included, and price. Comment on how many specific items from Figures 10-3 and 10-10 are addressed in the product's narrative description.

PAYROLL #1
Handles 200 employees in 99 departments. Employees can work in multiple states under five different pay rates. Also handles vacation, sick, and nontaxable pay rates. Included are federal and state unemployment tax and six deduction fields. (*List Price*: *$495, manual and demonstration disk $50*)
Requires: 64K (other requirements not available).
Payroll #1 Company
P.O. Box M1047
Mountain View, CA 94043
(415) 444-4444

PAYROLL #2
Stores 200 employee records on double-sided floppy disk. User manual included. Menu-driven. At additional cost, customizing is available. (*List Price*: *$49*).
Requires: 64K, one disk drive, printer.
Payroll #2 Company
3028 Silver Lane
Ann Arbor, MI 48106
(313) 333-3333

PAYROLL #3
This payroll program provides for 300 employees distributed to a maximum of 15 divisions. Thirty deduction types and five taxable categories are available. Federal and state income taxes for all 50 states are built-in through tax formulas. Updates are available at a modest charge. Printed output includes: checks, check register, W–2 forms, quarterly and summary reports. While it is written in UCSD Pascal, the UCSD Pascal system is not required. Hard disk compatible. (*List Price*: *$394*)
Requires: 64K, two disk drives, printer.
Payroll #3 Company
22 Hammel Dr.
Garden Grove, CA 92641
(714) 777-7777

PAYROLL #4
Provides for 150 employees for every 100K of disk storage. This allows space to copy the master file on the disk if automatic backup is used. Details of each pay period are retained through a self backup feature.

Handles situations like reimbursing employees for out-of-pocket expenses, paying bonuses, keeping track of vacation time, loans, advances and repayments. Includes custom state and local tax calculation programming. Programs are designed for rapid reprogramming. Original commented program source code is included, along with the tax tables.

To eliminate errors, input data go through a double-keying procedure, if necessary.

Other features include: up to 10 department names per disk, up to five automatic fixed deductions with a different amount for each department, and up to five special pay amounts or deductions for each employee each period. (*List Price*: *$400*)
Requires: 48K, two disk drives.
Payroll #4 Company
P.O. Box 735
Bellingham, WA 98226
(206) 222-2222

PAYROLL #5
Designed for novice users, includes five modules: payroll, contractor, restaurant, farm and piecework. Prints checks and W–2 forms. Allows automatic posting to the Job Cost and General Ledger programs by the same manufacturer. Users maintain federal tax changes, FICA limits and percentage changes, FUTA limit changes, state unemployment limits, and state income tax changes. (*List Price*: *Each module $595*)
Requires: 64K, two disk drives, 80-column monitor, 132-column printer.
Payroll #5 Company
P.O. Box 1301
Clearwater, FL 33575
(813) 888-8888

FIGURE 10-23
Simulated directory listings from a product-specific periodical

2. *Yates Health and Beauty Care Supply Center Case.* Yates Health and Beauty Care Supply Center wants to implement a payroll application on a microcomputer. Mr. Cooper, the company's financial officer, located the payroll listings given in Figure 10-23 in a software directory. The listings seemed little more than product announcements. He had to request literature and documentation to learn if applications were candidates for further evaluation. His specific payroll requirements include: 75 employees, 6 department/divisions, 5 fixed payroll deductions, and multiple-state tax calculations. Based only on the information available in Figure 10-23:

a. Which payroll packages do you think should be examined further?

b. Which package or packages address the following issues?
   Customization
   Source code availability
   Update

c. If Mr. Cooper's long-term intention is to integrate payroll with the general ledger package, which product should be investigated further?

3. *WMK Associates Case.*   Write to the companies identified in exercise 1. Ask for detailed information on their order processing package (unless information is already available from Chapter 9, exercise 2).

When literature is available, prepare a written or oral report on the differences in package
· Order entry types accepted
· Backorder handling
· Information displays provided
· Printed output provided

4. Arrange to have a demonstration of a sales order processing package. Before the demonstration, read the *User Guide* to learn about
· Setup tasks
· Operating procedures
· Printed and displayed output

After the demonstration, make an oral or written report about how the first two items were handled. Attach copies of any printed output to the report.

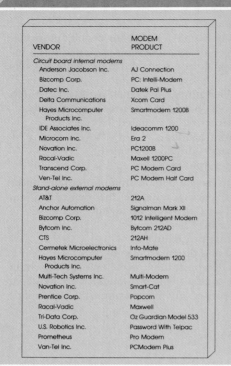

VENDOR	MODEM PRODUCT
Circuit board internal modems	
Anderson Jacobson Inc.	AJ Connection
Bizcomp Corp.	PC: Intelli-Modem
Datec Inc.	Datek Pal Plus
Delta Communications	Xcom Card
Hayes Microcomputer Products Inc.	Smartmodem 1200B
IDE Associates Inc.	Ideacomm 1200
Microcom Inc.	Era 2
Novation Inc.	PC1200B
Racal-Vadic	Maxell 1200PC
Transcend Corp.	PC Modem Card
Ven-Tel Inc.	PC Modem Half Card
Stand-alone external modems	
AT&T	212A
Anchor Automation	Signalman Mark XII
Bizcomp Corp.	1012 Intelligent Modem
Bytcom Inc.	Bytcom 212AD
CTS	212AH
Cermetek Microelectronics	Info-Mate
Hayes Microcomputer Products Inc.	Smartmodem 1200
Multi-Tech Systems Inc.	Multi-Modem
Novation Inc.	Smart-Cat
Prentice Corp.	Popcorn
Racal-Vadic	Maxwell
Tri-Data Corp.	Oz Guardian Model 533
U.S. Robotics Inc.	Password With Telpac
Prometheus	Pro Modem
Van-Tel Inc.	PCModem Plus

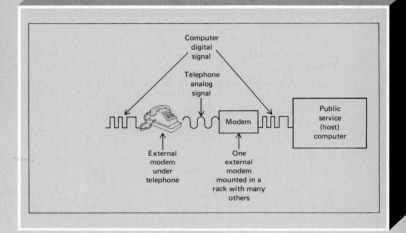

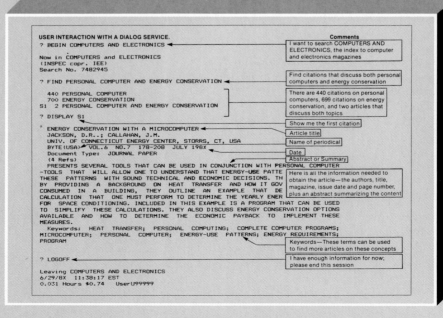

11

Communication Software and Services

AFTER READING THIS CHAPTER, YOU SHOULD BE ABLE TO

- Identify the hardware and software necessary for computer communications

- Describe services available to communicators, like electronic and voice mail, bulletin boards, and computer conferencing

- Identify some on-line databases

Personal computer users dramatically increase the value of their computers by using them for such communication services as

- Sending electronic or voice mail
- Maintaining electronic message centers or bulletin boards
- Participating in computer conferences
- Interrogating on-line databases in a public "on-line library" that contains information of interest to business and professional people

This chapter begins with a discussion of the hardware and software necessary to use a personal computer for communications. Then it describes some of the many services just listed. These services are all available on either a public or private basis using computers of all sizes.

MODEM

To send electronic mail to his salespeople, Frank Nelson of Interstate Distributing Company first had to equip his personal computer for communications. He had to buy a **modem** for linking his computer to a telephone line.

Modem is a short form for *modulate and demodulate*. **Modulation** is a process that takes discrete digital computer signals of 1's and 0's and endows them with sound to go through the telephone network, as shown in Figure 11-1. Telephone signals are called **analog** signals. Analog signals are **demodulated** back to digital computer signals on the receiving end.

Figure 11-1 illustrates use of an external modem, which is about the size of a 5-by-9-inch book, although some modems are even smaller. This one fits under a telephone, even though the telephone is not used once the modem power is turned on. The modem is connected with a cable to the telephone wall outlet. It is also cabled to the computer's so-called **serial port,** at the back side of the system unit. The cable is often called an **RS-232 cable,** or a **serial cable.** Bits are released from the computer's memory in a serial fashion, one digit after another, to the cable.

Mr. Nelson uses a less expensive **internal modem.** It eliminates an extra piece of hardware on the desktop. As shown in Figures 11-2 and 11-3, it is a special-purpose circuit board. It fits into a personal computer's expansion slot on the system board. A cable connects the circuit board directly with the telephone wall outlet. Computers with already built-in internal modems require only a cable to connect to the telephone wall outlet.

A sampler of modems, as well as communication software, appears in Figures 11-4 and 11-5. The software packaged with Mr. Nelson's

FIGURE 11-1
Computer communications using modems

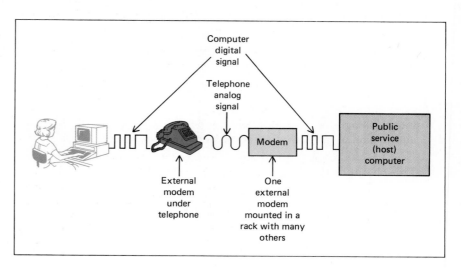

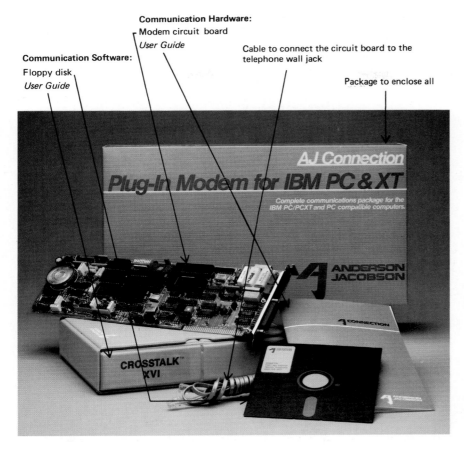

Communication Software:
Floppy disk
User Guide

Communication Hardware:
Modem circuit board
User Guide

Cable to connect the circuit board to the telephone wall jack

Package to enclose all

FIGURE 11-2
Components of an internal modem kit
(Courtesy of Anderson Jacobsen)

modem is what does the "computer-to-computer talking." The modem is just a service device to get the signals from one computer to the other.

One feature of communication software is an ability to dial automatically whatever telephone number is desired. **Auto-dial** phone numbers

FIGURE 11-3
An installed internal modem

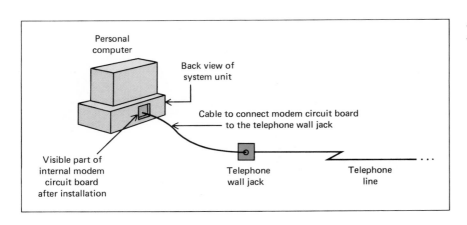

Personal computer

Back view of system unit

Cable to connect modem circuit board to the telephone wall jack

Visible part of internal modem circuit board after installation

Telephone wall jack

Telephone line

Access	MicroPhone	Procomm
ASCOM	*Omniterm	*RBBS-PC
ASCII Pro	PC Anywhere	Red Ryder
Asynchronous Communication Software	*PC Com-Plet	Reflection
*Conexus	*PC-Host	*Relay Gold
*CrossTalk	PC-MODEM	*Remote
In-Talk	PC-Talk	*Smartcom
Lotus Express	Personal Communications Manager	*Transcend
MEX-PC		

FIGURE 11-4
A sampler of communication software packages for personal computers

* Can be used to set up "do-it-yourself" private electronic mail or message systems.

FIGURE 11-5
A sampler of modems for personal computers

VENDOR	MODEM PRODUCT
Circuit board internal modems	
Anderson Jacobson Inc.	AJ Connection
Bizcomp Corp.	PC: Intelli-Modem
Datec Inc.	Datek Pal Plus
Delta Communications	Xcom Card
Hayes Microcomputer Products Inc.	Smartmodem 1200B
IDE Associates Inc.	Ideacomm 1200
Microcom Inc.	Era 2
Novation Inc.	PC1200B
Racal-Vadic	Maxell 1200PC
Transcend Corp.	PC Modem Card
Ven-Tel Inc.	PC Modem Half Card
Stand-alone external modems	
AT&T	212A
Anchor Automation	Signalman Mark XII
Bizcomp Corp.	1012 Intelligent Modem
Bytcom Inc.	Bytcom 212AD
CTS	212AH
Cermetek Microelectronics	Info-Mate
Hayes Microcomputer Products Inc.	Smartmodem 1200
Multi-Tech Systems Inc.	Multi-Modem
Novation Inc.	Smart-Cat
Prentice Corp.	Popcorn
Racal-Vadic	Maxwell
Tri-Data Corp.	Oz Guardian Model 533
U.S. Robotics Inc.	Password With Telpac
Prometheus	Pro Modem
Van-Tel Inc.	PCModem Plus

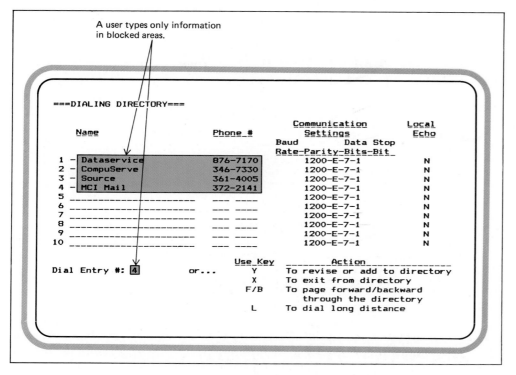

FIGURE 11-6
A sample dialing directory
(Adaptation of PC-TALK software, with permission of the Headlands Press, Inc.)

must be recorded in the software's **dialing directory,** like the one shown in Figure 11-6. Mr. Nelson typed into his directory the phone number of the electronic mail service he planned to use.

LINKING COMPUTERS

Before data communication can take place, compatibility must exist between computers. The settings shown in Figure 11-6 were preset because they are the common settings used for personal computers. A brief summary of what they mean helps to understand what is going on "under the hood" during communication exchanges:

Communication Setting	Meaning
1200	This is the number of bits that can theoretically be sent over a communication line per second. Common rates for personal computers are 300, 1,200, and 2,400. Modems that send data at higher **bits-per-second** (bps) rates are more commonly found in mainframe installations. Sometimes the bits-per-

second rate is called the **baud** (pronounced "bawd")
rate, which has a different meaning to the data
communication industry.

E   E stands for "even." If, as in Figure 11-7, all the "one"
bits in a character add up to an even number, like
two, then a zero is placed in the parity bit slot before
the character is sent. The **parity** bit provides a low
level of error checking. If the addition results in
an odd number, like 3, then a 1 is added in the
parity slot to "even" out the 1 bits. At the receiving
end, should the parity bit not be even, it signals a
transmission error.

7   Sets the number of bits that make up one character.
Seven is the number of bits in an **ASCII character**
(the ASCII characters are given in the chart in Appendix C).

1   Sets the number of stop bits that concludes the transmission of one character.

Asynchronous Communication

These settings reflect the most common way personal computers
communicate. It is called **asynchronous,** or character-by-character, **communication.** The term asynchronous means "not synchronized." It highlights the fact that characters are transmitted with a random idle period
between characters.

Asynchronous communication is also referred to as the "asynchronous protocol." **Protocol** is the data communication industry's term for
a set of rules or procedures established and followed by cooperating
devices. To communicate successfully, transmitting and receiving computers must follow the same set of rules, or protocols.

FIGURE 11-7
*Standard asynchronous (character-by-
character) communication*

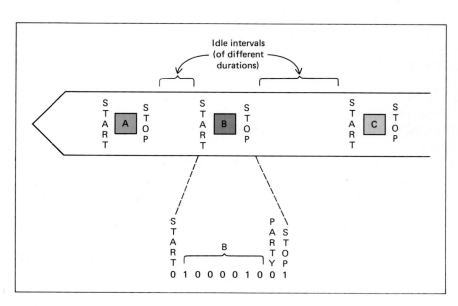

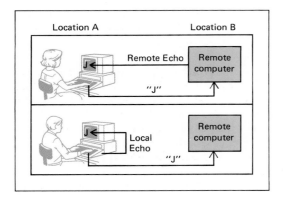

FIGURE 11-8
Remote and local echoing of keyboarded characters

Echo

In Mr. Nelson's package, the **local echo** setting refers to sending a keyboarded character simultaneously to the local display and to the remote computer. As illustrated in Figure 11-8, a local echo is not needed if a **remote echo** is supplied. Remote echoing occurs so quickly that a user has the sense that it occurs locally. It gives visual verification of the transmission accuracy.

Some users who enter a "yes" for the echo setting see two characters on the screen for every one keyboarded. It means that they are getting both a local and a remote echo. Just answering "no" to the local echo setting corrects this problem. (Sometimes, in place of "local echo," the term "half-duplex" is used.)

With the software set and the modem power turned on, Mr. Nelson is ready to communicate. He first types "4" to auto-dial the mail service. He can hear sounds from his modem as the software "dials" the phone number. The telephone ringing sound on the remote end is also audible. When the phone is answered, a high-pitched tone is heard. It is the familiar modem frequency **carrier** sound. Typing a carriage return in response to the tone establishes a link between the two computers. While the tone disappears, the carrier remains present on the line for the duration of the session.

Log-On and Public Services

With the communication link established, the remote computer takes control and prompts Mr. Nelson to log-on. A **log-on,** or sign-on, sequence validates a communicator to a host computer. It generally includes a request for a billing account number and a password. Both are stored on the public service company's database when Mr. Nelson originally subscribes to use the service.

Public service subscriptions are available at local computer retail stores and from other sources. Sometimes **public communication services** are called **videotex** services and provide, among other options:

- Electronic and voice mail
- Bulletin board services
- Computer conferencing
- On-line databases

The fee structures for two representative service companies are given in Figure 11-9. Some organizations that provide electronic mail services are listed in Figure 11-10.

Mr. Nelson answers most of the public service's log-on questions with a single keystroke because he preloaded his billing account number and other information into a message directory. Like the dialing directory, he can activate entire sequences with a single keystroke.

After log-on, he selects the service option desired. Services are offered in a menu, like the one in Figure 11-11.

Packet-Switched Service

When Mr. Nelson subscribed to a public communication service, he was given the local telephone number of three public packet-switched network companies: Telenet, Tymnet, and Uninet. Using any of them, he pays only for a local call, even though the service he uses is located many states away.

The diagram in Figure 11-12 shows how packet-switched networks operate. They have many **local nodes** in many cities to link users to

FIGURE 11-9
Sample fees for public communication services

FEES CHARGED	THE SOURCE	COMPUSERVE
One-time registration	$49.95	Executive service: None
		Consumer service: $39.95
Connect cost		
300 bits-per-second		
Day use	36¢ minute	21¢ minute
Evening use	14¢ minute	10¢ minute
1,200 bits-per-second		
Day use	43¢ minute	25¢ minute
Evening use	18¢ minute	21¢ minute
2,400 bits-per-second	(selected cities service)	
Day use	46¢ minute	
Evening use	20¢ minute	
Minimum monthly		
usage fee	$10.00	Executive service: $10 per month
		Consumer service: None

Note: Rates are often higher outside major metropolitan areas.

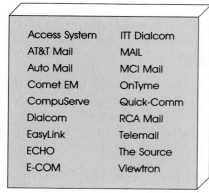

Access System	ITT Dialcom
AT&T Mail	MAIL
Auto Mail	MCI Mail
Comet EM	OnTyme
CompuServe	Quick-Comm
Dialcom	RCA Mail
EasyLink	Telemail
ECHO	The Source
E-COM	Viewtron

FIGURE 11-10
A sampler of public electronic mail services

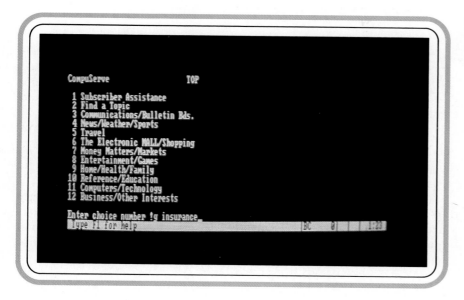

FIGURE 11-11
A sample menu for a public communication service
(*Courtesy of CompuServe*)

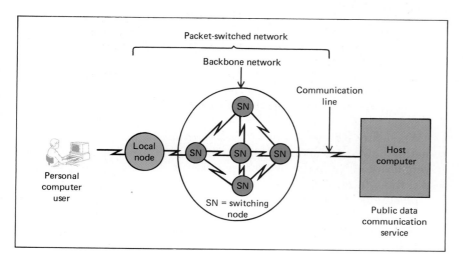

FIGURE 11-12
A packet-switched network has many local nodes in many cities that feed the backbone network which services various public and private host computers.

host public communication service computers. These public host computers are permanently attached to the network as a convenience to their customers. The hosts are billed by the packet-switching company for all transmissions made to them by customers. So a user only pays for the local phone call.

Inside the **packet-switched network,** data are routed in groups of characters called a **packet.** All user packets time share the same backbone network. Packets are "switched" from one node to another to reach their destination. Packet charges are included in a customer's monthly subscription bill from the public service. Charges are far less than if a direct toll call had been made to the host computer.

Many large and small companies have permanent connections with packet-switched networks. It is a convenient way to have an instant communication network. It is an alternative more organizations turn to, rather than develop their own data communication network.

ELECTRONIC MAIL

To eliminate telephone tag with his field sales representatives, Mr. Nelson uses electronic mail. Telephone tag results when one party calls another, who is not available, and leaves a message to return the call. Often the returned call finds no one in and results in another message. And so it goes wasting time, money, and effort.

Mr. Nelson prefers **electronic mail,** which is the transfer of messages by electronic methods. When logged on to the service, his display looks like the one in Figure 11-13. He types SCAN to review received mail quickly. Mail can be exchanged only by subscribers or sponsors of subscription accounts. Most letters cost under one dollar to send.

After typing READ to see a specific piece of mail, he is asked for its disposition. He can file or delete a letter, create a reply, forward it to another subscriber, or execute a combination of available options.

To send mail, Mr. Nelson types CREATE and the recipient's account number. He is prompted for a brief subject line before typing the body of the letter. When finished, he can, among other options:

· Add a command to send a carbon copy to another subscriber
· Save a copy of the letter in his own mailbox
· Request an acknowledgment that the letter is received

When Mr. Nelson began to use electronic mail, he felt there was something awesome about instant communication—typing a letter and having it instantly appear in another person's mailbox. There are drawbacks, though. He found that unsolicited junk mail pops up as it does in conventional mail. Also, when he wants to send a reply, he cannot simultaneously type new mail and display received mail. A solution requires first printing received mail to get a copy of it. To do this efficiently, he transfers mail from the service computer into his personal computer.

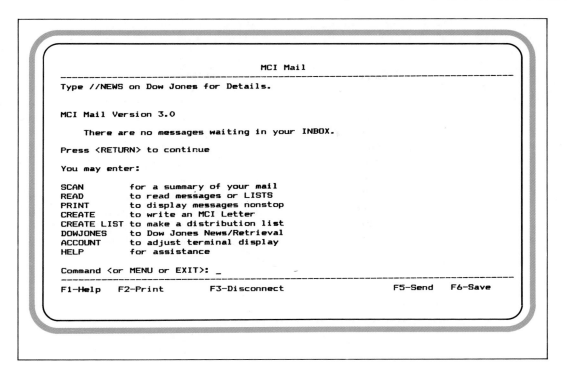

```
                                    MCI Mail
----------------------------------------------------------------------------
Type //NEWS on Dow Jones for Details.


MCI Mail Version 3.0

     There are no messages waiting in your INBOX.

Press <RETURN> to continue

You may enter:

SCAN          for a summary of your mail
READ          to read messages or LISTS
PRINT         to display messages nonstop
CREATE        to write an MCI Letter
CREATE LIST   to make a distribution list
DOWJONES      to Dow Jones News/Retrieval
ACCOUNT       to adjust terminal display
HELP          for assistance

Command <or MENU or EXIT>: _
----------------------------------------------------------------------------
F1-Help   F2-Print        F3-Disconnect             F5-Send   F6-Save
```

FIGURE 11-13
An electronic mail service menu of options
(Courtesy of MCI Communications Corporation. MCI Mail is a
registered service mark of MCI Communications Corporation.)

Uploading and Downloading

Bringing any computer file, like a letter, from a remote computer into one's own computer is called **downloading** a file. Conversely, sending a file to another computer is called **uploading** a file. A transfer takes only a few seconds for short files.

Mr. Nelson or his assistant usually prepares all documents for mailing at a personal computer. Then they upload them as a file transfer to their own electronic mailbox. In a final step, they forward mail to recipients' mailboxes. The efficiency of a file transfer is important, since billing is based on connect time.

Packages, such as Lotus Express, offer a feature that runs in the "background" while another application is in use. It monitors mail without interrupting "foreground" tasks, like a word processing document in progress.

At user-specified intervals, the software automatically logs on to an electronic mail service, retrieves incoming mail, and stores it on disk. An audio tone alerts a user that mail has been received.

The package can also send documents in their true form, without having to transfer them as ASCII text. The true form is usually a proprietary "binary" format. This means that word-processed documents and spreadsheets arrive with their format characteristics intact. This greatly simplifies the task of having to edit a communicated file.

FIGURE 11-14
An integrated voice/data computer
(Courtesy of Panasonic)

Private Service

A personal computer can be dedicated to function as a private electronic mail service. Most communication software packages provide this capability.

To accept mail, a personal computer must be in a ready state with an **auto-answer** feature enabled through the data communication software. To send mail, it can auto-dial and transfer files at designated times to designated phone numbers. In problem cases, it can retry to send mail until a successful transmission is achieved.

One organization, as an example, programs the auto-dial feature to collect branch sales orders at night. It takes advantage of reduced night telephone rates. The computers do their jobs without operators at either end.

Firms of all sizes set up private electronic mail systems. In one management consulting company, staff members spend most of their time working with clients outside the office. The company's private mail system helps to maintain communication between office and staff members. Anyone can send messages to selected individuals or to a distribution list of selected people on the system.

Voice Mail

Voice mail is an alternative to electronic mail. A personal computer, like the one shown in Figure 11-14, can be used. In some cases, an ordinary telephone serves as the input and output device. Whatever is used, a central computer controls voice traffic in digital mail systems, as shown in Figure 11-15. Its **voice digitizer** measures sound frequencies and assigns them values that can be stored as 1's and 0's. To play back voice mail, a **voice synthesizer** reads digital signals and converts them back to sound.

Some systems have a text-to-voice capability that enables a user to

FIGURE 11-15
Voice mail systems use voice digitizing and synthesizing.

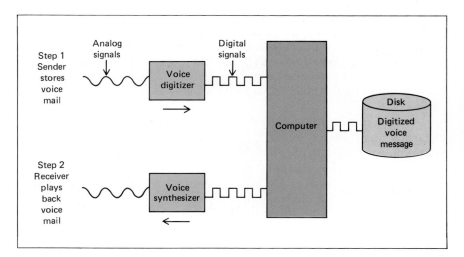

receive electronic mail messages over the telephone. Conversely, voice mail can be displayed and printed.

Users of voice and electronic mail systems claim that they

· Reduce phone bills because they promote more efficient communications
· Increase productivity because they reduce phone conversations and interruptions of the work routine
· Remove traditional time constraints because they are available at any hour of the day or night to leave or retrieve mail

BULLETIN BOARD SERVICES

While voice or electronic mail is sent to a specific recipient, **electronic bulletin board** messages are not. They are available for any caller to view. In addition, callers are free to add their own messages.

The electronic bulletin board at one public service is divided into about 75 categories. Categories correspond to user interests and include law, photography, astrology, and computer groups. The one for users of a popular personal computer contains messages left by private individuals, as well as companies, to

· Sell used equipment
· Ask for or provide advice
· Offer informal product reviews
· Make programs available to anyone who wants to download them

All messages are periodically deleted.

Some companies maintain bulletin boards on public service systems to get feedback on new products. Others maintain private systems. They dedicate a telephone number and a personal computer to the job. The system runs on "automatic pilot" in what is usually called **unattended mode.** It is often available 24 hours a day, 7 days a week. Any caller can leave a message about product deficiency, improvement suggestions, service, or whatever.

Many special-interest groups, like doctors, aviators, and community computer-user groups, have private personal computer-based bulletin board systems.

Bulletin board misuse, however, is a problem. This has led to a voluntary shutdown of some, and increased vigilance by others.

COMPUTER CONFERENCING

Computer conferencing is a restricted form of a bulletin board system. A computer conference is established by creating a pair of files:

· One for conference messages, called the **conference notebook file**
· One for a list of the conference members

In the case where a chemical company's project development team is geographically dispersed, a conference notebook file provides an electronic meeting place. If there are several topics to be discussed, separate conferences are established with different member lists.

When a key member of the project is transferred, the new replacement is able to get into the conference file and track its progress. Using "key word" searches, such as the former member's name, everything said about the member's area of responsibility is documented. It helped one replacement to avoid making a proposal that was previously rejected.

This tracking capability gives computer conferencing an advantage over telephone and face-to-face conferencing. In addition, it

- Is less expensive than a telephone conference call
- Allows users to get printed copies of the conference notebook file
- Does not require participants to be in designated places at predetermined times

The *Electronic Information Exchange System* (EIES, pronounced "eyes") has conducted controlled experiments of computer conferencing. One finding is that computer conferences result in at least as good a solution to a problem as could be expected from a group of people gathered in one room. More often than not, the quality of the solution is better.

Conferences on multiuser computers have an added advantage because many users can be on the computer simultaneously. This permits prearranging live-participation conferences, as the notebook file example in Figure 11-16 demonstrates.

Computer conferencing helps

- A government agency to coordinate its efforts with geographically dispersed members.

FIGURE 11-16
Printout of a notebook file from a "live" computer conference

```
Now joining: Randall (Tom)

114 Perez (Gil) 7-Oct-8X 10:21AM-PDT
Good morning, Tom! Have you had a
chance to read  my  analysis of  the
company's  long-range plan  yet?  The
section on the profit-sharing proposal
needs improvement.  Any ideas?

115 Randall (Tom) 7-Oct-8X 10:25AM-PDT
Hi, Gil. Yes I read it and have some
ideas that might interest you.  I need
more time to work on them. I  will  send
them before seven tonight.  Are we still
all planning to conference on Friday
morning?

Now joining: Stein (Sandra)

116 Perez (Gil) 7-Oct-8X 10:27AM-PDT
Hello, Sandra.  Have you heard whether
or not the Friday morning meeting is
on? Tom and I would like confirmation.

117 Stein (Sandra) 7-Oct-8X 10:29AM-PDT
Hello, Gil and Tom.  Yes, the meeting is
confirmed  for 9:30 a.m.  Gil, will your
rewrite of  the plan be ready by  then?
Tom, can you have some figures...
```

- A group of office automation consultants and corporate long-range planners in the United States, Australia, and other foreign countries to swap information on good and bad hardware, software, and service.
- An environmental group to keep abreast of regulatory issues.
- A nuclear power organization to swap information designed to prevent nuclear plant accidents. The conference also provides a forum for experts, should a crisis occur.

REMOTE COMPUTING

Remote computing packages tie two computers together so that both keyboards are active and both screens show the same thing. They allow users

- To operate their own computer from a distance—from a client's office, home, hotel room, or wherever there is another computer. This is useful to people who travel a lot and often wish that they could easily bring their computer with them.
- To collaborate with others on the same project, called **cocomputing,** such as a builder and a client working at opposite ends of the country. Both parties can view an evolving building design and make decisions either through a pop-up "chat" window or over another separate voice line.

These programs require that one computer function as a "host" and the other as a "remote" computer. The application program, such as a spreadsheet, word processor, or graphics program, must run on the host.

Cocomputing provides a valuable support tool for computer consultants and other computer troubleshooters. It requires putting "host-side" software on a customer's or client's computer. Then when a customer has a problem, the consultant calls the computer. Using the "remote-side" software, the consultant can explore the problem as if sitting in front of the computer. Alternatively, a consultant can have the customer demonstrate the problem while observing the same screens on the remote computer.

A remote computing feature is available in some full-featured communication software packages. It is also available in stand-alone packages such as those listed in Figure 11-17. While some, like TeleVision, handle graphics, others do not.

FIGURE 11-17
A sampler of remote computing software packages

ON-LINE DATABASES

Most organizations do not have the hardware, software, personnel, or other resources to maintain all the databases they desire. To fill the gap, they pay a fee to subscribe to **on-line database services,** such as those listed in Figure 11-18. These services are available to individual

Carbon Copy
Close-Up
In-Synch
PC Asynchronous
Remote
TeleVision

Automatic Data Processing	Dun and Bradstreet	Official Airline Guide/Electronic
Bibliographic	Federal Reserve Board	Standard and Poor's
Retrieval Services	General Electric	Telerate
Boeing	Information Services	The Source
Citicorp	G.T.E. (General Telephone	Time Inc.
CompuServe	and Electronics)	Warner Computer Services
Control Data	Harper and Row	Wharton Economic Forecasting
Data Resources	Interactive Data Corp.	Associates
Delphi	I.P. Sharp	Xerox
DIALOG Information Services	Mead Data	
Dow Jones News Retrieval	NewsNet	

FIGURE 11-18
A sampler of organizations that provide on-line database services

and corporate subscribers over private communication and public telephone lines.

Categories

On-line database services can be divided into three categories:

- Financial
- General business/research
- Special purpose

The Dow Jones News Retrieval is the best known of the financial services. It offers, among other services:

- Price quotes from the New York Stock Exchange, American Stock Exchange, and the over-the-counter market
- Full text of *The Wall Street Journal* and *Barron's* (financial newspapers)
- News, sports, weather, and a bridge, or "gateway," into the electronic MCI mail service

One service dominates the general business-research category. It is DIALOG Information Services, which has over 250 databases in the areas of

- Business
- Government and current events
- Law
- Medicine
- Engineering
- Science and technology
- Environment
- Arts, education, and social sciences

Some of DIALOG's **on-line databases** are listed in Figure 11-19.

Figure 11-20 gives an example of a DIALOG database search. It is typical of database searches in general. The search illustrated took about

- **Computer Database.** Comprehensive summaries of computer-related articles and publications from over 500 international sources spanning telecommunications, hardware, software, and services.
- **Laborlaw.** Authoritative summaries of U.S. legal decisions on labor relations, fair employment, wages and hours, and related matters.
- **BI/Data Forecasts.** Briefings on the economic, social, and political outlook for 35 major countries.
- **D&B—Dun's Market Identifiers.** Directory of over 1 million public and private companies with 10 or more employees, listing address, products, sales, executives, corporate organization, subsidiaries, industry information, sales prospects.
- **Disclosure/Spectrum Ownership.** Detailed ownership information for thousands of U.S. public companies.
- **Find/SVP Reports and Studies Index.** Summaries of industry and market research reports. Surveys from U.S. and international sources are used for market, industry, and company analyses.
- **PTS Prompt.** Primary source of information on product introductions, market share, corporate directions and ventures, and companies in every industry. Contains detailed summaries of articles from over 800 worldwide trade and industry sources for market planning and tracking.
- **ASI (American Statistics Index).** Summaries of government reports covering social, economic, and demographic data from over 500 federal agencies.
- **Newsearch.** Daily index to over 2,000 news stories and other features from newspapers, popular magazines, trade and industry journals, complete press releases from PR Newswire, business and management journals, legal periodicals, and newspapers.
- **Health Planning and Administration.** Nonclinical literature summaries on all aspects of health care, facilities, and planning.
- **Directory of Associations.** Directory of over 15,000 trade associations and other membership organizations.
- **REMARC.** Retrospective coverage of the cataloged collection of the U.S. Library of Congress.

FIGURE 11-19
A sampler of DIALOG's on-line databases

two minutes and cost under $1.00. Fees can mount rapidly, however, until search techniques are perfected.

DIALOG contains only abstracts of articles. By contrast, the LEXIS on-line database provides the full text of documents. It is one example of a special-purpose on-line database that services lawyers. Another example of a special-purpose service is one for airline travelers, the Official Airline Guide/Electronic. It allows subscribers to find direct and connecting flights to almost any point in North America.

Benefits

Most organizations, as well as traditional libraries, do not have on their shelves, indexed or cross-referenced, the breadth of material currently available in on-line databases. In addition, on-line databases

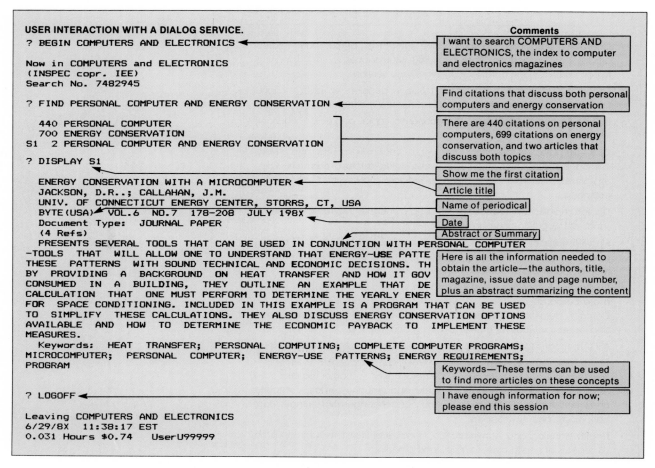

FIGURE 11-20
Example of an on-line database search using one of the DIALOG services
(Courtesy of INSPEC and DIALOG Information Systems)

are often more up to date because of weekly, or even daily, updates.

Some services provide an option to *flag* new items on topics of continuing subscriber interest. Every time a subscriber calls the service, it reports the addition of new items for the "flagged" topic. Managers use such flagging options to track

· Competition's new product announcements
· Changes in industry prices
· Personnel shifts
· New product patent filings

Problems

The effort required to learn how to conduct a successful search is a problem of using on-line databases. One analyst claims that it can take a month of regular practice, five or six times a week, before one feels comfortable with some services.

Specialized software products, like In-Search illustrated in Figure 11-21, provide tutorials that simulate search sessions. They help users to plan actual search strategies. Planning is done on a personal computer, before any on-line charges are incurred.

Specialized services, like InFact from Western Union and EasyNet from Telebase Systems, give subscribers easy access to a host of other vendors' database services

· Without having to subscribe separately to each desired service
· Without having to learn new and different commands to work with each service

This type of **gateway service** also helps subscribers to prepare search strategies. It will even select appropriate databases to search if desired. Should a subscriber type "SOS" for help, a human breaks in to chat "on-line" to help resolve search phrasing problems.

Costs

Searches can be expensive, especially if a search strategy is not pre-planned. But experts can do sophisticated searches while holding down costs. Two examples of searches and costs incurred by experts are

FIGURE 11-21
A simulated card catalog helps a user to develop an on-line database search strategy.
(Software: In-Search adaptation, courtesy of Menlo Corp.)

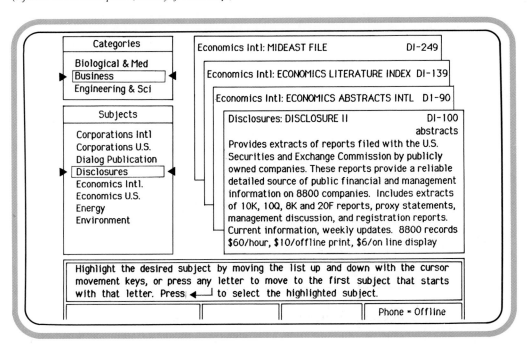

- $90 for a home health care firm seeking industry trends and forecasts (using five databases)
- $33 for a private person researching the potential growth of a company that offered him a job (using five databases)

These costs seem like bargains when compared with the cost of conducting laborious manual searches. In both cases, the searches took under one hour.

On-Line Database Alternative

Providers of CD ROM (compact disk read-only memory) databases offer an alternative to pay-as-you-go on-line searching. **CD ROM databases** are databases provided on a CD ROM disk that allow a user to browse through information at leisure without worrying about on-line charges. Some of the over 100 CD ROM databases available are

- Electronic Encyclopedia
- Compact Disclosure (a corporate financial index)
- Medline
- Aquatic Sciences and Fisheries
- Life Sciences Collection

Major users of this alternative, so far, are Fortune 500 companies, financial institutions, and government agencies that can afford to pay for it. As an example, the Electronic Encyclopedia costs $1,495 for the software and CD ROM player. To break even at this price, a user would have to spend more than 33.2 hours at $45 an hour, using the database on-line through DIALOG. Only then would it be more economical to buy the CD ROM version.

It is expected that as CD ROM databases become more popular, on-line services will be forced to redefine their services. Since historical information is the main feature of CD ROM, on-line services are expected to focus their efforts on what CD ROM cannot supply—up-to-the-minute reports.

Modem Alternative

While a CD ROM encourages less use of on-line services, another development is encouraging more use. It is a modem substitute under development by Pacific Bell Telephone. The company believes the hardware will make the modem obsolete.

Currently, a telephone line carries only one analog transmission through a modem. With Pacific Bell's new black box hooked into a single telephone circuit, however, signals are digitized at the source. It allows one phone line to carry seven distinct transmissions at once:

- Two voice channels (digitized voice)
- One 9600 bits-per-second data channel for high-speed access to information services and computer-to-computer connections
- Four lower-speed data transmission channels for data related to, for example, interactive building energy management, security systems, and community bulletin boards

The company hopes to position itself as the purveyor of the hardware, called a *multiplexer*, as well as the connecting link between information services and the user.

COMMUNICATION SOFTWARE EVALUATION

Almost any communication software package enables a user to connect to services providing

- Electronic mail
- Voice mail
- Electronic bulletin boards
- Computer conferencing
- On-line databases

A checklist to help evaluate communication software is given in Figure 11-22. Most of the listed items have already been covered. Others include include

- **Error correction.** This is a built-in method of catching and correcting errors in data, especially complete files, that are transferred between modems. Errors can be caused by static on telephone lines. Popular methods of detecting and correcting errors are called the *Xmodem, Ymodem, Kermit, MNP,* and *X.PC protocols*. Error detection and correction occur "under the hood." A user is not aware of the process.
- *Programming language*. This allows a user to create a so-called **script file** of procedures for further automating custom communication tasks. One example is a script file that logs a user on to a favorite communication service and enters the commands that get the user into the offering desired, such as a stock quotation service.
- **Multiple sessions.** This provides an ability to conduct more than one communication session at a time.

FIGURE 11-22
Communication software evaluation checklist

COMMUNICATION SOFTWARE

Are file transfers possible?
Can file transfers be checked for transmission errors?
Can a remote computer be dialed automatically?
Is remote computing possible?
Is there an unattended automatic answer capability?
Can a log-on response be reduced to a single keystroke?
Can more than one communication session be conducted at a time?
Is there a programming language to automate communication applications?
Is it possible to set up one or more private functions, like electronic mail,
    bulletin boards, and computer conferencing?

(Figure 3-25, General Software Evaluation checklist, is necessary to complete this evaluation.)

CASE STUDY: *Tracking Your Competition*

Marjorie Hill, director of national information for Laventhol & Horwath, tracks her company's competition by accessing on-line databases with her IBM PC. Hill's service became of critical importance to her firm in 1979, when the American Institute of Certified Public Accountants (CPAs) reversed a policy against advertising for accounting firms. As a result, competition for clients among accounting companies, such as hers, increased. "Some of the Big Eight (accounting firms) decided to focus on what has traditionally been our market, the middle-echelon companies and entrepreneurs," Hill says. Fearful that this would erode their client base, executives at 10th-ranked Laventhol & Horwath asked Hill's information center to evaluate the activity and strength of their competition.

Electronic Libraries.   Hill knew from past experience the databases that would give her indicators of competitor activity, including an increase or decrease in a competitor's revenue, domestic and worldwide sales, number of offices, number of employees, and number of partners.

Hill accessed two of DIALOG Information Services' data bases, ABI/Inform and The National Newspaper Index, to get that information. ABI summarizes articles on business practices, corporate strategies, and trends from business and management journals. The National Newspaper Index indexes articles from *The Wall Street Journal*, *The New York Times*, and *The Christian Science Monitor*, among others. Hill searched the databases by competitors' names to retrieve data on their marketing strategies and numbers.

Hitting the Data Bank.   Hill found that the Big Eight firms were actively soliciting new accounts. "We came up with quite a bit of information, articles in the data bank that talked about what CPA firms were doing from a marketing viewpoint," she says. "One thing Laventhol wanted to find out was how serious and specific these firms were and, within that, did they also become very specific—were they target-marketing our principal markets, which are: the leisure-time industry, health care and real estate? Were they going after entrepreneurs just by sales volume, or were they going after specific markets that we were established in? And which firms were doing that?"

Hill passed on the raw information she retrieved to company analysts who organized it into a confidential report for Laventhol's senior partners. They, in turn, used that report to decide on how to handle the emerging competition. "When (the executives) saw how some of the Big Eight were becoming more aggressive in trying to sell and market (their services)," Hill says, "Laventhol made the decision to market effectively and aggressively."

The end result was a fatter share of the accounting market for Laventhol. "I don't know what the exact figures are," Hill says, "but Laventhol has been increasing its accounts for the last four or five years."

(*SOURCE*: *Reprinted with permission from* Personal Computing, *May 1986, pp. 93–103. Copyright 1986, Hayden Publishing Company.*)

DISCUSSION QUESTIONS

1. Describe how on-line databases can provide business data that can help an organization make the right competitive decisions.

2. Since on-line databases generally provide information that is available elsewhere in a written form, why would anyone pay for something that is available at a much lower cost, or even free in many cases?

CHAPTER SUMMARY

- A *modem* modulates digital into analog signals, or demodulates analog to digital signals for data communications.

- Communication software can *auto-dial* phone numbers listed in its dialing directory.

- Common communication software settings are 1200 bits-per-second, even parity, 7 bits-per-character (ASCII), and 1 stop bit.

- *Asynchronous*, or character-by-character, communication is the most common way in which personal computers communicate.

- *Protocol* is the data communication industry's term for a set of rules or procedures established and followed by cooperating devices. To communicate successfully, transmitting and receiving computers must follow the same set of rules, or protocols.

- A *local echo* means that keyboarded characters are sent to the display and to the remote computer. A *remote echo* means that the keyboarded characters are first sent to the remote computer and then returned to the local display.

- When logging on to a remote computer, the high-pitched tone heard is the modem's frequency *carrier* sound. Although it becomes silent, the carrier remains present on the line for the duration of a communication session.

- A *log-on* validates a communicator to a host computer. It usually consists of typing a billing account number and a password.

- *Public communication services* might offer, among other options, electronic and voice mail, electronic bulletin boards, computer conferencing, and on-line databases. They are sometimes called *videotex* services.

- A *public packet-switched network* sends communication in groups of characters called a *packet*. Packets time-share the service's backbone network.

- *Electronic mail* is the transfer of messages by electronic methods.

- *Uploading* is sending a file to another computer. *Downloading* is receiving a file into one's own computer.

- An *auto-answer* feature enables a computer to accept incoming electronic mail or other data communication.

- In voice mail, a *voice digitizer* measures voice sound frequencies and assigns them values that can be stored as 1's and 0's. In playback, a *voice synthesizer* reads digital signals and converts them back to sound.

- An *electronic bulletin board* makes messages available to any logged-on communicator.

- When a computer is set to run on "automatic pilot" for data communication tasks, it is usually referred to as *unattended mode*.

- *Computer conferencing* is a restricted form of a bulletin board system. It has a *conference notebook file* and a member list control file.

- *On-line database* services provide databases of information over communication lines to subscribers for a fee.

- The DIALOG Information Service dominates the general business-research category of on-line database services.

- The effort required to conduct a successful on-line database search is a problem of using on-line databases. Specialized software and *gateway services* are supplying help for this problem.

- When evaluating a communication software package, it is useful to check if it also provides *error correction* (to detect errors during a file transfer), *script files* (to program data communication tasks), and *multiple sessions* (to do several communication tasks at once).

KEY TERMS

Analog
ASCII characters
Asynchronous communication

Auto-answer
Auto-dial
Baud

Bits-per-second (bps)
Carrier
CD ROM databases
Cocomputing
Computer conferencing
Conference notebook file
Demodulation
Dialing directory
Downloading
Electronic bulletin board
Electronic mail
Error correction
Gateway service
Host
Internal modem
Kermit protocol
Local echo
Local nodes
Log-on
Modem
Modulation

Multiple sessions
On-line database
On-line database service
Packet
Packet-switched network
Parity
Protocol
Public communication service
Remote computing packages
Remote echo
RS–232 cable
Script file
Serial cable
Serial port
Unattended mode
Uploading
Videotex
Voice digitizer
Voice mail
Voice synthesizer
Xmodem protocol

REVIEW QUESTIONS

1. What is a modem?
2. What is character-by-character communication called?
3. What does protocol mean?
4. Describe the communication settings "1200-E-7-1."
5. What does "log on" mean?
6. Describe some representative electronic mail commands.
7. How is a computer conference set up?
8. Compare the following:
   a. Electronic mail versus electronic bulletin boards
   b. Digitizing versus synthesizing voice
   c. Uploading versus downloading
   d. Local echo versus remote echo
   e. Auto-dial versus auto-answer
9. Identify the following:
   a. Public communication service
   b. Packet-switched network
   c. Gateway service
10. What are on-line database services?
11. Give an example of a database in each of the three common on-line database service categories.

EXERCISES

1. Visit your school or local public library to learn if any on-line database services are available for reference. Find out who can use the services and what are the restrictions to use. If possible, use the service yourself to research a term paper topic or to help supply information for the next exercise.

2. Prepare a research report that compares the features offered by three data communication software packages. Recent articles about packages should be available in the computer periodicals section of your library.

3. Find out what public electronic bulletin boards are available in your local area and the types of services they provide. Your local computer store or computer user's group should be able to give you some guidance. Try to arrange a demonstration of how to use one.

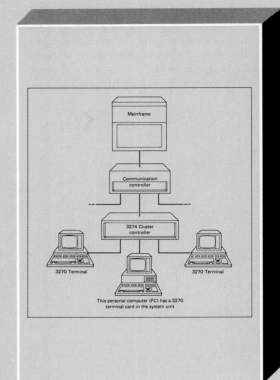

Mainframe

Communication
controller

3274 Cluster
controller

3270 Terminal

3270 Terminal

This personal computer (PC) has a 3270
terminal card in the system unit

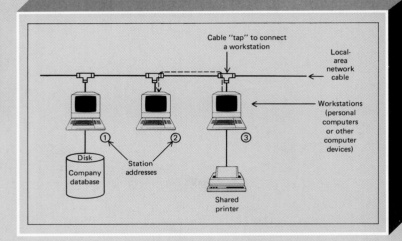

Cable "tap" to connect
a workstation

Local-
area
network
cable

Workstations
(personal
computers
or other
computer
devices)

① ②

Station
addresses

③

Disk

Company
database

Shared
printer

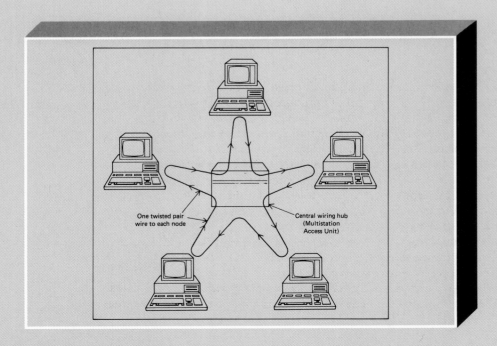

One twisted pair
wire to each node

Central wiring hub
(Multistation
Access Unit)

12

Networking

AFTER READING THIS CHAPTER, YOU SHOULD BE ABLE TO

- Describe why organizations install local-area networks
- Describe why organizations link small computers into wide-area networks
- Identify database and support issues that must be addressed when networking computers

Small computer users throughout organizations have an increasing need to share information and communicate. One generally accepted premise is that 80 percent of the information generated within a work group is used only by the work group. The other 20 percent of the information flow comes from outside the organization and is sent outside.

These figures suggest the reason progressive organizations install *local-area networks* (LANs). Their people need to communicate and exchange local information quickly, easily, and reliably. They also need to share application programs and output devices, such as expensive printers and graphic plotters.

This chapter begins by examining how a local-area network operates. Then it covers some technical and managerial issues related to installing and evaluating a local-area network.

A discussion about linking microcomputers to mainframes follows. These links allow users to access data stored in an organization's database on the mainframe. Often modems are used for these links which frequently cover great distances and connect *wide-area networks*.

All networks have similar problems. They are caused by many users sharing data and resources. A discussion of some of these networking issues concludes the chapter.

LOCAL-AREA NETWORKS

Local-area networks (LANs) consist mainly of connected personal computers and serve as the backbone of an *automated office*. They facilitate private group communication services in small companies and departments of large companies.

Figure 12-1 shows typical local-area network cabling that runs through an office. The most common environment is a single building. But local-area networks can extend throughout an industrial park, university, or other campuslike setting. Data traffic flows over the cable and is accessible to any personal computer or other device linked to the cable. Devices linked to the network are often called **workstations** or **nodes.**

Printers and hard disks attached to personal computers can be shared with others, as shown in Figures 12-2 to 12-4. But some local-area networks do not allow a personal computer to share its resources. Instead, they attach separate devices that are called *servers*, as shown in Figure 12-5.

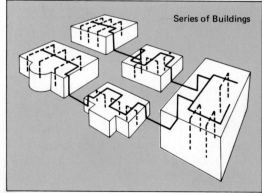

FIGURE 12-1
Local-area networks cabled throughout an office building and through a series of buildings in a campuslike setting
(Left: courtesy of Xerox Corp.; top: courtesy of Digital Equipment Corp.)

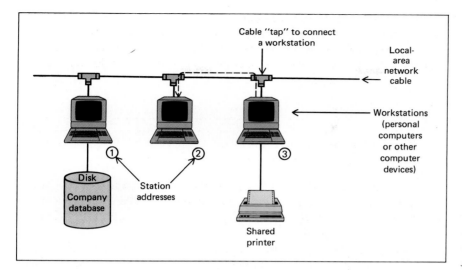

FIGURE 12-2
In this local-area network, workstation 3 sends electronic mail to workstation 2's floppy disk.

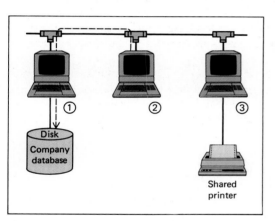

FIGURE 12-3
Workstation 2 sends a new record to the company's database which is stored on a hard disk.

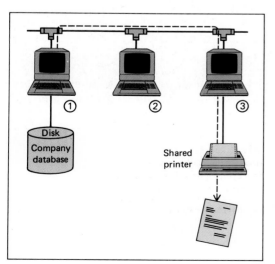

FIGURE 12-4
Workstation 1 sends a letter to be printed at the shared printer attached to workstation 3.

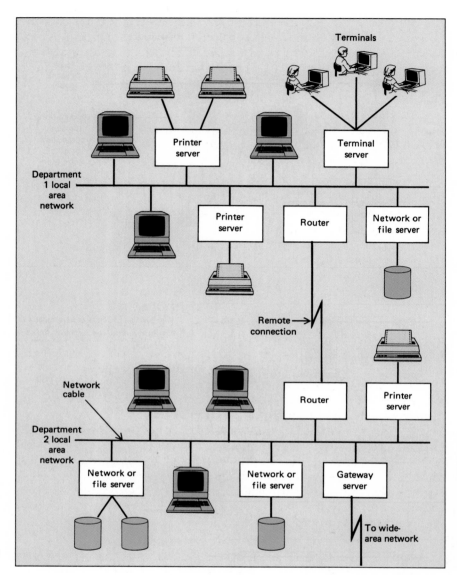

FIGURE 12-5
Connected local-area networks with
separate dedicated servers
(Adapted with permission of Digital Equipment
Corp.)

Every device on a network has a unique address. It enables one workstation to send a message or transfer a file to another attached device.

HOW A LAN WORKS

Figures 12-2 to 12-4 illustrate how users on Interstate Distributing Company's newly acquired local-area network

1. Exchange electronic mail
2. Share database information
3. Share hardware

Exchange Electronic Mail.   In Figure 12-2, user 3 creates a word-processed letter. It is essential that user 2 review a copy of the letter before it is circulated to others. By addressing user 2's workstation, the letter is sent as a file over the cable with a simple COPY statement. A few keystrokes could also send the letter to everyone on a stored distribution list.

Network software in each personal computer executes the file transfer. User 2 can interact with the letter as if it were created locally. The received file can be modified, and a copy saved, before being returned to its originator.

Share Database Information.   In the second example in Figure 12-3, user 2 adds a new customer record to the company's database. It is stored on a hard disk. Users access the company database according to privileges granted to them, such as

1. Read records only
2. Add and delete records
3. Update records only

Share Hardware.   In the third example in Figure 12-4, user 1 prints a letter on the shared printer attached to workstation 3. An address followed by the PRINT command suffices to accomplish this task. Typically, printer requests are queued and printed in sequence.

Sharing disks, as well as printers, helps to reduce computer hardware expenses. One or more large-capacity shared disks often eliminates the need for extensive disk storage at individual workstations.

Diskless workstations, or **LANstations,** are desktop computers without local disk storage. They retrieve all working files from the hard disk of a network file server. They take up less space and cost less than an ordinary desktop personal computer. Because a diskless workstation user has no facility to make copies of files, a company's database and software are less vulnerable to abuse. This improves security, which many companies require.

STAR NETWORK

When it shopped, Interstate Distributing Company had a choice of three LAN layouts, or topologies. **Topology** refers to the physical layout of personal computers and other devices connected to the network. The main types that dominated, as diagrammed in Figure 12-6, are

- Star
- Ring
- Bus

A **star network** has workstations clustered around a computer that acts as a central controller, or "switch." To communicate, a workstation must be switched, or temporarily connected at the controller, to another

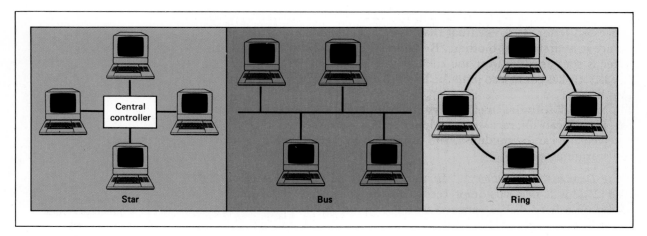

FIGURE 12-6
Three local-area network topologies

workstation. If the central controller fails, the network is down. Usually duplicate parts are built into central controllers to avoid such a disaster.

Sometimes the central controller in a star network is called a **private branch exchange (PBX), digital branch exchange (DBX),** or **computer branch exchange (CBX).** Often it is a minicomputer capable of linking or "switching" both voice and data calls. Some have served large companies for years as central switches in private telephone networks.

Newer technologies are the ring and bus layouts.

RING NETWORK

In a **ring network,** workstations are linked in an unbroken chain. The ring network that the Interstate Distributing Company's team considered came with software and hardware components similar to those shown in Figure 12-7.

The IBM Token Ring Network, as its name suggests, is a ring network, but when it is all wired, it looks very much like a star, as shown in Figure 12-8. A **central wiring hub** functions as the network's safety net if problems occur. As an example, if one workstation goes down, the central wiring hub immediately senses the problem, disconnects the problem workstation, and skips over it. To keep the logical ring "alive," it automatically attaches the two workstations on either side of the "dead" one. This restores the ring and keeps the network "up."

Data are transmitted in the network using a **transmission protocol** called **token passing.** When the network is idle, a message called a "token" is circulated around the ring to indicate its status. To send a message, a workstation

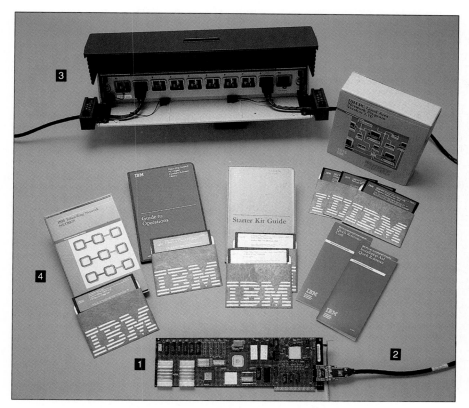

FIGURE 12-7
Hardware and software components of a token ring network. 1. A network adapter card (fits into a workstation's system unit). 2. Cabling (to connect the workstation to the MAU). 3. Multistation Access Unit (MAU) is the central wiring hub for up to 8 workstations. MAUs can be connected together to serve as many as 260 network nodes. 4. Software, which in this example, mainly consists of the IBM PC Local Area Network Program.
(Hardware and software: IBM Token Ring Network, courtesy of PC Magazine)

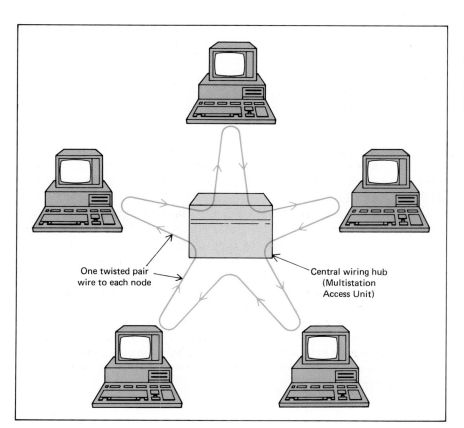

One twisted pair wire to each node

Central wiring hub (Multistation Access Unit)

FIGURE 12-8
The IBM Token Ring Network is physically a star (with the Multiple Access Unit at the center), but electrically and logically a ring. Follow the arrows in the diagram to observe the wiring pattern which forms an unbroken ring.

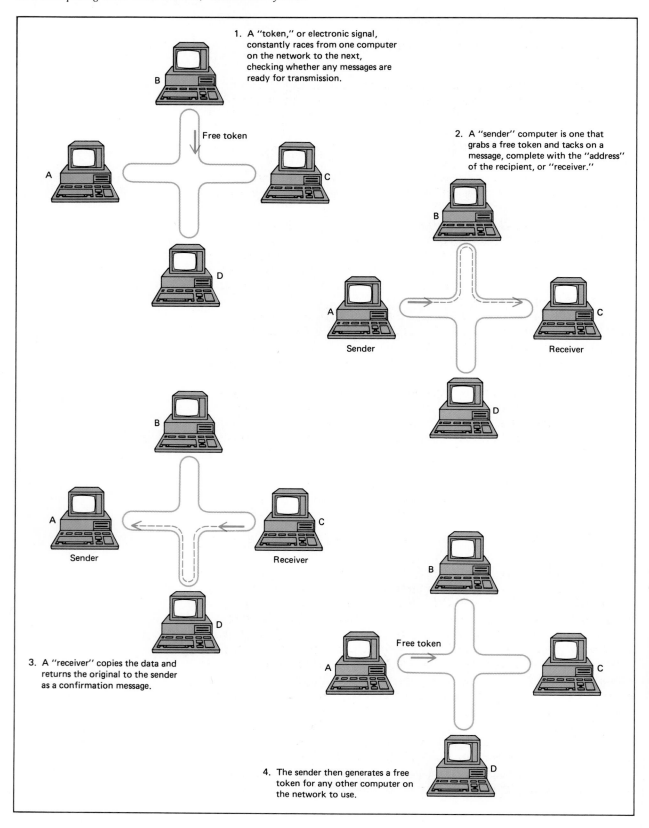

1. A "token," or electronic signal, constantly races from one computer on the network to the next, checking whether any messages are ready for transmission.

Free token

2. A "sender" computer is one that grabs a free token and tacks on a message, complete with the "address" of the recipient, or "receiver."

Sender

Receiver

Sender

Receiver

3. A "receiver" copies the data and returns the original to the sender as a confirmation message.

Free token

4. The sender then generates a free token for any other computer on the network to use.

- Captures the token
- Changes it to indicate a message is on the way
- Sends its information

A user is completely unaware that token passing is occurring at lightning speed "under the hood." In a well-designed network, a user cannot detect a difference between using a personal computer as a stand-alone unit or using it as a networked unit.

Figure 12-9 details how the unique electrical signal, called a token, circulates around the ring network until some computer grabs it. The sender, workstation A in this example, attaches a message to the token for workstation C. The message includes the address of the receiving workstation.

At the receiving end, workstation C copies the message and returns the original to workstation A as a confirmation message. During this entire exchange, or one complete ring cycle, the network is "busy" and cannot be used by any other node. Only after confirmation is acknowledged, and a free token is generated by the original sender workstation, is the network open once again.

If a free token becomes lost, possibly due to a power failure at one node, a workstation on the network that has supervisory status will detect the loss and regenerate a free token. With a large number of nodes on a network, more than one token can be regenerated and can cause problems.

The main benefit of token passing is that it prevents messages from interfering with one another, by guaranteeing that only one station at a time transmits. This is not true of another common type of local-area network that is built as a bus and uses a different transmission protocol.

BUS NETWORK

The second of the two major new local-area network technologies that the Interstate Distributing Company looked at was a bus network, much like the one in Figure 12-5. In a **bus network,** workstations are linked to a single cable, called a **bus,** and contend with each other to transmit a message. It works like a party-line telephone. If the line is not busy, a workstation is free to transmit its message. This method is variously called the **Ethernet, CSMA/CD,** or **contention** transmission protocol. Like token passing, this protocol works "under the hood" at lightning speed and is completely unobservable and unobtrusive from a user's vantage point.

Using this "listen before talk" method, all workstations on the network listen to the cable bus for a "carrier" signal which indicates that the line is free. If a workstation can "sense" that the line is free, it can siege or "access" the line to send its message. If another workstation also happens to sense the free line and sends its message, there is contention, or a "collision." If a collision is "detected," both workstations back off for a random time interval. Then they attempt to resend their message until success is achieved. This procedure gives meaning to the acronym CSMA/CD as follows:

C = Carrier
S = Sense
M = Multiple workstations (or many nodes)
A = Access (all want to access the network cable bus)
/ = (with)
C = Collision
D = Detection

Instead of CSMA/CD, this protocol is widely known as the **Ethernet standard.** It is one of the earliest of the formally accepted local-area networking standards. The **International Electrical and Electronics Engineers Association** approves standards. It has endorsed both the CSMA/CD and token passing protocols as local-area network standards. Hardware vendors that sell local-area network products generally conform to either or both of these standards.

The "listen before talk" scheme avoids the data transmission overhead found in token passing. It does not lock up the network during one entire send and receive acknowledgment cycle. It is efficient in environments with short and unevenly spaced messages, such as those in an administrative office. On the other hand, it cannot offer workstations an equal opportunity to transmit under heavily loaded conditions. Excessive contention degrades its performance.

The hardware and software to set up a bus network using CSMA/CD includes three main components. They are physically similar to those shown in Figure 12-7. They are the network adapter card, cabling, and software. A fourth component, called a **network server, dedicated network server,** or **file server,** is a small "black box" that runs the network software and contains the hard disk that is shared by everyone on the network.

The load the dedicated network server can handle varies greatly. It depends on the application the system is mainly used for and the load coming from each workstation. One network vendor offers these guidelines:

- Accounting—15 to 40 workstations
- Productivity (spreadsheets, word processing)—20 to 40 workstations

Using a dedicated network server is often preferable to using some employee's personal computer that does double duty as a shared hard disk. Often sharing duties degrades network performance for all users. Other local-area network hardware includes

- **Print servers** to allow sharing centrally located printers and to eliminate the need for individual workstations to have their own printers.
- **Terminal servers** to allow terminals access to any computing or information processing resource on the network.
- **Routing servers** to interconnect local-area networks.
- **Gateway servers** to interconnect local-area networks to wide-area networks.

Wide-area networks are usually associated with the use of modems and extend data communications beyond the range possible with local-area networks. They usually involve using the public telephone systems or private long-distance lines that are leased from the telephone company or other source. A gateway server provides the modem function and protocol conversion to seamlessly transform communication from the local-area network to the wide-area network. Local-area network users would use a gateway server, for example, to access on-line databases at public communication utilities.

Figure 12-5 diagrams a hypothetical local-area network using all optional components.

CONNECTIONS

Workstations can be connected by

· Twisted-pair wires
· Coaxial cables
· Fiber optic cables

Twisted-pair wire is easily recognizable as the line that connects a telephone to the wall jack. In addition to being economical, it is easier to install than coaxial cable.

Coaxial cable is often the same cable used to install home cable television. It is more expensive than twisted-pair wires, but it can handle higher data transmission rates. Data move along in most local-area networks at speeds in the millions of bits-per-second range.

As in other communication areas, **fiber optic cable** is the leading edge of transmission technology. It offers the highest data transmission rates possible. It is immune to electromagnetic interference. This makes it desirable for local-area networks that wander through factories or other heavy-duty work areas.

The speed at which data are transmitted along a communication path depends on its **bandwidth.** Local-area networks are either **broadband** or **baseband** systems. The difference between these two is similar to the difference between a four-lane highway and a single-lane street. Broadband can accommodate more data traffic than can baseband.

LAN EVALUATION

Interstate Distributing Company hired a consultant, who specialized in local-area networks, to assist in the evaluation and implementation of a local-area network. Some of the network evaluation criteria are listed in Figure 12-10. Some of the products considered are listed in Figure 12-11.

LOCAL-AREA NETWORK

Is the total cost reasonable and within budget?

Does it meet specific requirements?

Is it possible to start small, at a low financial risk, and gradually expand to meet more and more requirements?

Is it designed to prevent total network failure?

Does it interface with equipment supplied by more than one vendor?

Is it easy to install, maintain, interconnect to other networks, switch hardware around, and reset software controls without impacting other hardware and software?

(Figure 3-25, General Software Evaluation Checklist, is necessary to complete this evaluation.)

FIGURE 12-10
Local-area network evaluation checklist

A strategy evolved to set up a pilot test of a few workstations. The networking scheme used had to be modularly expandable without a lot of *downtime*, or idle time, to make alterations. It also had to have software that was uncomplicated and unintrusive so users could resume being productive almost immediately after installation.

Since several brands of workstations were already in use, the network had to accommodate their *multivendor* hardware situation. This might prove even more necessary in the long run when planned equipment is introduced that will almost certainly be from multiple vendors.

Finally, the new local-area network had to be reliable and affordable. Because of the wide differences in system capability, prices varied widely. It appeared that systems ranging from a few hundred to several thousand dollars per connection were available.

FIGURE 12-11
A sampler of local-area network products

3Com-Ethernet	IBM Token Ring Network
Apple Computer Appletalk Personal Network	Kimtron K-Net
	Nestar Systems
AST Research AST-Starsystem	Novell/S-Net
AT&T StarLan	Orchid Technologies PC Net
Banyan VINES	Proteon ProNet
Centram TOPS	Software Link Lanlink
Corvus PC/NOS	Standard Microsystems ARCnet
Fox Research 10-Net	Torus Tapestry
Hewlett-Packard HP-StarLAN	Ungermann-Bass Net/One PC
IBM PC Network	

LAN ALTERNATIVES

Some organizations that do not have a heavy investment in personal computers elect to use a minicomputer or a multiuser microcomputer instead of a local-area network. These computer systems offer all the shared hardware and data features available with a local-area network. Since they use terminals instead of personal computers as workstations, they can be less expensive to own and operate. As local-area networking matures, however, costs are expected to be less of a deciding factor in a decision to provide connectivity within a work group.

Some organizations elect to fill the gap between an expensive local-area network and no network at all with a **circuit-switching device.** One is shown in Figure 12-12. These devices, which are slightly larger than some external modems, are inexpensive and uncomplicated. They perform basic functions, like those diagrammed in Figure 12-13, with

FIGURE 12-12
A two-way circuit-switching device
(Courtesy of Global Computer Supplies)

FIGURE 12-13
A simple, inexpensive, hardware solution
to peripheral sharing
(Courtesy of Global Computer Supplies,
adapted with permission)

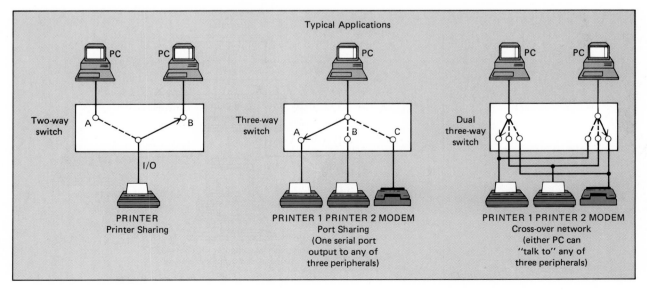

a flip of a switch. They are used by individuals and organizations that do not need the heavy workload and multiuser capabilities of a full-scale local-area network.

To give an example, one freelance journalist has one communication serial output port in his computer. He uses either of two printers for various printing tasks, and a modem for sending his stories electronically to his clients. All of his peripherals (two printers and a modem) require a serial input port. His simple solution is an ABC switch, as illustrated in Figure 12-13.

MICRO-TO-MAINFRAME LINKS

Employees of National Bank and other large organizations often want to access mainframe databases using their personal computers instead of terminals. Figure 12-14 illustrates one of several ways to achieve this so-called **micro-to-mainframe link** for an IBM mainframe connec-

FIGURE 12-14
This micro-to-mainframe link makes the personal computer appear to the mainframe as a 3270 terminal.

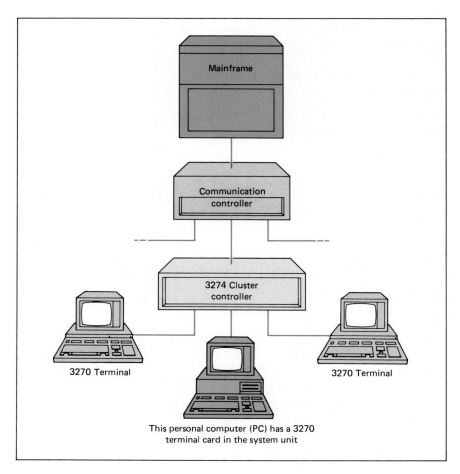

tion. It requires a **3270 terminal emulation card,** which resembles any LAN adapter card, to be installed in the personal computer's system unit. The card and related software make the personal computer function like a 3270 terminal that is permanently connected to the mainframe.

Synchronous Communication

The 3270 terminal emulation card takes care of the synchronous communication. As Figure 12-15 illustrates, it is different from the asynchronous communication shown in Figure 11-7. In **synchronous communication,** characters are sent in groups as a single bit stream. The bit stream follows a precise timing pattern that is set or "synchronized" by a master system clock in the front-end communication controller.

When several terminals or personal computers share one communication line, some strict rules must apply about who uses the line and when, or chaos would result. Typically, in micro-to-mainframe communications, a **front-end communication controller** assumes a "master" function at the mainframe end and "polls" terminals, one after the other, to see if they have data to send. All this happens "under the hood" at lightning speed without a user ever being aware of it.

If a terminal answers yes to a poll, it releases an entire bit stream of characters. Meanwhile, other terminals have to group characters until the poll arrives. Only one terminal is given permission to use the line at a time.

Many mainframe-oriented organizations use this **polling** method with synchronous transmission to

- Reduce line costs by having many terminals and adapted personal computers on one communication line
- Improve the quality of transmission, because more error control is available with synchronous, than with asynchronous, transmission

These organizations use very sophisticated front-end communication hardware and software, as well as special terminals, like the 3270 terminals, which are also known as **smart terminals.**

Organizations with local-area networks can use a less expensive solution to link personal computers to mainframes. This involves installing a gateway server, as shown in Figure 12-5. It could be set to perform the same functions as the 3274 cluster controller. This solution eliminates the need for terminal emulation cards in each personal computer.

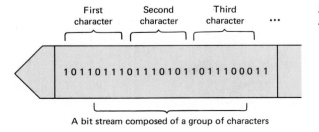

First character   Second character   Third character   ...

1011011101110101101011100011

A bit stream composed of a group of characters

FIGURE 12-15
Synchronous communication

Distributed Data Processing

National Bank's communication facilities support its distributed data processing. In **distributed data processing,** computers are networked throughout an organization to satisfy local data processing needs. Usually, distributed locations communicate management and control information to headquarters on a periodic basis.

National Bank's headquarters computer, called a **host** computer, is the hub of the company's star computing structure. It is a more elaborate multilevel version of the same star architecture found in local-area networking. Computers at each succeeding level become a host to those computers subordinate to them. This is a common structure in distributed data processing networks, which typically are also wide-area networks.

As the diagram in Figure 12-16 shows, the host computer is linked

FIGURE 12-16
A large organization's distributed data processing network

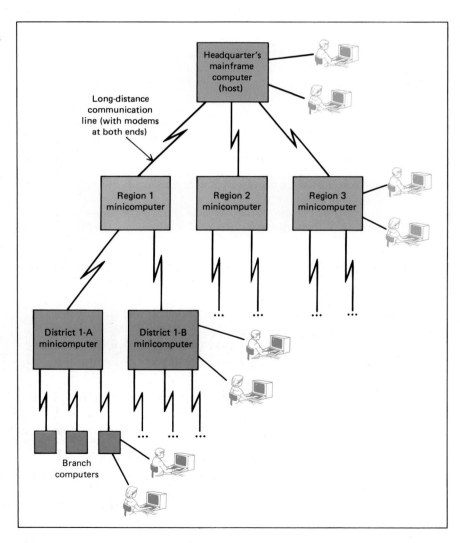

MAIN MENU

Account Information
Bill Payment
Transfers
Customer Service
Messages & Bulletins
Citibank Products & Services
Dow Jones News/Retrieval

CITIBANK PRODUCTS & SERVICES

Where to Get Cash
Product & Service List
Checking & Savings
Investment & Retirement
Credit
Sign Up for a Service

CUSTOMER SERVICE

Record a Mail-In Deposit
Link an Account to Direct Access
Stop a Check
Account Maintenance
Citibank Directory
Send Message to Customer Service

BILL PAYMENT

Make a Payment
Set Up Recurring Payments
Add a Payee
Payment Information
Recurring Payment Information
Payee Information
Update Payee Information
Cancel a Payment
Cancel Recurring Payments
Delete a Payee

TRANSFERS

Transfer Money
Set Up Recurring Transfers
Transfer Information
Recurring Transfer Information
Cancel a Transfer
Cancel Recurring Transfers

DOW JONES & COMPANY, INC.

Dow Jones Business and
 Economic News Services
Dow Jones Quotes
Dow Jones Text-Search Services
Financial and Investment Services
General News and Information Services
Mail Service and Free Customer Newsletter

MESSAGES & BULLETINS

Read Messages
Citibank Bulletins
Citibank Rate Hotline
Citibank Economic Forecasts
State of the Economy
Send Message to Customer Service

ACCOUNT INFORMATION

Balance Summary — All Accounts
Balances & Selected Activity
All Activity — Past 60 Days

by various interconnected communication lines to subordinate computers. The host can respond to both asynchronous and synchronous communications. To communicate with the headquarters office, remote computers use the bank's private modem wide-area network facilities.

The host computer compares with any public service computer that provides users with

- Electronic or voice mail
- Electronic bulletin boards
- On-line databases

The bank provides its employees with all these services on a private basis. It also provides its customers with the bank-at-home services shown in Figure 12-17. Customers can access the bank's computer using a modem and a personal computer.

NETWORKING ISSUES

Once networks of computers are installed, they require many of the features and servicing that are common in a traditional minicomputer or mainframe multiuser environment. This final section of the chapter considers four of these networking issues:

- Multiuser software
- User services
- Network maintenance
- Standards

Multiuser Software

Applications such as database management systems (DBMS), accounting, spreadsheet, graphics, word processing, and related software require multiuser features to be most effective when used in a networked environment.

As an example, at National Bank many people have daily access to any of a number of databases on branch minicomputers, local-area networks, and at the headquarters' mainframes. At all levels, data integrity and security are primary concerns. As a security measure, all the bank's database management systems automatically make the creator of a new file its "owner." Only an owner can grant authority to others to retrieve, add, change, or delete data in a file.

Another feature provides for shielding data from users who should not have access to all the data available in a database record. This involves creating a separate control or "view" file that contains the name of only those fields in a record that a user is authorized to view. In large organizations, a **database administrator** is responsible for determining views and settling all other user issues that relate to database access.

Database backup and recovery procedures must also exist to restore files in the event of a system crash. They involve complex logging and checking procedures that can be an entire subsystem within the DBMS. These procedures occur "under the hood" and are unobservable by a user.

Another subsystem must be present to avoid problems if two users try to update one record at the same time. The process is called **record locking** or **lockout** when one user is put on hold until the record is free for reuse.

User Services

At National Bank, technical support for nontechnical computer users is provided by a user services group called the **Information Center.** The center is staffed with

- **Information Center Specialists,** who concentrate on helping users with DBMS access, use, and programming
- **Decision Support Specialists,** who concentrate on helping users with model-building software, like spreadsheets and financial modeling software
- **Microcomputer Specialists,** who concentrate on researching the latest microcomputer hardware and software trends and introducing useful microcomputer technology into the organization

The group sponsors well-attended tutorial seminars on popular microcomputer software. It also advises individuals about personal software and hardware acquisition. Because the bank has volume purchase plans with major vendors, the group buys authorized software and hardware for bank users.

Providing support helps users to have positive first computing experiences. As an example, users do not have to concern themselves with such technical details as what software is needed to perform micro-to-mainframe links. Such problems are solved for them.

Network Maintenance

At National Bank, separate network maintenance groups monitor local-area and wide-area networks. Some are charged with handling such day-to-day operations as

- Starting up, and installing, new computer equipment
- Monitoring all equipment to avoid performance and communication bottlenecks
- Backing up disks and other storage media

A major responsibility of all network managers is computer site security and disaster planning. Some criteria used to handle this are listed in Figure 12-18. In the bank's case, security control is especially important because it must guarantee each depositor's right of privacy. The goal is to ensure that the computer system cannot be violated as a result of a criminal act or a simple accident.

EXAMPLES OF THREATS	PREVENTIVE MEASURES
Fire	Install fire extinguishers.
	Store disk and tape files in fireproof vaults.
Flood	Raise hardware and electrical wiring above floor level.
Sabotage	Install physical access controls, such as closed-circuit TV surveillance; voice, fingerprint, hand, or badge identification.
	Isolate and rotate jobs.
Natural disasters (earthquakes, etc.)	Store backup copies of software off-site.
	Establish an alternative emergency site (usually through a professional disaster recovery organization).
Illegal software access	Request user ID and passwords.
	Monitor use and maintain usage records.
Data	Require backup files.
	Encrypt or "scramble" data before storage.
Communication	Encrypt transmitted data.

FIGURE 12-18
Mainframe computer site security and disaster planning

In one form or another, these responsibilities are carried out in each network site. Whether a local-area network, minicomputer, or mainframe is in use, someone must take responsibility for its day-to-day operation and security.

One consultant warns that support and maintenance can account for nearly half the overall cost associated with running a networked computer environment. These often unanticipated costs of network administration are charted in the "hidden costs" identified in Figure 12-19 for local-area networking. Similar costs can also be involved with wide-area networks.

Standards

Everyone at National Bank, as well as most other organizations involved with a networked environment, is concerned about standards. **Standards** are specifications intended to facilitate data exchange between computers.

At present, National Bank must accommodate many standards. As an example, its mainframe communicates with personal computers using both the synchronous and the asynchronous transmission standards. Meanwhile, it has some local-area networks that use the token passing standard and others that use the Ethernet transmission standard. Computers using any one of these standards cannot "talk to" other computers that use a different standard without going through a protocol conversion process. This example represents a large organization's typical mix of standards that could benefit from consistency.

The future of computer communication standards includes goals

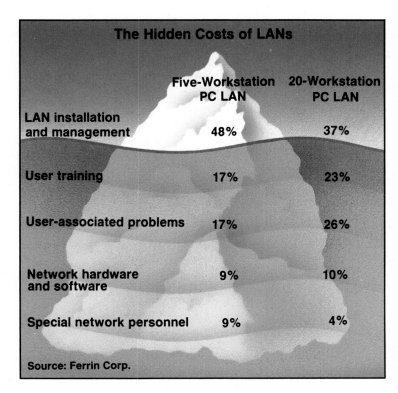

The Hidden Costs of LANs	Five-Workstation PC LAN	20-Workstation PC LAN
LAN installation and management	48%	37%
User training	17%	23%
User-associated problems	17%	26%
Network hardware and software	9%	10%
Special network personnel	9%	4%

Source: Ferrin Corp.

FIGURE 12-19
Some of the hidden costs and problems associated with networked environments (Source: PC Week, April 7, 1987)

- To allow any computer or terminal to "talk to" any other computer or terminal
- To have voice, data, and full-motion pictures flow simultaneously over the same public communication lines

To accomplish these goals requires that standards be established to build and use common communication facilities.

Communication engineers call the ideal network that carries simultaneous voice, data, and full-motion pictures that have been generated by any communicating or computing device an **integrated services data network (ISDN).** International committees are at work developing standard rules, or protocols, to make these networks possible.

While international networks may help to create a "global village," there are problems. Political and security concerns cause some countries to restrict the flow of data outside their borders. These governments avoid participation in an ISDN effort.

International standards are already in place for connecting to public packet-switched networks. The rules of connection are called the **X.25 standard** or *protocol*. It is part of a seven-layer structure for interconnecting communication devices established by the **International Standards Organization (ISO).**

A second emerging standard is called either **advanced program-to-program communications (APPC)** *or* **LU 6.2** (LU = logical unit). Both are IBM initiated standards. They allow one computer to communicate on a peer-to-peer basis with another computer that uses the same standard. At present, personal computers function in a "slave" relationship, as terminals do, when communicating especially with mainframes and minicomputers.

A third emerging standard is called **X.400,** which promises to connect electronic mail services around the world. It will enable a communicator to send messages anywhere, no matter what service is used to initiate the mail.

CASE STUDY: Cable Woes Cripple Network

Nearly a year after it hired a general electrician to wire up a high-speed token-ring local-area network, the sales and marketing arm of Hitachi America Ltd.'s computer division is finally on the way to getting its LAN working efficiently.

Wrong Assumptions.   "We assumed a lot of things when we were putting in the network," said Tim Ayres, office automation specialist and LAN manager at Hitachi's San Bruno, California, division. "One was that our electrician, who initially did all the electrical work for the office when we moved in, would be capable of putting in data communications cabling."

While the electrician did an adequate job of fitting the cables inside existing conduit pipes to meet local building codes, according to Mr. Ayres, he had little technical grasp for IBM's Type 1 cable, the heavily shielded twisted-pair wire used for Hitachi's LAN.

One result was very slow user response times. "The network would come down, and it would take two or three minutes to register a keystroke," said Mr. Ayres. "All of a sudden, it would just deteriorate in a matter of seconds to nothing." In addition, he said, the inadequate cabling caused users to often unexpectedly receive an "Abort, Retry, Ignore?" DOS message on their screens and, in many cases, to lose the data with which they were working.

"The stuff we use is, for lack of a better term, industrial strength," he said, describing his 10 million bit-per-second LAN from Proteon Inc. "If I had it to do all over again, we wouldn't go out and hire an electrician," he said. "We'd get a data communications specialist."

Hitachi chose Proteon's high-speed token-ring LAN because its network must support many stations (currently there are 30 users of IBM PCs, XTs and ATs) who run communications-intensive applications (including a lot of database queries using the Revelation package from Cosmos Inc.).

Support Barrier.   "Our dealer had just started carrying networking products," Mr. Ayres said. "I knew more than they did." In fact, he added, the dealer who sold Hitachi the LAN actually proved to be an obstacle to getting effective support.

"They got in the way," he said, "because the way these big vendors do their end-user support, you've got to go through your dealer, who goes through the distributor, who finally calls the vendor, and you've got all these people reinterpreting your problem. It's just a nightmare."

After seeking help from the dealer, the distributor and other semi-informed sources along the way, Hitachi finally decided to sign a service contract with Proteon to receive support and maintenance directly from the LAN manufacturer. "That has been our saving grace," Mr. Ayres commented. It eliminated the key problem, "multiple points of responsibility," to getting its LAN running.

An outside consultant was hired to install the LAN operating system, which is Novell Inc.'s Advanced NetWare 286. As a result, the system is now up and running, even though some kinks are still being worked out. Mr. Ayres concluded, "If we were doing it all over again, we would have the LAN vendor do as much of the installation as possible."

(*SOURCE: Don Steinberg, "Cable Woes, Lack of Support, Cripple Network Use at Hitachi," PC Week, May 19, 1987, p. 1. Adapted with permission.*)

Popping the Local Net Expectation Balloon.   The difference between what first-time buyers of local networks expect of their networks and what they actually get can be drastic. In fact, the less the buyer knows about networking and the less research done before buying, the greater the likelihood of disappointment.

With this in mind, the following list of what not to expect may help keep first-time buyers grounded in reality:

- Don't expect to install the net yourself unless you have lots of patience to contend with things like confusing directions. According to one industry executive, installing and configuring a local net is a black art. No one is really sure what the optimum configuration is.
- Don't count on your dealer's ability to install your network. While some dealers are qualified to install and maintain local nets, others aren't. Ask your dealer for names of their network customers. If the dealer measures up to the task, be prepared to pay for their expertise.
- Don't expect your local network to run itself. According to some estimates, managing a personal computer net requires 20 percent of a full-time person's time. Others say that is a conservative estimate. Regardless, it is important to realize that networks take time and effort to maintain. Even maintenance contracts don't usually include things like backing up the server, answering user questions and adding new net users.
- Don't expect the total cost of your network to equal the sum of the hardware, software, cabling and installation charges. One of the larger hidden network cost is time: the time it takes to train people to use, maintain and reconfigure the network.
- Don't expect people to work the same way after the network is installed. In sharing resources that were previously stand-alone, users need to change the way they do things. They need to become "network aware." Users need to purge old files to keep server space available for all users. As users realize productivity gains in a local network, they will use it more frequently, and others will want to access the network.

(*SOURCE: Paula Musich, Network World, March 30, 1987, p. 1. Adapted with permission.*)

DISCUSSION QUESTIONS

1. What kind of problems can surface if an electrician without LAN experience installs the cabling for a LAN?

2. Assume that you are given responsibility for the installation of a LAN in your company. Describe the things you could do to increase the possibility of a smooth and successful installation.

CHAPTER SUMMARY

- A *local-area network* (LAN) consists mainly of linked personal computers and serves as the backbone of an *automated office*. It allows users to exchange electronic mail and to share database information and hardware quickly, easily, and reliably.

- Devices linked to a LAN are often called *workstations* or *nodes*.

- *Diskless workstations*, or *LANstations*, are desktop computers without local disk storage.

- *Topology* refers to the physical layout of personal computers and other devices connected to the network. The three main types are star, ring, and bus.

- A *star network* has workstations clustered around a computer that acts as a central controller, or "switch." The central controller may be a *private branch exchange* (*PBX*), *digital branch exchange* (*DBX*), or *computer branch exchange* (*CBX*). Often it is a minicomputer capable of switching both voice and data calls.

- A *ring network* has workstations linked in an unbroken chain of many cable segments. It often uses a *token passing* transmission protocol. Its main benefit is to guarantee that only one station at a time transmits.

- A *bus network* has workstations linked to a single cable, called a bus. It often uses a "listen before talk" transmission protocol, which is also called the *Ethernet*, *CSMA/CD*, or *contention* protocol. It is efficient in environments with short and unevenly spaced messages.

- A *network server*, also called a *dedicated network server*, or *file server*, is a small "black box" that runs the network software and contains the hard disk that is shared by everyone on the network.

- Other local-area network hardware includes *print servers*, *terminal servers*, *routing servers*, and *gateway servers*.

- *Wide-area networks* are associated with the use of modems and the telephone system to communicate over greater distances than are possible with local-area networks.

- LAN workstations are connected by *twisted-pair wires*, *coaxial cable*, and *fiber optic cable*.

- The speed at which data are transmitted along a communication path depends on its *bandwidth*. Local-area networks are either *broadband* or *baseband* systems. Broadband accommodates more data traffic than baseband.

- LAN evaluation criteria include an ability to expand without a lot of downtime, accommodate multivendor hardware, and be reliable and affordable, among other concerns.

- LAN alternatives include *circuit-switching devices*, as well as minicomputers and multiuser microcomputers.

- *Micro-to-mainframe links* allow personal computer users to access mainframe databases. A *3270 terminal emulation card* inserted in a personal computer permits an IBM mainframe connection.

- In *synchronous transmission*, groups of characters are sent as a single bit stream that is timed, or synchronized, by a master system clock.

- A *front-end communication controller* at the mainframe end *polls* terminals to see if they have data to send.

- *Polling* is used with synchronous communication to reduce line costs and improve the quality of transmission.

- In *distributed data processing*, computers are networked throughout an organization to satisfy local data processing needs.

- Networked systems usually require multiuser software packages that provide for data security and integrity. As an example, they provide *record locking*, or *lockout*, to avoid problems if two users try to update one record at the same time.

- Networked systems usually require technical support for non-technical users.

- Network management includes responsibility for the network's day-to-day operation and security.

- *Standards* are specifications that are intended to facilitate the exchange of data between computers.

- An *integrated services data network* (*ISDN*) is an ideal network that carries simultaneous voice, data, and full-motion pictures which have been generated by any communicating or computing device.

KEY TERMS

3270 terminal emulation card	Central wiring hub	Dedicated network server
Advanced program-to-program communications (APPC)	Circuit-switching device	Digital branch exchange (DBX)
Automated office	Coaxial cable	Diskless workstations
Bandwidth	Computer branch exchange (CBX)	Distributed data processing
Baseband	Contention	Ethernet
Broadband	CSMA/CD	Ethernet standard
Bus	Database administrator	Fiber optic cable
Bus network	Decision Support Specialist	File server

Front-end communication
  controller
Gateway server
Host
Information Center
Information Center Specialist
Integrated services data network
  (ISDN)
International Electrical and
  Electronics Engineers
  Association
International Standards
  Organization (ISO)
LANstations

Local-area networks
Lockout
LU 6.2
Microcomputer Specialist
Micro-to-mainframe link
Network server
Nodes
Polling
Print server
Private branch exchange (PBX)
Record locking
Ring network
Routing servers
Smart terminals

Standards
Star network
Synchronous communication
Terminal server
Token passing
Topology
Transmission protocol
Twisted-pair wire
Wide-area networks
Workstations
X.25 standard
X.400 standard

REVIEW QUESTIONS

1. What is a local-area network (LAN) and why would an organization install one?

2. Describe how a LAN user might send electronic mail.

3. Describe how workstations are connected in a local-area network using the following topologies:
   · Star
   · Ring
   · Bus

4. Describe how data are passed around a ring network using token passing.

5. Describe how data are transmitted in a bus network using the Ethernet standard.

6. Describe the function of a
   · Network file server
   · Print server
   · Gateway server

7. List three kinds of media used to connect workstations together in a LAN.

8. Identify some criteria to consider when evaluating a LAN.

9. Identify two LAN alternatives.

10. Why would an organization install micro-to-mainframe links?

11. Describe one solution for achieving micro-to-mainframe linkages.

12. How is synchronous different from asynchronous data transmission?

13. What are the benefits of polling?

14. What is distributed data processing?

15. Describe two issues that surface once networks of computers are installed.

16. What is record locking?

17. What is an ISDN?

EXERCISES

1. Find out if there is a local-area network installed in school or at work. If you find an installation, ask the network manager for a demonstration of how a user
   · Sends a word-processed document to a printer on the network
   · Stores a word-processed document on a network file server
   · Accesses an on-line database at a public communication service
   Ask the network manager to demonstrate
   · How a user workstation is added to the local-area network
   · How a workstation is removed from the network

2. Locate three recent articles on local-area networking. Prepare an oral or written report on the products described and the advantages and disadvantages of each.

3. Locate articles that discuss integrated services data networks (ISDN). Prepare an oral or written report on the topics covered.

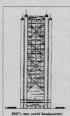

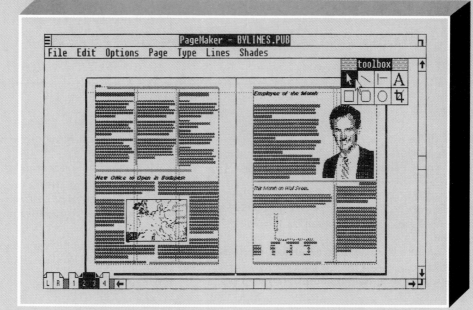

13

Desktop Publishing

AFTER READING THIS CHAPTER, YOU SHOULD BE ABLE TO

- Describe the steps necessary to assemble a page layout electronically
- Discuss related topics such as page description languages, publishing methods, and training requirements
- Initiate the evaluation of a desktop publishing system

Creating attractive and effective written documents is more of an art than a science. But a new class of software tools promises to make the job substantially easier. Especially when combined with laser printers, these software tools can increase the speed and efficiency of producing higher-quality documents ranging from business correspondence to newsletters, technical manuals, and even books.

After an introduction to some specialized terms used in desktop publishing, the main part of the chapter walks through the step-by-step procedure involved in using page composition software. Page composition software is the main ingredient in most desktop publishing systems. The hardware consists of the components shown in Figure 13-1.

The next section of the chapter describes how advanced word processing and form generator software also play a role in the desktop publishing arena. All the software covered is then summarized in a review of the

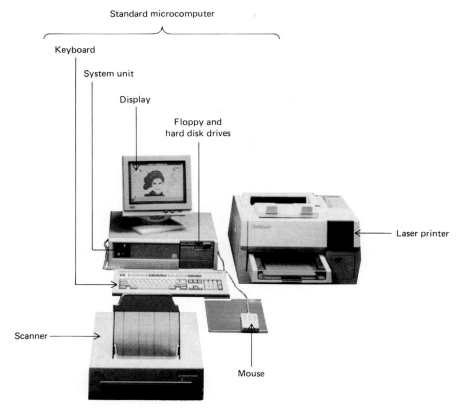

FIGURE 13-1
A turnkey desktop publishing system
(Hardware: AST Premium Publisher, courtesy of AST)

publishing software hierarchy. The review includes a contrast of traditional and modern publishing methods.

The chapter concludes with a discussion of training requirements and desktop publishing system evaluation considerations.

The chapter assumes a familiarity with concepts and terms presented in the chapters on word processing (Chapter 7), graphics (Chapter 6), hardware (Chapter 2), and networking (Chapter 12). All of these concepts converge in desktop publishing systems.

SPEAKING THE LANGUAGE

The Apple Macintosh microcomputer, along with Aldus' PageMaker software, launched the desktop publishing field in 1985. It was Paul Brainard, now the president of Aldus, who originated the term **desktop**

publishing. This refers to the use of microcomputers and other hardware, as well as software, to produce documents for publication purposes.

The main software used is called a **page composition package.** Its purpose is to replace a drafting table, scissors, and glue with electronic assembly of text and graphics. The composed page image, called a **page layout,** is then printed repetitively or reproduced using more traditional methods. Aldus' PageMaker is an example of a page composition package. It is included, along with many others, in the list of similar packages in Figure 13-2.

When the term *desktop publishing* is used, it generally refers to page composition software. This software does not, nor does related software, address publishing issues such as cost estimation, reproduction, binding, distribution, or financing. As more advanced software tools become available, something like a real publishing system is feasible. But the present application can more correctly be described as desktop page composition and layout.

The specialized field of desktop publishing has its own language that is new to an outsider. Some of the terms used are listed in the Desktop Publishing Glossary in Figure 13-3. A review of the glossary is recommended to get a glimpse of the range this area covers. All the important terms are discussed in the chapter.

To better understand what page composition software does and how it is used, the next several sections "walk through" an example.

FIGURE 13-2
A sampler of page composition software packages

ClickArt Personal Publisher	PageMaker
Compound Document Processor	Pagemaster
Crystal Publishing System	Page Perfect
DeskSet	Pagework
Display Ad Make-Up System	Pagewriter
Do-It	PFS:Personal Publisher
DP/Publisher	PS Compose
First Impression	Ragtime
FrontPage	Ready, Set, Go!
HALO Desktop Publishing Editor	Rim View
Harvard Professional Publisher	Solo
Impressionist	Spellbinder Desktop Publisher
Imprint	Superpage
LetraPage	The Newsroom Pro
MacPublisher	The Office Publisher
Newsmaster	Ventura Publisher
Pagebuilder	

DESKTOP PUBLISHING GLOSSARY

(Starred items are especially relevant to material in this chapter)

Alignment. How text lines up on a page or in a column: align left (flush left or ragged right), align center, align right (flush right or ragged left), or justify (flush on both the left and right).

˙ASCII file. Text saved without any type specifications or other formatting.

˙Bit map image file. Stores an image as a matrix of dots.

˙Bit-mapped font. A font composed of the actual dot sequence that forms each character. Since each character consists of a unique "map" of its data, a separate bit-mapped font file must be created for every member of a typeface family.

Built-in font. A font that resides permanently in a laser printer's ROM (read only memory).

CAP. Computer-aided publishing.

Continuous-tone image. An example is a black-and-white photograph that has continuous tone from black to white with many gradations in between.

Copy. Another name for text and graphics in the publishing industry.

˙Crop. To trim the edges of a graphic image, thereby removing part of it.

˙Desktop publishing. The use of microcomputers and appropriate software to create documents for publication purposes. The objectives are: to eliminate expensive typesetting and associated publishing costs; to retain control of a publication process; to save time.

˙Device independence. A feature of page description languages (PDL) which enables a document file to be printed on any printer or other device that accepts PDL-coded files. The device will provide the best output of which it is capable.

˙Dialog box. A window or full-screen display in response to a command that calls for setting options.

˙Document oriented. A term to describe a page composition package that is suited to handle long, consistently formatted texts, such as manuals and books.

Downloadable font. Same as **soft font.**

˙Drop cap. An oversized initial capital letter that begins a block of type.

˙Embedded code. Code inserted into text which defines its type specifications to a laser printer or typesetting machinery.

˙Flier. An advertising piece distributed in large numbers.

˙Flow (or pour) text or graphics. The process of filling in a column or other element with imported text or graphics. Text or graphics are "flowed," or "poured," into the layout's empty columns, boxes, or other elements.

Flush right or right justified. Text in which lines end at the same point on the right margin.

Flyer. Same as **flier.**

˙Font. One complete set of characters in the same typeface and size, including letters, punctuation, and symbols; 12-point Times Roman is a different font from 12-point Times Roman Italic, 14-point Times Roman, or 12-point Helvetica.

FIGURE 13-3
The desktop publishing vocabulary includes words from the computer and publishing worlds. Here are some of the basic terms and their definitions.

Font cartridge. An optional cartridge that contains font files and plugs into a laser printer to expand the printer's range of available fonts.

Footer. One or more lines of text that appear at the bottom of every page.

˚Format. The appearance of a document in terms of its number of columns, column width, column rules (lines), headline placement, headers, footers, and other standing design elements.

˚Form generator package. Used to design office and other forms electronically.

˚Generic font. A representation of alphanumeric characters on a screen that may not reflect what the final printed characters will look like.

˚Greeking. Conversion of text to symbolic bars or boxes that show the position of the text on the screen but not the alphanumeric characters.

Halftone. Traditionally, a photograph processed with an optical screen to strip information away in order to break it into dots. A computer creates similar dot patterns by creating an image from digitized data a dot at a time.

H and J. Short for hyphenation and justification, which are automatically applied to text in top-of-the-line computer-aided publishing software.

Header. One or more lines of text that appear at the top of every page of a document.

Hyphenation. Hyphenation can be achieved in several ways: some programs let you manually insert "discretionary" hyphens (hyphens that are visible only when they fall at the end of a line of text); some programs insert hyphens automatically based on a dictionary of words; some programs use a logic formula or algorithm to hyphenate words. Usually, dictionary hyphenation takes longer than logical hyphenation but is more accurate.

Icon. A functional graphic representation of a tool, a file, or a command displayed on a screen.

Invert. See **reverse.**

Justified text. Text that is aligned flush at both the left and the right edges. See also **hyphenation** and **H and J.**

˚Kerning. Amount of space between certain combinations of letters that must be brought closer together than others in order to create visually consistent spacing. See **tracking.**

Landscape printing. The rotation of a page design to print text and graphics horizontally across the 11-inch width of the paper. See also **portrait printing.**

˚Laser printing. Used to describe printing with one of the toner-based laser printers available for microcomputers, such as the Apple LaserWriter or Hewlett-Packard's Laserjet Plus. Some typesetters also use laser technology in conjunction with their photochemical processing, but these are usually referred to as phototypesetters rather than as laser printers.

˚Layout. The arrangement of text and graphics on a page.

˚Leading (rhymes with "bedding"). The space between lines. For example, 9-point type with a 12-point line height allows a 3-point leading.

Line art. A black-and-white illustration, or drawing.

Line spacing. See **leading.**

Linotronic. One of several brands of commercial phototypesetting equipment that accept PostScript documents and produce them at higher resolutions than possible on some personal laser printers.

⋅Master pages. In a page composition package, used to set column widths, margins, and any other items that appear in every left or right page.

⋅Object image file. Stores an image as formulas or instructions which describe the curves and lines that make up the images.

Offset printing. A printing process in which the inked impression is first made on a rubber-covered roller, then transferred to paper.

⋅Outline font. A font produced by instruction that describes the path (curves and lines) that makes up a character's outline. The instructions are written in a **page description language** that treats text as an object-oriented image which can be scaled (by using standard geometrical processes) to virtually any size while maintaining proportions. One outline font file can be used to produce the fonts for many typeface family members.

⋅Page composition package. Replaces a drafting table, scissors, and glue with electronic assembly of text and graphics in order to create a page layout.

⋅Page description language (PDL). A system for coding document files in order to make the files acceptable to laser printers, **typesetters**, or any other device that can read the coded "PDL" file. File coding is done automatically by many page composition packages. Three examples of page description languages are PostScript, Interpress, and DDL (Document Description Language).

⋅Page layout. An assembled page of text and graphics that is intended to be printed repetitively or reproduced using more traditional methods.

Page makeup. Composing a **page layout** including positioning text and graphics, and assigning type specifications.

⋅Page oriented. A term to categorize a page composition package suited to handling short documents that mix text and graphics in innovative ways on each page.

Pasteboard. A work area on the screen that surrounds the edge of the paper image.

Pasteup board. A piece of white cardboard used in the manual composition of a page layout. Typeset text is pasted on it and placeholders are positioned for a print shop to "strip" in graphic elements. A completed pasteup board is called a mechanical.

Photocomposition. A blanket term for a variety of technologies in which photographic processes are used to produce a high-quality page image composed of text, graphics, and fonts, on photosensitive paper, as when documents are printed on a Linotronic 100 or 300 typesetter.

Phototypesetter. Machinery that does **photocomposition**.

⋅Point. Smallest unit of measure in typographic measurement. There are 72 points in an inch.

Portrait printing. The normal printing orientation for a page: horizontal text on an 8½-inch-wide sheet of paper. See also **landscape printing.**

⋅PostScript. A **page description language** developed by Adobe Systems and used by Apple's LaserWriter and other high-resolution printers and typesetters.

⋅Printer fonts. Font files used by the printer which are different from the **screen fonts.** They can be **outline fonts** or **bit-mapped fonts.**

⋅Raster image processor (RIP). A separate microprocessor in a laser printer that converts outline fonts into bit-mapped images for laser printing.

FIGURE 13-3 (continued)

Reverse. The opposite of the normal appearance of text or a graphic image on the printed page. Normally, text and graphics are black on a white background. When reversed, they are white on a black background. Graphics can also be reversed. This option is called "invert" on some systems.

˙Resolution. The number of dots per inch used to represent an alphanumeric character or a graphic image. High-resolution images look smoother and have more dots per inch than do low-resolution images. The resolution of images displayed on the screen is usually lower than that of the final laser printout. Laser printers print 300 dots per inch or more; typesetters print 1,200 dots per inch or more.

Roman. Upright (nonslated) text styles, as distinguished from italic.

Ruler. Lines displayed on the screen that show measures against the page layout in, for example, inches or millimeters.

˙Rules or ruled lines. Black lines of various styles that can be drawn on a page and set to various thicknesses.

Sans serif. Typefaces without serifs, such as Helvetica, Avant Garde, and Geneva. See also **serif.** (This glossary is printed in Avant Garde, a sans serif typeface.)

˙Scale. Same as **size.**

˙Screen font. Since it is impossible to see the instructions that make up an **outline font,** developers must have some way of representing outline fonts on screen. The resulting "screen fonts" are bit-mapped fonts designed to approximate the look of corresponding outline fonts. Each outline font has a corresponding screen font.

Serif. Line crossing the main strokes of a letter. Typefaces that have serifs include Times Roman, Courier, New Century Schoolbook, Bookman, Palatino, and New York. See also **sans serif.** (The main text of this book is printed in Baskerville, a serif typeface.)

Size. To make a graphic image smaller or larger on a page.

˙Snap-to effect. A feature that appears like a magnet that pulls text and graphics in order to align them with a column edge or page margin. The snap-to effect can usually be turned on or off by a menu selection.

˙Soft font. A font that is transferred by software to a laser printer's RAM (random access memory), where it stays until a printing job is finished or until the printer is turned off.

˙Style sheet. A collection of type specs and format definitions that can be saved and used in many different documents.

˙Tag. A label inserted into text in order to identify its type specifications. Examples of tags are "@heading1" and "@bodytext." One tag can identify a group of detailed type specifications. Tags can often be inserted into a word processing document before the document is **flowed** into a page layout.

˙Template. In desktop publishing, refers to a prepared page layout containing ruler guides, placeholders, and ruled lines. Page composition software suppliers sell template packages for newsletters, manuals, and other types of publications, as "add-on" products.

˙Text wrap. The ability to wrap text around graphic images on a page layout. Some systems have an automatic text-wrap feature that will shorten lines of text when a graphic image is encountered.

Threaded or chained. Blocks of text that are connected together throughout the columns on a page and across pages from the beginning to the end of the article.

*TIFF (Tag Image File Format). A standard file format for scanned image files.

*Tracking. Measuring and controlling the overall tightness of letterspacing on a line to counteract the optical illusion of loose type. Used in addition to kerning. Also called white-space reduction.

*Typeface. A designed set of characters with a name, which is sometimes copyrighted, that describes their overall appearance. Examples are Times Roman and Helvetica. Typeface is used interchangeably with **font** in desktop publishing, basically because a typeface can be manipulated to get the elements that make up the fonts.

*Typesetter. Machinery that does **photocomposition**.

*Type specification. Type face, style, and size.

*Type style. A modification of a **typeface's** characters, such as **italic** or **roman**. Usually weight (light, medium, bold) is also considered an element of style.

Vertical justification. The ability to adjust the spacing between lines of text (leading) in fine increments to make columns and pages end at the same point on the page.

Word wrap. Automatic adjustment of the number of words on a line of text to match the margin settings. The carriage returns that result from automatic word wrap are called "soft" carriage returns to distinguish them from the "hard" carriage returns, which result when the Return key is pressed to force a new line.

Wrap. See **text wrap** and **word wrap**.

*WYSIWYG. What-you-see-is-what-you-get (pronounced "wizzywig") is a term used to describe systems that display full pages on the screen with text and graphics. Some programs are more WYSIWYG than others in the accuracy of the display. The term is also used to describe word processing programs that display different fonts on the screen.

Xerox PARC. Xerox's Palo Alto Research Center originated many of the standards for implementation of menus, windows, and icons that are now used by systems like *GEM, Microsoft Windows*, and the Macintosh, as well as programs like Software Publishing Corp.'s *PFS:ClickArt Personal Publisher*, Aldus Corp.'s *PageMaker*, and Ventura Software's *Ventura Publisher*.

FIGURE 13-3 (continued)

They cover the four steps that Clifford Layton follows to create a sample newsletter.

Mr. Layton works as a marketing assistant at Interstate Distributing Company. Ordinarily he works with a small advertising firm to create Interstate's sales catalogs, promotion pieces, price lists, and other items that are listed in Figure 13-4.

But Interstate is interested in doing some of the work in-house that is typically farmed out. The benefits it hopes to realize from using desktop publishing include

· Saving time by eliminating the communication delays of using outside services. Designs can be seen almost instantly instead of in days.

Advertisements	Low-volume specialty publications
Annual reports	Magazines
Appointment books	Newsletters
Awards	Operation guides
Books	Pamphlets
Brochures	Presentations
Business cards	Press releases
Calendars	Price lists
Catalogs	Product lists
Catalog sheets	Product specification sheets
Certificates	Programs for events
Circulars	Promotional material
Employee handbooks	Proof copies for commercial typesetters
Fliers	Proposals
Forms	Reports
Handouts	Stationery
Installation pamphlets	Stockholder certificates
Instruction manuals	Technical manuals and documents
Insurance policies	Training manuals
Labels	

FIGURE 13-4
Some uses for desktop publishing

- Saving money by eliminating the purchase of outside type and layout services.
- Regaining greater control of publishing projects by moving the entire process in-house. Interstate can better meet deadlines and use trial-and-error to stimulate creativity.

In addition, Interstate hopes to gain a competitive advantage, since promotions and other marketing projects do not have to be delayed because of unfinished promotional or support documentation.

Many organizations realize other benefits as their desktop publishing becomes part of larger systems through networking.

PAGE COMPOSITION EXAMPLE

Page composition software is the tool that allows Mr. Layton to design and lay out a newsletter, such as the one in Figure 13-5, or other document, right at his desk. To learn how to use page composition software, Mr. Layton created the sample newsletter shown in Figure 13-6. It was produced, from start to finish, in four steps. The steps cover the work flow shown in Figure 13-7.

One of many possible typefaces which range in size from 4 to 127 points.

This image was first digitized by a scanner and related software, then imported and placed on the page.

The image was trimmed (cropped) to fit.

Headlines and captions were typed with a built-in text editor. It enables correcting mistakes and typos right on the page.

Text was placed directly into columns from a word processing program with no additional typing.

Up to 20 different column widths per page are possible.

Line rules and bars in a variety of styles are available from a built-in design library.

Type can be created in bold, italics, outlined, shadowed, or reverse/inverted (as in this example) styles.

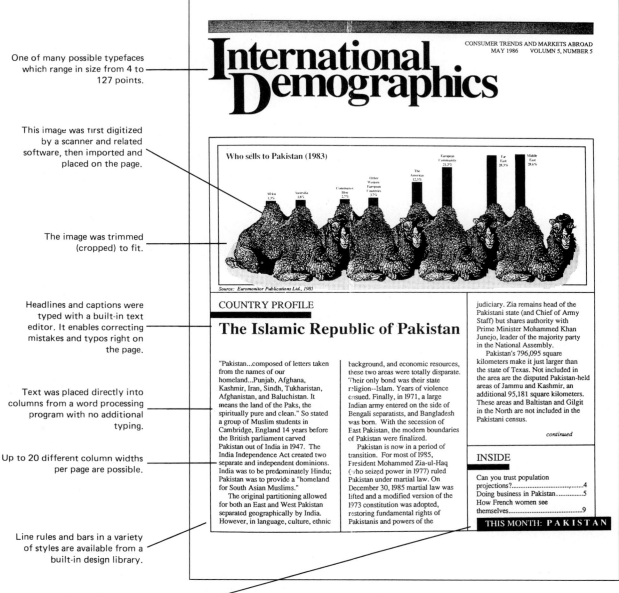

This page was first printed on a laser printer to get a proof copy. It was then sent on disk to a typesetter. Output from the typesetter is the same image on high quality resin-coated paper (RC paper), such as that used for black and white photography. This is then taken to a printer for reproduction on an offset press.

FIGURE 13-5

A newsletter created with the aid of a page composition package
(Software: PageMaker, courtesy of Aldus Corporation; Newsletter by Carol Terrizzi, American Demographics, Inc.)

1. The graphic logo first was created in a drawing package, then imported into a page composition package to create the page layout shown here.

2. The title Bylines was typed directly into the page layout using the Times Roman font in its largest size (127 points).

3. Text first was created in a word processing package, then imported into appropriate columns.

4. The drawing of the building first was scanned using an inexpensive scanner and saved in a popular drawing package file format acceptable to the page composition software. Once imported into this page layout, it was scaled down and a hairline border added using the page composition package's built-in "tools."

5. The text wrapped around the drawing is created by dividing the text into separate blocks and changing the width of each block.

6. The "text wrap" around at the large initial "drop cap" at the top of the third column required breaking the article and first paragraph into four different blocks of text.

Better Management, Inc

Ground-Breaking for New Headquarters Announced

It was all pomp and fanfare at the groundbreaking ceremonies for BMI's new corporate headquarters, held last Wednesday at the site on which the 27-story building will rise.

In attendance was BMI's entire Board of Directors, including Chairman Stephen W. Olsen, as well as a contingent of local dignitaries headed by the Mayor of Minneapolis and his wife. A cheering crowd of 1000 looked on, and all BMI employees were given the day off so that they could attend.

"This is an important day in the history of our company," Olsen said after he turned over a symbolic pile of dirt with a gold-plated spade. "Our spectacular growth has been making headlines for years. Now we will have a home that represents the status we have achieved in the management consulting industry."

After presenting Olsen with a key to the city, the Mayor commented, "As the leader of this great city, nothing is more exciting for me than to see another beautiful skyscraper thrust upward to signify to the world that Minneapolis is as dynamic and vibrant as ever."

(continued on Page 4)

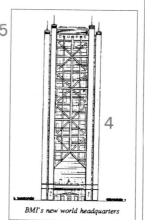

BMI's new world headquarters

A Message from Our President

This is an exciting time in the history of our company. I hope all of you enjoyed the groudbreaking ceremonies for our new headquarters. When the building is finished, it will be something to behold.

But the business of business continues, and I would like to address a concern that has been mentioned to me by several employees in recent months: the role of BMI in South Africa.

As many of you know, BMI has operated a South African office out of Durban since 1976. Ten years later, the situation in South Africa has deteriorated to such a state that every corporation that does business in that troubled country is being forced to evaluate what its next move should be.

Let me emphasize that BMI does no business with the government of South Africa. All of our sales are to private corporations. This does not mean, of course, that we feel no obligation to do what we can to help ameliorate the tragic

(continued on Page 3)

FIGURE 13-6

First page of a sample newsletter created with the aid of a page composition package
(Software: PageMaker; *Newsletter by Diana Burns and S. Venit, courtesy of* PC Magazine)

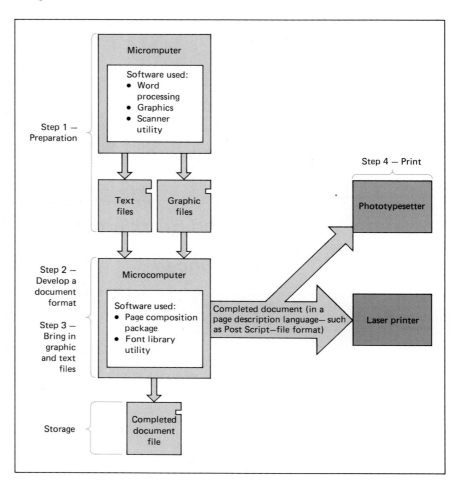

FIGURE 13-7
Typical desktop publishing work flow

STEP 1—PREPARATION

The first step of any desktop publishing project requires preparing text and graphics. Mr. Layton writes and edits all text, called **copy** in desktop publishing jargon, with a standard word processing package.

To prepare graphics, he uses a variety of packaged software. For instance, he uses a drawing package to create the logo for the sample newsletter. After the drawing is created, it is saved in a file that will be used later.

To create the image of the building structure requires a scanner and related scanner utility software. A scanner digitizes any image from a photograph, article, or other source. Once an image is scanned, it is also saved as a file that will be used later.

For page 2 of the sample newsletter, he uses a ready-made map image from a clip-art package. It is already available in a file for when it will be used later.

For page 3, he uses a spreadsheet package to create the bar chart shown in Figure 13-8. The chart began as a spreadsheet and was converted into a visual format with the spreadsheet package's built-in graphics feature. The chart is also saved as a file that is acceptable to the page composition software.

FIGURE 13-8
Third page of the sample newsletter created with the aid of a
page composition package
(*Software:* PageMaker; *Newsletter by Diana Burns and S. Venit,*
courtesy of PC Magazine)

7. The header and footer for page 1 and 3 were entered on a "master page" for odd-numbered pages, which included automatic page numbering and the shaded bars. A "master page" was also created for even-numbered pages 2 and 4.

8. The text was wrapped around the portrait (a scanned image) and the initial drop cap by dividing the text into eight different sections and changing the width of each column block. Text was reflowed into the shorter blocks.

9. The bar chart first was created in a spreadsheet package. It then was imported into the page layout.

10. The tab position settings for the table were carried over exactly as set earlier in the word processing package, but they could have been set or changed in this page layout.

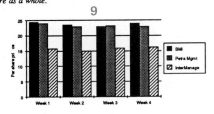

Page 3
7

Employee of the Month

Nicholas Kinnard was more than a little humble when he found out that he had been selected as the BMI Employee of the Month Award winner. "All I do is drive," he said.

Actually, Nicholas is one of the most important links between BMI's scattered Minneapolis offices. Every day he drives a company van from office to office, transporting employees, packages, letters, and messages and making sure everything and everyone gets to the right place.

Nicholas, 23, has been with BMI for almost two years. He started out at the central mail room, but when a driving position became available, he leapt at the chance to get outdoors.

"I've lived in Minneapolis all my life, but now I realize how little of it I had seen until I got in the van and started to drive all the time," he says. "Snow, rain, hail, ice, you see it all in this town, but I don't let it bother me. I just keep driving." And drive he does, sometimes 200 miles a day and more, without ever missing a stop on his rounds.

8

Like all employees of the month, Nicholas will receive three days paid vacation.

This Month on Wall Street...

Over the last month BMI's price-per-share stock value has risen along with the Dow Jones Industrial Average. The stock's performance is by no means stellar, but according to BMI's Stephen Laffey, it is "blue-chip" solid and destined to produce consistent advances no matter what the vagaries of the market are as a whole.

9

	BMI, Inc	Petra Mgmt	InterManage
Week 1	24.5	24	15.75
Week 2	23.5	23	15
Week 3	23	23.25	16
Week 4	24	23	16.25

10

(continued from Page 1)

situation that exists. But should we just close the office, cut our losses, and leave?

Those who oppose this kind of complete withdrawal make what I think is a convincing argument. They say that once a company leaves, it has virtually no chance to have any positive impact on the situation. BMI has several black South African employees in the Durban office, and we feel we owe them, as well as their white counterparts, the same kind of loyalty that all our employees get.

So for the time being we will not be closing the Durban office, but let me assure you that the Board of Directors will continue to monitor events closely.

All the newsletter's content is now prepared. It all exists as independent files on Mr. Layton's hard disk. The files now need some unifying element to bring them all together. That unifier is the page composition software. Its use begins step 2 of any desktop publishing effort.

STEP 2—DEVELOP A FORMAT

The first thing Mr. Layton does with the page composition software is to devise a format for the newsletter. A **format** defines the appearance of a document in terms of its number of columns, column *rules* (lines), headline placement, headers, footers, and other standing design elements.

For new projects, he often first uses pencil and tracing paper to create thumbnail sketches of possible arrangements of text and graphics on a page, called **layouts,** as shown in Figure 13-9. The tracing paper fits over a grid sheet that is the actual size of a document page.

Alternatively, he can use any one of a collection of over 20 **templates,** which are layouts prepared by graphic designers and consist of

- Ruler guides, to help align the various objects in a newsletter
- Placeholders, to identify the placement, type style, and size of text elements on a page
- Rule lines, to help separate the sections visually, as shown in the example in Figure 13-10

FIGURE 13-9
Hand-drawn thumbnail sketches of
possible page layouts
(Courtesy of PC World)

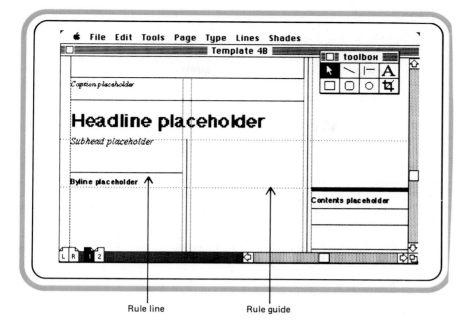

Rule line   Rule guide

FIGURE 13-10
A typical newsletter template contains
column and rule guides, as well as text
placeholders.
(Courtesy of MacWorld*)*

The supplier of the page composition package sells the templates as add-on packages. One template package is for newsletters, another is for manuals and other structured publications, and there are others. Each comes with a tutorial that explains things to consider when

- Laying out column-spacing guides
- Creating headlines
- Combining type styles for headlines and body text
- Adding artwork (graphics), lines, boxes, or shading
- Balancing the size and placement of text and graphics

The tutorials proved to be invaluable aids.

With a basic layout design in mind, Mr. Layton begins to exercise the page composition software. A typical screen resembles the one in Figure 13-11. It looks familiar to him. This is because it uses the common graphical icon-based, pulldown (or dropdown) menu structure that some of his other software uses. For every main menu bar item, there is a pulldown menu. Menu selections can be executed using a mouse or the keyboard. Although a mouse is optional, Mr. Layton finds it more convenient than keyboard equivalents for many functions.

He first selects File from the menu bar, then selects New from the pulldown menu of File options. The opening view is of a miniature blank page centered on the screen, and a toolbox in the upper right corner. The toolbox can be positioned wherever desired. It contains tools that are used to

- Create simple graphics (lines, boxes, circles, and so forth)
- **Crop** a graphic image by trimming its edges to remove part of it or **scale** an image by "stretching" or "shrinking" it
- Switch into text mode for editing or formatting text

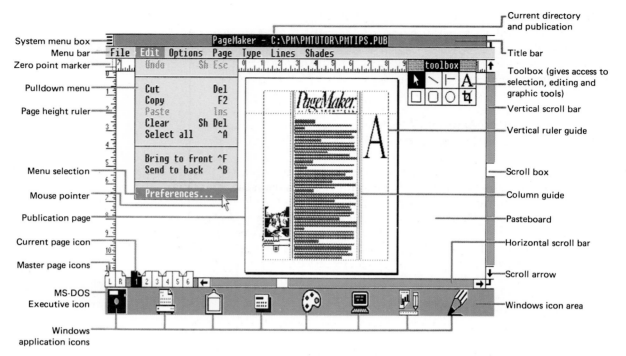

FIGURE 13-11
Screen from a page composition package
(Software: PageMaker, courtesy of PC World)

The lower left corner of the screen displays tiny icons labeled L(eft), R(ight), and 1, 2, 3, 4, 5, 6, or more. The Left and Right refer to so-called **master pages,** which are used to set column widths, margins, and any other item that appears on every left or right page. The numbered pages refer to their respective pages in the document. Clicking the mouse button with the mouse pointer placed on any of these icons causes the page to appear on-screen.

Defining a Master Page

Since the sample document is a four-page newsletter, Mr. Layton begins by designing the left and right master pages. He defines columns and other elements that will appear on every page, such as running headers, footers, and automatic page numbers. He can always suppress master page elements on individual pages as needed.

To define the right master (odd-numbered) page, he clicks the mouse button when the mouse pointer is on the menu item "Options." The action produces a pulldown menu with "Guides" listed. He selects it to cause rules to appear at the top and left of the screen. The rules help to position type or graphic elements.

From the "Options" menu, "Column Guides" is selected next, which causes a dialog box to appear. A **dialog box** is an on-screen window, or full-screen display, which appears in response to a menu selection or commands that call for setting options. At the option "Number of Columns," 2 is entered. Immediately the master page displays two equal-width columns delineated by light, dotted lines and a space between them. To create uneven column widths, the mouse pointer is placed on a column's right edge. Then the mouse button is pressed and the mouse is dragged to the right. This action stretches the column edge to the right. Once in position, the mouse button is released to lock the column edge in its new position.

The thin ruled line that appears between the columns is also placed into position. It requires selecting the line drawing icon from the toolbox and moving the mouse pointer into position.

A few nonprinting horizontal and vertical guide lines are also positioned where desired on the page. They will be helpful later because they have a **snap-to effect**—which resembles a magnetic pull—for aligning text and graphic objects. The snap-to effect can be turned on and off by a menu selection.

Finally, the header and footer are placed in the master pages. The header contains a page number that is incremented on every page. It is difficult for Mr. Layton to see the page number in the full-page view. This view is squeezed into whatever size screen the program is using. Usually text must be "greeked." **Greeking** converts text into symbols that show the position of the text on the screen, but not the actual characters.

To make text legible, it is necessary to enlarge the page with a selection under the View menu. Portions of pages can be seen in the same size as printed, reduced (to 50 percent, 75 percent, or a full-page view), or enlarged 200 percent. Selecting 200 percent enlarges the view to a small corner of the page at twice the size it will print. Using the scroll box on the right or bottom of the screen moves the desired portion of the enlarged page into position. In this case, it is the upper-right-hand corner.

Some users buy large-screen displays, like the one in Figure 13-12, to see legible text and a full page simultaneously. Such displays are ideal for viewing multipage documents that must have balanced layout designs on facing pages. Figure 13-13 gives an example of how facing pages 2 and 3 of the sample newsletter appear on a standard 12-inch display.

To get the word "Page" into the layout, Mr. Layton first clicks on the A in the toolbox, which is the icon for text selection. Then he clicks at the point where type is to be entered. From the Type menu he next selects Helvetica 9-point italic and then types the word "Page." He hits the space bar and then presses a three-key sequence: Control-Shift-3. A trio of zeros appears on the master page to hold space for the page number.

This entire process is repeated for the right-hand master page, with the appropriate layout variations.

FIGURE 13-12
A large-screen display shows a two-page document that must be viewed
in sections on a smaller screen display.
(Hardware: Amdek and IBM displays, courtesy of Amdek)

FIGURE 13-13
To show a two-page spread in the "full-page" view on a regular 12-inch
screen requires that smaller type sizes be "greeked" in
(Courtesy of PC Magazine)

Example of "greeking"
(illegible text)

Displayed pages

STEP 3—BRING IN TEXT AND GRAPHICS

Once the master page layouts are established, it is time to fill the empty pages. They are filled with text and graphics that are brought in from other programs or entered directly.

Mr. Layton prepares boxes and rules using tools from the toolbox. The boxes with graphics on page 1 are to be filled first.

Importing Graphics

Mr. Layton decides to begin with the graphics for the company logo in the upper left corner of the first page. When he selects the Place command from the File menu, a dialog box lists available graphic and text files. He selects the file desired by clicking the mouse button, and the mouse pointer shape changes to a pencil. It identifies the file as one created with a drawing package. He positions the pointer in the box reserved for the logo, clicks the mouse button again, and the graphic pops into place, sized to fit.

Graphics can be imported in a number of file formats. One is as a drawing or **object image file** in which images are stored as formulas or instructions that describe the curves and lines that make up the image. Another is as a painting or **bit map image file** in which the images are stored as a matrix of dots. Scanned images are also bit-mapped image files. Some packages adhere to the **TIFF** (Tag Image File Format) standard for scanned image files, which are also bit-mapped image files.

To change the position of an imported graphic, Mr. Layton places the pointer on the image and holds the mouse button down. Then he moves the mouse to tow the item to its new position. When he stops the mouse and releases the mouse button, the graphic remains locked in its new position.

Scaling is accomplished in much the same way. It requires selecting an appropriate tool from the toolbox to place small-boxed "handles" around the graphic. Then by placing the mouse pointer on a handle and towing or "pulling" it, the graphic dynamically stretches to fit the new space. "Pushing" the handles shrinks a graphic just as easily. A cropping tool is used to trim the edges off a graphic image.

Importing Text

With the graphics placed, Mr. Layton turns to importing text files. As before, he selects Place from the File menu, but now he chooses a text file. The mouse pointer shape changes to symbolize text pages. It is an inverted L partially enclosing what looks like tiny lines of type. By moving this symbol to where placement begins, he clicks the mouse button. The text gradually appears on the page within the column margins until the column is filled. Sometimes this is called **flow** or **pour** *text, or graphics*, into a column or layout.

A small icon that looks like a loop, which is called a "window shade," appears at the bottom of the text. If a plus is inside that loop, there is more text to be positioned. A loop with a pound sign (#) indicates the end of the file.

Imported text does not flow from first page to last, as it does in some other page composition packages. It stops when it hits the end of the column or page. To continue text onto the next column or page, Mr. Layton must click the pointer on the plus loop, place the pointer (which turns into a page icon) on the next column or page, and click again to insert the next block of text. This can be a liability in a long document.

Sometimes Mr. Layton likes to experiment with different page layouts. If he changes a column width to test a new idea, text must be reflowed into the column to force it to realign with the new margins. This is extra work compared with other packages that automatically reflow text to accommodate adjusted column width.

Ideally, a page composition package should **text wrap,** which is to flow text around any obstruction, such as the boxed graphic on page 1 of the sample newsletter, or the portrait on page 3. But some packages stop text dead in its tracks when they butt up against a graphic. To break up the logjam, the text must be broken into small blocks. Each block must be resized and towed into position around the obstructing graphic. This is a tedious and inexact process.

Some page composition packages cannot import some word processing files directly. The files must first go through a process to be converted to an **ASCII file** format. It is a standard file format and the conversion procedure is built into many software packages. But this conversion strips the file of such type format characteristics as line spacing, tabs, indents, boldfacing, and italics. These characteristics must be reinstated once the file is available to the page composition software. It is a wasteful duplication of effort.

Setting Type

Once Mr. Layton imports text, he can set it to some other font. A **font** is a complete set of characters in one typeface and size. Figure 13-14 gives examples of six fonts.

The examples in Figure 13-14 come from two popular typeface families: Times Roman and Helvetica. A **typeface** is a designed set of characters with a name that is sometimes copyrighted and describes their overall appearance. Every typeface variation is a separate font. All are "members" of the common typeface "family." Figure 13-15 illustrates other typeface families and some of their members. Mr. Layton selects Type from the main menu bar to review the font choices available.

A font's size, or height, is measured in **points.** There are 72 points in an inch. One of the menus in Mr. Layton's software lists about a dozen type point sizes from 6 to 72, but he can specify any point size from 4 to 127.

A font's characteristics are also indicated by style and weight. **Type style** refers to the modification of a typeface to italic, upright (called

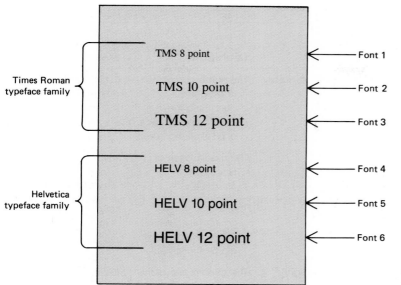

FIGURE 13-14
Examples of six fonts

HELVETICA LIGHT	OPTIMA. . . . .
HELVETICA LIGHT ITALIC	*OPTIMA ITALIC* . . . .
HELVETICA MEDIUM	**OPTIMA BOLD** . . . .
HELVETICA MEDIUM ITALIC	***OPTIMA BOLD ITALIC*** . . . .
HELVETICA BOLD	NEWS GOTHIC. . . . .
HELVETICA BOLD ITALIC	*NEWS GOTHIC ITALIC* . . . .
HELVETICA BLACK.	**NEWS GOTHIC BOLD** . . . .
HELVETICA BLACK ITALIC	***NEWS GOTHIC BOLD ITALIC***. . . . .
SOUVENIR LIGHT	NEWS GOTHIC CONDENSED . . . .
SOUVENIR LIGHT ITALIC	*NEWS GOTHIC CONDENSED ITALIC*. . . . .
SOUVENIR MEDIUM.	**NEWS GOTHIC CONDENSED BOLD** . . . .
SOUVENIR MEDIUM ITALIC	***NEWS GOTHIC CONDENSED BOLD ITALIC*** . . . .
CENTURY SCHOOLBOOK	PALANTINO . . . .
CENTURY SCHOOLBOOK ITALIC.	*PALANTINO ITALIC* . . . .
CENTURY SCHOOLBOOK BOLD.	**PALANTINO BOLD** . . . .
CENTURY SCHOOLBOOK BOLD ITALIC	KORINNA . . . .
MELIOR.	**KORINNA BOLD** . . . .
MELIOR ITALIC	TIFFANY MEDIUM . . . .
MELIOR BOLD.	TIFFANY DEMI . . . .
MELIOR BOLD ITALIC	

FIGURE 13-15
A collection of typeface families. A "member" of a typeface family is any variation on a basic typeface.
(Source: Francis X. Bolton, "Contrasting Faces," New York Personal Computer User's Group Newsletter, June 1987, p. 37)

roman), outline, or some other variation. Weight refers to the density of the characters, such as light, medium, or bold. Usually weight is understood to be simply another element of type style. The chart in Figure 13-16 lists all the characteristics that can be associated with a font.

In desktop publishing, typeface is used interchangeably with font, basically because a typeface can be manipulated electronically to get the characteristics that make up the fonts.

To change the font of imported text, such as an article title, Mr. Layton first highlights the text by dragging the mouse pointer over it. Then he makes a series of Type menu selections to implement the change. Every time a font characteristic is changed, he must highlight the text and indicate **type specifications** (typeface, style, or size) in a dialog box. Keyboard shortcuts are available to speed this process.

FONT CHARACTERISTIC	DEFINITION	EXAMPLES
Typeface or typeface family	The name, sometimes copyrighted, describing the overall appearance of a set of characters	Courier, Helvetica, Times Roman
Style	The modification of a typeface's characters	Italics, upright (also called roman), outline
Stroke weight	The density of the characters (which is often considered an element of style)	Bold, medium, light
Size (also called height)	The general size of the characters given in points (72 points in an inch)	10 point 12 point
Pitch	The number of characters per horizontal inch	10, 12
Spacing	The method of spacing between characters	Fixed, proportional
Orientation	How the character is placed relative to the page	Portrait (horizontal text on an 8½-inch-wide sheet of paper), landscape (horizontal text across the 11-inch width of the paper)

FIGURE 13-16
Font characteristics

Like the header and footer, the Bylines banner on page 1 is typed directly into the layout. It requires selecting the word "Times," for the Times Roman font, from the Type Spec (specification) menu. Then 127, the largest point size supported, is entered. Finally, the word Bylines is typed.

Setting type also involves some automatic procedures. For example, the space between certain combinations of letters is automatically adjusted in order to create visually consistent spacing. This process is called **kerning** by professional typographers. The letters AW, for example, may appear to have a wider gap between them than the letters MN unless there is a special kerning formula set up for the AW combination. Figure 13-17 shows how kerned text achieves a more refined typographic quality.

Kerning is one of many terms unique to the field of typography that describes the methods used to arrange letters on a page in a way

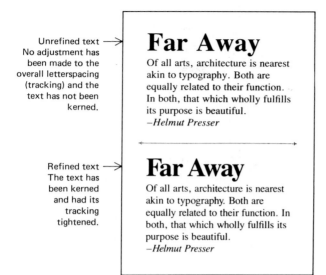

Unrefined text →
No adjustment has been made to the overall letterspacing (tracking) and the text has not been kerned.

Refined text →
The text has been kerned and had its tracking tightened.

Far Away

Of all arts, architecture is nearest akin to typography. Both are equally related to their function. In both, that which wholly fulfills its purpose is beautiful.
–Helmut Presser

Far Away

Of all arts, architecture is nearest akin to typography. Both are equally related to their function. In both, that which wholly fulfills its purpose is beautiful.
–Helmut Presser

FIGURE 13-17
Examples of kerning (adjust space between certain pairs of letters) and tracking (adjust letterspacing overall)
(Courtesy of PC World)

that is more than just pleasing to the eye. It also makes text easier to read. By their nature, such elements are unobtrusive—aesthetically laid-out type does not call attention to itself. But there is a lot going on behind the scenes.

Tracking is another automatic procedure that measures and controls the overall tightness of letterspacing. It counteracts the optic illusion of loose type. This and other automatic typographic features can be turned off or used selectively.

Hyphenation of text is also an automatic feature. It breaks words in order to space the text closely for enhanced readability. In Mr. Layton's software, hyphenation is based on a 110,000-word popular dictionary. In some packages, hyphenation is based on a logic formula. Usually, dictionary hyphenation takes longer than logical hyphenation but is more accurate.

Mr. Layton's software provides a prompted hyphenation mode. It lets him referee all breaks and add unrecognized words to a supplementary, user-specified 1,300-word dictionary.

After the four pages are laid out, Mr. Layton tries several different variations on the layout design. He positions articles and repositions them. He tries different typefaces and basically looks to get a good balance on each page. He does not want to leave one page, for example, with nothing but text or, more subtly, with one illustration overwhelming another.

STEP 4—PRINT

Once the pages look the way he wants, Mr. Layton is ready to print. To get the result desired requires a laser printer. As Figure 13-18 diagrams, he could run the laser printer to publish all the copies desired.

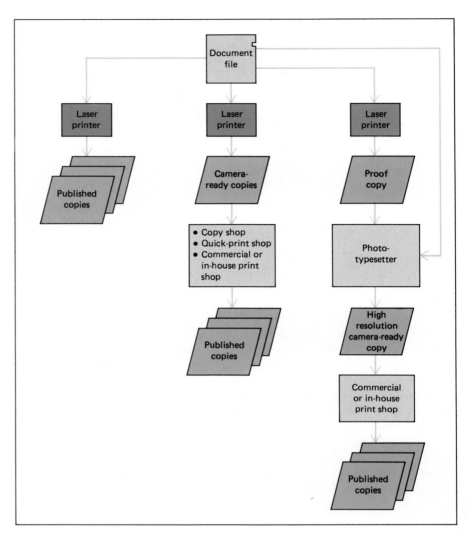

FIGURE 13-18
Alternative paths to publish document copies

More often, he takes the laser-produced original to a print shop for copies.

A complex page layout may take half an hour to print the first copy on a laser printer. Additional copies of the same original can be produced, on many laser printers, at eight or more copies a minute. Many people do not use their laser printer as a copy machine for high-volume jobs.

Figure 13-19 illustrates the comparative quality of output from a dot matrix printer, laser printer, and typesetter. The highest print quality is obtained from a typesetter. A **typesetter** (also called phototypesetter or imagesetter) is machinery that uses photographic processes to produce a page image on photosensitive paper. Examples are the Linotronic 100 and 300 typesetters. They print documents at a relatively high **resolu-**

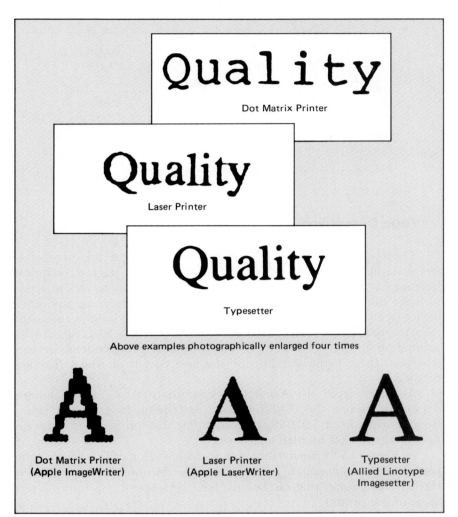

FIGURE 13-19
Samples show the comparative quality of output from a dot matrix printer, a laser printer, and a typesetter.
(*Courtesy of* PC Magazine)

tion, which is the number of dots per inch used to represent an alphanumeric character or a graphic image. Figure 13-20 lists the differences in printer output dot density.

More and more typesetters are being equipped to read a document file that has been produced with a microcomputer and page composition software. Because of this, Mr. Layton can upgrade the quality of his finished document without any additional effort except to print it on a typesetter.

The output from the typesetter is an image on resin-coated paper. It is similar to paper used in black-and-white photography. This output can then be taken to a print shop for high-quality reproductions.

Some typesetting services accept a page layout file that is sent to them by modem.

PRINTER OUTPUT DOT DENSITY	IMAGE QUALITY	PRINTER TYPE	EXAMPLE OF PRINTER COST
300 dpi (dots per inch)	Poor	Laser	$2,000
1,200 dpi	"Newspaper"	Typesetter	Begin at $25,000
2,540 dpi	Photographic	Typesetter	Begin at $50,000

FIGURE 13-20
Image quality related to dot density of output devices

Page Description Language

The magic that enables Mr. Layton's document file to drive a typesetter as easily as it drives a laser printer is called a **page description language (PDL).** A PDL is a system for coding document files in order to make the files acceptable to laser printers, typesetters, or any other device that can read the coded "PDL" file. File coding is done automatically by most page composition packages. Because a PDL file can be printed on a range of devices, it is called **device independent.** Devices that read these languages provide the best output of which they are capable.

As an example, the Allied Linotype Linotronic typesetter accepts document files in the *PostScript* page description language. It prints these documents at 1,270 dots per inch. Mr. Layton frequently has his documents run off by such a typesetter.

As Figure 13-21 demonstrates, a document is logically far from complete once the command to print is given. The document begins a journey through the printer that can be imagined as happening in four discrete areas of the printer.

The **laser printer** itself is a sophisticated computing device complete with its own microprocessor and random access memory (RAM). As mentioned, it can take as long as half an hour for it to "process" a complex document into a printed image. The journey begins once the print file is loaded into the printer's memory. Then the page description language interpreter "interprets" any printer instructions it finds in the document file. One instruction may tell it to retrieve a **built-in font,** which permanently resides in the printer's ROM (read only memory). Another instruction may tell it to scale the font up to 18 points. Another instruction may tell it to insert a graphic. All this activity occurs in a work area of memory.

The fonts retrieved by the printer are **printer fonts,** which are different from the screen fonts Mr. Layton saw earlier on the display during page layout. They can be **outline fonts,** which are produced by instructions that describe the path (curves and lines) that makes up each character's outline. These outlines are treated as object-oriented graphic images. By using standard geometrical processes, they can be scaled to virtually any size while maintaining their proportions. Because a single outline

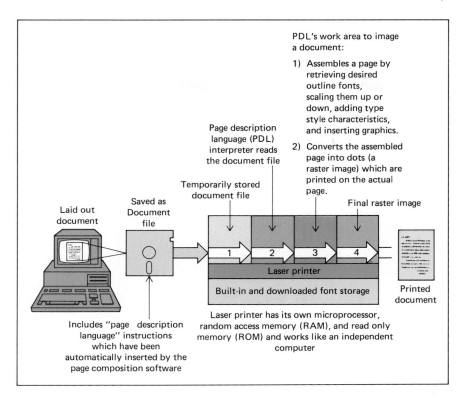

FIGURE 13-21
Work flow in a page description language printer

font can easily be scaled, or given bold, italic, or other type style characteristics, the need for many font files in the printer is eliminated.

Some printer fonts are **bit-mapped fonts.** They are composed of
the actual dot sequence that forms each character. Since each character
consists of a unique "map" of its data, a separate file must be created
for every member of a typeface family.

A **screen font** is a bit-mapped font designed to approximate the
look of the corresponding printer font. Some of these screen fonts are
generic fonts. They are general, not exact, representations of printer
fonts and so may not look on-screen like the final printed characters.
In such cases, the printed result can occasionally be surprising and can
cause many trial prints to be made until a desired appearance is achieved.

In desktop publishing, users try to get as close as possible to the
ideal of **WYSIWYG** (pronounced "wizzywig"), or "what you see is what
you get." As illustrated in Figure 13-22, it refers to a match of the
screen image with the printed image. In most cases, users settle for
"what you see is nearly what you get."

As the document is being assembled piece by piece in the printer's
work area, it must also be converted to dots by the **raster image processor
(RIP).** The dots of the final raster image are what get printed on
the paper.

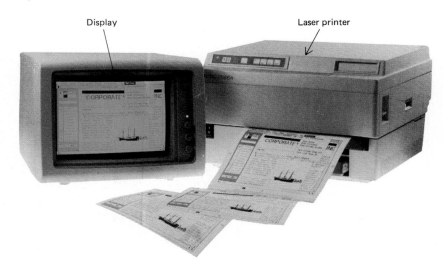

Display   Laser printer

FIGURE 13-22
In a WYSIWYG (what you see is what
you get) page composition program, the
screen display closely emulates a
document's printed appearance.
(Hardware: display, IBM; laser printer,
Hewlett-Packard; courtesy of PC World)

A laser printer like IBM's Personal Pageprinter is designed differently. It has all the printer's controlling circuitry located in the microcomputer's system unit. There the circuitry resides on a separate add-on circuit board called a laser controller. But regardless of where the electronics reside, the procedure to create printed output is similar.

PACKAGE ORIENTATION

Page composition packages can generally be classified by type, as follows:

Page Composition Package Type	Comments
Page oriented	Best suited to handle short documents that mix text and graphics in innovative ways on each page. An example is PageMaker.
Document oriented	Best suited to handle long, consistently formatted text, such as manuals and books. An example is Ventura Publisher.

Figure 13-23 compares these two types of packages when handling some common page layout tasks.

While a page-oriented package anticipates great variety from page to page, a document-oriented package expects consistency throughout a document. While the page-oriented package provides superior control over multiple elements with tricky layouts, the document-oriented package offers speedy reformatting and extensive support for such long document elements as table of contents creation, index generation, and section numbering.

| | HOW TASK IS HANDLED | |
Task	Page-Oriented Package	Document-Oriented Package
Flow text into a column	Stops at the end of a column or rule (line) barrier	Flows long text into the next or any other column on the page, or to any other page. A new page is automatically created if the text length requires it
Repeat the same paragraph specifications elsewhere	Manually reenter them	Define a "tag" and reuse them as needed
Make a change to layout text or graphic content	Change is made to the document layout file	Change is made to the original word processing or graphic file
Send the final document file to a typesetter	One file (except for bit-mapped images) must be sent	Many files must be sent (at least one file for each text and graphic item used)

FIGURE 13-23
Comparison of two types of page composition packages

The document-oriented package also supplies a slightly more automated environment. For instance, when the beginning of a word-processed document is placed on the page, a document-oriented package automatically flows the entire document across as many pages as the text requires. The page length of the document changes dynamically to accommodate the text. This feature is ideal for long, single-article documents, such as technical manuals and book chapters.

By contrast, in a page-oriented package, text must be manually continued from column to column or page to page.

As another example, the document-oriented package provides a method to involve work groups, such as technical writers, in the formatting task. They can insert, as an example, an @ symbol, followed by the name of a "tag," at the beginning of each different paragraph format. A **tag** is a label inserted into text in order to identify its type specifications. A tag such as "@ body text" can identify a group of detailed specifications that include

- Typeface
- Type size
- Type style
- **Leading,** which is the space between lines
- Paragraph alignment
- Indentation
- Tabs
- Spacing between paragraphs
- Rule lines above, below, or around a paragraph

Placing tags in word processing text makes long-document layout more efficient because it

- Spreads the format task among work group members
- Provides a way to use already defined specifications
- Reduces the time and steps necessary, using the page composition software, to lay out a document for publication

A problem is that group members must be trained to use tags and be kept current about valid tags. Also, they may not be very enthusiastic about the additional work necessary in order to distribute the formatting task.

A simple document might include tags to define body text, level 1 headings, level 2 headings, indented paragraphs, captions, and three-column tables. A more complex document might require more tags, one for each different combination of paragraph format, font, and tab settings.

Tags can also be selected from a list during the page layout process. Figure 13-24 shows a screen from a document-oriented package with some tag names listed on the left side. New tags can be added to or old ones deleted from this list. A collection of tags that are saved as a group and reused for many documents is called a **style sheet.** A style sheet resembles a template. A change to any tag will result in changes to all paragraphs that carry that tag.

Another fundamental difference between a document-oriented and a page-oriented package is how they handle files on disk. The page-oriented package assembles all files of text and graphics into one file that is sent to the printer, except for bit-mapped image files (from a scanner or paint package). They remain in a separate linked file.

By contrast, the document-oriented package contains many files. The page layout file acts as a control file. It holds page-formatting information and "pointers" to the original text and graphic files. Any changes

FIGURE 13-24

A screen from a document-oriented page composition package with a list of tag names

(*Software: Ventura Publisher, courtesy of Xerox Corp. Photo courtesy of PC Magazine.*)

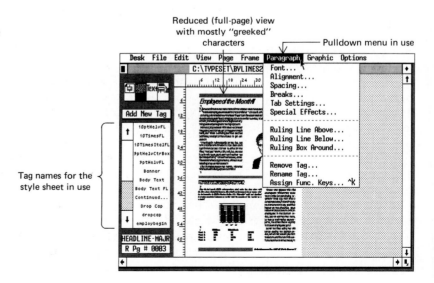

made to text or graphics in the page layout are actually made to original files. This method provides data integrity between the text shown in the page layout and the source text used to create the layout. It is ideal in work groups that can continue to update files during the page layout process.

The method has its drawbacks. Sending such a document to a typesetting service could be risky. A user must make sure that all component files are either communicated by modem or delivered on disks. A one-main-file-per-document system, on the other hand, reduces the likelihood of problems.

Mr. Layton found that his publishing projects required features from both types of packages. He expected that the best features of both would eventually be merged into a single package.

ALTERNATIVE SOFTWARE

Advanced word processing packages, such as WordPerfect and Microsoft Word, offer users an alternative to page composition packages. A personnel office in a pharmaceutical company uses such a word processor along with graphic and spreadsheet packages. This software combination is used to produce documents as complex as the example given in Figure 13-25.

Word processing packages are gradually acquiring more desktop publishing features. A common example, as Figure 13-26 illustrates, is to allow users to choose fonts. An example of the typesetting capabilities of several word processing packages, when used alone and with soft font packages, is given in Figure 13-27. **Soft fonts** or **downloadable fonts** are

- Purchased as software packages, rather than as a printer component
- Downloaded, whenever needed, from the system unit into a laser printer to expand its library of available fonts

Soft font packages are also used as accessory packages with one composition software to expand a printer's font library.

To create the sample newsletter in Figure 13-25, Janice Springer at the pharmaceutical company used a drawing package. It played the dual role of graphic generator and pasteup board. First she laid out the key design elements, such as title, borders, and subheadings. Then she created a bar chart with a spreadsheet package, and text with a word processing package. Next, both the text and bar chart were imported into the drawing package. The finished product was then printed on a laser printer.

This combination of common software and a laser printer is a satisfactory publishing solution for many individuals and organizations. Occasionally Ms. Springer finds, however, that the lack of large, bold headlines, and the drawing package's inability to maintain right justification of imported text, are significant limitations.

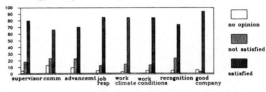

MESSAGE TO EMPLOYEES
Employee Review Results are Positive

Dear Fellow Mythical Employees:

Your responses to the Employee Review, summarized in this issue of The Printed Circuit, show your willingness to speak out about issues that concern you, and your interest in contributing to the success and growth of our Mythical Corporation.

More than 1,200 of you in the greater Xanadu area took the time to complete the questionnaire. You gave us worthwhile information that will help us improve our Mythical technology and productivity.

You told us that you like your jobs and you like working for Mythical. Most of you feel your contributions are recognized, but a few of you would like more Mythical feedback. You see quality as the issue most important to our continued success, not only in our Mythical products and services, but in every aspect of the jobs we do.

We have already taken steps to respond to some of your concerns and suggestions. In a recent letter to employees, Charles B. Unicorn, our Mythical president, pointed out his plan for maintaining Mythical's quality. Other Mythical activities and projects will address the remainder of your concerns.

Speaking for the senior management team, I want to thank each of you for your contributions to this year's review. Please continue to give us your ideas. They are vital to our continuing Mythical success.

Celestial Smith
Vice President/
Personnel and
Employee Relations

Celestial Smith

July 4, 1986
Volume 555
Issue 17632

Mythical
Corporation

The Printed Circuit
A Weekly News Service for Mythical Employees

FIGURE 13-25
This example newsletter was created without a page composition package.
It was created with a word processing package, a drawing package, and
a spreadsheet package which all worked with a windows package.
(Software: Microsoft Windows, Windows Write, Windows Draw, Lotus 1-2-3; courtesy
of PC World)

Some word processing packages also have limitations because they require the tedious process of **embedding** formatting **codes** into the text. For example:

    \p(icture) boat.gmf scale = .6\

This command inserts an image of a boat, contained in a file named BOAT.GMF, into a document when it is printed. The image is included at six-tenths the natural size of the picture.

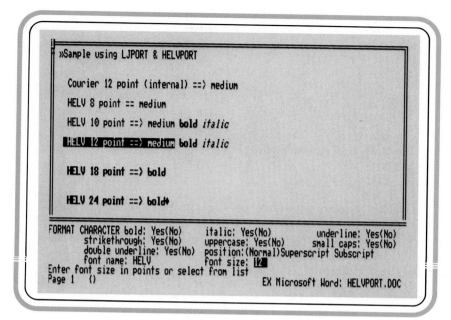

```
»Sample using LJPORT & HELVPORT

  Courier 12 point (internal) ==> medium

  HELV 8 point == medium

  HELV 10 point ==> medium bold italic

  HELV 12 point ==> medium bold italic


  HELV 18 point ==> bold


  HELV 24 point ==> bold♦

FORMAT CHARACTER bold: Yes(No)     italic: Yes(No)        underline: Yes(No)
       strikethrough: Yes(No)      uppercase: Yes(No)     small caps: Yes(No)
       double underline: Yes(No)   position:(Normal)Superscript Subscript
       font name: HELV             font size: 12
Enter font size in points or select from list
Page 1   {}                                EX Microsoft Word: HELVPORT.DOC
```

FIGURE 13-26
Choosing type fonts from a menu of a word processing program
(Software: Microsoft Word, courtesy of PC World)

FIGURE 13-27
Examples of the typesetting capability of several word processing packages

reflective
Lotus Manuscript

reflective
Microsoft Word 3.0 for the PC

reflective
Microsoft Works for the Macintosh

reflective
WordStar 4.0

reflective
Microsoft Word 3.0 plus SoftCraft Fancy Font

reflective
WordPerfect 4.2

reflective
WordStar 3.3 plus Polaris Ram-Resident PrintMerge

reflective
Microsoft Word 3.0 plus SoftCraft Fancy Font—dot matrix version

FORM GENERATORS

One of the mundane publishing projects most businesses undertake is the design of forms. Today they can save significant time and money by designing nearly every form used with a **form generator package.** Some of the packages listed in Figure 13-28 provide templates of common office forms. Templates can be printed out as is or can be modified as needed. Sometimes a word processing package can be used to generate simple forms.

FIGURE 13-28
A sampler of form generator software
packages

CLR Sprinter	FormWorx
Executive Office	FormWriter
EZ-Laser	iPrint
Formeasy	LaserForms PC
FormMaker	MegaForm
FormSet	Polaris Forms
FormTool	

The easier form generator packages work close to the "what you see is what you get" WYSIWYG ideal, as the example in Figure 13-29 shows. The form was created by Michael Beal, an assistant in the accounts payable department at a large east coast university. To create a box on the form in Figure 13-29, he

- Selects Box from the menu bar across the top of the screen
- Anchors the cursor, with a keystroke, to the upper left corner where the box should go
- Moves the cursor to the lower right corner and again anchors the cursor
- Chooses any of the half a dozen or so box styles (such as single line, double line, combinations of these, or thick lines), and the box is drawn automatically

FIGURE 13-29
A simple form design using a "what you
see is what you get" (WYSIWYG) package
(Software: FormWorx, courtesy of FormWorx Corporation)

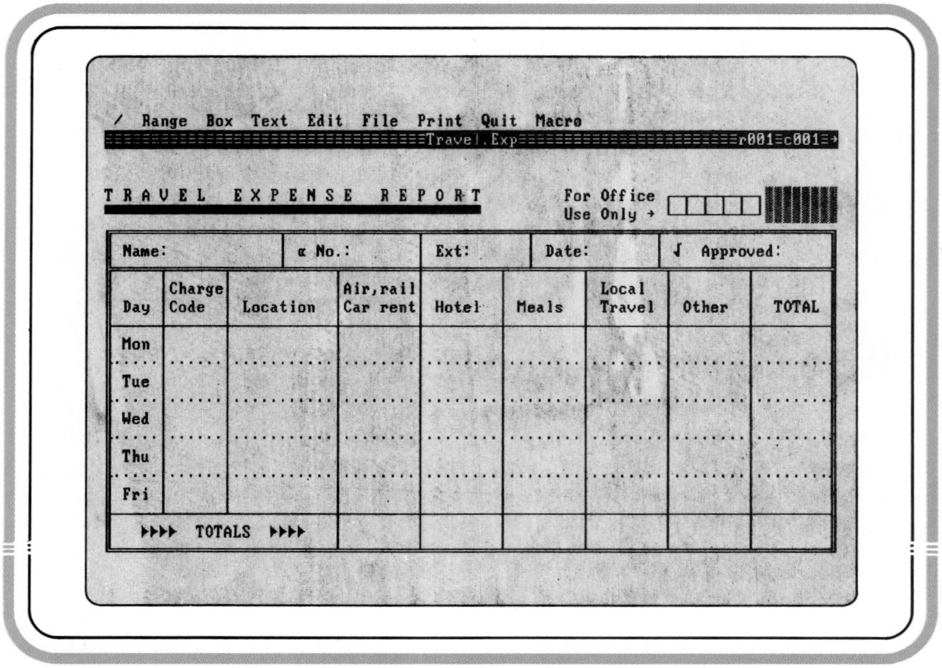

Another type of form generator package, such as Polaris Forms and FormSet, is command driven. It requires first writing a string of commands or instructions, such as those in Figure 13-30, with a word processing package. This is actually programming. After saving the instructions to the disk as a file, the form generator package must be loaded. It then processes the so-called *script* or *command* file. The example in Figure 13-31 is the output created from the script file in Figure 13-30.

A command-driven package requires programming skill. In return, it allows precision placement of elements specified to the maximum resolution of the printer. It appeals to individuals and organizations that are already comfortable with computer programming.

Forms generated by either type of package can be filled in

- On paper by hand
- On screen by using a mouse or keyboard
- In a batch by the computer using data drawn from a database program data file or from a word processor prepared data file

FIGURE 13-30

Portion of a script file from a command-driven form generator package
(*Software: Polaris Forms, courtesy of Polaris Software*)

```
.FC *
.. The first line must always be the FC command.
.. The * specifies that you are using soft fonts downloaded by
..   the Psetup utility.
..........................................................
..     Invoice form using Polaris Forms  (complete form)  ..
..     Filename is INV2.FRM                                ..
..........................................................
..   INVOICE box: Outline, then fill top.
.BX 0.33, 6.8, 0.83, 8.1, 1
.BX 0.33, 6.8, 0.50, 8.1, 0, 1, 2
..   INVOICE DATE box: Outline, then fill top.
.BX 1.00, 6.8, 1.50, 8.1, 1
.BX 1.00, 6.8, 1.17, 8.1, 0, 1, 2
..........................................................
..   Box around main body of form
.BX 2.67, 0.4, 6.67, 8.1, 1
..........................................................
..   First shaded horizontal bar containing 5 fields
.BX 2.67, 0.4, 2.83, 8.1, 0, 1, 2
..   Horizontal line at bottom of fields
.HL 3.17, 0.4, 7.7, 1
..   Four vertical lines to create the 5 fields
.RP 4, 0.0, 1.54
.VL 2.67, 1.84, 0.50, 1
.RP
..........................................................
..   Second shaded horizontal bar across top of columns
.BX 3.17, 0.4, 3.33, 8.1, 0, 1, 2
..   Horizontal line above SALES TAX field
.HL 5.67, 6.0, 2.1, 1
..   Horizontal line at the bottom of all columns
.HL 6.00, 0.4, 7.7, 1
..   Horizontal line above TOTAL field
.HL 6.33, 6.0, 2.1, 1
..........................................................
..   Vertical lines to divide columns
.VL 3.17, 1.0, 2.83, 1
.VL 3.17, 1.7, 2.83, 1
```

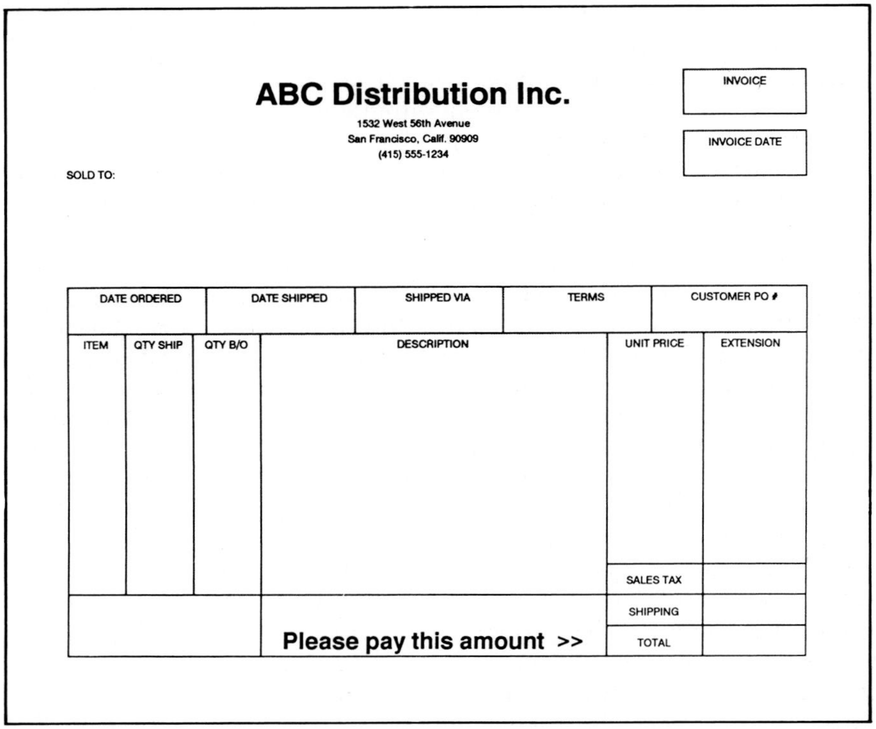

ABC Distribution Inc.

1532 West 56th Avenue
San Francisco, Calif. 90909
(415) 555-1234

INVOICE

INVOICE DATE

SOLD TO:

DATE ORDERED	DATE SHIPPED	SHIPPED VIA	TERMS	CUSTOMER PO #

ITEM	QTY SHIP	QTY B/O	DESCRIPTION	UNIT PRICE	EXTENSION

SALES TAX

SHIPPING

Please pay this amount >>   TOTAL

FIGURE 13-31
Printed form created by the script file in Figure 13-30
(Software: Polaris Forms, courtesy of Polaris Software)

With some packages, conditions can be inserted that automatically alter forms as they are being printed. This feature appeals to a large Ohio-based company that designs and constructs single-family modular homes. On report forms going out to the company's field sales staff, a bonus clause is inserted for those who sell over a certain amount in a given time.

The company finds that designing and managing forms with a microcomputer is considerably more cost-effective than the traditional method of

- Sketching out the design
- Giving the sketch to a graphic artist
- Circulating a copy of the pasted-up layout for approval
- Ordering a large quantity of the form to be printed in order to save the cost of frequent reprinting

When a form needs to be revised, someone in charge of publications edits it on a microcomputer. It is much faster and cheaper than a manual revision. In addition, by producing forms as needed on demand, the company conserves capital, storage, and handling. It no longer has to deal with throwing away stacks of obsolete expensive forms.

PUBLISHING HIERARCHY

The software available to support an individual or organizational publishing effort falls into a hierarchy of categories, as diagrammed in Figure 13-32. Categories overlap and are expected to do so even more in the future.

Word processing packages are expected to add more page composition features. Page composition packages are expected to add more word processing features. This change benefits users. As the two packages converge, the jostling between these packages will be eliminated.

In general, the higher the individual's or organization's needs in the publishing pyramid, the greater the complexity of the software that will satisfy those needs. Figure 13-33 graphs this relationship in terms of page layout complexity and document length. Longer documents, such as books, tend to be the most complex to lay out.

Some industry observers look at the publishing pyramid another way. They find that the lower levels concern individuals and the upper levels concern organizations. By and large, individuals care more about a document's content than its layout. They can usually be satisfied with a word processor's layout capabilities and instant printing. Work characteristics at this level usually concern time-urgent documents that are constantly changing, like memos, business correspondence, and price lists. Documents at this level are usually for internal, or very restricted, distribution.

FIGURE 13-32
Hierarchy of publishing requirements
(*Source*: Hewlett-Packard Co., *adapted with permission*)

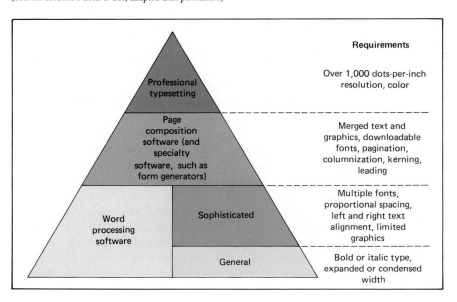

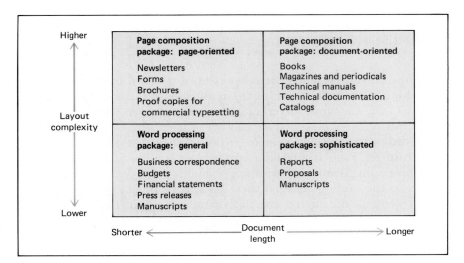

	Higher		
	Page composition package: page-oriented		**Page composition package: document-oriented**
	Newsletters		Books
	Forms		Magazines and periodicals
	Brochures		Technical manuals
	Proof copies for commercial typesetting		Technical documentation
			Catalogs
Layout complexity	**Word processing package: general**		**Word processing package: sophisticated**
	Business correspondence		Reports
	Budgets		Proposals
	Financial statements		Manuscripts
	Press releases		
	Manuscripts		
	Lower		
	Shorter ←	Document length	→ Longer

FIGURE 13-33
The relationship of document layout complexity to document length and appropriate software

Organizations, on the other hand, care a great deal about creating a high-quality impression through their published documents. At this end of the pyramid, requirements are considered to be layout driven. "High-quality" means a professionally designed and laid-out document that is printed at true typeset quality. Currently, that means at a resolution of over 1,000 dots per inch. It traditionally requires professional typesetting. Document characteristics at this level include, in addition to high quality, high volume and wide distribution.

Traditional Method

Many large organizations, like National Bank, maintain their own in-house publishing plant. This plant is complete with commercial typesetting machinery to meet their high-quality, layout-driven, document requirements. Both the publishing staff and the printing plant processed documents in a very traditional way before installing a desktop publishing system.

In the traditional process, a document goes from a word processor to the typesetter. Sometimes it is necessary to rekey documents into the typesetter manually. The typesetter then produces long columns of typeset text, called *galleys*. The galleys are given back to the writer or editor for proofreading. When all the necessary changes have been made to the galleys, and a final version has been prepared, a production artist begins a page layout or "paste-up" process. This involves arranging the galleys into multiple columns on a pasteup board. Space is allocated for graphics, which are pasted on separate boards. The completed boards are then sent to the print shop for reproduction.

The print shop photographs each page layout and each piece of artwork. Negatives of the artwork are then combined with negatives of the pages in a process called "stripping." The shop uses the negatives to produce a plate for the printing press, which reproduces the document in the quality desired.

Inevitably, last-minute changes occur in the assembly process. An author's alteration, for instance, usually must be typeset, pasted up, photographed, and so on. The publishing group has established that a 10 percent revision can account for 70 percent of a document's production time.

According to a study conducted by a research firm, changes boost the cost of producing technical manuals to as much as $400 per page over the course of several revisions. Other studies indicate that publishing costs rank second only to personnel as the greatest expense for most organizations. This expense, combined with the long document turn-around time of the traditional process, was completely unacceptable at National Bank.

Modern Method

National Bank acquired microcomputers to make its publishing effort more efficient and cost-effective. It created a local-area network and used a multiuser page composition package, such as Superpage. The software is designed to distribute separate functions, like text entry and editing, typographical formatting, and page composition. Functions are accessed by professionals at microcomputers connected to the local-area network.

Integration of the various skill groups on the local-area network has a favorable impact on the publishing process. It allows anyone in the publications department to view, adjust, and manipulate any combination of text and graphics. A group member can be at any workstation. The document can be at any stage of its development cycle.

Writers, for example, can enter text at a workstation and view it in typeset form, composed on the page as it will appear in the completed document. Indexes and tables of contents are generated automatically as the writer develops new chapters and sections.

Illustrators can scan images and create line art drawings including schematics and flowcharts. Designers can enter revised specifications on a style sheet to completely reformat a document. Designers have a greater opportunity to be more creative because experimenting with different layouts is now possible.

The traditional one-step-at-a-time process that inflexibly caused projects to move in a rigid progression from one skill group to the next (for example, from writers to illustrators to production people) is eliminated. Instead, this fragmented process is replaced by a system that joins all the players into a unified team—all the publication's professionals bring their skills to the project at the same time, or in parallel. As a result, the time needed to bring projects to camera-ready art is dramatically reduced. This in turn greatly reduces the cost of the publishing project on a per-page basis.

National Bank's publications manager has the opportunity to oversee in-house publishing with a greater degree of control. It is possible to monitor time, costs, and materials on a per-project basis. Delays due to approvals, revisions, errors, or modifications can be tracked.

Progressive companies, especially in the publishing and computer industries that are already comfortable around microcomputers, have installed in-house publishing systems. A Sausalito, California, software company, for example, uses such a system

- To reduce the cost of producing user manuals
- To give the company a competitive edge

The company can make a change to its software products and ship it with a changed user manual the same day.

At Hayes Microcomputer Products, a manufacturer of modems and data communication products, a networked publishing system has eliminated the work group's graphics and typesetting bottlenecks. If a document needs to go out quickly, they can turn it around in a day. Previously, it would have taken ten days if everything else was dropped.

Boeing Corporation, the aerospace giant that also markets computer products, publishes 2 billion pages a year. Around the Boeing offices, legend has it that the documentation for a 747 weighs more than the plane itself. The company now uses 200 Apple Macintoshs and other microcomputers to halve production costs for some of its reports and proposals.

Some organizations find microcomputer publishing software short of perfection. But all have discovered a relatively inexpensive and high-quality alternative to the costly, laborious process that has ruled the publishing world for generations.

Some large organizations are decentralizing some of their publishing work. National Bank's public relations department, as an example, is now expected to use its microcomputers and page composition software to produce news and press releases. The controller's department is responsible for the production of financial reports. The technical publications staff continues to develop technical manuals and other lengthy documents.

TRAINING

One major issue related to the use of desktop publishing is training. Simply buying a page composition package does not automatically imbue the purchaser with the skills, talent, and background of a layout artist or graphic designer. Ideally a user should be a designer, editor, writer, proofreader, and production expert all rolled into one.

One way around the apparently insolvable problem, according to experts in the field, is through training. While a series of classes or seminars may not turn a graphic illiterate into a Leonardo da Vinci, it will at least teach the basics of design and show how to use a particular piece of software. Software vendors and independent seminar organizers offer training and workshops, as do universities and other institutions.

Larger organizations often hire a trainer to teach in-house seminars.

All trainers seem to agree that mastering the basics of good visual communications is essential. Otherwise a document's message may be confusing, unappealing, or drowned in a sea of gray text.

The "page makeover" in Figure 13-34 illustrates how a document can be enhanced with good visual communication skills. The document is a one-page **flier,** which is an advertising piece that will be distributed in large numbers. It has no more than an instant to capture a reader's eye. It was submitted for a makeover to a professional layout artist.

Although the original appears organized, the artist finds it crowded and uninviting. The original type elements are too equal in weight. This makes it difficult to distinguish which information is the most important. Also, in the "before" image, the photo overshadows the headline beneath it. There is also an abundance of white space round the hand which does not serve any design purpose.

Changes to transform the document's visual impact are described in detail on the example. The "after" image demonstrates the kind of talent and skill necessary to develop such a document. For instance, it required the use of the following:

Hardware

- A microcomputer
- A scanner
- A laser printer

Software

- A scanning package
- A word processing package
- A page composition package
- Two printing utility packages

The makeover introduces more of the terminology used in this field. New terms are defined in the Desktop Publishing Glossary in this chapter.

Many publishing projects do not require the level of talent and skill brought to bear on the makeover example. Templates, for instance, are often adequate to achieve a professional-looking result.

EVALUATION

Interstate Distibuting Company began desktop publishing with a self-evaluation. This included asking such questions as

- What kind of documents are to be created with the desktop publishing system?

After

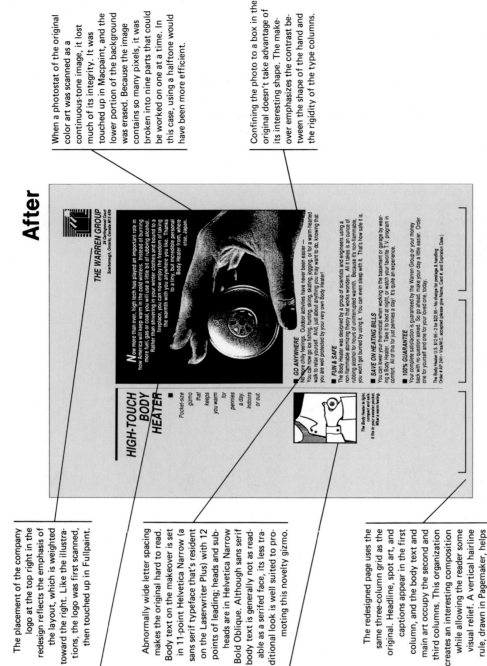

When a photostat of the original color art was scanned as a continuous-tone image, it lost much of its integrity. It was touched up in Macpaint, and the lower portion of the background was erased. Because the image contains so many pixels, it was broken into nine parts that could be worked on one at a time. In this case, using a halftone would have been more efficient.

Confining the photo to a box in the original doesn't take advantage of its interesting shape. The makeover emphasizes the contrast between the shape of the hand and the rigidity of the type columns.

The placement of the company logo at the top right in the redesign reflects the emphasis of the layout, which is weighted toward the right. Like the illustrations, the logo was first scanned, then touched up in Fullpaint.

The original text wasn't differentiated enough. The introductory text, now set in reverse type—white on a black background—stands out more and draws in the reader. The image of the hand had to be dropped in before the type was placed. The type was contoured around the hand using tabs and the space bar. The small boxes below the hand, drawn and then copied in Pagemaker, serve as bullets to emphasize the product's benefits.

Abnormally wide letter spacing makes the original hard to read. Body text on the makeover is set in 11-point Helvetica Narrow (a sans serif typeface that's resident on the Laserwriter Plus) with 12 points of leading; heads and subheads are in Helvetica Narrow Bold Oblique. Although sans serif body text is generally not as readable as a serifed face, its less traditional look is well suited to promoting this novelty gizmo.

The spot illustration was scanned as line art, touched up in Fullpaint, then placed in Pagemaker. Because the scanned art was based on a photocopy several generations old, some lines had lost their crispness. These lines were erased and replaced using the line drawing tool. In addition, the Fat Bits option was used to darken the background.

The redesigned page uses the same three-column grid as the original. Headline, spot art, and captions appear in the first column, and the body text and main art occupy the second and third columns. This organization creates an interesting composition while allowing the reader some visual relief. A vertical hairline rule, drawn in Pagemaker, helps divide the different levels of information.

Before

FIGURE 13-34

A page makeover

(Designer: Kimberly Mancebo; hardware: Apple Macintosh Plus, Apple LaserWriter Plus, Microtek scanner; software: Page-Maker, Versascan, Fullpaint, Macpaint, Microsoft Word; courtesy of PC Publish!, adapted with permission)

· What is the average length of the documents?

· What are the time and costs to produce documents using the current production process?

· What type of improvements over the present production method can be achieved?

With answers in hand, it was then necessary to evaluate available software and hardware. The main software component in most cases is a page composition package. An evaluation checklist, such as the one in Figure 13-35, was drawn up to support the software search. It focuses on topics covered in this chapter.

Hardware Considerations

Equally important is the hardware evaluation. Companies like Apple, IBM, AST, and others sell turnkey desktop publishing systems, such as the one shown in Figure 13-1. Systems usually come with a microcomputer, a laser printer, and a scanner.

Theoretically, such a bundled system should be able to "plug and play" without problems. But this is not always the case. One free-lance writer spent three days trying to get the scanner in a turnkey system to work. Only repeated calls to the vendor, and a new scanner software supplied by the vendor, solved the installation problem.

Graphic artists and production people use their microcomputers almost exclusively as dedicated desktop publishing workstations. But the larger group by far consists of individuals who use desktop publishing occasionally. Mr. Layton falls into this second category. He has many

FIGURE 13-35
Page composition software evaluation checklist

PAGE COMPOSITION PACKAGE

· Is the package WYSIWYG (what you see is what you get), which combines text and graphics on the screen and prints pages that match (or nearly match) the screen version?

· Does it provide both automatic and manual kerning, tracking, leading, hyphenation, and justification?

· Can the package import word processing files with format characteristics intact?

· Does text automatically wrap around a graphic and continue to the next column, page, or assigned location?

· Can both bit-mapped (painting package and scanner image) and vector (drawing package images) graphic files be imported?

· Can graphics be cropped and resized?

· What tools are available for creating rules, boxes, and so on?

· Are templates available? Can new templates or style sheets be created?

· Is hardware required at an affordable price?

· Are training and support available?

(Figure 3-25, General Software Evaluation Checklist, is necessary to complete this evaluation.)

other marketing department responsibilities that are not related to publishing.

Mr. Layton found that a hard disk, as well as a new, powerful 16-bit or 32-bit microcomputer, is necessary for satisfactory operating speed. An older floppy disk-based microcomputer, in all cases, provided disappointing performance.

Mr. Layton put together his own new system, component by component. It presented compatibility and integration problems. Components such as a large-screen display, a scanner, and a laser printer must be able to "talk to" each other. A sampler of suppliers of these products is given in Figure 13-36.

Mr. Layton had to be sure his laser printer was compatible with the page composition software. For example, the Apple LaserWriter

FIGURE 13-36
A sampler of laser printer, scanner, and
large-screen display suppliers

LASER PRINTER SUPPLIERS	
Apple Computer	Imagen Corp.
AST Research	NBI, Inc.
Canon	NEC Information Systems, Inc.
Citizen American Corp.	
Cordata	Office Automation Systems, Inc.
CPT Corp.	
Digital Equipment Corp.	
Epson America, Inc.	Okidata
Facit, Inc.	QMS
Genicom Corp.	Quadram
Hewlett-Packard Co.	Qume Corp.
IBM	Texas Instruments
	Xerox Corp.

SCANNER SUPPLIERS	
Abaton	Hewlett-Packard
Advanced Vision Research	IBM
Canon	Microtek
Datacopy	Ricoh
Dest	

LARGE-SCREEN DISPLAY SUPPLIERS	
Amdek	Princeton
E-Machines	Radius
Genius	Sigma Designs
MicroGraphic Images	Wyse
Moniterm	

will accept only files prepared by a package that supports the PostScript page description language.

Laser printers, he observed, take from a few minutes to an hour to print one page, depending on how complex the graphics are. So at half an hour per page, he could count on printing only sixteen original pages per day. Although copies ordinarily take far less time, he had to plan printing requirements carefully.

Scanners require lots of memory to store their digitized images. The typical working file for a scanned image is over a megabyte. When Mr. Layton realized that twenty scanned images, as an example, completely fill up a 20-megabyte hard disk, he decided on a larger-capacity hard disk drive.

The system that Mr. Layton put together cost the company about $10,000. It took over a week to get all the hardware working together. It involved wrestling with manuals from various sources and calls for help to vendors.

Training classes and lots of experimenting were necessary to learn how to use the system. After several weeks of working with it, Mr. Layton could turn out a high-quality document with ease.

In the case of large organizations, an evaluation includes networked microcomputers and multiuser page composition packages. Microcomputer-based systems are usually additions or replacements for established minicomputer or mainframe electronic publishing systems.

A package such as Impressionist runs on microcomputers, minicomputers, and mainframes. By standardizing on such a package, one large company minimized its investment in software, training, and support.

Cost Justification

Both Interstate Distributing Company and National Bank have experienced cumulative savings from decreased professional typesetting and printing costs. Their desktop publishing systems easily justified the purchase of, at a minimum, a laser printer and page composition software.

Most experience a saving in printing costs. Typeset copy occupies about 40 percent less space on the page than standard word processing monospaced type.

Some find that only a new laser printer is necessary. When it is coupled with word processing software, it suffices for a great deal of the printed material that is currently being typeset.

But the economy of these new systems is not the only force, in many cases, for motivating an upgrade to desktop publishing. Typeset copy is easier to read than monospaced dot matrix output, and it conveys a more professional image.

In the future, desktop publishers will be able to buy famous-designer templates. Also, amateur graphic designers will be helped by expert systems to make layout and typography decisions. New systems will even scan a document and intuit rules to turn a formless jumble of text and graphics into a tasteful, visually interesting document.

CASE STUDY: Application: Setting Up For Desktop Publishing

As Aretha Franklin's song, "I Knew You Were Waiting" charged up the pop music charts, Arista Records sent out weekly flyers to its dealers around the country, keeping them apprised of Franklin's concert tours and chart-topping hits. But when, some time later, Arista released several records in one week from the likes of Whitney Houston and Billy Ocean, the record maker wasn't able to generate its artists' flyers fast enough. Designers in Arista's Creative Services department found themselves staying until 8 or 10 o'clock at night waiting for type to come back from the company's in-house typesetters or for someone to paste a photo on a board.

Needing a quick and efficient way to produce flyers, Creative Services invested in a desktop publishing system that would develop and print them in-house. While the system met the goals of speed and efficiency, setting it up turned out to be more work than staff members anticipated.

Arista first had to decide whether to go with a Macintosh- or MS-DOS-based system. According to Millie DeFino, administrative assistant to the vice-president of finance and administration, "Everyone was pushing for Apple. But everything here is IBM, including a network. We decided we wanted software compatible with our existing system."

Initially, Arista installed Front Page from Studio Software. This was the beginning of the company's problems.

"We learned that in order for the program to work with the Mergenthaler typesetting equipment we have, we needed to upgrade to Front Page Plus," DeFino says. That meant paying $600 on top of the $695 already spent. But shortly after the new software arrived, Studio Software, the program's publisher, declared bankruptcy. On the recommendation of an outside consultant, Arista switched to Ventura Publisher from Xerox Corp.

"Then we couldn't print," recalled DeFino. (The computer was hooked to a QMS-PS 800, a serial laser printer with PostScript.) "At first we thought it was the printer. We went crazy hooking it up and taking it apart. When we realized there was nothing wrong with the printer, we called Ventura. The problem was something called handshaking. We had to put another command in the system file. It took us a week to figure all this out."

As for the mouse necessary to command Ventura, DeFino says, "I couldn't get used to the mouse. My hand is too heavy. I have to develop that touch." Amy Finkle, an assistant in the Creative Services department, now produces the flyers, as well as promotional literature enclosed with record albums sent to radio stations. "Everyone is giving her stuff to do. Her job is getting bigger and bigger," explains DeFino.

(*SOURCE: Michael Antonoff, "Setting Up for Desktop Publishing,"* Personal Computing, *July 1987, pp. 75–82. Reprinted with permission.*)

DISCUSSION QUESTIONS

1. As Arista discovered, you cannot just buy a desktop publishing system, plug it in, and start producing documents. What kind of advice do you think would have helped Arista to go about setting up for desktop publishing in a more realistic way?

2. Do you think that existing hardware should influence a software purchase decision, as it did at Arista? What arguments can you offer for and against such a decision?

CHAPTER SUMMARY

- *Desktop publishing* refers to the use of microcomputers and other hardware, as well as software, to produce documents for publication purposes.

- A *page composition package* replaces a drafting table, scissors, and glue with electronic assembly of text and graphics. The composed page image, called a *page layout*, is then printed repetitively or reproduced using more traditional methods.

- The four steps necessary to assemble a page layout electronically are: prepare text and graphic files, develop a document format, bring in graphic and text files to the page layout, and print.

- A *format* defines the appearance of a document in terms of its number of columns, column rules, headline placement, headers, footers, and other standing design elements.

- *Templates* are layouts prepared by a graphic designer.

- Graphics can be imported into a page composition package formatted as drawing (object oriented), painting (bit-mapped oriented), and scanned (bit-mapped or TIFF, Tag Image File Format) files.

- Importing text is sometimes called *flowing* or *pouring* in text.

- *Text wrap* occurs when text automatically flows around any obstruction, such as a graphic.

- A *font* is a complete set of characters in one typeface and size. A *typeface* is a designed set of characters with a name that describes their overall appearance. In desktop publishing, typeface is used interchangeably with font, basically because a typeface can be manipulated electronically to get the characters that make up the fonts.

- *Type style* refers to the modification of a typeface to italic, upright (roman), outline, or some other variation.

- *Kerning* is the adjustment of the space between certain combinations of letters. *Tracking* measures and controls the overall tightness of letterspacing.

- A *typesetter* is machinery that uses photographic processes to produce a page image on photosensitive paper.

- A *page description language (PDL)* is a system for coding document files in order to make the files acceptable to laser printers, typesetters, or any other device that can read the coded "PDL" file. Because a PDL file can be printed on a range of devices, it is called *device independent*.

- *Printer font files* are used by the printer and are different from *screen fonts*. They can be *outline fonts*, which means that they are produced by instructions that describe the path that makes up each character's outline. They can also be *bit-mapped fonts*, which are composed of the actual dot sequence that forms each character.

- A *screen font* is a bit-mapped font that is designed to approximate the look of the corresponding printer font.

- *WYSIWYG*, or what you see is what you get, is an ideal in desktop publishing that refers to a match of the screen image with the printed image.

- *Page-oriented* page composition packages are best suited to handle short documents. *Document-oriented* packages are best suited to handle long documents.

- A *form generator package* is used to design office and other forms electronically.

- In the publishing pyramid, the low-end requirements of an individual's content-driven publishing needs are often satisfied with word processing packages. Page composition packages and professional typesetters often satisfy the layout-driven high-end requirements of organizations.

- Traditional publishing methods involve a rigid progression from one skill group to the next. Modern methods involve flexible parallel tasks executed on local-area networks.

- Mastering the basics of good visual communications is essential training for successful desktop publishing.

- A desktop publishing system evaluation includes software and such hardware considerations as disk capacity and printer speeds.

KEY TERMS

ASCII file
Bit map image file
Bit-mapped font
Built-in font
Copy
Crop
Desktop publishing
Device independence
Dialog box
Document oriented
Downloadable font
Drop cap
Embedded code
Flier or flyer
Flow text or graphics
Font
Format
Form generator package

Generic font
Greeking
Hyphenation
Kerning
Laser printer
Layout
Leading
Master pages
Object image file
Outline font
Page composition package
Page description language (PDL)
Page layout
Page oriented
Points
PostScript
Printer fonts
Raster image processor (RIP)

Resolution
Roman
Scale
Screen font
Snap-to effect
Soft font
Style sheet
Tag
Template
Text wrap
TIFF
Tracking
Typeface
Typesetter
Type specification
Type style
WYSIWYG

REVIEW QUESTIONS

1. What is desktop publishing?

2. What is a page composition package used for?

3. Briefly describe the steps necessary to assemble a page layout electronically.

4. How are graphics imported into a page composition package?

   Contrast the following:

5. · Font and typeface

6. · Kerning and tracking

7. · Printer and screen fonts

8. · Outline and bit-mapped fonts

9. · Page-oriented and document-oriented composition packages

10. · Content-driven and layout-driven ends of the publishing pyramid

11. · Traditional and modern methods of publishing

12. What is a page description language?

13. What does WYSIWYG mean in desktop publishing?

14. List important considerations in an evaluation of a desktop publishing system.

EXERCISES

1. *Alton College Case.*   Assume that you are a student assistant in the registrar's office at Alton College. The registrar asks you to research and recommend the purchase of a suitable page composition package. The office's publishing needs are mainly for long, text intensive documents, such as a schedule of courses and classes for each term, and various shorter documents. The office already has IBM PC microcomputers, so any package must be compatible with them. Examine package reviews in current microcomputer periodicals and make a comparative report of two suitable packages. End the report by recommending the one that would be the better purchase, and justify your recommendation.

2. *Alton College Case.*   The registrar is convinced by your recommendation to buy a page composition package. But the office does not have a laser printer. You are asked to do another research study to recommend the purchase of a laser printer. Examine hardware reviews for laser printers in the current microcomputer periodicals and make a comparative report of two suitable printers. End the report by recommending the one that would be the better purchase, and justify your recommendation.

3. *Alton College Case.*   The registrar wants to learn more about the subject of page description languages. He asks you to prepare a report that compares the differences among the three dominant languages: PostScript, Interpress, and DDL (Document Description Language). End the report with your choice about which one, if any, you think is most likely to survive as a standard. Justify your choice.

14

Knowledge-Based Systems and Other Applications

AFTER READING THIS CHAPTER, YOU SHOULD BE ABLE TO

- Explain what a knowledge-based system is and how it is used
- Describe uses for microcomputer knowledge-based packages like "shells," personal advisory, and decision assistant software
- Describe how a programmable robot performs useful tasks

Artificial intelligence, often referred to as "AI," is the branch of computer science that makes computers imitate human behavior. Other disciplines, among them psychology, linguistics, mathematics, business, education, and philosophy, contribute to AI's development.

AI is used as an umbrella term for the collective research that has produced, among other efforts:

- Knowledge-based systems
- Programmable robot systems
- Natural language systems

This chapter covers knowledge-based and robot systems. Natural language systems are covered in Chapter 8, "Database and File Management Packages."

Knowledge-based systems act as assistants, colleagues, or even expert consultants to users in specialized areas. Examples explored in this chapter include locomotive maintenance troubleshooting, infectious disease diagnosis, and telephone service selection.

Microcomputer knowledge-based systems have spun off new software categories. This chapter includes a discussion of "shells," personal advisory, and decision assistant software.

Probably the most exotic of the systems explored here are programmable robots. The chapter concludes with a discussion of what they are and how they work. It also covers controversial issues related to robots in society.

KNOWLEDGE-BASED SYSTEMS

This section of the chapter looks at examples of established knowledge-based systems. Although some of these well-known systems have been developed on special-purpose hardware, today comparable systems are being developed on ordinary desktop computers.

Software and engineering skills required to create knowledge-based systems are examined next. The section concludes with a discussion of how to develop knowledge-based systems from scratch.

Knowledge-based systems capture, magnify, and distribute access to judgment. They function as assistants, colleagues, or experts, as the diagram in Figure 14-1 implies.

Examples of established knowledge-based systems and the kind of assistance they provide include

CATS—it helps diesel locomotive repair engineers solve maintenance problems.

R1 or XCON—it helps Digital Equipment Corporation's sales representatives put together computer systems that meet a customer's needs at the lowest cost to the customer. It saves the company an estimated $200,000 a month in staff costs.[1]

PROSPECTOR—it helps geographical engineers to locate minerals. In 1983, it accurately predicted a molybdenum deposit worth millions of dollars in Washington State.[2]

---

[1] Elizabeth Horwitt, "Exploring Expert Systems," *Business Computer Systems*, March 1985, p. 49.
[2] "Artifical Intelligence," *Business Week*, March 8, 1982.

FIGURE 14-1
Knowledge-based systems function like an assistant, or an expert, or anything in between.
(*Source*: Artificial Intelligence Satellite Symposium Notebook, *Texas Instruments, 1985. Adapted with permission.*)

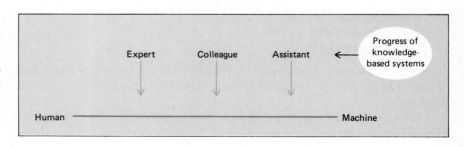

SACON—it assists civil engineers in structural analysis.

TAXMAN—it assists tax consultants with estate-planning tax problems.

ACE—it helps AT&T's service staff to resolve glitches in communications equipment.

PROMOTER—it helps advertisers to analyze the effects that promotions have on sales in the packaged goods industry.

MYCIN—it helps doctors to diagnose infectious blood diseases.

PUFF—it helps doctors to diagnose lung problems.

Some systems are still at the beginning, assistant level. Others have progressed over time to become expert systems. Progress comes from capturing more and more knowledge in the knowledge base.

Knowledge Base

A knowledge-based system has three main parts: the knowledge base, inference engine, and explanation facility, as diagrammed in Figure 14-2. The **knowledge base** is a stored collection of facts and rules about a specific area of knowledge. As an example, the Digital Equipment Corporation's system stores 500 facts in its knowledge base. Facts, in this case, are descriptions of computer parts, engineering constraints, and hardware specifications.

FIGURE 14-2
Essential parts of a knowledge-based system

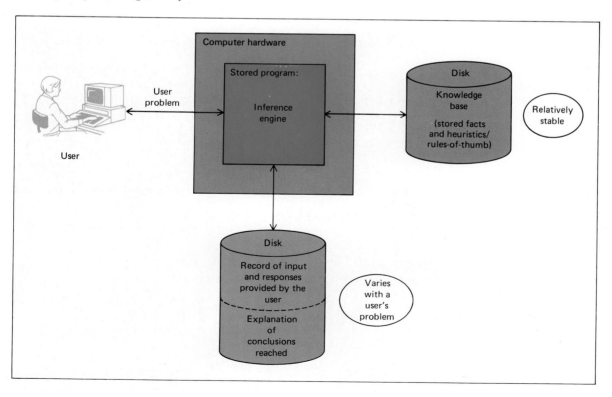

Although it is possible to compare a knowledge base with a database, they are different because the knowledge base contains heuristics. **Heuristics** are rules-of-thumb about the task at hand. One expert calls heuristics the knowledge of good judgment. **Knowledge engineers** have special skills to mine heuristics out from human experts and to transfer them into a computerized knowledge base.

Heuristics often end up as "rules" in the knowledge base. Digital's system contains 5,000 rules for putting together a "least cost" computer system. When done, it is expected to contain over 100,000 rules. The rules deal with how, when, and where the parts, engineering constraints, and specifications are to be applied. A simple example rule might be: If a customer orders five or more of part X, then a part Y will also be needed. This kind of information is the important part of a knowledge base. In some systems it represents years of judgment and experience that is the essence of a human expert.

David Smith, who appears in the photo in Figure 14-3, is a General Electric Corporation expert who transferred his 40 years of experience to the CATS (*Computer-Aided Troubleshooting System*) knowledge base. He is one of only a handful of people who understand the mechanical and electric systems used in diesel-electric locomotives. By transferring his special expertise to the CATS knowledge base, it is available to many people in an area that has a scarcity of experts. Now the CATS system is routinely used to help General Electric repair engineers diagnose diesel locomotive maintenance problems. It also helps to train maintenance workers.

FIGURE 14-3
Dr. Piero Bonissone (left) and Mr. David Smith using General Electric Company's CATS expert system
(*Courtesy of General Electric Company*)

Using a Knowledge-Based System

Using CATS involves typing in responses to questions concerning the malfunction displayed on the screen. The program tries to pinpoint the source with such questions as

- Is the fuel filter clean?
- Are you able to set fuel pressure to 40 pounds per square inch?

At appropriate points in the question-and-answer session, a user can call up detailed drawings of the locomotive's various components (screen at right in Figure 14-3). Eventually, the troubleshooting system identifies the cause of the malfunction and, if necessary, demonstrates repair procedures on another screen (at left in Figure 14-3).

Although sections of the CATS system are still in development, it is expected to reduce locomotive downtime significantly. When complete, it is expected to solve 80 percent of all maintenance and repair problems and to reduce maintenance and repair costs significantly.

To simplify user interaction with a knowledge-based system, often a natural language program is used. Like those discussed in Chapter 8, they can be separate software packages that interface users to the knowledge-based systems. A user then can converse with the knowledge-based system in a natural language, like English. The MYCIN dialogue in Figure 14-4 shows a natural language exchange.

MYCIN helps doctors to diagnose infectious blood diseases. It also recommends therapy. It has about 450 rules and 1,000 facts in its knowledge base.

Knowledge Engineering

To transfer Mr. Smith's expertise to the CATS knowledge base required the services of Dr. Piero Bonissone, a knowledge engineer. He is skilled in the art of extracting heuristic knowledge from an expert.

To put the extracted knowledge into the computer, Dr. Bonissone had to quantify it. He transferred Mr. Smith's knowledge into a set of IF–THEN rules, as shown in Figure 14-5. A structured set of interlocking rules is called a *rule tree*, a **decision tree,** or a *search tree*. It is only one way to represent knowledge in a computer system. It took about one-and-a-half years to develop about 1,500 rules in the CATS system.

The IF–THEN rule approach is called a **production system.** It is the most commonly used method to represent knowledge in a computer system. Some other ways to represent knowledge are called *semantic networks*, *frames*, and *first-order predicate logic*.

Inference Engine

Whenever maintenance engineers use CATS, they work directly with the inference engine. An **inference engine** is a program that makes a knowledge-based system work. It retrieves facts and rules from the knowledge base. It also has a facility to explain, and store, its reasoning or conclusions.

- What is the patient's name?
  John Doe.
- Male or Female?
  Male.
- Age?
  He is 55.
- Have you obtained positive cultures indicating general type?
  Yes.
- What type of infection is it?
  Primary bacteremia.
- When did symptoms first appear?
  May 5, 1975.
- Let's call the most recent positive culture CULTURE-1. From what site was CULTURE-1 taken?
  From the blood.
- When?
  May 9, 1975.
- Let's call the first significant organism from this blood culture ORGANISM-1. Do you know the identity of ORGANISM-1?
  No.
- Is ORGANISM-1 a rod or a coccus or something else?
  Rod.
- What is the gram stain of ORGANISM-1?
  Gramnegative.
- Have there been positive cultures from sites which are not associated with infections about which you are seeking advice?
  No.
- Did ORGANISM-1 grow aerobically?
  Yes.
- Did ORGANISM-1 grow anaerobically?
  Yes.
- What is the suspected portal of entry of ORGANISM-1?
  The gastrointestinal tract.
  .
  .

NOTE

When satisfied that it has a reasonably good feel for the situation, MYCIN starts a short line of questions in preparation for recommending a course of treatment:

- My recommendation will be based on the opinion that the identity of ORGANISM-1 may be 1 Pseudomonas aeruginosa, 2 Klebsiella pneumoniae, 3 E. coli, 4 Bacteroides fragilis, 5 Enterobacter, or 6 Proteus nonmirabilis. On a scale of 0 to 4, where higher numbers indicate greater severity, how would you rate the patient's degree of sickness?
  3.
- Does the patient have a clinically significant allergic reaction to any antimicrobial agent?
  No.
- How much does the patient weigh?
  70 kilograms.
- My first recommendation is as follows: In order to cover for items 1, 2, 3, 5, and 6, give Gentamycin using a dose of 119 mg (1.8 mg/kg) q8h IV [or IM] for 10 days. Modify dose in renal failure. And in order to cover for item 4, give Clindamycin using a dose of 595 mg (8.5 mg/kg) q6h IV [or IM] for 14 days. If diarrhea or other gastrointestinal symptoms develop, check for pseudomembranous colitis.
- Do you wish to see the second choice?
  .
  .
  .

FIGURE 14-4
A sample MYCIN session
(*Source*: *Peter G. W. Keen and Michael S. Scott Morton*, Decision Support Systems, © 1978, Addison-Wesley Publishing Co., Reading, MA, pp. 42–43. Reprinted with permission.)

As an example, assume that one maintenance engineer responds "no" to a question like "does the engine start?" As evident from Figure 14-5, the rule tree leads to the goal or conclusion that the "fuel tank is empty."

To find the answer to subsequent "if" clauses, the program simply recasts its facts into user questions like "Is the fuel filter clean?" *If* the answer is "yes," *then* the program seeks an answer to the next question: "Are you able to set fuel pressure to 40 pounds per square inch?" *If*

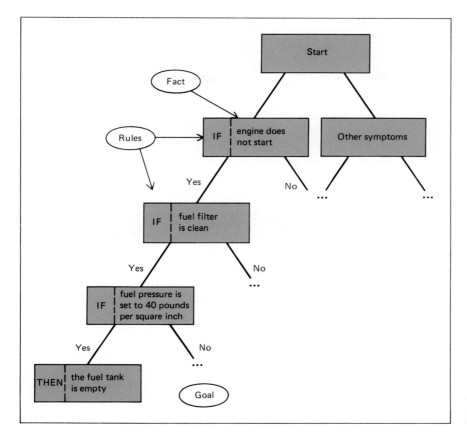

FIGURE 14-5
IF–THEN rule tree in a knowledge-based system

the answer is "yes," *then* the program keeps moving forward until it finds the THEN clause that gives the probable cause of the problem.

The inference engine program and knowledge base in CATS were created using **LISP** (for *LISt Processing*). It is one of two programming languages used for knowledged-based systems. The other is called **PROLOG** (for *PROgramming in LOGic*). An example of the simpler PROLOG language appears in Figure 14-6. Some versions of these languages run only on specially dedicated and expensive machines. One LISP machine, as an example, costs $80,000. These same programming languages are now available, some for under $100, for use on ordinary desktop computers.

Testing

Before any knowledge-based system is put into use, it must perform at an acceptable level. In the case of MYCIN, its developers tried to achieve 90 percent accuracy at diagnosing a disease and selecting a therapy. It was assumed that the program could not achieve perfect performance in its field of expertise.

To test MYCIN's performance level, ten actual cases of meningitis from hospital records were run through the system. The same cases

A 1-minute course in Prolog programming

Prolog programming is based on declared facts and conditional rules that programmers can manipulate in a declarative fashion. A fact consists of a relationship or a predicate and an object or objects. Standard Prolog notation for the English statement "John is father of Mary" would be

Father (John, Mary).

A simple query to a knowledge base with this fact stored in it of

? - father (X, Mary).

meaning "Does Mary have a father?" will produce the answer

X = John.

Once Prolog finds a fact that satisfies the desired goal, it stops searching the knowledge base unless asked to continue searching for additional facts that also meet the criteria. Conditional rules are declared by the notation ":-" which can be read as "if." The rule

Parent (X, Y):-father (X, Y)

would mean "X is the parent of Y if X is the father of Y." Prolog can logically apply such rules to facts in the knowledge base to answer more complicated queries. For example, after a program states the following facts, Prolog can logically answer questions about relationships described in them.

Prolog statement	**English meaning**
Father (John, Mary).	John is the father of Mary.
Father (Paul, John).	Paul is the father of John.
Grandfather (X, Y):-parent (Z, Y), father (X, Z).	X is grandfather of Y if some Z is parent of Y, and X is father of Z.
Parent (X, Y):-father (X, Y).	X is the parent of Y if X is the father of Y.

When the following question is asked

? - grandfather (X, Mary).	Is there an X that is grandfather of Mary?
then Prolog will answer	X = Paul

Applications that lend themselves to such declarative programming can be relatively quick and easy to write. However, it is difficult to know whether the answer the program provides is necessarily the best solution to a problem. This drawback is magnified in a large knowledge base.

FIGURE 14-6
A one-minute course in Prolog programming
(*Copyright 1984 by Cahners Publishing Company, Division of Reed Holdings Inc. Adapted with permission from* Mini-Micro Systems, *May 1984.*)

were given to eight infectious disease experts. The therapies selected by MYCIN, the experts, and the actual therapy given patients were then sent to eight more evaluators. Evaluators were infectious disease experts who had published papers on meningitis diagnosis and treatment.

Evaluators rated the prescribed therapies without knowing who, or what, had selected which therapy. In this test, using all eight evaluators' ratings to arrive at a definition of "correct," MYCIN scored only 69 percent. While this was short of the 90 percent target, it was better than any of the human experts. The best human expert scored 68 percent.

In spite of MYCIN's reliability, it is not commonly used by physicians. That is because its question-and-answer approach could take a physician almost an hour to arrive at a diagnosis. The time is unacceptable in the real-world conditions of a hospital.

By contrast, another medical expert system, developed jointly by Stanford University and Pacific Medical Center in San Francisco, is in regular use at Pacific Medical. It is reported that doctors sign 85 percent of PUFF's reports without a change. PUFF analyzes 250 factors that determine pulmonary dysfunction. Within 90 seconds, it issues a printout that may, in its own words, "indicate" or "suggest" what is wrong with the patient. Because it solves 85 percent of all cases, physicians have more time to solve the 15 percent of problem cases that remain.

Explanation Facility

For one or a combination of moral, ethical, and legal reasons, a professional is unlikely to accept the advice or conclusions produced by a knowledge-based system unless the logic and chain of reasoning are available for review. To satisfy this need, most knowledge-based systems have an **explanation facility** that reports exactly how they arrived at a given conclusion or line of reasoning. Explanation facilities provide a listing of the rules that contribute to a conclusion. Some also identify rules that were rejected and explain why.

A common feature is to give a **certainty factor** to a conclusion. One MYCIN conclusion, as an example, indicated:

> The identity of the organism is streptococcus (with a certainty factor of .7).

That is, the conclusion is not 100 percent certain in this case, it is given with only a 70 percent certainty. The factor is stored in the knowledge base along with the conclusion. Sometimes the certainty factor is the net figure accumulated along the way of chaining through a rule tree. Each rule may contain its own certainty factor.

System Development

This explanation facility helped Dr. Bonissone and Mr. Smith to ensure that the CATS system did not arrive at a correct result from the wrong rules. During the development of CATS, they constantly used this facility to determine which rules were used and when. Rules were added or modified to bring the system to correct conclusions. This process of incremental development is normal. It is the basis for increasing the performance and reliability of a knowledge-based system.

Most knowledge-based systems begin very small. The objective is to create a system that works only at the "assistant" level. In time, as new rules are added, it reaches a "colleague" level. Only a few systems operate at the expert level.

Most new system development projects are for very specialized areas of knowledge, like locomotive repair or specific disease diagnosis. These systems have none of a human expert's so-called "deep knowledge" about the world and the structural and physical principles behind it. This is why a medical expert system, when confronted with a new disease or symptom, will fail. Its knowledge base lacks the new or novel association. Even if available, it cannot tell the user why the symptom is associated with a disease. It will only explain a conclusion with the so-called "shallow knowledge" available in its specific knowledge base.

It is much more difficult to capture a broad knowledge base, such as one for a business manager. As an example, for a single product pricing problem, a manager may need to consider facts and rules about the way employees, customers, suppliers, and other affected parties will react to the change. The many behavioral variables that must be considered have retarded development of knowledge-based systems in the general business management area.

To simplify developing knowledge-based systems, organizations are using so-called **shell,** *framework*, or *generator* packages. These packages contain an inference engine program without the knowledge base. The knowledge base can be entered by a knowledge engineer or, in some cases, directly by an application or "domain" expert, like a manager or decision maker. Shell packages are the predominant way to develop knowledge-based systems on microcomputers.

1st-Class	Level Five
Arby	M.1
ES/P Advisor	Micro Expert
ESP Frame Engine	Nexpert Object
Expert Edge	REVEAL
EXSYS	Rule-Master
Guru	TIMM-PC
KDS 3	TI Personal Consultant
KES	

FIGURE 14-7
A sampler of knowledge-based system development tools or "shells" for personal computers

Some microcomputer shell packages, like those listed in Figure 14-7, cost a few hundred dollars and others can cost as much as $12,000. The more expensive packages include

- Several days of formal customer training on how to develop a knowledge-based system
- The services of a consultant to help load proprietary knowledge into the knowledge base

The next section of the chapter looks at an example of a microcomputer knowledge-based system created with a shell package. It also looks at two other kinds of microcomputer software that demonstrate various characteristics identified with knowledge-based systems. They are personal advisory and decision assistant software packages.

SHELL PACKAGES

Microcomputer shell packages are used by both application experts and knowledge engineers to build knowledge bases. Once the knowledge is captured, then other, less knowledgeable users can run the applications.

Some microcomputer shells have the following shortcomings:

- User input procedures are unnecessarily tedious.
- The knowledge base is restrictively small.
- A natural language interface for noncomputer users is not provided or is awkward to use.
- No explanation facility is available.

These technological limitations are expected to disappear as this software matures on ever-more-powerful microcomputers.

One industry specialist believes that purchasing the latest technology should not be the issue when deciding on a knowledge-based system project. More important is whether an application will be worth the cost of development. The hours required to develop and constantly enhance a knowledge base make payback especially important.

Telephone Services Application

Frank Derfler planned a simple application that would easily pay for itself in a short time. In addition, he had the microcomputer skills to develop the application himself. He is responsible for ordering millions of dollars of commercial telephone services a year for the federal government.[3]

The application he developed transfers his expertise at ordering telephone services to a large number of account managers in the government. He says that "an account manager now needs to have the acumen of a lawyer just to determine where to send orders for telephone service. Formerly, they needed only a knowledge of telephone technology and a familiarity with business practices to be effective. The split-up of AT&T and the telephone industry restructuring by the government, however, have created a situation where technical skills and a knowledge of business practices aren't enough."

The knowledge base Mr. Derfler built, as shown in Figure 14-8, contains 14 examples of telephone service orders. The knowledge base entry format resembles a familiar spreadsheet layout. Columns represent factors bearing on the choice of a telephone service company, or "carrier." Factors include

- Type of telephone service desired, such as direct distance dialing (DDD)
- Geographical category desired, such as the continental United States (CONUS)

The last column can be thought of as a conclusion when given the preceding factors. The last column lists either the name of a telephone carrier or a reference to a list of names. All should be solicited for bids to provide telephone service.

The software is designed on the principle that if given enough examples, it will "learn" to recognize rules and patterns. From given examples, it constructs a decision tree that it uses to reach its conclusions. Figure 14-8 shows the rules inferred from the examples given in the same figure.

Unlike classic knowledge-based systems, no rules need to be entered into the program. Rules are, instead, automatically generated from the several example cases given. This type of knowledge-based system shell, which automatically constructs rules from examples, is called an **induction system.**

After the rules are generated, Mr. Derfler's role as the application developer is over. But, should any rule conflicts appear, they must first be resolved. The software prompts the developer through problems.

Figure 14-9 shows what users, in this case account managers, see when they use the application. They are asked for answers to short multiple-choice questions. The program continues to ask questions until all its decision tree logic paths have been satisfied. Then it presents its final answer, as the example in Figure 14-9 shows. A user can ask to

---

[3] Frank J. Derfler, Jr., "Expert-Ease Makes Its Own Rules," *PC Magazine*, April 16, 1985, pp. 119–124.

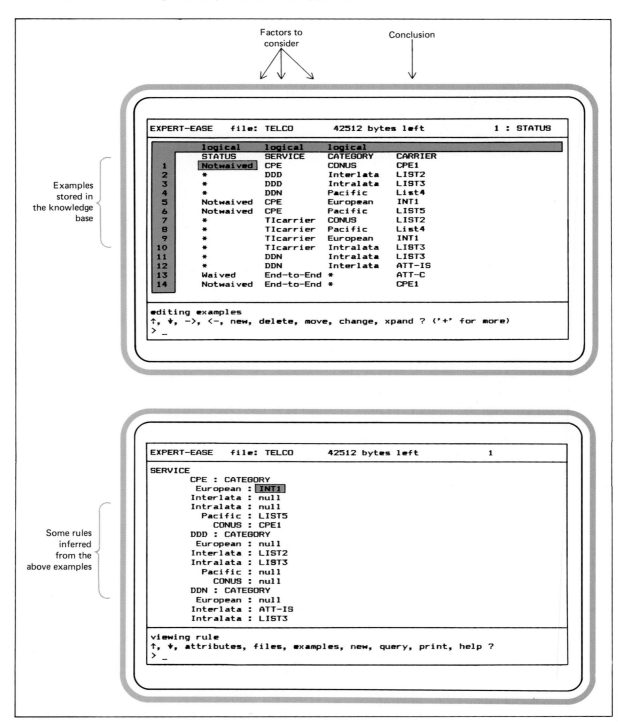

FIGURE 14-8
Building a knowledge base using a microcomputer "shell" program
(*Software: ExpertEdge, courtesy of Human Edge Software*)

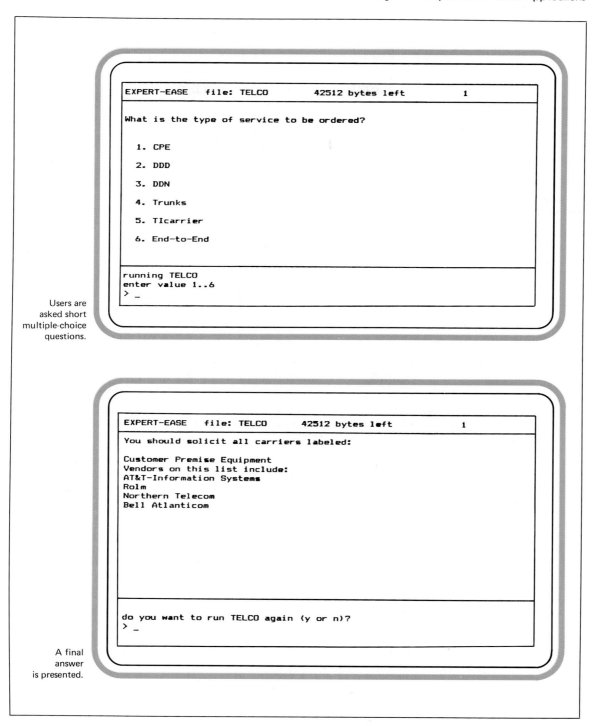

Users are asked short multiple-choice questions.

```
EXPERT-EASE    file: TELCO          42512 bytes left           1

What is the type of service to be ordered?


   1.  CPE

   2.  DDD

   3.  DDN

   4.  Trunks

   5.  TIcarrier

   6.  End-to-End


running TELCO
enter value 1..6
>  _
```

A final answer is presented.

```
EXPERT-EASE    file: TELCO          42512 bytes left           1

You should solicit all carriers labeled:

Customer Premise Equipment
Vendors on this list include:
AT&T-Information Systems
Rolm
Northern Telecom
Bell Atlanticom




do you want to run TELCO again (y or n)?
>  _
```

FIGURE 14-9
A user's view of the microcomputer system "shell" program
(Software: ExpertEdge, courtesy of Human Edge Software)

see the logic path followed to arrive at an answer. But the program cannot supply any more-detailed explanations about how a conclusion was reached.

Package Limitations and Benefits

Mr. Derfler found the package to be limited. It could not deal with slight variations of a single example. Also, it provided no way for experienced users to shortcut the tedious dialogue process.

The application Mr. Derfler developed is typical of a user's first attempt at fashioning a knowledge-based system. It is built with inexpensive and technologically limited software that enables a user to

- Develop a simple project with the modest goal of creating a knowledgeable assistant.
- Experiment with knowledge-based system development in the hope of gaining incremental knowledge for later, more ambitious projects. Failed first projects are common and expected as part of the learning process. Learning is often equated with the medieval guild system where progress is measured in stages as one moves from an apprentice to a journeyman and finally to a master builder.

All microcomputer shell packages work differently. All provide a different set of limitations. Mr. Derfler's package, for instance, holds 255 examples with a maximum of 31 factors in an example.

Another shell package, Guru, allows about 1600 rules in a so-called "rule set." One rule set can link to another as needed. The package also provides all the standard microcomputer applications associated with an integrated package:

- Spreadsheet
- Word processing
- Database management
- Graphics
- Communications

A spreadsheet cell can consult a rule set to arrive at its value. A word processing project might be prepared to call on a rule set to decide whether to include a particular paragraph in a form letter.

This type of flexibility and interconnectivity of software tools holds great promise for building usable business and other systems. Having access to traditional databases alone provides many exciting expansion possibilities. To date, a variety of shell packages have been used to create useful applications for the following:

- Statistical consultant
- Linear programming expert
- Weld selector
- Material handling selector
- Health care billing adviser
- Bankruptcy adviser
- Library reference expert
- Kidney disease expert
- Chest pain expert
- Real estate expert
- Computer purchasing expert
- Optical systems design expert
- Stock market adviser

Some developers of these knowledge bases are packaging and selling them as personal advisory software.

PERSONAL ADVISORY SOFTWARE

Personal advisory software seems to be the closest thing to "off-the-shelf" knowledge-based systems that one can get. These packages, like the examples listed in Figure 14-10, can be bought in retail stores and come with a built-in knowledge base.

The intent of most **personal advisory software** is to extend a person's judgment and intellectual capabilities. Packages are available, as an example, to help close a sale, negotiate a contract, and manage a business.

Sales Consultant

The Sales Edge is a package that exemplifies software in this category. It gives a salesperson personal advice about how to deal with a specific customer to make a sale. The advice is the kind one might expect from an assistant or a colleague.

Dr. James Johnson, a clinical psychologist and the developer of the package, explains how the knowledge base evolved. He, and other staff members, went through volumes of sales-oriented literature. They gleaned, he says, "every piece of advice that any expert has ever offered" on the subject of selling. Using established rules-of-thumb, the program figures out a best course of action to recommend in a user's sales situation.[4]

Dan Bronski, a salesperson on Interstate Distributing Company's staff, uses the package to help close sales. The package has three parts:

· Assessing yourself
· Assessing your customer
· Putting both together into a Sales Strategy Report

---

[4] Abbey Salomon, "Electronic Advisors," *Inc.*, March 1984, p. 131.

Sales Edge
Management Edge
Trigger
Negotiation Edge
The Art of Negotiating
Communication Edge
Thoughtware Products:
  Management Diagnostic Series
    Assessing Personal Management Skills
    Evaluating Organizational Effectiveness
    Understanding Personal Interaction Skills

Management Training Series
  Leading Effectively
  Motivating to Achieve Results
  Defining Goals and Objectives
  Improving Employee Performance
  Performance Appraisal
  Managing Time Effectively
  Conducting Successful Meetings
  Managing by Exception

FIGURE 14-10
A sampler of personal advisory software packages for personal computers

The software begins by asking Mr. Bronski whether he agrees or disagrees with a series of statements. Eighty-five statements, such as those listed here, are flashed on the screen one at a time:

- I like to take charge of situations.
- I am somewhat impulsive.
- I work for others around me rather than for myself.
- I easily accept substitutes.

To agree, he hits a left arrow key. To disagree, he uses the right arrow key. The approach resembles taking a psychological profile test.

The process to assess the customer is similar. Only this time Mr. Bronski agrees or disagrees with a series of 50 traits that are listed on the screen, as shown in Figure 14-11. The traits are stored in a separate file that Mr. Bronski updates as he gets to know the customer better. Occasionally he makes adjustments to his own stored profile.

Strategy Report

Mr. Bronski took under half an hour to do the assessments. Then he printed a Sales Strategy Report, similar to the one shown in Figure 14-12. Alternatively, the report could have been displayed. It is composed of six sections, combining information from the two assessment files. It reports

- What to expect from a customer, based on the customer's interests and style of doing things
- How to lead the customer through the sales process in a mutually beneficial way
- Reminders about what areas to concentrate on for the sales meeting
- Guidelines for getting a presentation off on the right foot
- A strategy to deal with the actual presentation
- Techniques to close the sale

The report does not provide an explanation for how it arrives at a given strategy.

FIGURE 14-11
Assessing customer traits using personal advisory software
(*Software: The Sales Edge, courtesy of Human Edge Software*)

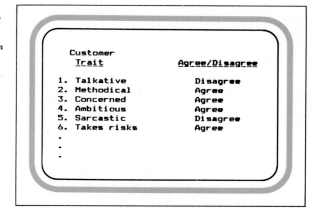

SELLING MR. J.R.

WHAT TO EXPECT:
You will find many interactions with Mr. J.R. difficult. You are involved with plans and ideas. Mr. J.R. is concerned with his own inadequacies. You perform well under stress while his performance deteriorates markedly. You think up projects and use initiative to carry them through. He will worry excessively over difficulties and be unable to take action. You welcome the opportunity to be creative and work independently. Mr. J.R. prefers to work under an authority with daily routines involving concrete details. You enjoy status and monetary rewards. He prefers to be recognized for hard work.
Exercise caution when dealing with this person. Behave in a reserved manner, use a soft voice and always avoid threats or criticism. Remember, Mr. J.R. is uncomfortable in groups. He is a hard worker, but needs quiet praise.

CUSTOMER SPECIFIC PREPARATION STRATEGY

PREPARE TO PRESENT INFORMATION IN DETAIL:
You tend to focus on the "big picture" while Mr. J.R. is more concerned with details. Prepare to give a relatively detailed presentation. The actual amount of detail you present depends on the level of detail Mr. J.R. introduces in the needs analysis phase of your meeting.

CUSTOMER SPECIFIC CLOSING STRATEGIES

IT'S THE LITTLE THINGS:
Get your customer to agree on the details and minor points of the sales agreement. It is not necessary to
.
.
.

FIGURE 14-12
Excerpts from a Sales Strategy Report
(Software: The Sales Edge, courtesy of Human Edge Software)

At first, Mr. Bronski rebelled against the whole idea that people's personality types could be neatly pigeonholed. He also questioned whether it was even possible to devise "formulas" that dictate optimum human behavior.

Yet he finds the reports remarkably on target. Sure, he discards some advice. But he finds out other advice that often is crucial to a successful sales call. He figures that at the very least, using the program forces him to examine all his assumptions carefully before a sales call. He prefers the software to using "how-to" books and tapes, or going to sales seminars. It gives him the ability to interact with the package to customize his own sales plan.

Improve Management Skills

Related packages provide for assessing an individual's

- Management skills
- Organizational effectiveness
- Interaction with others in a work group

Assessed strengths can be enhanced or weakness corrected with another series of training packages. Sample screens from various training packages appear in Figure 14-13.

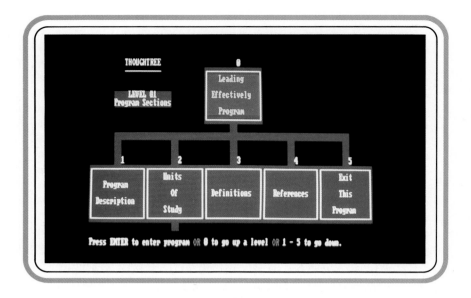

FIGURE 14-13
Sample screens from a series of management training programs
(*Software: Thoughtware Management Training Series, courtesy of Thoughtware, Inc.*)

Individuals like Sharon Weisman, a quality-control manager for a small manufacturing firm, use management training software. Two of several programs that Ms. Weisman uses are

· *Leading effectively.* It helps to assess her own management style and to compare it with the self-perception of other managers.
· *Defining goals and objectives.* The program helps her to distinguish between long-term objectives and short-term goals.

The programs all have limitations. Ms. Weisman cannot, for example, evaluate the composition of the group against which she is being compared. Topics in some programs, she thought, could have been better presented in a book. She finds it easier to read a book than to read the display.

Regardless of the software's present limitations, individuals as well as small and large organizations are buying libraries of it to improve management skills. Some of the reasons they give:

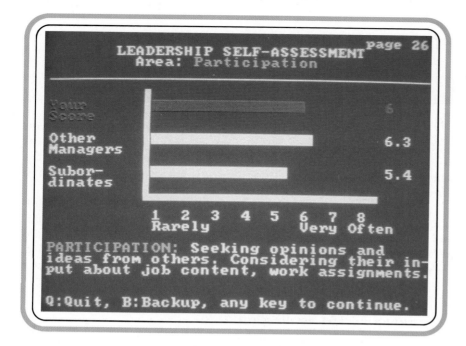

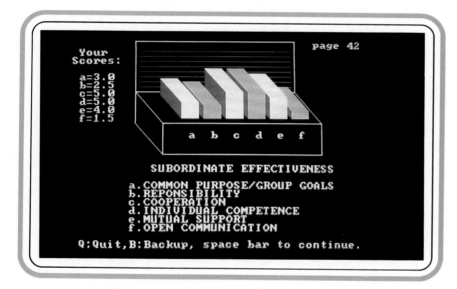

FIGURE 14-13 (continued)

- Training costs are substantially cut. The software eliminates the need for classroom facilities and travel expenses for trainer and trainee.
- Training time is shorter, sometimes by 30 percent, than with traditional methods. It reduces the amount of time an employee has to spend away from the job.
- Employees are free from dependency on expensive seminars, instructor availability, and a rigid training schedule.
- Employees are free to evaluate and improve their skills at whatever pace they choose—in the comfort and convenience of their office or home.

Companies like Exxon and General Electric, among many others, make such training software available to employees.

DECISION ASSISTANT SOFTWARE

Decision assistant software is the opposite of personal advisory software. A starting premise of this software is that it does not know answers to problems. It assumes that the user is the best determiner of the answer to a problem. What it does know is how to lead a user through the problem analysis process to arrive at an answer.

Some users like to contrast decision assistant software with spreadsheet and financial modeling software. Spreadsheets are ideal for "number crunching" problems. **Decision assistant software,** by contrast, handles both quantitative (numeric) and qualitative (nonnumeric) problems. The following example demonstrates this dual capability, while Figure 14-14 shows how this software relates to knowledge-based systems.

Product Pricing Application

The president of a small computer software development company, Janet Whitestone, uses decision analysis software. She must decide how to price a new software product. Traditionally, companies know the price of their new products by using a simple formula. It is to multiply the cost of making the product by 3 or 3.5 to get the retail price. With decision assistant software, a number of other alternatives can be conveniently evaluated.

As shown in Figure 14-15, Ms. Whitestone types in the six alternative prices among which she expects to make a choice. The same figure shows other steps as well:

- Step 1 establishes evaluation criteria. This example is simple, because only six criteria are used to determine the final pricing point for the new software product. Criteria are also ranked by weight to show their importance to a final decision.

FIGURE 14-14
A comparison of knowledge-based system elements and microcomputer decision assistant software

KNOWLEDGE–BASED SYSTEM ELEMENTS	RELATIONSHIP TO DECISION ASSISTANT SOFTWARE
Facts	Requires a user to think clearly about facts, or alternatives, which are input for the decision session.
Rules-of-thumb (heuristics)	Allows a user to establish rules-of-thumb for arriving at a decision.
Certainty factors (confidence weights)	Allows a user to weight decision criteria.
Decision tree of interlocking rules-of-thumb	Provides, in many cases, an underlying decision tree to structure the decision data (which may not be displayed in some software).

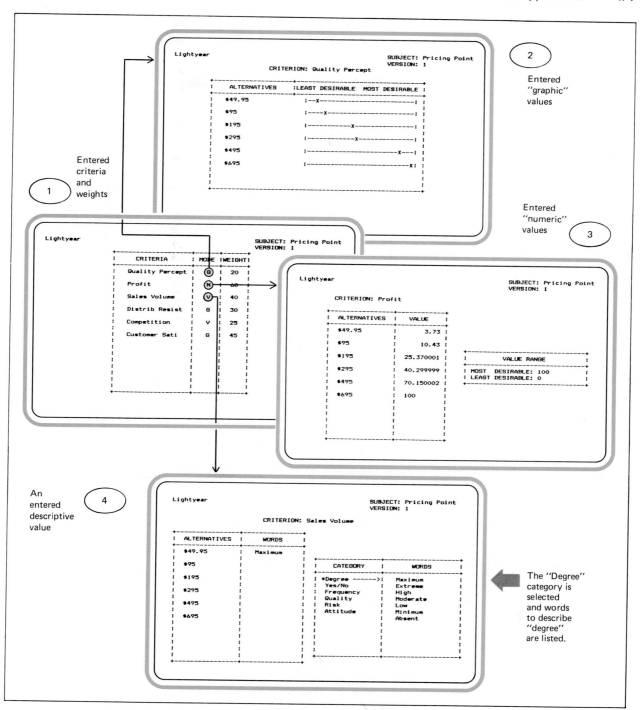

FIGURE 14-15
Different kinds of values can be entered for division criteria.
(*Software*: *Lightyear, courtesy of* Business Software)

The evaluation shows that the first two alternatives pass the profit rule.

A detailed analysis of the $495 price option

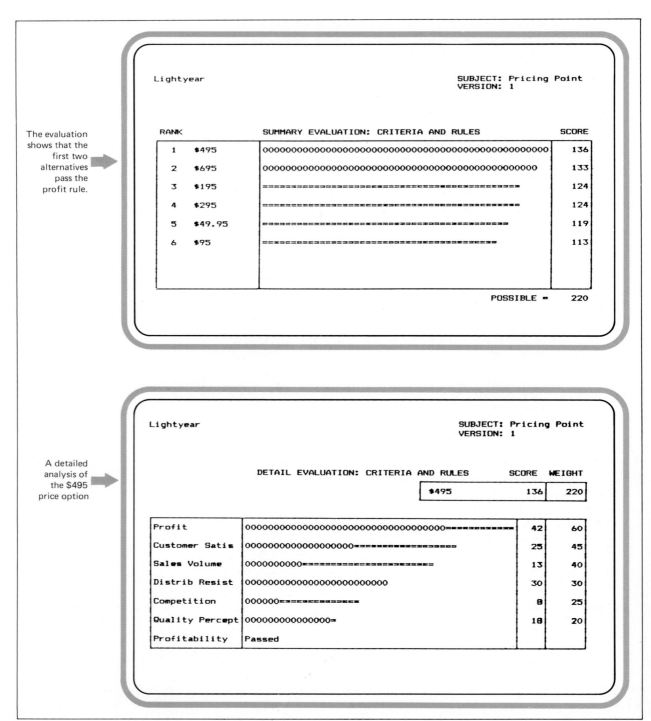

FIGURE 14-16
Evaluating results

- Steps 2, 3, and 4 establish values for each criterion:
    —For quality perception, a bar graph appears on the screen. Typing a right arrow key moves the X indicator on the scale to indicate a value from most to least desirable.
    —For profit, an amount from 0 to 100 indicates the desirability of each alternative.
    —For sales volume, a two-step process is required. First, a CATEGORY like "Degree" is selected. Then WORDS that describe "Degree" are displayed and used as appropriate.

After all values are entered Ms. Whitestone enters rules that the model must obey to arrive at a result. For this example, she types only one rule: "Profit must return at least 45." It means that for a price alternative to be acceptable, it must return at least 45 percent profit.

Evaluating Results

Eventually Ms. Whitestone is presented with a screen similar to the first one in Figure 14-16. It shows that only the $695 and $495 price alternatives pass the profitability rule. A bar of 0's across the screen indicates this result.

From the winning scores of 136 and 133, it looks like a "close call." So a detailed analysis, like the second screen in Figure 14-16, is requested. It shows, among other things, that the $495 price alternative

- Will create no distributor resistance
- Will not produce the sales volume that other options could

At this point, Ms. Whitestone may decide to redo the analysis. She may combine two criteria, profit and sales volume, into a single criterion, called gross profit. Such variations help her to understand better the impact of the pricing decision on different variables.

Ms. Whitestone finds that the decision assistant software helps to make her own thoughts clearer, more organized, and more presentable to others. In other words, it helps her to analyze objectively and present her own intuitive feelings about the decisions she makes.

It also serves a bonus purpose where group decisions are required. It forces everyone in a meeting to concentrate on the issues at hand.

FIGURE 14-17
A sampler of decision assistant software packages for personal computers

Limitations and Uses

One problem is using decision assistant software is not thinking carefully about all elements of a problem. Sloppy thinking generates meaningless and misleading results. The software is demanding and requires more than average knowledge to use. But by using the software, a user potentially can acquire desirable decision-making analytical skills.

Decision assistant packages, like those identified in Figure 14-17, are being used for the following:

- Evaluating job candidates to fill newly opened positions.
- Evaluating other software packages. At Bank of America world headquarers

Arborist
Brainstormer
Decision Aide
DecisionMap
Deciding Factor
Expert Choice
Light Year
The Confidence Factor

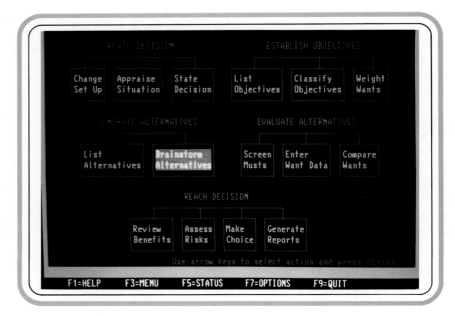

Many options are available to a decision maker.

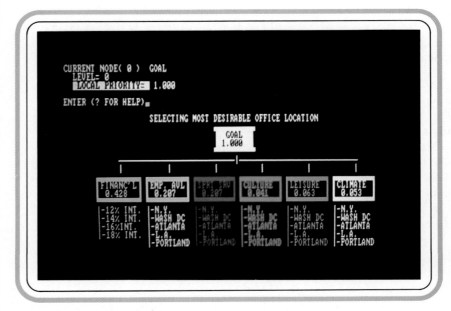

An inverted tree format organizes the
information on which a decision is based.

FIGURE 14-18

Decision assistant software screens

(*Top software:* Decision Aide, *courtesy of Kepner-Tregoe, Inc.; bottom software:* Expert
Choice, *courtesy of E. Forman, T. Saaty, M. Selly, and R. Waldron,* Expert Choice,
Decision Support Software, Inc. *1983–86.*)

in San Francisco, System Consultant Dick Lowell says, "We compare lots of software here with a long list of criteria. This makes the decision really easy." [5]

· Evaluating bank customer loan applications.
· Evaluating a site for the Navy's fourth annual microcompuer conference.
· Evaluating:

Acquisitions	New products
Advertising choices	Policy alternatives
Career choices	Proposals
Contracts	Relocation sites
Employees	

Figure 14-18 gives examples of alternative approaches to the analytic process used by two other decision assistant packages.

FIGURE 14-19
The Star Wars *movie robot, Artoo Detoo*
(Courtesy of Lucasfilm Ltd.)

ROBOT SYSTEMS

This final section of the chapter looks at robot systems. Robots are controlled by the smallest up to the largest types of computers. The discussion begins by comparing romantic with realistic images of robots. Then it "walks through" the computer-programmed steps that a robot might follow to do an assembly-line job. The sequence contrasts a robot's primitive capability with intuitive human capability. Several steps focus on using a robot's sensory subsystems, like vision and touch.

By definition, a **general-purpose robot** is a mechanical device that can be taught to do a variety of complex jobs. Considerations about how to "teach" a robot and how to evaluate its flexibility are covered. The section concludes with arguments used to cost justify robots and an assessment of their social impact.

ROBOTS IMAGES AND REALITY

The only contact most people have with robots is through the movies. Many are charmed by robots like Artoo Detoo, shown in Figure 14-19, who appears in the movie *Star Wars*.

This image stretches the current limits of reality. Real robots are far more predictable. A simplified illustration of one robot appears in Figure 14-20. Its primary function is to pick a small part from a bin and place it in a hole on the disk drive's metal casting. Parts of the step-by-step procedure to do this are illustrated in Figure 14-21.

FIGURE 14-20
Major structural components of a robot
(Courtesy of Robotics Age)

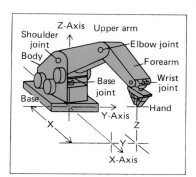

---

[5] Jim Bartino, "Aiming for the Executive Suite," *InfoWorld*, November 19, 1984, p. 32.

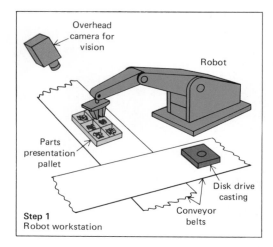

Step 1
Robot workstation

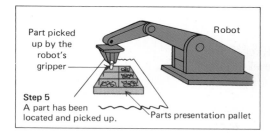

Step 5
A part has been
located and picked up.

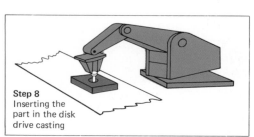

Step 8
Inserting the
part in the disk
drive casting

Summary of computer program steps

Step 1
Wait for a disk drive casting to enter
the robot workstation.

Step 2
Take a photograph or image of the
parts presentation pallet (an egg
carton arrangement that separates
parts). One or more overhead cameras
photograph the egg carton to get an
image.

Step 3
Locate a part in the image. A vision
subsystem, often sold separately from
the robot, does all image related work.

Step 4
If the egg carton is empty, move the
empty carton to the stacking area and
signal the conveyor belt controller to
move a fresh egg carton into position.
Go to step 2.

Step 5
A part has been located in the egg
carton. Pick up the part and position
it in the visual inspection station.
Take a photograph to get an image of
the part. Determine the orientation
of the part.

Step 6
If an incorrect part is detected by the
vision subsystem, deposit the part in
the reject bin. Go to step 2.

Step 7
The part is correct. Adjust the robot
hand angle according to the observed
orientation of the part. Move the part
to a point just above the insertion
location on the disk drive casting.

Step 8
Insert the part in the disk drive
casting, by moving it vertically
downward while monitoring the force.
When the vertical force reaches a
specified value, stop the robot vertical
motion.

Step 9
Check the vertical position of the
robot hand when it stops moving. If
it is at a height that indicates the part
was inserted, release the part from the
gripper and retract the robot hand.

Step 10
The part was not inserted correctly.
Move the robot hand in the plane of
the floppy disk casting by a small
increment along a prescribed path. Go
to step 8.

FIGURE 14-21
A robot's programmed sequence

PROGRAMMING CONSIDERATIONS

The program to control the robot's movements, summarized in Figure 14-21, reveals that

· All relevant actions must be programmed completely and unambiguously
· There is no intuitive knowledge present, such as that possessed by human workers

A human worker, especially one with experience in production-line assembly, can be instructed to do the task in a few minutes. A worker also knows, without further instruction, what actions to take for the unforeseen conditions that occur.

As shown, the steps in Figure 14-21 do not accommodate the many things that can go wrong. For example, what if the disk casting does not have a hole for the part to be inserted? The program also presupposes significant capabilities in the robot and its vision subsystem. They require that the vision subsystem and robot movements be calibrated.

SENSORY SUBSYSTEM

A vision subsystem is only one of several possible **sensory subsystems.** Others include voice and touch subsystems. They allow a robot to sense its surroundings and modify its actions to carry out specified tasks.

Vision

A vision subsystem that supports a robot's activity consists of a video camera mounted above the robot workstation. The camera records two-dimensional images that are digitized, much like they are in a graphics imaging system. But in a sensory subsystem, the image is analyzed for content. Figure 14-22 shows a typical industrial robot that is supported with a vision subsystem to work on parts. An analysis provides answers about a part's location, orientation, and quality. The answers are passed to the robot controller which activates the robot's movement. The relationship of the sensory subsystem to the robot is diagrammed in Figure 14-23.

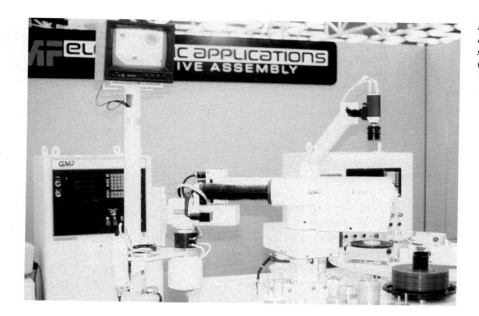

FIGURE 14-22
Robot with a two-dimensional vision subsystem
(Courtesy of GMF Robotics)

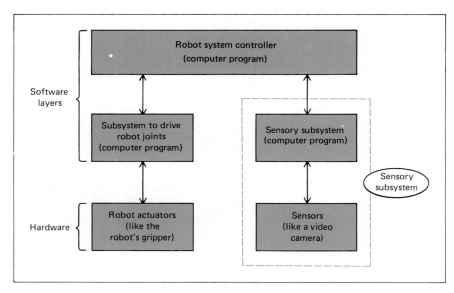

FIGURE 14-23
Relationship of a sensory subsystem to a robot system

The visual-tactile robot, shown in Figure 14-24, attains a touch sensitivity almost equal to a human hand. Its sensors detect size, shape, and pressure.

One manufacturer uses a three-dimensional vision-guided robot to weld parts together. Three-dimensional vision is obtained by mounting two cameras, 30 inches apart, on the robot arm, as shown in Figure 14-25. Fancier vision is needed in the welding application because

- Parts weight more than 1,000 pounds each, so there is little hope of placing them accurately.
- Parts are made by a number of manufacturers and vary in size and shape. After the cameras record the images, the vision subsystem determines part position and orientation from the stereo image pair.

Touch

Touch subsystems complement vision subsystems in robot installations. One automobile company puts touch sensors on a robot's wrist or hand. Its objective is to determine force and torque that arise from contact with an object. Such information is used to guide a robot to follow car door seams or other special surfaces.

Another company's touch subsystem uses "artificial skin." With this method, a robot's finger tips, also called *end effectors*, are composed of an array of pressure sensors. They enable robots to recognize, inspect, and locate objects from the pressure sensed.

FIGURE 14-24
A visual-tactile sensing robot handles objects as fragile as eggs.
(Hitachi robot, courtesy of Hitachi America, Ltd.)

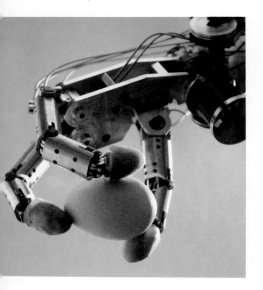

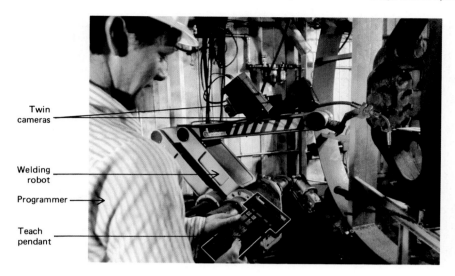

Twin cameras

Welding robot

Programmer

Teach pendant

FIGURE 14-25
A robot equipped with two cameras for three-dimensional vision
(*Product: Automatix robot, courtesy of Automatix*)

Sonar Sensor

Some robots are now being outfitted with senses that no human being has: the perception of infrared light and ultrasonic sound. The new breed of **homebots,** or personal robots, typically has ultrasonic transmitters/sensors. To determine where objects are located, a robot's sensor sends out an ultrasonic wave signal and detects its feedback. Then it sends a second sensor signal. By computing the time taken for individual signals to go out and return, the robot can determine where objects are located. Such a sonar sensor is used with great effect during demonstrations of "follow-me," where a personal robot automatically rolls behind its demonstrator who walks from room to room.

COMPUTER–AIDED MANUFACTURING

General Motor's highly flexible and completely **computer-aided manufacturing (CAM)** facility in Michigan makes adjustments to parts of different sizes in minutes. The emphasis is on manufacturing that accommodates rapid design changes and product customization. It has abandoned the old concept of long production runs of one thing, and only one thing.

The plant produces not one but a family of axles for different models of cars. In its pilot phase, 50 robots move parts within 40 manufacturing and *assembly cells.* Driverless robot-driven carts move parts between cells and transport products to shipping areas.

The robots in this flexible environment are mainly general-purpose robots. A general-purpose robot can be *taught* a task through programming. Once a task is learned, the robot can repeat it endlessly. But should a new task be required, the same robot can easily be reprogrammed to do the new task. Theoretically, a general-purpose robot, programmed to assemble axles, could easily be reprogrammed to assemble TV sets, or electric motors, or just about anything.

TEACHING

Teaching a robot its task refers to the process of

- Leading a robot through a sequence of moves.
- Recording the coordinate geometric and other data necessary to reproduce the movement sequence. Once the coordinate data are known, they can be included in the robot controller program.

As an example, to teach the robot how to function in the disk drive assembly operation, a programmer uses a **teach pendant,** like the one in Figure 14-25. The device allows a programmer to take a robot through movements by pushing appropriate buttons to

- Move robot joints
- Adjust movement speeds
- Record coordinate locations

During the teaching phase, the teach pendant is attached to the robot controller program. Only those motions and coordinates that the robot programmer wants are recorded.

Robot programming languages are proprietary, and each robot manufacturer supports its own language. Most require skilled programmers.

Axes

The complexity of a robot program is related to the number of axes that need to be controlled. A robot's *axes* or *degrees of freedom* (*DOF*) define its flexibility. For maximum flexibility, a robot needs six axes.

Six geometric parameters are required to specify completely the location and orientation of a rigid body, the robot, within some coordinate system. Three coordinates, the X, Y, and Z axes, locate the robot's center of gravity, as shown in Figure 14-20.

The robot that the disk drive manufacturer bought had five axes. Three axes control the base joint, shoulder joint, and elbow joint; two axes control the wrist joint, which rotates the gripper. Eventually the company upgraded to a robot with six axes. Such a robot has a wrist that provides three-axes control and is called a **fully articulated robot.** This type is often used in applications that directly duplicate manual tasks. But, compared with the human hand and arm, which have an estimated 22 degrees of freedom, six axes seem minimal.

With a seventh movement axis, a robot can roll across the floor along a preprogrammed path. At one major New York City bank, a robot mail-cart delivers office mail by following a track sprayed on the carpet.

COST JUSTIFICATION

The factors driving a decision to modernize a facility are often labor related. At a Ford Motor plant, shown in Figure 14-26, robots measure openings for windshields, doors, and lights. They work ten times as fast as humans and require no fringe benefits.

At the disk drive manufacturing facility, one operator oversees two robot systems. They do work that formerly required six people. The system is expected to pay for itself in two years.

The list in Figure 14-27 from *Business* magazine identifies the productivity advantages of robots over human workers. These advantages have been used to cost justify robots for such applications as the following:

- Assembly
- Forging (example: removal of white-hot metal from a furnace)
- Inspection
- Materials transfer

- Packaging
- Parts sorting
- Product testing
- Quality control

FIGURE 14-26
Robots measure openings for windshields, doors, and lights.
(*Courtesy of David Franklin*/Time Magazine)

Work more reliably:
    Set standards of 95% uptime.
    Can work three shifts.
    Take no vacations.
    Take no coffee breaks.
Work more consistently and accurately:
    Improve product quality.
    Reduce scrap rates.
    Make production more predictable.
    Contribute to higher capital utilization.
    Self-diagnose departures from efficiency.
    Can design improved work methods.
Work less expensively:
    Eliminate need for worker's compensation.
    Eliminate need for retirement plans and social security.
    Eliminate need for insurance programs.
Work in less controlled environments:
    Work in poor climatic conditions.
    Ignore noise.
    Do hazardous or dangerous jobs.
Work solely for the organization:
    Do not moonlight.
    Do not engage in industrial espionage.
    Do not sabotage operations.
    Do not become proselytized.
    Do not commit internal theft.

FIGURE 14-27
Productivity advantages of robot workers over human workers
(Source: Reprinted by permission from Business *magazine, "Robots—Coming to Work in America," by Michelle J. Gengler and Richard J. Tersine, April–June 1983. Copyright 1983 by the College of Business Administration, Georgia State University, Atlanta.)*

General-purpose robots that do these jobs can start at $7,500. They are made by General Electric, Unimation, Cincinnati Milicron, and Automatix, among others. Sensory subsystems often are created by robot or other companies like Object Recognition Systems and Robot Vision Systems.

SOCIAL IMPACT

The impact of robots on a society can be measured in economic, personal, and psychological terms.

Economic

Research studies suggest that people will lose their jobs to robots in greater numbers in the future. Yet the argument is raised that, if robots are not used, industries in the United States will not be able to compete with foreign producers. Then more jobs will be lost.

One observer suggests that for workers, a choice between robots and foreign competition is merely a choice between hanging and the electric chair. It is a bind society must resolve.

Others argue that the loss of jobs is not the most difficult economic challenge posed by robots. One robot expert claims that retraining is the major social problem created by robotization. He claims that massive retraining programs will be needed to prevent the creation of an oversupply of workers whose skills have become obsolete.

At the moment, little is being done to create retraining programs. Nor are strategies being developed, such as shorter work hours, to stabilize a robotized economy.

Personal

While robots are driving people out of work, people are bringing robots into their homes. One two-and-a-half-year-old child learned the alphabet from a four-and-a-half-foot robot, like one shown in Figure 14-28. The child considers the robot a companion and talks to it and kisses it. The parents fret when the child occasionally kicks it.

The mother likes the robot better than a pet—it doesn't eat or mess. Also, unlike a guest, she can turn it off. It also has a vacuum cleaner attachment to off-load some of the cleaning chores.

The father likes the robot to function as a house security guard. He bought security hardware components, including intrusion sensors, passive infrared detectors, and smoke sensors. Because he is a computer software developer, he uses the robot to develop his own programming skills. The robot has its own computer, keyboard, and display built into its head. Like his own personal computer, the robot can be programmed by him or by packaged commercial software.

Computer industry experts believe that a typical consumer may be disappointed with a homebot. Most are still awkward pioneers, unlike fictional movie robots. Personal robots are manufactured by Androbot, Heath, and Robotics International, among others.

Psychological

Along with the fear of unemployment, robots trigger some odd anxieties at home. One mother feels that her daughter would rather have the robot help her with homework than the mother. A child who has a robot feels neglected because his friends play with the robot more than him. Some psychologists firmly expect such outcomes when robots replace parents, friends, and teachers in people's affections.

There are, of course, more primordial fears, like the apprehension over robot terrorism. Consider a scenario in which a mad electrician seizes control of the robots and marshals them into squadrons of killer troops guided by a central computer. Most experts view such an eventuality as highly improbable. They base their opinion on the fact that robots really behave like severely retarded children that require continuous attention from their parents to solve or deal with the most trivial problem.

FIGURE 14-28
Personal robots, or "homebots"
(Top: courtesy M. Waythons/Black Star;
bottom: courtesy Favert/Gamma-Liaison)

CASE STUDY: Campbell's Keeps Kettles Boiling with Personal Consultant

At Campbell Soup Company plants around the country, soup is "cooked" in giant product sterilizers—commonly called cookers. Plant operators and maintenance personnel handle day-to-day cooker operations, but on occasion, difficulties arise that require the attention of an expert—someone thoroughly versed in the design, installation, and operation of the equipment.

Unfortunately, there just aren't enough experts to go around. So, when problems arise, the cookers can be shut down for long periods of time while an expert is flown in. To ease that time pressure, while freeing the experts for design improvements and other work, company officials decided to try a knowledge-based system. They wanted the system to diagnose possible problems and recommend specific solutions. And they wanted it to help train new maintenance personnel.

Because the company wanted a system in each plant, it decided to try personal computers. The system picked was the Texas Instruments (TI) Professional Computer, with 768K memory, 10-megabyte hard disk, and color graphics display.

Campbell and Texas Instruments agreed to work together to produce a system using TI Personal Consultant, a knowledge-based system "shell." Campbell provided the experts, and TI provided the knowledge engineer to enter that expertise in the computer.

System development took about six months, with a cooker expert and knowledge engineer getting together for three or four days each month at Campbell.

TI developed the prototype system with about 30 rules. Although this system didn't have much depth to its knowledge, it served as a catalyst for uncovering a wealth of knowledge about the cooker, which the human expert had not previously considered relevant.

The system was enlarged and refined over the next several months. Each revision produced more refined questions and new steps in the rules. The complete system has 150 rules plus start-up and shutdown procedures for the cookers. It has been demonstrated to plant personnel and has been well received. The system is now being installed in Campbell plants for use in diagnosing problems.

(SOURCE: "Campbell's Keeps Kettles Boiling with Personal Consultant," AI Interactions, *August 1985, pp. 3–4. Adapted with permission.*)

DISCUSSION QUESTIONS

1. Describe the motivations for developing a knowledge-based system.

2. Originally the Campbell cooker expert was reluctant to have a computer program capture his knowledge. His resistance was slowly overcome after he saw positive system results. What suggestions can you make about how to deal with experts who are reluctant about transferring their knowledge to knowledge-based systems?

CHAPTER SUMMARY

· *Artificial intelligence* is the branch of computer science that makes computers imitate human behavior. Many disciplines contribute to AI's development.

· AI is used as an umbrella term for, among other things, programmable robot systems, knowledge-based systems, and natural language systems.

- *Knowledge-based systems* capture, magnify, and distribute access to judgment. They can function as assistants, colleagues, or experts.
- Classic examples of knowledge-based systems are CATS, R1 or XCON, PROSPECTOR, MYCIN, and PUFF.
- The three main parts of a knowledge-based system are the knowledge base, inference engine, and explanation facility.
- A *knowledge base* is a stored collection of facts and rules about a specific area of knowledge.
- *Heuristics* are rules-of-thumb about a task at hand. One expert calls heuristics the knowledge of good judgment.
- *Knowledge engineers* have special skills to mine heuristics from human experts and to transfer them into a computerized knowledge base.
- An *inference engine* is a program that makes a knowledge-based system work. It retrieves facts and rules from the knowledge base. It also has a facility to explain, and store, its reasoning or conclusions.
- LISP and PROLOG are programming languages used for knowledge-based systems.
- An *explanation facility* reports how a knowledge-based system arrives at a given conclusion or line of reasoning.
- A *shell* package contains an inference engine program without a knowledge base. It is the predominant way to develop knowledge-based systems on microcomputers.
- Shell packages are used by application experts and knowledge engineers to build knowledge bases. Then other less knowledgeable users can run the application.
- *Personal advisory software* is intended to extend a person's judgment and intellectual capabilities. Packages are available, as an example, to help close a sale, negotiate a contract, and manage a business.
- *Decision assistant software* can help a user to analyze problems that are not based on numbers alone.
- A *general-purpose robot* is a mechanical device that can be taught to do a variety of complex jobs.
- A *sensory subsystem* allows a robot to sense its surroundings and modify its actions to carry out specified tasks. Examples are vision, voice, and touch subsystems.
- A goal of *computer-aided manufacturing* is to make rapid design changes and to customize products.
- *Teaching* a robot involves leading it through its task with a *teach pendant* and recording the coordinate geometric and other data to reproduce the movement sequence. All collected data must be included in a robot controller program.
- Advantages used to cost justify robots for industrial applications include the following: they work faster than humans, they require no fringe benefits, and they do dangerous tasks.
- Robots have an economic, personal, and psychological impact on society. For example, they can put people out of jobs, they can enter the home as companions and pets, and they can replace parents, friends, and teachers in people's affections.

KEY TERMS

Artificial intelligence	General-purpose robot	LISP
Certainty factor	Heuristics	Personal advisory software
Computer-aided manufacturing (CAM)	Homebot	Production system
	Induction system	PROLOG
Decision assistant software	Inference engine	Sensory subsystem
Decision tree	Knowledge base	Shell
Explanation facility	Knowledge-based system	Teach pendant
Fully articulated robot	Knowledge engineer	

REVIEW QUESTIONS

1. What is artificial intelligence?
2. List three examples of classic knowledge-based systems.
3. Describe the three parts of a knowledge-based system.
4. What does a knowledge engineer do?

5. What is a "shell" package? How are they used?

6. What is personal advisory software? Give an example.

7. What is decision assistant software?

8. What is a general-purpose robot?

9. What is a sensory subsystem? Give an example.

10. Identify the main goal of computer-aided manufacturing.

11. How is a robot taught to do useful tasks?

12. List three advantages used to cost justify robots for industrial applications.

13. Lists three impacts of robots on society.

14. What is a knowledge-based system?

EXERCISES

1. Locate articles on three knowledge-based system "shell" packages. The articles will probably call the packages "expert system" shells or development packages. Prepare an oral or written report that compares the packages.

2. Most knowledge-based system ("expert system") shell packages have demonstration programs, and even tutorials, included on the distribution disk. Locate a package and run the "demo" and the tutorial.

3. Identify a situation that you think would benefit from a knowledge-based system. Write a report that describes the situation and justifies the benefit of having a knowledge-based system. Include a section that addresses problems that might arise. Describe how the problems could be handled if the system were implemented.

Appendix A

History and Social Impact of Computing

AFTER READING THIS APPENDIX, YOU SHOULD BE ABLE TO

- Identify the major computing milestones that led to today's information society

- Give examples of how computers are affecting varoius areas of society, like the home, health care, and education

- Describe social issues that concern a computer-based society

Few contest the idea that society has evolved

- From an original agricultural society
- Through an industrial "smokestack" society
- Into an information society based on computing.

How did it happen? What are the milestones along the way that mark this change? This appendix begins with a look at the historical milestones in computing that led to the present information society.

Then it examines ways that computers are affecting various areas of society. Computers in the home, education, community, health care, entertainment, sports, music, art, and dance are among the areas covered.

The last part of the appendix addresses social issues that concern a computer-based society, like employment, personal privacy, computer crime, and ethics.

COMPUTING MILESTONES

Computers, as we know them, began in early 1940 with the so-called ABC computer. Before then, computing traces a historical line that begins with counting on fingers and progresses through the Roman and Arabic numerical systems.

User demand for improved speed of calculation fired the early development of modern computing.

1940s—The Beginnings

John V. Atanasoff, a mathematics professor at Iowa State College, required a calculating device to perform mathematical operations for 20 masters and doctoral students. None of the mechanical calculators available served his needs. With an assistant, Clifford E. Berry, he designed and named their machine the *Atanasoff-Berry-Computer,* or the **ABC Computer,** as shown in Figure A-1.

The design of the ABC Computer influenced the design of the **ENIAC** (*Electronic Numerical Integrator and Computer*), shown in Figure A-2. It was the first large-scale computer ever built.

John W. Mauchley and J. Presper Eckert, Jr., of the University of Pennsylvania, built the ENIAC. It was designed to respond to the U.S. Army's need for a machine to compute artillery trajectories. In the early 1940s, the United States was engaged in World War II.

The ENIAC weighed 30 tons and required the floor space of a house. Its bulk is attributed to the use of 18,000 **vacuum tubes** that resemble slim light bulbs in size and shape, as shown in Figure A-3. They registered the on and off electronic pulses that are the essence of digital computing.

Considerable pessimism surrounded the ENIAC's design. One mathematician calculated that a vacuum tube would fail every 15 minutes. Since it would take 15 or more minutes to find the tube, no useful

FIGURE A-1
John V. Atanasoff and Clifford E. Berry
(left and middle), inventors of the ABC
Computer; the Atanasoff-Berry-Computer
(or ABC Computer, right)
(Courtesy of Iowa State University)

FIGURE A-2
THE ENIAC computer with its co-
inventors, J. Presper Eckert, Jr. (front,
left), and John W. Mauchly (center)
(Courtesy of UPI/Bettmann Newsphotos)

Vacuum tubes used in first
generation computers (1 tube
equals 1 circuit element)

Transistors used in second
generation computers
(1 transistor equals
1 circuit element)

FIGURE A-3
The shrinking size of computer
electronic circuitry
(Left: courtesy of IBM; right: courtesy
of Raytheon Company)

Integrated circuits on a silicon
chip used in third and fourth
generation computers
(1 chip equals over 15,000
circuit elements)

FIGURE A-4
John von Neumann
(Courtesy of Princeton University)

work could be done. But the ENIAC worked. It computed mathematical problems 1,000 times faster than any machine before it. Today, however, a desktop personal computer is more powerful than the ENIAC.

Also in the 1940s, another University of Pennsylvania pioneer, John von Neumann (in Figure A-4), developed the **stored program concept** of reading a program into memory for processing. Several historians suggest that Mr. Eckert, a colleague of Dr. von Neumann, generated the idea before it was published in a 1945 paper by Dr. von Neumann.

Although reading programs into memory is standard today, it was different on the ENIAC. The ENIAC was **hard-wired.** All its circuitry was wired to perform one specific job. If the job changed, wires had to be changed. Loading and storing a new program in memory for execution, instead of rewiring the computer, were major computing milestones.

1950s—Business Computers

Dr. Mauchly and Mr. Eckert formed a private company that was bought by Remington-Rand. Their first business contract was to deliver a computer for use in the 1950 national census. The **UNIVAC I,** shown in Figure A-5, was the first computer devoted to nonmilitary work.

The UNIVAC I was then used to predict the outcome of the 1952 presidential election. With only 5 percent of the votes "tallied," it correctly predicted that Dwight Eisenhower would defeat Adlai Stevenson. This was the beginning of wide public awareness of computers.

During this time, **IBM,** which made punched card machines, lost some business because of UNIVAC. IBM's punched card machines had

FIGURE A-5
The first commercial-use computer, the UNIVAC I, predicted the winner of the 1952 presidential election.
(Courtesy of Sperry Corporation)

Examples
of
program
code

COBOL Language
MULTIPLY HOURS-WORKED BY PAY-RATE GIVING GROSS-PAY
ROUNDED

Machine Language

```
11110010 01110011 1101 001000010000 0111 000000101011
11110010 01110011 1101 001000011000 0111 000000101111
11111100 01010010 1101 001000010010 1101 001000011101
11110000 01000101 1101 001000010011 0000 000000111110
11110011 01000011 0111 000001010000 1101 001000010100
10010110 11110000 0111 000001010100
```

FIGURE A-6
*Program code that compares a single line
of COBOL with machine language
(Source: T. J. O'Leary and Brian K. Williams,
Computer and Information Processing,
Benjamin/Cummings, 1985, p. 171.)*

been handling the census count work. The company soon turned around to become the dominant force in the computer industry.

By 1956, IBM delivered 76 machines, to become the computer industry leader. By 1960, the company produced business computers that had **transistors,** instead of vacuum tubes, for its controlling circuitry. It marked the emergence of a **second generation** of computers that were faster, smaller, more reliable, and less expensive than **first-generation** vacuum tube computers.

The transistor was not new, but it took time to understand its mathematical physics. Three scientists at Bell Laboratories invented it in 1947 and later received the Nobel prize for their work. It eventually led to building tiny radios that could fit in a person's pocket.

Program Languages

Dr. Von Neumann wrote programs in **machine language,** the **program language** that computer hardware "understood." As the example in Figure A-6 shows, it is difficult for humans to read, as well as to write, machine language programs.

Efforts developed to simplify programming. Languages like **FORTRAN** (*FOR*mula *TRAN*slation) and **COBOL** (*CO*mmon *B*usiness *Ori*ented *L*anguage) were developed.

Grace Hopper, a former commodore in the United States Navy, was a pioneer in the field of computer languages. She was a member of the committee that explored solutions to the problem of transporting programs written for one computer to another different computer. The result was a standardized COBOL for which Dr. Hopper, who is shown in Figure A-7, wrote the first practical program.

In 1958, John McCarthy invented the LISP (*LIS*t Processing) programming language. It is suitable for symbol and list manipulation required for programming projects based on artificial intelligence research.

1960s—Minicomputers

By the 1960s, a number of computer companies began to introduce smaller computers. Among them, the largest company is Digital Equip-

FIGURE A-7
*Computer program language pioneer,
Grace Hopper, retired U.S. Navy
(Courtesy of U.S. Department of the Navy, official photo)*

FIGURE A-8
The first successful minicomputer, the
DEC PDP-8
(Courtesy of Digital Equipment Corp.)

ment Corporation (DEC), which opened the **minicomputer** market. Figure A-8 shows the DEC PDP-8, the first successful minicomputer.

In 1964, IBM announced its System 360, a large mainframe computer shown in Figure A-9. It launched the **third generation** of computing. It used **integrated circuit** technology, which is still used today. In this technology, on and off circuits elements are first etched, then burned, into a **silicon chip.** Figure A-3 shows a silicon chip.

The IBM System 360 is primarily a **batch processing** system. Users leave jobs for processing and come back later to pick them up when done. There is no human interaction during computer processing. But

FIGURE A-9
The IBM System 360, a third-generation
computer
(Courtesy of IBM)

John Kemeny, a mathematics professor at Dartmouth College, did not want students to wait for batch processing delays. It motivated his and Thomas Kurtz's development of **time sharing** software. The software allowed many students with terminals to work interactively with a computer during its program processing. Students could enter data and get feedback almost instantly. This **interactive** method of computer use dominates today.

The software inventors also created the interactive **BASIC** (*Beginner's All-purpose Symbolic Instruction Code*) program language. It allowed nontechnical people, like students, to program the computer.

By late 1960, software companies emerged. But software continued to be plagued with errors that stimulated publicity about their unreliability. The problems remain today but are being addressed by automated program generators.

1970s—Microcomputers

By 1970, IBM introduced its System 370. This mainframe computer looked much like its predecessor, the System 360. But it used integrated circuit chips that contained over 15,000 circuit elements on a single chip. The chips are called **LSI** (for **large-scale integration**) chips. Some industry analysts consider this the beginning of the **fourth generation** of computer systems. Earlier integrated circuits had as few as 22 circuits on a chip.

In 1971, Intel introduced its first **microprocessor** chip. It contained all the major logic circuitry of a computer on one chip. Intel called it a "computer on a chip." Today such chips cost a few dollars each and are found in many things, including toys, appliances, cars, satellites, and microcomputers.

The first commercial **microcomputer,** which had a microprocessor as its "brain" or "engine," appeared in 1974. It was offered by mail order in kit form and was called the Altair. By 1977, Apple Computer, Radio Shack, and Commodore sold completely assembled microcomputers, also called **personal computers,** like the one in Figure A-10.

FIGURE A-10
One of the earliest completely assembled microcomputers, the Apple II
(*Courtesy of Apple Computers, Inc.*)

FIGURE A-11
*Steve Jobs (top left) and Steve Wozniak
(bottom, left), co-inventors of the Apple
II microcomputer
(Courtesy of AP/Wide World Photos and Apple
Computer, Inc.)
Dan Bricklin (top, right) and Bob
Frankston (bottom, right), co-developers
of the VisiCalc spreadsheet program
(Courtesy of Lotus Development Corporation)*

The inventors of the Apple, Steve Jobs and Steve Wozniak, shown in Figure A-11, were members of the Homebrew Computer Club in California. Club members, impressed with their assembled computer, wanted to buy a copy. So the two entrepreneurs borrowed money and assembled the first Apple computers in a garage.

Microcomputers did not attract business users until 1979 when the first electronic spreadsheet program, **VisiCalc,** appeared. The idea for VisiCalc came from Dan Bricklin, a Harvard student who had a complex business analysis assignment that required lots of calculations. He had seen word processing programs and so set out to do something similar to manipulate numbers. He developed his spreadsheet program with a friend, Bob Frankston. Both men are also shown in Figure A-11. The program ran only on the Apple II microcomputer. Industry researchers claimed it was the first time that a software program promoted the sale of computer hardware.

The 1970s saw many other computer firsts, among them:

- First program to understand **natural language.** It allows a user to talk to a computer in plain English.
- First **expert system** completed. It allows a computer to function as a consultant to a user, in a specific problem area (like diagnosing a medical problem).
- First **supercomputer** shipped. They are high-speed computers used for advanced military, scientific, and other projects.
- First **local-area network** installed. The networks mainly allow one personal computer to communicate with another in small companies, as well as in departments of large organizations.
- First moves to **distributed data processing.** It is an approach to decentralizing computing in an organization.

1980s and Beyond

The Apple personal computer was eclipsed in the early 1980s by the IBM Personal Computer. Today there are many brands of personal computers, but most remain compatible with standards established by the IBM products.

Apple introduced its new Macintosh microcomputer in mid-1980. It had many novel features, like

- Windows
- Mouse pointer
- Visual user interface with icons instead of commands

These innovative ideas stemmed from research at Xerox's Palo Alto Research Center. Xerox's Star computer, the prototype of the Macintosh style, was introduced in 1981 and never became successful. But the impact of its style is being felt in many computer offerings.

The mid-1980s saw the microcomputer eclipse the mainframe and minicomputer in market dominance. Hardware, in turn, is being eclipsed by software dominance. Microcomputer software entrepreneurs like Mitch Kapor, formerly of Lotus Development Corporation, and Bill Gates, of Microsoft Corporation, command as much media attention as does IBM. Mr. Kapor wrote Lotus 1-2-3, the spreadsheet program that succeeded VisiCalc. At the age of 23, Mr. Gates was responsible for marketing PC–DOS, the operating system used in almost every IBM Personal Computer sold. At the age of 32, he heads his own billion dollar company, Microsoft Corporation. Both men appear in Figure A-12.

FIGURE A-12
Bill Gates, (top), marketer and developer of the PC–DOS operating system for the IBM Personal Computer and chairman of the board of Microsoft Corporation; Mitch Kapor (bottom), author of the Lotus 1-2-3 spreadsheet program
(Top: courtesy of Microsoft Corp.; bottom: courtesy of Lotus Development Corp.)

COMPUTERS IN SOCIETY

Computers, especially personal computers, have become a part of almost every aspect of modern society. This section presents "snapshots" of how computers are used in health care, by handicapped people, and in the home, community, education, research, entertainment, sports, music, art, and dance.

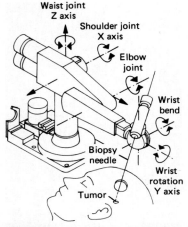

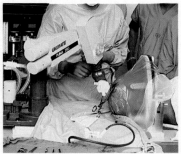

FIGURE A-13
A robot arm assists in a brain operation.
(Courtesy of Long Beach (CA) Memorial Medical Center)

Health Care

For the first time in medical history, doctors have used a computerized robotic arm to help with actual surgery on the human brain, as Figure A-13 shows.[1] The robot arm holds and directs a surgical drill and biopsy needle, during specialized brain surgery. The robot's program calculates movements while doctors apply pressure on the arm to penetrate the skull and brain.

The robot helps surgeons to remove tissue samples from suspected brain tumors that are difficult to reach by conventional means. "The robotic arm is safer, faster, and far less invasive than current surgical procedures," says the device's inventor, Yik San Kwoh. The robotic arm's great accuracy

- Eliminates the need for general anesthesia
- Reduces trauma to the brain
- Allows patients to go home the day after brain surgery, instead of a week or more later

In the future, Dr. Kwoh says, "the device may be used to repair blood vessels, guide laser beams to tumors, and help orthopedic surgeons repair ruptured discs, torn ligaments, and cartilage."

Also in the future, computer communication, combined with robotic technology, is expected to allow physicians to provide long-distance surgery assistance in remote or inaccessible locations. This could positively affect the health outlook in Third World nations. Such nations could also benefit from so-called expert systems that would work side by side with paramedics to help diagnose and treat medical problems.

Handicapped

Scott Luber is a young accountant with muscular dystrophy. He works for Nankin, Schnoll and Company, an accounting firm in Milwaukee, Wisconsin.[2] He is one of hundreds of men and women who are employed because of their proficiency with adapted computers.

Paul L. Hazen of Johns Hopkins University claims that "innovation, coupled with the leverage of personal computing, can transform the dedication and drive of millions of handicapped individuals into a significant human resource. It should be an important social objective," he claims, "because the number of people afflicted with mental and physical handicaps typically represents about 10 percent of a nation's population."[3]

For the visually impaired, a voice synthesizer can be attached to a computer to read words that appear on a display. A similar device can

---

[1] Sandra Blakeslee, "A Robot Arm Assists in Three Brain Operations," *New York Times*, June 25, 1985, p. C1.

[2] Sherry Sontag, "For Disabled, Computers Are Creating New Lives," *New York Times*, August 24, 1985, p. 1.

[3] Paul L. Hazen, "Micro Computing in the 80's," *Computer*, October 1984, p. 142.

be programmed to speak for people who cannot talk. Alternatively, software can translate the text appearing on a display into printed Braille, which visually impaired persons can read.

People with limited mobility can use keyboards with oversize keys or devices that can replace keyboards altogether. For the deaf, computer electronic mail can replace office telephones. Electronic mail transmits typed messages instantly to and from other computers. All these possibilities and adaptations of computers are enabling the handicapped to enter today's work force.

Home

Some studies of the impact of computers in the home offer reassuring results. Trika Smith-Burke, an investigator in one study, said "the use of home computers [like the one shown in Figure A-14] in the families studied seems consistent with the social organization. If a family was highly cohesive, it remained so. The computer was thought of as a family machine. If a family was individualistic, that was the nature of the home-computing behavior. Where prominent sibling rivalries existed among children, that pattern was sustained in arguments over use of the computer. If the computer took the place of anything, it was TV."[4]

While children primarily use home computers for playing games and programming in BASIC, adults find it useful for other things. They prepare home budgets and do personal investment and tax planning with it. Many software packages are available for these standard chores.

FIGURE A-14
A home or family computer
(Courtesy of IBM)

---

[4] Glenn Collins, "Study Finds Computers and Family Mix," *New York Times*, September 10, 1984, p. 27.

Some subscribe to **public communication services.** Various offerings include

- Electronic financial and brokerage services
- Electronic live "chats" or conferences
- Electronic bulletin boards
- Games
- Electronic shopping, and other options

Some offerings are less than ideal. As an example, electronic shopping does not provide for the visual inspection of items. Many would consider this undesirable when shopping for certain goods, such as clothing.

Computers in the home are also used to pursue interests in education, arts, sports, and entertainment. But in many cases, the cost of owning a home computer restricts its use to only a small percentage of the potential market. As the cost comes down, this is expected to change.

Community

Computers play a role in delivering community and other social services. Daniel Walker, a firefighter technician for a Louisiana community, uses a computer to chase fires. The computer is in a van that follows the fire engine to the scene of a fire. On the way, Mr. Walker retrieves the floor plan of the burning building. It has information vital to firefighters, such as types of doors, presence of hazardous materials, and location of ventilation systems and utility shutoff valves.

The software that stores the floor plan is an ordinary **computer-aided design (CAD)** graphics package. Mr. Walker updates the plans from notes the firefighter staff gathers on regular inspection tours.

Tending to a community's spiritual needs is also more manageable with computer assistance. A pastor in Long Island, New York, created a database management system to handle church accounting, census, and collection records.[5] Other clergy use their computers with word processing software to prepare sermons. One minister prints and duplicates his sermons for distribution to interested congregation members.

Education

The variety of ways that computers have changed education and training are evident everywhere. Computer literacy courses are now mandatory in most colleges and a number of high schools. Some colleges require all freshmen to own a personal computer. Some places like the University of Mexico, shown in Figure A-15, even offer such specialized courses as robotics.

---

[5] "The Newest Testament: Churches Turn to Computer Management," *Business Computer Systems*, October 1983, pp. 156–162.

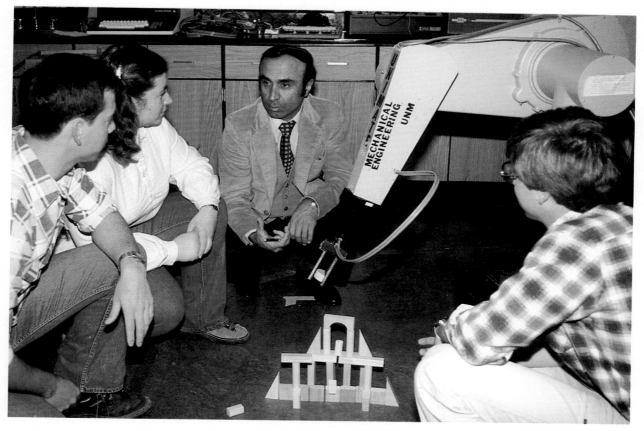

FIGURE A-15
College students at the University of New Mexico learn to program robots.
(*Courtesy of the University of New Mexico*)

The computer has changed some of the ways students learn. Interactive videodisk courses allow a student to

- Select subjects from a display menu
- Follow a video image and sound presentation on a TV set
- Interact with the video through computer keyboard input

Developers claim that the method can be a quicker and more effective way to learn than with traditional methods.

Figure A-16 shows Nelson Whitney creating an interactive videodisk lesson for a biology course.[6] The course is prepared with an **authoring system.** This is a software package that allows nonprogrammers, like

---

[6] Wayne Parker, "Interactive Video: Calling the Shots," *PC World*, October 1984, pp. 99–108.

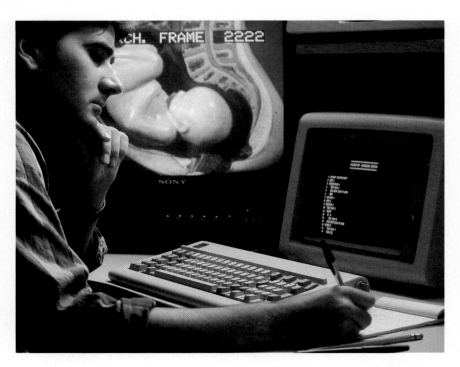

FIGURE A-16
Nelson Whitney creates an interactive video display lesson that combines text and graphics
(Courtesy of George Steinmetz)

many teachers, to create or "author" computer-based instruction programs. When students take the course, they will be experiencing **computer-assisted instruction (CAI).**

The software Mr. Whitney customizes for his course will interact with a student by

- Asking questions
- Keeping track of answers
- Illustrating points
- Adjusting its presentation of information to a student's demonstrated knowledge and level of experience

Some educators are using the computer's capacity for simulating real-life situations to teach such subjects as anatomy and genetics. One microcomputer package allows students to experiment with genetics by providing a simulation of the breeding of cats. The program uses the laws of genetics to determine the characteristics of the offspring that would be born to a hypothetical pair of cats described by the student. The program successfully creates an environment in which a student must act like a scientist to discover the principles of genetics.

Computer-assisted instruction requires equipment that is often too expensive for many financially pressed schools. Also, to integrate sophisticated computer instruction into the classroom requires computer-literate educators. Formal programs at all educational levels are addressing this retraining job.

Several computer manufacturers are helping to train educators. One is helping to develop curriculum materials for elementary grade-schoolers.[7] The program uses computers, typewriters, and tape recorders to teach students to read and write. The "writing to read" program has been successful. Children in test groups learn to type narratives, stories, and poems—at an age when other children are learning how to write their names.

The program is very expensive to implement. It offers a radical departure from the normal way in which early childhood education is currently conducted. Early results, nonetheless, are encouraging.

The educational possibilities of computers are not restricted to formal classrooms. From their homes, students with personal computers can take continuing education and college credit programs through public communication services. There are also programs available for those who attend elementary and secondary schools.

Inexpensive personal computer software packages make the pursuit of self-education possible on an even less formal basis. Speed-reading packages, like the examples shown in Figure A-17, cost under $200. They claim to help users read at double or triple their present speed without sacrificing comprehension. They are only one of a growing list of self-help and self-education software packages available to anyone with access to a personal computer.

Research

Figure A-18 shows Robert H. Schwartz, a professor at the University of Rochester, New York, who uses a personal computer for his research.[8] Previously he relied on standard genealogical flowcharts to trace the inherited disease cystic fibrosis. The fatal illness is one of the "most commonly inherited diseases in the United States," he says.

With his personal computer, Dr. Schwartz now can store and organize the personal, demographic, and genetic records of approximately 850 people more efficiently. One large "kindred" group that he traced descended from a couple who lived in France in the mid-1700s. He located 37 cases of cystic fibrosis that occurred in that kindred for his study of the genetics related to the disease.

Registrar Rose Scola at Chicago's Brookfield Zoo uses a personal computer for a different kind of genetic search.[9] She works with a database system called ARKS (Animal Records Keeping System). It links, through communication lines, into another database called ISIS (International Species Inventory System). ISIS contains an inventory of nearly every zoo animal in North America and at 26 zoos in Europe and Asia—in all, more than 70,000 live animals and tens of thousands of their forebears.

The inventory was developed by a team at the Minnesota Zoo, sponsored by national zoo organizations and the U.S. Department of the

[7] Doran Howitt, "Experimental Software Boosted," *InfoWorld*, October 29, 1984, pp. 29–30.
[8] "Genetic Research," *PC World*, February 1985, p. 31.
[9] Janet Goldenberg, "Animal Trackers," *PC World*, February 1986, pp. 158–161.

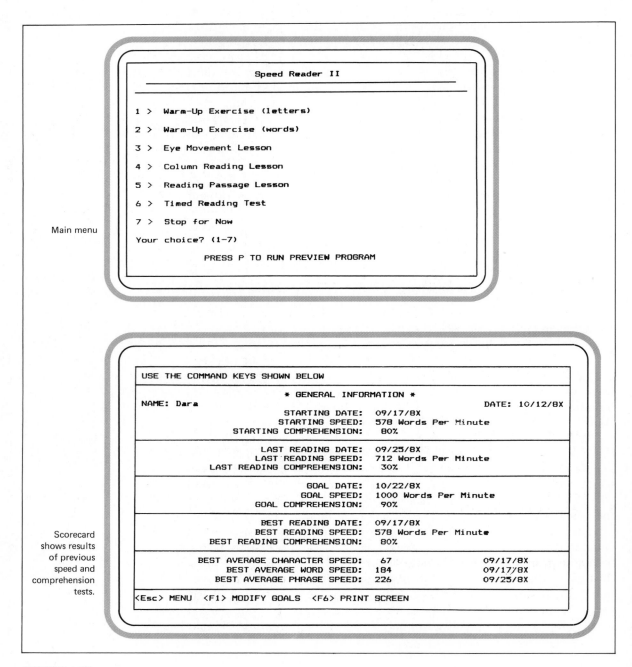

Main menu

Speed Reader II

```
1 >   Warm-Up Exercise (letters)

2 >   Warm-Up Exercise (words)

3 >   Eye Movement Lesson

4 >   Column Reading Lesson

5 >   Reading Passage Lesson

6 >   Timed Reading Test

7 >   Stop for Now

Your choice? (1-7)

        PRESS P TO RUN PREVIEW PROGRAM
```

Scorecard
shows results
of previous
speed and
comprehension
tests.

```
USE THE COMMAND KEYS SHOWN BELOW

                  * GENERAL INFORMATION *
NAME: Dara                                    DATE: 10/12/8X
                   STARTING DATE:   09/17/8X
                   STARTING SPEED:  578 Words Per Minute
            STARTING COMPREHENSION: 80%

               LAST READING DATE:   09/25/8X
               LAST READING SPEED:  712 Words Per Minute
        LAST READING COMPREHENSION: 30%

                      GOAL DATE:    10/22/8X
                      GOAL SPEED:   1000 Words Per Minute
              GOAL COMPREHENSION:   90%

               BEST READING DATE:   09/17/8X
               BEST READING SPEED:  578 Words Per Minute
        BEST READING COMPREHENSION: 80%

        BEST AVERAGE CHARACTER SPEED:   67        09/17/8X
           BEST AVERAGE WORD SPEED:    184        09/17/8X
         BEST AVERAGE PHRASE SPEED:    226        09/25/8X

<Esc> MENU   <F1> MODIFY GOALS   <F6> PRINT SCREEN
```

FIGURE A-17
Displays from two speed-reading software packages
(Software: Top, Speed Reader II, courtesy of
Davidson and Associates; bottom, The Evelyn
Wood Dynamic Reader, courtesy of Timeworks, Inc.)

FIGURE A-18
Robert H. Schwartz uses a personal
computer for his genealogical research.
(Courtesy of Jon Reis/The Stock Market)

Interior. The database is helping to promote zoo-based breeding programs that seek to preserve and replenish endangered species.

In the humanities area, Eleanor Prosner of Stanford University is using a personal computer for Shakespearean research. She is classifying Shakespearean lines under their metric types and has identified about 12 types.[10] Another humanities professor, Harley Balzug of Georgetown University, organized a nationwide computer conference of Soviet studies experts on a public communication service computer.[11]

Research of still another type occupies computer scientists and military strategists at the Defense Advanced Research Projects Agency. One project is to develop a new generation of computerized land and air defense systems.[12] Two prototype vehicles are shown in Figure A-19. The hexapod walks with the aid of 16 on-board computers. The computers get their information from sensors and use it to guide the vehicle forward, backward, or to the side.

The autonomous land vehicle is another experimental military-use vehicle. It is a robotlike, driverless device that "sees" through a television camera linked to a built-in computer. The computer matches images to data in its memory and decides which way the vehicle should go. Both vehicles could not have been developed without computer components.

Entertainment and Sports

The computer's impact on the ways people find entertainment is evident in any computer arcade in any town. While many applaud the ability of video games to sharpen a player's hand-eye coordination, others deplore their heavy "kill-the-opponent" content.

---

[10] Jonathan Littman, "Computing the Classics," *PC World*, June 1983, Vol. 1, No. 6, pp. 266–274.

[11] Patricia Mandell, "Georgetown University: A School Full of Diverse Applications," *PC Week*, October 16, 1984, pp. 41–45.

[12] John Greenwald, "Over Hill, Over Dale . . . ," *Time Magazine*, August 19, 1985, p. 18.

FIGURE A-19
Top: the hexapod is designed to cross
terrain that would bog down a jeep;
bottom: prototype of a driverless tank,
called an autonomous land vehicle
(Top: courtesy of Ohio State University, Office
of Communications Services; bottom: courtesy
of Martin Marietta Corporation)

More educationally inclined are the simulation games sold for use on home computers. Probably one of the most familiar is Flight Simulator, shown in Figure A-20. It lets users fly under bridges and make crash landings without messing up a hair on their heads. The program provides a credible example of real-life flight training simulators that cost about $3 million each.

Some of the best of the adult game simulators are those that recreate the stock, real estate, and commodities markets. They are startlingly realistic. They let players dip their feet into the volatile market for stock options without having to take a real financial drubbing.

Computer technology now offers a way to bring more pleasure to viewers of old movies. Methods have been devised for turning black-and-white reels from the golden ages of television and Hollywood into so-called *colorized movies*. An example of the transformation is shown in Figure A-21.

Computers have also penetrated the way sports are run. This year's baseball season found more computers in major league dugouts than ever before. The Chicago White Sox team uses it to develop coaching

FIGURE A-20
This flight simulator puts users in the cockpit of a Cessna 182.
(Software: Flight Simulator, courtesy of Microsoft Corp.)

FIGURE A-21
Hollywood movies are transformed from black-and-white originals to new "colorized" versions.
(Courtesy of Colorization, Inc.)

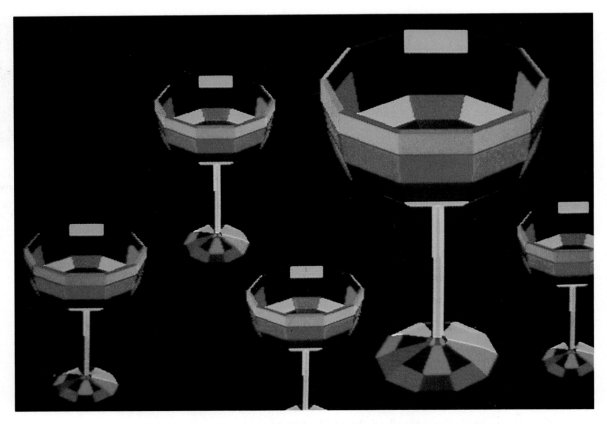

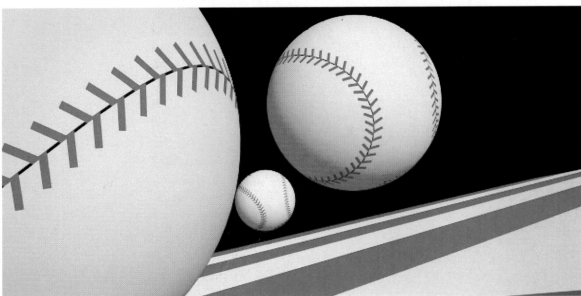

FIGURE A-22
Computer art
(Top: courtesy of PC World; *bottom: courtesy of Cranston/Csuri Productions, Columbus, OH)*

strategies. The New York Yankees use it for scouting activities. Almost all teams use it to compile their players' and teams' statistics.[13]

Amateur sports people use their personal computers in other ways. For example, they can

· Play 18 holes of golf indoors during the winter
· Monitor their running and weight-reduction progress on a regular basis
· Improve their tennis with programmed instruction

Music, Art, and Dance

FIGURE A-23
Eddie Dombrower, inventor of a notation scheme for the preservation of dances using a personal computer (Courtesy of Jerry Stoll/InfoWorld).

One of the newest revolutions in musical computing is occurring in classrooms. Computers serve as teachers, and software replaces the piano that schools cannot afford. More students have hands-on exposure to the strains of Mozart or the refrains of the newest "pop" artist. The only equipment needed is a personal computer with an attached music synthesizer that resembles a piano keyboard.

In another area, computer artists are turning out images like those shown in Figure A-22. The images are as sharp as photographs, yet as free from the bounds of reality as animated cartoons.

A personal computer is helping Eddie Dombrower, who appears in Figure A-23,[14] to develop a visual language to record dance movements that dancers and choreographers can understand. The language is called Dance on Microcomputer (DOM) Notation.

Mr. Dombrower's notation system presents new possibilities for the preservation of dances. The traditional notation system, called Labanotation, is made up of symbols that are difficult to learn. It takes a choreographer who knows Labanotation about six hours to record one minute of dance on paper. Most dance artists do not know or use it, so it is rare to find a dance recorded for posterity.

Mr. Dombrower is still refining his notation system. Eventually he hopes to produce disk libraries of classical repertoire.

INFORMATION AGE CHANGES

While the preceding examples demonstrate some of the good effects of computers on a society, there is another side. The final section of this appendix looks at changes that take place as a society becomes more computerized. Areas covered include the work environment, privacy, and computer crime.

Research shows that about two-thirds of the U.S. work force is now made up of information workers. These are white-collar professional and clerical workers. While "technology America" is growing rapidly,

---

[13] "Baseball Stats," *PC World*, September 1984, p. 34.
[14] Denise Caruso, "Computerized Choreography," *InfoWorld*, March 5, 1984, pp. 29–30.

"smokestack America" is not. The blue-collar work force is not growing as fast as the white-collar work force. One reason is that information and other services are given more and more attention in our society than is manufacturing. Another reason is that, increasingly, manual labor is being replaced by robots and other forms of automation.

Both these economies create unemployment because of computers. Studies of information workers, as an example, indicate that the percentage of middle managers is being reduced. So is the percentage of staff people whose main function has been getting information prepared for managers, to help them in their decision making. Companies are saying that, with the computer, managers can get and prepare their own information.

Social scientists predict that these changes are as significant to this generation as the Industrial Revolution was to an earlier generation. But no one alive today remembers firsthand the upheavals of that first industrial revolution. One historian suggests that its remembrance would cause all thoughtful people to give pause: What is to happen to the dispossessed? This problem must be addressed to ensure the vitality of a nation and the enlargement of its human and other resources.

One optimistic study predicts that the economy, as a whole, will prosper. Growth is expected to come from creative and innovative smaller companies. Within the past ten years, virtually all new jobs have been created by small businesses. They seem to adapt more quickly to new customer demands. They also have faster communication channels and often better information systems.

Work Environment

In a computer-based economy, workers are no longer bound to the traditional office. The term **telecommuting** has been used to describe homebound workers reporting to the office through their computers. The term **electronic cottage** describes a home where paid work is done with the help of a computer. It could be independent work or work done for an organization.

Right now this phenomenon resembles an evolution—one that is happening on an experimental basis. Blue Cross, the hospital insurance company, is more than satisfied with its cottage program.[15] Part-time employees work at home terminals to enter insurance claims. Some key about 2,000 claims a week. They are paid at a fixed rate for each claim.

Other companies are experimenting with the idea. But managers worry about employee productivity—how to get it, how to measure it. Employees fret over the possibility of stunted careers and the lack of outside human contact.

Some feel that business must first figure out how to dismantle its current way of organizing work. The concept of going to work came

---

[15] Ann Lallande, "Probing the Telecommuting Debate," *Business Computer Systems*, pp. 102–112.

about because people had to be together in one location to accomplish work. To manufacture, you went to the plant. To manage information, you went to the office. Telecommuting now allows an individual's ideas to go to work while the individual stays at home.

Electronic Watchdogs

Managers are solving the problem of measuring employee productivity in ways that are worrying some union, government, and labor officials. They claim that the **electronic monitoring** systems being used are causing stress and dehumanizing employees.

As an example, Vaughn Forter has a black box the size of a dictionary that sits in a compartment above his truck's right front tire.[16] At the end of his trip, his boss at Leprino Foods Company in Denver, Colorado, pulls a cartridge out of the box and pops it into a personal computer. In seconds the computer prints out a report showing all the times the truck was speeding.

Leprino's monitoring system was installed only after repeated urgings about speeding failed. Truckers who drive too fast

- Strain engines
- Get too few miles per gallon
- Run up undue maintenance bills

Now a trucker gets 3 cents a mile bonus for every trip made without breaking the 55 miles-per-hour speed limit. After three offenses of driving over 65 miles per hour, a trucker is fired.

While the truckers do not like the "watchdog," supervisors find that they save the company three times their investment in one year. The reduction includes lower insurance costs because of the declining accident rate. The objectives of Leprino's workers and supervisors, as well as those in other organizations, are expected to continue to clash while ironing out an equitable way to serve both ends.

PRIVACY

A personal concern of many individuals in an information society is privacy. Figure A-24 identifies only a few of the many databases, or *data banks*, that currently exist about residents in the United States.

People have a natural concern that information about them

- Is used properly
- Is protected against improper access
- Contains accurate facts

---

[16] Michael W. Miller, "Computers Keep Eye on Workers and See If They Perform Well," *Wall Street Journal*, June 3, 1985, pp. 1, 15.

Laws that help people to protect their privacy include

- *Federal Privacy Act* (1974)—prohibits the government and its contractors from keeping secret personal files on individuals.
- *Freedom of Information Act* (1970)—allows anyone access to any federal agency records kept about them.

FIGURE A-24
Some federally owned data banks with
information about U.S. citizens
(Source: Office of Management and Budget)

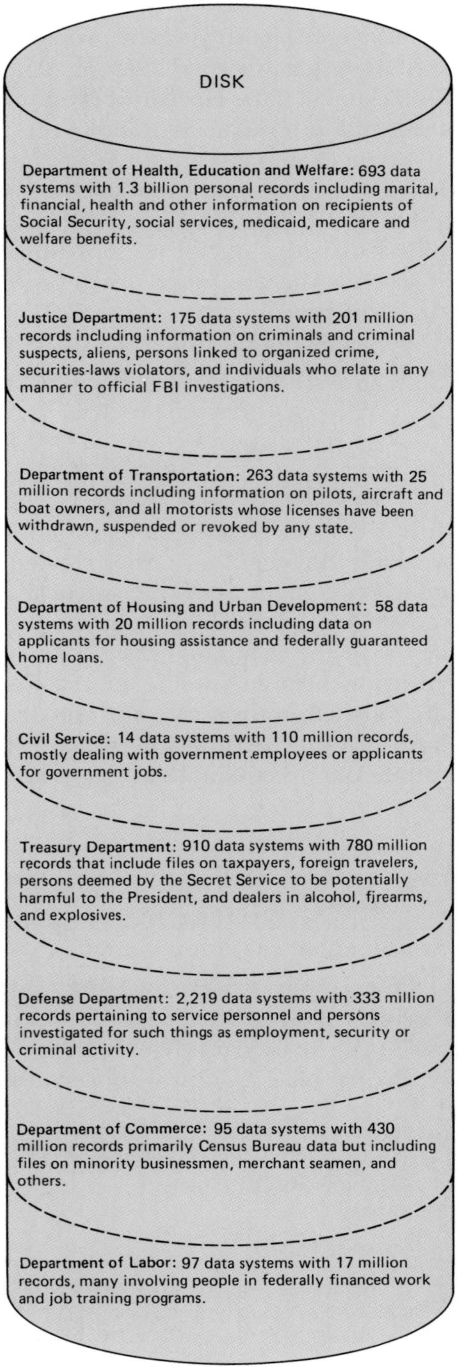

DISK

Department of Health, Education and Welfare: 693 data systems with 1.3 billion personal records including marital, financial, health and other information on recipients of Social Security, social services, medicaid, medicare and welfare benefits.

Justice Department: 175 data systems with 201 million records including information on criminals and criminal suspects, aliens, persons linked to organized crime, securities-laws violators, and individuals who relate in any manner to official FBI investigations.

Department of Transportation: 263 data systems with 25 million records including information on pilots, aircraft and boat owners, and all motorists whose licenses have been withdrawn, suspended or revoked by any state.

Department of Housing and Urban Development: 58 data systems with 20 million records including data on applicants for housing assistance and federally guaranteed home loans.

Civil Service: 14 data systems with 110 million records, mostly dealing with government employees or applicants for government jobs.

Treasury Department: 910 data systems with 780 million records that include files on taxpayers, foreign travelers, persons deemed by the Secret Service to be potentially harmful to the President, and dealers in alcohol, firearms, and explosives.

Defense Department: 2,219 data systems with 333 million records pertaining to service personnel and persons investigated for such things as employment, security or criminal activity.

Department of Commerce: 95 data systems with 430 million records primarily Census Bureau data but including files on minority businessmen, merchant seamen, and others.

Department of Labor: 97 data systems with 17 million records, many involving people in federally financed work and job training programs.

- *Fair Credit Reporting Act* (1970)—allows anyone access to credit bureau records kept on them. It also allows a person to challenge the records if they are inaccurate.

But the concern over the misuse of computer-based information continues to be an issue. As an example, political groups, private companies, and others take information from sources like telephone directories, voter registration rolls, and land ownership records. Often the records, once stored in a computer, are used for purposes different from those for which the information was originally gathered. The potential for misuse looms as a serious threat to a society devoted to freedom.

COMPUTER CRIME

Misuse of computer information can be extended to include computer crime. **Computer crime** refers to all uses of computers to

- *Steal money or goods*—like the bank teller who uses knowledge of the bank's system to embezzle money from inactive customer accounts.
- *Steal information*—like the accountant who steals a list of selected customer names for personal profit-making purposes.
- *Industrial espionage*, or stealing proprietary business information—like taking or selling trade secrets or product formulas to a rival company or nation.
- *Steal computer time*—like the administrator who uses access to a company computer to keep personal records for his social club's bowling league, or more seriously, uses the company's computer to run a side business.
- *Steal software*—like anyone who illegally copies a friend's or company's software for private purposes. This is typically called **piracy.**

Computer criminals are usually people employed in positions of trust. They have no prior criminal record and are well educated. Their profiles superficially make them desirable employees.

Hackers

The slang term **hacker** means anyone whose hobby is studying how computers work. Often hackers are young people who find penetrating someone else's computer a challenge. They do not see themselves as criminals, although they are aware of the malicious nature of their intent.

Four 13-year-old boys, as an example, gained access to two Canadian firms' computers through dial-up public networks. They blocked out legitimate users and destroyed files. The Royal Canadian Mounted Police and the United States Federal Bureau of Investigation cooperated in tracking and apprending the hackers.

Laws and Ethics

Federal and state laws are emerging to deal with computer crime. One state imposes a $20,000 fine and five years in jail for most of the cases already described that involve stealing. Hackers come under a different penalty plan.

Professional organizations in the information industry, like the Data Processing Management Association, require members to maintain and support ethical behavior. Since computing has spread well beyond computer professionals, an ethical attitude toward computing concerns a much greater population. All computer users must consciously monitor and assess their own actions to prevent criminal behavior.

FUTURE

Edward A. Feigenbaum, Stanford University professor and author, says of the future of computers in society:

> Knowledge is power, and the computer is an amplifier of that power. Those nations that master new knowledge technology will have a cultural and political ascendancy. The information processing industry, which is destined to be the world's largest industry by the year 2000, exists to serve human information processing needs. But very few of those needs involve calculating numbers or storing and retrieving data. Most human work involves knowledge, reasoning, and thought.[17]

The promise of artificial intelligence underlies Dr. Feigenbaum's comment. Future computer hardware and software are expected to amplify human knowledge and thought processes. Some early versions of these products are already in service.

---

[17] Quoted in "PC World View," *PC World*, September 1984, p. 34.

CASE STUDY: Examining Megatrends

We are living in a time of parentheses, according to John Naisbitt, author of the best-seller *Megatrends*. It is the time between eras. "Amid the sometimes painful and uncertain present, the restructuring of America proceeds unrelentingly," he writes. Nevertheless, "We have not quite left behind the America of the past—centralized, industrialized and economically self-contained. We are clinging to the known past in fear of the unknown future."

Naisbitt's Washington, D.C.-based consulting firm conducts research on social, economic, political, and technological movements in the United States. Among his clients are AT&T, United Technologies corporation, Control Data Corporation, and Atlantic Richfield Company.

Naisbitt's research group uses a trend extrapolation methodology consisting of three components:

- *Content Analysis.*   About 6,000 newspapers, both United States and foreign, are examined each month. Content analysis effectively monitors social change because the news hole is a closed system. When something new is introduced, something else must be omitted.
- *Analysis of activities in bellwether states.*   In interpreting its research data, the Naisbitt group learned that there are five states in which most social innovation occurs in this country. The other 45 are, in effect, followers. The key indicator state is California, with Florida a close second. The other three trend-setting states are Washington, Colorado, and Connecticut.
- *Extrapolation.*   "Trends, like horses, are easier to ride in the direction that they are already going," Naisbitt says. "You may decide to buck the trend, but it is still helpful to know it is there."

Three of Naisbitt's ten megatrends are summarized here.

Megatrend #1: *Although we continue to think we live in an industrial society, we have, in fact, changed to an economy based on the creation of information*. For the first time, our economy is based on a key resource that is not only renewable but self-generating. The telephone, computer, and television have merged into an integrated communications system. It will fuel the information society the way energy (electric, oil, nuclear) kept the industrial society humming and the way natural power (wind, water, and brute force) sustained the agricultural society.

For example, between 6,000 and 7,000 scientific articles are written each day. Scientific and technical information now increases 13 percent per year. That means it doubles every 5¼ years. But the rate will soon jump to perhaps 40 percent per year. This is attributed to new, more powerful information systems and an increasing population of scientists. That means the data will double every 20 months.

In the information society, we have systematized the production of knowledge and amplified our brainpower. To use an industrial metaphor, we now mass-produce knowledge. This knowledge is the driving force of our economy.

Computer skills will be needed in up to 75 percent of all jobs by 1990. Being without computer skills is like wandering around the Library of Congress with all the books arranged at random, with no card catalog and no friendly librarian to serve your information needs.

Megatrend #2: *We are moving in the dual direction of high tech/high touch, matching each new technology with a compensatory human response*. When we moved from an agricultural to an industrial society, we moved more industry into our farms. In about 1800, 90 percent of our population produced 100 percent of the food. Today, only 3 percent of the population produces 120 percent of the food we need.

We will increasingly run our factories with information rather than laborers. Robots will play a big role.

We must learn to balance technology with human spiritual demands. Indeed, something else has been growing alongside the technological invasion. For example, as hospitals become environments of fluorescent lights, stainless steel, and computers, home births are growing more common. An increasing number of chronically ill patients are choosing hospice care. The more technology we introduce into society, the more people will want to be with other people.

Megatrend #3: *No longer do we have the luxury of operating within an isolated, self-sufficient, national economic system. We must acknowledge that we are part of a global economy*. During the past decade, the Third World has begun to take up most of the world's industrial tasks. By the year 2000, Third World countries will manufacture as much as 30 percent of the world's goods.

Rather than reinvest in the industries that once made this country, the United States must move toward enterprises of the future.

(*SOURCE: John Naisbitt,* Megatrends, *Warner Books, New York, 1984. Adapted with permission from Warner Books, New York, and Macdonald/Futura, London.*)

DISCUSSION QUESTIONS

1. What evidence suggests that we have changed to an economy based on the creation of information?

2. Do you agree that the United States must move toward enterprises of the future rather than rein-vest in the industries that once made the country? Why? What would you recommend to future entre-preneurs?

CHAPTER SUMMARY

- Computers, as we know them today, began in early 1940 with the *ABC Computer*. It influenced the de-sign of *ENIAC*, the first large-scale computer ever built.

- Early computers were designed for military pur-poses.

- *Vacuum tubes* provided the electronic circuitry in *first-generation* computers.

- The *stored program concept* is to read a program into memory for processing. It is a standard today. Early computers were *hard-wired*. If their job changed, wires had to be changed.

- The first business computer, the UNIVAC I, was delivered to process the 1950 national census.

- *IBM* emerged as a computer industry leader in 1956.

- *Second-generation* computers used *transistors* instead of vacuum tube circuitry. They were faster, smaller, and less expensive than first-generation computers.

- During the 1950s, programming languages like *COBOL*, *FORTRAN*, and *LISP* were developed.

- The first minicomputer appeared in the 1960s.

- *Third-generation* computers used *integrated circuit* technology which is still in use today.

- The motivation for the development of *time-sharing* software was the delay associated with waiting for *batch processing*. Time sharing, in turn, spurred the development of the interactive BASIC progam-ming language which allowed nontechnical people to program the computer.

- *Large-scale integration* (LSI) chips contain over 15,000 circuits on a single chip. Some industry analysts consider their use, in the 1970s, to mark a *fourth generation* of computers.

- A *microprocessor chip* contained all the major logical circuitry for a computer on one chip. Intel made the first chip in 1971. It served as the "brain" of the first assembled *microcomputer*, also called a *per-sonal computer*, by 1978.

- *VisiCalc* was the first software, an electronic spread-sheet program, responsible for the sale of computer hardware.

- Examples of how computers are used in various areas of today's society include the following:
  Health care: A robot arm helps with brain surgery that is safer, faster, and less invasive than current surgical procedures.
  Handicapped: Adapted computers are transforming the dedication and drive of millions of handicapped individuals into a significant human resource.
  Home: Families are using computers in the home for replacing TV, preparing budgets and taxes, playing games, pursuing education, and subscrib-ing to electronic services.
  Communities: Computers are helping firefighters in towns and in forest ranges to provide better levels of services.
  Education: Computers are changing the way stu-dents learn through computer-assisted instruction and simulation programs.
  Research: Computers are facilitating research in such diverse areas as hereditary diseases, Shake-spearean metrics, and military vehicles.

- While "technology America" is growing rapidly, "smokestack America" is not.

- *Telecommuting* has been used to describe home-bound workers reporting to the office through their computers.

- The *electronic cottage* describes a home where paid work is done with the help of a computer.

- Electronic monitoring of employees and their prod-uctivity is causing a labor problem.

- People are concerned about the misuse of com-puter-based information held in *data banks*. Laws help individuals to protect their privacy.

- *Computer crime* includes stealing information, computer time, and software. Illegally copying software is called *piracy*.

- A *hacker* is anyone whose hobby is studying how computers work.

KEY TERMS

ABC Computer
Authoring system
BASIC
Batch processing
COBOL
Computer-aided design (CAD)
Computer-assisted instruction
  (CAI)
Computer crime
Distributed data processing
Electronic cottage
Electronic monitoring
ENIAC
Expert system
First-generation computers
FORTRAN
Fourth-generation computers
Hacker
Hard-wired
IBM
Integrated circuit
Interactive

Large-scale integration (LSI)
Local-area network
Machine language
Microcomputer
Microprocessor
Minicomputer
Natural language
Personal computer
Piracy
Program language
Public communication service
Second-generation computers
Silicon chip
Stored program concept
Supercomputer
Telecommuting
Third-generation computers
Time sharing
Transistors
UNIVAC
Vacuum tube
VisiCalc

REVIEW QUESTIONS

1. When were computers, as we know them, first developed?

2. What provided the electronic circuitry of the first computer?

3. Why was the invention of the *stored program* concept significant?

4. What was the first task of the first business computer in 1950?

5. What marked the emergence of second-generation computers?

6. What were some of the programming languages developed during the 1950s?

7. When did the first minicomputer appear?

8. What marked the emergence of third-generation computers?

9. What motivated the development of time-sharing software and the BASIC language?

10. What does LSI mean?

11. When did assembled microcomputers, or personal computers, first appear?

12. What was the first type of software program that was responsible for the sale of computer hardware?

13. Give one example of how computers are used for each of the following:
   a. Health care
   b. Handicapped people
   c. Home
   d. Community service
   e. Education
   f. Research support

14. Identify one social issue related to the impact of computers in each of the following areas:
   a. Workplace
   b. Privacy
   c. Crime

EXERCISES

1. Borrow a copy of John Naisbitt's *Megatrends* (New York: Warner Books, 1984) from your library. Read it to prepare an oral or written report on the seven megatrends not covered in the Case Study, "Examining Megatrends."

2. Examine your local newspaper and clip any computer articles. After doing this for two weeks, prepare an oral or written report that summarizes each social issue addressed. Each summarized issue should be followed by your own analysis and opinion about the issue addressed.

3. Research how personal computers are being used in your community. Select one example to do a researched written or oral report that answers the following questions:
   - Who uses the computer?
   - What is it being used for? (Provide specific examples and even computer printouts, if available.)
   - When is it used?
   - Where is it used?
   - Why is it used?
   - What hardware is used? How much did it cost?
   - What software is used? Where did it come from? Did someone program it? What language was used to program it?
   - What training was necessary to use the hardware and software?
   - What problems have been experienced?
   - What benefits have been experienced?
   - How has the computer changed the way things are done?

Include anything else that would be relevant to "flesh out" your report. This could include profiles of the computer users and their reaction to learning about and using computers.

Appendix B

Number and Code Systems

How does the computer do arithmetic when all it works with are 1's and 0's? This appendix examines the characteristics of the binary, or base 2, number system. It looks at how *binary digits*, or "bits," perform addition and are converted to decimal numbers. It covers the same topics again with the hexadecimal number system. It concludes with a review of computer code systems.

BINARY NUMBER SYSTEM

The binary number system that does all the calculation inside a computer can be thought of as the collection of lights diagrammed in Figure B-1. Each light can be turned "on" or "off." When a light is "on," it is a signal to use the number, or value, equal to its position.

As an example, look at the binary representation for a number 7. It consists of three "on" signals. Reading from right to left, it is interpreted as follows:

Column Position	Positional Value
1	1
2	2
3	4

The sum of positional values is $1 + 2 + 4 = 7$.

Conventional form uses the shorthand symbol of "power" or "exponent" to express position. A power is shown as a raised number next to a base number, like 2^2, which represents 4.

Although the binary system is built on a base of 2, it only uses the numbers 0 and 1. It is similar in concept to the familiar decimal system, which has a base of 10 but uses only the numbers 0–9.

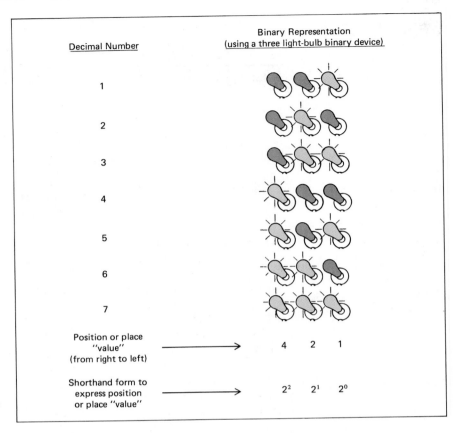

FIGURE B-1
Characteristics of the binary number system

FIGURE B-2
Number systems use positional "values."

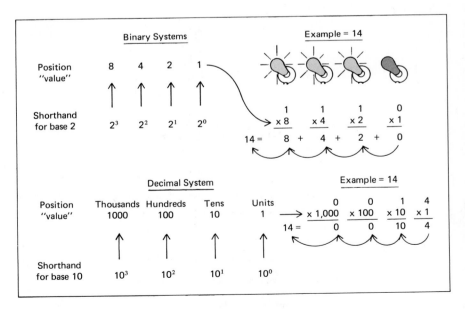

As Figure B-2 shows, both the decimal and binary number systems use positional values. Some decimal system positions follow:

Position	Position Value
1	Units
2	Tens
3	Hundreds
4	Thousands

The decimal number 14, as an example, consists of 4 unit values and 1 tens value.

By contrast, to represent the number 14 in the binary system requires that positions 2, 3, and 4 be "on." The sum of the positional values is $2 + 4 + 8 = 14$. Figure B-3 identifies, in more detail, some positional values associated with the binary number system.

FIGURE B-3
Incremental positional values in the
binary number system

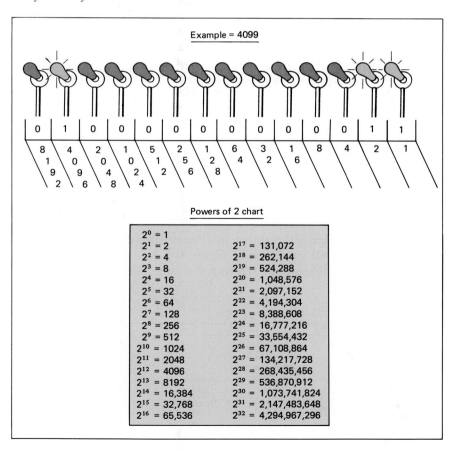

Example = 4099

| 0 | 1 | 0 | 0 | 0 | 0 | 0 | 0 | 0 | 0 | 0 | 0 | 1 | 1 |

Powers of 2 chart

$2^0 = 1$
$2^1 = 2$
$2^2 = 4$
$2^3 = 8$
$2^4 = 16$
$2^5 = 32$
$2^6 = 64$
$2^7 = 128$
$2^8 = 256$
$2^9 = 512$
$2^{10} = 1024$
$2^{11} = 2048$
$2^{12} = 4096$
$2^{13} = 8192$
$2^{14} = 16,384$
$2^{15} = 32,768$
$2^{16} = 65,536$

$2^{17} = 131,072$
$2^{18} = 262,144$
$2^{19} = 524,288$
$2^{20} = 1,048,576$
$2^{21} = 2,097,152$
$2^{22} = 4,194,304$
$2^{23} = 8,388,608$
$2^{24} = 16,777,216$
$2^{25} = 33,554,432$
$2^{26} = 67,108,864$
$2^{27} = 134,217,728$
$2^{28} = 268,435,456$
$2^{29} = 536,870,912$
$2^{30} = 1,073,741,824$
$2^{31} = 2,147,483,648$
$2^{32} = 4,294,967,296$

Binary Addition

Some binary arithmetic processes, like the addition shown in Figure B-4, are similar to decimal arithmetic. But the binary addition may look confusing because there are no symbols beyond 1 and 0 to use.

To see how addition works in the binary number system, it helps to review the ordinary process of decimal addition. As an example, to add 7 + 7, which is 14:

1. Put down the 4 in the units column.
2. Carry the 1 to the tens column.
3. Since there are no numbers in the tens column, just "bring down" the 1 that is "carried over" to complete the result.

To apply the same process to the binary example, work from the right to the left column and

1. Add 1 + 1, which is 2 and is represented in binary as 10. Put down the 0 in the first column and carry the 1.
2. Add 1 + 1, which is 2 plus the "carry over" of 1, which results in 3 and is represented in binary as 11. Put down a 1 and carry the other 1.
3. Repeat step 2.
4. Since there are no numbers to add the last "carry-over," just "bring down" the 1 that is "carried over" to complete the result.

The binary example in Figure B-2 provides evidence that the binary addition answer in Figure B-4 is correct.

While this provides an example of how binary arithmetic works, it does get more complex. Even having more than two numbers to add can prove confusing for humans. Fortunately, humans do not have to do binary arithmetic to work effectively with computers.

Decimal Conversion to Binary

To convert a decimal number to a binary number, the "remainder method" can be used, as shown in Figure B-5.

The "remainder method" requires dividing a decimal number by 2

FIGURE B-4
Binary addition is similar to decimal addition.

BINARY ADDITION		EQUIVALENT DECIMAL ADDITION
111	⟶	7
+111	⟶	+7
1110	⟶	14

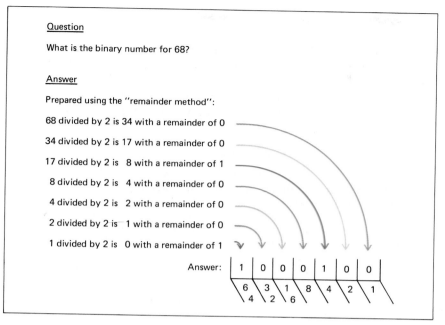

FIGURE B-5
Converting a decimal to a binary number

through several iterations. When no more answers are left to divide by 2, the process is finished. The binary value is made up of the collection of "remainders" that result. The most significant digit of the binary value is the final remainder.

This "remainder method" is useful to convert decimal numbers to any other number system. It requires only changing the number system base as the divisor. Some other number systems that computer professionals work with are octal (base 8) and hexadecimal (base 16).

HEXADECIMAL NUMBER SYSTEMS

Humans are not as good as computers when working with page after page of all 1's and 0's. Computer scientists and others prefer to work, instead, with the hexadecimal number system. It has a base of 16, as shown in Figure B-6.

Hexadecimal numbers range from 0 to 9 and then switch to the alphabet at decimal 10. Ten to 15 are conveniently represented by a single alphabetic character.

The hexadecimal number system is often encountered when examining a snapshot of memory, called a *memory dump*. It is a printed listing of the computer's memory at any given moment of time. It is often used to investigate processing problems. The printout consists of row

Decimal Number	Hexadecimal (Base 16) Equivalent	Binary Equivalent
0	0	0000
1	1	0001
2	2	0010
3	3	0011
4	4	0100
5	5	0101
6	6	0110
7	7	0111
8	8	1000
9	9	1001
10	A	1010
11	B	1011
12	C	1100
13	D	1101
14	E	1110
15	F	1111

Binary digits in memory ⟶ 1 1 1 0   4 digits

Decimal equivalent   1 4

Hexadecimal equivalent   E   1 digit

Binary numbers are easier to interpret if they are separated into groups of four digits and then converted to a hexadecimal equivalent.

FIGURE B-6
Binary-to-hexadecimal conversion

on row of hexadecimal numbers. As the example in Figure B-7 implies, one 8-bit byte of memory is represented on a memory dump as two hexadecimal numbers. This represents a 4 to 1 reduction of data, which makes the investigation into memory problems more manageable.

Consulting a chart, similar to the one in Figure B-6, is a convenient way to convert groups of four binary digits to hexadecimal equivalents.

FIGURE B-7
One byte requires two hexadecimal numbers.

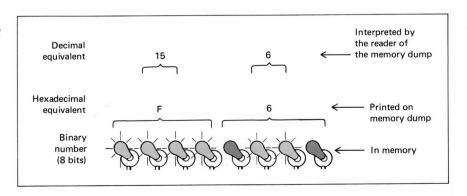

Hexadecimal Arithmetic

To solve memory dump problems often involves adding and subtracting hexadecimal numbers. An easy way to do this:

1. Convert the hexadecimal value to decimal.
2. Add or subtract in decimal.
3. Convert the answer back to hexadecimal.

Some examples are given in Figure B-8. The first addition example is fairly straightforward, using the chart in Figure B-6 as a reference:

- Hexadecimal B converts to decimal 11.
- Hexadecimal 4 converts to decimal 4.
- Adding 11 + 4 results in decimal 15, which the chart shows is equivalent to hexadecimal F.

In the second addition example, each column is treated separately. When hexadecimal C(11) and B(12) are added, the result is 23. For any number above 15, the procedure is to

1. Subtract 16, which is the base of the hexadecimal number system, from the sum (in this case, it is 23 − 16 = 7)

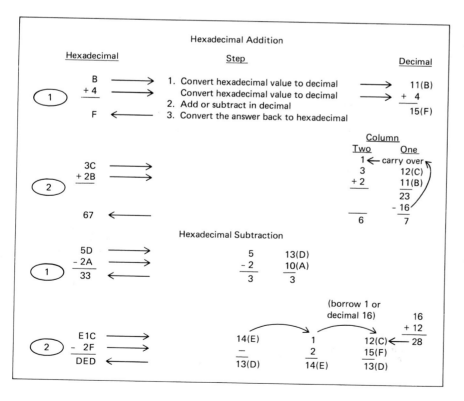

FIGURE B-8
Hexadecimal addition and subtraction

2. Place the answer, in this case 7, in the column and carry a 1 to the next column

Each column is treated in the same way.

Subtraction is similar, as the examples indicate. The second subtraction example shows that when a "borrow" occurs, it is for the decimal value 16, the base of the hexadecimal number system.

Contrast to Code Systems

Generally, numeric data are processed in memory using the binary number system. But some numbers never have arithmetic operations performed on them. An example may be a zip code like 12491. This zip code is stored in memory as an *alphanumeric* character, and not a number.

Programmers tell the computer how to treat numbers. Using the BASIC programming language as an example, a programmer might indicate the following data for computer entry:

BASIC Data Name	*Actual Data*
ZIP.CODE$	Zip Code
TAX.AMOUNT	Taxes

In BASIC, the $ symbol in a data name tells the computer that the actual data, like zip code, are to be stored as "character" data. The data will not be used for arithmetic operations.

By contrast, the absence of a $ symbol in a data name tells the computer that the actual data, like taxes, are to be used in arithmetic calculations. Such data are stored as binary numbers ready for all arithmetic operations.

The two most common code systems that computers use to store "character" data are the following:

Code System	*Description*
ASCII (pronounced AS key)	American Standard Code for Information Interchange. It is a 7-bit code scheme that adds an eighth check bit to get a regular 8-bit byte (pronounced *bite*). Personal computers and most data communications use the ASCII code to represent character data.
EBCDIC (pronounced eb SEE dick)	Extended Binary Coded Decimal Interchange Code. It is an 8-bit code scheme developed by IBM and is used mainly on IBM mainframe computers.

Examples of binary bit patterns for both coding systems are given in Figure B-9.

FIGURE B-9
Computer code system bit patterns

CHARACTER	ASCII 7-BIT CODE	EBCDIC 8-BIT CODE
A	1000001	11000001
B	1000010	11000010
C	1000011	11000011
D	1000100	11000100
E	1000101	11000101
F	1000110	11000110
G	1000111	11000111
H	1001000	11001000
I	1001001	11001001
J	1001010	11010001
K	1001011	11010010
L	1001100	11010011
M	1001101	11010100
N	1001110	11010101
O	1001111	11010110
P	1010000	11010111
Q	1010001	11011000
R	1010010	11011001
S	1010011	11100010
T	1010100	11100011
U	1010101	11100100
V	1010110	11100101
W	1010111	11100110
X	1011000	11100111
Y	1011001	11101000
Z	1011010	11101001
0	0110000	11110000
1	0110001	11110001
2	0110010	11110010
3	0110011	11110011
4	0110100	11110100
5	0110101	11110101
6	0110110	11110110
7	0110111	11110111
8	0111000	11111000
9	0111001	11111001

REVIEW QUESTIONS

1. How are the binary and decimal number systems similar?

2. Explain the process of binary addition, using 101 + 111 as the example.

3. How is the "remainder method" used to convert a decimal number to a binary number? Use 67 as the example.

4. What is the base of the hexadecimal number system?

5. What is a memory dump used for? What number system is it printed in?

6. What is a convenient way to convert binary numbers to hexadecimal equivalents, or vice versa?

7. Explain the process of hexadecimal arithmetic, using 2A + 3C as an example, and hexadecimal subtraction, using D1C − 2E as an example.

8. How are character data different from numeric data in a computer's memory? Write your first name using first the ASCII and then the EBCDIC code systems. The table in Figure B-9 should be used for guidance.

Appendix C

ASCII Code Chart

The ASCII, American Standard Code for Information Interchange, character set shown with its three-digit so-called "decimal" code, which is a "shorthand" for the seven-bit binary representation of each character.

ASCII CODE	CHARACTER	ASCII CODE	CHARACTER	ASCII CODE	CHARACTER	ASCII CODE	CHARACTER
000	Null	032	(space)	064	@	096	
001		033	!	065	A	097	a
002		034	"	066	B	098	b
003		035	#	067	C	099	c
004		036	$	068	D	100	d
005		037	%	069	E	101	e
006		038	&	070	F	102	f
007	beep or bell	039	'	071	G	103	g
008		040	(	072	H	104	h
009	tab	041	)	073	I	105	i
010	line feed	042	*	074	J	106	j
011		043	+	075	K	107	k
012		044	,	076	L	108	l
013	carriage return	045	–	077	M	109	m
014		046	.	078	N	110	n
015		047	/	079	O	111	o
016		048	0	080	P	112	p
017		049	1	081	Q	113	q
018		050	2	082	R	114	r
019		051	3	083	S	115	s
020		052	4	084	T	116	t
021		053	5	085	U	117	u
022		054	6	086	V	118	v
023		055	7	087	W	119	w
024		056	8	088	X	120	x
025		057	9	089	Y	121	y
026		058	:	090	Z	122	z
027		059	;	091	[	123	{
028	right	060	<	092	\	124	¦
029	left	061	=	093	]	125	}
030	up	062	>	094	∧	126	~
031	down	063	?	095	—	127	⬦

Codes 028–031 (right, left, up, down) are grouped as "cursor movement".

Glossary

ABC Computer The Atanasoff-Berry-Computer from 1940, the forerunner of the first large-scale computers.

accelerator board or card A circuit board with a newer microprocessor on it than the one already installed. Accelerator boards enable owners of older computers to upgrade without purchasing all new hardware.

accounting package Commercially available software that automates the routine accounting functions of small-to-medium sized organizations; usually provides management information.

add-ins *See* add-ons.

add-ons Packages created to add value to other, more widely used packages; also called add-ins.

advanced program-to-program communications (APPC) An IBM standard for communication between computers.

aged trial balance A common report produced by accounting packages which lists customer balances according to how old the balance is since the billing date.

alignment *See* Chapter 13, Desktop Publishing Glossary.

analog graphics standard A color display standard characterized by an ability to display as many as 256 colors simultaneously.

analog signals The signals sent over normal telephone lines.

analytic graphics Use of graphics for personal data analysis.

animation Continuous movement graphics.

application development software packages Computer programs that guide users in developing custom software.

application software Software that makes the hard-

ware perform a meaningful user task, such as word processing or order processing.

architecture A term that refers to the overall design of how a computer is built to handle its input-processing-output functions.

arithmetic/logic unit A component of the central processing unit that calculates and compares data when instructed by the control unit.

arrow key *See* cursor control key.

artificial intelligence Term used for computer systems that mimic human behavior, such as robot systems, knowledge-based systems, and natural language systems.

ASCII American Standard Code for Information Interchange, a 7-bit code system that dominates microcomputer hardware.

ASCII file *See* Chapter 13, Desktop Publishing Glossary.

asynchronous communication Communication in which characters are transmitted with random idle periods between characters.

authoring system Software package permitting nonprogrammers to create instructional programs.

auto-answer A feature of data communication software which allows a computer to accept incoming data communications.

auto-dial The capability of communication software to automatically dial a phone number listed in its dialing directory.

automated office An office with linked computers that facilitates the exchange of information.

backup The process of copying a file or an entire disk so that data are not lost when a disk is damaged.

backward compatibility *See* downward compatibility.

balance sheet An accounting document that provides a snapshot view of a company at a fixed moment in time.

bandwidth   The bits-per-second transmission capacity of a data communication line.

baseband   A communication system operating within a narrow frequency, thus limiting the number of signals it can transmit at one time.

BASIC   Acronym for Beginner's All-purpose Symbolic Instruction Code, a popular computer language developed in the 1960's.

basic input/output system (BIOS)   A set of operating system programs that controls the flow of data into and out of the computer.

batch processing   A data processing system in which input data are stored and processed as time becomes available; processing is not interactive and usually entails waiting.

baud rate   The bits-per-second (bps) transmission rate of data over a communication line.

binary system   A two-state system.

bit   One binary digit.

bit map image file   *See* Chapter 13, Desktop Publishing Glossary.

bit-mapped font   *See* Chapter 13, Desktop Publishing Glossary.

bit-mapped images   Images stored by painting packages; the location of each dot making up the image is recorded, allowing for the individual manipulation of the pixels.

bits-per-second (bps)   A measure of the information that can be transmitted by a communication device.

bootstrap program   The part of a system that operates when the computer is first turned on.

broadband   A communication system which can transmit many signals simultaneously.

bugs   Errors in a computer program.

built-in font   *See* Chapter 13, Desktop Publishing Glossary.

built-in function   Prepared formulas, like sum, average, and count, that are built into software.

bus   (1) A single cable which links workstations in a bus network. (2) The electronic roadways that are etched into a circuit board.

bus network   A local area network topology which links workstations to a single cable; normally workstations must contend with each other for use of the transmission line.

business graphics   Analytic and presentation graphics.

byte   A group of 8 bits creating the fundamental unit with which a computer works.

CAP   *See* Chapter 13, Desktop Publishing Glossary.

caption bar   The top line across the top of each window on the screen that indicates the currently loaded program name.

carrier   (1) Plastic unit that houses integrated circuit chips. (2) Characteristic high-pitched sound produced by a modem.

cathode ray tube (CRT)   The display technology used by color and monochrome monitors; it is the same technology that is used in ordinary television sets.

CD ROM databases   Databases provided on a CD ROM disk that allow users to browse through information at leisure without incurring charges associated with on-line database use.

cell   The intersection of a column and a row on a spreadsheet; also called coordinate.

cell pointer   A visual indication of which cell is currently activated.

cell range   A group of linked cells.

central wiring hub   A component of a ring network which functions to keep the network "up" by detecting problems with connected workstations.

certainty factor   Margin of confidence included in a conclusion derived by knowledge-based system.

central processing unit (CPU)   The "brain" of a computer that works on, or processes, input and generates output.

chart of account   An account numbering system used in a general ledger application.

circuit board   A web of electronic components and pathways designed to perform one or more functions, such as a display circuit board; the common way to attach devices to the system unit.

circuit-switching device   An inexpensive hardware device that serves as an alternative to expensive local area networks; it is most appropriate for organizations that do not need heavy workload and multiuser capabilities.

clip art   Prestored symbol libraries used in preparing graphics.

clipboard   A mechanism in a window package which allows two applications to exchange data through "copy" and "paste" selections.

clone   *See* compatible computer.

coaxial cable   A high-frequency transmission cable.

COBOL (*COmmon Business Oriented Language*)   A third-generation programming language widely used for business applications on large computers.

cocomputing   Collaborating with others on the same project using a remote computing package.

cold boot   A term for starting a personal computer that has been off.

color gun   The component of a cathode ray tube (CRT) which shoots an electron beam at the phosphor dots on the back of the display screen; a monochrome display uses one color gun and a color display uses three.

command   An instruction to a computer to perform a function.

command key   A keyboard key used to issue a command.

command mode   The absence of menus in a software application.

communication software   Software that enables sharing computer file information and hardware. It also enables the use of on-line databases and other services.

compatibility   The capability of application software written for old operating system versions to be used on newer versions.

compatible computer   A personal computer that mimics the PC standard; also called clone.

compiler   One type of language processor; it translates source code into machine language.

composite monitors   Computer displays that use a simple composite video color signal.

computer-aided design (CAD)   Type of program used to create and manipulate precision-drawn objects.

computer-aided manufacture (CAM)   Production of goods by robots that can accommodate rapid design changes and product customization.

computer-assisted instruction (CAI)   Instruction in which students learn with the aid of computer programs.

computer branch exchange (CBX)   *See* private branch exchange.

computer conferencing   A restricted form of bulletin board system with a conference notebook file and a member list control file.

computer crime   Stealing data, computer time, or software through illegal access to or manipulation of a computer system.

computer programmer   A professional who specializes in coding and debugging programs.

computer system   A group of interrelated items considered as a unit, consisting of hardware, software, people, and procedures.

conference notebook file   A file established in a computer conferencing system to hold conference messages.

consolidation   A spreadsheet feature that allows for the combination or merging of several spreadsheets to get a summary spreadsheet.

constant data   Items, like headings on a report, that do not change from report to report.

contention protocol   *See* ethernet.

context-sensitive help   A feature of word processing and other software which provides assistance appropriate to the action the software "senses" is causing a user to seek help.

continuous-tone image   *See* Chapter 13, Desktop Publishing Glossary.

control key   A key that triggers a command key sequence.

controller   A mainframe hardware device designed to off-load certain processing tasks from the CPU.

control unit   The component of the central processing unit that carries out program instructions.

conversion   Changing from one system to another.

copy   *See* Chapter 13, Desktop Publishing Glossary.

copy protected   A manufacturing procedure that prevents the copying of software or detects an unauthorized copy.

crippled copy   Disk supplied by its manufacturer for testing by a potential user; it is limited to a few records.

crop   *See* Chapter 13, Desktop Publishing Glossary.

CSMA/CD (Carrier Sense Multiple Access with Collision Detection)   *See* ethernet.

cursor   A tiny underscore on the screen which indicates the position where the next typed character will appear.

cursor control key   A key that moves the cursor around the current display, also called arrow key.

custom application   Software developed exclusively to suit a user's specific automation needs.

customer statement   A listing of a customer's unpaid invoices. Statements are usually generated once a month by a sales order processing application.

customizing   Introducing program modifications to tailor a package for a user.

cut and paste   Another name for a block move; the highlighting and moving of a block of text.

cut over   The switch to a new system at the end of the parallel testing period.

database   Collection of related files.

database administrator (DBA)   Individual in charge of overseeing all of an organization's database activity.

database management system (DBMS)   File management package that can work on several files at one time.

data file   Stores data that are created by, and used by, a program file.

data flow diagram A graphic model of a computer system.

data processing system Computer-based system for manipulating data to process routine transactions.

DBMS accounting package An accounting application that is built on top of a database management system (DBMS) package.

debugging The process of correcting programming errors.

decision assistant software Programs designed to analyze quantitative and qualitative problems.

Decision Support Specialist Helps users with model-building software, like spreadsheets and financial modeling software.

decision support system Programs designed for large organizations to support middle-level tactical and upper-level strategic managers in decision-making tasks.

decision support tool Applications such as financial modeling and spreadsheet packages which provide information to decision makers.

decision tree A structured set of interlocking rules, also called a "rule tree" or "search tree."

dedicated network server *See* network server.

defaults Preselected choices that simplify data entry.

demodulation The process of converting analog signals to digital signals.

desktop organizer An application that includes such things as a notepad, appointment book, clock, calendar, calculator, index card file, and telephone directory.

desktop publishing The use of microcomputers and appropriate software to create documents for publication purposes.

device independence (1) A software feature that allows an application to run with a variety of hardware peripherals. (2) *See* Chapter 13, Desktop Publishing Glossary.

dialing directory Stores the auto-dial phone numbers in communication software.

dialog box *See* Chapter 13, Desktop Publishing Glossary.

DIF (Data Interchange Format) A general spreadsheet file exchange format.

digital branch exchange (DBX) *See* private branch exchange.

digital graphics standard A color display standard characterized by a display of 16 simultaneous colors; all digital displays require a compatible display circuit board.

digitizer tablet A grid used to send X-Y coordinates to the computer.

digitizing Recreating an image into a series of computer readable dots.

direct access A method of sorting information in a computer system that allows it to be accessed in a random order.

directory A listing of all the files on a disk.

diskcopy A utility command which allows the user to make backup disks of programs and data.

disk drive A hardware component that houses, and physically provides access to disks during use by a program.

diskless workstation Desktop computers without local disk storage; also called LANstations.

disk operating system (DOS) Special software that manages a computer, preparing the hardware to accept application software, among other things.

disks Magnetic storage media for data and programs.

display TV-like screen or monitor.

distributed data processing A system in which computers are located throughout an organization.

document content architecture (DCA) An IBM internal format standard for document exchange; the two types are Revisable Form Text (DCA RFT) and Final Form Text (DCA FFT).

document header A feature that allows word processing users to describe a document and list the date created, author, typist, and any relevant comments desired.

document oriented *See* Chapter 13, Desktop Publishing Glossary.

document review package A stand-alone package that allows reviewers to create and attach notes in an organized manner to a word processing document.

dot-matrix printer A printer that arranges dots to form characters.

downloading Transmitting a file from a remote computer into one's own computer.

downward compatibility The ability of newer model microcomputers to run software which was designed for older standards.

drop cap *See* Chapter 13, Desktop Publishing Glossary.

drop-down menu *See* pull-down menu.

dynamic data exchange (DDE) A window package feature that automates data transfers between applications.

echo Simultaneous transmission of keyboarded character to a local display and a remote computer.

editing The process of revising or correcting a document.

editor A programmer tool which facilitates the typing and correction of lines of program code.

electronic bulletin board A communication system that makes messages available to any logged-on computer.

electronic conferencing A communication service that allows conferees to be in any place and to participate in an on-going conference at any time.

electronic cottage Home where paid work is done with the aid of a computer.

electronic mail The transfer of messages by electronic methods.

electronic monitoring A system used by some organizations to monitor employee productivity.

electronic spreadsheet A convenient tool to explore problems that can be defined numerically in row and column format.

embedded code *See* Chapter 13, Desktop Publishing Glossary.

English language command interface An add-on package which allows a user to type commands that resemble natural-language English.

ENIAC Acronym for Electronic Numerical Integrator And Computer, the first large-scale computer.

error correction A built-in method of catching and correcting errors in data that are transferred between modems.

ethernet protocol The "listen before talk" transmission protocol used in a bus network.

exception reports Reports that call a manager's attention to information that falls outside specified parameters.

executive subsystem A component of the operating system that makes all hardware and software work harmoniously.

expansion slots Places on a system board for inserting circuit boards that attach peripherals to the computer.

expert system A computer system that contains a knowledge base of facts and relationships contributed by experts and has the ability to make inferences on that knowledge base.

explanation facility Part of knowledge-based system that explains the line of reasoning behind conclusions.

export A file conversion function that transports a copy of a file in a format for use on foreign software.

family of products A group of related stand-alone products used to integrate applications.

fault-tolerant computing A feature of newer PC architecture which kicks in a duplicate hardware component the instant a failure is detected in a primary component.

feasibility report A formal, written report that details the economic, technological, and operational feasibility of a proposed development project.

feasibility study Formal analysis of a firm's computing requirements.

fiber optic cable A cable immune to electromagnetic interference over which a laser can transmit data.

field Slot in a record to hold data.

file A collection of records about one subject.

file and database management software Enables users to create file-based applications without programming.

file conversion *See* translation.

file locking A feature which prevents users, except the file owner, from destroying a file.

file management package File manager that works on only one file at a time.

file server *See* network server.

financial modeling package Software used to handle problems that have more dimensions and complex formulas that can easily be handled by spreadsheet packages.

first-generation computers The earliest computers, including the ABC computer and ENIAC.

flat-panel display A monitor that lies flat rather than standing upright; usually found on small portable microcomputers.

flier or flyer *See* Chapter 13, Desktop Publishing Glossary.

floppy disk A flexible disk used to store information in a microcomputer.

flow text or graphics *See* Chapter 13, Desktop Publishing Glossary.

flush right or right justified *See* Chapter 13, Desktop Publishing Glossary.

font *See* Chapter 13, Desktop Publishing Glossary.

font cartridge *See* Chapter 13, Desktop Publishing Glossary.

footer *See* Chapter 13, Desktop Publishing Glossary.

format (1) To partition a disk into sectors and tracks. Blank disks are not usable until they have been formatted. (2) *See* Chapter 13, Desktop Publishing Glossary.

formatting The process of specifying a document's final appearance on the printed page.

form generator package   *See* Chapter 13, Desktop Publishing Glossary.

FORTAN (FORmula TRANslation)   (1) A third-generation programming language widely used in scientific and mathematical applications. (2) Acronym for Formula Translation, a high-level computer language developed in the 1950s.

fourth-generation computers   Computers developed in the early 1970s; they use chips that can contain over 15,000 circuits each.

fourth-generation language (4GL)   Very-High-Level Language (VHLL) currently used in database management systems, decision support systems, and application development packages; programming language resembles normal English.

front-end communication controller   A hardware device used in a micro-to-mainframe link that polls terminals to see if they have data to send.

fully articulated robot   A robot with six axes.

function keys   Keys in a separate part of the keyboard that are programmed to perform various tasks.

gateway server   Local area network hardware which interconnects local area networks to wide area networks.

gateway service   A specialized communication service to help subscribers prepare on-line database searches.

general ledger application   The heart of an integrated accounting package that produces the balance sheet and the income statement.

general-purpose robot   A mechanical device that can be programmed to perform a variety of jobs.

generic font   *See* Chapter 13, Desktop Publishing Glossary.

goal-seeking   A spreadsheet add-on package feature which allows a user to indicate a desired result, then identify the numbers that can and cannot be manipulated in order to achieve the goal.

grammar checker   Software that spots errors that would be ignored by a spelling checker, such as redundancies, incorrect forms of words, and so on.

graphics adapter   *See* graphics board.

graphics board   A separate circuit board required by digital displays; also called graphics adapter.

graphics package   Application software that produces images.

graphics user interface   *See* window package.

graphics workstation   A grouping of hardware and software required to meet an organization's graphic needs; typically includes a personal computer, graphics software, plotter, and slide-making hardware.

greeking   *See* Chapter 13, Desktop Publishing Glossary.

H and J   *See* Chapter 13, Desktop Publishing Glossary.

hacker   One whose hobby is studying how a computer works; can involve illegal access to others' systems.

halftone   *See* Chapter 13, Desktop Publishing Glossary.

hands-on test   Using candidate software on a computer to check that it is appropriate for the intended use.

hard copy   A printed copy of computer output.

hard disk   A rigid metallic disk encased in a sealed box, and used for data storage; also called fixed disk.

hard-dollar saving   Actual reduction in out-of-pocket costs to a firm accrued by the use of automated data processing through, for example, reduction in payroll.

hardware   The physical part of a computer.

hard-wired   Wired to perform one specific job, as the ENIAC. A new program required rewiring.

header   *See* Chapter 13, Desktop Publishing Glossary.

heuristics   Empirical reasoning or rules-of-thumb used to solve problems.

homebot   Personal robots, often designed to perceive ultrasonic sound.

horizontal package   An accounting package that is generalized enough to be used by many industry types; also called a general or cross-industry package.

hypertext   An electronic system for organizing and presenting information nonsequentially.

hyphenation   *See* Chapter 13, Desktop Publishing Glossary.

IBM   Leading company in computer industry.

icons   Symbols used to indicate commands.

imaging   Software that allows for digitization of a photograph or any printed (or live) images.

import   A file conversion function that retrieves an exported file and converts it into its native format to make it available for use.

income statement   A financial document which shows an organization's income and expenses over a period of time.

independent system vendor (ISV)   *See* value added reseller.

index File by means of which a specific record can be located.

indexed sequential access method (ISAM) A method of data storage offered with COBOL and other computer languages.

induction system A knowledge-based system shell that automatically constructs rules from examples.

industry-specific package Software that combines data processing and management information functions and is geared to a specific industry.

inference engine A program that makes a knowledge-based system work.

Information Center Center through which the user services group provides computer technical support to nontechnical computer users.

ink-jet printer A printer that projects drops of ink on to the surface of the paper.

input Computer jargon for putting something into a computer as well as a name for anything put into the computer.

input form Prepared input formats available with some graphics packages to simplify creating graphic images.

integrated accounting system The name given to a package consisting of several accounting functions.

integrated circuit A circuit etched onto a silicon chip; also, the technology that makes use of this technique. Use of integrated circuits marked third-generation computers.

integrated circuit chips A computer device consisting of miniaturized electronic components etched onto a silicon surface.

integrated package A package that usually includes word processing, spreadsheet, graphics, database management, and communications. It provides for easy movement among applications.

integrated services data network (ISDN) A communication network that carries simultaneous voice, data, and full-motion pictures.

interactive Method of computer use in which a user interacts with the computer.

internal modem A special-purpose circuit board that fits into a personal computer's expansion slot and is connected directly to the telephone wall outlet by a cable.

International Electrical and Electronics Engineers Association An organization that approves networking standards.

International Standards Organization (ISO) Organization which sets rules for international communication.

interpreter One type of computer language processor; it translates source code into machine language during program execution.

invert *See* Chapter 13, Desktop Publishing Glossary.

justified text *See* Chapter 13, Desktop Publishing Glossary.

kerning *See* Chapter 13, Desktop Publishing Glossary.

keyboard The hardware unit of a personal computer with which a user most commonly enters and manipulates data.

keyboard oriented A data entry style that uses keystrokes, often to select items on menu bars or to type commands (versus a mouse-oriented style).

keyboard template A plastic or cardboard cutout which overlaps the function keys and has a place to write memory-jogging labels for function key actions.

key field Any important lookup item in a record.

key glossary A list of short-form key stroke combinations used to call up frequently used text.

knowledge base A stored collection of facts and rules about a specific area of knowledge.

knowledge-based systems Software systems that capture, magnify, and distribute access to judgment.

knowledge engineers People who specialize in transforming heuristics into a computerized knowledge base.

landscape printing *See* Chapter 13, Desktop Publishing Glossary.

language processor Programs that translate common programming languages, such as BASIC or COBOL, into machine language.

LANstations *See* diskless workstation.

large-scale integration (LSI) Etching of more than 15,000 circuits on a single computer chip; marked the fourth-generation computers.

laser disk Same as optical disk.

laser printer An extremely fast printer that uses photocopying techniques to produce high quality text and graphic output.

laser printing *See* Chapter 13, Desktop Publishing Glossary.

layout *See* Chapter 13, Desktop Publishing Glossary.

leading *See* Chapter 13, Desktop Publishing Glossary.

letter-quality printer A printer that produces high-quality printing often used for formal correspondence.

line art *See* Chapter 13, Desktop Publishing Glossary.

line items   Lines of information which identify each actual item ordered on a sales order data entry screen.

line spacing   *See* Chapter 13, Desktop Publishing Glossary.

linking   A method of combining spreadsheets.

linotronic   *See* Chapter 13, Desktop Publishing Glossary.

LISP   A programming language used for knowledge-based systems, abbreviated from "List Processing."

local-area network   A network linking two or more personal computers and computerized devices which allows them to share software, hardware, and communication services.

local node   A connecting point in a packet-switched network that helps to link users to various public and private host computers.

lockout   *See* record locking.

log book   Record of computer system malfunctions.

log-on   A sequence that validates a communicator to a host computer.

LU 6.2   Standard developed by IBM for communication between computers.

machine language   Binary language used by digital computers.

macros   A block of program code that allows a user to replace a block of keystrokes with a simple entry key.

mail merge   An application used to merge a form letter file and a data file to create personalized form letters.

mainframe computer   A large computer; also known as a mainframe.

management by exception   A management approach which advocates spending time on exceptional conditions and not wasting valuable time on things that are performing as expected.

management hierarchy   The three levels of management—operational (lowest), tactical (middle), and strategic (upper)—found in most organizations.

management information system (MIS)   A collection of software programs that produce information to help managers make business decisions.

markup copy   A copy of a style checked document with comments and suggestions inserted throughout.

master pages   *See* Chapter 13, Desktop Publishing Glossary.

memory   One of two major components of the processor unit, used for temporary storage of data and programs.

memory address   A unique number in a computer's memory which identifies a storage location.

memory bank   A memory management technique that partitions memory into sections, called "banks," and switches among them, as needed.

memory-resident utilities   Utilities that are loaded into memory and that can be called up without disrupting the main task.

menu bar or line   A line of menu items on the screen that are selected by using a mouse or by pressing selected keys.

menu mode   A software package that runs with lots of menu screens; this mode is slow, but helpful for novices.

menu pointer   Used to highlight one of several command choices on a display.

micro-channel architecture (MCA)   A microcomputer architecture which allows other processors, besides the central processing unit, to co-exist and perform various processing tasks.

micro-channel connectors   The expansion slots in the PS/2 microcomputer which tether various physically separated components to the system unit.

microcomputer   A small computer with a central processing unit contained on a single microprocessor chip.

Microcomputer Specialist   Researches latest microcomputer hardware and software and introduces new technology into a firm as appropriate; usually works in a company's Information Center.

microprocessor   A miniature central processing unit on a single integrated circuit chip.

micro-to-mainframe link   Control software that enables a microcomputer user to exchange information with a mainframe.

minicomputer   Smaller, less powerful, less costly computers than mainframes. Usually do not require special rooms and can be installed anywhere. Considered a medium-sized computer between a smaller microcomputer and a larger mainframe.

mnemonic commands   Easily remembered keystrokes that perform built-in functions; for example, P to "print" and C to "copy."

model   A simulation of an activity.

modeling   Processing of representing, through mathematical equations and logical expressions, aspects of an organization's business activities; simulation.

modeling language   Fourth-generation programming language used to create a model.

modem   A device that transmits data over a telephone wire. It can connect a terminal to a mainframe, or one microcomputer to another, despite physical distance.

modulation   A process that takes discrete digital computer signals of 1's and 0's and endows them with sound to go through telephone lines.

monitor   *See* display.

monochrome display   Monitor that presents data or graphics in one color.

motherboard   *See* system board.

mouse   A device used to control the movement of a pointer around a screen; usually involves pointing to selections on a pull-down menu.

mouse oriented   A data entry style that uses a mouse and pull-down menus. (versus a keyboard-oriented style).

multidimension   A spreadsheet feature which allows for the organization and analysis of data by whatever criteria are appropriate, such as budget category, time period, and departments.

multifunction board   A single circuit board which provides the functions of several separate boards.

multiple session   The ability to conduct more than one communication session at a time.

multiscan monitors   Computer displays that accept a range of graphic standard scan rates from various display boards; also called multisync monitors.

multisync monitors   *See* multiscan monitors.

multitasking operating system   Allows several programs to be run simultaneously.

multiuser computer   A computer supporting several people simultaneously, with users often working at terminals.

multiuser microcomputers   Microcomputers with a processor unit that can be shared by multiple users.

multiuser spreadsheet   A centralized spreadsheet that allows many users access at once.

natural language   Any language spoken by humans; distinguished from program language. User communicates with a computer in user's own language, English, for example.

natural language package   Software that enables a user to ask search questions in plain English.

natural language systems   Enable users to carry on a computer dialogue in plain English.

near letter quality printer   A type of dot matrix printer which produces both rough-draft and letter-quality output.

networking   Linking computers, such as personal computers, for sharing software, information, and resources.

network server   A small black box that runs the network software and contains the hard disk that is shared by everyone on a network.

nodes   *See* workstations.

normalizing files   Rules that can be used to create smaller, more manageable files from unorganized larger files.

notepad   A feature of a desktop organizer that allows a user to cut and paste data from one application to another.

numeric keypad   Special keys designed to speed data entry in numerical-oriented applications.

object code   The machine code image of compiled source code.

object image file   *See* Chapter 13, Desktop Publishing Glossary.

object library   *See* symbol library.

object-oriented images   Images produced by CAD packages and stored as formulas which are always sharp and clear when enlarged; also called vector images.

offset printing   *See* Chapter 13, Desktop Publishing Glossary.

on-line database service   Provides information over communication lines to subscribers for a fee.

on-line help   A word processing application feature instantly available to provide aid to a user.

open order report   A beneficial report generated by a sales order processing package which helps management to determine which customer orders have not been shipped and which items are causing backlogs.

Operating System/2 (OS/2)   The operating system designed to optimize the performance of the Intel 80286 microprocessor and the Personal System/2 line of microcomputers.

operating systems   System software that manages data input and output, program execution, and memory.

optical disk   A new computer storage medium which interacts with the computer through a laser beam, also called a laser disk.

optimization   Software which helps a user to select the "best" option from a series of "what if" possibilities.

order header   The data-entry screen in a sales order processing application which accepts all order data except line items.

outline font   *See* Chapter 13, Desktop Publishing Glossary.

outline processor   An application that is used to organize elements on a screen in outline form.

output Computer jargon for getting something out of a computer as well as for what comes out.

overhead transparency Plastic sheets that contain data or illustrations that can be projected by an overhead projector.

override A sales order application feature that allows a user to overwrite order header data which is automatically supplied from the customer database record.

packaged application Application software that is sold already programmed.

packaged software Ready-made software.

packet A group of characters sent in a packet-switched network.

packet-switched network A system which sends communication in pieces of information called "packets."

page composition package The main software ingredient in most desktop publishing systems which replaces a drafting table, scissors and glue with the electronic assembly of text and graphics in order to create a page layout.

page description language (PDL) *See* Chapter 13, Desktop Publishing Glossary.

page layout *See* Chapter 13, Desktop Publishing Glossary.

page makeup *See* Chapter 13, Desktop Publishing Glossary.

page oriented *See* Chapter 13, Desktop Publishing Glossary.

painting software Software that allows for the creation of free-form images.

parallel processing The ability to harness the power of several coprocessors for a single computing task.

parity bit A character bit used to provide a low level of transmission error checking.

pasteboard *See* Chapter 13, Desktop Publishing Glossary.

pasteup board *See* Chapter 13, Desktop Publishing Glossary.

PC-DOS The industry standard single-tasking operating system.

PC standard A term which identifies the fact that there are more IBM PC's and compatibles in use than any other type of microcomputer.

peripherals Devices like printers, disk drive, and display that are connected to a microcomputer's system board.

personal advisory software Programs designed to extend the user's judgment and intellectual capabilities.

personal computer A small, desktop-sized computer; technically called a microcomputer.

personal productivity software Computer applications that help people accomplish some of their most important everyday professional functions. Examples are word processing, spreadsheets, and graphics.

Personal System/2 (PS/2) The new line of IBM personal computers which use 3 ½-inch floppy disks and offer advanced processing capabilities.

phosphor The coating on the back of the display screen which glows when struck by light beams.

photocomposition *See* Chapter 13, Desktop Publishing Glossary.

phototypesetter *See* Chapter 13, Desktop Publishing Glossary.

picking/packing slip A document which is provided by an automated sales order entry procedure that is used in gathering (picking) order items, as well as shipping (packing) them.

piracy Illegal copying of software.

pixel A term for one picture element.

plotter A device used to print paper charts or transparencies.

point *See* Chapter 13, Desktop Publishing Glossary.

pointer A highlighted area on the screen which a user can move around to make menu and other selections.

polling A transmission procedure used with synchronous communication to reduce line costs and improve the quality of transmission; only one terminal is allowed use of the line at a time.

pop-up windows *See* dialog box.

portrait printing *See* Chapter 13, Desktop Publishing Glossary.

PostScript *See* Chapter 13, Desktop Publishing Glossary.

presentation graphics The use of graphics for presentation to others.

previewing Permits a user to examine a graphic before printing.

primary data Cannot be computed; are the usual items included in a file.

printer fonts *See* Chapter 13, Desktop Publishing Glossary.

printing spooling A feature that allows a user to start a new project while printing is going on.

print server A local area network device which allows workstations to share centrally located printers.

private branch exchange (PBX) Another name for the central controller in a star network; also called computer branch exchange (CBX) and digital branch exchange (DBX).

processing What occurs to transform input to output.

processor Computer hardware that interprets and executes instructions and communicates with the input, output, and storage devices.

production system An approach to problem solving based on the "if-then" rule.

program A set of instructions for a computer, telling it what to do; another word for software.

program coding The step in the programming process concerned with writing code that instructs the computer to carry out the logic design.

program design The design of a program's overall structure and detailed processing logic.

program file Stores lines of program code for execution (occasionally also stores data).

program listing A computer-printed copy of program source code.

programmer-analyst A dual-function professional, usually found in smaller organizations, who performs all program design and coding work.

programming language Used to code computer programs; examples are BASIC and COBOL.

program overlay Allows a programmer to write programs that chain, or link, one program segment to another.

program statements Lines of program code.

PROLOG A programming language used for knowledge-based systems, abbreviated from "Programming Logic."

prompts *See* user prompts.

proportional spacing A professional class word processing feature that allocates printing space according to character size; for example, more room is allowed for an uppercase "M" than for a lowercase "i."

protected mode A mode of operation with the 80286 and 80386 microprocessors which runs the newer Operating System/2 and makes multitasking through hardware servicing possible.

protocol A set of transmission rules in data communications.

prototype A rough model of a user application.

prototyping approach When a systems developer works with a user to create a rough version of a computer system without adhering to the system development life cycle.

public communication service A center where electronic mail and other types of information are received and sent utilizing a mainframe computer.

public-domain software Software of interest primarily to hobbyist computer users that is often distributed by user groups free, except for the cost of distribution and the floppy disk.

pull-down menu A menu of command options that appear to "pull-down" on a display, like a window shade, once a main menu line command is selected.

random access File processing that allows records to be manipulated in a random order. It is the opposite of sequential access.

random access memory (RAM) The place in the computer where programs and data must reside before they are processed by the central processing unit.

raster image processor (RIP) *See* Chapter 13, Desktop Publishing Glossary.

raster scan The process of refreshing the phosphor dots on a display screen.

read-only memory (ROM) Permanent storage areas that contain utility programs.

real mode An operating mode supported by the 80286 and 80386 microprocessors which uses only the first 640 Kbytes of available memory, it is used for running traditional DOS programs because it mimics the old 8088 microprocessor memory addressing limitation.

record locking or lockout Process whereby one user is put on hold if two users attempt to update one record at the same time.

relational DBMS Database management system that links files to each other through a key field.

remote computing packages Data communication applications which link two computers together so that both keyboards are active and both screens show the same thing.

report generation A feature of database software that generates custom reports without programming.

report layout A hand-drawn layout of a desired report.

requirement analysis The first step in the systems development life cycle, this is the investigating stage.

resolution The number of distinguishable points or dots on the display.

response time Time after a user types the last key of an entry to the time the computer displays the last letter of a reply.

reverse *See* Chapter 13, Desktop Publishing Glossary.

RGB monitor A monitor that uses a refined color separation technology to produce high-quality color images.

ring network A local area network topology which links workstations in an unbroken chain of many cable segments. Ring networks often use a token passing transmission protocol.

robot systems A field of artificial intelligence that develops and uses computer controlled robots to perform specific mechanical tasks.

roman *See* Chapter 13, Desktop Publishing Glossary.

RS-232 cable A cable that connects an external modem to a computer; also called serial cable.

ruler *See* Chapter 13, Desktop Publishing Glossary.

rules or ruled line *See* Chapter 13, Desktop Publishing Glossary.

sales history report A report generated by a sales order processing application that can help managers to set marketing strategies.

sales order processing application An application of accounting packages which allows orders to be entered into the computer as soon as they are received from a customer.

sans serif *See* Chapter 13, Desktop Publishing Glossary.

scale *See* Chapter 13, Desktop Publishing Glossary.

screen font *See* Chapter 13, Desktop Publishing Glossary.

screen painting Process of designing a form or other graphics on a screen.

script file A file created by some programmable communication software which holds procedures for further automating custom tasks.

scrolling Moving text up and down so that the desired portion of the text appears in the display.

search Process of retrieving a record or data.

search and replace Functions used to find a word or phrase in a word-processed document and replace it with another word or phrase.

secondary data Any variable that can be computed from other variables.

second-generation computer Faster and more reliable computer developed in the late 1950s and early 1960s that used transistors for its circuitry.

sensory subsystem A part of a robot's design that enables it to perform activities that normally require human senses, for example, vision.

sequential access File processing that begins with the first record and progresses sequentially through the entire file.

serial cable *See* RS-232 cable.

serial port A port in the back side of a personal computer which provides the connection, via a cable, between the computer and an external modem.

serif *See* Chapter 13, Desktop Publishing Glossary.

shell A package containing an inference engine program without the knowledge base; also called "framework" or "generator" packages.

silicon chip Chip on which circuits are etched. Use marked the third generation of computers. See integrated circuit.

single-task operating system Accommodates one user and is only used on personal microcomputers.

size *See* Chapter 13, Desktop Publishing Glossary.

slide show software A program which allows personal computer users to create simulated "slides" for presentations.

smart terminal A terminal with a certain level of memory and some editing capability.

snap-to effect *See* Chapter 13, Desktop Publishing Glossary.

soft copy Display computer output, especially graphics.

soft-dollar saving Benefits to a firm accrued by the use of automated systems other than in out-of-pocket costs, such as increased productivity of managers.

soft font *See* Chapter 13, Desktop Publishing Glossary.

software The nonphysical part of a computer; the programs that run on a computer, telling the hardware what to do.

software development house *See* software houses.

software directories Publications containing information about software packages, including what the software does, hardware supported, operating system requirements, pricing, number of current users, contact information, and geographic area serviced by the supplier.

software houses Companies devoted to developing new software; also called software development companies, software suppliers, and software vendors.

software supplier *See* software houses.

software vendor *See* software houses.

source code A programming language, which is translated by a language processor into object or machine code.

spelling checker Software used to match words in a document with words in its dictionary for mismatches. It displays suspect words and suggests corrections.

spreadsheet   A grid containing rows and columns; the common name for a program that computerizes spreadsheet use.

stand-alone accounting package   An accounting software application which performs one function, such as sales order or accounts receivable processing.

standardizing on software   Requiring everyone to use the same package, for example, a spreadsheet package. It occurs in multiuser environments to facilitate file exchange and to simplify training and maintenance support.

standards   Specifications intended to facilitate the exchange of data between computers.

star network   A local area network topology with workstations clustered around a computer that acts like a central controller, or "switch."

storage   The keeping of data on disks rather than just in a computer's memory.

stored program concept   Concept of temporarily storing programs in a computer's memory.

structured methods   Used to analyze, design, and program computer systems; it starts from an overview of the problem and then focuses on increasingly smaller details.

style checker software   Used to spot errors that would be ignored by a spelling checker. Also called a grammar checker.

style sheets   (1) Prepared formats that come with a word-processing package; some enable users to create custom style sheets. (2) See Chapter 13, Desktop Publishing Glossary.

supercomputer   High-speed computer used for advanced military, scientific, and other projects.

symbol library   A library of prestored symbols that can be used in the preparation of graphic presentations.

synchronous transmission   The transmission of data one byte after another in regular intervals synchronized by a master clock.

synonym finder   Software that performs the role of a thesaurus, also called electronic thesaurus.

system analysis   The investigative phase of what has to be done to develop a new application.

system analyst   A person who analyzes, designs, and implements computer systems.

System Application Architecture (SAA)   The plan intended to allow all of IBM's diverse line of computers to "talk to one another."

system board   The main circuit board of a personal computer on which the main chips reside.

system design   A description of how a computer system should be developed to serve a specific purpose.

system development life cycle   The steps from initial analysis through implementation and maintenance involved in developing a new computer system.

system documentation   A collection of all the documents created to develop and install a new system.

system flowchart   A graphic model showing the flow of control through a computer system.

system integrator   See value added reseller.

system software   A collection of software which consists of operating systems, utility programs, and program language processors.

system unit   A hardware component of a personal computer that houses the components that perform the actual processing.

tag   See Chapter 13, Desktop Publishing Glossary.

teach pendant   Device used to program desired motions and coordinates of a robot.

telecommuting   Working at home and communicating with one's office or company via computer.

template   (1) A master spreadsheet without numbers or data. (2) A small plastic cut-out of memory jogger labels for the function keys. (3) See Chapter 13, Desktop Publishing Glossary.

terminal   An input device connected to a computer, consisting of a keyboard, a video display, and a communications link.

terminal server   A local area network device which allows terminals to access any computing or information processing resource on the network.

text-based data manager   A package which allows a user to write notes marked with keywords for later search, retrieval, and organization.

text wrap   See Chapter 13, Desktop Publishing Glossary.

third-generation computer   Computer developed in the 1960s that used integrated circuitry and silicon chips.

third party   A computer industry term for independently developed products and services.

threaded or chained   See Chapter 13, Desktop Publishing Glossary.

3270 terminal emulation card   An adapter card (or circuit board) used to achieve a micro-to-mainframe link for an IBM connection.

TIFF   See Chapter 13, Desktop Publishing Glossary.

time sharing   (1) System in which separate computer terminals are connected to and dependent on a central computer. (2) Multiple programs are resident in memory at once and each user's program is executed in allocated time slices.

titles A spreadsheet package feature which locks in a row or a column on the display.

token passing A method for controlling transmission in a local area network.

topology The physical layout of personal computers and other devices connected to a network.

touch-sensitive display An alternative to a keyboard used on some personal computers that is activated by touching the screen and blocking light beams.

tracking *See* Chapter 13, Desktop Publishing Glossary.

transistors Devices that replaced vacuum tubes for computer circuitry and that marked the second generation of computers.

translation A spreadsheet feature that allows different packages to share files by importing and exporting them using file exchange formats; also called file conversion feature.

transmission protocol The set of rules used to transmit data in a network.

turnkey system Combination of hardware and software packaged for sale by a value added reseller, theoretically ready to be turned on and used.

turnkey vendor *See* value added reseller.

twisted-pair wire The line that connects a telephone to the wall jack; used for data communication.

typeface *See* Chapter 13, Desktop Publishing Glossary.

typesetter *See* Chapter 13, Desktop Publishing Glossary.

type specification *See* Chapter 13, Desktop Publishing Glossary.

type style *See* Chapter 13, Desktop Publishing Glossary.

type through A word processing feature which enables a user to type directly to the printer.

unattended mode The feature that allows a computer to run on "automatic pilot" for data communication tasks.

undelete A feature that restores the last deletion made in a word processing document.

undo A feature that cancels a mistake or allows a change of mind.

UNIVAC The Universal Automatic Computer, the first business computer, used in the early 1950s.

Unix operating system Operating system software with both multitasking and multiuser capability.

uploading Transmitting a file from one's own computer to a remote computer.

user An individual or an organization that uses computers.

user-developed systems Computer systems that are custom-developed by the people who will be using them.

user groups Formal or informal gatherings of computer users to share information, software, and other matters of interest.

user guide The part of a software application package that contains instructions about how to use the software.

user prompts Messages displayed on a computer monitor asking questions of or giving instructions to the user of a software program to facilitate its operation.

utilities Programs that help to keep track of files and perform disk housekeeping chores. Often called DOS commands, they include format a disk, copy a disk, copy a file, examine file directory content.

vacuum tube Device for basic computer circuitry used in first-generation computers; resembles a slim light bulb.

value added reseller (VAR) Retailer who combines hardware and software, often from various manufacturers, for resale as a turnkey system.

variable data Items that can be split into primary and secondary data and that can change each time the report is run.

vector images *See* object-oriented images.

vertical justification *See* Chapter 13, Desktop Publishing Glossary. .

vertical package *See* industry-specific package.

virtual 86 mode A mode of operation with the 80386 microprocessor which allows a user to run many DOS applications at the same time.

virtual machine The capability of one computer to perform as if it were many computers running different operating systems simultaneously.

virtual memory Using disk space as an operating memory even though it is not actual memory.

VisiCalc The first electronic spreadsheet program.

voice digitizer A component necessary for voice mail service that measures voice sound frequencies and assigns them values that can be stored as 1's and 0's.

voice mail A communication system that uses a voice digitizer and voice synthesizer to transfer messages by sound.

voice recognition A computer that operates by sound input rather than a keyboard.

voice synthesizer A component necessary in voice mail service that reads digital signals and converts them back to sound.

warm boot Restarting a program with the computer already on.

wide-area network A network that uses modems and the telephone system to communicate over long distances.

widow and orphan control A word processing feature which prevents one line from being separated on a page from the rest of the paragraph on another page.

wild card Characters, such as question marks, that are used, for example, in a search and replace process, to symbolize ambiguous characters.

window package Used by microcomputers to display multitasking sessions. A window is one area of a divided display screen.

word processing software A program that helps the user to create, edit, and store text.

word wrap A function that moves any word that crosses the right-hand margin to the next line.

workstations Devices linked to a local area network; also called nodes.

wrap *See* Chapter 13, Desktop Publishing Glossary.

WYSIWYG Acronym for "What you see is what you get." Word-processing software whose display shows exactly what a printed document will look like.

Xmodem protocol An example of a popular method of detecting and correcting errors in data communication.

X.25 Rules for connecting to public packet-switched networks.

X.400 A standard to connect electronic mail services around the world.

zoom function A painting software feature which improves graphic detail by causing an enlarged dot-by-dot pattern of a drawing section to be displayed.